BIG GAME OF NORTH AMERICA
Ecology and Management

BIG GAME

OF NORTH AMERICA

ECOLOGY AND MANAGEMENT
A Wildlife Management Institute Book

Compiled and edited by
John L. Schmidt and Douglas L. Gilbert

Illustrated by
Charles W. Schwartz

Technical Editors
Richard E. McCabe and Laurence R. Jahn

Published by STACKPOLE BOOKS

BIG GAME OF NORTH AMERICA, Ecology and Management

Copyright © 1978 by
Wildlife Management Institute,
except pages 207–225.

Second Printing, revised, 1980

Published by
STACKPOLE BOOKS
Cameron and Kelker Streets
Harrisburg, Pa. 17105

Library of Congress Cataloging in Publication Data
Main entry under title:

Big game of North America.

   Bibliography: p.
   Includes index.
   1. Big game animals—North America.   2. Wildlife
management—North America.   3. Mammals—North America.
I. Schmidt, John L., 1943-   II. Gilbert,
Douglas L.
QL715.B53   639'.979   78-14005
ISBN 0-8117-0244-8

Design and Layout by
Richard E. McCabe and Kenneth J. Sabol

FOREWORD

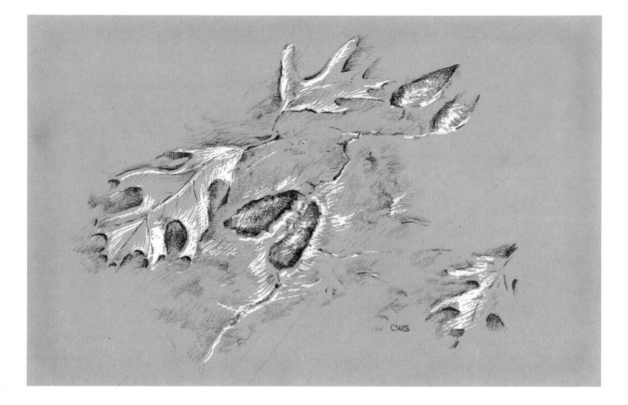

The knowledge and insights of many prominent wildlife scientists have been joined in this publication on North America's large mammals, their status, management and future. That this was done reflects the wildlife profession's recognition of the need for such an authoritative volume. Drawing on years of personal study and observation and the published writings of hundreds of other scientists, the authors and editors have produced a book that long will stand as a major reference on the ecology and management of large mammals.

This book will be of value to practicing wildlife managers and to those engaged in research, administration and education. It should be accepted widely as a textbook for the thousands of young people who year-ly undertake courses of study in wildlife sciences at North American colleges and universities. The methodologies and relationships it emphasizes will be useful abroad as well. Serious-minded outdoor enthusiasts will find much of interest in its chapters, including both the accounts of individual species and those dealing more broadly with predation and predator control, animal behavior, habitat changes, nutrition, carrying capacity and other subjects.

Aside from its importance as a modern and comprehensive summary of the management of North America's interesting and spectacular large mammals, the book, taken as a whole, has still another dimension. Its many chapters testify to the fact that, given public support, cooperation and adequate funding, the wildlife profession is fully capable of maintaining populations of native wildlife within the capacity of natural habitats to supply needed food, water and shelter. The record attests to that fact. Many of the species covered in this book, now abundant, once were at perilously low population levels.

It cannot be noted too frequently that the most severe threat to the well-being of all North American wildlife is this continent's expanding human population. Man and his works continue to occupy more and more living space needed by wildlife. And what land man does not occupy himself or build on, he oftentimes decreases in terms of its utility to wildlife. Man significantly alters vegetative cover, creates obstacles to animal movements, or makes other uses of the land, including for recreation, that displace or disturb animals during such critical periods as calving seasons or in winter when their energy reserves are depleted. Secure habitat is the keystone to diversity and abundance of all wildlife, both large and small.

As this book makes clear, more sophisticated research will help to refine the wildlife profession's understanding of the forces and events that affect these valuable large mammals, for good and for bad. As new understanding is gained, it will be blended into management strategies and field programs. In some cases, this may involve only relatively simple changes. More extensive management adjustments may be required in others. But in all cases, the objective of wildlife management and all that it entails is to replace unplanned events and uncertain results with planned actions and known results. For only in this way will the animals and mankind's interest in them be benefited alike.

Daniel A. Poole, President
Wildlife Management Institute

ACKNOWLEDGEMENTS

The authors and editors gratefully acknowledge contributions of the following individuals to the book's completion: Donald E. McKnight, Karl B. Schneider, Dolores A. Moulton, P. J. Bandy, David C. Kradel, John M. King, Kenneth C. Nobe, Einar Alendal, David R. Gray, Henning Thing, Mary Jean P. Currier, Steven Sheriff, Leonard V. Hills, William Samuel, Robert J. Hudson, Dale A. Wade, Bart O'Gara, Charles Trainer, Ron Smith, Helenette Silver, David B. Mertz, Kathy E. Freas, Morris G. Southward, James D. Nichols, Fred Bunnell, Gayle Joslin, Norbert V. DeByle, Phillip J. Urness, Thomas McCabe, L. Jack Lyon, James M. Peek, Robert Pratt, Phyllis Turner, Pamela D. Joseph, Maurice G. Hornocker, Robert S. Hoffmann, George Calef, James Davis, Eugene Mercer, Linda Garrett, Daniel A. Poole, Lonnie L. Williamson and Kenneth J. Sabol.

CONTENTS

LIST OF TABLES

LIST OF FIGURES

BIG GAME OF NORTH AMERICA

Ecology and Management

Chapter 1

EVOLUTION AND TAXONOMY

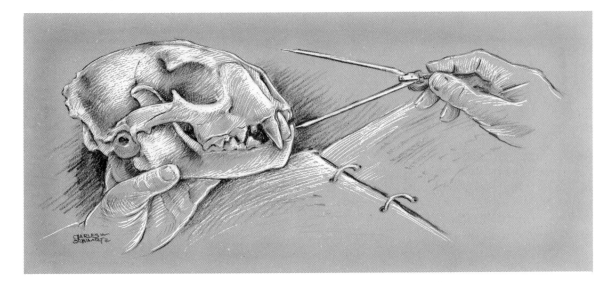

Douglas L. Gilbert
Professor and Head
Department of Fishery and Wildlife Biology
Colorado State University
Fort Collins, Colorado

Evolution is the change of species or that a species undergoes over long periods of time. It usually results in complexity or a "higher" organism. Morphological, anatomical, physiological and behavioral characteristics may be involved. Natural selection, generally caused by predation and competition, dictates which animal types remain in a population. Evolution of animals has been well-documented in most mammalogy and ornithology texts and, thus, will be treated very briefly in this book. Vertebrate classes in their simplest form may be diagrammed as in Figure 1.

Marsupial animals appeared during the early Cretaceous Period of the Mesozoic Era,

approximately 125 million years before present (B.P.). Most placental mammals originated in Europe and Asia in the early Cenozoic Era and in the late Paleocene epoch, more than 70 million years B.P. Development and rapid change occurred in the Oligocene and Miocene epochs, 40–25 million years B.P. The Cenozoic Era is known as the "Age of Mammals." The order Carnivora (meat-eaters, including cats and bears) preceded Artiodactyla (all of which are herbivores, including deer, sheep, etc.) from mid- to late Paleocene (Table 1).

Fossil records show that most of our big game species migrated to North America via the Bering Strait land bridge which con-

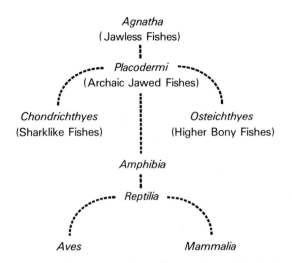

Figure 1. Diagram of vertebrate classes in their simplest form.

nected Siberia at Cape Van Koren to Alaska near Nome. Migration took place during the Miocene and Pliocene epochs (10 million years B.P.) and the Pleistocene epoch (1.5 million years B.P.). Exceptions are the peccary, pronghorn and musk-ox. Apparently, the pronghorn and peccary originated and remained in North America. Musk-oxen originated in North America, migrated to Asia, then returned to North America.

TAXONOMY

Taxonomy simply is the identification and classification of organisms. For most big game animals, identification is little or no problem. Classification is necessary to assure that everyone is talking or thinking about the same animal. For example, the elk of Europe is essentially the same animal as the moose in North America. Thus, the term "elk" can be confusing. But the generic name, *Alces,* can only refer to the moose, and no one can mistake it for anything else. The generic name for the elk of America and the red deer of Europe is *Cervus.*

Scientific nomenclature is necessary to identify species exactly and is vital for communication among persons interested in animals. For this reason, it is advisable for persons to memorize the scientific names

Table 1. The geological time scale since animal life became abundant. Mammals or their ancestors typical of each Period are shown (after Romer 1970).

Era	Period	Estimated time since beginning of each Period (Millions of Years)	Epoch	Mammals and Ancestors
Cenozoic (Age of Mammals)	Quaternary	2	Recent	Modern species and subspecies. Extinction of some mammals. Dominance of man.
			Pleistocene	Appearance of modern species and subspecies. Extinction of some large mammals, widespread glaciation.
	Tertiary	65–70	Pliocene	Appearance of modern genera.
			Miocene	Appearance of modern subfamilies.
			Oligocene	Appearance of modern families.
			Eocene	Appearance of modern orders.
			Paleocene	Primitive marsupials and placental mammals dominant.
Mesozoic	Cretaceous	130		Appearance of marsupial and placental mammals. Extinction of large reptiles.
	Jurassic	180		Archaic mammals, reptiles dominant.
	Triassic	225		Therapsid reptiles, first dinosaurs.
Paleozoic	Permian	275		Appearance of therapsid reptiles from which mammals evolved.
	Carboniferous	350		First reptiles.
	Devonian	400		Age of fishes.
	Silurian	450		Archaic fishes.
	Ordovician	500		Appearance of vertebrates.
	Cambrian	575		Appearance of invertebrates.

(genus and species) of animals in which they are interested. Once a pattern of identification and classification is established and the scientific name is used repeatedly, most individuals will use the scientific name rather than the common name.

Taxonomy can be very complicated, especially if one tries to distinguish between races or subspecies. In recent years, however, the tendency has been to lump groups together, rather than split them into smaller categories. The approach in this text is to keep taxonomic information simple and restricted to that which is practical. Subspecies or race designations will be found in the chapters for individual species.

It is recommended that serious students of mammalian taxonomy take a course in mammalogy or at least read a text on the subject. Taxonomic detail is included in virtually all of them. One must be cautious, however, because classifications change and a taxonomic chart may be out-of-date before it is printed.

Obligatory classification of animals is listed in Figure 2. Not included are most "sub-" and "super-" classifications. Also omitted are infra-designations, cohorts and tribes. The scientific names included in this chapter are those presented by Jones et al. (1973).

Order Carnivora

In this book, all animals are included in two orders, Carnivora (Figure 3) and Ar-

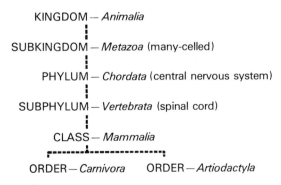

Figure 2. Obligatory classification of North American big game mammals.

tiodactyla (Figure 4). Major characteristics for Carnivora are:

1. Digits with claws;
2. No fewer than four toes;
3. Dentition modified for flesh diet—conical canines, tuberculate molars and premolars adapted for shearing flesh;
4. Brain highly developed;
5. Mostly terrestrial, but may be partly aquatic, arboreal, or fossorial;
6. Simple stomach;
7. Long pelage, consisting of underfur and guard hair; and
8. Great variance in size.

In Carnivora, big game species are found in two families: Ursidae (bears) and Felidae (cats). Major characteristics of the Ursidae are:

1. Plantigrade feet, with five toes;
2. Carpals and metacarpals touching the ground;
3. Claws not retractile;
4. Robust, large and heavy body;
5. Small and insignificant tail and ears;
6. Teeth of an omnivore—carnassial teeth not well-developed; and broad, flat or bunodont molars;
7. Dentition—$3/3 + 1/1 + 4/4 + 2/3 \times 2 = 42$;
8. First three premolars often missing; and
9. Baculum or os-penis present.

Genera and species to be included are *Ursus americanus* (black bear), *U. arctos* (brown or grizzly bear) and *U. maritimus* (polar bear). Grizzly and Kodiak bears are now considered subspecies of *U. arctos* (Jones et al. 1973). The polar bear was in a separate genus, *Thalarctos,* but recently has been included in *Ursus*. All of the bears exhibit dormancy to some extent during winter months. This is not true hibernation because the animals can be easily aroused. Body temperature and physiological processes are not greatly reduced.

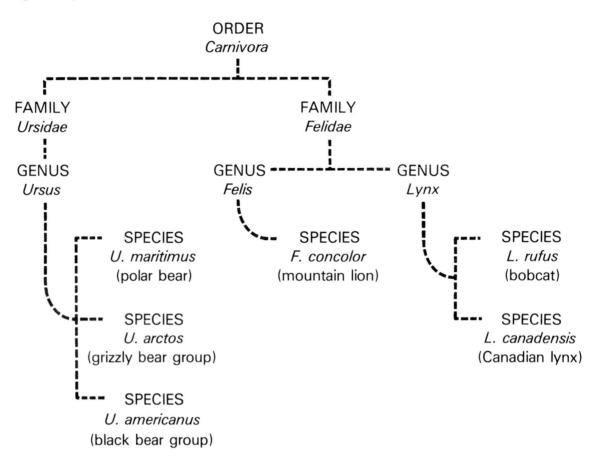

ORDER
Carnivora

FAMILY
Ursidae

FAMILY
Felidae

GENUS
Ursus

GENUS
Felis

GENUS
Lynx

SPECIES
U. maritimus
(polar bear)

SPECIES
F. concolor
(mountain lion)

SPECIES
L. rufus
(bobcat)

SPECIES
U. arctos
(grizzly bear group)

SPECIES
L. canadensis
(Canadian lynx)

SPECIES
U. americanus
(black bear group)

Figure 3. Obligatory classification of Carnivora order.

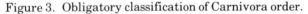

Black bears also can be color phases of brown, cinnamon, black or in combinations. Gray and blue color phases are found in some locales. Black bears have shorter, stronger recurved claws than the grizzly bears. Hence, the statement can be made that adult black bears can easily climb trees while adult grizzly bears cannot. Characteristics of black bears are:

1. Skull profile nearly straight, or convex from nose to forehead;
2. High point of body over rump;
3. Color highly variable;
4. Short and strongly curved claws; and
5. Back upper molar never more than 57 millimeters (2.25 inches).

The grizzly group is all lumped under *U. arctos,* which includes the large brown bear, Kodiak bear and grizzly. These great bears are the largest land mammals in North America. Distinguishing characteristics are:

1. Skull profile concave from nose to forehead;
2. High point of body at front shoulders, denoting power;
3. Color always brown-to-tan, or some variation;
4. Relatively straight and long claws, up to 76 millimeters (3 inches); and
5. Back upper molar never less than 57 millimeters (2.25 inches).

The great white bear of the North, or polar bear, is well known by nearly every American who visits the zoo. Recent management practices, curtailment of some harvesting methods, and agreements with other countries have assured continuance of population numbers. Characteristics are:

1. White-to-yellowish color with black nose, lips and pads of feet;
2. Long neck adapted for aquatic mobility and maneuverability;
3. Extremely large feet adapted for aquatic and snow environments;
4. Carnivorous diet, mainly seals and fish; and
5. Liver poisonous to man—high concentration of vitamin A.

Characteristics of Felidae, the cat family, include the following:

1. Digitigrade feet, haired below except the pads;
2. Short, curved and retractile claws;
3. Five toes on the front feet, four on hind feet;
4. Short and round skull, with short rostrum;
5. Short tail, to one-half of body length;
6. Dentition—$3/3 + 1/1 + 3/2 + 1/1 \times 2 = 30$ (except *Lynx* where premolars are 2/2); and
7. Canines grooved and carnassial teeth well-developed.

The only North American big game species in the Felidae family that will be discussed elsewhere in this text is *Felis concolor* (mountain lion). This large cat is not spotted except when very young and is usually gray-to-tan in color. The tail is approximately one-half the body length. Smaller species of this family include species of *Lynx* (lynx and bobcat), which remain spotted to some extent throughout life and have short tails.

Order Artiodactyla

Characteristics of the order Artiodactyla are:

1. Generally even-toed and hooved (unguligrade);
2. Main axis of foot between third and fourth toes—first toe (inner) suppressed or vestigial, and second and fifth toes may form dew hooves commonly called dewclaws;
3. Herbivorous diet; and
4. Os-penis absent.

The suborder Suina includes Suidae (pigs), Tayassuidae (peccaries) and Hippopotamidae (hippopotami). Common characteristics of these families are:

1. Simple stomach (nonruminant);
2. Thick and robust body;
3. Bristlelike hair;
4. Thick skin;
5. Omnivorous diet;
6. Bunodont and wrinkled molars;
7. Tusklike, enlarged and curved canines;
8. Two or four toes (except peccary which has three on hind foot);
9. Metacarpals and metatarsals not fused (no "cannon bone"); and
10. Upper incisors present.

Suidae includes swine or domestic hogs, old world pigs, and introduced European wild boar *(Sus scrofa)*. Family characteristics are flaring tusks or canines, large size and a relatively rough appearance. Teeth vary in number from 34–44. The European wild boar has been introduced into many states, including Tennessee, North Carolina and California, where they are hunted.

The collared peccary, or "javelina," belongs to the family Tayassuidae, and is restricted to the Americas. They are found from the southwestern United States to Central America. These gregarious animals are less carnivorous than true pigs; much herbaceous material is eaten. The genus and species found in the United States is *Dicotyles tajacu*. Until recently, the genus for collared peccary was *Tayassu*. Characteristics are:

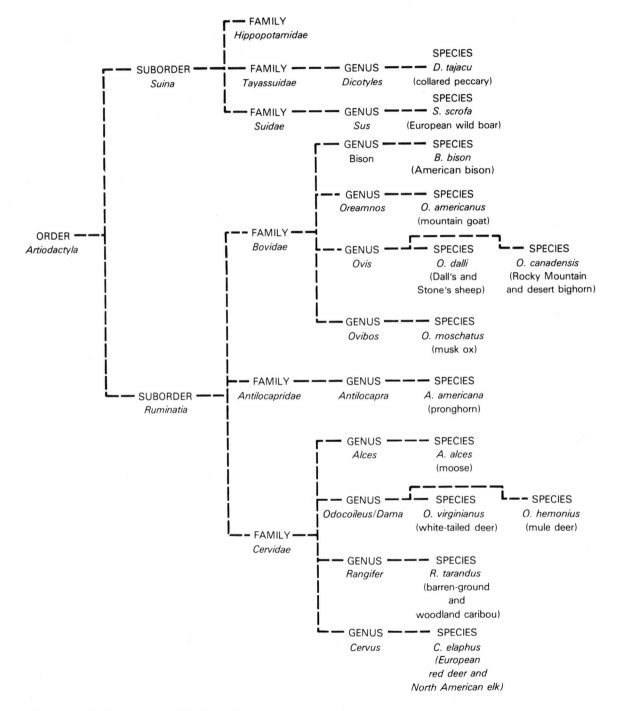

Figure 4. Obligatory classification of Artiodactyla order.

1. Smaller than Suidae;
2. Canines less flared than in *S. scrofa;*
3. Molars not wrinkled and squarish, with four cusps;
4. Four toes in front, three behind;
5. Musk gland on mid-dorsal rump; and
6. Dental formula—2/3 + 1/1 + 3/3 + 3/3 × 2 = 38.

The suborder Ruminantia includes camels, giraffes, true antelope, pronghorn, deer, sheep, cattle and goats. Common characteristics of those species found in North America include the following:

1. Four-chambered, complex stomach;
2. Cud chewed and regurgitated once to several times before the final swallowing;
3. Metacarpals and metatarsals fused into a cannon bone;
4. Horns or antlers usually present, at least in one sex;
5. Incisors and canines usually absent in upper jaw;
6. 32 or 34 teeth, depending on presence of upper canines; and
7. Brittle and hollow hair, shed twice annually.

This suborder includes the families Bovidae (bison, true antelope, sheep and goats), Antilocapridae (pronghorn) and Cervidae (deer, elk, moose and caribou). Common characteristics of Bovidae are:

1. Both sexes horned;
2. Unbranched horns with bony core, and ectodermal sheath not shed;
3. Gall bladder present; and
4. Dental formula—0/4 + 0/0 + 3/3 + 3/3 × 2 = 32.

Relative to dental formulae, one of 0/4 + 0/0 + 3/3 + 3/3 × 2 = 32 can be written 0/3 + 0/1 + ... The variance is whether or not the fourth incisor should be called a canine. Zoologists believe that it should.

Antlers differ from horns in that the former are shed annually, usually in mid-winter. In addition, they are solid bone with no outer sheath. Horns consist of a bony core and an outer sheath made of keratinlike material or agglutinated hairs. Horns grow from the base, and an annual ring will show on the outer sheath each year. Pronghorn shed the outer sheath each year and show no annual rings. Annual rings can be counted and used for age determination.

Genera of Bovidae in North America are *Bison* (bison), *Oreamnos* (mountain goat), *Ovis* (sheep), and *Ovibos* (musk-ox). There is but one species of mountain goat, *Oreamnos americanus*. *Ovis canadensis* includes the Rocky Mountain and desert bighorns. *Ovis dalli* includes the Dall's and Stone's sheep of northern North America. *Ovibos moschatus* is the musk-ox. *Bison,* or the American buffalo, are no longer important as a game species.

Mountain goats are found farther above timberline than any other North American big game mammal. It has been introduced into many areas, including Colorado and South Dakota. Although hunted, it is mainly a trophy animal. The major challenge for those who pursue goats is simply reaching the area where they are found. Mountain goat characteristics are:

1. White-to-yellowish color and shaggy appearance;
2. Black, slender and slightly recurved horns, not shed;
3. Horns essentially the same size for both sexes;
4. Scent gland immediately posterior to each horn;
5. Laterally compressed and squarish appearance;
6. Large, black hooves with protruding pad; and
7. Rounded to squarish track, less pointed at tip than other hooved big game species.

The wild sheep of North America are in the genus *Ovis*. *O. canadensis* includes both the Rocky Mountain bighorn and the desert bighorn. They look alike except that the horns of the Rocky Mountain ram are less flared than those of the desert bighorn ram. The desert bighorn is more angular and generally less sleek than the Rocky Mountain bighorn. Common characteristics of wild sheep are:

1. Horns of males massive and curled;
2. Horns of females slender and recurved;
3. Habitat generally rocky crags and cliffs;
4. Generally gray-to-tan color, with white rump patch and light-colored nose;
5. Large hooves with protruding pads in posterior part; and
6. More-or-less pear-shaped track.

Musk-oxen, *Ovibos moschatus,* sometimes called "musk bison," are the small bison of the far North. This member of Bovidae, with its heavy, shaggy coat and a diet of tundra vegetation, is well-adapted to life in that environment. Distinguishing characteristics include:

1. Both sexes horned;
2. Horns nearly meet at bos or base on top of head;
3. Long hair or mane, extends to the knees;
4. Woollike underfur;
5. Body highest over front shoulders;
6. Circular herd defensive formation, with weaker individuals inside and stronger outside; and
7. Dark brown-to-black color, with lighter-colored face.

The Antilocapridae, the pronghorn family, includes but one genus, *Antilocapra,* and one species, *A. americana.* The commonly used name "antelope" is a misnomer. True antelope do not have forked horns. Pronghorns are characterized by the following:

1. Horn "pronged" in front;
2. Outer sheath annually deciduous, in late fall or early winter;
3. Females sometimes horned;
4. Females' horns shorter than ears;
5. Gall bladder present;
6. No "dew" hooves or lateral digits;

7. Erectile hair on rump (heliographic);
8. Dental formula same as Bovidae;
9. Eye orbits large, well back and high in skull; and
10. Great speed and endurance.

The Cervidae family includes four genera: *Odocoileus* (deer); *Alces* (moose); *Cervus* (elk); and *Rangifer* (caribou). Common characteristics of this family are:

1. Antlers only on mature males (except *Rangifer*—both sexes antlered);
2. No gall bladder;
3. Dew hooves show, thus feet are four-toed;
4. Lachrymal depression present in front of eye;
5. Dental formula—$0/3 + 0/1 + 3/3 + 3/3 \times 2 = 32$ (except *Cervus* and *Rangifer*).

The most commonly used generic name for deer is *Odocoileus* although *Dama* is the correct taxonomic name. Apparently, the animal was first called *Dama,* and the oldest name is theoretically correct. However, *Odocoileus* is the most widely used. The black-tailed deer of the Pacific Coast once was considered a separate species *(O. columbianus).* In recent years, it has been classified as a subspecies under *O. hemionus.* The western deer, or "mule" deer *(O. hemionus),* is distinguished from the white-tailed deer *(O. virginianus)* by the following:

1. Short and "ropelike" tail with black tip;
2. Long ears, hence the name "mule" deer;
3. Metatarsal gland on the outside of the lower hind leg approximately 76 millimeters (3 inches) long;
4. Dichotomously branched or "bifurcate" antlers;
5. Bouncing gait;
6. Black coloration on face; and
7. White rump patch visible, because of the small tail.

White-tailed deer, or "whitetails," are found in eastern forests and along deciduous forest habitat in river bottoms of the West. Whitetails are of smaller average size than mule deer. Distinguishing characteristics of whitetails are:

1. Antlers not dichotomous after the first fork;
2. All points from main beam;
3. Comparatively small metatarsal gland, 25–50 millimeters (1–2 inches);
4. Large tail, "flaglike" when erected and white on underside;
5. Much white on face and underbody;
6. Comparatively short ears;
7. Reclusive behavior—skulks and hides; and
8. Comparatively more running and less bouncing gait.

The genus *Cervus* includes both the European red deer and the North American elk. Both now are considered *Cervus elaphus*, although the elk was called *C. canadensis* for many years. Elk are larger than mule or whitetail deer, but smaller than moose. The history of elk in North America is a classical story of exploitation and reintroduction. Populations now are hunted over much of the western United States. Perhaps a better common name is "wapiti," as the animal was called by Indians. Use of this term prevents confusion with the "elk" or moose of Europe. Distinguishing features of wapiti are:

1. Large antlers, not dichotomous after first fork;
2. All points from one beam;
3. Neck and gait often camellike in appearance;
4. Canines in upper jaw of all males and some females ($0/3 + 1/1 + 3/3 + 3/3 \times 2 = 34$);
5. Gregarious and generally migratory; and
6. Mature males lighter in color than mature females.

Moose *(Alces)* are the largest of the Cervidae found in North America. Exploited over much of their eastern range, these large deer are still abundant in northern North America, including a portion of the northwestern United States. There is but one species, *A. alces*. It can be distinguished by the following:

1. Large and palmate antlers;
2. Points shorten with advanced age;
3. Long and bulbous muzzle;
4. Upper lip prehensile or capable of grasping;
5. Dewlap, or "bell," common;
6. Dark coloration, with older animals often black in appearance;
7. Very long legs;
8. Humped appearance of front shoulders; and
9. Less gregarious than other deer.

The northernmost member of Cervidae is the caribou *(Rangifer)*. Currently, all are lumped under one species, *R. tarandus*. Generally, there are considered to be two subspecies, the barren-ground caribou of the far northern tundra and the woodland caribou. Distinguishing features of the species are:

1. Both sexes antlered, with males' antlers generally larger;
2. Irregular antlers with spatulate segments;
3. One or two brow tines or "spades" extend down and over the face;
4. Upper canines may or may not be present ($0/3 + 1/1 + 3/3 + 3/3 \times 2 = 34$);
5. Large feet with prominent dew hooves;
6. Clicking sound by tendons when animals walk;
7. Most aquatic, migratory and gregarious of Cervidae family; and
8. Striking color dimorphism between lighter and darker parts of the body.

In this brief chapter on evolution and taxonomy, no attempt has been made relative to specific detail. The serious student of either is referred to a text on those subjects. Detail relative to subspecies and races is included in these chapters for each species.

Chapter 2

AMERICAN ELK

Raymond J. Boyd
Wildlife Management Biologist
U.S. Bureau of Land Management
Rawlins, Wyoming

In the study of pioneer times in North America, there are many accounts of the abundance of game animals. American elk, or "wapiti," figure prominently in these accounts. It was sought as a source of meat and was one of the most widely distributed members of the deer family in North America.

However, as man moved westward, elk disappeared from settled regions until they virtually vanished from most of their historic ranges. Remnant herds were scattered in the Rocky Mountain region and parts of the Pacific Northwest and Canada. With elk numbers steadily decreasing and elk habitats being settled, farmed or logged, the American people became aware of the problem, and management and research programs were started to restore elk populations.

This chapter is an assemblage of facts and insights about the American elk that have been brought to light since Olaus J. Murie's classic work, *The Elk of North America,* was published in 1951. Most of the data presented are derived from reviews of vast amounts of literature concerning elk research and management, and from new and on-going research efforts. It will present some suggested guidelines for elk management and a number of questions that, so far, remain unanswered by research.

IMPORTANCE

The importance of the American elk cannot be overemphasized. Its economic value to communities near hunting areas is tremendous. Dollars to the community during the short elk hunting season may exceed the money flow for the rest of the year in these communities.

Estimated by the Colorado Division of Wildlife, the amount of money spent by elk hunters in Colorado during 1975 reached more than $36 million. That same year, license fees resulted in more than $3.8 million to the Division for its programs. Of the dollars spent by elk hunters in Colorado, it is estimated that 75 percent, or more than $27 million, is distributed in the vicinity of elk hunting areas. According to Waters (1964), "hunting and fishing rank with mining, agriculture and manufacturing in Colorado's economy."

Estimates of the economic value of elk hunting to the various states and provinces are shown in Table 2.

TAXONOMY

During the Pleistocene epoch, there were ten subspecies of the genus *Cervus* in North America. Of these, six are extinct: the

Table 2. Economic value of elk hunting to various states and provinces, 1975.[a]

State or province	Number of hunters		Amount spent by elk hunters[b]		Amount to wildlife agencies from license sales		Total harvest
	Resident	Nonresident	Resident	Nonresident	Resident	Nonresident	
Arizona	7,530	185	no data	no data	$ 203,310	$ 19,425	1,090
Colorado	91,614	35,895	$24,154,947	$12,020,159	1,145,175	2,692,125	22,632
Idaho	49,382	6,748	no data	no data	641,966	1,012,200	8,981
Montana	72,671	18,002	no data	no data	236,181	2,718,302	14,619
New Mexico	6,500	646	2,385,500	323,000	97,500	48,450	1,805
Oregon	108,113	2,797	16,531,559	no data	1,081,130	97,895	15,351
Utah	18,803	101	no data	no data	376,060	15,150	2,389
Washington	102,785	830	no data	no data	1,798,738	76,360	12,730
Wyoming	43,501	5,765	5,842,184	3,541,785	625,515	720,625	20,970
Alberta	16,171	225	no data	no data	145,539	23,400	850
British Columbia	6,890	339	2,294,370[c]	200,010	68,900	33,900	1,172
Saskatchewan	2,282	0	384,266[c]	0	34,230	0	190

[a]Data provided by John P. Russo, Arizona; Richard N. Denney, Colorado; Errol E. Nielson, Idaho; Eugene O. Allen, Montana; James F. Johnson, New Mexico; Paul Ebert, Oregon; Homer Stapley, Utah; L. D. Parsons, Washington; James D. Straley, Wyoming; Harold D. Carr, Alberta; Ray A. Demarchi and W. C. Macgregor, British Columbia; and Hugh Hunt, Saskatchewan.

[b]Exclusive of license fees.

[c]Based on all big game hunting expenditures.

Eastern elk (*C. canadensis canadensis* Erxleben); the Merriam elk (*C. canadensis merriami* Nelson); *C. whitneyi* Allen, a fossil from Wisconsin; *C. lascrucensis* Frick, from New Mexico; *C. aguangae* Frick, from southern California; and an unknown subspecies from a fossil in Alaska (Murie 1951).

A recent reclassification of *Cervus* (Jones et al. 1973) has changed the familiar species name *canadensis* to the European form, *elaphus*. This will be the nomenclature used throughout the balance of this chapter. Listed under the type species are the four living subspecies:

1. Rocky Mountain elk *(C. e. nelsoni* Bailey*)* are located in the central to northern Rocky Mountains, including northern Saskatchewan, most of Alberta and eastern British Columbia, as well as in eastern Oregon and Washington, Idaho, western Montana, Wyoming, Colorado, Utah, Nevada, New Mexico and Arizona;
2. Roosevelt or Olympic elk *(C. e. roosevelti* Merriam*)* are found in the coastal areas of the Pacific Northwest;
3. Manitoba elk *(C. e. manitobensis* Millais*)* are found in the southwestern corner of Manitoba, the southern half of Saskatchewan and southeastern Alberta; and

4. The Tule or "dwarf" elk *(C. e. nannodes* Merriam*)* are restricted to west-central California.

Although the American elk will be referred to as such in this chapter, the more appropriate name is "wapiti"—a Shawnee Indian word meaning "white deer," in reference to elk's bleached spring coats (Madson 1966). "Elk" is a colloquialism derived from the German word "elch," which refers to the European moose. In other parts of the world, outside North America, "elk" is used to designate a number of species of the Artiodactyla order, including the Sambar deer of Ceylon.

DISTRIBUTION

At one time, the American elk was the most widely distributed member of the deer family on the North American continent. It was found from Atlantic to Pacific coasts, and from Mexico to northern Alberta with the exception of the southern coastal plains and the Great Basin (Hall and Kelson 1959).

Elk disappeared from the eastern United States early in the 1800s, and Western herds shrank to a total population low about 1900 under the impacts of market hunting and agriculture. At present, huntable herds of elk are found mainly in the western United States and southwestern Canada (Figure 5). Herds also may be found in several states east of the Mississippi River, including Michigan, Virginia and Pennsylvania.

DESCRIPTION

Elk are the second largest member of the deer family in North America, surpassed only by moose. Largest of the American elk

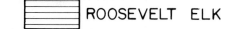

TULE ELK

MANITOBA ELK

ROCKY MOUNTAIN ELK

ROOSEVELT ELK

Figure 5. Distribution of American elk in 1975.

is the Roosevelt elk of western Oregon and Washington. Weights for mature bulls of this subspecies range from 318–499 kilograms (700–1100 pounds), while mature cows average 265–284 kilograms (584–621 pounds).

Data indicate that Manitoba elk are next in size, with mature bulls averaging 353 kilograms (777 pounds) and cows averaging 275 kilograms (606 pounds) (Blood and Lovass 1966). Rocky Mountain elk average approximately 318 kilograms (700 pounds), while a mature cow averages from 227–239 kilograms (500–525 pounds) (Murie 1951). Tule elk of California are smallest of the species. Mature bulls weigh about 182 kilograms (400 pounds), and cows range from 148–159 kilograms (325–350 pounds).

Like all members of the deer family in northern latitudes, elk have distinct summer and winter coats. In the winter, an elk's head, neck and legs are dark brown, while its sides and back are gray-brown and much lighter in color. Elk also have a distinct yellowish rump patch bordered with a dark brown or black stripe. Both sexes have heavy, dark manes extending down to the brisket area. The summer coat, which is complete by July 1, is a deep reddish-brown color, with little or no undercoat, giving the animals a very sleek appearance. By early September, the summer coat is changing to the winter form.

Roosevelt elk are usually darker than Rocky Mountain elk, and in some cases, the neck of the former is black. Tule elk are generally lighter than the other species and may even be a claylike color.

Elk have no functional teeth in the forward part of their upper jaw, with only

Tooth-hunters once were a major problem for elk managers. This elk, killed in 1923, was left after only its two "bugler" teeth were removed by poachers. A Wildlife Management Institute photo.

Typical six-point bull elk during the rut. Photo by author.

a heavy dental pad to oppose the lower incisors. Premolars and molars are present in both upper and lower jaws. However, unlike other North American deer, both sexes of elk regularly have a pair of incisiform canine teeth in the forward part of the upper jaw. These are the well-known "elk teeth," "whistlers" or "buglers," and are almost as highly prized as a trophy by hunters as are antlers.

The dental formula for elk is as follows:

$$I \frac{0}{4} \ C \frac{1}{0} \ PM \frac{2}{2} \frac{3}{3} \frac{4}{4} \ M \frac{1}{1} \frac{2}{2} \frac{3}{3} \times 2 = 32.$$

The typical antler of the adult Rocky Mountain bull elk consists of a long, round beam sweeping up and back and usually bearing six tines. The brow tines and the bez tines are close to each other near the base of the beam and extend out above the muzzle in a formation of four points that now commonly are called "lifters." The trez tine rises higher up on the beam and the fourth point rises still higher. The latter is the royal or "dagger" point which is a heavy tine and usually the dominant one. The remaining points, called the sur-royals, result from forking at the end of the beam (Murie 1951).

The first antlers normally begin growth in May when the young bull is nearly one year old. Generally, they are single spikes 254–

610 millimeters (10–24 inches) long, but occasionally with small forks at the tips. In an examination of 1,839 yearling bulls from Colorado's White River herd, 28.4 percent had more points than the typical spike formation, with some bulls having four to five tines per side (Boyd 1970). According to Murie (1951), only occasionally do yearling bull antlers fork or have extra points. Studies of other elk herds in Colorado tend to agree with Murie's contention, and do not show large percentages of yearling bulls with antlers having more points than a typical spike formation (Boyd 1966, 1967). It would seem, therefore, that there is some genetic or nutritional factor in the White River herd that induces the production of more antler material.

The second set of antlers approaches the typical six-point form but ordinarily carries only four or five points on a side. The beams, however, usually are small and slender. Antlers of bulls in their third year are still likely to have less than six points, usually four or five, but the beams are heavier than those of two year olds. Succeeding antlers are usually six-point and occasionally seven-point, and form annually until the bull passes his prime, after which they may degenerate.

Antlers of other species of American elk are similar in form to the Rocky Mountain elk with the possible exception of some Roosevelt elk bulls, which may have a "crown" of three or four points where the sur-royals are usually located. This antler formation also is common to the red deer.

LIFE HISTORY

Elk calves usually are born in early June, after a gestation period of 8–8.5 months. At birth, a calf weighs approximately 13 kilograms (28.6 pounds). The usual birth is a single calf, with twins being extremely rare (Murie 1951). Although arguable, it is believed that cows seek calving areas near the upper reaches of winter ranges which offer open brush and grassy areas, dense timber for cover, and water.

After a calf is born, the cow tends to stay apart from other elk for two to three weeks until its young is able to travel. The cows and calves then begin to congregate and, by mid-July, herds of up to 400 animals are common on some summer home ranges. In many instances, a few cows act as "babysitters" for as many as 20 calves while the mothers are grazing elsewhere.

On their summer ranges, fully mature bulls are alone or in small groups of up to five or six animals. They tend to favor high, windy points where they can rest, protect their growing antlers and utilize any breeze to ward off bothersome flies and other insects. Younger bulls usually are mixed in with the cow-calf herds until early September.

By early August, the bulls' antlers have completed their growth, and "velvet" covers are stripped off by sparring and by thrashing against trees and bushes. In early September, bulls are ready for the rut, and bugling and harem formation start. Younger bulls are driven from the cow-calf groups as the older "herd" bulls attempt to eliminate all competition for their harems. Harem size may be as many as 30 cows, but 15–20 cows seems to be the usual size. Younger bulls driven from the harems tend to hang around the fringes, with the apparent intent to steal a cow without being seen by the herd bulls. In fact, many people think most breeding is done by the younger bulls because the herd bulls are preoccupied chasing other bulls away or driving reluctant cows back to the harem.

While there can be no doubt that yearling (15-month old) bulls are sexually mature (Conaway 1952), these bulls generally do not participate in the breeding. It is rare that yearlings or "spike" bulls have harems and, in many instances, 10–15 spike bulls may be found together during the rut, acting as if they are not sure just what is going on. There have been instances, however, when yearling bulls have established harems of as many as 17 cows in areas of Colorado where heavy hunting pressure reduced mature bull numbers by about 47 percent in four or five years (Boyd 1970).

Bull elk with harem of 11 cows, in Rocky Mountain National Park, Colorado. Photo courtesy of the U.S. Department of Interior.

While the bull is the "boss" of the harem, it is the older cows that are the true leaders in an elk population. An older cow usually gives the alarm and leads the rest of the group away from real or imagined danger.

By the second week of October, most breeding has been accomplished, and the bulls resume their solitary ways and try to gain strength for the coming winter. When early winter snows begin to accumulate, cows, calves and most bulls begin to migrate down to winter ranges where they usually spend December through March. A few older bulls, however, stay in higher areas and often winter in snow as deep as four feet (Madson 1966) or more. As the winter period ends in late March, the cows, calves and young bulls start a gradual migration back up to summer ranges, and the whole cycle begins again.

POPULATION DYNAMICS

Population dynamics involve the study of changes in an elk population and the influences that produce those changes. This section will examine just the basic population parameters which affect the size of an elk herd or population.

Productivity

Of vital interest to wildlife managers is the growth rate of elk herds. This rate is a

Adult bulls often winter in areas with snow covering in excess of 1.2 meters (4 feet). A Wildlife Management Institute photo; taken by L. Doyle Mathews.

most difficult statistic to ascertain, and probably in no other phase of big game ecology are there greater discrepancies of data and estimates. While the rate of increase can be expressed in several ways, probably the most convenient is to express calf production as the ratio of calves per 100 cows at a specific time of year. This ratio includes all cows other than calves. As such, it includes many yearling cows that cannot have calves.

Productivity generally is estimated by two factors: pregnancy rates and cow-calf ratios after postnatal mortality. Pregnancy rates can be determined by inspection of reproductive tracts for embryonic material and for corpora lutea of pregnancy. These reproductive tracts can be collected from recreational hunters who have been instructed to collect the proper organs, or directly from elk killed in reduction programs. Data from these sources can be very useful in estimating reproductive success.

While there is considerable disparity in the number of calves recorded in September prehunt counts, most recorded data concerning pregnancy rates in different herds are remarkably similar. From the limited data presented in the literature, it appears that Rocky Mountain elk incur relatively large prenatal and postnatal losses. This apparently is due in large measure to restrictive forage conditions on winter ranges and, to a lesser degree, to disease and predation. However, it must be remembered that a large calf crop will lower prehunt productivity counts the following year because of a larger number of nonbreeding yearling cows present in the herd.

Pregnancy rates for adult Roosevelt elk in western Oregon have been calculated to be one-half to two-thirds those reported for Rocky Mountain elk. Analyses of Roosevelt elk reproductive tracts show that infertility in this species is a result of ovulation failure or embryonic mortality (Harper 1971), and may be a result of improper nutrition.

As mentioned, elk usually have only one calf. The probability of twinning is rare, averaging one-third of 1 percent and probably lower. The low birthrate is balanced by the fact that cows carefully protect their young through their first year.

Breeding season

Field observations of rutting activities indicate that bugling is usually heard first about mid-August and may continue into November. Actual rutting activities probably do not start until mid-September and may last to near the end of October.

Dates of conception generally range from September 15 to November 4; about 75 percent of the conceptions occur between September 26 and October 10, with a median date of about October 5 (Morrison et al. 1959, Boyd and Ryland 1971). Struhsaker (1967) placed the peak of the rut for elk in Alberta, Canada, between September 8–21.

Behavior and movements

Elk are restless animals, possibly due to their size and daily requirements of large amounts of forage for maintenance and growth. Once elk settle on their seasonal home ranges, daily movements are dictated by the availability of food, water and cover and, to some extent, external harassment.

In certain areas, some elk remain year-round on their summer range, but the majority migrate to lower winter ranges when snow becomes deep. Some migrations are only a short altitudinal movement, while others cover 48–64 kilometers (30–40 miles). As a general rule, larger bulls start their migration to summer ranges before the cows, calves and younger bulls, often "pushing" the retreating snowline.

Some elk movements are remarkable in terms of distances traveled and time taken to complete them. In one instance, a neck-banded cow was observed in early June in the Rio Grande River drainage of Colorado. Two and one-half months later, the cow and its calf were observed 177 kilometers (110 miles) to the northwest.

Hazards of winter are not limited to food scarcity, deep snow and predation. Photo courtesy of the National Park Service.

Daily movements of Roosevelt elk generally follow a pattern of resting, feeding and watering at various intervals of the day or night. They tend to feed moving uphill from bottomlands during the early morning and to bed down in the middle of the day. They resume feeding in mid- or late afternoon, moving in a downhill direction until after dark. There are many recorded instances of elk feeding by moonlight, and many elk hunters seem to find better hunting during the dark phase of the moon.

Herding characteristics

Elk are gregarious and, in the summertime, often gather in herds of up to 400–500 animals. Larger congregations of more than 1,000 animals can be observed on some winter ranges. While it is not a normal situation in any sense, gatherings of more than 15,000 elk have been recorded on the Jackson Hole National Elk Refuge during severe winters (J. Straley, personal communication).

In the summer, older bulls generally remain by themselves or in small groups of five or six animals. During the rutting season, large summer herds are separated into the breeding harems.

As with other herd species, elk often panic and stampede en masse. They take their cue from other animals in the herd and run away from real or imagined danger that may have been noticed by only a few. These mass stampedes rarely cover long distances and end very quickly. When a few animals stop, the rest progressively slow down and stop as well.

Elk often are playful and many times can be observed kicking and splashing in shallow ponds evidently with great enjoyment. This activity is vastly different, however, from wallowing in sloppy mud, which usually only occurs during the rut and appears to be indulged in only by rutting bulls.

Territoriality

Groups of elk do not appear to remain constant either in size or sex and age makeup. Because of this, most elk researchers do not subscribe to the theory that elk groups establish, hold and defend territories. Whether bull elk establish territories is a matter of argument among many elk managers. Picton (1962) reported that some Montana bulls establish and defend territories ranging in size from 1.1–1.6 kilometers (0.67–1.0 square mile). Struhsaker (1967) reported no indication of territoriality in his studies of elk breeding behavior in Banff National Park, Alberta, Canada. He stated that a herd bull defends the area his harem occupies, but that this area is not geographically fixed. In studies of the Roosevelt elk in coastal Oregon, Graf (1956) contended that these animals were territorial, but he did not show the exclusive use of an area by either individuals or herds that is necessary to demonstrate territoriality.

Communication

A newborn calf has a loud squeal which is high pitched and piercing and, if no danger is present, is moderately short. If the calf is frightened, it usually gives forth with a series of squeals and longer screams. Cow elk reply to their calves with barks, grunts and sometimes a similar imitation of a calf call. During the summer, a traveling group of cows and calves can be located easily by the noisy squealing which goes on almost continuously. When alarmed or suspicious of danger, all elk older than calves can give a sharp bark which can be heard a considerable distance. Penned and trapped elk or those faced with severe stress will grind their teeth in warning. This produces a distinctive sound, much like bone splintering.

The main call of the elk, and its most famous, is the bugle of a bull during the rut. This call varies greatly, but generally begins on a low-pitched bellow and scales upward until it reaches a high pitched, distinct, loud trimodal note which is held until the bull runs out of breath. The "bugle" then drops quickly to a grunt or a series of grunts.

Bugling is not restricted to bulls, however, as there is ample evidence that cows bugle, especially in May and early June during the period of parturition. Why cows bugle is unclear, but it may be expressions of feeling caused by the approach of parturition (Murie 1951).

HABITAT NEEDS AND PREFERENCES

Food

The elk is a herbivore, and its year-round food sources can be categorized into three primary types of plants—browse, grass and forbs. A great deal remains unknown about the variety of preferences elk have for foods on summer and winter home ranges.

Plant growth in late April or early May causes elk to turn away from coarse browse forage of winter ranges and avidly seek out new grasses—83.2 percent of their May diet in the White River area of Colorado was grass (Figure 6). Rumen analyses for June and July showed 91.7 percent of the elk diet to be grass and grasslike plants. Snowberry, currant and low huckleberry made up most of the 8.3 percent of browse food in stomachs. No forbs were present (Boyd 1970).

In Arizona, 60 percent of midsummer elk forage was grass and forbs, the rest being browse. In Idaho, up to 85 percent of the midsummer diet was grass and forbs.

Taking the summer months as a whole, grasses and sedges are the primary forage plants, constituting more than 75 percent of the diet of Colorado elk. In Montana, only 30 percent of the summer elk diet was grasslike plants, with 64 percent forbs. Studies in Manitoba revealed the summer elk diet to consist of 22 percent grasslike, 52 percent browse and 26 percent forbs. Of all the grasses and grasslike plants reported eaten by elk, bluegrass appears to be the most palatable.

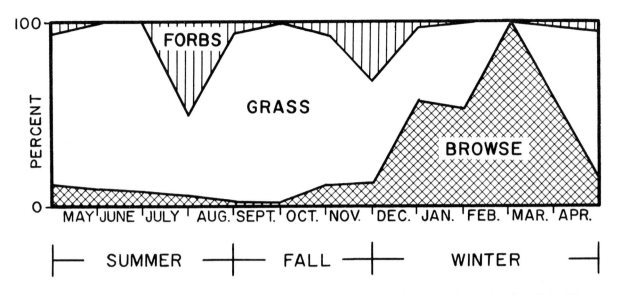

Figure 6. Proportions of grass, browse and forbs found in rumens of Rocky Mountain elk, White River area, Colorado.

Concerning year-round use of grass and grasslike plants by elk, winter food composed of grass ranged from 84 percent on Montana's predominately grass ranges, 65 percent in Idaho, and 22 percent in New Mexico, Manitoba and Colorado (Kufeld 1973). Primary use of grass in the fall was indicated in Montana studies where grass consumption averaged 73 percent. A high percentage of grasses in elk diets also was found in Colorado where they constituted 92 percent of the fall forage. Grasses and sedges comprised 37 percent and 40 percent of the fall diets for elk in Manitoba and Idaho, respectively (Kufeld 1973).

In a Colorado study (Boyd 1970), browse of all types represented 56.9 percent of the plants consumed during the period from December through April. Oakbrush ranked first among the woody species consumed during the winter, followed by aspen, serviceberry, big sagebrush and snowberry in this study.

During the summer, woody species such as aspen, currant, snowberry and huckleberry comprised 10.3 percent of the elk diet. During the fall months, aspen and currant made up the bulk of the browse diet in the White River area of Colorado (Boyd 1970).

In one study in the Blue Mountains of Oregon, bitterbrush, snowberry, mountain mahogany and western juniper were preferred winter foods. Shrub use on Montana's grass winter ranges averaged 9 percent, while elk in Idaho and northeastern Washington consume shrubs at a 15 percent rate in the winter. The summer diet in Montana averaged 6 percent shrubs, while Idaho studies indicated 55 percent shrubs and Manitoba reported 52 percent shrubs in the elk diet.

Forbs (weeds), consisting primarily of peavine and various composites, constituted 12.1 percent of all elk rumen contents examined during summer months in Colorado. Forbs appeared in highest percentages during August when 43.6 percent of the diet was this class. During September, October and November, forbs such as penstemon, vetch, peavine and various composites comprised only 1.7 percent of the rumen contents.

The summer diet in Montana averaged 64 percent forbs, while one study recorded a

100 percent forb diet. Elk in Oregon appeared to take 80.9 percent weeds during summer months in one study. Fall diets are primarily grasses, but a New Mexico study reported a 2 percent intake of forbs.

In summary, grass or grasslike plants were found in rumen samples throughout the year. Browse of some kind was present every month, although volumes generally were low during summer. Forbs were consumed primarily during midsummer and late fall.

On a frequency basis, grass and grasslike plants (mostly sedges) represented 65.6 percent of the plants consumed during an annual period. Woody species averaged 26.8 percent and forbs 7.6 percent of diet composition reported by Kufeld (1973).

Water

Water does not seem to be lacking in any of the elk habitats in North America, and elk make regular use of springs, ponds and lakes in their various ranges. Elk also get much of their moisture needs from vegetation, especially during the summer months. During the winter, their need for water is satisified by consuming snow.

Cover and climate

Cover actually may not be a necessary habitat requirement for elk. Rocky Mountain elk can be found bedded down on open hillsides in very heavy snowstorms. On the north side of the same mountain, other elk can be found bedded in heavy spruce-fir timber apparently trying to escape the storm. During very cold, clear weather, wintering elk seem to favor bedding down in aspen groves or on oakbrush hillsides. According to Murie (1951), healthy elk do not mind the cold and do not seek shelter from it.

Elk apparently are very susceptible to hot weather. They can be found bedded down on snowbanks in late spring and into early summer as long as the snow lasts. After the snow disappears, many elk can be found bedded down in very dense timber on north slopes apparently taking advantage of the shade. However, during some hot days, many elk—especially bulls with growing antlers—can be found on high open points with no cover at all, taking advantage of any breeze to help reduce the torment caused by flies. Heavy winds do seem to cause elk to seek shelter.

ESTIMATING POPULATION PARAMETERS

Enumerating various components (sex and age ratios, mortality rates and total population size) of an elk population is a difficult, but important task of the wildlife manager. These data tell the manager much about the dynamics and general health of the herd. All these data are difficult to obtain but, with adequate sample sizes, they provide the information needed for proper management of elk populations.

Estimating age structure

Essential to the role of wildlife managers dealing with elk is an understanding of the age structure of elk populations and of harvests. Structure refers to the division of a population into various age classes, such as calf, yearling, two year old, etc. This allows managers to determine the number of sexually mature females, the number of calves, and losses in succeeding age classes. From these data, the production and the survival of young can be estimated—information necessary for understanding the dynamics of a given elk population.

There are two methods of primary interest to a wildlife manager for determining age structure in an elk population. The first involves checking ages of elk killed by hunters. This is done by examination of tooth wear and replacement. Aging by this method is based on the sequence of tooth eruption and wear. There are several aging guidelines available, but techniques developed by Quimby and Gaab (1957) are used by many wildlife managers and researchers.

One problem associated with this method is obtaining a large enough sample to enable the manager to make an accurate estimate of a herd's age structure. In order to increase samples, hunters can be invited to remove the lower jaws from their kills and bring them to check stations. Requests for jaws can be stamped on special licenses or permits, and instructions for removing the lower jaw from dead elk can be included in the information section of big game information folders furnished by the various state conservation agencies to all elk hunters. It must be remembered, however, that ages obtained by this method are not necessarily representative of herd age composition. For example, many elk killed by hunters have to be packed out on horseback and in order to save weight and space, the jaws are often left in the field. Also, relatively few persons bring out the head or jaw of cow or calf elk.

If the wildlife agency is willing to spend the time and money, rather large sample sizes of jaws can be gathered by setting up several check stations around one herd area. In the White River area of Colorado, 3,061 elk jaws were obtained over a five-year period by using five check stations each year.

The check station method of collecting elk jaws is very effective for special research areas or extremely important herds, but is not satisfactory for statewide age-structure estimations. Age samples from all elk herds in a state can be greatly increased by using the dental cementum-aging procedure which utilizes only an incisor tooth from a harvested elk (Keiss 1969). The tooth is sectioned with a special sectioning saw, put through various staining procedures and then examined through a microscope for cementum annuli which can be counted in a manner similar to counting rings in a tree stump.

By sending every hunter, or a statistically reliable sample of hunters who draw a special permit or license, a small postage-paid

Cross section of an incisor from an unknown age elk killed in October; age estimated at six years by cementum annuli.

envelope in which to collect and mail an incisor, sample sizes can be increased substantially. The hunter has a much easier task removing an incisor than the whole jaw and can carry the tooth in his pocket rather than pack out a lower jaw. This system, utilizing envelopes for collecting teeth samples, has been used successfully in Colorado since 1972, and has enabled wildlife managers to obtain age data from herds that were not sampled otherwise. Laboratory technicians in Colorado now age more than 3,500 elk each year from throughout the state.

Estimating sex and age ratios

Two general methods of estimating sex-age ratios in elk herds are by ground counts and aerial counts. Ground counts are useful in areas where elk congregate in large numbers, such as feed grounds or on winter ranges. If the terrain is rough or if heavy brush makes visibility difficult, aerial classification is the only technique for obtaining these estimates.

While fixed-wing aircraft are satisfactory for obtaining counts on winter ranges, low and slow flying with helicopters is necessary to do an accurate sex ratio-classification count. In most instances, a larger, more representative sample can be obtained by use of these specialized aircraft.

Prehunt sex-age ratio counts should be made in mid-September at the peak of the rut when the largest percentage of bulls can be observed. Elk can be classified as spike bulls, young bulls (typical antler conformation, but light beams and usually four to five points), mature bulls (typical antler conformation, but heavy beams), cows and calves. Calves can be distinguished from yearling cows primarily on the basis of face or nose conformation, but color, relative thickness of the neck and comparative size are other criteria.

Classifications can be facilitated by using tape recorders to tally the various categories and, later, to extract the data. This method allows the observer to watch the elk continually while recording the sex or age of each animal. Prehunt counts in Colorado using helicopters have routinely collected data on more than 1,000 elk from selected herds each fall and winter (Boyd 1970).

Sex-age ratio counts in early December, before the larger bulls have pulled back to high and isolated wintering areas away from the main herd, are made to estimate changes caused by fall hunting. Techniques and criteria of posthunt counts are not different from prehunt counts.

Total population estimates

To an elk population, it is vital for the wildlife manager to estimate the total elk population on a given range. There are several censusing methods available for making these estimates.

Aerial counts of elk on winter ranges have been done since about 1946. These sample counts, for the most part, are accomplished by use of fixed-wing aircraft but, in spite of statements to the contrary, do not account for all elk in a survey area. Research concerning the percentages of deer or elk observed from the air, compared to the total population present, were done in Colorado for several years. Only about 37 percent of the elk present on a sagebrush-oakbrush-serviceberry wintering area actually were

seen by aerial observers (Boyd 1958). Winter counts are used by many wildlife management agencies to evaluate the population trends and to set annual hunting seasons and regulations.

Indirect census methods that have been used successfully by several management agencies are contrasts of prehunt and posthunt sex ratio counts and harvest estimates (Boyd 1970). While there are many excellent references concerning these censusing methods, one excellent review applicable to elk is by Hanson (1963), in which calculating abundance of vertebrates from sex-age ratios is discussed.

While the population figures resulting from these methods are extremely valuable, they do not elucidate the entire story of elk herd dynamics. Data missing are estimates of nonhunting mortality and formulas to calculate the consequences of future management on elk populations. In addition, it is just as difficult to reconstruct the effects of past management efforts on elk populations.

There also is a vital need for the wildlife manager to set management goals for the herd. In fact, there always has been a need to set goals and priorities for managing wildlife populations. The difficulty of obtaining reliable information on which to base these objectives has long been realized by wildlife managers. Because there were no tools or methods to assist in gathering and analyzing data, this deficiency was ignored in setting harvest limits, regulations and management priorities.

With the development of computer technology, a modeling method became available that allows wildlife managers to estimate various elk population parameters that cannot be determined otherwise. This method is the computer population simulation approach. Most data needed to conduct a simulation are contained in a calendar of biological events in the life cycle of an elk population (Boyd et al. 1975).

This computer approach to wildlife management is just beginning to be accepted and should become the primary, future management tool. But, simulations are not the only

Cow (second from left) and two calves are identified during an aerial survey. Calves are distinguished from yearling cows primarily on the basis of nose or face conformation (a calf has short, blunt nose). The neck on a calf appears to be shorter and heavier than that of a mature elk. A calf also has a fuzzy, rounded patch on its forehead and in general has a "puppylike" fuzzy appearance. Photo by author.

answer to elk management and, in fact, they will require the wildlife manager to gather more field data. More important, however, computers will furnish a place to store and evaluate essential data.

HARVEST MANAGEMENT AND OBJECTIVES

Elk management is the effort to maintain an optimum supply of elk for both the hunter and the nonconsumptive user. Management includes, but is not restricted

to protection, hunting regulations, grazing policies on public lands, and habitat analyses. The basic methods, however, are annual appraisals of elk herds and plans for harvesting surplus animals.

Part of herd appraisal is a careful evaluation of biological factors and physical characteristics of elk. This information is needed to determine acceptable hunting periods. Specifically, herd appraisal involves the determination of: (1) breeding, gestation, parturition and weaning periods; (2) reproductive data in terms of numbers of calves born per female, calf survival, and normal sex ratios in the prehunt and posthunt populations; and (3) the best time of year to obtain a quality animal from the standpoints of trophy, size, population protection and other criteria.

To identify an acceptable hunting period, the earliest starting and latest ending dates are projected relative to the method of hunting and the sex and age classes of elk to be harvested (Table 3). Then, within that period, a specific schedule can be established based on local environmental and elk population conditions.

Referring to the data in Table 3, it can be seen that cow elk should not be hunted prior to September 1, but bulls may be hunted as early as August 1. However, it would be better if neither sex were hunted until the peak of the rut had passed—about October 1. Strictly from a trophy criterion, bulls could be taken as late as December 31.

Once the acceptable schedule for each type of harvest has been established, a suggested framework for the various hunting seasons can be decided upon (Table 4). This will enable the wildlife manager to determine where and when seasons overlap, and whether or not hunting periods should be modified within constraints posed by the

biological and physiological data shown in Table 3.

The framework of hunting seasons shown in Table 4 is taken from Colorado elk hunting season data and serves to illustrate the effects of various constraints. In this case, the regular elk hunting season cannot open earlier than the first Saturday after October 9 because of an agreement between the Colorado Division of Wildlife and the Colorado Cattlemen's Association. Another constraint occurs during the archery season when only antlered elk are legal until September 1. After that date, any elk can be taken by bow because of the accepted fact that calves are self-sufficient by then.

Beginning dates for elk hunting seasons in various states and provinces range from about September 1 in Saskatchewan, September 10–15 in Idaho, Wyoming and Alberta, to the last week of September in Arizona. Opening dates in other states are: October 1 in Utah, October 9–16 in Colorado, October 20–25 in Montana, and as late as November 1 in Washington. Season lengths vary from six or seven days in Arizona to more than five weeks in Montana. It is difficult to give average opening or closing dates for elk hunting because there are so many variations in season lengths, permit numbers, special hunt areas and harvest objectives from one area to another. Some states, in an effort to spread out hunting pressure, have set Monday or Wednesday opening days, while others require the hunters to choose a designated period within the season in which they can hunt. The other-than-weekend opening date has been opposed by labor unions in several states. Arguing that such openings discriminate against certain working groups of people, the unions have influenced agencies to open hunting seasons on weekends despite sound management arguments favoring other-than-weekend openings.

The harvest objective is sustained yield— a concept aimed at taking surplus elk so that wintering animals will have ample resources for maintenance and growth. Most states and provinces in which elk hunting is

Table 3. Biological factors and physiological characteristics of elk needed to determine acceptable hunting seasons.

Characteristic	Date(s) or data
Breeding season	9/1 to 10/15
Gestation period	249–262 days
Parturition	5/15 to 6/15
Approximate maternal independence date	9/1
Reproductive data	Prehunt sex ratio: bulls cows calves
	35–45/100/35–65
	Posthunt sex ratio: bulls cows calves
	8–25/100/45–65
Best period for trophy	9/1 to 1/31
	Antler shed 3/1 to 4/15
Best pelage	10/1 to 12/30

Table 4. Elk hunting season framework in Colorado.

Type of season	Jan.	Feb.	Mar.	Apr.	May	June	July	Aug.	Sept.	Oct.	Nov.	Dec.
Rifle												
Early								23■7				
Regular										9■21		
Late											Late Nov. & Dec.	
Muzzle-loading rifle												
Regular									13■21			
Late											Late Nov. & Dec.	
Archery												
Regular								16■21				
Late											Late Nov. & Dec.	
Special (damage)		(As needed)										

permissible establish "bull-only" seasons for unrestricted numbers of hunters, but some set "any elk" hunts (either sex, plus calves) and no restriction as to the number of hunters.

When some control of the total harvest is needed, the usual procedure is to set a limited number of "any elk" permits. This system reduces the harvest of cows, yet allows unrestricted bull hunting. The only drawback to this system is the fact that hunters can take either an antlered or an antlerless elk on a special permit. Trying to set the number of special permits is complicated by the fact that, in some years, a majority of the hunters holding these permits take antlerless elk. By not knowing how many hunters will take an antlerless elk, proper management on the antlerless or producing portion of the herd is difficult.

As agencies move toward more scientific elk management, the "antlerless-only" permit has begun to replace the "any elk" permit. When a hunter applies for a quota-regulated antlerless elk permit, he knows he cannot take a bull; thus, more control is achieved in the harvest of a herd's female population. A final step in control of harvesting is the specified permit system used very successfully in Colorado. This system predetermines the number of antlered and antlerless elk to be harvested each year. It also specifies a desirable number of permits to be issued for hunting of each type. This system is based upon many years of experience of calculating and then evaluating hunter success using various types

of permits. In the Colorado system, for example, an average of 24 percent of the antlered elk permit holders and 75 percent of the antlerless elk permit holders take an elk (Colorado Division of Wildlife 1975).

HABITAT PROBLEMS AND IMPROVEMENT TECHNIQUES

Much of our elk habitat was created by natural processes including plant succession after fires. Man-induced activities, such as agriculture, grazing and forestry, have modified natural elk habitat. Some modifications have been favorable and others extremely unfavorable to the elk. To date, there has been little deliberate elk habitat development. Certain lands of the United States Forest Service, Bureau of Land Management and state wildlife agencies have been reserved for grazing exclusively by game animals, but this practice is not widespread, especially on federal lands. Proper timber-harvest practices and controlled burning can be used to improve elk habitat on winter ranges that are gradually becoming climax forest.

The problems of decreasing winter ranges and overgrazing of forage plants by elk are not restricted to public lands. Elk often graze on private land and damage haystacks, fences and crops at certain times of the year. This problem can be so severe that wildlife management agencies must face the choice of either eliminating the offending elk or enhancing winter home

When elk browse juniper to this extent, all forage on that particular range is scarce. Like most browse, juniper can be cropped only once, after which a new stand must provide the next forage. Here, however, even the seedlings have been eaten. Photo courtesy of the U.S. Park Service.

ranges. Land for winter ranges has been purchased throughout the western United States with funds furnished through the Pittman-Robertson Act of 1937. Land acquisition for game animals has progressed slowly, however, because of financial and political constraints. Each area purchased supports varying numbers of elk and other wildlife and will continue to do so indefinitely as long as the wildlife management agencies maintain control of these lands. In some instances, where outright purchase of land was not possible, grazing rights have been secured for elk and other big game animals. The future of elk and elk hunting may well depend on additional purchases or leases of winter ranges.

As implied previously, a primary and continuing role of wildlife managers is to adjust elk numbers to forage supplies. Elk herds that are too numerous for the available winter habitat destroy natural forage plants and frequently damage private property. A major elk management problem is that of achieving annual harvests that provide a sustaining balance between herd size and its forage supply. Appropriate harvest quotas often are difficult to attain because of opposition by public groups who misunderstand the principles of elk management, or of wildlife management in general. There is a great need for an improved public understanding of the rationale, methodology and basic objectives of big game management.

OTHER MANAGEMENT PROBLEMS

When forage supplies on elk winter ranges become depleted, public demand invariably arises for winter feeding of elk. This demand often is the basis for heated discussion and controversy. At first, winter feeding of elk would appear to be a simple solution to a simple problem. But, when all facets of the problem are considered, the problem is complex and the solution is anything but simple.

Heavy winter mortality is a symptom of a serious problem—insufficient forage for the number of elk present. It is not true that winter feeding benefits elk or their habitat. Winter feeding only serves to compound the problem by artificially holding more animals in a particular area than the carrying capacity of that area can support. Not only does a winter-feeding program adversely affect the goal of sustained yield, but it entails considerable expense without any assurance that the well-being of individual animals or an entire herd is enhanced. Winter feeding is simply a means of imposing dependence on wild animals in an unnatural setting or circumstance. As a rule, feeding programs work to the detriment of elk and their habitat. A good example is the Jackson Hole elk herd and range in Wyoming. After 65 years of expensive winter feeding, that herd is considerably smaller than when feeding began.

Large congregations of elk on feeding grounds do not result in a healthy herd. Without exception, reproduction in artificially fed herds is lower than in naturally subsisting herds. Disease and stress inevitably result from overcrowding of animals on feeding grounds.

CONCLUSION

As the American public becomes more affluent and has more time to spend for recreation, increased demand for multiple uses will be placed on western public lands where many big game animals in general, and elk in particular, spend their lives. Demand may increase to the extent that recreation will replace cattle and sheep on big game summer ranges. Summer recreation by backpackers, campers and others can force elk from favored summer home ranges to less desirable areas. In the near future, elk harvests in the back country areas of Colorado, Idaho, Montana, Wyoming and British Columbia will increase as more hunters secure access to these areas. From an elk management standpoint, there is not enough hunting at the present time in the wildest of our elk ranges. Elk management in the wilderness areas will become more and more of a problem for wildlife management agencies.

Ways to resolve conflicts of elk with grazing, forestry and agriculture need to be explored. Manipulation of timber stands to produce elk forage may improve conditions, but this may be compounded by harrassment of elk as a result of logging roads being constructed in their summer home ranges. There is little doubt that habitat acquisition will be of more value than feeding programs to the elk. The western distribution of elk cannot be increased appreciably, but more intensive management of elk and their habitat should allow maintenance of remnant populations and even a surplus to be harvested annually for recreation.

Wapiti are basically wilderness animals and should be treated as such. With sound management programs, opportunities will continue to be available to those persons wishing to hunt, observe or listen to elk in their natural habitat.

Chapter 3

MULE AND BLACK-TAILED DEER

Olof C. Wallmo

Principal Wildlife Biologist
U.S. Forest Service
Juneau, Alaska

TAXONOMY AND DISTRIBUTION

Mule deer and black-tailed deer are sufficiently different to justify distinct common names, yet similar enough to be included in one species, *Odocoileus hemionus*. It seems apparent, as has been speculated, that they are diverging genetically, but taxonomy must recognize organisms at the current stage in the evolutionary stream. As recognized today, *O. hemionus* consists of 11 subspecies (Cowan 1956a) which, together, inhabit every major vegetative type in western North America and every climatic zone except arctic and tropic (Figure 7). However, only 7 of the 11 are clearly viable subspecies (Table 5). The burro deer *(O.h. eremicus)* was rejected by Hoffmeister (1962) as being inseparable from desert mule deer *(O.h. crooki)*. The Inyo mule deer *(O.h. inyoensis)* was considered a questionable entity by I. McT. Cowan, A. S. Leopold, and W. G. Macgregor (personal communications: December 1975, October 1977 and November 1977, respectively), probably representing periodic mixing of *O.h. hemionus* and *O.h. californicus.* Tiburon Island mule deer *(O.h. sheldoni),* described by Cowan (1956a:353), is "closely similar to burro deer," based on specimens from Tiburon Island off the coast of Sonora, Mexico, 2.5 kilometers (1.5 miles) from the main body of range of *O.h. crooki.* Cedros Island

mule deer *(O.h. cerrosensis),* reportedly distinctly different in color from other coastal subspecies (Cowan 1956a), occur on Cedros Island off the west coast of Baja California, and have dwindled to near extinction (Cowan and Holloway 1978). These comments do not constitute a taxonomic revision.

The range of Rocky Mountain mule deer *(O. h. hemionus)* is larger than that of all the other subspecies combined. It occupies all of the Rocky Mountain and intermountain regions, with scattered populations extending as far east as Manitoba, Minnesota and Iowa, and as far north as southern Yukon Territory.

Wherever necessary, mule deer and blacktails are migratory, but this seasonal behavior is most conspicuous in the high ranges of the Rockies where deer may move 80 kilometers (50 miles) or more from summer to winter ranges. Snow depth, as it affects deer mobility and forage availability, is considered by some to be the dominant factor in population dynamics, particularly along the cordillera from Colorado and Utah into Alberta and British Columbia. It commonly is believed that other influences accounted for a decrease in mule deer numbers until early in this century, followed by an increase until the late 1950s and early 1960s, and a subsequent decline. Some of the possible causes are discussed later.

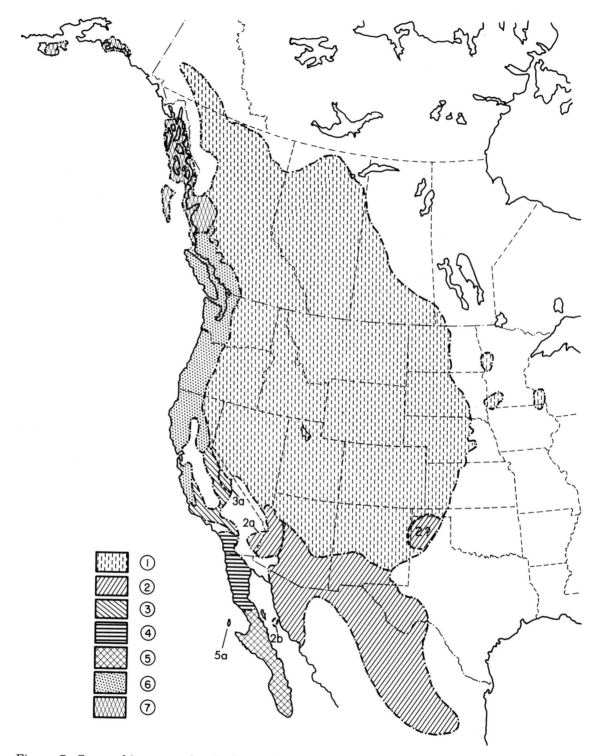

Figure 7. Geographic range of mule deer subspecies: (1) *O. h. hemionus;* (2) *O. h. crooki;* (3) *O. h. californicus;* (4) *O. h. fuliginatus;* (5) *O. h. peninsulae;* (6) *O. h. columbianus;* and (7) *O. h. sitkensis.* Current documentation was not found for *O.h. eremicus* (2a) and *O.h. sheldoni* (2b), and *O.h. inyoensis* (3a) is in doubt. *O.h. cerrosensis* (5a) is in threat of extinction.

A Rocky Mountain mule deer, approximately two years old. Photo by Don Domenick; courtesy of the Colorado Division of Wildlife.

Discontinuous populations of Rocky Mountain mule deer across the plains offer testimony to their remarkable adaptability. There, only the occasional escarpments, buttes, draws and stream bottoms provide enough forage diversity and cover to support deer. Mule deer nearly disappeared from the plains by the late 1930s, probably due to the combination of excessive hunting, several periods of severe drought complicated by overgrazing by domestic livestock, and several extremely severe winters. The deer since have reestablished themselves on the plains and are spreading eastward.

The southern subspecies—desert (*O. h. crooki*), California (*O. h. californicus*), southern (*O. h. fuliginatus*), and peninsula (*O. h. peninsulae*) mule deer—are influenced more by extended seasonal droughts than by severe winters. Abundant supplies of succulent vegetation are available for brief periods only. In Arizona, New Mexico and western Texas, these periods normally occur in late summer and winter. In California, the period normally is restricted to winter.

Vast amounts of desert and California mule deer habitat have been and continue to be lost in housing development, urban sprawl and agriculture in Arizona and California. If the assessment by Baker (1956) is correct, the desert mule deer range in Mexico may be much less extensive than indicated in Figure 7, which is based on Leopold (1959).

The range of California mule deer overlaps that of Rocky Mountain mule deer and Columbian blacktails on the north, southern mule deer on the south, and nearly reaches that of desert "mulies" (and perhaps *O. h. eremicus*) to the east. Thus, the California subspecies might be less a discrete taxonomic entity than representative of a transition in characteristics from *O. hemionus* to other subspecies. In fact, the range for California mule deer includes desert, chaparral, woodland and montane habitats used by other subspecies.

There is little evidence to suggest that individual subspecies are habitat specific. They seem to adapt readily when transplanted to ranges of other subspecies. Blacktails, which are commonly associated with temperate coniferous rain forests, also thrive in chaparral and woodland habitats of California and tundra in Alaska. Moreover,

33

Table 5. Subspecies of *Odocoileus hemionus*.

O. h. hemionus (Rafinesque)	—	Rocky Mountain mule deer
O. h. californicus (Caton)	—	California mule deer
O. h. fuliginatus (Cowan)	—	Southern mule deer
O. h. peninsulae (Lydekker)	—	Peninsula mule deer
O. h. crooki (Mearns)	—	Desert mule deer
O. h. columbianus (Richardson)	—	Columbian black-tailed deer
O. h. sitkensis (Merriam)	—	Sitka black-tailed deer

it can be misleading to associate mule deer with climax vegetation types only. In many cases, subclimax or successional stages are preferred habitat. In other cases, climax vegetation may be essential. For blacktails, from northern Vancouver Island northward, old-growth forests provide the only respite from extreme snow depths on winter range. And in many areas, regrowth on cutover areas soon becomes so dense as to preclude deer use in summer.

The northern Pacific Coast is no doubt the latest region to be reoccupied by deer since retreat of the last glacier. Sitka blacktails (*O. h. sitkensis*) occurred only to the north end of the Alexander Archipelago until transplants beginning in 1917 extended their range along the Alaskan coast to Yakutat, Prince William Sound, and Afognak and Kodiak islands. Suitable habitat has developed there during the past few hundred to few thousand years. By transplanting, man may have accelerated inevitable reoccupation of these areas.

It is easy to speculate about the factors that limit the northward extension of mule deer and blacktail range. However, ready hypotheses are not available for eastern and southern limits. Beyond those limits, whitetailed deer have exclusive domain, although they share the geographic range of mule deer from Mexico to northern Alberta. This geographic coexistence has been attributed to different habitat preferences, but the nature of those respective preferences has yet to be defined fully.

REPRODUCTION AND GROWTH

Cervids in the Northern Hemisphere breed in fall or winter and bear their young in spring and summer. Transplanted to the Southern Hemisphere, they can adapt their reproductive behavior to opposite seasonal conditions (Caughley 1971). It is hypothesized that seasonal changes in the relative length of night and day provide the stimulus to adjust the reproductive pattern. Further adjustments—probably to local habitat phenology—result in a considerable time span over which the stages of the reproductive process of *O. hemionus* occur.

Columbian and Sitka blacktails are reported to breed from September to November, peaking a month earlier than most mule deer (Brown 1961, Olson 1952, Taber and Dasmann 1958). Research indicates that Rocky Mountain mule deer tend to breed in November and December, and most fawns are born in June (Anderson and Medin 1967). Desert mule deer breed even later, primarily during December and January, and bear fawns in July and August (Lang 1957, Swank 1958, Wallmo 1962). Southern mule deer may breed as early as northern blacktails (Bischoff 1957).

It is intriguing to examine reasons for these phenological differences. In the cool rain forests of the north Pacific Coast, the early arrival of fawns avails them of the driest months—May, June and July—to develop sufficiently to withstand the wet weather that follows. In the Rocky Mountain-Intermountain region, parturition in June and early July minimizes exposure of fawns to late spring or early fall snowstorms. Desert mule deer fawns are born in mid- to late summer, after the normally prolonged spring drought, and when there is an adequate supply of forage to sustain milk production, but this would be the driest period of the year for southern mule deer. Whether or not these are significant reasons for regional variations of reproductive events, it seems reasonable to assume that such variation is not simply accidental.

Both extrinsic and intrinsic factors stimulate the complex endocrine system that manipulates various physiological processes involved in reproduction. In males, these factors are manifested in growth of antlers during spring and summer, swelling of the neck and shoulder area prior to the rut and, then, in hyperactivity, belligerence and a pronounced drop in food intake during the rut. Though it is not apparent to an observer, sexual recrudescence in females is underway several months prior to heat. At the time of ovulation, the peak of estrus or heat, does are receptive for only a short period—reportedly, a few hours to less than a day. If not bred, however, they go through additional estrus cycles, each cycle being three to four weeks in length. Males are capable of fertilizing females during the entire period that does are fertile and receptive. However, judging from the time span over which fawns are dropped, most breeding occurs in a few weeks. A Colorado study (Anderson and Medin 1967) showed that about 70 percent of breeding took place within a 20-day period. The mean length of gestation is 203 days, with individual variance of as much as 30 days (Anderson and Medin 1967, Robinette et al. 1973).

From a sample of 482 Rocky Mountain mule deer does in Utah, Robinette et al. (1955) obtained the following distribution of fetal litter sizes: no fetuses—2 percent; one fetus—37 percent; two fetuses—60 percent; and three fetuses—1 percent. Under favorable conditions, neonatal productivity may average two fawns per breeding female, but little is known of the survival of new-born fawns in the wild; the necessary observations have been too difficult to obtain.

There are few data on the birth weights of fawns in the wild. In a study by Robinette et al. (1973), the average weight of 79 pen-born male Rocky Mountain mule deer was 3.7 kilograms (8.3 pounds), and the average weight of 93 females was 3.6 kilograms (8 pounds). The average weight of nine pen-born male Columbian blacktails, reported by Cowan and Wood (1955), was 3.1 kilograms (6.85 pounds). At 135 days of age, the average weight of the mule deer fawns was 27–36 kilograms (69–80 pounds), and of blacktails 27–32 kilograms (60–70 pounds). At about this age, puberty occurs and the rate of increased growth slackens. Thereafter, the animals exhibit an annual growth cycle—increasing in weight from spring to fall and decreasing from fall to spring. A growth peak for females is reached at about two years of age, while males may continue to grow larger until their ninth or tenth years (Anderson et al. 1974).

Deer capitalize on abundant and nutritious forage for growth and weight gain in summer and fall, and minimize energy intake and expenditure in winter when energy costs are high and forage supplies poor. Anderson et al. (1972) indicated that male Rocky Mountain mule deer in northern Colorado store fat rapidly from April to October but deplete most of it by December, reaching a low weight in March. Females put on fat more slowly from June to December and also lose it more slowly than males, reaching a low weight in May (Figure 8). For all mule and black-tailed deer, the net result is an undulating growth curve (Figure 9). The phenology of the annual cycles no doubt differs somewhat from one area to another, but the patterns would be similar.

Adult mule deer doe. Courtesy of the Colorado Division of Wildlife.

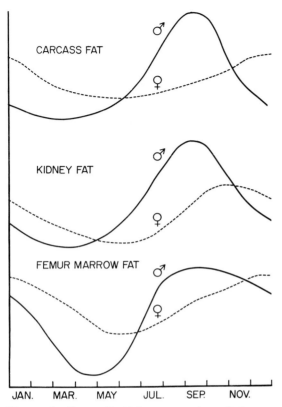

Figure 8. Generalized interpretation of the annual cycle of fat storage and depletion for mule deer in Colorado, depicted originally by Anderson et al. (1972). Vertical scale is the same for each parameter; they range from the lowest to the highest during the year.

FOOD HABITS AND SEASONAL NUTRITION

It is an oversimplification to categorize mule deer as browsers. Woody plants are neither uniquely palatable to deer nor uniquely suited to their nutritional requirements and digestive capacity. It probably is more accurate to call them "intermediate feeders," according to the classification of Hofman and Stewart (1972), because the deer adapt to a wide range of forage types and phenological conditions. The list of foods that they eat seems to be limited only by the persistence of the investigators. Kufeld et al. (1973) found at least 673 species of plants reported to have been eaten by Rocky Mountain mule deer. The inventory included only those plants for which there were estimates

of amounts consumed. Much additional information on food habits is available for California and Inyo mule deer (Leach 1956), Columbian blacktails (Brown 1961, Leach and Hiehle 1957), desert mule deer (Anderson et al. 1965, Brownlee 1971, Mc-Culloch 1973), and Rocky Mountain mule deer (Leach 1956, Neff 1974).

There are two important criteria for evaluating forages. First, they must be palatable. Second, they must be digestible

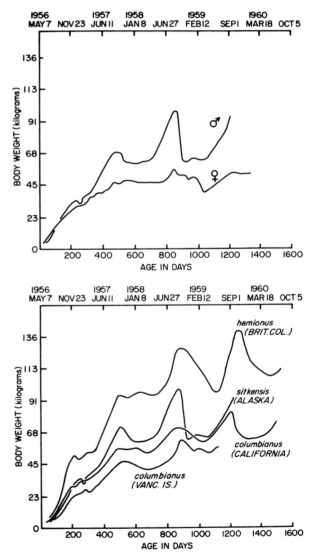

Figure 9. Growth patterns of a male and female Sitka deer (top) and males of four geographic origins (bottom), all maintained on a high nutritional plane (after Bandy et al. 1970).

by and beneficial to rumen microorganisms. Assuming a forage species is palatable—the basis of which is not well-understood—the quality of forage is determined largely by the proportion of cell contents (especially proteins and soluble carbohydrates) to cell wall, or fiber. Cell contents are digested rapidly by rumen microbes, yielding the nitrogen and chemical energy needed for their own proliferation. The by-products, microbial protein and volatile fatty acids, are the source of nitrogen and chemical energy for deer.

Cell wall material, the substance of plant fiber, is digested slowly by rumen microbes, so metabolites required by deer are yielded more slowly. Lignin, which is most abundant in woody stems, is particularly resistant to microbial digestion. It is important to recognize, however, that winter twigs of live deciduous shrubs and trees contain living cells which offer more protein and soluble carbohydrates than do dead forbs or grasses. But the latter have a lower lignin-cellulose ratio.

Under severe conditions, palatability is an expression of a deer's choice between a poor assortment of forages. Deep snow on winter ranges may require a deer to browse on forage that is relatively palatable, but metabolically inadequate. Long-term study of the food habits of mule deer in California led to the conclusion that high mortality in severe winters was associated with dependency on browse, and low mortality during mild winters was related to a more diversified diet that included green grass (Leach 1956).

On all mule deer and black-tailed deer ranges, seasonal temperature and moisture regimes regulate the annual nutrition cycle. Information on crude protein content and digestibility of seasonal diets in several regions is presented in Figure 10 and Figure 11, respectively. In the Colorado Rockies, the mule deer diet appears to be nutritionally inadequate during at least one-half of the year. The period of inadequacy is shorter in northern Arizona because spring growth begins several weeks earlier. For

Forage for these Rocky Mountain mule deer must be palatable, digestible by and beneficial to rumen microorganisms, particularly during winter stress periods. Photo by Ray C. Erickson; courtesy of the U.S. Fish and Wildlife Service.

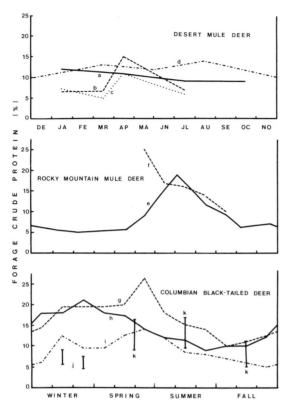

Figure 10. Seasonal levels of dietary crude protein in (a) southwestern New Mexico (Boeker et al. 1972); (b,c) central Arizona (Swank 1958); (d) central Arizona (Urness and McCulloch 1973); (e) northern Colorado (Wallmo et al. 1977); (f) northern Arizona (Urness et al. 1975); (g,h,i) western Washington, the range of nine browse species (Brown 1961); and (k) western Oregon, the range of four browse species (Hines 1973).

desert mule deer, protein may be above the assumed critical level (7 percent crude protein) throughout the year or somewhat deficient during the spring dry period. The diets of blacktails in mature chaparral in northern California may be deficient in protein from September to December, while in managed chaparral areas ("shrubland") protein intake may meet or exceed needs throughout the year.

Only recently has appropriate attention been given to energy values of deer forage. Unfortunately, estimates of the amount of energy in foods available to deer or the energy requirements of mule deer are not easily obtained. Several research institu-

tions in Canada and the United States are making progress in this area. It is hoped that these efforts will result in practical methodology for determining the potential of seasonal forage to meet seasonal energy requirements. Information now available suggests that diets of mule deer fail to meet energy requirements for body maintenance during a considerable portion of the year (Wallmo et al. 1977). Most winter browse is a conspicuous limiting factor. While the inherent seasonal reduction in metabolic rate and forage intake of mule deer is a survival adaptation, if there is an energy deficit, it must be met by tissue catabolism. Survival of mule deer, therefore, is a matter of adapting to prolonged periods of nutritional stress. But this is the situation in which they have evolved in North America.

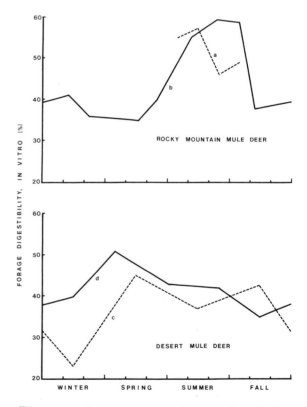

Figure 11. Seasonal levels of forage digestibility in (a) northern Arizona (Urness et al. 1975); (b) northern Colorado (Wallmo et al. 1977); (c) southwestern New Mexico (Boeker et al. 1972); and (d) central Arizona (Urness and McCulloch 1973).

Box traps constructed of wood, aluminum or nylon mesh, such as the above "Clover Trap," are used to capture deer for marking, transplanting or measuring a variety of morphological and physiological characteristics. Photo by Don Domenick; courtesy of the Colorado Division of Wildlife.

HABITAT MANAGEMENT

Each vegetational complex is dynamic and, no doubt, more suitable for deer in one stage of its annual development than in others. Habitat alterations that have been interpreted as beneficial to mule deer, including those applied specifically in deer management, are too numerous to list here. They are based generally on three axioms:

1. Early stages of plant succession are more beneficial than climax vegetation;
2. A mixture of plant communities provides better habitat than any single community; and
3. More browse is preferable to less browse.

With regard to the first axiom, fire and logging generally are considered to be favorable influences—the improvement being attributed to the abundance and diversity of forage that occurs in the secondary suc-

cession. This principle has been applied to all the forest types of the West, except the coastal temperate rain forest from northern Vancouver Island northward. The exception is due to use of the forest as winter range. Wherever forest cover is removed from local sites, snow accumulations can be excessive for deer. But, in winters when snow accumulations are relatively light, the additional food provided for 5–10 years after logging may be beneficial. Wildlife managers must guard against being misled by such temporary conditions. Permitting large deer populations to develop as a result of a series of mild winters could result in crowding the many animals in remaining old-growth forests during severe winters. High winter mortality could be expected. Moreover, the brief period of habitat enhancement in early vegetative successional stages usually is followed by a century or more of essentially unusable habitat. Outside the coastal temperate rain forest, logging and fire may improve habitat conditions for deer for one-quarter century or longer. Large burns and cutovers of the past purportedly have resulted in appreciable increases of deer populations (Brown 1961).

In principle, clearing pinyon-juniper woodland or chaparral stands also can improve mule deer habitat by increasing the abundance and diversity of forage. The most extensive improvement program in the West is being conducted on pinyon-juniper stands in Utah winter range by the Utah Division of Wildlife in cooperation with the U.S. Forest Service. The conversion of chaparral stands to "brushland" has long been advocated on blacktail range in California, and more recently has been proposed as a desirable practice for desert mule deer and Coues white-tailed deer in Arizona. Several workers, however, still question whether or not the benefits to deer from pinyon-juniper or chaparral conversion will justify the inherent costs (Clary et al. 1974, McCulloch, 1974, Terrell and Spillett 1975, Urness 1974).

In forest, woodland and chaparral, it is recommended that clearings be small and not comprise a majority of the total area. For the pinyon-juniper type in Arizona, Mc-Culloch (1974) suggested cleared areas 30–183 meters (100–600 feet) wide interspersed with uncleared strips of comparable width. He also suggested that the total cleared area amount to less than one-third of the home range of each deer, adding the qualification that adequate tree cover must be left for shelter and emergency browse during severe winters. For Arizona chaparral, it is recommended that clearings be no more than 91–122 meters (300–400 feet) wide, and total no more than 50 percent of the area (Urness 1974). To benefit black-tailed deer on California's chamise brushland, Biswell et al. (1952) prescribed scattered small clearings of about 2.2 hectares (5 acres) each, leaving at least 30 percent of the area in well-distributed dense brush.

Patch-cutting ponderosa pine to benefit mule deer in the Southwest was recommended by Patton (1974). He further recommended a maximum opening size of 18.2 hectares (45 acres), or a maximum width of 488 meters (1,600 feet). In subalpine coniferous forest, small clearcut strips 20–122 meters (66–400 feet) wide, alternating with comparable uncut strips, were found to increase deer use (Wallmo 1969) and improve forage supplies (Regelin et al. 1974). Similar conclusions were drawn for mixed-conifer habitat in northeastern Oregon, with the reservation that information concerning optimum size, shape and distribution of cutting units is incomplete (Edgerton 1972). Along the northern Pacific Coast, clearings may be beneficial during summer, but this does not compensate for their loss as winter range. Wherever populations are restricted by habitat conditions on winter range, improvement of summer range is of limited value.

In the Rocky Mountain and Intermountain regions, high mortality frequently occurs on sagebrush winter ranges. Some contend that sagebrush is a major source of sustenance for deer (Smith 1959), while others believe that its volatile oils severely limit its value as deer food (Longhurst et al. 1968, Nagy et al. 1964). Recent experiments suggest that the forage complex can be improved by partially suppressing sagebrush and encouraging the increase of herbaceous vegetation (Carpenter 1976). However, on these ranges, snow can prohibit deer from obtaining a diversified diet. Snow fences have been used experimentally in Colorado to displace snowdrifts and make available necessary forage stands that occur in the lee of ridges and gulleys (Regelin 1976).

The habitat improvement axioms seem to include the philosophy that variety of habitat conveys benefits to deer by giving them more opportunity to select the most favorable situations. With increasing habitat diversity, deer have opportunity for more beneficial forage selection. The advantages have been discussed theoretically by Freeland and Janzen (1974), Longhurst et al. (1968) and, perhaps in a more practicable sense, by Leach (1956). The principle applies logically to cover as well as to food but, at present, there exists only a rudimentary comprehension of the relationship of cover to the needs of mule deer. This is an important subject for future research.

POPULATIONS: PAST, PRESENT AND FUTURE

In rating the hooved mammals in North America, Young (1956) said deer are "the most serviceable to man in providing meat for his food, skin for his clothing, and sport for his recreation." Such serviceability may have resulted in the extinction of many other large mammals of this continent, but deer have survived splendidly.

The effect of man's activities on mule deer populations is not easily measured, though it is commonly believed that it has been significant. Seton (1937) estimated that there were about 10 million mule deer in North America at the time of the arrival of white man, and 0.5 million in 1908. Cessation of range and forest burning by Indians, overhunting and overgrazing on mule deer ranges possibly contributed to the early decline. By 1930, the U.S. Forest Service estimated 750,000 deer, including whitetails, on western national forests and, by 1965, more than 3 million (U.S. Forest Service 1930–1965). Hunting regulations, predator control, forest fires and logging (by setting back plant succession) are suggested reasons for population recoveries until the late 1950s and 1960s. Thereafter, the reversal of such influences and the increasing usurpation of habitat for human uses are blamed for a general decline of mule deer population throughout the West, giving rise to a symposium on this subject at Logan, Utah in 1976.

Unfortunately, actual effects are not supported by accurate population inventories. Rarely is it possible to document influence of one or a combination of environmental pressures on populations. As pressures on mule deer populations and habitat increase, more and better data are needed. It has been projected that urbanization and related uses of the land in the 48 contiguous states of the United States will increase 35 percent from 1969–1984 (Bormann 1976). Non-

urban uses may increase even more. From 1960–1974, the acreage in highway rights-of-way in Colorado increased about 43 percent and, in 1973, the area in platted mountain home developments totaled nearly 283,290 hectares (700,000 acres) (Wallmo et al. 1976). In 1974, in seven of the western United States, more than 18,000 mule deer and black-tailed deer were reported to have been killed in collision with automobiles (Wallmo et al. 1977). The current rush to utilize coal, oil shale and uranium deposits in the West portends continuing reductions in the amount and quality of deer habitat.

To determine equitable compensation for habitat losses, some advocate that wildlife values be translated into the language of industry—dollars. Certainly, mule deer have significant economic value. During the past decade, nearly 2 million hunters annually harvested more than 0.5 million mule and black-tailed deer. Dressed carcasses amounted to something on the order of 22.5 million kilograms (50 million pounds) of meat. Based on estimates from numerous economic surveys, the money spent on goods and services incidental to this hunting constituted a yearly "flow" of perhaps $500 million in the United States and western Canada. Such data can be used to obtain dollar values for harvested deer and for the productivity of deer habitat, but they cannot account for the personal value of experiences derived from wildland and deer.

For at least the near future, man apparently can be expected to continue depleting natural resources in the effort to sustain his own interminable growth. Consequently, wildlife management will be conducted on an ever-decreasing land base. Each hectare of mule deer range that is lost to the encroachment of human populations represents an erosion of the very qualities that attract such movement in the first place. The effectiveness of mule deer management in the future will be determined by the extent to which society comes to understand and appreciate the delicate relationship between the deer and dwindling habitat.

Chapter 4

WHITE-TAILED DEER

Lowell K. Halls

Project Leader
Southern Forest Experiment Station
U.S. Forest Service
Nacogdoches, Texas

The white-tailed deer (*Odocoileus virginianus* Rafinesque) is the most popular big game animal in North America. It thrives in a wide range of climatic and habitat conditions, withstanding adversity and quickly adapting to changes. It reproduces rapidly, its antlers are highly prized trophies, and its elusiveness challenges even the most experienced hunters.

For centuries, the whitetail has played a significant role in man's existence. To the Indian, it was a prime source of food and clothing. Antlers were used as ornaments, chipping tools, headdresses and awls; sinews were used for bow strings, fishing lines and thread; brains were used for tanning and bleaching (Calhoun and Loomis 1974). To the early settler, the deer was a ready source of income, food and clothing. Today, the whitetail is primarily an object of recreation. In 1974, more than 8 million hunters in the United States harvested 2 million whitetails (Wilcox 1976).

Yet, in overall perspective, the whitetail is more than an object of the hunt. It is a factor in the nation's economy—money generated by deer hunting extends into the billions of dollars annually. It is a source of food for human consumption—70.9 million pounds of boneless, edible meat were contributed by harvested whitetails in 1975 (Wilcox 1976). It is aesthetically appealing—many regard it as a symbol of the outdoors, a portrait of serenity in the woods. No wildlife species exceeds the whitetail in long-time influence on the entire field of conservation. Hunting laws have been enacted, conservation policies promulgated, wildlife restoration begun, and public attitudes toward environmental issues swayed by ecological principles developed in the long history of whitetail management.

TAXONOMY AND DISTRIBUTION

The white-tailed deer is a member of the Artiodactyla order, the Ruminantia suborder, the Cervidae family, and the Odocoileinae subfamily (Baker, In press). It inhabits every state in the United States, with the possible exceptions of Alaska and Utah. The northward range extends into all southern provinces of Canada from Nova Scotia to British Columbia and into the Northwest Territories. To the south, its range extends through Mexico and Central America into South America as far as 15 degrees south latitude. Thirty subspecies (races) are recognized in North and Central America (Figure 12) and eight in South America (Figure 13).

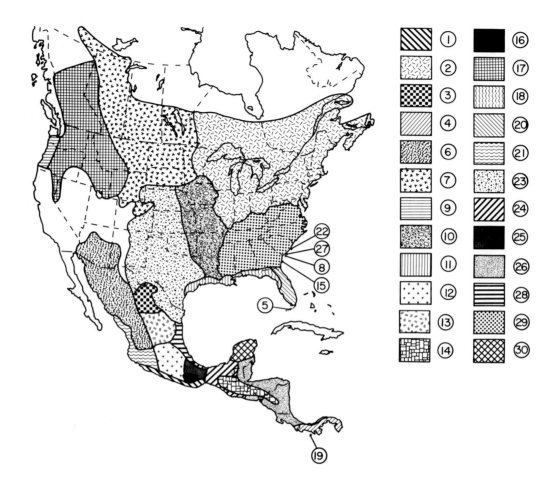

Figure 12. Distribution of white-tailed deer subspecies in North and Central America.

1. *O. v. acapulcensis* (Acapulco)
2. *O. v. borealis* (Northern woodland)
3. *O. v. carminis* (Carmen Mountains)
4. *O. v. chiriquensis* (Chiriqui)
5. *O. v. clavium* (Florida Key)
6. *O. v. couesi* (Coues, Arizona or Fantail)
7. *O. v. dacotensis* (Dakota)
8. *O. v. hiltonensis* (Hilton Head Island)
9. *O. v. leucurus* (Columbian)
10. *O. v. macrourus* (Kansas)
11. *O. v. meilhennyi* (Avery Island)
12. *O. v. mexicanus* (Mexican Tableland)
13. *O. v. miquihuanensis* (Miquihuana)
14. *O. v. nelsoni* (Chiapas)
15. *O. v. nigribarbis* (Blackbeard Island)

16. *O. v. oaxacensis* (Oaxaca)
17. *O. v. ochrourus* (Northwest)
18. *O. v. osceola* (Florida Coastal)
19. *O. v. rothschildi* (Coiba Island)
20. *O. v. seminolus* (Florida)
21. *O. v. sinaloae* (Sinaloa)
22. *O. v. tareinsulae* (Bulls Island)
23. *O. v. texanus* (Texas)
24. *O. v. thomasi* (Mexican Lowland)
25. *O. v. toltecus* (Rain Forest)
26. *O. v. truei* (Nicaragua)
27. *O. v. venatorius* (Hunting Island)
28. *O. v. veraecrucis* (Northern Veracruz)
29. *O. v. virginianus* (Virginia)
30. *O. v. yucatanensis* (Yucatan)

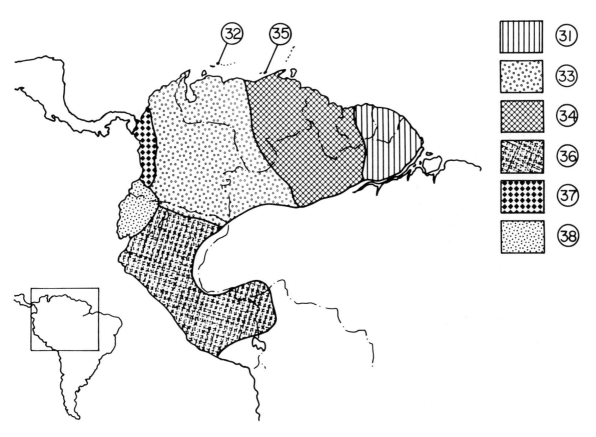

Figure 13. Distribution of white-tailed deer subspecies in South America (Whitehead 1972).

31. *O. v. cariacou*
32. *O. v. curassavicus*
33. *O. v. guodotii*
34. *O. v. gymnotis*

35. *O. v. margaritae*
36. *O. v. peruvianus*
37. *O. v. tropicalis*
38. *O. v. ustus*

The classification into subspecies is somewhat confusing because of integration among subspecies, instability of characteristics and widespread transplanting of subspecies into geographical ranges belonging to others. For example, introductions of deer from Texas, Wisconsin and North Carolina have completely clouded the taxonomic picture of whitetails in Florida (Harlow and Jones 1965). There are, however, visibly distinct differences between widely separated subspecies. Generally, the larger forms are found in the North and the smaller in the South. In South America, the whitetail is commonly referred to as "Venado," and previously was considered a separate species, *Odocoileus cariacou* (Whitehead 1972).

DESCRIPTION

Collectively, several physical features distinguish the white-tailed deer. At birth, male fawns from northern subspecies usually weigh 3.2–3.6 kilograms (7–8 pounds). Fawns from southern subspecies weigh considerably less. The higher the nutritional level of does, the larger the fawns are at birth and the faster they grow while nursing. The weight of fawns may double in the first 15 days and quadruple in 30–40 days. Skeletal growth is most rapid during the first seven months, followed by a fairly rapid growth the next summer. Gains in weight follow the same pattern.

Body weight continues to increase slightly until 5.5 or 6.5 years of age, and at full maturity males in the northern United States and southern Canada generally weigh 90–135 kilograms (200–300 pounds), and females 25–40 percent less. The Coiba Island and Florida Key deer may weigh 22.5 kilograms (50 pounds) or less. Variable body weights within subspecies are mainly a reflection of nutrition. For example, deer in Llano County, Texas were approximately 30 percent smaller than deer of the same subspecies in the Rio Grande Plain (Teer et al. 1965). In fertile bottomland-hardwood forests of Louisiana, 2.5-year old bucks weighed 23 kilograms (51 pounds) more than bucks of the same age in the less fertile upland forest (Short et al. 1969).

Body height and length correspond in general with weight. These measurements range from approximately 102 centimeters (40 inches) in height and 242 centimeters (95 inches) in length for the northern subspecies to 61 centimeters (24 inches) in height and 122 centimeters (48 inches) in length for Central American subspecies.

At birth, the rust-colored fawn is white spotted and remains so until the first shedding, three to four months later. Yearlings and adults change pelage twice annually. In spring, May–June, the winter coat is shed and replaced by reddish-brown hair. In fall, September–October, winter hair grows up through the summer hair to form a gray or grayish-brown coat. The air trapped inside the hair acts as a layer of insulation in winter. Sickly animals may shed late, and fawns shed later than adults.

Underparts are white, such as the lower surface of the tail, chin and throat. So, too, are the band around the muzzle and the ring around the eyes. The upper body of tropical whitetail subspecies may be vividly colored, ranging from tawny to orange-cinnamon.

The distinctive tail of the adult is about 28 centimeters (11 inches) long, broad at the

Female (doe) white-tailed deer. Photo by James D. Yoakum.

Figure 14. Comparison of antlers and facial characteristics, rump patches, tails and metatarsal glands in white-tailed deer (top), black-tailed deer (center) and mule deer (bottom).

base and brown above, with a prominent white fringe (Figure 14). In some subspecies, there may be dusky areas on top of the tail. When the whitetail is in flight, its tail is raised and moves from side-to-side with each bound. Melanism and albinism are rare, but mottled or white deer are seen occasionally.

Antlers develop from two permanent stumps of bone generally referred to as pedicels. Buck fawns have small bumps (buttons) on their brow the first year and spikes or branched antlers each year thereafter. A typical antler is one main beam that arises from the brow, curves slightly backward, then out and forward. Unbranched tines arise from the beam.

Antlers are borne by bucks (rarely by does) usually from April through February. Antler growth is initiated by the pituitary gland, which is stimulated by increasing hours of daylight. The growing antler is covered with "velvet," a membrane containing small blood vessels which supply nutrients to the bony structure. As the "rack" attains full size in August and September, the male hormone testosterone is released into the bloodstream and inhibits further antler development. The blood supply to the antlers is cut off, the velvet dries up and is shed. Velvet shedding is accelerated when bucks rub their antlers against trees, posts and brush. During the rut, the antler is a hard polished bone with sharp tines. As long as testosterone is pumped into the bloodstream the antlers remain fixed, but when production of this hormone decreases in winter, the antler base dissolves and racks are broken or fall off (Calhoun and Loomis 1974).

Older bucks shed antlers before young bucks do. Immature or unhealthy bucks may not shed their antlers until March or April. In South America, the cycle of antler growth is irregular (Brokx, In press). Bucks in velvet may be seen at almost any time of year. This is caused by seasonal temperature variations and the consequent irregular breeding season.

Antler size and shape is a reflection of age, heredity and nutrition (Davis 1973, Calhoun

Whitetail buck with typical, symmetrical antlers. Photo by E. P. Haddon; courtesy of U.S. Department of Interior.

and Loomis 1974). Yearling bucks that are nourished adequately will grow antlers with four to eight tines. Undernourished bucks are likely to produce a single unbranched antler (spike) or a poorly formed antler. Antler growth is influenced by nutrition at any age, but proper nutrition is most important in young deer because body growth takes precedence over antler growth. Antlers usually reach their maximum size when the bucks are about five years old. Thereafter, new antlers may lack symmetry, develop many small tines, or become malformed in some other way. Northern subspecies carry larger antlers with more numerous tines than those of smaller subspecies. In any locality, whitetail bucks that attain the greatest body size tend to develop the largest antlers.

Whitetails have four sets of external glands (Taylor 1956). Interdigital glands are located in the split of all four hooves. This gland secretes a musky-smelling, waxy substance. The metatarsal gland is located on the outside of the hind leg above the hoof and is ringed with white hairs. In whitetails from southern Mexico to South America, the size and features of the metatarsal gland are poorly defined. The tarsal gland is located inside the rear leg at the hock. Both sexes of deer, including fawns, deliberately urinate on the tarsal gland tufts. The preorbital glands, located in the corner of each eye, secrete a cleanser for the eyes.

The dental formula for whitetails is: incisors 0/3, canines 0/1, premolars 3/3, molars $3/3 \times 2 = 32$.

HISTORY AND CURRENT STATUS

The history of white-tailed deer in the United States is one of near tragedy and triumph (Trefethen 1975). When settlers first came to North America the whitetail, although it was not necessarily abundant, occupied a wide geographical range. During the period of land clearing and forest exploitation, forage supplies became plentiful and deer numbers increased proportionately. But, with repeated burning of cutover forests, market hunting, agricultural development and a lack of game laws, the whitetail experienced difficult times. By the end of the Nineteenth Century, whitetail populations were at their lowest number in recorded history, totaling less than 500,000 animals. Remnant herds remained only in protected and isolated habitats. Some of the first efforts to restore whitetail populations were successful, but most were not. Since the 1930s, and especially since World War II, the whitetail has made a remarkable comeback. Principally as a result of forest rejuvenation, better law enforcement, public awareness and support, and successful stockings into previously occupied habitats, the deer have increased steadily throughout most of their range. Today's white-tailed deer population in the United States numbers approximately 12 million (Wilcox 1976), more than ever recorded.

In Mexico and Central America, the whitetail has played an important part in cultural development (Mendez, In press).

Deer have served as a major source of protein for people, as well as supplying bones used in various forms as tools. In 1958, whitetails were common in remote mountain districts of Mexico but had largely disappeared from lowlands of northern Mexico, primarily because of restricted habitat, unrestricted hunting and public indifference. Today, deer still are found in Mexico and Central America. They are common in some areas but practically eliminated in others.

In Canada, white-tailed deer originally occurred in the most southern parts of a few provinces (Passmore 1970). During the early exploration period, there were no deer in Nova Scotia and only a few in New Brunswick. Whitetails were found in the southern regions of Quebec, Ontario and southcentral Manitoba. Most of the other Prairie Provinces were populated by mule deer only. Because of forest cutting and burning and curtailment of prairie fires, white-tailed deer extended their range northward, in some cases into the Northwest Territories. To a large extent, whitetails in Canada are living in marginal habitat. Thus, severe winters are apt to cause marked declines in population levels throughout most of the currently occupied range.

Transplanting of whitetails abroad has met with varying degrees of success (Baker, In press). Whitetails released in the British Isles have fared poorly. In Czechoslovakia, a sizable herd has grown from an 1852 transplant of two males and four females. Whitetails have survived and expanded greatly in Finland. Recent introductions are doing well in Yugoslavia. Probably the most notable stocking success has been on South Island and Stewart Island of New Zealand. The present status of whitetails released in Cuba, Curacao and other Caribbean islands is unclear.

LIFE HISTORY

North American whitetails mate in the fall. The peak of the breeding season (the rut) is usually in November, but depending on climate, nutrition and latitude, it may occur from October to January. Inadequate nutrition can cause a late and irregular rut, and prevent mating of animals in poor health (Verme 1969). In South America, the rut varies according to locality; fawns are born throughout the year (Brokx, In press).

The doe is in heat (estrus) for approximately 24 hours, and if not serviced or if she fails to conceive, she will come into heat once or twice again at 28-day intervals. A buck may follow a doe for two or three days before the heat period, and then accompany her for three or four days after mating. Thus, a buck is not likely to service more than three or four does during a 28-day period.

Fawns are born after a gestation period of approximately 202 days, but gestation can range from 195–212 days. Most fawns are dropped in late May or June.

At birth, the ratio of males to females is approximately 1:1. There is some evidence that more males are produced when mature females are undernourished, whereas well-fed and well-nourished does are likely to produce more female than male fawns (Verme 1969).

Does can breed when six to seven months old, but most breed for the first time at 1.5 years of age. The initial breeding age largely depends on health. Bucks are about 1.5 years old at the time of their first participation in the rut.

Rust-colored and white-spotted fawn will remain hidden for most of its first few months. Photo by Marvin Lee; courtesy of U.S. Department of Interior.

Life expectancy of white-tailed deer varies widely across North America. Hunting pressure and habitat conditions are the major determining variables. There are records of whitetails living more than 20 years, but few live more than 10. In hunted herds, only a small percentage of the harvested bucks are older than 4.5 years. In Illinois, for example, the life expectancy was 2.5 years (Calhoun and Loomis 1974). In Pennsylvania, the average age was two years for males and three years for females (Forbes et al. 1971). Only 3 percent of males and 20 percent of females reached an age of 4.5 years.

BEHAVIOR

The first few days following birth, fawns seldom move more than 1–2 meters (3.3–6.6 feet), mostly remaining isolated and bedded. Dams seek out their fawns to nurse and groom a few times during the day. During their first few months, fawns do not wander far and usually remain hidden. As they grow older, fawns accompany their mothers for gradually longer distances and periods of time. By fall, mother and fawn are nearly always together. In Illinois, 74 percent was the average frequency of association for a doe and her fawns from autumn until the next fawning season (Hawkins and Klimstra 1970).

Daily movements of adults are associated closely with feeding routines. Deer feed most actively early in the morning and during the evening. Unhunted bucks are apt to feed for short periods during midday. Deer occasionally feed at night, especially when food is in short supply or hunting pressure is heavy. In daily search of food, deer may travel several kilometers within their normal home range. In Florida, the maximum distance traveled by deer during a 24-hour period was 2.4 kilometers (1.5 miles) (Jeter and Marchinton 1967). In Georgia, the average distance traveled was 2.5 kilometers (1.55 miles) (Marchinton and Jeter 1967). Deer may move beyond their home range in search of food, but they usually return.

In the South and wherever winters are not severe, deer remain on their home range. In Florida and Alabama studies, the minimum home range varied from 59.5–98.3 hectares (147–243 acres) (Marchinton and Jeter 1967, Byford 1971); in Texas, 24.3–137.6 hectares (60–340 acres) for does and 97.1–356.1 hectares (240–880 acres) for bucks (Thomas et al. 1964); in Missouri, about 65 hectares (160 acres) (Progulske and Baskett 1958); and in South Dakota, about 259 hectares (640 acres) (Richardson and Petersen 1974). Summer ranges for deer in Minnesota ranged in size from 70.8–190.2 hectares (175–470 acres) (Rongstad and Tester 1969); and in New York, they averaged 202.4 hectares (500 acres). Food scarcity tends to increase the size of the home range.

In the North, there is a fall movement to winter range in response to snow depth and cold weather. Distances traveled depend on severity of weather, adequacy of shelter and availability of food, but the usual distance is 16.1–32.2 kilometers (10–20 miles). They seek shelter and concentrate in "yards" that may hold anywhere from a few deer to hundreds. The yarding period usually occurs from late December to mid-April, and deer generally remain within a radius of 0.4 kilometer (0.25 mile) of coniferous cover. In Minnesota, winter home ranges varied from 161.9–485.6 hectares (400–1,200 acres) and decreased with increasing snow depths (Rongstad and Tester 1969). Travel within yards is influenced primarily by the arrangement of stands offering either food or cover. Daily activity is modified by weather and snow conditions. The spring return of deer to summer range coincides with weather conditions and availability of green food in March and April.

Home range familiarity can be conveyed from one generation to another as long as food remains available (Byford 1971). Deer enlarge their ranges or leave them at times because of hunting or other disturbances. For example, deer chased by dogs may leave their home range, but usually return within a few hours or days (Marchinton et al. 1971).

Where deer are transplanted into new territory they usually stay within 1.6–3.2 kilometers (1–2 miles) of the point of release. In southern Texas, the average movement of live-trapped deer was 2.0 kilometers (1.4 miles) (Ellisor 1969). In Illinois, 68 percent of transplanted deer later were killed within 3.2 kilometers (2 miles) of the release area (Hawkins and Montgomery 1969). Occasionally, deer move long distances when released. In Indiana, some adults were found 24.1 kilometers (15 miles) and fawns 9.7 kilometers (6 miles) from the release site (Hamilton 1962).

Individual and group behavior

The most common family group is an adult doe, her female yearling and two fawns (Hawkins and Klimstra 1970). Leadership is matriarchal. At fawning, adult does separate socially and spatially from all other deer. Yearling siblings usually stay together during the summer and break up during October and November. Yearling does often regroup with their mothers after fawning season, and they remain together until the next fawning season. Yearling bucks seldom regroup with their mothers but may group with other bucks during winter and spring. Adult bucks are gregarious from February through August, usually in groups of two to four. During the rut, adult bucks tend to stay alone when not chasing does. In winter and spring, deer of both sexes and all ages are intermingled. They may form social groups which are more or less together, but are not necessarily families. Yearling bucks may migrate to nearby ranges, wander out and return to original range, or remain sedentary. Bucks usually become permanent residents of areas established as yearlings.

During the rut, does and bucks exhibit distinctive behavioral patterns associated with "rubs" and "scrapes" (Moore and Marchinton 1974). With the hardening of antlers

and at the beginning of velvet-shedding and neck-swelling, bucks vigorously rub small trees, presumably to remove the velvet and, perhaps, to practice combat. Rubs also may serve as visual expressions of dominance and as olfactory signposts. Scents from the rubs can be detected for several days. Rubs usually are made when a dominant buck encounters other males. There may be several rubs within the range of a mature buck, and he may return to them in successive years. Combat is common among dominant bucks during rutting but not against subordinate bucks that may occupy the same area. Rubbing is most intense prior to the peak of the breeding season.

Scrapes are formed by the buck pawing a 0.1–0.2 square meter (1–2 square foot) area on the ground and then urinating either in or behind the scraped area. The buck may urinate on the tarsal glands to produce a very pungent odor, and then lick the same area. The scrapes are made in conspicuous places and usually within areas where there are many rubs. Bucks may return to the scrapes, rework them and physically defend them against other bucks. Does frequently approach the scrapes and urinate in them and, thus, establish contact with a buck to increase the probability of mating.

A buck may defend an area immediately surrounding a doe in heat by rubbing and with sneezelike sounds. Combat may result when a dominant buck accompanies a doe out of his own area of dominance.

Communication

Whitetails communicate by sight, sound and scent (Taylor 1956). A mother's voice conveys some meaning to her fawn at birth. She may call softly to locate it. The fawn may vocally express fear or discontent, and bleats to attract attention. The sense of smell enables the dam and fawn to recognize each other.

A buck trailing a doe in the fall often gives a short, repeated "bla," "ma" or "ba" sound. When with females in estrus, dominant bucks may produce a rapid sneezelike sound towards the other bucks that try to approach the doe. This action often is accompanied by antler rubbing or a threat display.

When startled, adults alert other deer within hearing to possible danger by a loud "blow" or "snort." When in pain or accosted by a predator, the doe often bawls loudly like a calf in pain.

Whitetails soon learn to ignore common recurring sounds such as distant cars, tractors and whistles, but any new or unnatural sound is cause for alarm. The deer quickly detects sounds, but often is perplexed by the direction from which it comes.

Odors are an important means of communication. Whenever excited by fear or hostility, the deer elevates the tuft of hair on the tarsal gland so that it stands out at right angles and emits a penetrating odor of musk. Does discharge a scent to warn fawns, and bucks are especially odiferous when in the rut.

The fawn leaves an individual odor by urinating down the inside of its hind legs so that the fluid saturates the hairs of the tarsal gland. Increased frequency of urination by a doe is an early indication of approaching estrus. In the presence of a buck, the doe may urinate every one or two minutes.

The interdigital glands actively secrete at all seasons and scent the animal's tracks, enabling deer to find one another or to retrace their steps.

PRODUCTIVITY

Potential productivity is the rate at which a species can increase if no deaths occur. Theoretically, one mature whitetail buck and one doe could increase to 22 animals in 5 years and to 189 in 10 years. Rarely, however, does a herd in the wild approach this potential.

Net productivity is the actual yearly rate of increase after mortality from all causes, except legal hunting, has been deducted. Net productivity should run between 20–35 percent of the population in a designated

area or about one-half of potential productivity. In Texas, the net productivity ranged from 12–44 percent over a period of eight years (Teer et al. 1965).

Productivity is related to age of the female. In most cases, only a small percent of female fawns breed but, in some cases, they contribute substantially to herd increases. In Nova Scotia, 15 percent of fawns bred (Patton 1976a); in North Carolina, 37.5 percent (Chiavetta 1958); and in Illinois, 41 percent (Roseberry and Klimstra 1970). On a good range in Pennsylvania, approximately one-third of female fawns bred at six months of age (Forbes et al. 1971). In Iowa, as much as 82 percent of fawns have bred (Kirkpatrick 1975). Usually a fawn that produces has only one offspring the first year. In the 2.5–7.5 year old classes, most does give birth to two or more fawns annually. Twin fawns are the rule and triplets occasionally occur. On good ranges in Texas, fully mature adults produced 65 percent twins, 3 percent triplets and 32 percent singles (Teer 1963). In Nova Scotia, 85 percent of adult does bred annually (Patton 1976a). They produced 59 percent twins, 5 percent triplets and 21 percent singles. Beyond 7.5 years, the annual number of fawns per doe declines.

The female's ability to produce healthy fawns is substantially affected by nutrition (Verme 1963, 1965a). Stillbirths, fetus resorptions and postnatal deaths increase when does are poorly nourished. Digestible energy intakes one or two months prior to breeding seem to regulate ovulation rates. Deficiency of energy or protein during the latter one-half to one-third of pregnancy lessens the chance of fawn survival. Reduced productivity usually is in proportion to the severity of nutritional stress, and the reproductive process of young does is more sensitive to nutritional deficiencies than that of mature does.

Production of fawns is fairly sensitive to differences in habitat quality. In Kentucky, natality rates dropped 47 percent as the range became overpopulated (Dechert 1968). In Pennsylvania, there was an average of

1.8 fawns per doe on good range, but 1.2 fawns or fewer per doe on poor range (Forbes 1963). Therefore, on good range, there was 50 percent greater production per doe than on poor range. The capacity of a deer herd to increase is governed by the number of fawns which survive the first winter. And the ability of fawns to live through the winter is dependent primarily on the availability of an adequate food supply.

MORTALITY FACTORS

The main causes of death—excluding legal hunting—are predation, automobile accidents, diseases, parasites, starvation, crippling from gunshot and arrow wounds, getting caught in fences, poaching and old age.

Predation

The extent of kill or harassment by predators varies by location. Wild dogs are a serious menace. In Pennsylvania alone, they kill an estimated 500–1,000 deer annually (Forbes et al. 1971). Dogs are most perilous to young fawns, to pregnant does immediately prior to fawning, and to heavily parasitized and undernourished animals. They are especially dangerous to deer in the North when snow is deep or crusted. In some areas, however, hunting with dogs is not considered a limiting factor in deer populations (Marchinton et al. 1971). When coyotes are numerous, they readily prey on fawns. In an unhunted deer herd in south Texas, 82 percent of fawn mortality was attributed to coyotes (Barron and Harwell 1973). Bobcats occasionally kill fawns. Lions and bears rarely are prevalent enough to be significant predators. However, in Ontario, wolves reportedly killed 9–11 percent of the deer herd during a five-month winter period (Kolenosky 1972). Foxes, eagles and ravens seldom kill fawns.

In some cases, predators serve a useful purpose by removing inferior animals and by acting as a natural population control. Bounty hunting to control predators generally is considered to be biologically and economically unsound.

Automobile accidents

Automobiles are a major threat to deer, particularly along well-traveled highways. Nearly 22,000 deer are killed annually by motor vehicles in Pennsylvania, at a cost to motorists of about $5.2 million (Forbes et al. 1971). In Vermont, 1,765 deer were killed by motor vehicles in 1963 (Day 1964); in Iowa, 2,635 during 1974 (Gladfelter 1975); and in Nova Scotia, 455 out of 715 deer deaths were attributed to roadkills (Patton 1976b). Most kills occur during the rutting season and in spring, at sunrise and two hours after sunset, and on weekends (Allen and McCullough 1976).

Diseases

Infectious viral diseases are potentially devastating to deer, particularly the acute epizootic hemorrhagic disease (EHD), sometimes diagnosed as "bluetongue" (Trainer and Karstad 1971). The mode of transmitting the disease is unknown, and there is no effective treatment or control. Its occurrence and identification were reported first by Shope (1967). Outbreaks, resulting in many deaths, can occur annually in southeastern states and periodically in most other states and Canada. Usually, the disease is associated with high deer densities. It commonly occurs in late summer and early fall, and ceases after the first frost.

Deer are vulnerable to many bacterial diseases such as anthrax, enterotoxemia, brucellosis, leptospirosis and salmonellosis. Anthrax has the greatest potential for reaching epizootic proportions in the Southeast since it is most prevalent in areas that periodically flood (Hayes and Prestwood 1969). Enterotoxemia is associated with the sudden availability of a high protein or high carbohydrate diet following a maintenance ration. It may produce deaths when deer move from native forage to heavily fertilized pastures (Runge and

Wobeser 1975). Leptospirosis and brucellosis also occur in deer, but to a lesser extent. In Texas, salmonellosis reportedly may be a serious cause of fawn mortality; and theileriasis, a hemoprotozoan disease, may be expected to cause or contribute to large scale deer losses where extreme weight loss occurs (Marburger et al. 1971).

Fungal infections usually occur as secondary invaders to other diseases. Actinomycosis, or "lumpy jaw," probably is the most prevalent of the fungal infections.

Parasites

Internal parasites can cause significant mortality. Several types of stomach worms are widespread in deer and can be deadly when deer populations exceed habitat carrying capacity (Kellogg 1976). The meningeal worm, *Parelaphostrongylus tenuis,* is widespread and found in many deer when populations are high. Infection rates were 100 percent for deer in dense populations in Maine (Behrend and Witter 1968), and 70–80 percent in West Virginia (Dudak et al. 1966). Normally, the meningeal worm does not cause neurologic disturbances except in unusual hosts, namely, moose, pronghorn, elk and mountain sheep. Other deer parasites include liver flukes, tapeworms, lungworms, muscle worms, nasal bots and coccida.

Infections of some parasites, such as the stomach worms, vary with deer densities and can indicate habitat carrying capacities and nutritional status of herds. As deer numbers increase, more immature parasites are deposited on the ground in droppings and are available to infect more deer. As deer numbers increase above carrying capacity, food shortages occur and deer weaken, allowing internal parasites to dominate and eventually kill.

The most common external parasites are ticks, lice, mites and flies. External parasites are mainly nuisances and seldom cause death by themselves. However, they can reduce vitality and seriously affect health and productivity of deer under stress conditions. Also, they can transmit certain diseases that can cause problems. For example, the cattle fever tick, *Boophilus annulatus,* can live on white-tailed deer. It is a carrier of piroplasmosis which is a deadly blood disease of cattle.

Starvation and weather

Either starvation or inadequate nutrition may cause death at any age, but young deer are most likely to die. In south Texas, 16 percent of a fawn crop died as a result of starvation and disease (Cook et al. 1971). Also in Texas, starvation was the main factor in a 16 percent natural mortality of deer over a six-year period (Teer et al. 1965). In northern climates, the competition for food within yards is intense and, if crowded conditions persist over a prolonged period, high losses occur, particularly among fawns and old deer (Severinghaus 1972).

Except in extreme northern habitats, weather alone rarely is a debilitating factor to deer. However, when associated with poor nutrition, it causes moderate to heavy mortality and a decrease in productivity. In New York, when the accumulated snow level was 38.1 centimeters (15 inches) or more for 40 days, fawns began to die (Severinghaus 1975). And after a 50.8-centimeter (20 inch) snow depth existed for about 60 days, adult deer began to die. The extent of mortality can be predicted from an index which includes a windchill and snow-hazard rating (Verme 1968).

Other factors

Deer attempting to cross a fence may become entangled in the wire and remain until death, or become crippled during extrication and later die as a result of these injuries. It is difficult to estimate the number of these deaths, but it may be as much as 5 percent of total mortality.

A variety of insignificant tumors have been reported for deer. Toxic substances such as arsenite, chlorinated hydrocarbons

Entanglement in fences is one cause of accidental mortality. A Wildlife Management Institute photo.

and petroleum products may be serious in some places.

Poisonous plants may contribute to deer mortality since the flora of virtually all white-tailed deer habitat includes one or more species of them. Deer eat many of the plants containing toxic substances, but there are no confirmed reports of poisoning.

Pesticide residues often are found in deer tissue but usually at levels below the maximum tolerance limits established by the Food and Drug Administration (Barrier et al. 1971, Cotton and Herring 1971).

It is impossible to get an accurate count of deer killed by poaching or of wounding losses by legal hunting. However, in some areas, illegally killed deer may equal or exceed the legal kill (Richardson and Peterson 1974). Researchers in Maine estimated wounding loss alone at 8 percent (Banasiak 1961).

In hunted populations, bucks seldom die of old age. But any deer, male or female, be-

comes increasingly susceptible to debilitating factors after 8.5 years of age. Congenital and genetic abnormalities are rare in whitetails and exert little influence on populations.

HABITAT NEEDS AND PREFERENCES

Food

Immediately after birth, the fawn exists entirely on its mother's milk. The change to other foods is gradual. When two or three weeks old, fawns begin to forage, and at about one month they manage to eat hard foods such as acorns and seedy fruits. By September, many fawns are on full forage and fruit diets, and by October or November, most no longer nurse.

Daily dry matter consumption by deer is approximately 2–4 percent of live body weight but varies seasonally. For mature bucks, daily consumption of air dry feed (2.0–2.9 kilograms: 4.4–6.4 pounds) is greatest during spring. It falls off during summer and then increases again after velvet is shed from the antlers. Bucks lose weight during the rut, but normally without harmful effects. During the winter, they eat about one-half the normal amount eaten in spring and summer (Forbes 1963). They may lose 15–30 percent of their body weight in fall and winter, even when ample food is available (Long and Cowan 1964).

Does have their highest food intake in the fall prior to the breeding season. Food consumption drops slightly during winter then slowly increases in spring, and reaches a peak in early fall. The decrease in food consumption and corresponding weight loss in winter seems to be associated with physiological changes which occur in sexually mature deer during the breeding season (Long and Cowan 1964).

Food consumption in sexually immature deer increases as body weight increases, without regard to the season of the year (Long et al. 1965).

Nutrient requirements of deer vary with age class, reproduction cycle and weather.

Several studies have established nutritional levels that can be used as general guidelines in management (French et al. 1956, McEwen et al. 1957, Ullrey et al. 1970 and 1971, Verme 1963 and 1969).

Young growing deer require high levels of crude protein (16–20 percent of dry matter intake), phosphorus (0.2–0.3 percent), and calcium (0.25–0.5 percent). Maintenance requirements for adults are 6–8 percent protein, 0.16–0.25 percent phosphorus, and 0.2–0.3 percent calcium. Pregnant and lactating does have about the same requirements for minerals and crude protein as do growing animals.

Mature animals have a special need for high energy foods during the breeding season and in cold weather. In prolonged periods of extremely cold weather, many deer—especially fawns—die as a result of energy deficiencies. A diet that contains a digestible energy concentration of 2.75 kilocalories per gram is considered adequate for deer (Ullrey et al. 1971). If the available winter forage contains less than 2.2 kilocalories of digestible energy per gram (a digestion coefficient of 50 percent), the chances of fawn survival are slim. In Michigan, the winter maintenance requirements for pregnant does were 158 kilocalories of apparent digestible energy and 131 kilocalories of metabolizable energy per kilogram of body weight$^{0.75}$ per day (Ullrey et al. 1970). On a full-feed diet in winter, deer are able to maintain a positive energy balance, but are unable to do so on a maintenance diet (Moen 1968a). Even though nutrient deficiencies are apt to be critical during the winter period, winter feeding usually is not recommended (Kelsey 1973).

The deer's diet depends primarily on what food is seasonably available (Kohn and Mooty 1971). The greater the variety of plants, the greater the chances are for the whitetail to achieve its productive potential.

Browse (leaves, stems and buds of woody plants) is considered by many to be the mainstay of deer diet, mainly because of its year-round availability (Halls 1973). Many plant species are eaten, but the relative utilization—especially of evergreen species—usually is highest in late fall and winter. Browse consumption is highest when acorns are scarce and lowest when acorns are abundant (Harlow et al. 1975). Browse species vary considerably in quality (Mautz et al. 1976). They usually are adequate in protein and minerals during the spring but below or at deer maintenance levels the remainder of the year. The quality is particularly low when only the twigs of deciduous species are available and when deer are forced to eat the older and more fibrous parts of the plant (Short 1971). In such cases, digestive disorders can cause death even though the deer have full stomachs and appear to be in good condition. Deer on overbrowsed range are much more apt to consume less protein than deer on good range.

Forbs usually are eaten most heavily in the spring or whenever they are succulent and green (Short 1971). When available in ample quantities, they may constitute 50 percent or more of the deer's diet. Forbs, such as legumes, contain 25 percent or more crude protein, with the digestion coefficients exceeding 60 percent.

With few exceptions, native grasses are of little consequence in the deer's diet, although the young green shoots are eaten in late winter and early spring (Halls 1973).

Deer eat fleshy fungi but only rarely are the fungi abundant enough to contribute a major portion of the diet. Fleshy fungi are high in phosphorus and protein (Miller and Halls 1969).

Deer relish many kinds of fruits and, even though they significantly influence deer condition and productivity, the fruits usually are not considered a staple or a dependable source of food because of their sporadic occurrence. Many fruits have high contents of protein, phosphorus and calcium, and the kernels of nuts have fat contents up to 75–80 percent (Short and Epps 1976). Acorns are an especially good source of energy.

Deer definitely prefer certain species of plants and plant parts. Succulent plants are more palatable than dry plants. The more nutritious plants usually are preferred, but not always. Browse leaves usually are more palatable than twigs, and twig tips more so than older growth. Evergreen plants are preferred to deciduous plants during the winter. Agricultural crops, such as soybeans, and winter pastures of annual grasses and legumes are readily eaten by deer whenever they are in close proximity to forest habitats (Nixon et al. 1970).

Water, salt and cover

Deer drink free water when it is available but can go for extended periods without it. In northern climates, deer can use snow as a source of moisture. Deer also are good swimmers. They like to play in water and will quickly take to water to escape predators and man.

Deer apparently maintain a positive sodium balance throughout most of the year at intake levels far lower than that required by domestic animals (Weeks and Kirkpatrick 1976). However, a high turnover rate of water in the spring may lead to a temporary, negative sodium balance. Thus, deer use natural salt licks and salt blocks relatively frequently in the spring. Salt is used to bait deer into traps at this time of the year.

In the South, there is seldom a lack of adequate cover for deer except, perhaps, in large tracts of recently clearcut forest lands or in areas where brush is cleared to favor grass. In the North, cover is a critical factor in providing adequate protection from extreme winter weather. Deep snow, cold temperatures and lack of protective cover on summer ranges encourage deer to concentrate in coniferous yards. Without ample cover for protection, deer cannot exist in northern forests. Even in the Midwest, cover is a prime habitat requirement in the winter (Stoll and Donohoe n.d.). Deer on a depleted range require heavier cover than do deer on good range (Moen 1968b). Physiologically,

cover becomes important to deer only when its presence is necessary to enable the deer to meet their basal energy requirements (Moen 1968a).

HARVEST OBJECTIVES AND POPULATION CONTROL

Deer are hunted to provide recreation and meat, and to control the density, structure and health of herds. The questions of how many and what kind of deer to harvest are extremely complicated because of the interplay of many biological, economical and political factors.

Potentially, the deer harvest will increase proportionately with an increase in herd density. But beyond a certain threshold point of herd density, the harvest decreases rapidly. Likewise, reproductive rates decrease sharply when deer densities become high in relation to habitat carrying capacity. Thus, the greatest reproductive rate and harvest potential are achieved at population densities below the maximum.

Techniques by which the wildlife manager can control herd density to obtain an optimum harvest, if that is the management objective, are many and varied. In recent years, several simulation models have been proposed. In Colorado, Gross (1972) suggested a model based on the relationships among reproductive and mortality rates, harvest, and population density as a guide to making management decisions. The basic feature of this process is that reproductive rate declines as population density increases; that is, changes in reproduction are density dependent. Walls (1974) used a simulation model to show that the harvests should include both antlered and antlerless deer, and that long-term stability could be achieved by management practices designed to promote specific sex ratios. The harvest ratio of antlered to antlerless deer changes with the level of reproduction; thus, the desired ratio varies among populations. Davis (1967) constructed a mathematical model for resource allocation by varying the coefficients of deer mortality, productivity and harvested values. The analysis conformed reasonably well with the general behavior of actual deer populations and provided estimates of optimum size and structure of the annual harvest and residual herd.

An analysis technique that allows determination of both recruitment and mortality, and that relates these dynamic functions to deer population size and trends has been developed by Downing (In press). This technique requires an estimate of the number of deer that die in each sex and age class for at least two consecutive years. Since losses occur for many reasons and throughout the year, some of the data have to be estimated or adjusted. If hunter harvest is the major mortality factor, data can be obtained cheaply through check stations and modeled to predict what likely would happen under any desired management strategies. The main advantage of the technique is that it yields current information on herd structure and population trends.

Virginia is a good example of regulating deer densities by controlling the doe harvest (Gwynn 1976). Basic data are obtained from check stations to determine the proportion of fawns and adults of each sex. The percentage of total female mortality is controlled by manipulating the number of days that doe deer can be hunted. If the herd is below its habitat's carrying capacity and the goal is for a population increase, bucks only are harvested. When the herd is at carrying capacity and the goal is to keep the population steady, the number of doe-days is adjusted to provide 30–40 percent females in the harvest. When the herd exceeds carrying capacity and the goal is to reduce the population, the hunting season is designed to include 40–50 percent females in the harvest.

A similar procedure is used in Pennsylvania (Lang and Wood 1976). The whitetail population is calculated on the basis of harvest reports, sex ratios, and attrition and recruitment rates. The strategy is to estimate the herd size at the end of the hunting season in one year, predict the recruitment and prehunting season population for the next year, and determine the number of antlerless permits to be issued. The percentage of does to be removed is defined by the management objectives: whether to maintain, increase or decrease the herd size.

A basic premise in most contemporary hunting systems is that antlerless deer must be considered in the total harvest. Buck-only hunting rarely represents a harvest in excess of 10 percent of the total population (Forbes 1963, Neal 1968). This usually is less than the net productivity and fails to achieve a balance between deer numbers and habitat. If a herd is to be held stable, all surplus deer should be harvested annually, including a designated number of females. If a herd is to be increased, some of the surplus should be left for additional breeding stock. If a herd needs to be reduced, the entire surplus and some of the breeding stock should be harvested (Forbes 1963).

Hunting pressure largely determines the age-class structure in the hunted herd. Heavy hunting pressure will produce an early-age harvest with few animals exceeding 2.5 years of age. An early-age harvest maximizes the return in deer numbers and flesh per unit of forage consumed, and is most applicable when habitat quality is less than excellent. In contrast, late-age harvest permits a larger proportion of deer to attain maximum size, but it results in a less proficient use of food (Short 1972). This form of management requires a selective-harvest schedule or deer numbers may get out of hand. It is most practical in high quality habitats where trophy bucks are a premium.

Telltale evidence appears when deer are underharvested and the population exceeds the carrying capacity. Some of the signs, such as animals dying from malnutrition, are obvious and appear quickly. Others, such as low reproductive rates, are subtle and may go unnoticed for several years.

Signs of too many deer are: (1) the most palatable plants are heavily grazed and may disappear; (2) the use of "stuffer" foods increases; (3) browse lines appear; (4) deer reproductive rates decline, and there are more single fawns and fewer twins; (5) fawn death losses are high; (6) mature animals show a decline in size and weight; (7) antler size declines and there is a high percentage of spike bucks; (8) deer are in poor physical condition and more susceptible to disease and insects; and (9) the sex ratio at birth may favor bucks.

HABITAT MANAGEMENT AND IMPROVEMENT TECHNIQUES

To exhibit their full biological potential, whitetails must have access to suitable habitat. Home ranges must include an adequate source of food and cover, daily and seasonally for an indefinite number of years. The destruction or deterioration of habitat has been and will continue to be the most serious obstacle to optimum production of deer.

There are many ways in which habitat management can benefit deer at little or no expense to other resources. The practical decisions involve politics, economics and aesthetics as well as biological and ecological relationships. Throughout most of the whitetails' range, habitat is largely a reflection of timber stand conditions and management practices.

Timber stands

An interspersion of hardwood and evergreen tree-cover types is most likely to meet the year-round needs of white-tailed deer. The main contribution of hardwoods to deer is fruit and browse for food, but in the farm woodlots of the Midwest they also are the main source of winter cover (Nixon et al. 1970). Oaks usually are the main component of hardwood stands, and when they produce ample crops of acorns, the deer fatten rapidly in the fall and a high percentage of does conceive and bear healthy fawns. The big disadvantage of oak is that acorn yields are not consistent; thus, oaks are an undependable source of food. A mixture of

species in the white and black oak groups helps to balance acorn yields, since acorns of white oaks mature after one year and those of black oaks mature after two years.

To produce most acorns, the oaks should be at least 20.3–25.4 centimeters (8–10 inches) in diameter at breast height, have fully developed crowns and maintain a dominant or codominant position in the stand (United States Forest Service 1971). Trees which bear heavily in a good year are likely to do so again in succeeding good years. Expected acorn yields per square foot of oak tree basal area usually range from 0.9–3.6 kilograms (2–8 pounds). Acorn yields are favored by maintaining oak trees in long rotations and periodically thinning the stands in which they are located. In the South, good deer habitat should contain approximately 47 oaks per hectare (19 oaks per acre). Other hardwoods, such as beech, dogwood, cherries, haws and gums, contribute significant quantities of fruits readily eaten by deer.

Hardwood trees, especially sprouts, also are important sources of browse. Water oak and willow oak sprouts are eaten readily by deer in the South (Halls and Ripley 1972); pin-cherry and sugar maple in Pennsylvania (Marquis 1974); aspens in South Dakota (Richardson and Petersen 1974); mountain maple, dogwood and beaked hazel in Minnesota (Wetzel et al. 1975); and maple, apple, sassafras, dogwood, staghorn sumac, witch hobble and basswood in New York (Severinghaus 1974). In hardwood forests, as in most habitats, a wide variety of species is needed to create stability in the food regime.

Evergreen trees are essential for adequate cover in deer yards of the North during severe winters. In Michigan, a densely stocked, even-aged stand of native swamp conifers offered deer the best protection from cold weather (Ozoga 1968). In Minnesota, conifer-dominated stands—especially those containing balsam fir and white cedar— were used more frequently than hardwood stands in late winter (Wetzel et al. 1975). In Ontario, white birch, balsam fir, and alder types and stands combining aspen, white birch, maple and balsam fir were used most frequently from October–April (Kearney and Gilbert 1976). Even though evergreen trees seldom are a major source of deer food, they may be the sole source of emergency food available to whitetails in extreme cold and snow conditions of northern climates. Species such as hemlock may be browsed to the extent that they are eliminated from a stand.

A combination of evergreen and hardwood trees provides the best winter habitat in northern climates. In Michigan, it is recommended that deer yards consist of even-aged mature evergreen timber as prime winter cover, and be interspersed with pole-size and sapling conifers, mixed hardwood-conifer, northern hardwoods and upland openings to provide adequate food and cover (Ozoga 1968).

Size, shape and distribution of cutting units

Timber-cutting units should be distributed into a pattern of many different-aged stands to provide year-round habitat within the home range. For an 80-year rotation in the South, it is recommended that 20 percent of the even-aged stands be in young-age classes (less than 15 years), 30 percent in intermediate (16–49 years), and 50 percent in older-age classes (more than 50 years) (United States Fish and Wildlife Service 1976a).

Roach (1974) suggested converting large tracts of even-aged stands into a balanced distribution of age classes by dividing the tracts into 50 stands and regenerating 5 stands at 10-year intervals. Older stands are cut first. To avoid a severe loss of timber values in the short-term process, the cutting schedule would have to be executed over a long period of time. Some of the units cut first may be immature; some of the units cut last may be overmature. The loss of timber values would be small.

Ideally, timber-cutting units should be small enough to enable deer to utilize them fully without overbrowsing, yet large enough to be economical as a lumber resource. The exact size and shape are flexible and interrelated. For example, an 80.9-square hectare (200-acre) block would provide less "edge" and be less desirable than a strip two or three times as long as it is wide. Cutting units of less than 20 hectares (50 acres) in size are recommended in Ohio (Nixon et al. 1970), and 8 hectares (20 acres) in Pennsylvania (Roach 1974). In Michigan, Verme (1968) recommended that openings be no more than 181 meters (200 yards) wide. Emphasis should be given to creating the maximum edge by arranging cutting units into irregular or rectangular shapes.

Timber stand density

Dense stands of conifers are needed to protect deer against severe weather; however, dense stands of conifers or hardwoods produce little food. Crowded trees with their narrow, restricted crowns seldom bear much fruit, and there is a strong negative correlation between tree density and understory food production for deer.

Timber stands should be open enough to produce good quantities of deer food, yet dense enough to grow commercial crops of timber. Density can be controlled by regulating the seedling spacings at regeneration and by thinning. In the South (Halls 1973), a seedling spacing of at least 1.8 meters by 2.4 meters (8 feet by 10 feet) is suggested as a reasonable compromise between deer habitat and timber production. To be of maximum benefit to deer, the timber stand should be thinned heavily and at an early age. The heavier the thinning, the greater the response of forage. Optimum tree density, of course, will vary according to tree species, site quality and product to be grown. In the South, a residual tree basal area of 16–18 square meters per hectare (70–78 square feet per acre) is suggested for upland pine-hardwood stands. Repeated thinnings should be a standard practice in timber stands with sawlog rotations. In forested areas where cutting is forbidden, forage yields and deer numbers are likely to decline.

The effects of timber cutting on forage production are temporary. In the South (Halls 1973), herbaceous plants quickly respond to cutting, and the yields peak in a year or two. Browse yields peak within three to five years after a timber thinning. Yields then decline as the tree crowns close in and many of the understory plants grow beyond the reach of deer. Essentially the same relationship exists in northern forests, but the changes occur at a slower rate (Pengelly 1961).

Prescribed burning

Foresters prescribe burn to prepare seedbeds, restrict growth of hardwood sprouts, control disease and reduce fuel accumulation. Prescribed burning also affects deer habitat (Halls 1973). The first year after a fire, crude protein and phosphorus content of forage is increased. Burning improves the palatability of forage, and deer often concentrate in newly burned habitat. Fire causes browse plants to resprout close to the ground, and for several years, depending on climatic conditions, most of the current season's growth is within reach of deer. Fire also favors the growth of herbaceous plants, many of which are eaten by deer.

To benefit deer most, timber stands should be burned in late winter when plants are dormant. At this time, fire seldom kills browse plants, and little palatable forage is destroyed. Occasionally, however, winter fires get hot enough to kill desirable midstory hardwoods that provide mast. Summer fires should be avoided because they kill many desirable browse plants and eliminate forage that is needed by deer during the subsequent fall and winter.

Fires should be excluded from young pine stands until the trees are about 4.6 meters (15 feet) tall. Thereafter, burning should be done periodically, as needed to keep most browse plants within reach of deer. An interval of three to five years is recommended in southern pine forests.

Forest openings

Openings within the forest, either temporary or permanent, add to the variety of food and cover, provide a consistent and abundant source of food, and increase the "edge" (Halls 1973). Temporary openings usually are the result of a clearcut timber harvest or a catastrophe such as a tornado or wildfire. They are productive for only a few years and, with timber regeneration, develop into stands where food is likely to be sparse. If openings are to be retained permanently, they must be mowed, burned or cultivated. The frequency of practices that must be applied to keep openings productive and attractive to deer primarily depends on the rate of plant growth. This may vary from seasonal mowing or annual burns in the South to several year intervals in northern climates.

Intensively managed openings that serve a special need for deer may merit cultivation, seeding and fertilization (Halls and Stransky 1968). Such openings can provide highly nutritious food at critical times of the year when both quality and quantity of native foods in the forest are low. Food plots are expensive, ranging from a few dollars to $247 or more per hectare ($100 or more per acre). Their justification depends on the adequacy of food in the surrounding forest and their cost in relation to benefits derived.

Openings are usually 0.4–2.0 hectares (1–5 acres). They probably should comprise at least 2 percent of the total forest area to be of any significance to the deer herd. Any area in excess of 5 percent is likely to be too expensive and, therefore, unacceptable to the timber grower. The primary purpose of the openings is food production; thus, they should be well-distributed throughout the deer's home range and on relatively fertile sites.

In the selection of openings, the landowner should take advantage of existing conditions and timber-cutting practices. Abandoned homesites are especially good because they often contain several high quality deer food species such as plums, honeysuckle, grapes, blackberries, haws and oaks. Utility rights-of-way, roadsides and firebreaks should be included and managed as part of the opening system. After a final timber harvest, specified plots can be designated as permanent openings and excluded from timber regeneration.

DAMAGE PROBLEMS AND CONTROL

Deer often cause damage in areas where native foods are scarce or unpalatable, usually in late winter or early spring. In forested areas, tree seedlings are susceptible to damage by deer. Consistent heavy browsing seriously restricts vertical growth, causes malformation and, in some cases, kills seedlings and saplings of desirable timber species. Deer have caused regeneration failures of pin-cherry and sugar maple in 25–40 percent of several areas in Pennsylvania (Marquis 1974). Satisfactory regeneration occurred only where there were abundant seedlings in advance of a timber harvest. Deer nip the terminal buds of pine seedlings, especially from planted stock, and reduce vertical growth. Usually, browsing is not intensive enough to cause a significant loss of pine seedlings.

When in close proximity to forest cover, orchards and agricultural crops such as soybeans, corn and small grains are consumed readily and sometimes damaged by deer. In Pennsylvania, crop damage is considered the major cost of deer production, amounting to $0.5 million or more annually (Carroll 1963). It costs several dollars per hectare to protect citrus groves against deer in some areas of Florida (Beckwith and Stith 1968).

The most effective means of controlling damage by deer is to keep animal numbers in balance with native food supplies, but in critical areas additional measures are warranted (Calhoun and Loomis 1974). Prescribed burning and food plots can be used to entice deer away from tree seedlings, but are not always successful. Several commercial repellents and mixtures of blood meal and bone meal or meat scraps provide

effective but expensive protection. Commercial repellents usually are sprayed on the crop, whereas meat scraps or meal are placed in bands around the crop. In some cases, the repellents simply may force deer to move to another field. Noise-makers and lights sometimes help for a short time, but deer soon become accustomed to them.

Physical barriers such as high fences are necessary for permanent exclusion of deer along major highways. Windrowing of debris and slash to the outer edges of a planting site was one means of temporarily excluding deer from expensive cottonwood plantings in the Mississippi Delta.

MISCELLANEOUS MANAGEMENT PROBLEMS

Cattle compete with deer when there is a shortage of food, mostly during winter when both are seeking green feed. Some common use of browse may extend into spring, but rarely is there any overlap during the summer and fall. Competition for forbs usually occurs in late summer but seldom is serious. Competition for grass exists only in late winter or early spring and usually is light. Both cattle and deer heavily graze fertilized food plots; thus, if the plots are to provide supplemental food for deer, cattle must be excluded from them.

Whitetails compete with goats for browse at all seasons, especially in the winter and on heavily stocked ranges. Sheep compete directly with deer for forbs, usually during the summer, but whenever else forbs are available.

The ranges of white-tailed deer, moose and elk overlap, mostly near the northern edge of the whitetail's range (Baker, In press). Whitetails and moose use similar plant communities in summer and autumn. In Ontario, the heaviest competition occurred in the alder type from May–June (Kearny and Gilbert 1976). Normally, there is little overlap in the use of winter range. However, under severe climatic conditions, both deer and moose seek shelter in dense

Box traps baited with salt are an effective and relatively inexpensive means of capturing deer. Photo by Don Domenick; courtesy of the Colorado Division of Wildlife.

coniferous stands. Whitetails and elk coexist in summer along forest edges (Moran 1973). In winter, deer prefer newly cutover areas and swamp conifers, whereas elk occupy varied forested habitats, seemingly without discrimination. In late summer, elk may eat browse forage that is needed by deer in winter. However, competition usually is not severe because elk can subsist mainly on grass. Even when mule deer and whitetails occupy the same general area, they seldom compete for food because they tend to remain segregated in their choice of habitats.

Occasionally there is a need to capture deer in the wild. Trapping with box traps is probably the most efficient means of capture (Hawkins et al. 1967). Salt is a favorite bait. Corn, apples and other food items are used but they often attract other animals. Nets can be dropped from helicopters, or used over baited plots as drop or cannon nets placed along travelways and deer driven into them. In most cases, several deer can be captured at one time with a minimum of casualty.

When used with bait, tranquilizers such as Diazepam (Tranimul) make it easier to handle and transport deer and to retain them in close quarters without undue excitement (Thomas et al. 1967). Usually, there are some deaths associated with the use of tranquilizers.

Projectile syringes loaded with various drugs are effective at close range. Malfunctioning equipment, incorrect doses, poor placement of darts and animal reaction to chemicals cause variable success. When injected with nicotine salicylate, 50 percent of the deer captured in a Texas project were immobilized, 15 percent escaped and 35 percent were killed as a result of massive hemorrhage or head damage (Thomas and Marburger 1964). Of 101 deer injected with succinylcholine chloride in Pennsylvania, 76 were immobilized satisfactorily, 14 were not affected because of an underdose or malfunc-

tioning equipment, and 11 died from overdose or injuries (Liscinsky et al. 1969). In Virginia, injections of succinylcholine chloride resulted in a capture rate of 63.6 percent for adults and 65.5 percent for fawns (Wesson et al. 1975). Mortality rate was 8.6 percent for adults and 13.8 percent for fawns.

Chapter 5

MOOSE

Albert W. Franzmann
Research Biologist
Kenai Moose Research Center
Alaska Department of Fish and Game
Soldotna, Alaska

The moose, *Alces alces,* is the largest member of the deer family and is one of North America's largest land mammals. Early explorers of this continent were fascinated by this majestic inhabitant of northern (boreal) forests, and many accounts of moose appear in their writings. To those persons who lived or traveled through our boreal forests, moose were an important source of food, clothing, tools and recreation. Moose continue to provide the basic staples for a decreasing number of people who live from the land. However, many people still depend on moose meat as a supplement food source and basis for recreation.

Mature bull moose produce the world's largest antlers and they are highly prized as trophies. In addition to the experience of the hunt, there may be the reward of up to 318 kilograms (700 pounds) of delicious meat. It is impossible to place a value on the experience of observing or photographing a bull moose in his prime, standing in solitary assuredness, or a cow moose quietly leading her twin calves through a forest.

DISTRIBUTION AND TAXONOMY

Past distribution and abundance of moose in North America were related to the dynamics of glacial epochs and associated pres-ence of boreal forests. Moose once ranged over a broad belt of the then-forested Great Plains and eastern United States (Peterson 1955). They spread northward with the retreat of glaciers and extension of the boreal forest. The present distribution of moose is limited in the North by the absence of woody food plants on the tundra; in western mountain ranges by excessive snow depth and lack of woody plants; on the prairies and arid valleys of the South and West by absence of shade, water and suitable food; and in the Southeast by neurological disease (Kelsall and Telfer 1974). Local distribution and abundance are related to successional stages of vegetation resulting from natural disturbances such as lightning-induced wildfires, flooding, glacial movement and volcanic eruptions. They also are related to man-induced actions such as forestry practices, land clearing, homesteading, farming, construction and fires. These vegetation successional forces and related natality and mortality characteristics of a population are responsible for the dynamic nature of moose populations.

Moose also inhabit the boreal forests of northern Europe and Asia and, in the past, were believed to be a species separate from "New World" moose. However, all moose are now considered a single species represented

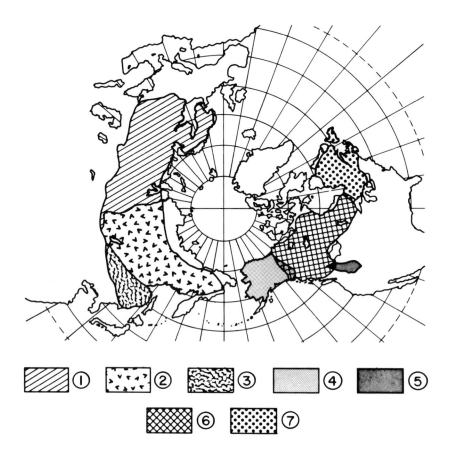

Figure 15. Circumpolar distribution of moose (Peterson 1974a): 1 = *A. a. alces*, 2 = *A. a. pfizenmayeri*, 3 = *A. a. eameloides*, 4 = *A. a. gigas*, 5 = *A. a. shirasi*, 6 = *A. a. andersoni*, 7 = *A. a. americana.*

by a number of geographically distinct subspecies (Figure 15) (Peterson 1952). The European and Asiatic subspecies are commonly called "elk," and this has been a source of confusion since the North American elk is a different genus.

Four subspecies of moose are recognized in North America. Eastern moose *(A. a. americana)* inhabit the northeastern United States and eastern Canada, including Newfoundland, westward to the Great Lakes. Northwestern moose *(A. a. andersoni)* are found from the Great Lakes north and westward to the Pacific coast and into the Yukon Territory. Western Yukon Territory, northern British Columbia and Alaska are the ranges of the Alaskan moose *(A. a. gigas),* largest of the North American subspecies. Shira's moose *(A. a. shirasi)* occupy

the northern Rocky Mountains of the United States and extend northward into southern Alberta and British Columbia.

DESCRIPTION

Newborn moose pelage is light red to reddish-brown in color with shades of gray-to-black on the lower abdomen, chest and legs. The muzzle, hooves, eye rings and ears also are shaded black. White hairs may be seen in the inguinal area and inside the ears. After two to three months, this juvenile coat is replaced by a darker coat with similar but darker patterns of shading. In spring, moose shed their winter coat, which is rather dull in appearance. It is replaced by a new coat of short, fine, nearly black hair. As summer progresses, these guard hairs, which are of scalelike structure, grow rapidly and generally attain a lustrous red-brown general appearance with shading toward black, particularly in the low extremities. Some moose in prime coat, particularly males, appear nearly black. White hair around the vulva on females generally is characteristic, but may be absent. Guard hairs, which may grow to 25.4 centimeters (10 inches) on the shoulder hump of Alaskan moose, provide these color patterns, but an undercoat of grayish, fine wool provides the insulating qualities necessary to live in cold regions. Color variations from black to very light brown or gray occur throughout the range of moose, and albinism may occur.

The "bell" and the large, flexible, overhanging upper lip of the moose are distinguishing characteristics. The "bell," a pendulous dewlap of skin and hair dangling from the throat area, has no known function. On mature bulls, bells may be up to 38.2 centimeters (15 inches) in diameter at their base and average about 25.4 centimeters (10 inches) in length. Bells are present in a variety of shapes and forms, but all tend to decrease in length with age.

An adult moose has 32 teeth—12 in the upper jaw and 20 in the lower jaw. The dental formula is (Peterson 1955):

$$I \frac{0}{3} + C \frac{0}{1} + P \frac{3}{3} + M \frac{3}{3} \times 2 = 32.$$

Mandibular tooth wear has been used as an index to age of moose (Passmore et al. 1955), but this technique generally has been replaced by counting cementum layers in sectioned incisor teeth (Sergeant and Pimlott 1959).

Moose lack metatarsal and interdigital external glands, but have a pair of lachrymal glands below the eyes and a pair of relatively small tarsal glands on the medial aspect of the hind legs.

Antler growth of male moose begins in spring and continues through summer. During this growth period, the antlers are covered with "velvet" which contains an extensive vascular system providing nutrients for antler development. As maximum antler

Bull moose in rutting season. Photo by Len Rue, Jr.

development is attained, generally by late August, the blood supply decreases and the velvet dries and is shed. Butting and rubbing antlers against trees and shrubs assists in the shedding process and is the first evidence of the approaching rut.

Maximum recorded Boone and Crockett Club measurements for moose antlers are: spread—204.8 centimeters (80.6 inches); palm length—142.2 centimeters (56 inches); palm width—75.7 centimeters (29.8) inches; beam circumference—32 centimeters (12.6 inches); and greatest number of points (single antler)—24 (Nesbitt and Parker 1977). These measurements are not from the same moose, but all are from Alaskan moose. Bubenik (1973) described two main palmicorn-type antlers (shell-like palm and split palm) and the basic cervicorn or branched antler whose structure can be traced in the palm (Figure 16).

Growth rates and size of antlers are a function of genetic potential and nutrition which, in turn, are influenced by many

Figure 16. Typical shapes of moose antlers (Bubenik 1973): (top) *A. a. alces,* full palmicorn; (center) *A. a. alces,* cervicorn; (bottom) *A. a. gigas,* split-palm butterfly-type.

variables in the general realm of habitat and climate. Most males shed their antlers from late November through December, but it is not uncommon to see antlers on young bulls as late as March.

Both male and female moose attain maximum weights during fall. They may increase their late winter-spring weights by 21–55 percent before entering the rut (Franzmann et al. 1978). Meaningful weight comparisons between subspecies and populations of moose would require comparisons of whole body weights at the same time of year. The only data available for this type of comparison are for 6 adult female Alberta moose whose October mean live weight was 418 kilograms (919.6 pounds) (Blood et al. 1967), and 17 adult female Alaskan moose whose mean October weight was 448.5 kilograms (986.7 pounds) (Franzmann et al. 1978). Heaviest individual

recorded live adult weights come from an Alaskan moose and are 490 kilograms (1,080 pounds) for a female and 595.5 kilograms (1,310 pounds) for a male. Higher weights have been estimated and undoubtedly exist, but lack confirmation.

Adult female moose (n = 23) from a highly productive, expanding population in Alaska had a mean total length of 301.5 centimeters (120.6 inches); chest girth of 201.3 centimeters (80.5 inches); hind foot measurement of 81.5 centimeters (32.6 inches); and a shoulder height measurement of 185.5 centimeters (74.2 inches). Mean measurements of five adult males in this population were obtained for total length— 305.5 centimeters (122.2 inches), and chest girth—204.1 centimeters (81.6 inches). Significantly lower measurements were recorded from other populations in Alaska (Franzmann et al. 1978). Measurements of Alberta moose (Blood et al. 1967) allowed comparisons and Alaskan moose, as would be expected, were considerably larger.

ECOLOGY

Reproduction and growth

The life cycle of a moose begins with the breeding season or the rut, which extends from early September to late November with the peak period occurring in late September and early October. Markgren (1969) indicated that the duration of estrus or "heat" is characterized by cows being receptive for about 7–12 days, but the actual estrus period lasts less than 24 hours. The interval between heats is approximately 20– 22 days (Edwards and Ritcey 1958). It appears that the peak of moose breeding season falls within one estrus period, with one earlier and perhaps one or two later periods accounting for only small percentages of total pregnancies (Peterson 1974b). Edwards and Ritcey (1958) reported that 89 percent of the moose were conceived within a two-week period in British Columbia.

Female moose can potentially breed as yearlings (16–18 months age) and reproduce yearly until 18 years of age. However, their maximal reproductive potential is between 4–12 years of age. Most moose produce single calves, but twins are not uncommon and triplets have been reported.

Reproductive performance as reflected by ovulation and pregnancy rates has been widely accepted as a function of nutrition. Ovulation rates of yearlings have been reported from 0 percent (Peek 1962) to 82 percent (Rajakoski and Kovisto 1966). Reported pregnancy rates for adult females varied from 59.5 percent (Franzmann et al. 1976) to 93 percent (Rausch and Bratlie 1965).

The gestation period for moose is approximately eight months, with the peak of calving occurring in late May and June. As parturition approaches, the pregnant female seeks seclusion and, if still associated with her young of the previous year, will aggressively drive it (them) away. The year-

ling generally does not stray far from its mother and may reassociate with her within several weeks after birth of her next calf or calves.

Moose generally give birth lying down and may nurse their young in that position. The calf, weighing 11–16 kilograms (25–35 pounds) often is up the first day and standing fairly easily by the third or fourth day. Calves are licked copiously soon after birth and this activity continues regularly, establishing and maintaining the cow-calf bond.

Moose calves derive a substantial proportion of their early nutritive requirements from milk. Knorre (1961) concluded that wild moose cows produced about 150 liters (40 gallons) of milk during a lactation period; however, domesticated moose in Russia were capable of producing 430 liters (113 gallons) per season (Yazan and Knorre 1964). Cows lactate until fall, then

Moose calves vie for cow's milk, a significant nutritional portion of their early diet. Photo by William E. Ruth.

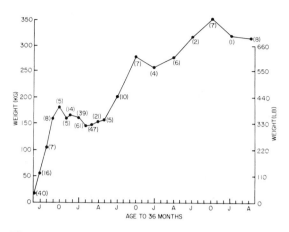

Figure 17. Weights of moose by month to 36 months of age (Franzmann et al. 1977). Sample sizes are in parentheses.

gradually wean their calves. Attempted nursing has been observed in January, although significant lactation has ceased by that time.

Moose calves begin experimentally chewing on plants within a few days after birth and start foraging regularly by two weeks of age. Development of the rumen depends on this forage intake. Calves grow rapidly during their first five months, and Alaskan calves average 181.4 kilograms (399 pounds) by October (Franzmann et al. 1978). Monthly weights of moose to 36 months of age are shown in Figure 17. From October to May, calves maintain their weight or may

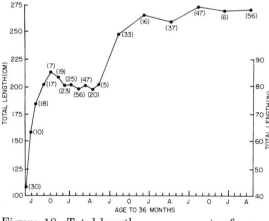

Figure 18. Total length measurements of moose by month to 36 months of age (Franzmann et al. 1977). Sample sizes are in parentheses.

actually decrease in body weight. As forage becomes available in abundance in spring, they again grow rapidly and attain weights of 278.9 kilograms (613.6 pounds) by 16–18 months of age. Total length measurements follow a growth pattern similar to the weight curve (Figure 18). No significant differences in weight or body measurements are detected between male and female moose until 36 months of age (Franzmann et al. 1978).

Although the potential maximum natality rate of moose populations is great, it is seldom achieved. Data on realized natality, reflecting prenatal and postnatal mortality, are lacking for moose populations because of extreme difficulties associated with censusing spring calf production. Nevertheless, information that reflects calf production and survival to fall is obtained regularly. In the Nelchina Basin, Alaska, fall ratios of calves to 100 cows ranged from 13:100 in 1972 to 89.8:100 in 1953 (Bishop and Rausch 1974). Recruitment of young at the 1972 rate is not

Rapid growth of calves during their first eight months of age depends, to a great extent, on the availability of succulent forage, such as aquatics. Photo by Leonard Lee Rue III.

adequate to sustain the population. Realized production of calves in the fall population is the product of ovulation and pregnancy rates, and prenatal, postnatal and summer mortality. Mortality factors acting upon the fall calf population further depress it for another year before it potentially becomes a reproductive segment of the total population.

Mortality

Populations of moose in good habitat respond with high initial calf production and, in most instances, can absorb mortality from severe winters, predation, regulated hunting, poaching, disease, competition and accidental deaths. However, moose populations in poor habitat with low initial calf production and survival cannot absorb significant natural and hunting mortality.

Winter mortality results from a complex of several factors related primarily to snow depth, density, hardness and persistence of these conditions over time. These factors affect mobility of moose and the availability of food which, in turn, influence energy balance. Adverse snow conditions were responsible for a nearly 100 percent calf mortality on the Kenai Peninsula, Alaska during winter of 1971–1972 (Franzmann and Arneson 1973).

Predation by wolves is a mortality factor that may affect moose over large parts of its North American range. Peterson and Allen (1974) indicated that snow conditions were related to wolf predation in that increased snow density and crusting enabled wolves to maneuver better. In addition, increased snow depths often resulted in moose herd concentrations, making individuals more accessible to wolves. Lowered moose nutritional status—associated with snow conditions—also increased vulnerability. Rausch et al. (1974) stated that the relationship of wolves to moose populations is not clear at this time but, in situations where severe winters result in moose population decreases, wolf populations may contribute further to this decrease. Continued predation undoubtedly slows the recovery of popu-

lations depleted by severe winters. On ranges where hunting pressure is sufficient to use the annual moose surpluses, wolves compete directly with man for this resource.

Black bears prey upon moose calves, primarily in spring. Chatelain (1950) concluded that on the Kenai Peninsula, Alaska a large black bear population was responsible for substantial calf mortality, but that its effect on the welfare of moose populations was unknown. Brown bears can potentially kill moose of all ages, but the effect of this predation on the welfare of moose populations also is unknown.

A peculiar case of moose mortality occurs in eastern and central North America where moose and white-tailed deer are in close association. Anderson (1964) reported that the causative agent of "moose disease" or neurological disease was the parasite *Parelaphostrongylus tenuis*. White-tailed deer are the normal primary host of this parasite and suffer no apparent harm from its presence. However, when moose pick up the parasite, it invades the brain area and causes incoordination, lameness, stiffness, weakness, circling associated with blindness, and eventually paralysis and death (Anderson 1964). This disease has been associated with marked declines in moose populations of Nova Scotia and New Brunswick, and may have been responsible for similar declines in Maine and Minnesota (Anderson 1972). The parasite is common in southwest Ontario (Anderson 1964) and has been found in Manitoba (Bindernagel and Anderson 1972).

Liver flukes *(Fascioloides magna)* in white-tailed deer produce no clinical disease. However, moose in close association with these deer may become infected, with some adverse results. Liver lesions from this parasite, often called "liver rot," frequently have been observed in moose (Anderson and Lankester 1974).

The moose tick *(Dermacenter albipictus)* is well-distributed over most of the range of North American moose populations except that of Alaskan moose. Many researchers have reported great numbers of these ticks on moose and suggested that the ticks may have a definite detrimental effect, perhaps even fatal (Anderson and Lankester 1974).

Although many other parasites and diseases have been reported in moose (Anderson and Lankester 1974), most are not associated with significant mortality. One must consider that the potential always exists for a major disease situation in moose populations and, as man and his domestic animals further encroach upon moose habitats, the probability of such a situation increases.

Direct competition for forage between moose and white-tailed deer, mule deer, elk, domestic animals and snowshoe hares has been documented (Wolfe 1974). In general, these forms of direct competition are minimal except for remaining vegetation in areas where forage has been extensively depleted or when weather conditions are severe.

Hunting and poaching are mortality factors which, when unchecked or improperly regulated, may have a detrimental impact on a moose population—particularly a declining one. Conversely, a moose population can benefit from the culling influence of properly regulated hunting.

Motor vehicles and railroad trains are the primary sources of accidental deaths to moose. On the Kenai Peninsula, Alaska, highway losses averaged 125 moose per year and exceeded 250 moose during 1971 (Paul LeRoux, personal communication). Annual fatalities approaching several hundred moose were experienced on a 120-kilometer (75-mile) segment of the Alaska Railroad (Rausch 1957). Winter severity and lack of available browse influenced the number of highway and railroad moose fatalities. Moose are inclined to seek the relatively stable surfaces of roads and railbeds for movement during periods of inclement weather or food scarcity.

BEHAVIOR

Moose are essentially solitary and have one or several seasonally distinct home ranges to which they are strongly attached (LeResche 1974, Houston 1968, Geist 1963). These ranges are consistently small throughout North America, and no matter how far moose habitually move, home range during a given season seldom exceeds 5–10 square kilometers (3.1—6.2 square miles) (LeResche 1974). Movement information may be obtained by immobilizing and placing visual and/or radio collars on moose and plotting resightings.

Although cows with calves may be an exception (Altmann 1958, LeResche 1966), moose are not considered territorial (Geist 1963). The relative strength of the cow-calf bond may influence territorial tendencies. This bond is extremely strong through the first weeks of the calf's life, but during summer, the calf becomes increasingly independent. This bond increases the calf's chance of surviving its first year of life. The cow provides defense against predation, and the calf may benefit from the cow's experienced habitat selection. Although the cow-

Placing individually identifiable collar on an immobilized moose. Photo by Spencer Lindermann; courtesy of the Alaska Department of Fish and Game.

Cow moose with four-month old calf. Photo by James Keith Rue.

calf bond may benefit the calf's chances for survival, there is evidence that it is not essential. In Alaska, several moose introductions were accomplished by using calves alone (Burris and McKnight 1973).

The close cow-calf association is the rule in habitats where food supply is limited. Exceptions occur where the food supply is locally abundant. This was evident on the Kenai Peninsula, Alaska in an area of maturing moose habitat where the trees were crushed during winter to set back plant succession and rehabilitate the habitat mechanically (Oldemeyer 1977). Large groups of all age classes of moose in close association, including many cows with calves, utilized the available browse (Sigman 1977).

Altmann (1959) outlined special behavior patterns of the rutting bull which may include:

1. The build-up, challenger, swaying gait. The heavy antlers dip from side-to-side.
This is executed in stiff, long strides, usually in formal circles around the rival bull.

2. The mock-battle. During hitting and shredding trees and shrubs before the fight, it is possible for the rival to withdraw.

3. "Displacement" feeding. Either browsing or grazing with hasty, jerky movements and exaggerated intensity takes place; eyes are fixed on the opponent.

4. Reinforcement of drive. This stage is characterized by (a) occasional return to the cow, sniffing her and curling up the upper lip, head raised high; (b) activation of a wallow or making a new wallow and rolling in it; and (c) hitting and rubbing shrubs and young trees with the antlers.

5. The fight, or the rival's decision to yield. Pushing antler action of aggressor is received by yielding movements of the opponent, but after six to eight steps or

more backwards, the yielding bull braces himself and pushes forward. If one of the opponents slips or stumbles, he may be hit in the ribs or flank. The battle may end with rapid withdrawal of the beaten individual (in most cases) or a gradual stalemate. In the latter case, the two rivals begin displacement activities— browsing, grazing or tussling in the shrubbery and keeping each other under tension for hours or, in some cases, for days until one of them leaves the area. The cow stands quietly or browses nearby during the entire ritual and conflict.

6. The driving and mating stage. The bull drives the cow, mounts her, and, if she stands, breeds her repeatedly over a period of one or two days.

Variations of this behavior pattern have been recorded. An encounter between two males, in some cases, only goes as far as a "sizing-up" of one another's antler development, size and condition followed by one or both moving off (Lent 1974b). Also, fighting

may be extremely aggressive once an encounter goes that far. Peterson (1955) and Markgren (1969) cited numerous occurrences of violent and even fatal fights.

During the rut, cows are very aggressive toward one another. In contrast to other antlered species, they assume an active and independent role during the rut. Lent (1974b) discussed three aspects of this behavior: (1) the lack of male control over female activities; (2) the unusual use of vocal signals by females; and (3) under certain conditions, the great mobility of females. This mobility and aggressiveness has been observed at the Kenai Moose Research Center, Alaska, where females actively have attempted to get into enclosures where mature rutting males are present.

Lent (1974b) described male vocalization during the rut as a "croak" to distinguish it from the simple "grunt" emitted by cows communicating with the calves. Adult cows produce a long, quavering moan during the breeding season, and Lent (1974b) attested that the sound can be heard at a distance of

These two bulls locked antlers in an encounter at Farewell Lake, Rainy Pass, Alaska on December 20, 1939. They were spotted from an airplane by state wildlife agents. After landing, the agents approached the bulls, sawed the antlers and freed them. One moose died from wounds received in the fight. The other, after attempting to attack his rescuers, wandered off. A U.S. Bureau of Biological Survey photo; courtesy of the National Archives.

3.2 kilometers (2 miles). Lent also described a whine of appeasement used by both sexes until two years of age, and a "bark" by males associated with large aggregations and during active fights or chases. A "roar bellow" has been heard from moose under extreme stress, such as being confined in a trap or pursued on foot.

HABITAT

The primary limiting factor of moose populations throughout their range in North America is habitat. Food and climate are the most important aspects of habitat for moose. Seasonal weights of rumen contents varied from 18–51 kilograms (40–112 pounds) (Gasaway and Coady 1974). It is apparent that large quantities of forage must be produced to maintain moose. The quality of forage is an additional factor which must be considered. Deficiencies in any part of the vast complex of nutrient needs of proteins, fats, carbohydrates, minerals and vitamins may detract from optimum population maintenance. Such factors as digestibility of forage, volatile fatty-acid production in the rumen, water balance, trace element metabolism and behavioral considerations also influence utilization of nutrients.

Food habits of moose vary considerably over their North American range but are characterized in general by use of early successional woody browse, such as early stages of regrowth following disturbances by fire, logging, clearing and others. Peek (1974) concluded that willows are important to

Bull moose in predominantly willow habitat. Photo courtesy of the Alaska Department of Fish and Game.

Young female moose in predominantly birch habitat. Photo courtesy of the Alaska Department of Fish and Game.

Shiras and Alaskan moose and that balsam fir, quaking aspen, and paper birch are important to Canadian moose, but local variations in forage preferences are important as well. Moose are a pioneering-type animal and adapt to a variety of available forage. However, certain plant species are preferred and moose respond with improved reproductive success when these plants are available. This accounts, in part, for the historic population fluctuations experienced by moose.

The potential variety of edible forage for moose throughout the year may be significant in balancing nutritional intake. During summer, moose utilize forbs and aquatic plants in many areas. Ground vegetation, such as low bush cranberry, is highly

utilized in winter on the Kenai Peninsula, Alaska (LeResche and Davis 1973). Plants of this type have high nutritive value and aid in balancing and supplementing the moose diet in these areas.

Depth, density and hardness of snow in most of the North American range of moose is an important factor limiting suitability and availability of certain habitats for moose during the critical winter months. Moose activity in winter is regulated by snow conditions. Coady (1974) indicated that although snow may not cause moose migrations, it does influence the timing and distance of movements. In addition, snow may alter the energy balance of moose by increasing metabolic demands for locomo-

Moose trailing through deep snow. Photo courtesy of the Alaska Department of Fish and Game.

tion and by decreasing energy reserves through limitation of access to otherwise available food.

There is no evidence that extreme cold for short periods has adverse effects on moose if they can obtain shelter from wind (Kelsall and Telfer 1974). Moose winter successfully in some of the coldest regions of the world. Climates exceeding 27 degrees Centigrade (82 degrees Fahrenheit) for long periods without shade or access to lakes or rivers do not support moose (Kelsall and Telfer 1974).

MANAGEMENT

Cumming (1974) outlined the progression in approaches to moose management in Ontario as: (1) protection from suspected overexploitation, (2) development of some regulated use, (3) increased use of an underutilized resource, (4) sustained yield and optimum use of a resource, and (5) recrea-

tional and economic benefits to people. This outline, with minor modifications, provides a framework of moose management progression in most states and provinces. To this list could be added the developing trend to consider moose population needs in total resource planning for forest management units.

Moose numbers in North America are estimated to range between 0.8–1.2 million, with an annual average harvest near 90,000. Difficulties of assessing total numbers of moose in most areas permit management based on estimates rather than precise numbers. It can be stated generally that moose populations are stable or increasing in available habitat. Local declines are experienced from the single impact or combined impacts of severe winters, predation, neurological disease and excessive harvest.

The ultimate measures of a population's well-being are its production and recruitment of young; mortality rates are a by-product of these assessments. Moose management decisions today are based primarily on assessment of these population characteristics by aerial survey (Rausch et al. 1974). Population modeling may be employed using the survey data for status and predictive information. Fall transect surveys in selected habitats with adequate snow cover, and prior to bulls shedding antlers, provide the best estimates of population composition. Moose populations are counted and classified by sex and age composition (adult bulls, yearling bulls, cows and calves). The white vulva hair patch on females aids in sex determination if antlers are shed.

The number of moose seen per hour provides some insight about population size and trend if surveys are conducted in a comparable fashion each year. Spring surveys have been employed before calving to assess winter survival of calves and after calving to assess natality (Bishop and Rausch 1974). Stratified random square blocks censused with intensive search of small areas improved opportunities for observing moose (Evans et al. 1966). Straight-line transects allow greater area coverage. However, the

proportion of animals seen is reduced. The type, timing and intensity of aerial surveys will vary with topography, climate, funding and goals. Timmermann (1974) concluded that, because of the many variables associated with aerial surveying, the data obtained are treated best as trend indicators and not absolute numbers.

Other population-related assessments sometimes used to help formulate management decisions are range condition evaluations (such as range productivity and utilization of key species), vegetation succession, digestibility of forage, and forage-nutrient analysis. Pellet group counts have provided information on relative use of habitats and assessment of population trends. Some lesser used, but supplemental information has been obtained from direct ground counts, track counts, aerial photography and infrared thermal imagery (Timmermann 1974).

The principle that an animal living in an environment best reflects the condition and quality of that environment is being used to assess the relative health among moose populations. Rumen volatile fatty-acid (VFA) production (Gasaway and Coady 1974) and

Dart gun immobilization of moose from helicopter. Photo by Ed Klinkhart; courtesy of the Alaska Department of Fish and Game.

physiologic (blood and hair) information (Franzmann et al. 1976) are being used as relative quality criteria. Increased blood calcium, phosphorus, total protein, hemoglobin and packed cell volume values were correlated with improved condition of moose. Hair sampling and analysis for mineral elements may be used to determine and monitor past and present mineral element uptake in moose which, in turn, reflects nutritional status of a population (Franzmann et al. 1975).

Harvest data are assembled from mandatory harvest tickets, questionnaires and check stations. Examination of harvested animals may provide pregnancy rates (also obtained by palpation of immobilized moose), age structure of the herd by sectioning incisor teeth (Sergeant and Pimlott 1959), and the relative condition of animals as reflected by visceral, marrow and cover fat, body growth, and antler development.

Moose harvest objectives vary from limited harvest for trophy males to optimum sustained-yield harvest of either sex. Application of these systems depends on location, access and productivity of populations, as well as tradition, legal authority and associated moose-harvest plans and regulations for other game animal populations. Management procedures for harvest may vary according to objectives, by utilizing such mechanisms as season length and schedule for one or either sex, limited licenses, controlled access, controlled method and means of taking moose, and special announcements of openings and closures. As the dynamics of moose populations become better known, flexibility in employing management options to meet objectives will become more important. Correspondingly, increased enforcement of regulations is required. To be valid, regulations must be coordinated with realistic enforcement.

Good moose habitat is essential for the moose resource and its utilization, be it for maximum recreational opportunity or optimum sustained yield. Habitat protection may consist of setting aside large areas that are dedicated primarily for moose habitat, such as the Kenai National Moose Range, Alaska. Limitation of construction and other activities that restrict moose migrations and movements between traditional seasonal home ranges and within critical-use areas of a seasonal home range also may be employed. Increasing demands on the total resource make it imperative that moose management objectives be incorporated into land-use planning.

Preference of moose for early successional vegetation makes it possible to manipulate selected habitats to improve carrying capacity for moose. Prescribed burning, logging in small blocks, selected land clearing and mechanical rehabilitation (Oldemeyer 1977) are practices which result in returning vegetation to early successional stages generally favorable to moose. These practices must be compatible with other resource management considerations and should be subject to total resource planning. In some instances, they may prove detrimental to moose, such as in areas where white-tailed deer are in close association with moose. Logging and associated settlement benefited white-tailed deer, but their subsequent expansion northward brought neurological disease to moose in eastern North America (Karns et al. 1974).

The primary problem moose managers face today and in the future is the maintenance of adequate habitat. In some areas, heavy harvests combined with increasing losses to wolves and other predators may be equally important limitations to moose populations. Knowledge of the particular ecological requirements of each moose population and its associated species is essential to sound management. Undoubtedly, resource agencies will continue to have problems financing the necessary research to obtain this knowledge and to implement adequate moose management programs. Improved public awareness of and appreciation for the aesthetic, commercial and recreational values that the moose resource offers will be beneficial in improving the priority of managing it.

CHARLES
SCHWARTZ

Chapter 6

CARIBOU

A. T. Bergerud

Honorary Associate Professor
Department of Biology
University of Victoria
Victoria, British Columbia

In May, 1792, an explorer, David Thompson, described the caribou crossing the Nelson River (Parker 1972a): ". . . the herd the first day to one hundred and twenty miles in length and the herd of the second day to half as much more, making the whole length of the herd to be one hundred and eighty miles in length, by one hundred yards in breadth . . . by the above space, allowing each deer, ten feet by eight feet, an area of eighty square feet, the number of Rein Deer that passed was 3,564,000 an immense number."

Such assemblages still can stagger the imagination. Each July the bulk of the Porcupine caribou herd gathers on the Arctic plain adjacent to the Beaufort Sea, where densities reach 19,000 animals per square kilometer (50,000 per square mile). This postcalving aggregation must be one of the great remaining natural marvels of this world—equal to zenithal flights of the passenger pigeons and massings of American bison. Such sights, or even knowledge thereof, add perspective to our lives, a tonic and humbling experience. Surely our stewardship on Earth requires our continued coexistence with this splendid animal.

ECOLOGY

Life history

Caribou *(Rangifer tarandus)* have roamed the North for more than one million years. The earliest evidence is from central Germany about 440,000 years ago (Banfield 1961). At present, five subspecies are recognized in North America and a sixth, formerly of the Queen Charlotte Islands, British Columbia, is extinct (Figure 19).

Caribou belong to the deer family (Cervidae) in the Order Artiodactyla. They are an even-toed ruminant with a four-compartment stomach. Caribou are medium-sized deer, with males larger than females. Males of the larger subspecies, found in central Alaska, northern British Columbia and Ungava, Quebec, weigh 181–272 kilograms (400–600 pounds), and those of the smaller subspecies in the Northwest Territories and the Arctic Slope of Alaska, 124–169 kilograms (275–375 pounds). Respectively, females usually weigh about 91–136 kilograms (200–300 pounds) and about 91 kilograms (200 pounds). The above represent average fall weights. Males can

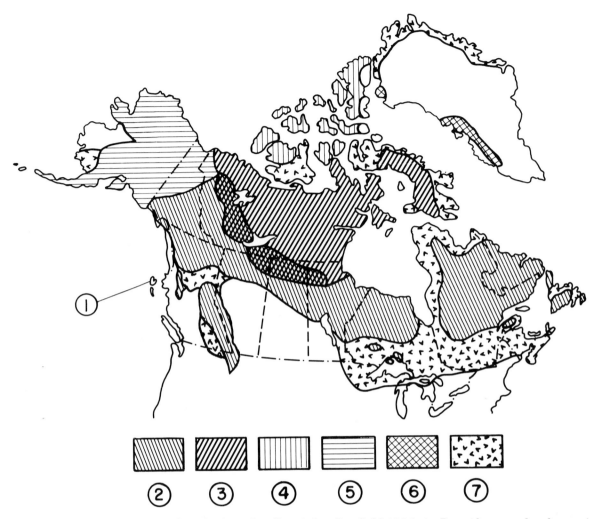

Figure 19. Past and present distribution of caribou (after Banfield 1961): 1. *Rangifer tarandus dawsoni* (extinct); 2. *R. t. caribou;* 3. *R. t. groenlandicus;* 4. *R. t. pearyi;* 5. *R. t. granti;* 6. *R. t. eogroenlandicus;* and 7. former range.

lose as much as 25 percent of their weight during the autumn rut, as do females during some winters.

Caribou are unique among deer in that both females and males commonly have antlers. In northern populations, nearly all females have antlers, but many females in Ontario, Quebec and Newfoundland are "bald." As many as 95 percent of females in one Newfoundland herd had no antlers. The antlers of males are tall, commonly 102 centimeters (40 inches) or longer, often with beams flattened (palmate) and as many as 40 or more points. A brow tine is recognized as the "shovel" over the face. The bez tine is

a handlike structure that forks from the main beam above the brow tine.

The caribou breeding season is much shorter than that of other deer. Actually, the majority of breeding occurs in a one-week period in either the middle or end of October. If a female fails to conceive, she can experience a second or third heat period at intervals of 10–12 days. Gestation is about 227–229 days, with the calves born in May or June. About 90 percent of the young are born during a 10-day period. Dates of breeding and parturition vary among herds, but are remarkably constant within herds. For example, in the Nelchina herd in Alaska the peak of calving always has been from May 24–28; in the Interior herd, Newfoundland, from May 28–June 1; and for various herds in the Northwest Territories, from about June 10–14.

Caribou calves weigh about 5–9 kilograms (11–20 pounds) at birth and are precocial and able to follow their dams within one hour of birth. This mobility is an important adaptation which reduces mortality, since calves are highly vulnerable to predation at birth on the exposed tundra. The first few weeks of life are critical ones; often 25 percent or more of calves die before one month of age.

Population dynamics

The productivity of caribou is low compared to the other cervids in North America. Twinning is almost unknown, and puberty in females is normally not reached until 29–41 months of age. Age-specific pregnancy rates for the Kaminuriak herd were the following: yearlings, 2 percent; two years, 48 percent; three years, 82 percent; and four years or older, 91 percent (Dauphine 1976). However, the pregnancy rate is high for mature females and constant among geographical regions: Kaminuriak herd, 90 percent pregnant; Beverly herd, 78 percent; Nelchina herd, 89 percent; Western Arctic herd, 78 percent; and the Interior herd, 85 percent.

The pregnancy rate remained high in Newfoundland over an 11-year period, even though winter nutrition varied greatly. In one year, some calves starved and in another winter females lost 26 percent of their November weight by June. To the contrary, adult Peary caribou on some Arctic islands starved during the winter of 1973–1974 and again in 1975, and subsequently had low reproductions with only 7 percent pregnancy rates both years (Parker et al. 1975, Thomas et al. 1976).

The most interesting finding comes from the introduction of 29 reindeer—a semi-domestic relative of caribou—to St. Matthew Island, Alaska, in 1944. These 29 animals increased to 1,350 by 1957, then to 6,000 by 1963. This herd increased at a rate of 34 percent per year from 1944–1957, and 28 percent per year from 1957–1963. During the entire period 1944–1963, density increased from 0.08–18 caribou per square kilometer (0.2–46.7 per square mile). This population increase was quite constant and did not follow the normal sigmoid growth curve for animals "pushing" and exceeding their food resources. Even survivors of the eventual "crash" continued to ovulate. In the winter of 1963–1964, the entire herd starved and only 42 animals remained in 1965 (Klein 1968). Until then, the herd did not demonstrate an appreciable increase in mortality or decrease of reproductive rate, despite the dramatic increase of density and depletion of food supplies over the 19-year period. This study strikingly identifies the degree to which some caribou populations have achieved a reproductive rate independent of food supply.

The reproductive rate of caribou is low, but the mortality rate is high. An average of only 50 percent of calves in many herds live to 12 months of age. Calf mortality can exceed 90 percent in herds located where there are high densities of wolves and/or grizzly bears. Adults fare better. The natural annual mortality of adults is about 4–6 percent with few natural predators. In Newfoundland, males had a higher mortality rate (9 percent) than females (4 percent). The natural mortality rate of adults when there are normal densities of predators has not been determined yet, but it probably will average 7–13 percent, depending on predator densities.

At birth, approximately 51–55 percent of calves are male. In Newfoundland where lynx selectively killed male calves, the sex ratio favored females by five to six months of age. However, in the Kaminuriak and Nelchina herds, males predominated in the yearling class. They also were most abundant in the two-year age class of the Kaminuriak herd (Bergerud 1971a, Miller 1974, Skoog 1968). The mean percent of adult males was 39 for eight populations which either were not hunted or were hunted nonselectively (Bergerud 1974a). Frequent segregation of the sexes makes it difficult to obtain a representative sample of a caribou population.

The percentage of calves in a herd, at birth, is normally about 27–30. Herds with calves representing less than 10 percent of their populations in April probably are declining; herds with 17 or more calves per 100 animals in April likely are increasing (based on the assumption of hunting mortality near 5 percent).

Mortality factors

Caribou calves die from a multitude of factors, including birth defects, accidents, social interactions such as trampling, wind chill, desertion and predation. By far, predation is the most important natural cause of death. On calving grounds in the Northwest Territories, Miller and Broughton (1974) reported that 32 percent of the calves they found dead were killed by wolves. During an 11-year study in Newfoundland, lynx were found responsible for 75 percent of the calves I located dead or dying. When wolves and possibly grizzly bears are abundant, calf mortality during the first year can be about 85 percent; I believe that miscellaneous deaths can account for 30 percent of this loss and that predators cause the remaining 55 percent. Wind chill is the second most common cause of death of newborn calves during inclement weather (*cf.* Kelsall 1968). This cause of mortality can deplete an entire calf crop. The Kaminuriak herd lost much of its 1962 calf crop from this factor (Miller 1974). The extent of this form of mortality depends on both the severity of weather plus the vigor of calves at birth. Following hard winters, the weight of pregnant females is reduced which, in turn, results in calves of reduced size at birth. These small calves have reduced viability and increased susceptibility to mortality from harsh weather; thus, the two variables are involved (Bergerud 1974b, Dauphine 1976). Desertion is

possibly the third most common cause of death. Females in large moving herds tend to abandon their calves more frequently than do nonmigratory dams.

Causes of death for adults include drowning, social interactions during breeding, death in parturition, disease, starvation and predation. There now is considerable evidence that white-tailed deer transmit the parasitic meningeal worm *Parelaphostrongylus tenuis* to caribou with fatal results. The declines of caribou in Minnesota, Maine, New Brunswick and Nova Scotia may have been due in part to the northward spread of deer when settlement practices cleared forest lands. The only viable caribou population now coinhabiting range with high densities of deer is in the Shickshock Mountains, Gaspé, Quebec. Altitudinal stratification, with caribou living higher than deer, may be the reason that contact is minimized. If caribou could become resistant to this disease, it might be possible to restore them to many former ranges. This should be an important area of research for wildlife departments.

Starvation is another cause of death, especially on the Arctic Islands and the Alaskan Peninsula. Skoog (1968) predicted that snow and ice cover would limit populations on the Arctic Islands, and his prediction has been proven correct. In 1972–1974, a large portion of the Peary caribou population died. The population on 20 islands was estimated to number 24,320 in 1961 (Tener 1961), but in 1974, only 2,676 caribou remained (Miller et al. 1977)—a 90 percent loss. This die-off resulted because snow and/or ice prevented the animals from reaching food.

Predation is omnipresent. Recent studies in Alaska showed males more vulnerable than females and that caribou in small groups faced greater risk than more aggregated individuals. Wolves were able to secure an animal from nearly 50 percent of the groups they tested or chased (Haber 1977). Caribou have but one strategy besides herding: running. A 50 percent mortality rate per wolf encounter for single animals leaves something to be desired.

Behavior

We can presume that the extrinsic environment has shaped the behavior of the species. Important environmental factors have been the weather (snow and wind), other animals (insects and wolves), visibility in the habitat (mostly open views for many populations), and the flora (slow-growing lichens). First, the open habitat plus the presence of wolves likely has fostered the caribou's gregarious behavior. Grouping reduces predation (Bergerud 1974c), but is not compatible with a sedentary mode of life because of the slow-growing flora and the variability of food supplies due to snow and wind. Thus, the caribou is a gregarious but nomadic denizen of the Arctic prairies.

Caribou are always moving, usually in large groups. We might say caribou constantly move but pause periodically where there is an abundance of requisites. A brief outline of the annual cycle of movement and aggregating behavior is presented in Table 6 (for details on behavior and movement, see Bergerud 1974c).

Table 6. Annual cycle of behavior and movement of caribou.

Time of year	Life cycle, pause-shift schedule[a]	Group size and composition	Habitat utilized	Factors affecting aggregating and movement behavior
April–May	Spring migration, spring shift	Long columns, pregnant females at front, few males, some yearlings drop out, 50–1,000 per group	Natural channels, areas free of snow, south slopes	Movement starts with bare areas, move faster if start later, 19–55 km/day (10–30 mi/day); move to familiar areas to produce young, tradition involved
Late May–early June	Calving, calving pause	Scattered over calving grounds, alone at birth, yearling and female groups less than 10 per group	Tundra, sedge meadow, drier uplands	Pause to give birth to calves, immediately join other females with young calves; period for female to learn to recognize her offspring
July	Post-calving aggregation, post calving shift	Huge groups of females, yearlings and young calves, up to 80,000 per group	Tundra, new willow-birch growth, wind-swept hills, snow fields	Huge herds form, with sharp boundary line; herds reduce wolf predation on offspring; animals often together because of discontinuous nature of insect-relief habitat
August	Summer dispersal, summer shift	Scattered small groups everywhere, less than 100 animals together	River flats, alpine tundra, birch-willow stands	Insects abate; animals can scatter to find most palatable food, move and then pause
September	Fall shuffle, fall shift	Females start to group, males join female groups	Tundra, open lichen-conifer forests	Movement to bring sexes together
October–November	Rut, fall pause	Random assortment males and females, herds 5–400 per group	Open lichen-conifer forests, bushy areas	Pause for breeding; can start moving while breeding if snow occurs
November	Fall migration, fall shift	Long columns, groups up to many thousands	Open lichen-conifer forests, bushy areas	Movement triggered by first heavy snow; move to areas where food will be easier to find later in winter
December–March	Winter, winter pause	Scattered over range 20–100 per group, males segregated	Sedge lake margins open forests, wind-swept mountains	Little movement if snow cover does not change; widely scattered if little snow and food can be detected over wide area; concentrated and aggregated if area where food can be detected is discontinuous

[a]Pause-shift sequence from Skoog (1968).

HABITAT NEEDS AND PREFERENCES

Caribou have universal tastes, eating a wider variety of plants than other deer species. A partial list of the plants eaten includes 62 lichens and 282 kinds of seed plants (Bergerud 1977). However, caribou show preference for green vascular plants and mushrooms. When these plants cannot be secured, caribou are opportunistic and will eat whatever plants are available. Relative availability then is the prime factor in species utilization.

As the spring thaw advances, caribou quickly change their diet to include new vegetative growth. In mountainous regions, caribou can continue to find new plant growth by shifting altitude and visiting receding snowfields. Grasses, sedges and cottongrass are the most important plant groups eaten. The animals also seek other newly sprouting plants such as willow catkins, larch needles, leaves of alder and Solomon's seal, and sweet gale buds.

The most important food in the summer diet are green leaves of deciduous shrubs, especially those of willow, shrub birch and blueberry. Caribou are fastidious feeders, stripping leaves from woody stems and picking only new sprouts and finer stem tips of sedges, herbs and horsetail. In late summer, they actively search for mushrooms.

After the first hard frost, leaves quickly become unavailable and the animals switch to terrestrial lichens and leaves of evergreen shrubs. The most important fruticose lichens eaten include *Cladonia alpestris, C. rangiferina* and *C. mitis.*

In winter, snow depth dictates food availability. Winter greens are especially important if caribou can find them by digging holes in the snow (called feeding craters). The animals also seek the fine twigs of birch, willow and blueberry. Where a sun crust that can support caribou develops on the snow, they will shift from open habitats to forest cover seeking arboreal lichens growing on coniferous trees.

Two environmental needs stand out above all others: (1) to escape or find relief from flying insects in summer; and (2) to find food through deep snow in winter. These two needs largely dictate where caribou will be found.

Caribou are bothered especially by warble and nostril flies. The warble fly lays its eggs on the flanks of caribou. When the larvae hatch, they burrow through the skin and move to the region of the back. The nostril fly lays live larvae in the nostrils of caribou. To reduce insect attacks, caribou seek hilltops with strong winds, snow and ice fields, and cool and shady forests. If the environment does not provide insect-relief habitat, then the animals keep moving, at times running and stampeding. They often stand in dense clumps on hilltops with their heads down and together, hindquarters out. Apparently the simple obstructions of caribou bodies reduce attacks. Animals continually wheeze and shake to ward off insects.

In winter, finding food through deep snow is the all-important need of caribou. We should distinguish between "absolute abundance" of food (the actual food amount present; often what we see and measure on summer range studies) and "relative abundance" of food (the amount of food the animals can find through snow cover). In winter, caribou often are found where there is limited absolute abundance of food, but because of reduced snow depths there is high relative abundance. Caribou seek areas of reduced snow cover, south slopes and windswept mountains to locate food.

Caribou can smell the presence of food under snow, probably to depth no more than 15–18 centimeters (6–7 inches) of continuous snow. They often visit shrubs sticking through the snow because air vents adjacent to the stems let them scent down to greater depths. Even when covered by snow, shrubs bridge the detection gap between the snow surface and buried ground flora.

Summarizing the condition suitable for winter feeding:

1. Irregular terrain—because of wind currents and, thus, variable snow depths—is superior to uniform terrain;

2. Habitats with three vegetation strata (ground, shrub and tree) are superior to ranges with only one or two strata (the trees should be well-spaced);

3. Regions with shallow snow are superior to those with deep snow; and

4. Terrain with hard snow (that will support caribou) is superior to terrain with soft snow if it is deep.

DISTRIBUTION AND STATUS: PAST AND PRESENT

The caribou of the Nearctic are distributed throughout Canada and Alaska in the tundra and taiga biomes (Figure 19). They no longer frequent New Brunswick, Nova Scotia, Maine or Minnesota. A small herd of 20–30 still frequents the Selkirk Mountains in southeastern British Columbia and northern Idaho (Freddy 1974).

How many caribou were there originally? This presumes that there was an upper carrying capacity, a view I question. Populations likely rose and fell. Murie (1935) estimated an Alaskan herd at 568,000 animals in 1920, or 2.2 per square kilometer (5.6 per square mile). Also, in 1962–1967, the Nelchina herd approached 1.9 animals per square kilometer (5 per square mile). Thus, based on habitat available and a density of 1.9 animals per square kilometer (4.9 per square mile), Alaska may have reached 1–2 million caribou (Murie 1935) and northwestern Canada may have had 3.8 million (Clarke 1940). However, numbers were probably much lower, perhaps 0.4–0.6 per square kilometer (1–1.5 per square mile) (Calef 1974), or 3–5 million caribou for all North America.

There were perhaps 1.3 million caribou in the mid-1960s, and in 1977, about 1.1 million. Three large populations now exist, each composed of several subpopulations or herds that have different calving grounds:

1. The Ungava population, ranging over about 260,000 square kilometers (100,000 square miles), calving at three or more locations and numbering perhaps 150,000 adults and yearlings in 1976 (S. Luttich, personal communication)

2. The barren-ground population found from the Mackenzie River to Hudson Bay, ranging over about 1.6 million square kilometers (610,000 square miles), calving at at least seven locations and now numbering at least 547,000 animals (Thomas 1969, Parker 1972a, Calef 1977) (see Figure 20); and

3. The Alaskan population (west of the Mackenzie River), ranging over 1 million square kilometers (400,000 square miles) and calving at 15 or more locations and numbering about 600,000 animals between 1964–1970 (Hemming 1971), but reduced to 238,000 animals by 1977 (Davis 1977).

Since about 1964, 7 of the 11 major caribou herds in Alaska have declined by approximately 362,000 animals, or 60 percent (Table 7). These herds were monitored, and why management failed is an extremely important question.

I believe the Alaskan herds declined because of heavy hunting of adults in the absence of satisfactory survival of young. The most significant cause of calf mortality was predation by wolves and possibly grizzly bears. Of the seven herds that declined, six were heavily hunted (10–20 percent annual harvest) while the seventh, the Mount McKinley herd, was only lightly hunted. The decline of the McKinley herd is probably explained by egress to the Mulchatna herd (Haber 1977). This egress would explain the increase of the Mulchatna herd, the only important herd to have increased in recent times except for the Alaska Peninsula herd (Figure 20). The Nelchina herd was the most intensively studied of the herds that declined. Figure 21 shows the increase of this herd from 1955–1962, after the wolves had been reduced, and the subsequent decline of the herd from 1963–1972. Note in Figure 21

Table 7. Population estimates of caribou since 1960 (herd numbers correspond with Figure 20).

Herd number	Herd	Year counted	Census estimated	Method of census	Reference source
1	Queen Elizabeth	1961	26,000	winter aerial transect	Tener 1963
1	Queen Elizabeth[a]	1974	2,700		Miller et al. 1977
2	Banks Island	1972	12,000	winter aerial transects	Urquhart, Unpublished
3	Western Arctic	1970	195,000[b]	aerial photo extrapolation	Hemming 1971
3	Western Arctic	1976	40,000[b]	aerial photo extrapolation	Davis 1977
4	Porcupine[c]	1972	110,000	aerial photo extrapolation	Calef 1974
4	Porcupine[c]	1976	110,000		D. McKnight[c]
5	Beaver	1963	3,000		Hemming 1971
6	Mt. McKinley	1966	8,000	ground count at migration	Haber 1976
6	Mt. McKinley	1976	1,000	aerial census	Haber 1977
7	Delta	1963	5,000		Hemming 1971
7	Delta	1973	2,000		D. McKnight[c]
8	Fortymile	1969	20,000		LeResche 1975
8	Fortymile	1975	4,000	aerial photo extrapolation	Davis 1977
9	Chisana	1963	3,000		Hemming 1971
9	Chisana	1976?	1,000		Davis 1977
10	Mentasta	1965	5,000		Hemming 1971
10	Mentasta	1977	2,700	aerial photo extrapolation	Davis 1977
11	Nelchina	1962	71,000	random quad-rats winter	Siniff and Skoog 1964
11	Nelchina	1977	14,000	aerial photo extrapolation	Davis 1977
12	Mulchatna	1963	5,000		Hemming 1971
12	Mulchatna	1976	9,000	aerial photo extrapolation	Davis 1977
13	Kenai	1976	250	direct count from air	Davis 1977
14	Alaska Peninsula	1968	14,000		Hemming 1971
14	Alaska Peninsula	1977	16,700	aerial photo extrapolation	Davis 1977
15	Adak Island	1976	275	direct count from air	Davis 1977
16	Spatsizi	1976	2,000	direct count rutting groups	Hazelwood[c]
17	Bluenose[e]	1967	19,000	air photo and transect count	Thomas 1969
17	Bluenose[e]	1975	90,000	transect count	Calef 1977
18	Bathurst[e]	1967	144,000	air photo and transect count	Thomas 1969
18	Bathurst[e]	1974	174,000	transect count	Calef 1977
19	Beverly[e]	1967	159,000	air photo and transect count	Thomas 1969
19	Beverly[e]	1974	124,000	aerial transects	Calef 1977
20	Kaminuriak[e]	1968	68,000	transects, blocks, photo	Parker 1972a
20	Kaminuriak[e]	1976	45,000	aerial transects	Calef 1977
21	Coats Island	1975	2,000		Parker 1975
22	Baffin Island[e]	1963–1973	10,000–30,000	transects, general observation	Rippen, Unpublished MacPherson, Unpublished
23	Ungava	1976	150,000	count of females on calving grounds	S. Luttich[c]
24	Mealy Mt.	1963	800	winter aerial transects	Bergerud 1967

Table 7.

25	Avalon Pen	1967	720	direct aerial count, autumn	Bergerud 1971a
26	Interior	1966	7,700	winter aerial transects	Bergerud 1971a
27	Slate Islands	1976	200+	walking transects, Lincoln Index	Bergerud[d]
28	Ontario	1959–1964	13,000	winter aerial transects	Simkin 1965
29	Nipigon Islands	1975	75	walking transects, pellet count	Bergerud[d]
30	Selkirk Mts.	1974	20–30	ground observation	Freddy 1974
	Melville Peninsula[e]	1976	45,000	aerial transects	Calef 1977
	Wager Peninsula[e]	1976	12,000	aerial transects	Calef 1977
	Lorriland Refuge[f]	1976	17,000	aerial transects	Calef 1977
	Baffin Island	1974	20,000	aerial transects	Calef 1977
	Kaudy Plateau	1977	1,700	direct aerial count	Bergerud[d]
	Itcha Mts.	1977	250	direct aerial count	H. Mitchell[c]
	Wells Gray	1970	350	snow field census	R. Ritcey[c]
	Waco	1972	8,000	aerial transect	I. Juniper[c]

[a]Does not include all the islands identified by Tener (1961).

[b]Excludes calves.

[c]Personal communication.

[d]Personal files.

[e]See Figure 22.

[f]There also are large numbers of woodland caribou in the Mackenzie Mountains at the Yukon and the Northwest Territories, perhaps 10,000–20,000 (Calef, personal communication).

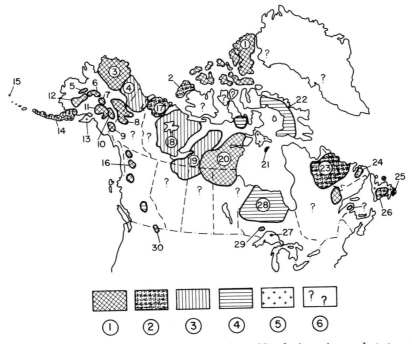

Figure 20. Location of some of the major caribou herds in North America and status since the 1960s. Numbers identify herds listed in Table 7. Population estimates may be known by local biologists for "?" areas but are not to the author: 1. decreased; 2. increased; 3. stable; 4. unknown; 5. introduced; 6. no population trend known.

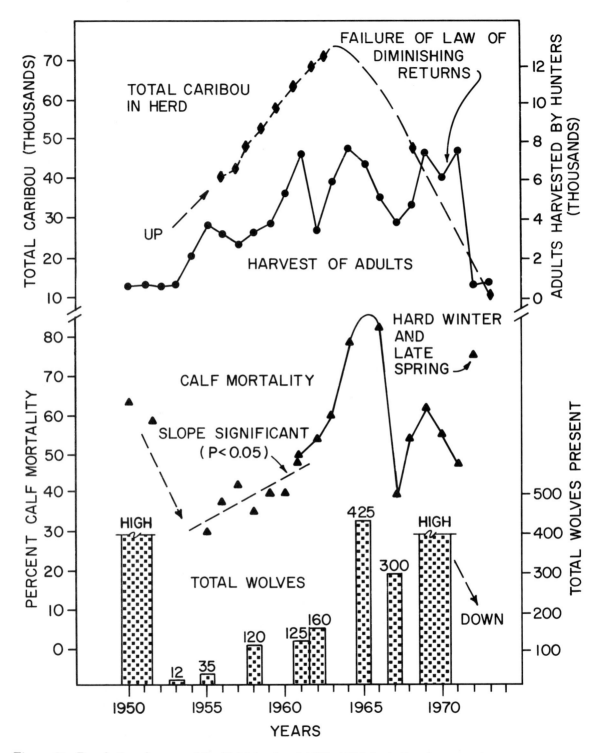

Figure 21. Population changes of the Nelchina herd 1950–1972, including harvest of adults, survival of calves and abundance of wolves (after Rausch 1967, 1969, Skoog 1968, Bos 1975). Calf mortality (1961–1969) is calculated from the percentage of two-year old females in the harvest of the total females two years of age and older, and is believed to underestimate calf mortality by 10–15 percent.

that as wolf numbers increased, survival of the calves decreased. When wolf numbers declined from illegal hunting in 1966, calf survival showed a marked improvement. After 1968, wolves again increased and calf survival was reduced. These data suggest that predation played a dominant role in calf survival in this herd. Calves also may have died from starvation in the winter of 1970–1971 and/or from wind chill in 1972 (Bos 1975). In the other herds, annual calf survival to 12 months of age was known to be poor, often only 15 percent in at least four of the five other herds during their declines. Wolf numbers also were high in the areas of these herds. In summary, these herds had population parameters similar to other herds in North America that declined when hunting was heavy and predator numbers high.

The Porcupine herd did not decline like the seven other herds, yet calf survival was poor; an average of only 19 percent of the calves survived annually in the years 1972–1977 (calculated on the basis that 75 percent of the females gave birth). The one difference between the dynamics of the Porcupine herd and the other herds that declined was that the Porcupine was only lightly hunted—a harvest of less than 5 percent annually. This contrast with the other herds strengthens the view that the other herds declined because of a combination of heavy adult losses from hunting plus a high mortality of calves; adult losses were not replaced.

The decline of the Alaskan caribou population appears to have resulted from overhunting in the absence of adequate recruitment. The same factors were responsible for declines in the Northwest Territories from 1949–1955 (Banfield 1954, Parker 1972) (Figure 22), and in Newfoundland from 1915–1930 (Bergerud 1971a).

I believe that three points of view held by some wildlife biologists in Alaska contributed to the management failure experienced there. They were: (1) that large herds would not be overharvested; (2) underestimation of the extent of calf

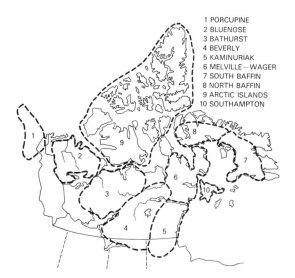

1 PORCUPINE
2 BLUENOSE
3 BATHURST
4 BEVERLY
5 KAMINURIAK
6 MELVILLE—WAGER
7 SOUTH BAFFIN
8 NORTH BAFFIN
9 ARCTIC ISLANDS
10 SOUTHAMPTON

Figure 22. Major caribou ranges in the Northwest Territories (G. Calef, personal communication).

mortality when predator numbers were high; and (3) that food supplies set carrying capacity for caribou populations which, consequently, had to be hunted heavily to prevent the animals from overgrazing habitat and declining in number. There is recent evidence of considerable shifts relating to the first and second views, but the food supply-carrying capacity notion still persists. As a result, some Alaska herds continued to be harvested heavily, with the intent of preventing ranges from becoming overgrazed.

Mathematically, in a herd of 100 animals, approximately 61 will be females. If the herd has had poor prior recruitment of calves, many of the females will be older animals and sexually mature. These females (80 percent pregnant) should produce 49 calves. But, if only 15 percent of these calves live to one year, only seven animals are added to the herd. Seven calves are just about sufficient to equal the annual natural mortality of adult caribou living in areas with few predators. Thus, there is no surplus for hunters and any hunting will reduce future populations.

In addition, population declines are difficult to halt. The law of diminishing returns works neither for men nor wolves (Figure

21), at least initially. Hunters can still find caribou because of the open terrain and their conspicuous habits. Wolf numbers are adjusted only slowly to reduced caribou herds (called predator lag); thus the same number of wolves hunt a smaller supply of game for a time.

If herds are to be harvested heavily, it is essential to determine the percentage of calves in the herd each March–April. Counts made during autumn may not provide an accurate assessment of recruitment if wolf predation is extensive on the winter range. The loss of just one calf crop can be extremely serious. Several herds that declined in Alaska were not monitored as to calf survival for several consecutive years. When they were checked, it was too late; the herds already were reduced substantially.

MANAGEMENT

Estimating population parameters

Caribou, because they usually live in open habitats, are relatively easy to census. Various herds have been estimated by:

1. Aerial transect counts in winter (Bergerud 1963);
2. Aerial census of quadrats selected at random from stratified density strata in winter or on the calving grounds (Siniff and Skoog 1964, Parker 1972a);
3. Tag-resighting methods (Lincoln Index) (Parker 1972b);
4. Aerial photographic techniques (Parker 1972a); and
5. Actual counts of animals or tracks where they intersected roads or rivers.

At present, the most common technique is to photograph females in July when nearly all of them gather in huge postcalving aggregations. Males, calves and yearlings then are prorated to the July female count based on classification counts of the herds during the autumn rut when all age-sex classes are represented proportionally. Census results should not be accepted unless two independent methods show agreement. The most comprehensive treatment of census procedures is Parker's (1972a) census of the Kaminuriak herd in 1968.

For animals that live in forested habitats, I have used the King strip census in May and June. A tally of carcasses from winter mortality was conducted concurrently. Also, diagrams of male antlers of forest-dwelling races have been drawn to identify individuals for a total count of males (Bergerud 1973). The other components of the herd can be added based on autumn composition counts.

Animals can be aged as calves, yearlings and adults by comparing body size and antler growth. The short face of young animals contrasts well with the longer horse-face of adults. Until 12 months old, calves can be distinguished from adults during aerial surveys, and during ground observation until the animals are 17 months old. Collected animals should be aged by noting wear on the mandibular teeth or by cross-sectioning incisors and counting annulations in the cementum (Skoog 1968, Miller 1974).

The sexes usually can be distinguished by the larger size of males (thick neck, white mane and large antlers in the autumn) and the Roman nose of males in contrast to the straight profile of females. The best method is to ignore all other characteristics and observe the animals from the rear for the presence or absence of the vulva (Bergerud 1961). The sex of animals killed by hunters can be checked by measuring the length of the lower mandible or the diastema length of the mandible (Miller 1974).

The pregnancy rate of caribou can be estimated by field counts (air or ground) of antlered females in May. Nonpregnant females shed their antlers in March or April, whereas pregnant females shed their antlers at the time of calving (Skoog 1968, Bergerud 1976). This technique requires that the observer know the percentage of females in the population that have the antler characteristics, which can be determined by counts in

This photograph, and the next two, illustrate the sequence of events during caribou-tagging operations at Duck Lake, Manitoba. Here, a bull caribou (antlers shedding velvet) is approached. Extended shepherd's crook will be used to pull the animal safely to the canoe for marking.

A live caribou is held momentarily while metal tag and yellow streamer are attached to the ear.

A tagged caribou swims toward shore moments after its release. It and other barren-ground caribou were tagged to provide information on intermingling among herds, eastward and westward movements, and rate of travel. Photos by E. F. Bossenmaier; courtesy of the Manitoba Wildlife Branch.

autumn. It also is possible to tell whether a female has given birth by the presence or absence of a large milk udder immediately postcalving (Bergerud 1964). If a female is seen with a large udder and no calf, it can be concluded that her calf died, since calves invariably follow their dams in populations that calve in open habitats. Microtechniques are now well-advanced for determining past pregnancies of a female based on counts of corpora lutea of pregnancy in the ovaries (Dauphine 1976).

Harvest objectives

The data seem clear; men and predators compete for a common resource. If wolf and/or grizzly bear numbers are high—one predator per 65–130 square kilometers (25–50 square miles) hunting moose and caribou, or one predator per 259–311 square ki-

lometers (100–120 square miles) hunting mostly caribou—only 10–20 percent of caribou calves may survive to 12 months of age. Also, the natural mortality of adult caribou when predators are present is possibly 7–10 percent or more. In these situations, there can be practically no human harvest; the balance is too fine. If a harvest is required for subsistence hunters, wolf populations in those areas must be reduced. In the absence of wolves, possibly 15–20 percent of a caribou herd can be cropped in years when there is no extensive wind chill mortality of calves.

Managers charged with supervising recreational hunting probably can permit a harvest of 10–15 percent of the males even in the presence of moderate wolf numbers; for example, one wolf per 518 square kilometers (200 square miles). The harvest probably can be only 5 percent if both sexes are taken (Parker 1972a). Hunting of only males will alter the sex ratio. Annual harvests of 11 percent of male caribou in Newfoundland for nine years reduced the male-female ratio from 1:2 to 1:3 (Bergerud 1971b). Fertility remained high and females continued to conceive in their first heat period. If the sex ratio is unbalanced to 1:5–9, possibly not all the females will be bred in their first estrus. Calves born 10–12 days later than the majority of calves will be at a survival disadvantage.

A growing segment of the public wants unharvested ecosystems. They wish to view ungulates and wolves interacting in their natural setting. Even in this setting, I believe that many caribou populations are below desirable densities (*cf.* Walters et al. 1975). A valuable experiment would be to remove whole wolf packs as suggested by Haber (1977). This removal would test Haber's hypothesis that intrapack social restraints suppress reproduction in wolves. In any case, the caribou population should increase, the wolf population would bounce back, and the ecosystem then could proceed on its own course of evolution, but at higher equilibrium densities of predator and prey.

Habitat problems

Range destruction of climax lichens by forest fires has long been considered the nemesis of caribou (Scotter 1964). Leopold and Darling (1953) were the first to formalize this hypothesis. After a four-month tour of Alaska, they postulated that caribou were climax animals requiring climax lichens, and concluded: "Caribou have been . . . very much reduced in central and southern Alaska by burning over the winter range." To the contrary, Skoog (1968) thought fires had little impact on caribou in Alaska. Edwards (1954) published that caribou had declined in British Columbia because of habitat destruction by fires. Cringan (1957) expressed a similar opinion with respect to woodland caribou in Ontario. Hunting, predation and disease were presented as alternative reasons for declines in British

Columbia and Ontario (Bergerud 1974b). Lastly, Scotter (1964, 1967) studied forage supplies of the Beverly herd in Saskatchewan and argued that fires were one of the principal causes of decline and that the vast destroyed range would not permit a caribou population increase for several years. However, he later changed his view that fires were harmful and said that effects were equivocal (Rowe and Scotter 1973). In yet another paper, he agreed in conjunction with the several authors that a 5-times increase in area covered by fires would have little influence on caribou numbers and that the range could support a 6.5-times increase in numbers (Bunnell et al. 1975).

About 1967, caribou ecologists began to recognize the beneficial effects of forest fires. Ahti and Hepburn (1967) recommended controlled burning in Ontario of peatlands, bogs and spruce muskegs to increase lichen supplies. Bergerud (1971c) argued that forest fires had increased lichen forage in Newfoundland by opening up forest canopies and destroying stunted alpine conifers. Bergerud (1972) also felt that caribou did not require lichens and often ate other foods in winter. Heinselman (1973) argued for the need to restore fire to its natural role in the forests of northern Minnesota. Johnson and Rowe (1975) studied fire on the winter range of the Beverly herd and reported that lightning accounted for 99.9 percent of the area burned from 1966–1972. They felt that fires probably improved the caribou range by mineralizing nutrients and renewing the growth of sedges, forbs, shrubs and even lichens. They concluded: "If it is accepted that fires are part of the boreal forest ecosystem then it follows that the vegetation has never existed in a climax state . . . over wide areas. The mosaic of vegetation of all ages visible today is probably close to the norm. The carrying capacity of the land may well be similar to what it always has been."

Miller (1976) concluded after a three-year study of caribou range in northern Manitoba that forest fires benefited caribou by maintaining the heterogeneity of habitat types. I have also noted this fire-created heterogeneity in Labrador and Ontario. Many heavily utilized lichen-woodland winter ranges owed their existence to repeated burning.

Debates about the values and use of fire on caribou ranges in the boreal forest finally have brought action. In 1976, the Canadian federal government ceased fire-fighting operations in the Northwest Territories in large areas of noncommercial forest (caribou range).

On this question of limiting factors on caribou populations, Leopold and Darling (1953) stated: "We cannot agree with the viewpoint expressed by Green (1950) that because Alaska is large and funds . . . small it necessarily follows that the game program must be directed towards controlling the action of predators, both men and wolves, rather than improving the range. To ignore range limitations for caribou is to ignore the crux of the problem. One fire easily could undo the work of decades in protecting a local population from men and wolves."

Hindsight indicates that Green was right, and that Leopold and Darling were wrong. Consequently, caribou habitat management was misdirected for nearly one-quarter of a century. It has not been demonstrated that an absolute shortage of food has caused caribou declines, but "men and wolves" clearly have been implicated.

Another dated argument is that caribou will overgraze their range and crash. The decline of free-ranging caribou due to an absolute shortage of foods caused by high populations has not been documented. Again, it was Leopold and Darling (1953) who formalized this concern. They hypothesized on the basis of declines of closely herded reindeer in Alaska and deer populations in the United States that overgrazed their ranges and starved in winter. Caribou, however, are not like sedentary reindeer and deer. As caribou numbers increase, their movements become more pronounced, their ranges expand and grazing pressure is distributed over larger and larger areas.

As to the question of full range occupancy, Skoog (1968) thought it almost axiomatic that no caribou herd has ever occupied all of its potential range. Snow cover prevented caribou from utilizing but a fraction (2–10 percent) of their range (Skoog 1968, Miller 1976). As a result, some areas may be denuded of lichens while a few feet away lichens are lush. This happens regardless of caribou density. Range overutilization, in a botanical sense, in areas of reduced snow cover should be considered the norm for caribou range (Bergerud 1974d).

Caribou ecologists have attempted to measure range carrying capacity since the start of management efforts. Estimates of maximum sustained densities have ranged from one reindeer per 8.1 hectares (20 acres) to one caribou per 109 square kilometers (42 square miles). Presently, I am investigating a population on the Slate Islands, Lake Superior, Ontario, where there is about one caribou per 14 hectares (35 acres). Similar high densities have existed there since at least the 1940s. There are no terrestrial lichens available, and the only substantial arboreal lichens are above a 1.5-meter (5-foot) browse line; in fact, there is hardly any food at all in the winter. Ahti (unpublished), a lichenologist, estimated in 1958 the carrying capacity of that section of Ontario at one animal per 109 square kilometers (42 square miles). The actual sustained density is 768 times the estimated carrying capacity. I do not know of any studies of the range of free-ranging caribou that have resulted in (1) increased numbers, (2) improved animal quality, or (3) a predicted decline where it could be shown that birth or death rates were altered due to an absolute shortage of food.

There is no answer to the perennial question of how many caribou a given range can support. Range has not yet been shown to limit numbers. In 1963–1965, the Nelchina herd reached the highest density of any major caribou herd in recent times (1.5–1.9 caribou per square kilometer: 4–5 per square mile). However, after several years of study when the population was peaking, Skoog (1968) felt that there were no problems of food shortage, then or in the future.

He said: "In reality, caribou populations in Alaska seem to have maintained densities much lower than the maximum dictated by food alone." He was speaking of both the past and present.

Caribou populations reach various unpredictable population levels. This is the Andrewartha and Birch (1954) theory of population regulation. Predator-prey oscillations appear to be a major factor in the rise and fall of caribou populations (Bergerud 1971a, 1974).

The flora cannot be measured to determine maximum stocking, but caribou can be collected to measure their health and sizes and, thus, the quality of their range. For example, reindeer introduced to a virgin, high quality range on St. Matthew Island, Alaska showed increased body-growth rates and ultimate body size compared to the genetic stock from which they originated (Klein 1968). Part of their superior performance may relate to the lack of harassing insects on the ocean island, but since average size declined at high stocking levels, nutrition also must have been involved.

Wildlife managers might be well-advised to collect animals in May and June to assess the annual impact of winter nutrition, and again in September for statistics on oversummering conditions. Collected animals would provide a wealth of data. Some examples are: (1) nutritional quality of forage (Klein 1962), (2) fat deposits (Dauphine 1976), (3) growth rates, (4) disease and parasitism, and (5) blood parameters (LeResche et al. 1974). Population data available from such collections would include age structure, pregnancy rates and reproductive history.

Another habitat problem is that of unstocked ranges. For a long time, managers did not feel that it was feasible to restock caribou because of the belief that caribou were wilderness animals that required climax lichen stands far removed from civilization. This not being so, opportunities exist for reestablishing old herds and establishing new ones, even if the flora is not as it was.

Two potentially serious limitations are disease if deer are present and excessive wolf or lynx predation. Releases should succeed on islands without wolves, lynx or deer. When wolves are present, island archipelagoes should be considered. Here the releases of caribou could "island hop" to escape wolves.

From 1961–1964, the Newfoundland government introduced caribou to 18 sites. Success varied but, to date, animals have been harvested legally from four of these sites. A major problem was keeping the animals on the habitats where they were introduced (Bergerud 1974c).

Excellent results were achieved from the release of 23 calves on Adak Island in the Aleutians in 1958 and 1959. Harvests have been as high as 30 percent of the population (in 1973), a record for sustained yield. Another record was that one of the harvested males weighed 318 kilograms (700 pounds), the largest caribou recorded. Islands without predators offer substantial opportunities for population growth, maximum survival and high yields.

Other management problems

There are a multitude of possible or imagined problems associated with increased human use of the North. These include illegal hunting, construction of barriers to movement, abandonment of ranges, human harassment and disturbed predator-prey interactions. The susceptibility of caribou to overhunting is becoming well recognized. There is no solution except more intensive management, including better law enforcement and less poaching.

Large caribou herds need vast space to make suitable range adjustments to winter food shortages, insect attacks and predators. Experiments have been conducted to determine if caribou can navigate pipelines and roads which recently have been constructed. Results have been inconclusive, in part because of faulty experimental design and logistic limitations. It has been noted that caribou sometimes stand under elevated pipelines and in the shade of adjacent buildings to escape insect attack. It is likely that caribou will habituate to these artificialities; they have shown no fear of human construction in the past. If we could step back in time and travel with Lewis and Clark across the vast shortgrass prairie, would we have predicted that pronghorn would adapt to super highways, trains and even barbed wire? Caribou probably are more adaptable than pronghorn.

Furthermore, there is not any good evidence in the literature showing that caribou abandon their ranges as a result of disturbance, with the possible exception of calving areas. To the contrary, a small herd in Ontario winters each year on an active airstrip because of good lichen stands favored by open forest canopies on the runway approaches. Skoog (1968) indicated that there was not sufficient evidence to suggest that Alaskan caribou deserted ranges adjacent to roads in areas where hunting occurred. However, many ranges have been vacated simply due to the attrition of caribou populations. Clearly, if all animals of a population or herd are eliminated, a valuable tradition of uses of the landscape also is eliminated. But if caribou populations are allowed to increase, former ranges may be occupied again.

Also, I think the adverse effect of human harassment of herds has been overstated. Such harassment cannot be condoned, and caribou ecologists may be among the worst offenders. However, the additive effect of such harrassment to the natural stresses of the extrinsic environment are not measurable. In summer, caribou are harassed by insects to the extent that feeding ceases, entire herds stampede and weights remain static. The animals have the ability to cope with this sort of stress. The same applies to the winter season when caribou can lose up to 25 percent of their fall weights and, at times, exist in wretched physical condition. Harassment is serious when young calves are present; herds stampede and the young can be trampled or separated and abandoned by their dams. Human activity should be avoided near calving grounds.

Another more subtle, adverse effect of man is modifying the interaction between predators and caribou. Banfield (1974b) reported that caribou travel down seismic lines, and that wolves may be having increased hunting success by ambushing along these routes. In a new national park in Canada, a road and trail through a key caribou range are now being planned. If these routes are completed and traveled in the winter by snowshoers or snowmobilers, wolves will travel on the routes of compacted snow and enter this winter range more frequently. Wolves need to be studied in greater detail in order to predict how man will adversely affect the complex predator-prey relationships in changing ecosystems used by caribou.

A lone caribou of the Mount McKinley Herd in lush vegetation near the base of Mount McKinley, Alaska. Photo by William E. Ruth.

THE FUTURE

In general, there is reason to be very hopeful for the future of caribou. They are highly adapted to their environment and also adaptable. *Rangifer* is the only ungulate that can use the lichen pastures of the North. Densities of two caribou per square kilometer (5.2 per square mile) or higher might be achieved. The ultimate question for caribou is the same as that once posed for bison—can the land be theirs to wander?

Chapter 7

PRONGHORN

James D. Yoakum
Wildlife Management Biologist
U.S. Bureau of Land Management
Reno, Nevada

For eons, the vast central grasslands of North America supported a tremendous biomass of grazers—pronghorn, bison, elk, deer and bighorn sheep. The numbers of pronghorn and bison are legendary; each population is estimated to have been 30–40 million. Thus, the American prairies can be rated historically as one of the greatest productive big game regions of the world.

Early records often referred to the pronghorn as "antelope," a term handed down through generations, resulting in its common use today. Therefore, use of "antelope" is acceptable, but "pronghorn" is the accurate common name for this species. In Mexico, pronghorn are called "berrendo" which means "pinto," in reference to their tan and white coloration.

TAXONOMY

Pronghorn belong to the family Antilocapridae, indigenous only to North America and with a geological history from the Middle Eocene epoch (approximately 17–70 million years B.P.) to the present. During the Pleistocene epoch (1 million years B.P. to present), there were many genera. However, only one genus existed when Lewis and Clark collected the first specimen for science in 1804 (Thwaites 1905). It was from this

collection that George Ord (1818) gave the pronghorn its scientific name, *Antilocapra americana*. Thus, pronghorn maintain a unique distinction among North American big game due to scientific classification of a single family, genus and species. Classification is based primarily on the annual shedding of horn sheaths. However, this classification currently is being questioned by some scientists (O'Gara and Matson 1975).

At present, there are five recognized subspecies:

1. American pronghorn *(A. a. americana)* (Ord 1818) is the most abundant subspecies, ranging throughout the Great Plains of Canada and the United States, and inhabiting the Great Basin and adjacent mountainous states;
2. Oregon pronghorn *(A. a. oregona)* (Bailey 1932) is found on sagebrush steppes of southeastern Oregon, but its total range has not been determined;
3. Mexican pronghorn *(A. a. mexicana)* (Merriam 1901) has limited ranges in southern Arizona, New Mexico, and from Texas to central Mexico;
4. Peninsular pronghorn *(A. a. peninsularis)* (Nelson 1912) has original range in southern California and Baja California, Mexico, and was listed as endangered in 1972; and

5. Sonoran pronghorn *(A. a. sonoriensis)* (Goldman 1945) ranges from the west central plains of Mexico to southern Arizona and, in 1967, was first listed by the United States Department of Interior as endangered.

DESCRIPTION

The physical characteristics of the pronghorn are listed by Walker and Paradiso (1968). Both sexes have permanent horns covered with a sheath. The male's horn sheath is shed annually after the breeding season. Average male horns are 30 centimeters (12 inches) in length and have a short branch, often termed the "prong," arising from the upper one-half of the horn and directed forward. Females may have no horns or small horns, which generally are shorter than the ears.

Head and body length range from 1.0–1.5 meters (40–60 inches). Their tails are 7.6–

Adult doe pronghorn. Note ears are longer than horns, and absence of black cheek patch. Photo by author.

An adult pronghorn buck on the Malheur National Wildlife Refuge, Burns, Oregon. Note the horns are much longer than the ears, and the black cheek patch. Photo by author.

10.2 centimeters (3–4 inches) long. Shoulder height varies from 79–102 centimeters (31–40 inches). Adult males vary from 41–64 kilograms (90–140 pounds); adult females generally weigh 20–30 percent less.

Upper parts of the body are reddish-brown to tan. The neck has a black mane, and the underparts, rump and bands under the neck are white. Males have black cheek patches on both sides of the neck, but females do not. Females have four mammae. The dental formula for pronghorn is: I 0/3; C 0/1; PM 3/3; M 3/3 × 2 = 32.

Pronghorn possess large eyes, approximately 5 centimeters (2 inches) in diameter. Only the third and fourth digits are developed on their feet, and lateral toes are lacking—hence no "dew-claws."

ECOLOGY

Life history

Mating occurs during late summer when bucks fight for harems of as many as 15 does. Often the mating season lasts only two to three weeks. After a gestation period of 250 days, does give birth in solitude during May or June. A doe usually has a single fawn at the first birth and twins thereafter.

At birth, fawns weigh 2.3–3.2 kilograms (5–7 pounds). Does' milk is extremely rich in nutrients. During the first week of life, fawns remain inactive, growing and gaining strength. However, at about five days of age, they can outrun a man. Within three weeks fawns begin nibbling vegetation, and by three months they have acquired adultlike pelage. Although fawns occasionally breed, pronghorns usually mate for the first time at 15–16 months and apparently breed annually thereafter for the duration of their lifetimes, which may be 7–10 years.

Population dynamics

Pronghorn natality averages 180 fawns per 100 breeding does. Fawn survival is highest for herds on high density ranges where summer doe-fawn ratios of 100:100

Three-day old pronghorn fawn. Photo by author.

Two pronghorn fawns approximately three weeks old. Note the developing horns on the fawn on the right. Photo by author.

are common. Low density ranges frequently have summer ratios of less than 100:50.

Mortality rates of two thriving herds in Oregon were studied intensively for a three-year period (Yoakum 1957). It was estimated from 225 carcasses with known-age deaths that 38 percent died or were killed between the time they were born until two months of age. Twelve percent of the mortality was represented by those 3–6 months of age, 8 percent was represented by those 7–11 months old, and 42 percent by those 1–10 years old.

Sex and age ratios over a 10-year period for an increasing pronghorn population in Colorado averaged 66 adult bucks: 100 adult does: 86 fawns (Hoover et al. 1959). Buck numbers no doubt would have been higher in a non-hunted area. The figure for does includes all adult females, making the proportion of fawns seem small. Ratios from a relatively static population in Oregon averaged 40 bucks: 100 does: 26 fawns over a seven-year period.

Pronghorn at four months of age. Photo by author.

Mortality factors

Factors affecting the survival of pronghorn have been studied extensively for the past three decades. Of these, predation has been researched most. Coyotes and bobcats are recorded as the most consistent predators, especially on newborn fawns. Raptor predation is recorded as nominal.

Pronghorn diseases also have been investigated intensively. Pronghorn are noteworthy for their relative lack of epizootic diseases. Even though blood from hundreds of pronghorn has been analyzed from Texas to Wyoming to Oregon for brucellosis, leptospirosis and anaplasmosis, no positive results of these common bovid diseases are on record. Two fairly common diseases are keratites (pinkeye) and actinomycosis (lumpy jaw). Parasites, both external and internal, likewise are uncommon for pronghorn. Some reasons for the infrequency of diseases and parasites are the animals' behavior of not concentrating in large numbers, infrequent use of moist areas, and constant daily movements—thereby changing feeding and bedding locations.

Natural accidents, such as miring in muddy lakes, drowning and locking horns, take a small toll each year. Severe winters with deep snows are probably the greatest cause of accidental mortality affecting pronghorn. Deep snows decrease the availability of sufficient nutritional forage.

Man-influenced accidents, such as roadkills, take a larger number of animals each year, especially on high speed roads. Barbed wire and woven wire fences create one of the most serious problems today for pronghorn. Although local pronghorn herds adapt to fencing, other herds forced to make seasonal movements because of deep snows on traditional winter range experience significant mortality. It is these herds, forced to move to forage grounds at lower elevations, that become victims when fences limit their mobility and, thereby, restrict forage availability.

Since the highest death loss is within a few weeks following birth, wildlife managers are investigating neonatal factors. It is postulated that during the last three months of pregnancy females lack nutritional forage needed to produce and maintain healthy fawns at birth. This appears to correlate with high numbers of fawns to does on the more succulent and diversified vegetative ranges in the Plains states compared to low numbers of fawns to does on the sagebrush steppes of the Great Basin ranges.

BEHAVIOR

Movements

The timing and length of pronghorn movements vary with altitude, latitude, weather and range conditions. These movements invariably are related to seeking the basic habitat requirements of quality forage and water. These various behavioral influences are demonstrated by three separate herds which live within sight of the Hart Mountain National Antelope Refuge in south-central Oregon:

1. The first area has a diameter of 8 kilometers (5 miles) in Warner Valley. The site has sufficient forage and a year-round water supply. Snow depth rarely, if ever, exceeds 15.2 centimeters (6 inches). This situation supports a small herd that does not migrate.

2. The second area is the adjacent Drakes Flat tableland, 24 kilometers (15 miles) in length. Food and water are abundant throughout the year. Pronghorn use the higher elevations (80 percent or more of the area) all year; however, deep snows may force the animals to move to lower elevations. As soon as snow depths recede, the herd moves back to higher elevations where preferred plants are more available. This situation results in a herd with altitudinal seasonal movements.

3. The third area is on Hart Mountain where differentiation among summer and winter home ranges is pronounced. Extent of pronghorn travel is related to

the amount of snow. The deeper the snow, the further the herd travels to lower elevations with less snow. These travels are not true migrations, such as those of the caribou, since the pronghorn movements differ each year, but are related to annual snow depths.

The majority of pronghorn in North America now exist in herds with ranges 8–16 kilometers (5–10 miles) in diameter. Possibly less than 10 percent of all pronghorn herds travels 80–160 kilometers (50–100 miles). However, many of the latter herds have exhibited this extent of annual movement for hundreds of years and continue to do so in order to survive. Man-made barriers—such as fences, interstate highways and railroads—often seriously handicap movements and can reduce the carrying capacities of some ranges.

Pronghorn daily movements vary with season of year primarily due to forage availability and behavioral patterns. During the spring and summer, daily movements are generally 0.1–0.8 kilometers (0.06–0.5 miles) as forage and water are usually plentiful. However, distances traveled daily are greater during the fall and winter. This is the mating season and a time of reduced quantity of preferred forage. Average movements per day during this time of year are 3.2–9.7 kilometers (2–6 miles).

Pronghorn may be the swiftest mammals in North America. They are able to run 65 kilometers per hour (40 miles per hour), and are capable of bounding 3.5–6.0 meters, (12–20 feet) (Walker and Paridiso 1968). Their "cruising" speed is approximately 48 kilometers per hour (30 miles per hour) with fast, short runs of 4.8–6.4 kilometers (3–4 miles) common. Exhaustion occurs rapidly during these short sprints.

Social groups and territories

Pronghorn are gregarious. This is most noticeable in northern populations where winter concentrations often number 200–

1,000. When spring approaches, dominant males establish territories with small bands of does, yearlings and fawns. Areas that are not defended territories contain bands of bachelors and nondominant single males.

Bucks exhibit territorial dominance from March to October. Territories are small areas with intervening ridges and larger ones in flatter terrain, established in close proximity to needed habitat. In Montana, territories included both sufficient forage and open water during the rut period (Bromley and Kitchen 1974). Territorial bucks defend their ranges against intrusion from other males and mark tall vegetation with subaricular gland secretions, urine and large piles of feces. Intruding bucks challenge the defending male by (1) staring at the intruder, (2) vocal displays, (3) approaching the intruder, (4) interacting with the intruder, and (5) chasing, or withdrawal by the intruder.

Occasionally fights occur. Rare occasions have been noted where challenging bucks locked horns, resulting in the death of both bucks (Yoakum 1957).

Territorial behavior of pronghorns is beneficial to the species for the following reasons.

1. It insures that the largest, healthiest and most aggressive bucks do most of the breeding (Bromley and Kitchen 1974).
2. It provides defended havens where does can escape harassed courtship from bachelor bucks during parturition, lactation and the rut (Cole and Wilkins 1958).
3. It decreases competition between non-breeding bucks and pregnant or lactating does for ranges with better quality forage and water supplies (Gilbert 1973).

HABITAT

Population-vegetation relationships

Recent pronghorn population distributions and densities have been related to vegetative communities (Yoakum 1972,

Sundstrom et al. 1973). This was accomplished by overlaying state wildlife agency pronghorn census data with a vegetative community map developed by Kuchler (1964). It became readily apparent that Great Plains states maintain a high percentage of the world's pronghorn population (Table 8).

Table 8. Estimated pronghorn populations for the major vegetative communities of North America (after Yoakum 1972).

Vegetative community	Pronghorn population	Percent of total
Grasslands		
Short grasslands	190,210	49
Mixed grasslands	71,750	19
Total	261,960	68
Brushland-grassland		
Sagebrush-grassland	103,810	27
Mesquite-grama	4,600	1
Woodland-galleta	10,950	3
Total	119,360	31
Desert	4,170	1

Habitat requirements

Frequently the question is asked, "What are the characteristics of a range that allow it to produce and maintain more pronghorn than an adjacent range?" This question led to a 20-year study evaluating sagebrush-grassland communities in six states (Yoakum 1974). Based on the findings of this study and a review of published reports, pronghorn habitat requirements were classified into two categories: abiotic (nonliving) and biotic (living).

Pronghorn occupy land typified by low, rolling, wide-open, expansive terrain. Some small herds occupy ranges with sparse stands of ponderosa pine or juniper, although rarely. The latter sites generally have low understory vegetation that permit distant visibility and allow rapid mobility. The size of a home range is dependent on the quality and quantity of habitat characteristics during the time it is occupied every year.

Natural barriers affect pronghorn movements and, therefore, the occupancy of habitat. Natural barriers include large bodies of water, wide rivers, abrupt escarpments and mountain ridges, dense high brush and trees, deep canyons and others. Einarsen (1948) cited examples of such barriers when he referred to two situations (one being the Columbia River and the other a heavily forested area) in which pronghorn did not settle on or relocate to nearby favorable ranges.

Pronghorn inhabit ranges from sea level to 3,353 meters (11,000 feet) in altitude. Only a few pronghorn in Mexico occupy ranges at sea level. Likewise, small herds use alpine meadows in Oregon and Wyoming. By far, the greatest densities occur on rangelands between 1,200–1,830 meters (4,000–6,000 feet) above sea level. The highest densities appear to be in habitats averaging 25–38 centimeters (10–15 inches) of precipitation per year. Where pronghorn have been transplanted to areas of higher precipitation, production and/or survival rates declined. Pronghorn do live in areas of less precipitation, but population densities likewise are less.

Most pronghorn ranges receive some snow. However, when snow accumulations exceed 25–30 centimeters (10–12 inches), they may have a difficult time obtaining necessary forage. Prolonged winters with deep snows are especially harmful when combined with factors such as (1) low quantities or qualities of forage, (2) excessive wind that increases chill factors, and (3) man-made obstacles impeding free movement to areas with less snow cover.

Temperatures do not appear to be a significant limiting factor. Pronghorn adapt to hot deserts or alpine plateau conditions.

Extensive ranges that produce and maintain high pronghorn densities have water available every 1.6–8.0 kilometers (1–5 miles). Small herds can be found farther than 8 kilometers (5 miles) from water, but studies in Wyoming disclosed that 95 percent of more than 12,000 pronghorn were within a 4.8–6.4 kilometer (3–4 mile) radius of water (Sundstrom 1968).

Herd of pronghorns in a desert-shrub community of southern Nevada. Photo courtesy of the U.S. Bureau of Land Management.

Pronghorn obtain water from springs, streams, lakes, water catchments, metal troughs and snow. When succulent forage is available, about 1 liter (approximately 1 quart) of water per day per pronghorn seems sufficient. During dry summers, 3.8–5.7 liters (1.0–1.5 gallons) per day may be needed per animal (Sundstrom 1968).

Quality and quantity of vegetation appear to be the major factors affecting pronghorn densities. The following characteristics of the sagebrush-grassland community were found on preferred ranges:

1. Ground cover averaged 50 percent living vegetation and 50 percent nonliving vegetation.

2. The general composition of vegetation was 40–60 percent grass, 10–30 percent forbs and 5–20 percent browse.

3. Within the vegetative community, there was a variety of species. This often included 5–10 species of grasses, 20–40 species of forbs and 5–10 species of shrubs.

4. Succulent plants were much preferred. Dietary studies disclosed that during wet springs or summers producing an abundance of succulent forbs, pronghorn utilized more forbs than during dry springs or summers.

5. Open rangelands having a variety of vegetative types were preferred to monotypic vegetative communities. Such areas provided grass sprouts and an abundance of succulent forbs.

6. Vegetation on pronghorn ranges averaged 38 centimeters (15 inches) in height. Rangelands with vegetation more than 61 centimeters (24 inches) in height are less preferred, and those with vegetation over 76 centimeters (30 inches) are used infrequently. Pronghorn occasionally will seek taller vegetation for forage,

such as saltbrush. They may pass through the taller brushy areas while traveling to or from more preferred ranges; however, their total year-round use of areas with vegetation 76 centimeters (30 inches) or higher is minimal. This may be due to factors of limited visibility or decreased mobility, both of which are paramount to pronghorn survival.

Pronghorns historically grazed with herds of bison, elk, deer and bighorn sheep. There appears to be little problem of tolerance or competition when and where forage is abundant.

It must be emphasized that optimum habitat is directly related to proper amounts, qualities and distributions of all essential requirements in ecosystems occupied by pronghorn. Too little or too much of any one requirement may become the major factor limiting pronghorn production or survival.

Implicit in optimum habitat is the right combination of abiotic and biotic factors.

DISTRIBUTION AND STATUS: PAST AND PRESENT

Distribution

The range of pronghorn during the early Nineteenth Century included most of the Great Plains, high sagebrush steppes, and grass valleys in the Great Basin states, parts of southcentral Canada and northern Mexico (Nelson 1925, Einarsen 1948) (Figure 23). By the 1920s, the ancestral range had been drastically reduced. Actually, pronghorn did not inhabit all the area outlined by Nelson and Einarsen. These early publications documented a general distribution pattern. There were areas within the general range not in-

Herd of pronghorns on the grasslands of South Dakota. Photo by author.

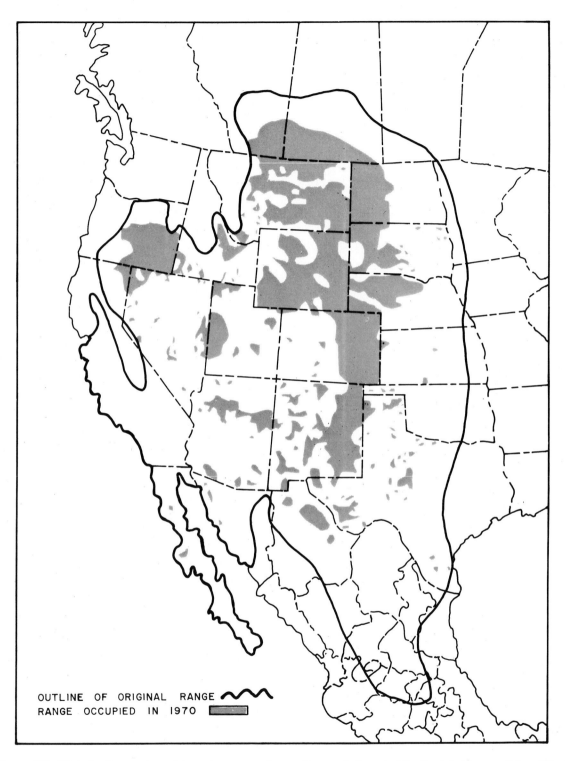

Figure 23. Distribution range of American pronghorn. Range delineated for "original range" (modified from Nelson 1925) denotes only the peripheral boundaries; not all areas within the boundaries were occupied by pronghorn. Range occupied in 1970 graphically modified from Sundstrom et al. (1973).

habited by pronghorn, such as the Rocky Mountain crest. On early maps, however, these locations were not delineated. Another example comes from a recent report disclosing that there is no documented evidence that pronghorn existed north of the Columbia River prior to transplants of this century (J. B. Lauckhart, personal communication).

Ranges occupied by pronghorn today have been identified from reports received from state and provincial wildlife agencies (Figure 23). Pronghorn occupy most of their historic range except lands along the Mississippi River. Reintroductions since the 1920s have extended the range to some previously unoccupied regions of South Dakota and Texas. In addition, pronghorn have been translocated to Florida, Washington and Hawaii, which never had pronghorn populations in the past. The stocking efforts in Hawaii and Florida were unsuccessful.

Abundance

Just how many pronghorn roamed the continent prior to the arrival of white man is not known for sure, but the pre-Columbian population was estimated to have been 30–

40 million or more. It also has been speculated that pronghorn numbers once exceeded those of bison (Nelson 1925).

During the early Nineteenth Century, herds began to decrease gradually. By the latter part of the century, numbers declined at an alarming rate. By the 1920s, the total pronghorn population in the United States was estimated at 13,000 (Hoover et al. 1959). This was the population's lowest level. From 1922–1924, Edward Nelson conducted the first extensive census and recorded 26,700 pronghorn in the United States. Within a decade, the population increased to more than 130,000. The population rose to 246,000 by 1944, to 360,000 in 1954, and 406,400 in 1976. This is well over a 1400 percent increase from the original Nelson census of 1924 (Tables 9 and 10).

Population estimates for pronghorn in Canada follow a similar pattern. Actually, the counts jumped from 1,300 in 1924 to 22,300 in 1976—a remarkable increase of about 1600 percent (Table 10).

Data for pronghorn populations in Mexico—where the animals were first seen by European explorers—are lacking in detail compared to those for Canada and the United States. However, in 1924, it was esti-

Table 9. Estimated pronghorn populations 1924–1976 and recorded harvests 1934–1976 for the United States.

Area	Population 1924[a]	Population 1976	Percent increase	Recorded total harvest 1934–1976
Arizona	700	7,300	943	18,200
California	1,100	5,000	355	5,100
Colorado	1,200	31,000	2483	102,100
Idaho	1,500	13,300	787	34,000
Kansas	10	1,100	10900	200
Montana	3,000	71,200	2273	485,700
Nebraska	200	9,800	4800	22,300
Nevada	4,300	6,500	51	6,200
New Mexico	1,700	26,900	1482	45,000
North Dakota	200	8,100	3950	43,100
Oklahoma	20	200	900	100
Oregon	2,000	11,300	465	18,200
South Dakota	700	33,500	4686	152,900
Texas	2,400	10,500	338	27,500
Utah	700	2,600	271	2,700
Washington		50		
Wyoming	7,000	168,000	2300	999,200
Total	26,700	406,400	1422	1,962,500

[a]Data from Nelson (1925). All pronghorn population numbers rounded to closest 100, except for Kansas, Oklahoma and Washington.

Table 10. Comparison of estimated pronghorn populations in North America, 1924–1976.

| Region | 1924[a] | 1976 | Change from 1924–1976 | |
			Number	Percent
Canada	1,300	22,300	+ 21,000	+ 1615
Mexico	2,400	1,000	− 1,400	− 58
United States	26,700	406,400	+ 379,700	+ 1422
Total	30,400	429,700	+ 399,300	+ 1313

[a]Data from Nelson (1925). All population estimates rounded to closest 100.

mated that 2,400 pronghorn ranged throughout Mexico (Nelson 1925). The most reliable current data indicate the population in 1976 is one-half or less of the 1924 estimate. It was documented that herds in Mexico have been and still are declining (Baker 1958, Dalquest 1953, Guzman 1961, Leopold 1959). Within the past decade, the Mexican government has pursued efforts to increase numbers by translocating several herds from the United States to various areas in Mexico.

It appears that the pronghorn population in North America is presently stabilizing at around 400,000.

Why did the pronghorn population in North America decrease from 40 million during the early 1800s to less than 13,000 in 75 years? It is apparent the population decreased rapidly as the North American continent was being settled (Bailey 1926, Buecher 1960b, Leopold 1959, Ligon 1927, Newberry 1855, Villa 1951).

The vast central valley of California is an example of where pronghorn herds vanished when white men settled the land. Speaking about pronghorn, Newberry (1855) stated, "Though found in nearly all parts of the territory of the United States west of the Mississippi, it is probably most numerous in the valley of the San Joaquin, California. There it is found in herds literally of thousands. . . ." But only two decades later, after the gold rush days brought a mass human migration to that area, Caton (1877) wrote, "It [pronghorn] was very abundant in California twenty-five years ago. . . . They are very scarce, if any exist in that state now." Although historical reports document the San Joaquin Valley pronghorn density as once being greatest in the world,

pronghorn were extirpated in that area. Extensive agricultural and ranching practices and other human developments were the reasons for loss of ancestral habitat.

Other pronghorn populations experienced similar declines. The basic reasons were always the same, although expressed in different terms—market hunting, railroads, highways, livestock competition, homesteaders, changes in land-use patterns, poaching, agriculture, etc. It was the advance of settlement that directly and quickly decreased the pronghorn herds by relentless year-round shooting for food and pleasure. Settlers also contributed to the population decline by occupying pronghorn habitats (Yoakum 1968).

Natural mortality factors, such as hard winters (Allred 1943), predation (Nelson 1925) and droughts (Beer 1944), played a part in annual losses to pronghorn herds. But these factors were present during pre-Columbian times and the herds remained in the millions. It was only when white man and his civilization came to North America that the herds decreased to a fraction of their pristine abundance.

A review of literature indicates there are three important reasons why pronghorn have increased at a record rate within the past 50 years (Yoakum 1968): (1) regulated hunting (Buechner 1960b, Mathisen 1962, Rush 1944); (2) return of historical range and habitat (Leister 1932, Benson 1956); and (3) accelerated application of wildlife management practices (Buechner 1960b, Forsyth 1942, Russell 1937, Barker 1948, Wilcox 1963).

The regulation of hunting activities is without doubt the greatest single factor contributing to pronghorn increases. Although laws prohibiting the killing of pronghorn were passed by state legislatures in the late 1800s and early 1900s, they did not correct the problem. When state wildlife agencies actively began enforcing these laws in the 1920s and 1930s, herds began to increase.

At about the same time the herds began to increase, former rangelands reverted to pronghorn habitat. Early homesteaders and settlers, not successful on their small, open-prairie farms and ranches, simply abandoned their properties, which went unclaimed. In time, the lands again accommodated pronghorn. This phenomenon took place in Canada as well as in the United States, to the pronghorn's benefit.

By the 1940s, North Americans were laying groundwork for the science of wildlife management. Practices and techniques were developed for purposes of increasing wildlife numbers and improving habitats. One outstanding management practice developed was the method of trapping pronghorn and reestablishing them to former ranges. This method was used in practically every western state, and many thousands of pronghorns today are products of these efforts.

As of July, 1976, two subspecies of pronghorn are listed as endangered (U.S. Fish and Wildlife Service 1976b). These are the Sonoran and the Peninsular pronghorn. These subspecies occupy the fringe of pronghorn range and probably never were abundant. They now are considered endangered as a result of excessive and uncontrolled hunting, and losses of habitat to agriculture.

SPECIES MANAGEMENT

Sex and aging methods

One of the most important tools of pronghorn and other big game management is a basic understanding of the division of populations into age and sex classes. Such understanding allows for fundamental analyses of population dynamics, such as determination of breeding females, fawns produced, and percentages of bucks, does and fawns. Most wildlife agenices now present sex and age ratios using a mathematical base of 100 does. For example, if a known population has 25 bucks, 50 does and 50 fawns, the correct way to list these ratios would be 50:100:100.

Field identification of adult pronghorns usually is easy. Mature males have horns longer than their ears. Most males have a black "mask" covering their faces up to the horns, and they always have black cheek patches on both sides of their heads. Adult females have horns that are 2.5–7.6 centimeters (1–3 inches) in length (most often much shorter than the length of their ears). When present, their facial masks are smaller than those found on adult males; and adult females do not have black cheek patches (Einarsen 1948).

Age determination is best accomplished by examination of tooth replacement and wear (Dow and Wright 1962). The height of teeth above the gumline is not a good index of age because molars and premolars erupt throughout most of adult life, at the rate they are worn down. During the course of tooth wear, the infundibula (or recesses in the grinding surfaces of the teeth) gradually are reduced in height and eventually disappear. Consequently, tooth wear and size allow for age determination on the basis of the number of infundibula present (Table 11).

Census techniques

Most pronghorn are counted from the ground, air or both. Ground counts often are used on sparsely inhabited ranges during late summer or early fall. These surveys provide accurate data on annual fawn survival, but are time-consuming and expensive. Aerial counts cover much more area in less time. Aerial surveys are made during summer and fall in some states, and during

Table 11. Tooth eruption and replacement in the lower jaw of pronghorn (after Dow 1952, Dow and Wright 1962): milk or deciduous tooth-D; permanent tooth-P.

Age	Incisors			Canine	Premolars			Molars		
	1	2	3	1	2	3	4	1	2	3
Birth	D						D			
6 weeks	D	D	D	D	D	D	D	P		
17–17 months	P	D	D	D	D	D	D	P	P	P
27–29 months	P	P	D	D	P	P	P	P	P	P
39–41 months	P	P	Pa	Pb / P	Pc	Pc	Pc	P	P	P
4.5 years	P	P	Pa	Pb / P	18–20 infundibula					
5.5 years	P	P	Pa	Pb / P	13–16 infundibula					
6.5 years	P	P	P	10 infundibula						

aUncertain.
bTooth is in process of eruption.
cTotal of 24 infundibula.

An aerial photo of 27 pronghorns gives a good record of sex and age ratios. There are 17 bucks, 9 does and 1 fawn in this herd. Photo by author.

winter in others. Early morning and late evening are best for aerial censuses at elevations of 46–91 meters (approximately 50–100 yards). Some states accomplish censuses on an area rotational basis, thereby counting one-third or one-fourth of the state's herds each year. Since pronghorn live in open country and are easily seen, counts are often more complete and accurate than for other big game species, such as deer or elk, that normally live in taller, more dense vegetation.

Trapping and translocations

The New Mexico Department of Fish and Game originated procedures for capturing and transplanting pronghorn in 1937 (Russell 1964). The primary objectives were to capture small bands of pronghorn on ranges where herds were abundant and transplant them to historic ranges from which herds had been extirpated. Wildlife biologist T. Paul Russell is credited with developing capture techniques based on past experiences with trapping wild horses. Other states readily adopted similar procedures, resulting in many transplants in most western states during the past three decades. For example, Colorado biologists successfully transplanted almost 1,000 pronghorn to 24 different sites during a 10-year period (Hoover et al. 1959). Another example is Texas, where 5,000 pronghorn were captured and released there from 1939–1975 (Hailey, In Press).

Capturing methods include herding the animals into a trap by aircraft. Figure 24 details the construction of a trap. Such a trap is expensive, but once built, it can be used for several years. Detailed construction plans for the trap may be found in Hoover et al. (1959) and Russell (1964).

Transplanting techniques have improved greatly since the earliest efforts. Suggested methods are well-documented by Hoover et al. (1959). Special attention should be given to this report's "Survey for Selection of Antelope Transplant Sites." Compilation of data plus a review of "Habitat Requirements," as stated in this chapter, should be examined thoroughly prior to selection of release sites. Recent, unsuccessful introductions to nonhistoric ranges are good examples of improper release site selection. However, when proper sites were chosen carefully, herds have been reestablished successfully, which is one of the reasons why pronghorn now are comparatively plentiful.

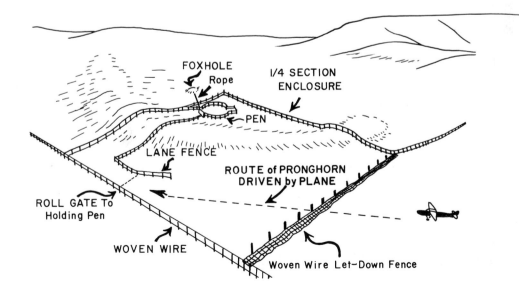

Figure 24. A pronghorn trap (adapted from Hoover et al. 1959).

Harvests

When data have been collected on such factors as sex and age ratios, population trends, range conditions, carrying capacity and mortality factors, it is possible to estimate whether pronghorn populations can be harvested on a sustained-yield basis.

Pronghorn harvest data for 1934–1976 are presented in Table 9. It is apparent that regulated harvesting has not impaired pronghorn population increases. Within the past 50 years, pronghorn in the United States increased more than 1400 percent. During the same period of time, more than 2 million pronghorn were harvested. Most states permit adult bucks-only harvests. Some states with abundant populations permit pronghorn harvests of all sexes and ages.

An example of harvest considerations is provided by Griffith (1962):

1. A ratio of one buck to five does is adequate for breeding purposes. Excess bucks constitute a harvestable surplus.
2. Harvest should be by management units. This distributes hunting pressure to allow maximum harvest of animals consistent with surpluses within a given geographic boundary.
3. Drawings for permits constitute the most successful method for administering controlled hunts. Legal animals should be "pronghorn with horns longer than ears" until such time as either sex seasons are warranted.
4. Hunts should be held in late August and early September to take advantage of prime condition of animals, and prior to shedding of horns and loss of weight, which decrease trophy value.

HABITAT MANAGEMENT

Vegetation

It is postulated that pronghorns thrive best on ranges in a subclimax vegetative condition. Such conditions were brought about in historic time through (1) wildfires caused by natural phenomena, such as lightning, and (2) seasonal grazing by herbivores, such as bison, elk and deer. Consequently the vegetative community was in constant change which, in turn, produced mixed stands of grass, forbs and browse.

Where habitat conditions for pronghorn are suitable, every effort should be made to retain them in a healthy and productive condition. Vegetative type conversions should be attempted only on ranges in poor condition. Degraded vegetative changes have resulted from man's activities or from lack of one or more of the required natural habitat features. An example of historic range that now is poor habitat for pronghorn is the vast dominant sagebrush area of the Great Basin sagebrush-grassland steppes with less than 5 percent grasses and/or forbs. Monotypic shrub lands maintain few pronghorn. However, when range conversion projects have been properly planned and implemented, improved habitat supports healthy pronghorn populations. Conversely, improperly planned projects that change the vegetation from a dominant shrub community to a monotypic grassland without forbs and browse is not desirable or beneficial for pronghorn.

The condition and structure of the vegetative community probably are the most important characteristics of pronghorn habitat, and so too of pronghorn management.

Water

The Wyoming Department of Fish and Game determined that areas of the Red Desert were lacking in available water for pronghorn. Therefore, its personnel constructed water catchments (Figure 25) specifically for use by pronghorn. The water facility collects, stores and makes available runoff from rains and melting snows. Other species of wildlife benefit directly from these catchments as well.

The Oregon Department of Fish and Wildlife recognized the lack of water in pronghorn's sagebrush-grassland steppes habitat. To remedy this deficiency, the De-

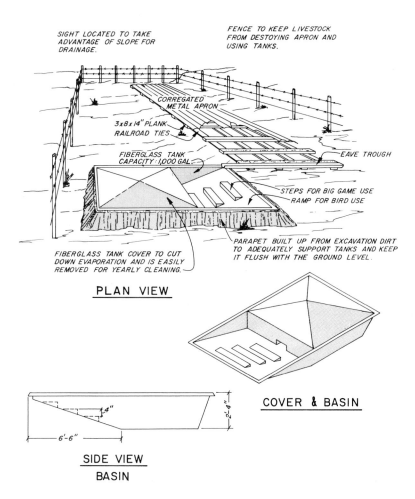

Figure 25. Water catchment designed for pronghorn use on the Red Desert, Wyoming.

partment granted funds to the United States Department of Interior's Bureau of Land Management to construct small reservoirs for the purpose of collecting runoff water for both domestic livestock and wildlife. These reservoirs were used readily by pronghorn and proved a wise investment.

Basic principles for water management to meet pronghorn needs are:

1. Maintain water supply every 1.6–8.0 kilometers (1–5 miles), depending on the range.
2. Water needs to be available in all seasons, except when snow is present.
3. Precipitation catchments specifically designed for big game use are successful in water deficient ranges.
4. When water supplies are made available for other uses such as windmills and troughs for livestock, they should be designed so that excess water overflows into a pond at ground level. This creates a source of water that can be used by pronghorn and other wildlife.

Fences

Pronghorn have difficulty jumping or going through fences constructed to control livestock because, historically, habitat occupied by pronghorn contained no similar obstacles. Fences can be a significant factor of pronghorn mortality when they restrict the animals' movements to procure food or water, or to escape from deep snows.

Studies indicate that the following measures should be taken to reduce pronghorn mortality caused by fences (Spillet et al. 1967, Zobell 1968, Interstate Antelope Conference 1962, United States Bureau of Land Management 1974):

1. Net-wire fences generally are barriers, so their construction on pronghorn ranges is discouraged.
2. For barbed-wire fences on cattle ranges:
   a. the bottom strand should be at least 41 centimeters (16 inches) above the ground;
   b. the bottom strand should be smooth because pronghorn tend to crawl under fences;
   c. the middle strand should be 25 centimeters (approximately 10 inches) above the bottom strand, and the top wire 25 centimeters (approximately 10 inches) above the middle wire, for a total top wire height of 91 centimeters (36 inches) from the ground;
   d. no stays between posts, which allows for loose wiring;
   e. there should be low-height or lay-down panels, or pass structures for heavily travelled pathways and/or migration routes; and
   f. fenced areas should be as large as possible, to minimize subdivisions of pronghorn habitats.

Background data and rationale for these recommendations are well-documented in a report of the Regional Fencing Workshop held in Cheyenne, Wyoming in March, 1974. Participating in this workshop were representatives of state and federal agencies, conservation organizations, user groups such as stockmen, plus concerned individuals.

Lands for pronghorn

According to a study at Colorado State University (1969), approximately 45 percent of the pronghorn population in the western United States was on federal lands, and the remainder on state and private lands. These data were based upon information received from state wildlife agencies, and the reported accuracy varied from 75–95 percent. The same study reported that 82 percent of the federal lands inhabited by pronghorn were under the jurisdiction of the Bureau of Land Management. Twelve percent was managed by the Forest Service, 3 percent by the Corps of Engineers, 2 percent by the Fish and Wildlife Service, and 1 percent by other federal agencies.

Einarsen (1948) reported that pronghorn inhabited 12 United States Department of Interior National Wildlife Refuges. Of these, two were specifically set aside for restoration of this species. These two refuges were the Hart Mountain Antelope Refuge in Oregon and the Charles Sheldon Antelope Refuge in Nevada. These refuges plus several others, such as the National Bison Range in Montana, are excellent sites to see and photograph pronghorn in natural habitats. There are a number of national parks and monuments that also provide viewing opportunities for those interested in these native animals. Yellowstone National Park and Wind Cave National Monument have good populations of pronghorn on native ranges and provide scenes not unlike what Lewis and Clark might have seen during the early 1800s.

There are a number of state parks with good populations of pronghorn for public viewing. One of the most outstanding is Custer State Park in South Dakota. Here visitors can see pronghorn and bison on open grasslands just as Indians witnessed them hundreds of years ago.

Management organizations

There are two organizations that meet on a scheduled basis to coordinate and disseminate information on the American pronghorn. The Interstate Antelope Conference was originally instituted in 1949 to coordinate census techniques among wildlife agencies of California, Idaho, Nevada and Oregon. Annual meetings have been conducted ever since, making this one of the earliest and most continuous organizations devoted to management of a single wildlife species. During the past two decades, the conference has changed in scope and accomplishments. Personnel of cooperating wildlife agencies recognized mutual management problems. Consequently, joint research projects have been developed and various aspects of animal and habitat management practices discussed. Land management agencies and university research associates have joined and contributed. Other state resource agencies attend to share and benefit from the pooling of knowledge and experience. These yearly meetings result in presentations of agency progess reports and scientific papers that are published in annual transactions. The host wildlife agency, selected on a rotating basis, is responsible for publication and distribution of the transactions.

The Pronghorn Antelope Workshop originated in 1965 and now meets on a biennial basis. Usually, 50–75 persons attend, representing state and federal agencies, private individuals and companies, universities and colleges, and conservation organizations. The workshop is sanctioned by the Western Association of State Fish and Game Commissioners. To date, eight workshops have been conducted, primarily in Rocky Mountain states. It is international in scope since representatives of two Canadian provinces and of Mexico participate. The most important accomplishment of this workshop is its proceedings. These volumes include much of the recent field data available on the ecology, biology and management of pronghorn and its habitat. Copies of these proceedings are printed and distributed by the host wildlife agency.

THE FUTURE

Seventy-five years ago, prominent conservationists warned of the possible extirpation of pronghorn. Their warnings came as the world's pronghorn population dwindled to a dangerous low of less than 13,000. But during the past 50 years, the pronghorn did not go the way of Dodo birds and passenger pigeons. In fact, the population increased to 400,000. There are two reasons for this remarkable comeback. First, pronghorn are adaptive—they can live compatibly with cattle just as they did with bison. Their habitat requirements can be met in the sagebrush steppes as well as the grassland prairies. Second, man has learned to harvest pronghorn wisely. He has learned to apply scientific management techniques to reestablish the condition of historic ranges and construct habitat improvements, particularly water areas, beneficial to pronghorn herds.

Today, the western ranges are testimony to the pronghorn's adaptiveness and the foresight of man in recent decades. Man has realized that if he controls use of pronghorn and manages pronghorn habitat, the animal can live on a sustained basis.

In many respects, the American pronghorn is a classic example of how wildlife and man can coexist beneficially. The current status of the pronghorn populations attests to their remarkable restoration.

Chapter 8

BISON

Margaret Mary Meagher

Research Biologist
National Park Service
Yellowstone National Park, Wyoming

Among ungulate species classified as game animals, the bison is something of an anachronism; it provides few hunting opportunities. Most bison are managed for aesthetic, scientific and commercial reasons; they are the only native large mammal now being raised predominantly in semidomestic situations.

Today, bison evoke a mystique not shared by any other large North American mammal. This mystique probably is derived from our Indian and frontier heritages (McHugh 1972). The vanished millions of "American buffalo" from the Great Plains pique our imaginations but have left little tangible information about the species (Roe 1951). Historical accounts are fascinating but often conflicting and incomplete (Dary 1974, Haines 1970). Although research is increasing (Miller 1977), there still is much to learn about bison.

DISTRIBUTION AND TAXONOMY

With only a few exceptions, free-ranging bison—existing in some kind of dynamic equilibrium with their environment—no longer exist. Only in and near Wood Buffalo National Park, Northwest Territories, Canada (Stelfox 1976) and in Yellowstone National Park, Wyoming (Meagher 1973)

are there free-ranging bison populations subject entirely to natural regulatory processes, neither cropped nor hunted by man. Aesthetically and scientifically, these herds are the most important in existence today. Most other herds in state or federal ownership also are managed primarily for aesthetic and scientific values. However, the latter herds are subject to cropping and varying kinds and intensities of management, including ranching practices such as culling, sex and age structure manipulation, pasture rotation, winter feeding and brucellosis control.

In recent years, the commercial value of bison has increased. There are private herds throughout the United States managed as livestock enterprises with meat sold as a speciality item. Hides, heads and other parts also find a ready market.

Bison usually are hunted in intensively controlled situations that vary from commercial hunting on private ranches to reductions of state-owned herds by hunters who take preselected animals. In few locations (Alaska and Canada) is there opportunity for hunts in the traditional sense.

Two North American subspecies of modern bison currently are recognized according to cranial evidence (Skinner and Kaisen 1947): *Bison bison bison* (plains bison) and *B. b. athabascae* (wood bison). A third form, the mountain bison, often is mentioned in historical accounts of the Rocky Mountains of the United States. Skinner and Kaisen placed mountain bison with wood bison. Also, the existence of a Pennsylvania subspecies cannot be substantiated.

DESCRIPTION

Bison are generally dark brown in color, with massive-appearing forequarters. The head, forelegs, hump and shoulders are covered with longer hair than on the flanks. Hair on the hindquarters is short and woolly. As the coat ages, the longer hair over the hump and shoulders may lighten considerably, becoming almost tan, especially on old bulls.

Calves are reddish-tan at birth, changing to brown-black at about three months. Adult males and females are sexually dimorphic but otherwise resemble each other in color, shape and presence of permanent horns (Table 12).

Detailed comparisons of wood and plains bison are difficult to make because of the disappearance of most wild populations of both forms well before this century, followed by hybridization of remnants. Historical accounts generally agree that, compared to plains bison, the wood bison was larger, darker, hardier, more fleet and wary, and lived in smaller bands (Roe 1951). Descriptions using the term "mountain bison" sometimes characterized wood bison as smaller in size than plains bison. This discrepancy in descriptions of size among subspecies may

A bison bull. Photograph by James D. Yoakum.

Table 12. Comparison of physical characteristics of adult bull and cow bison *(B. b. bison)*.

Characteristic	Bull	Cow
Weight	± 900 kilograms (± 2000 pounds)	± 450 kilograms (± 1000 pounds)
Height at shoulder	1.67–1.98 meters (5.5–6.5 feet)	1.37–1.67 meters (4.5–5.5 feet)
Hump	Massive, sometimes very angular	Smaller, more rounded
Head	Broad, triangular frontal appearance	Narrow, linear frontal appearance
Horns	Proportionately thicker at base, simple curve	Proportionately thin, often recurved in side view
Head hair	Thick, long "mop" on top	Less dense, shorter
Beard	Lengthy	Relatively short
Cape and pantaloons on forelegs	Pronounced	Relatively short

be due to the sex and age of animals seen. Cranial evidence, however, indicates that wood and mountain bison both are *B. b. athabascae,* and are larger than animals of the plains bison subspecies (Skinner and Kaisen 1947).

LIFE HISTORY

Single bison calves usually are born in spring, after an approximately 9.5-month gestation period. The majority are born during May, with peaks varying somewhat among areas. Occasional late calves are seen in most herds.

The rut begins from mid- to late July and essentially is over by late August or early September.

Longevity of bison varies. In wild populations, relatively few bison attain old age, which begins at about 12–15 years. However, an occasional bison will attain more than 20 years of age. Personal observations suggest that more cows than bulls live to be very old. On ranches and in small public herds, few animals reach advanced age. Because of the difficulty of keeping mature bulls within fences, few are allowed to reach full physical maturity.

POPULATION DYNAMICS

Productivity

Sexual maturity of individuals varies from herd to herd. While an occasional female breeds as a yearling, and others mature as two year olds, most breed for the first time at age three. In Yellowstone National Park, however, the majority of females reach sexual maturity at four—later than reported for other herds. Sexual maturation (the capability of reproducing) of males appears to be comparable to females: a few males mature as yearlings, one-third as two year olds, and probably all others by age three. Regardless of sexual maturity, most breeding is done by fully mature males (seven to eight years old).

Although cows theoretically are capable of producing a calf every year, production is much less except with intensive management. This probably results from a variety of factors (Meagher 1973). Populations which are not cropped or culled will have a higher proportion of older and otherwise nonproducing females. Disease, particularly brucellosis, is a factor which appears to lower productivity in Wood Buffalo National Park, but not in Yellowstone. In both areas, a complex of factors related to harsh environment may be important, with lowered productivity being an important natural regulatory mechanism.

Sex and age ratios

Fetal sex ratios consistently show that males slightly outnumber females. Data are lacking for calves at birth. In Yellowstone, female bison appear to be more numerous than males in the 10-month to 3.5-year age range. Thereafter, male survival predominates until the bison reach full maturity and the females again outnumber males (Meagher 1973).

Mortality rates

While mortality rates are variable over time and from place to place, certain patterns emerge. Realized natality in wild populations is lower than observed pregnancy rates. It is not known if most mortality occurs just before or just after birth. For practical purposes, calf production in a wild population usually is expressed as a percentage of a herd. Peak calf percentages have been about 20 percent (Meagher 1973, Stelfox 1976). These percentages may decline steadily through the year by one-third to one-half in Wood Buffalo National Park (Fuller 1962), or hold at a consistent level through most of the first year of life in Yellowstone National Park. In both cases, there is considerable mortality by the end of the first year.

Bison mortality in Yellowstone National Park also is appreciable for yearlings and two year olds. By the third year, 50 percent of a calf crop for a given year may have disappeared. Thereafter, mortality rates vary according to severity of winters.

MORTALITY FACTORS

Only natural mortality factors will be discussed, recognizing that today's intensively managed bison herds are little affected by such.

Predation

The physical structure of bison, with massive frontquarters, and its stolid temperament, suggest that as a species it evolved to face danger rather than flee, making them quite vulnerable to the modern rifle. Only two predators other than man have been associated with bison: the grizzly bear and wolf. We cannot evaluate fairly their historic relationships to the bison, but instances of grizzly predation must have been opportunistic and infrequent. Judging by some accounts, bears were losers as often as winners in direct conflicts with bison. Rare circumstantial evidence for grizzly predation in Yellowstone has been found. More important, winter-killed bison provide carrion for grizzlies emerging from winter dens.

Wolves prey on bison in Wood Buffalo National Park. They act as culling agents, but do not regulate the bison population. At present, wolves are too few in Yellowstone to exert significant predation; historical records suggest that elk would be more likely prey in this locale.

Diseases

Important diseases in free-roaming bison herds include tuberculosis, brucellosis and anthrax. Wood Buffalo National Park bison are affected by all three diseases (Stelfox 1976); Yellowstone National Park bison have only brucellosis (Meagher 1973).

Tuberculosis causes some mortality and acts as a factor in population regulation in Wood Buffalo National Park. It is not known if brucellosis is endemic or was introduced among North American bovids. With brucellosis, bison in susceptible herds may abort a first calf, although subsequent pregnancies appear normal. Brucellosis apparently acts as a population regulation factor in Wood Buffalo National Park, but not in Yellowstone. Several outbreaks of anthrax occurred in bison of Wood Buffalo Park from 1964–1967. While usually fatal in two to seven days, anthrax has affected only a small percentage of the population. Although transmission of any of the three diseases to cattle probably is physiologically possible, this is precluded by lack of contact.

Internal parasites do not appear significant in any population, although a large variety have been found. External parasites, such as biting flies, influence bison distribution and movement during some seasons of the year.

Other factors

History recounts such events as mass drownings when bison plunged into rivers swollen with snow melt, or broke through ice. Such drownings have occurred most recently in Wood Buffalo National Park (Fuller 1962). Otherwise, accidents are a minor factor in population regulation.

Large-scale mortality from adverse weather, such as extensive crusting of deep snow, also was reported historically. Today, periodically severe winter weather appears to be important mainly in Yellowstone (Meagher 1973, 1976). Winterkill probably results from the combined effects of climatic stress, forage availability and physiological conditions of individual animals. Aged and otherwise weakened animals can be expected to die every year. Such deaths usually occur after prolonged weakening, often in late winter and early spring. In more severe winters, some subadults also die. Subadult mortality may be differential, with more males surviving than females. Size, together with social standing in the population, may explain this. Severe spring weather also can cause appreciable calf mortality.

BEHAVIOR

Individual behavior patterns—a function of sex and age characteristics—such as communication and breeding, are fairly consistent among bison herds. Behavior strongly influenced by environmental factors or management practices will vary.

Social organization

Bison are basically gregarious. Cows, calves, yearlings and spike-horned bulls two to three years old remain in herd groups of varying sizes throughout the year, although cows usually separate briefly to calve. A base unit of perhaps 11–20 animals is common (Fuller 1960), with larger herds formed by temporary bunching of these smaller units. There is no evidence that these base units are composed of blood relatives. One or more mature bulls—but not necessarily the same bulls—commonly are seen with herd groups throughout the year. Otherwise, bulls separate except during the rut, when most of them spend a large part of their time within or peripheral to herd groups. Bulls not with herds often form small and temporary bachelor groups. Solitary bulls seem to be so by choice; many of them are just reaching maturity rather than old age (Fuller 1960).

Bison are dominance-organized rather than territorial. Dominance relationships among bulls are most obvious during the rut. The relationships are mainly linear, resembling a peck order, but are not necessarily stable—reversals and triangles can occur (Lott 1972). This allows subordinate bulls to do some breeding. Dominance relationships also may influence use of foraging sites and space.

Bison bulls are polygamous but do not form harems during the breeding season. Instead, they form temporary pairs called "tending bonds," and breed a number of cows sequentially. Fights among males during the rut usually involve head-shoving matches to establish or reinforce dominance rather than to possess certain females, although the more dominant bulls also are more successful in passing on their genes.

Communication

Cow-calf and intraherd communications consist mostly of nasal grunts and snorts, audible only at relatively short distances.

The roar or bellow of a rutting bull, audible for a considerable distance, is the most distinctive sound bison make. Bulls also use snorts and stamping as auditory threats (Lott 1974). There is a broad repertoire of visual signals, varying from subtle to overt, which affect dominance relationships. These include aggressive signals such as head-on threats, nod threats (a kind of stylized head-bobbing) and broadside display postures. Submission signals consist of turning the head away, moving away or grazing.

Movements

Seasonal movements in the large areas follow regular, repetitive patterns. In Yellowstone and Wood Buffalo parks, such movements are truly migratory between winter and summer ranges.

In Yellowstone, although unfenced, few bison cross the park boundaries. Mature cows, which provide the herd group leadership, apparently have strong affinities for specific winter ranges (Meagher 1973).

Short-term movements are less predictable. Solitary bulls move least, often staying in the same place for days, especially in winter. Herd groups move more widely and frequently, although winter movements are more circumscribed.

HABITAT NEEDS AND PREFERENCES

Bison are predominantly grazers. Although grasses are the main food in most places, sedges provide the major source of forage in Wood Buffalo and Yellowstone national parks. Recent studies comparing bison and cattle on the shortgrass plains indicate that bison have a greater preference for warm season grasses, and feed less selectively and in different areas (Peden et al. 1974). Bison appear to have greater digestive ability for low-protein, poor quality forage, and may eat more. Thus, not surprisingly, they perhaps are better able than cattle to exploit more fully the shortgrass plains. In all areas presently inhabited by bison, snow or open water is available at all times and apparently is utilized daily.

Bison use forested areas when available. Such use may be for shade, or to escape insect pests. They also may forage more successfully in forests during periods of crusted or dense, deep snow. During severe winter conditions, forested areas and topographical variations may provide some degree of shelter (Meagher 1973, 1976). Fairly extensive forests may be traversed from one foraging area to another.

Bison require large areas to be maintained as free-ranging, naturally regulated populations. They can be kept successfully in small pastures as semidomestic animals.

Although an eminently successful inhabitant of historic grasslands, the bison is truly a Pleistocene mammal, able to survive in places where no other large ungulate can (Meagher 1976), including open valleys covered with several feet of snow and subjected to frequent wind and storm conditions for at least one-half of the year. Yellowstone National Park appears to present the harshest winter environment where bison populations have been able to persist over time under natural conditions. Protected by dense woolly pelts, and foraging like animated snowplows with a side-to-side head swinging motion, the largest bulls can feed in several feet of loose snow. Scattered thermal sites—particularly warm ground with less snow—apparently provide a margin for survival for bison in the harshest wintering areas of Yellowstone. In Yellowstone, selection pressures related to the harsh winter environment have led to the production of some bulls with an exceptionally high and sharply angled hump structure. These bulls can forage successfully in snow which is too deep and dense for lesser bison. Even some cow bison in Yellowstone National Park appear to have somewhat more hump development than do cows elsewhere, where the snows are not as deep and long-lasting.

Virtually all areas inhabited by bison have readily accessible sources of water. Photo by E. P. Haddon; courtesy of the U.S. Fish and Wildlife Service.

Bison cows and calves in Hayden Valley, Yellowstone National Park. Photograph by Nancy Rudolph.

Bison feed in scattered thermal areas of Yellowstone National Park, where warm ground prevents deep snow accumulations. Photo by author.

MANAGEMENT

Commercial management practices vary among owners, according to locale, sizes of herds and commercial objectives. Publicly owned herds usually are presented in as natural a setting as possible within the management constraints under which they operate. Manipulative management usually is practiced to some degree since almost all of these herds are fenced-in.

History of management

After the elimination of free-ranging plains bison in the last century, various semidomesticated herds provided a nucleus for most of the present herds. In Yellowstone National Park and Wood Buffalo National Park, free-ranging wood bison survived.

Plains bison were subsequently introduced into both parks. In the past, managers in both areas regulated some of their bison population units, but not at present. Management objectives for both areas are to maintain free-ranging populations, naturally regulated to the greatest extent possible.

The early history of bison in Yellowstone National Park provides insight into the evolution of park wildlife management philosophy (Meagher 1973). At the time the park was established in 1872, camp hunting was permissible. Only wanton destruction was prohibited, but market hunting and poaching were rampant. Hunting was prohibited in 1883, but legal means for enforcement did not exist. In 1894, the Yellowstone Park Protection (Lacey) Act provided enforceable protection, but poaching continued until about 1900. At the time, bison numbers everywhere were at very low levels. Plains bison from private herds were introduced in 1902 because extinction of the remaining native bison was feared.

From 1902–1930, the introduced bison were intensively managed. Herding, rotation of pastures, castration of bull calves, separation of calves for weaning, round-ups, haying and winter feeding were part of the operation at various times. During this same period, predator populations were controlled. The wild herd in Yellowstone Park was virtually ignored. As bison increased elsewhere, the Yellowstone herd became less important as a restocking source. The need for cropping became apparent about 1930 when more than 1,000 bison were being maintained at the park's Buffalo Ranch.

With reestablishment of the bison population in Yellowstone Park, administrators began to realize that parks were important as natural areas, and that artificial devices for bison management should be eliminated as much as possible. Intensity of bison management gradually decreased, but regulation of population sizes continued into the mid-1960s.

Since then, cropping of bison has terminated in Yellowstone National Park. It was realized that cropping to provide a sustained yield for harvesting and to maintain certain levels of vegetative production was not necessarily consistent with objectives of a national park administered as a natural area.

Intensive ecological studies have been directed toward understanding the degree to which Yellowstone still offers ecological completeness for bison and the degree to which the bison population is regulated by natural factors. Pending completion of these studies, no manipulative management of either bison or vegetation is planned. Concurrently, understanding of bison's role in sustaining a large variety of dependent meateaters—coyotes, bears, an occasional wolf, ravens and magpies—has increased. For example, in Pelican Valley and Hayden Valley, where other ungulate species do not

winter, winter-killed bison may be a vital food source for grizzly bears that emerge from dens when snow still covers these areas to depths of 0.6 meter (2 feet) or more. Any program of manipulation must consider such predator-prey relationships.

The degree to which other parks and refuges provide adequate year-round ranges for bison, in part, must govern their management.

Distribution

Historic distribution of the two subspecies (Figure 26) overlapped along the east slope of the Rockies. Ranges for historic times are based on early accounts plus limited paleontological data. Fenced-in herds of bison are found throughout parts of the United States and Canada.

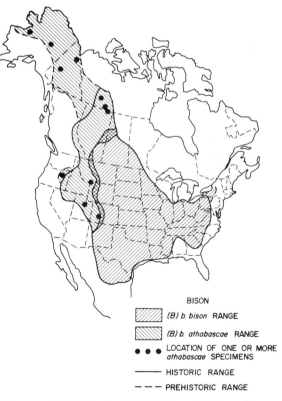

BISON

▨	(B) b. bison RANGE
▨	(B) b. athabascae RANGE
● ● ●	LOCATION OF ONE OR MORE athabascae SPECIMENS
——	HISTORIC RANGE
– – –	PREHISTORIC RANGE

Figure 26. Historic distribution of *Bison bison bison* and *B. b. athabascae* (after Skinner and Kaiser 1947).

Population status

Bison today are thriving. In addition to the many fenced-in herds, derived mainly from plains bison stock, large numbers of plains-wood hybrids are found in Yellowstone and Wood Buffalo national parks. Pure-blood wood bison inhabit the McKenzie Bison Sanctuary in the Northwest Territories, and another small group was placed at Elk Island, Alberta, where they are fenced-in and disease-free (K. Baker, personal communication). Alaska maintains several small, free-ranging plains bison herds which originated from introductions made in 1928.

Estimating population parameters

Commercial herds and all but the largest public bison herds may consist of known-age and known-sex animals. Total population is determined by periodic round-ups. Frequently, the sex ratio of a herd is manipulated by removal of bulls.

When age and sex must be estimated, ages usually are approximated by size comparisons, although large calves sometimes can be confused with small yearlings. Discernible categories for experienced observers are calves, yearlings, spike-horn bulls, adult cows and adult bulls. Ratios of calves to total herd numbers usually are used for long-term population information.

Bison population levels are determined best by aerial censuses, rather than sample estimates. Censuses are conducted most effectively during winter. Total and calf production counts from aerial photographs have been used successfully in Wood Buffalo National Park (Stelfox 1976). Visual counts are used in Yellowstone, where smaller numbers make this technique feasible.

Harvest objectives and season framework

Animals are not harvested in Wood Buffalo and Yellowstone national parks. Harvest objectives vary in other areas. Removal of annual increment is usual. Removal of bulls may be made to control fence-breaking problems, or for trophies. Meat production or live sale is emphasized commercially.

Other management problems

The presence of certain disease organisms influences the management of bison in both parks. Wood Buffalo presently manages

Bulls and some cows in Yellowstone National Park have greater hump development than do bison elsewhere as a result of selection pressures related to the harsh winter environment. A Wildlife Management Institute photo.

In contrast to many of the animals in Yellowstone, bison in other herds have hump structures that are neither as high nor as acutely angled. Photo by E. P. Haddon; courtesy of the U.S. Fish and Wildlife Service.

for as large a free-roaming, disease-controlled population as possible. The present program includes anthrax vaccination to protect a nucleus population in the event of an outbreak (Stelfox 1976). Yellowstone Park managers maintain a boundary-control program to prevent bison contact with cattle and potential transmission of brucellosis. Long-term ecological studies presently are being conducted in both areas, directed toward solving these problems, if possible, as well as toward monitoring and understanding the bison populations and their natural relationships.

FUTURE NEEDS

Missing among the array of bison herds restored in North America is a Great Plains population, free-ranging on mixed prairie habitat and subject only to natural influences—including predation by wolves. Such a population would help maintain the species' full genetic variability. Generally, in the words of William Hornaday, such a population would restore "a grandeur and nobility of presence which is beyond comparison among ruminants" (Stone and Cram 1902).

A free-ranging bison population on the Great Plains is not a likely prospect due to economic pressures, especially those related to agriculture, and to spatial demands for human occupation. Constraints, therefore, are indirectly associated with bison population growth and movement, and directly related to limitation of prairie restoration.

In recent decades, historic plains bison habitats—virgin shortgrass, tallgrass and mixed grass prairies—have been recognized for their multiple benefits for man and wildlife. Efforts by private interests to salvage remnant tracts and prairies and to reclaim lands for prairie restoration have been fairly successful. And though the federal government and state governments usually have not taken the lead in preserving relic prairies, they have helped considerably in purchases and other acquisitions (Betz 1977). But with respect to bison, small relic and remnant prairies are not enough to restore a free-ranging wild population.

Chapter 9

MUSK-OX

Peter C. Lent

U.S. Fish and Wildlife Service
Anchorage, Alaska

TAXONOMY

Modern taxonomic treatment of musk-oxen began with the study of Allen (1913) who recognized a single species with three subspecies: *Ovibos moschatus moschatus* (Zimmerman), *O. m. niphoecus* (Elliott) and *O. m. wardi* (Lydekker).

In a detailed examination and statistical treatment of all available material, Tener (1965) concluded that *O. m. niphoecus,* the Hudson Bay musk-ox, was not a valid subspecies and that the differences between *O. m. wardi* of the High Arctic and *O. m. moschatus* of continental Canada were "suggestive of incipient subspeciation." Based on his detailed review of the literature, Harington (1961) similarly concluded that there were "at most" two valid subspecies.

DESCRIPTION

The pelage of musk-oxen is most striking. Long guard hairs reach down to the ground, especially on mature bulls. Individual hair strands of 62 centimeters (24.4 inches) in length have been taken. These hairs also form a beard under the chin and, particularly on bulls, there is a mane that accentuates the hump formed by the forequarters. Under this coarse, dark outer layer is the lighter-colored, extremely fine underhair, now widely known as "qiviut," a name derived from a Greenland Eskimo word. This underhair is shed from May through August. During this period, the animals often have a strange patchy appearance and may be seen with long streamers of qiviut waving in the wind. There is a tendency for individual musk-oxen from the Canadian Arctic Archipelago and Greenland to have whiter faces, saddles and "stockings" than those from the Canadian mainland.

The combination of long, heavy outer hairs and insulating qiviut is, of course, an important adaptation for the severe cold and strong winds of the Polar deserts. However, under sub-Arctic or cold maritime conditions, this extreme development may be disadvantageous. Numerous observers have seen musk-oxen weighted down with large balls of ice and snow hanging from the guard hairs. On Nunivak Island, evidence has suggested that musk-oxen have perished by being frozen to the ground, presumably as a result of a rapid thaw-freeze cycle (Spencer and Lensink 1970).

The long, thick pelage of adults leads the casual observer to over-estimate the weight of these animals. By way of comparison, mature males tend to weigh about three-fifths as much as mature male bison. Very few weights are available from wild musk-oxen, except for the introduced population on

Table 13. Average weights of musk-oxen from Nunivak Island, Alaska[a]. The numbers in parenthesis are sample size.

	11 months old[b]		23 months old		35 months and older	
	Kilograms	Pounds	Kilograms	Pounds	Kilograms	Pounds
Males	74 (29)	163	116 (5)	256	269[c] (3)	593
Females	69 (43)	152	107 (10)	234	172 (6)	379

[a]Based upon author's unpublished data and unpublished records on file at the U.S. Fish and Wildlife Service, Bethel, Alaska and the Alaska Department of Fish and Game, Fairbanks, Alaska.

[b]Most weights were obtained during transplant operations in late March and early April, assumed to be one month before peak calving period.

[c]Butchered weights, not corrected for blood loss. All three were thought to be four years or older.

Nunivak Island, Alaska (Table 13). Tener (1965) reported an average weight of four adult males from the Canadian mainland of 341 kilograms (750 pounds). Bulls from Nunivak Island do not reach as great a weight. No adult female musk-oxen weights are available from Canadian populations. Adult females reach about 60 percent of the weight of adult males (Nunivak data). In captivity, bulls have reached approximately 650 kilograms (1,430 pounds) and cows nearly 300 kilograms (660 pounds). Calves weigh 10–14 kilograms (22–31 pounds) at birth.

Horns are present in both sexes. However, from about the end of the first year of age, sex-related differences in horn morphology become increasingly pronounced. The horns of females remain slender and generally shorter than those of males. Curvature (deflection) is generally greater and the horns pass closer to the bones of the malar region. In males, the deposition of bone at the base of the horn cores and the corresponding expansion of a horny sheath leads to development of a massive base that covers parietal regions to the midline. This horny base does not fully coalesce; a narrow hairline remains. On females, the bases enlarge but a small whitish patch of hair persists between them, even in the oldest cows.

The patterns of horn development, together with other clues, provide the trained observer with a means of sexing musk-oxen two years and older in the field and estimating their ages up to four or five years (Allen 1913, Bos 1967, Smith 1976). The horn cores in calves and yearlings are weakly attached,

and great care must be exercised in handling captive animals to prevent damage.

POPULATION DYNAMICS

Traditionally, musk-oxen have been considered to exhibit low productivity, perhaps lower than any other ungulate species. This consideration has been attributed to three characteristics: (1) lack of twins, (2) high age of sexual maturity (cow first giving birth when age four), and (3) capability of producing calves only in alternate years. Of these characteristics, only the first can be considered to be well-documented. The birth of viable twins never has been reported from either captive or wild populations. Pedersen (1958) believed that twins occur in favorable years but provided no documentation to support his contention. The lack of viable twins even under high planes of nutrition in captivity makes his contention a dubious one.

Age of first breeding in females is highly variable, depending on environmental conditions and, perhaps, also on social factors. In captivity, females have bred as yearlings and produced offspring at the age of two (Oeming 1965). Among a group transplanted from Nunivak Island to nearby Nelson Island, Alaska, all females gave birth at three years of age and possibly one gave birth at two. Two year olds have given birth in a free-ranging group in Norway. For the Nunivak Island population there is increasing evidence that three-year-old cows contribute significantly to productivity rates (Lent, Unpublished). So far as the true Arctic of Greenland and the Canadian Archipelago is concerned, it must still be assumed that few, if any, cows conceive before their third year.

The old belief that females can produce offspring only in alternate years is not based on any substantive information (*cf.* Tener 1965). What is now well-documented is that total reproductive failure (zero calf crop) occurs frequently in High Arctic populations (Vibe 1958, 1967, Tener 1965, Gray 1973, Parker et al. 1975). Domestication project personnel at University of Alaska have weaned calves artificially to ensure successive-year breeding, but there is no evidence that this weaning is necessary. On Bathurst and Nunivak islands, cows with calves are courted and show every indication of estrus. In the wild Norwegian group, one cow produced five calves in five successive years.

An accurate picture of productivity is not available for most musk-ox populations because calf numbers almost always have been expressed as a percentage of total numbers seen or as a percentage of groups excluding lone bulls. Very little information on sex ratios or age structure is available, except for the Nunivak Island population (Spencer and Lensink 1970, Lent, Unpublished). Tener (1965) commented that the proportion of calves to total population is generally lower than in other northern ungulates, such as caribou, bison and Dall's sheep. However, in favorable years, such as 1971 on Banks Island (Urquhart, Unpublished) and 1973 on Nunivak Island, the proportion of calves fell within the normal range for caribou. In four years for which sufficient data are available (Table 14), the estimated early summer proportions of calves to cows

Musk-ox group on Nunivak Island. Left to right: mature male, yearling male, calf and mature female. Photo by T. Smith.

137

Table 14. Musk-oxen calf production on Nunivak Island, 1966–1971[a].

Year	Month of composition count	Number of females three years and older	Month of postcalving aerial count	Estimated adult mortality between surveys[b]	Number of calves and percent of total population	Estimated number of calves per female three years and older
1966	March	172	July	10 percent	110 (19 percent)	0.64
1968	April	202	July	9 percent	100 (14 percent)	0.50
1970	February	184	July	25 percent	50 (10 percent)	0.27
1971	March	109	September	4 percent	71 (13 percent)	0.65

[a]Data for four years when both a precalving census by snowmachine and a postcalving aerial survey were accomplished. Aging and sexing of adults is accurate only from precalving census.

[b]Based on total population counted in precalving census compared to total in summer counts excluding calves. Assumes, for purposes of estimate, that mortality rates are equal for all age and sex classes.

three years and older were 65, 50, 27 and 65 percent.

Like natality rates, calf survival rates tend to fluctuate greatly. Most available information, however, provides only crude estimates of calf survival, because adult mortality rates are unknown. Furthermore, the data of Tener (1965) were based on ratios in mixed-sex herds only, excluding the variable portion of adult males outside such groups. Tener estimated that survival among calves in the Thelon Game Sanctuary averaged better than 50 percent. More recent data from the Canadian Arctic islands suggest that mortality often is higher. Total or near total mortality has been reported by Vibe (1958) and others.

Some accurate successive counts of total numbers of calves in summer and short-yearlings (about 11 months old) the following year are available for Nunivak Island. Average mortality based on five counts is 15 percent. With these figures, one may tend to underestimate mortality because aerial surveys in summer tend to miss some of the small young calves. These limited data suggest that greatest mortality occurs in years following high winter-spring adult mortality. Presumably, calves were born in poor condition, or their mothers were in poor condition and could not provide adequate nourishment or care.

Other age-specific mortality rates and age-structure information are available only for the Nunivak Island population. It is important to keep in mind that this introduced population is not subject to predation but is subject to severe subarctic, maritime winter

weather with deep snowcover and ice conditions, quite different from that normally occurring within the natural distribution range of musk-oxen. The lush summer vegetation on Nunivak Island is equally atypical for natural musk-ox range. The approximate composition of this population, based on a sample of 555 of 673 animals in 1968, is reproduced from Spencer and Lensink (1970) in Table 15. Subsequently, age at death was determined from cementum annuli of 29 recent skulls found on the island (Lent, Unpublished). The average age at death for those surviving their first year was 5.5 years. Maximum age was 13, but only three musk-oxen survived past 9 years. In contrast, the potential for longevity in the wild is 23 years (Buckley et al. 1954), and it is believed that several individuals in the original transplant to Nunivak Island survived to about 20 years of age. From examination of 48 recently-dead animals from the Parry Islands, Canada, 56 percent were found to be more than 10 years old at death. One was nine and the rest were less than three years old. Males made up 69 percent of the 42 animals of identifiable sex (Parker et al. 1975).

Aside from man, wolves are the only significant predators of musk-oxen. Hone (1934) and Tener (1965) cited and summarized the many anecdotal descriptions of predation. Gray (1970) provided a detailed description of a lone wolf killing a lone musk-ox bull. Most recorded accounts are of predation on lone bulls. According to Freeman (1971), wolf predation was implicated in about 50 percent of musk-ox mortality in

Table 15. Composition of Nunivak Island musk-ox population in April, 1968[a].

Age class	Number[b]			Percent		
	Male	Female	Total	Male	Female	Total
4 years or older	209	150	359	31.0	22.3	53.3
3 years	44	52	96	6.5	7.7	14.2
2 years	63	45	108	9.4	6.7	16.1
Yearling			110			16.4
Total	316	247	673	56.1	43.9	100.0

[a]A total of 555 musk-oxen was classified by age and sex during the census; 99 unclassified animals, consisting of a few individuals in larger groups and three inacessible herds of 22, 29 and 33 were prorated on the basis of the composition in herds of similar social structure. Adapted from Spencer and Lensink (1970).

[b]Data are adjusted to include one 2-year old female and 17 yearlings removed just prior to the census. Not adjusted for removal of 23 calves in 1964, 10 in 1965 and 12 yearlings in 1967.

the Jones Sound area of the Northwest Territories. Effective use of the circular group defense formation against wolves and dogs has been described by many authors.

Deep snow cover and ice layers often result in massive mortality, particularly when dense snow and ice lie immediately over vegetation. Vibe (1958) believed that warming conditions and more maritime winters occur in cycles in Greenland. These maritime winters closely resemble the typical winters on Nunivak Island, where widespread mortality due to starvation also has occurred. Femur marrow analyses on 12 carcasses found there in 1972–1973 showed seven cases with extractable lipid content under 17 percent ($\bar{x} = 13$ percent), whereas three apparently healthy females killed accidentally in the spring of 1969 averaged 89.5 percent extractable lipids (Lent, Unpublished). Similarly, Parker et al. (1975) found lipid content below 7 percent in 19 of 22 femurs examined from carcasses found in the Parry Islands following the population crash in 1973–1974. Record snow depths and hard drift conditions were believed to be responsible. Mortality was particularly severe on Bathurst Island where the number of musk-oxen counted declined from 446 in spring of 1973 to 285 in March 1974, and then, to 105 in August 1974 (Miller and Russell 1975). The timing of this decline is reminiscent of observations from Nunivak that indicate the peak of mortality due to malnutrition usually occurs late in spring, around the calving season.

Accidental deaths have been reported frequently. Falls from cliffs, drownings or losses on sea ice are the most common. Among 113 recorded cases of natural mortality on Nunivak Island, Spencer and Lensink (1970) listed 4 from falls off cliffs, 14 lost on sea ice or washed ashore 8 mired in bogs or drowned in rivers, and 4 of unspecified injuries. They believed the most common unrecorded cause of mortality was loss of animals that wandered out onto the sea ice. The ice surrounding the island is not as stable as that in the true Arctic. Since the Spencer-Lensink compilation, I observed a young calf fall from a cliff to its death on Nunivak. Other observers have also reported deaths due to falls. Mortality due to parasitic infections or diseases is extremely rare in the wild but has occurred frequently in captivity (Samuel and Gray 1974).

MOVEMENTS AND BEHAVIOR

In comparison to their cervid counterparts in the Arctic, the caribou, musk-oxen are relatively sedentary and occur in smaller, more stable groups. Seasonal movements tend to be less than 80 kilometers (50 miles) in length, usually considerably less, even on the mainland of Canada and Alaska. Movements as far as 300 kilometers (186 miles) have occurred following transplants in Alaska. Little is known about daily rates of movement. Lent and Smith both tracked identifiable groups during the rut (Smith 1976). One group moved over a circuit of 11

Table 16. Seasonal changes in mean group size of musk-oxen.

Location	Winter	Summer
Thelon Game Sanctuary[a]	19.7	11.3
Fosheim Peninsula[b]	15.1	9.6
Nunivak Island[c]	14.9	7.8

[a]Excludes lone males which comprised 0.5 percent of population in winter, 9.0 percent in summer.

[b]Excludes lone males which were absent in winter, but comprised 3.9 percent of total population in summer.

[c]Excludes lone males and all-male groups (winter $\bar{x}$ = 5.2; summer $\bar{x}$ = 1.3).

kilometers (6.8 miles) in a two-week period, returning nearly to the point of origin. The average distance between consecutive day sightings for three harem groups was 1.5 kilometers (0.93 miles).

Information on group sizes for musk-oxen observed at various seasons and locations are summarized in Table 16. There is a universal tendency for larger groupings to occur in winter than in summer. However, such winter groups may be especially large if disturbances have occurred. It is likely that the presence of active predators in an area would promote large gatherings, but this has not been documented. Nunivak Island musk-oxen continue to form large groups and defensive formations despite more than 40 years without contact with wolves.

Smith (1976) concluded that smaller groups exist in May and June before males enter into rutting activities. Males then take possession of existing groups and exclude all other males from the groups during the rut. They do not gather a harem of females in any sense, but after they take possession of a group they promote stability by discouraging egress of females and ingress of males. Lone males and small groups of males become more frequent as the rut commences in July.

Musk-oxen exhibit polyphasic activity with relatively short periods of feeding and resting-rumination. Gray (1973) indicated these periods are about 150 minutes in duration. Synchrony of activities is pronounced in small groups.

During the rut, from early July through September, bulls with harems spend up to 50 percent of their time in sexual and antagonistic activities. The behavioral repertoire of musk-oxen in the rut has been described in detail by Gray (1973) and Smith (1976). Behavior patterns are basically similar to those seen in other bovids, and presumably function to deter egress of females from the harems, test estrus condition and promote receptivity to mounting. Actual copulation was observed only during the first week of September on Nunivak Island. Similarly, five copulations in captive groups were observed between August 30 and September 12.

The usual culmination of encounters between harem males and mature challengers is the charge and clash. After the preliminary displays, contestants select level ground and charge at speeds of at least 40 kilometers per hour (25 miles per hour), clashing directly on the horn bosses. Twenty or more such clashes have occurred in single fights. Bulls in possession of harems were estimated by Smith (1976) to be 6–10 years old.

Musk-ox calves normally are born from late April through May. Extremes of births recorded on Nunivak Island are April 5 and June 19. One birth occurred in late July in the free-ranging population in Norway.

The mother-infant relationship is clearly of the "leader-follower" type (Lent 1974a). Close physical contact and frequent interactions for nursing prevail, particularly during the first two weeks of life. Mother and infant remain within a group. This tendency is not only advantageous in respect to predation, but also may be useful to reduce windchilling of the infant. After the first month, calves begin to interact frequently with one another in social play. They may associate with one another and cows other than their own mothers for entire activity periods. This behavior may explain some of the observations of alleged twinning.

There have been no indications of territoriality in musk-oxen at any season, nor have home ranges been defined. However, inten-

Cow and calf at domestication project near Fairbanks, Alaska. Note browsed condition of shrubs. Photo by author.

sive studies with marked individuals are lacking. During the rut, there is a tendency for harems to avoid one another and distribute themselves over available habitat, interspersed with lone males or all-male groups. Gray (1973) reported linear dominance hierarchies among males in groups observed outside the rutting period.

ECOLOGY

Food habits

In summertime, musk-oxen show a general preference for moist habitats and riparian vegetation. Information on the principal forage species reported by various authors is summarized in Table 17. Selection of green, new-growth plant parts has been noted by several authors (Tener 1965, Bos 1967, Alendal 1976). Leaves of low shrubs, especially willow and dwarf birch,

have been reported to be important wherever they occur. Musk-oxen at the domestication farm in Fairbanks browse on aspen and have learned to bend over stems up to 5 meters (16.4 feet) in height, using a foreleg to hold them while they strip off leaves. Musk-oxen show a predilection for lush, fertilized vegetation adjacent to colonies of cliff-nesting birds, wherever these occur. This preference accounts for some of the mortality from falls off cliffs.

Selection of winter forage species seems to be determined largely by the characteristics and distribution of snow cover. Snow-free areas or areas of shallow snow depth and easily fractured crusts inevitably are preferred (Lent and Knutson 1971). The frequent occurrence of certain shrubs and woody species such as Labrador tea, crowberry, dwarf birch and willow in winter diets relates to the tendency of these species to grow on hummocks of exposed relief.

Similarly, on Nunivak Island the vegetation of coastal sand dunes is relatively accessible. The major species occurring there, beach rye grass, is the most important winter forage species. Other species such as woodrushes and sedges are grazed heavily where they occur on the windswept edges of marine escarpments. In contrast to the more mobile, light-grazing behavior in summertime, winter feeding of musk-oxen usually is concentrated and can result in close cropping of accessible plants.

Responses to snow and other physical factors

The importance of snow cover conditions to the well-being of musk-oxen has already been alluded to. Generally speaking, areas

Table 17. Summary of preferred food species and of plant species avoided by musk-oxen.

Location and season	Preferred species[a]	Avoided species[b]
Ellesmere Island— summer (Tener 1965)	sedges blue grasses Alkali grasses fescue broad-leafed fireweed cottongrass bladder campion willow	dryas saxifrages wheatgrass Lapland cassiope
Banks Island— summer (Wilkinson et al. 1976	sedge hairgrass pendent grass polar willow	
Nunivak Island— summer (Bos 1967)	sedges narrow-leafed cottongrass horsetails bluejoint grass fescues alpine foxtail cloudberry nagoon-berry diamond leaf willow dwarf birch	
Thelon Sanctuary— winter Tener (1965)	Labrador tea crowberry blueberry shrub birch	lichens wheatgrass

Table 17.

Bathurst Island— winter (Parker et al. 1975)	willow purple mountain saxifrage grasses and sedges poppy	
Nunivak Island— winter (Bos 1967)	beach rye grass sedge wood rushes fescue grass crowberry dwarf birch	snow wood rush dwarf cornel wild parsley lovage
Nunivak Island— winter (Utermohle in Lent, Unpublished)	unidentified grasses crowberry Labrador tea birch willow unidentified forbs	
Svalbard— season not specified (Alendal 1974)	alpine foxtail blue grass fescue grass mountain sorrel (no willows or birch present on Svalbard)	

[a]Based on field observation except Parker et al. (1975) data which were based on rumen analyses and listed in order of abundance.

[b]Species indicated to be eaten less than would be expected if selection were random.

with mild, wet climates have proven unsuitable for transplants. Reports of heavy mortality and low recruitment always have been associated with winters of deep snow and icing conditions. Within limits, these relationships appear to be density-independent. On Nunivak Island, snow depths of more than 30 centimeters (11.8 inches) were avoided entirely except by a few mature males.

Hot summer conditions do not seem to be directly adverse to musk-oxen. In Fairbanks, Alaska, they are able to cope well with summer temperatures above 30 degrees Centigrade (86 degrees Fahrenheit), given shade and water. Such warm conditions may be conducive, however, to parasites not normally found in musk-oxen. Drinking of water is rare among adults in the wild. Snow consumption is observed occasionally.

Distribution and numbers

Although musk-oxen frequently have been referred to as endangered in popular literature and occasionally in scientific papers, there is no reason to consider any major population in danger of extirpation. Throughout their range, populations either are increasing or fluctuating in response to climatic conditions. In either case, they are functional parts of relatively stable ecosystems. Transplants have introduced musk-oxen to areas where they formerly occurred, as well as into locations where they were not present within recent geologic time (Table 18). The approximate boundaries for the present circumpolar distribution of the species as well as points of introduction are shown in Figure 27. The species also has been bred successfully in captivity, in connection with domestication experiments and at locations such as the Alberta Game Farm (Oeming 1965).

The worldwide free-living musk-ox population is approximately 25,000. The population in East Greenland is believed to have increased to about 15,000 in recent years as a result of favorable conditions for several winters (H. Thing, personal communication). Populations were estimated to number about 10,000 in the Canadian Arctic, including 8,500 in the Arctic Islands and 1,500 on the mainland (Tener 1965). No current information is available for the mainland. However, numbers presently are lower on some of the major islands but greatly increased on Banks Island. In Alaska, the total number at the various introduction locales is close to 1,000 (Table 18).

Table 18. Musk-ox introductions and transplants, 1929–1976.

Location	Source	Year(s)	Number introduced	Status
Svalbard	E. Greenland	1929	17	36–50 in 1959, 30 in 1974
Norway	E. Greenland	1947–1953	27	Approximately 45 in 1973 including 7 that moved to Sweden
W. Greenland (Sondre Strømfjord)	E. Greenland	1965, 1967	27	60–80, little dispersal
Nunivak Island, Alaska	E. Greenland[a]	1935, 1936	31	Peak of 750 in 1968; now about 600
U.S.S.R. (Taimyr Peninsula)	Banks Island, Canada	1973	10	Apparently doing well
U.S.S.R. (Taimyr Peninsula)	Nunivak Island	1975	20	Only one died first winter
U.S.S.R. (Wrangel Island)	Nunivak Island	1975	20	Apparently doing well
Nelson Island, Alaska	Nunivak Island	1967, 1968	23	Rapid increase, now over 50
NE Alaska-Arctic Natl. Wildl. Range	Nunivak Island	1969, 1970	65	Initial heavy mortality and dispersal; now good recruitment
Seward Peninsula, Alaska	Nunivak Island	1970	36	Dispersed but slowly increasing
Cape Thompson, Alaska	Nunivak Island	1970	36	Heavy mortality and dispersal, few recent observations
Fairbanks, Alaska[b]	Nunivak Island	1964	33	Good production
Ft. Chimo, Quebec[b]	Ellesmere Island	1967	15	Some production, released in wild North Quebec
Bardu, Norway[b]	E. Greenland	1969	41	Poor success, later moved to offshore island
Unalakleet,[b] Alaska	Fairbanks, Alaska	1976	49	Viral disease problem in herd

[a]Thirty-four animals were brought from Greenland to Fairbanks in 1930; survivors and young born in Fairbanks were moved to Nunivak in 1934 and 1935.
[b]Domestication herds.

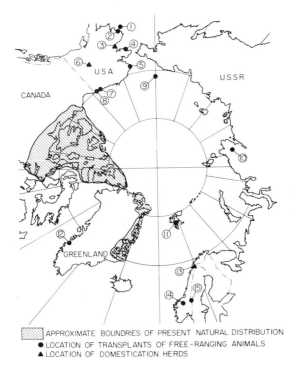

Figure 27. Current distribution of musk-oxen including recent transplant sites and domestication stations: 1 = Nunivak Island; 2 = Nelson Island; 3 = Unalakleet; 4 = Seward Peninsula; 5 = Cape Thompson; 6 = Fairbanks (entire herd moved to Unalakleet in 1978); 7 and 8 = Arctic National Wildlife Range; 9 = Wrangel Island; 10 = Taimyr Peninsula; 11 = Syalbard; 12 = Sondre Stromfjørd; 13 = Bardu; 14 and 15 = Norway.

MANAGEMENT

Harvesting

In the Nineteenth Century and the first two decades of the Twentieth Century, numbers of musk-oxen decreased dramatically as a result of heavy harvesting by explorers, whalers, trappers, native peoples using firearms and market hunters taking hides. Market hunting was particularly significant after the demise of the North American bison herds (Hone 1934, Tener 1965). In Alaska, musk-oxen were limited in distribution to the Arctic coastal plain and extirpated before the establishment of effective regulations. Initial management efforts in Canada were directed toward achieving near total prohibition of hunting. Hunting of the introduced Nunivak Island musk-ox population also was prohibited until 1974. Then, following several years of controversy, the United States Fish and Wildlife Service agreed to permit limited recreational hunting on this National Wildlife Refuge to reduce the musk-ox population. After issuance of an environmental impact assessment, the State of Alaska implemented a carefully controlled recreational hunting program on the island, open to a limited number of residents and nonresidents selected by a drawing. In the fall of 1976, 27 males and 2 females were taken on Nunivak. Each hunter was transported and guided by an Eskimo resident of the island, using either boats or snowmachines, thus providing considerable input to the village economy.

In Canada and Greenland, restrictions on hunting by native peoples have been eased somewhat in recent years. Quotas for native (Inuit) hunters in Canada permit taking of approximately 70 musk-oxen per year. In East Greenland, hunting is permitted only by local residents in the Scoresbysund area. Based on a complex quota system, as many as 80 animals per year have been taken. There is believed to be a significant number of illegal kills in this area.

Transplanting

Throughout the Twentieth Century, musk-oxen have been transplanted frequently (Lønø 1960, Andersen 1966, Lent 1971, Unpublished). The reasons for these operations have varied, including: (1) reintroduction to ranges where musk-oxen had been extirpated; (2) introductions to ranges outside the natural distribution of the species; (3) establishment of herds for domestication experiments; and (4) in the case of removals from Nunivak Island, to alleviate population pressure and overgrazing of winter range. A summary of transplant activities is given in Table 18.

Original musk-ox herd brought from Greenland in 1930 and held near College, Alaska until 1935. Photo courtesy of the National Archives.

Habitat degradation

Problems of habitat degradation have been documented only for Nunivak Island where the introduced population is limited by snow cover to a restricted winter range, mainly within the coastal dune system. Intensive grazing and trampling of the dunes have altered the vegetative cover and decreased the stability of certain dune systems. Competition among musk-oxen and reindeer or caribou generally has not been considered to be significant or to present management problems. However, Alendal (1976) suggested that musk-oxen on Svalbard (Spitzbergen) Islands may have declined in recent years due, in part, to competition for winter forage with a reindeer population that has increased dramatically during the same period. In this respect, it may be significant that woody species used heavily elsewhere by musk-oxen in winter are absent on Spitzbergen.

Domestication

Management of musk-oxen as domestic animals has remained largely experimental for several years. The purpose of domestication has been the production and utilization of qiviut for sweaters, scarves and other products (Wilkinson 1971, 1974). Good success in breeding musk-oxen has been achieved at the University of Alaska in Fairbanks. In 1975, 50 animals were transferred from the Fairbanks farm to establish the first Eskimo village herd at Unalakleet, Alaska. In 1977, the remainder of the Fairbanks herd was moved to Unalakleet. Qiviut shed from wild animals also has been collected and utilized in products for sale by the Eskimos of Nunivak Island.

Censusing and capturing

Censuses in the Canadian Arctic have employed standard techniques for fixed-wing

Eroded coastal dune on Nunivak Island. The crest of the dune is snow-free or nearly so in normal winters. This leads to severe trampling and close cropping of vegetative cover. Photo by author.

Capture of musk-ox for transplant using net. Photo by Jerry L. Hout.

aircraft and helicopters (Miller et al. 1973, Miller and Russell 1974). On Nunivak Island, the restricted winter distribution of musk-oxen has permitted the use of snow-machines for censuses. This provides not only accurate determination of total numbers but also good information on the sex and age composition of the population.

Jonkel et al. (1975) have had some success immobilizing musk-oxen using succinyl-choline chloride administered by a "Cap Chur" gun fired from a helicopter. However, the techniques and dosages need further refinement. Transplants from Nunivak Island also were accomplished initially with the use of helicopters and drugs. Calves have been captured using airplanes and boats, driving animals into bodies of water. More recently, however, use of snowma-chines has been developed and refined. Captures for a 1975 transplant to the Soviet Union were accomplished entirely by six-men crews on snowmachines. Eleven-month old animals were caught by hand and with ropes. Two-year olds were captured by entangling them in large nets made of nylon shroud cord. No drugs were employed at any stage of capture or transport to the Soviet Union. Fifty-four animals were captured and tagged, 40 of which actually were trans-planted. A pregnant two year old was the only casualty.

All capture and similar operations with musk-oxen should be avoided during the period when calves in their first two weeks of life are likely to be present. Considerable evidence from Alaska, Canada and Norway reveals that abandonment and desertion of such young calves occurs readily as a result of harassment or disturbance (Lent 1971, Alendal 1976, Jonkel et al. 1975). Even the techniques developed on Nunivak Island may result in considerable stress to noncap-tured animals, especially pregnant ones, since groups frequently are run by snow-machines until severe exhaustion is evident in many individuals.

THE FUTURE

Development of energy resources in the North American Arctic soon may bring to an end the relatively undisturbed status that musk-oxen and their habitats have enjoyed for the last one-half century. Exploration for oil and gas deposits already is underway on some musk-ox ranges in the Canadian Arctic (Urquhart, Unpublished, Miller and Russell 1974). Proposals for extraction of these resources involve plans for pipelines that pass through areas utilized by musk-oxen, including the Arctic National Wildlife Range in Alaska (Lent 1976). To meet possible conflicts, wildlife biologists need increased understanding of musk-ox behavior, particularly of responses to distur-bance. The potential for abandonment of calves and stress on adults as a result of habitat disturbance and herd harassment already has been pointed out in this chapter. Improved information is needed on indi-vidual musk-ox movements, degree of indi-vidual adaptability on specific ranges, and rates of interchange among populations on islands in the Canadian Arctic.

Throughout the North American Arctic, native people are organizing and demanding greater voice in resource policies and alloca-tions. It is, of course, risky to predict what the consequences of this could be. However, it could result in increased pressures for con-sumptive utilization of musk-oxen through subsistence or recreational hunting, or in expansion of reindeer or musk-oxen hus-bandry in the Arctic. Any of these changes could have major repercussions on the status of wild musk-oxen. If the present trend continues, shifting away from an essentially protectionist mode of management toward regulated harvests, then undoubtedly there will be an increased need for better under-standing of musk-ox population dynamics and movements.

Chapter 10

MOUNTAIN GOAT

Chester B. Rideout

Assistant Professor
Indiana University Northwest
Gary, Indiana

Of the big game animals in North America, the Rocky Mountain goat *(Oreamnos americanus)* is probably the least known by the American public. Because of their rugged and remote habitat, mountain goats seldomly are seen in their native ranges. They also have a poor survival record in captivity and, therefore, are not common in zoological parks. Wild mountain goats often are confused with the better-publicized bighorn sheep.

The mountain goat has been hunted for many years, primarily as a trophy animal, and is a valuable game species throughout its range. It is also important as a symbol of the spirit of rugged mountain wilderness areas in the West, and as inspiration for wilderness preservation.

TAXONOMY

Mountain goats are rupicaprines, or goat antelopes. They are related closely to the chamois of Europe but not to any species in North America. Some recent articles incorrectly claim that the mountain goat is a close relative of the pronghorn, which is the sole surviving species of family Antilocapridae.

Four subspecies have been named from the mountain goat: *Oreamnos americanus*

americanus, O. a. kennedyi, O. a. missoulae and *O. a. columbiae* (Rideout and Hoffmann 1975). Cowan and McCrory (1970) indicated that no distinct cranial characteristics of the mountain goat can be used to categorize subspecies. Because of this fact and the small number of specimens available (only 167 skulls could be examined by Cowan for this study), subspecific categories remain to be confirmed or abandoned based on additional scientific data for this species.

DESCRIPTION

The mountain goat is stocky, with a short tail and slender neck. The black horns are thin and pointed, ranging in length for adults from 200–305 millimeters (7.9–12 inches). The coat is made up of white wool and white guard hairs and sometimes includes dark brown hairs on the back and rump. On kids, these hairs often form a brown line along the back. The winter coat is quite long and includes a pointed beard approximately 130 millimeters (5.1 inches) in length. Molt of the winter coat begins in June, and adult males have their summer coats by mid-July. Females and juveniles complete their molt later, by mid-August; this difference is useful in sexing goats during summer months. The skin varies in

Table 19. Mean measurements of 28 mountain goats in the Sapphire Mountains of Montana (after Rideout 1974a).

| | Kids | | | | Yearlings | | | |
| | Male | | Female | | Male | | Female | |
	mm.	in.	mm.	in.	mm.	in.	mm.	in.
Total length	907.9	35.7	851.0	33.5	1194.0	47.0	1182.0	46.5
Tail	70.4	2.8	102.0	4.0	86.0	3.4	91.7	3.6
Hind foot	238.6	9.4	248.0	9.8	292.0	11.5	280.0	11.0
Ear	87.8	3.5	95.0	3.7	95.0	1.8	98.3	3.9
Neck (minimum)	235.9	9.3	210.0	8.3	300.0	11.8	289.7	11.4
Girth	623.9	24.6	578.0	22.8	876.0	34.5	841.0	33.1
Height at shoulder	519.5	20.5	470.0	18.5	692.0	27.2	685.7	27.0
Horn curve	15.8	0.6	13.0	0.5	162.0	6.4	130.3	5.1
Weight[a]	16.0	(35.3)	15.0	(33.1)	33.6	(74.1)	32.4	(71.4)

[a]In kilograms (pounds).

Molt of adult goats' thick and long coats takes place from June through mid-July, during which time the animals frequently rub against obstacles and leave clumps of discarded wool on shrubs and trees. Photo by Don Domenick; courtesy of the Colorado Division of Wildlife.

Table 19.

	Two year olds			Three year olds				Four year olds and older			
	Male		Female		Male		Female		Male		Female	
mm.	in.	mm.	in.	mm.	in.	mm.	in.	mm.	in.	mm.	in.
1342.5	52.9	1286.0	50.6			1363.0	53.6	1539.7	60.6	1410.1	55.5
98.5	3.9	81.0	3.2			104.0	4.1	91.0	3.6	107.6	4.2
296.5	11.7	294.5	11.6			316.3	12.5	328.3	12.9	307.7	12.1
108.0	4.3	105.0	4.1			109.0	4.3	113.0	4.4	115.7	4.6
337.0	13.3	301.5	11.9			345.0	13.6	421.0	16.6	373.9	14.7
946.0	37.2	908.0	35.7			970.3	38.2	1140.0	44.9	1070.0	42.1
698.5	27.5	740.0	29.1			734.3	28.9	890.3	35.1	796.6	31.4
176.5	6.9	140.0	5.5			192.7	7.6	228.7	9.0	206.4	8.1
41.5	(91.5)	38.6	(85.1)			49.6	(109.4)	68.6	(151.3)	56.5	(124.6)

thickness, especially in adult males, being thickest on the flanks (Rideout and Hoffmann 1975). Puncture wounds received during lateral displays occur primarily on the stomach and flanks. "Dermal shields" in these areas may be as much as 22 millimeters (0.9 inches) thick in old males. Mountain goats bleed very little when injured, perhaps due to an efficient blood clotting mechanism (Geist 1967b, 1971a, 1975a).

The hooves of the mountain goat are large and oval in shape, and include prominent dew hooves. As a result, mountain goats are better able to travel through snow than the mountain sheep, which have smaller hooves (Geist 1971a). The hoof consists of cushion-like pads surrounded by a hard shell. These pads are sensitive to touch and provide a much better grip on smooth rock surfaces than do the hooves of other North American ungulates.

Adult males exhibit the following measurements: total length—1,245–1,787 millimeters (49–70.4 inches); length of tail—84–203 millimeters (3.3–8 inches); length of hind hoof—300–368 millimeters (11.8–14.5 inches); weight—46.2–136 kilograms (101.6–299.2 pounds) (Rideout and Hoffman 1975). Males are from 10–30 percent larger than females in weight and linear measurements (Table 19).

A newborn kid in Montana weighed 2.95 kilograms (6.5 pounds), and measured 559 millimeters (22 inches) in length and 343 millimeters (13.5 inches) in height at the shoulder (Brandborg 1955).

The skull of the mountain goat differs from that of mountain sheep in being quite fragile (Schaffer and Reed 1972). This can be related to differences between the antagonistic behaviors of mountain goats and sheep. Black glands lie behind the horns in both sexes of the mountain goat. These glands are swollen and active in males during the rut, and are used to mark vegetation with distinctive odors as plants are drawn behind the horns (Geist 1964, DeBock 1970).

ECOLOGY

Life History

Mating begins in early November and usually ends by mid-December. Geist (1964) reported matings as late as January 3. The gestation period has been estimated at 178 days by Brandborg (1955) and 147 days by Asdell (1964), who also reported that successful breeding can occur in two-year old goats.

Kids are born in late May or early June (Brandborg 1955). Single births are most common, although twins have been reported frequently. Lentfer (1955) reported seeing triplets in the Crazy Mountains of Montana during rapid population growth following the introduction of mountain goats.

Kids are precocial; they follow the mother shortly after birth and nurse approximately

An adult female mountain goat with a two-month old kid in Montana in August. Nanny is in summer coat. Photo by author.

once every hour. Females give birth in isolation in areas of steep cliffs. Some nursing occurs in September, but it is rare at that time. Kids follow their mothers until the next year's kids are born; females then become quite aggressive toward yearlings.

Mountain goats leave characteristic signs, including well-used trails, white wool hanging from shrubs and trees, and droppings. Pellets are about the same size as those from deer, but are concave on one end and pointed on the other. The track matches that of deer and mountain sheep in size, but is wider and more oval (Brandborg 1955).

Population dynamics

Mountain goat productivity varies considerably among areas and in response to weather conditions preceding birth of young

(Brandborg 1955). Estimates of production also may vary because of the small sample sizes available. In Black Hills, South Dakota, 86 kids and 52 yearlings were reported per 100 adult females (Hanson 1950). This study was done 20 years after mountain goats were introduced to the area and is the highest productivity reported in literature. Kid to female ratios ranged from 77:100 to 84:100 in Montana (Rideout 1974a). Values of 73:100 for Washington, from 22:100 to 79:100 for Idaho, and 45:100 for Jasper National Park, Alberta have been reported (Anderson 1940, Cowan 1944, Brandborg 1955).

Mortality of mountain goats is high during their first winter, varying from 27.3–72.6 percent in Alberta, Montana and Idaho ranges (Cowan 1944, Brandborg 1955, Rideout 1974a). A greater mortality of kids and yearlings during a severe winter has been reported (73 percent and 59 percent respectively) than during a mild winter (27 percent and 2 percent) (Rideout 1974a).

Rideout (1974) and Chadwick (1973) reported that adult male to adult female ratios in Montana from 1971–1973 ranged from 23:100–56:100. The lowest male to female ratios followed winters with excessive snowfalls, which indicated that mortality of males exceeded that of females' during severe winters (Rideout 1974a). Accurate sex ratio data are lacking in most studies due to the difficulty in determining sex of goats in the field and to their inaccessibility.

Mortality factors

The most significant predators of mountain goats are mountain lions and golden eagles. Mountain lions are able to attack and kill mountain goats, and golden eagles have been observed carrying off newborn kids and knocking yearlings from cliffs. Other predators of the mountain goat are the bobcat, coyote, black bear and grizzly bear (Rideout and Hoffmann 1975).

Parasitism is thought to be a major limiting factor in the mountain goat population of the Black Hills. Infections of helminths,

Table 20. Age classes (by years) of mountain goats captured in Idaho and Montana (after Brandborg 1955, Rideout 1974a), and shot in South Dakota (after Richardson 1971).

Study	Kids	1	2	3	4	5	6	7	8	9	10	11	12	13	Total
Brandborg	3	9	11	7	10	3	5	1	3			2	1	1	56
Rideout	9	5	4	3	2	3	3			1					30
Richardson	1	15	11	13	10	9	11	9	5	6	3	1			94
Total	13	29	26	23	22	15	19	10	8	7	3	3	1	1	208

lungworms *(Protostrongylus stilesi* and *P. rushi)* and nematodes *(Nematodirus maculosus)* are extremely heavy in this introduced population (Boddicker et al. 1971). Mountain goats also suffer from wood tick infestations (Cowan 1951, Brandborg 1955).

Researchers studying mountain goats seldom report goats exceeding 11 years of age (Table 20). The oldest individuals reported in the literature include an 18-year old female and a 14-year old male (Cowan and McCrory 1970).

BEHAVIOR

Movements

Daily movements vary from a few hundred meters to 3.2 kilometers (2 miles).

August movements are as much as 20 times greater than those during January (Brandborg 1955, Chadwick 1973). Activity occurs at all times of the day and night, but long distance movements do not occur during dark nights (Rideout 1974b). Activity usually increases at dawn and dusk (Figures 28 and 29). Mountain goats are well-known for their climbing ability; they can travel across the steepest of cliffs with ease, and can gain 460 meters (1,509 feet) in altitude in 20 minutes with little apparent effort (Holroyd 1967).

Migration to wintering areas occurs with the first heavy snowfalls. Preferred winter habitat includes the lowest possible south-facing cliffs, as well as high ridges where snow is removed by the wind. Winter ranges may be extremely small. Brandborg (1955)

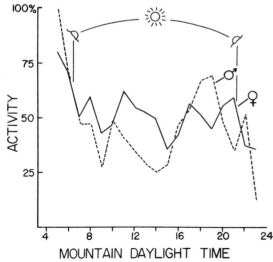

Figure 28. Percent of activity of radio-collared male and female mountain goats in the Sapphire Mountains of Montana during July and August of 1971 and 1972 (after Rideout 1974b).

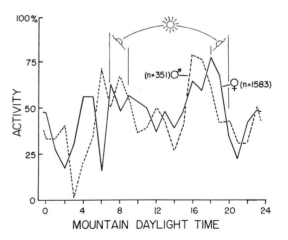

Figure 29. Percent of activity of radio-collared male and female mountain goats in the Sapphire Mountains from September through November, 1972 (after Rideout 1974b).

153

observed goats which occupied a winter range of 80.9 hectares (200 acres) for three months in the Salmon River area.

The choice of winter habitat also depends on snow depth. Rideout (1974b), working in the Sapphire Mountains of Montana during the severe winter of 1971–1972, found that winter locations of radio-collared goats seldom were within the area occupied during summer and fall. There was much less snow the next winter, and radio-collared goats were usually at higher elevations within the summer-fall ranges (Figure 30). In the same study, yearly home ranges of 21.5 square kilometers (8.3 square miles) for adult males, 24 square kilometers (9.3 square miles) for adult females, 31.1 square kilometers (12 square miles) for two year olds, and 48.3

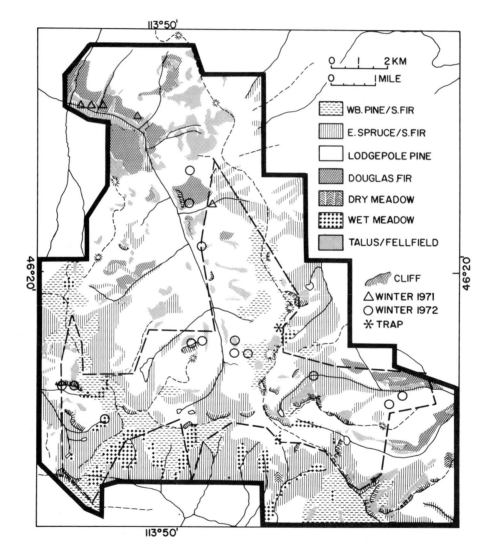

Figure 30. The summer-fall ranges used by radio-collared goats in the Sapphire Mountains, from May 16 to November 15 of 1971 and 1972 is indicated by the dashed line (after Rideout 1974b, In press). Goat locations during the winter period (November 16 to May 15) are indicated by triangles for the severe 1971–1972 winter, and by circles for the mild winter of 1972–1973. Note that winter locations during the mild winter are usually within the summer-fall range, whereas much lower elevations were needed in 1971–1972.

square kilometers (18.7 square miles) for yearlings were calculated by the maximum polygon method (Rideout 1974a, In press).

Individual and group behavior

Mountain goats usually are found in groups of two to four during the summer and fall (Figure 31). Larger groups occur on bedding grounds during winter storms (Holroyd 1967) and at salt licks during summer.

Mountain goats exhibit a number of comfort movements, including scratching with the hind foot and horns, rubbing against ground and vegetation, and biting or licking wool. They dig bedding depressions and toss dust back over their coat, which most likely is a reaction to discomforts of heat, ectoparasites and shedding (DeBock 1970).

Goats usually rest on their sides with their legs extended. Often the eyes are closed, and the head may be folded back along the body. On hot days goats bed in the shade or on snowbanks where irritation from insects is reduced (Brandborg 1955).

Social behavior

Mountain goats do not butt heads together in their fighting behavior like sheep do, probably because the skull is much more fragile. Threats include: (1) the "horn threat," in which the head is rotated in a forward direction to display the horns; (2) the "rush threat," where the threatening goat rushes toward the opponent while performing a horn threat; (3) the "horn swipe," which is an upward swipe with the horns; (4) the "stare threat," in which one goat stares intently at another; and (5) the "present threat," which is a lateral display in which goats line up head-to-flank and slowly march in a circle (Geist 1964, DeBock 1970).

Blows are delivered to the flanks and rump from the present threat in mountain goat kids. Similar blows by adults, especially by females during the mating season, have resulted in serious injury or death. Aggression toward yearlings demonstrated by adult females following the birth of their new kids may be due in part to the possibility of injury to the kid, since yearlings' horns are 130–160 millimeters (5.1–6.3 inches) long. The play of kids includes neck fighting, where one kid places his neck over another's neck and tries to force the other kid to its knees. They also exhibit mounting behavior, and play "king of the mountain" on top of a rock or stump (Geist 1964, 1967b, DeBock 1970).

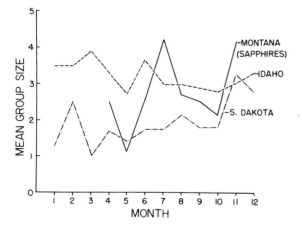

Figure 31. Monthly group sizes for mountain goats from Montana, Idaho and South Dakota (after Hanson 1950, Brandborg 1955, Rideout 1974a).

Mountain goat kids delivering blows to the abdomen from the "present threat." Photo by author.

Adult male mountain goats in present-threat display. Photo by author.

The dominance hierarchy of the mountain goat outside of the rut is variable. Some studies report females and juveniles are dominant over males (Geist 1964, Chadwick 1973), while others indicate males are dominant in most contests (DeBock 1970, Rideout 1974a). Aggressiveness by females during the summer appears to be stimulated and intensified when food resources are limited (Rideout 1974a).

As the mating season approaches in October, male-female interactions increase. Males feed less often while tending females and show decreased activity. Males mark vegetation with their horn glands and dig rutting pits; these pits are often soaked with urine. Wet soil, which is tossed back along the sides and belly of the male goats, stains the wool. Males can be identified from a considerable distance during the rut by their stained coats (DeBock 1970).

In courtship, the male approaches the female in a low-stretch position, with the legs bent and body parallel to the ground. The male's approach stimulates urination by the female. The urine is examined by the male, whose upper lip then is drawn back. The male then performs a foreleg kick between the hind legs of the female, which is followed by repeated mountings (Geist 1964, DeBock 1970).

Communications

Mountain goat vocalizations are produced at low intensity, and most observers have not been close enough to hear them (Rideout 1973, 1974a). However, several vocalizations have been reported. These include a low-pitched grunt, a buzzing or humming sound produced during low-stretch demonstrations, a warning snort and a bleat by a male, and bleats by kid and mother when separated from each other (Rideout and Hoffman 1975).

HABITAT NEEDS AND PREFERENCES

Mountain goats have very broad food tolerances. Cowan (1944) found that mountain goats in Alberta ate 77 percent grasses and herbaceous vegetation and only 23 percent willow in summer months. Casebeer (1948), on the other hand, found that grazing provided only 4 percent of the summer diet in Montana; the other 96 percent consisted of grouse whortle-berry.

Mountain goat diets also are varied on winter home ranges. In the Black Hills, the winter diet consisted of 16 percent mosses and lichens, 30 percent woody plants and 10 percent unclassified (Harmon 1944). Shrubs were a small portion of the winter diet in Montana, Colorado and Alaska, and grasses made up 90 percent of the winter diet in Washington. Foods used heavily during the winter months included beargrass in Montana, ponderosa pine in Montana and Alberta, alpine fir in British Columbia, and fern rhizomes in Alaska (Rideout and Hoffmann 1975).

Mountain goats prefer steep slopes or cliffs, since they offer an untapped food source and protection from predators. Sun and wind limit snow depths on southern and western exposures, so snow accumulations are greatest on north- and east-facing slopes. As a result, food availability is greatest on steep south- and west-facing slopes in the winter months, whereas north- and east-facing slopes have the greatest supply of snow, water and succulent forage in summer (Figure 32). During severe weather, mountain goats seek caves and overhanging ledges (Brandborg 1955, Rideout 1974a).

Mountain goat ranges encompass alpine tundra and subalpine areas of the northern Rocky Mountains—habitats associated with low temperatures and heavy snowfalls. Details concerning the effects of weather in different ranges are provided by Hanson (1950), DeBock (1970), Geist (1971a), Chadwick (1973) and Rideout (1974a).

Water is not a significant limiting factor for mountain goats in most ranges. Snow-

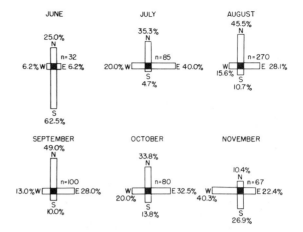

Figure 32. Direction of slope area used by mountain goats in the Sapphire Mountains (1971–1972) as determined by radio telemetry. Open bars indicate the percentage of observations in each compass direction (n = total monthly radio locations) (after Rideout 1974b).

banks usually are present at high altitudes all year, and goats have been seen eating snow. Anderson (1940) thought that water limited the distribution of goats in Washington, whereas Brandborg (1955) saw no evidence of daily movements to reach water in Idaho or Montana.

Salt licks are used extensively by goats during the summer, and travel to salt licks frequently occurs. Stockstad et al. (1953) reported that sodium is preferred over other minerals by goats in Montana, and Hebert and Cowan (1971) concluded that increased sodium consumption in spring and fall is due to lack of sodium in a lush diet. Sodium concentrations at salt licks range from 20–5,500 parts per million (Brandborg 1955, Hebert and Cowan 1971).

MANAGEMENT

Distribution and status

Mountain goat populations have been managed for a considerable period of time. Restrictions of one mountain goat per hunter began as early as 1903 in Idaho and 1905 in Montana. During the 1930s and 1940s, regulations on hunting season length were established, and some areas in Montana were closed to mountain goat hunting (Brandborg 1955, Foss and Rognrud 1971).

Mountain goats have been introduced successfully into the Black Hills of South Dakota, several areas of Montana, the Gore, San Juan and Collegiate Ranges of Colorado, the Wallawa Mountains of Oregon, Olympic National Park in Washington, and Baranof, Chichagof and Kodiak islands of Alaska (Figure 33). Introductions on Vancouver Island in British Columbia and the Twin Peaks area of Utah were not successful (Rideout and Hoffmann 1975).

Successful mountain goat introductions have expanded hunting opportunities in some states. In 1965, 29 percent of the mountain goat permits issued in Montana

INTRODUCED HERDS

NATIVE POPULATIONS

Figure 33. Distribution of *Oreamnos Americanus.*

were for restored populations; and mountain goats now are hunted on a permit basis in Colorado and the Black Hills (Hibbs et al. 1969, Foss and Rognrud 1971, Richardson 1971).

Mountain goat populations were estimated at 2,785 in Idaho, 4,451 in Montana prior to Fish and Game Department transplants, and 5,000 in Washington (Casebeer et al. 1950, Brandborg 1955). Populations of 300–400 goats in South Dakota, 390 in Colorado, and 12,000 in Alaska also have been reported (Klein 1953, Hibbs et al. 1969, Richardson 1971).

Estimating populations

The age of a mountain goat can be determined by counting rings that encircle its horns. The first ring is formed during the second winter at 22 months of age, and others are formed each successive year. The teeth also are indicators of age: the innermost pair of incisors (I1) are replaced at 15–16 months, the second pair (I2) at two years, the third pair (I3) at three years of age, and the canines in the fifth year (Brandborg 1955, Geer 1971).

Mountain goats are difficult to sex, particularly during the winter. Differential molting patterns and the greater bulk of males can be used to sex during the summer. The horns of males are thicker at the base than those of females and they curve evenly back along their entire length. Those of females bend more sharply several centimeters from the tip. During the hunting season, females can be identified because they usually are accompanied by kids and because they tend to be more gregarious than males. They also lack the dirty coat of the male during the mating season.

Mountain goats can be counted with least difficulty in spring on their winter ranges. Counts are best obtained by ground surveys or from slow-flying aircraft. Population estimates also have been made in Montana with the Lincoln Index (Rideout 1974a), but this technique has not proven accurate with the small sample sizes available in most herds.

Harvest objectives and season framework

Unlike many members of the deer family, mountain goats cannot be managed over large geographical areas (Foster 1976). They are hunted on a limited basis in most mountainous areas of their total range. Mountain goat hunting seasons originally ran from mid-September to late November in Montana and Idaho. These dates have been variable, however, involving as few as 10 days in some cases. Hunters often are urged not to take females accompanied by young, but compliance is not mandatory. In Idaho, the carcass must be recovered from the field as in the case of other big game species (Brandborg 1955, Foss and Rognrud 1971).

Habitat problems and improvement techniques

Mountain goats have overused many desirable browse plants in South Dakota's Black Hills (Richardson 1971). Habitat destruction occurs during repeated trail use and through construction of bedding depressions. No significant effort has been made to improve mountain goat habitat. Because of the wide variety of plants consumed by mountain goats, major considerations for introductions appear to involve the prevalence of south-facing cliffs at low altitudes and the condition of habitat in the proposed transplant area. In the Wallawa Mountains of Oregon, such cliffs are lacking and heavy grazing by domestic sheep preceded the largely unsuccessful introduction of mountain goats (M. Vaughan, personal communication).

Other management techniques

Mountain goats have been captured with Clover deer traps, rope-mesh traps, rope nooses and woven-wire pen traps (Rideout 1974c). They have been marked with sheep branding paint, colored eartags and plastic collars. Radio tracking studies were conducted in the Sapphire and Swan mountains of Montana (Chadwick 1973, Rideout 1974a, 1974b).

Because of difficulty in obtaining whole weights of mountain goats, weight estimation formulas have been derived from girth and length measurements. The best weight-estimation formulas are:

Weight (kilograms) = 0.0000315 length (centimeters) × girth^2 (centimeters) + 5.36; or,

Weight (pounds) = 0.0011 length (inches) × girth^2 (inches) + 11.5.

These formulas estimate weight more accurately than do formulas based only on girth and require only one more linear measurement (Rideout and Worthen 1975).

FUTURE NEEDS

More detailed studies of mountain goat populations must be made before many herds can be managed more intensively. Unless wildlife managers have the opportunity to increase their knowledge of mountain goat population dynamics and habitats, goat populations in some areas potentially face extermination, such as occurred in southern British Columbia during the 1960s (Foster 1976). This experience emphasizes the need and urgency for more adequate data on which to base sound management decisions.

In other geographic areas, logging at high elevations has resulted in loss of a number of goat herds (Brandborg 1955, Chadwick 1973). Nevertheless, mountain goats have sustained fewer losses than any other big game species in North America. This is due to the remoteness of mountain goat habitat (Rideout 1973). It is the careful, knowledgeable management of that habitat that primarily will determine the future well-being of mountain goats.

Chapter 11

BIGHORN SHEEP

William Wishart

Wildlife Research Biologist
Fish and Wildlife Division
Edmonton, Alberta

The bighorn sheep is one of the most highly esteemed big game species in North America. There are few people, if any, who cannot be impressed at the sight of a large bighorn ram bearing its crown of massive horns. Thus it was with Pedro de Castadena, a soldier in Coronado's army in 1540, when he sighted bighorns at the confluence of the Gila and San Francisco rivers in Arizona. He described them as "Sheep as big as a Horse, with very large horns and little tails. I have seen some of their horns, the size of which was something to marvel at" (Seton 1929).

TAXONOMY

Asia generally is accepted as the ancestral home of North American sheep since they have characteristics closely related to the primitive Siberian snow sheep of northeastern Asia (Cowan 1940). It is probable that wild sheep reached North America by way of the Bering Strait land bridge during the Pleistocene epoch. Ice age influences divided the population into two groups that evolved independently into the thinhorn species *Ovis dalli* of the north and the bighorn *Ovis canadensis* to the south.

The bighorn group is comprised of: (1) the "type" species Rocky Mountain bighorn (*Ovis canadensis canadensis* Shaw); (2) the California bighorn (*O.c. californiana* Douglas); and (3) the desert bighorns (*O.c. nelsoni* Merriam), (*O.c. mexicana* Merriam), (*O.c. cremnobates* Elliott) and (*O.c. weemsi* Goldman) (Cowan 1940).

DESCRIPTION

The first detailed description of bighorns, including their excellent eating qualities, was written by Franciscan missionaries on the California peninsula in 1702. However, it was not until 1804 that the species was described and named *Ovis canadensis* by Dr. George Shaw of the Royal Society of London, from a specimen that was collected and preserved by Duncan McGillivray near Banff, Alberta in 1800 (Seton 1929). David Thompson, a Canadian explorer and cartographer, described McGillivray's discovery on November 30, 1800 as follows:

> Our road lay along the Bow River, which to the very mountains has beautiful meadows along its banks. Mr. McGillivray, a man, and the Indian set off ahead to hunt the mountain goat [sheep]. Several herds of them were feeding a little distance before us in our road, and three of them were killed by the Indian and a large old buck by Mr. McGillivray, which we skinned round. We found their meat to be exceedingly sweet and tender and

Rocky Mountain bighorns are distinguished from other subspecies, in part, because of shorter ears and larger body size. A Wildlife Management Institute photo.

moderately fat. The she-goats might weigh from about 120 to 140 pounds [54–63 kilograms] alive. The buck that was killed might weigh about 190 or 200 pounds [86 or 91 kilograms], thirty of which may be the weight of his enormous horns, which measured along the curve were 3½ feet [1.07 meters] long and 15 inches [38.1 centimeters] in circumference (Hopwood 1971).

Generally, the Rocky Mountain bighorn is distinguished from other subspecies by shorter ears, shorter rows of teeth and larger body size (Cowan 1940). Coat color is extremely variable in all subspecies, from dark brown to light brown or grayish-brown with a white trim outlining the back of all four legs. They also have a conspicuous white rump patch that appears to diminish in size from northern to desert subspecies.

Weights of mature bighorns vary considerably among subspecies. Desert big-

horns are the lightest, with adult rams *(O.c. nelsoni)* weighing 57.6–86.2 kilograms (127–190 pounds) and adult ewes weighing 33.6–51.7 kilograms (74–114 pounds) (Blood et al. 1970). Intermediate in weight is the California bighorn. Adult males of this subspecies weigh 82.1–93 kilograms (181–205 pounds), and adult females weigh 48.1–65.8 kilograms (106–145 pounds). Rocky Mountain bighorns are heaviest. According to Blood et al. (1970), mature rams weigh 72.6–143.3 kilograms (160–316 pounds), while mature ewes weigh 53.1–90.7 kilograms (117–200 pounds).

Horns of adult Rocky Mountain bighorn rams generally are longer, more massive, taper more gradually and are less divergent than those of the desert and California rams. In contrast, the slender recurved horns of desert bighorn ewes are longest, up to 305 millimeters (12 inches), and heaviest (Cowan 1940). Boone and Crockett records for trophy big game animals provide representative comparisons of horn measurements of desert and Rocky Mountain bighorn rams (Nesbitt and Parker 1977). Average horn dimensions (using only the right horn, inasmuch as both horns generally are nearly equal in size) for the 30 largest desert bighorns harvested and recorded in North America include: length, 1,022.8 millimeters (40.3 inches); and base circumference, 393.7 millimeters (15.5 inches). Those average horn dimensions for Rocky Mountain bighorn rams are the following: length, 1,106.4 millimeters (43.6 inches); and base circumference, 403.4 millimeters (15.9 inches).

Horn lengths are somewhat misleading, since bighorns characteristically "broom" or break off horn tips up to several centimeters

during head-on clashes with other rams (Shackleton and Hutton 1971). The dried skull and horns of Rocky Mountain rams more than eight years old typically average 11.3 kilograms (24.9 pounds) and range from 8.2–13.6 kilograms (18–29.9 pounds) (Blood et al. 1970). Seton (1929) reported that a dried skull and horns of a large ram weighed 19.7 kilograms (43.5 pounds). An elaborate support and protective structure developed in the skull of bighorn rams, probably as a result of horn weight and frequent head-on clashes.

Gradation of horn and body sizes within the species provides a general external guide to the sex and age classes (Figure 34). At birth, lambs range in weight from 3.6–4.5 kilograms (8–10 pounds) and stand from 381–432 millimeters (15–17 inches) at the shoulder. Height increases and weight gains

Desert bighorns exhibiting characteristic horn size differential for adult ram and ewe. Photo by James D. Yoakum.

| yrs | lamb
0.5 | ♀
1.5 | ♀
adult | ♂
1.5 | ♂
2.5 | ♂
3-5 | ♂
5-7 | ♂
8-16 |

Figure 34. Sex and age classes of bighorn sheep. Note that the animals form a cline in body and horn size and that the adult female is very similar in external appearance to the yearling ram (after Geist 1968).

are rapid, so that by the end of six months an average lamb stands about two-thirds of its mother's height and is approximately one-half her weight. Long yearlings (15–18 months) are nearly as large as adult females which stand about 915 millimeters (36 inches) at the shoulder. Ewes approaching three years of age generally are indistinguishable from adult ewes during field observations. Mature rams stand about 1,015 millimeters (40 inches) at the shoulder.

Following their first winter, both sexes exhibit rapid horn growth. Maximum horn growth for ewes occurs in the first two or three years and for rams during the first four or five years. By that time, horns have grown about 75 percent of their potential length and have reached virtually all of their basal circumference. The horns of long yearling males often closely resemble those of the adult ewes, making it difficult to distinguish sex and age classes under field conditions. Although growth rates of horns are extremely variable due to genetic and age factors, ultimate size largely depends on forage quality and availability (Shackleton 1973).

The horn sheaths are epidermal in origin and grow over conical bony cores of frontal bones to form permanent structures. The bony cores contain a rich vascular network that perform a thermoregulatory function. The disproportionate size of horns of desert bighorns, such as large horns on small-bodied sheep, may be explained by a possible trend toward larger horns in both sexes, hence greater heat loss from horns of desert bovids throughout the world (Taylor 1966).

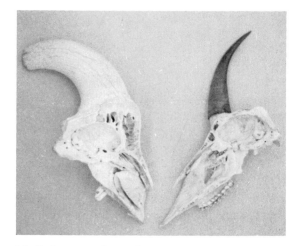

Medial section through skulls of an adult bighorn ram (left) and an adult mountain goat male (right): massive protective bone roof for the brain of the clashing bighorn in contrast to thin bone of the thrusting mountain goat.

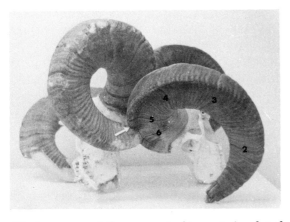

Clash posture at the moment of impact simulated with two ram skulls, showing the breakage or "brooming" area (white arrow) of the horn tip of one ram meeting the horn base of the other. Numbers indicate location of annual rings and age of the ram on the right. The first annulus has been "broomed" away.

that gradually wear and fade with exposure, becoming lighter and whiter by late winter and spring.

ECOLOGY

Reproduction

Both male and female bighorns subsisting on high quality forage mature sexually at 18 months of age. However, most ewes first breed at 2.5 years of age. Young rams have to compete with older rams in order to participate in the rut. For northern bighorns, breeding activity is concentrated in November and December, while desert subspecies breed from July to December (Russo 1956, Hansen 1967). The latter have the most prolonged breeding season of native North American ruminants.

The species is promiscuous, and although an estrus ewe may be pursued by a number of rams, the order of male dominance prevails from earlier battles. Consequently, the heaviest horned rams perform most of the breeding (Geist 1971a). However, young rams complete the breeding activities where older males are not present (Streeter 1970).

The gestation period is from 175–180 days; thus lambing occurs in May and June for northern bighorns and from January to June for desert subspecies. Single lambs are the rule. However, an unusually high incidence of twinning was reported in British Columbia, where 4 of 11 pregnant California bighorns were carrying twin fetuses (Spalding 1966). Longevity of both sexes can be 14–17 years, while life expectancy appears to be about 10–12 years (Geist 1971a).

Each year, generally during the rut, an annulus is formed on the horn sheath of rams, leaving a conspicuous permanent record of age. The number of annuli on the cementum from an extracted tooth plus knowledge of sequential tooth development (Table 21) provide more precision than do horn annuli in determining ages of adult ewes older than three or four years (Armstrong 1965).

The pelage of bighorns is a dense outer layer of coarse, brittle hair underlain with a loose layer of fine wool. The annual spring shedding, usually in unsightly mats of hair, is a bilateral process that takes place in the nonproductive cohorts first, followed by postpartum ewes and other sheep that generally are in poor condition. New hairs have whitish cellular shafts with dark tips

Table 21. Sequence of tooth eruption in lower jaws of Rocky Mountain bighorns (after Taylor 1962).

Age	Incisors 1	2	3	Canine 1	Premolars 2	3	4	Molars 1	2	3
5 months	D	D	D	D	D	D	D	1/2		
18 months	P	D	D	D	D	D	D	P	P	
30 months	P	P	D	D	P	P	3/4	P	P	3/4
42 months	P	P	P	D	P	P	P	P	P	P
44 months	P	P	P	P	P	P	P	P	P	P

D = Deciduous; P = Permanent.

Losses appear to be largest during the first year of life. Desert subspecies characteristically have high initial survival of lambs, followed by a greater mortality rate. Lambs in warm climates apparently survive the first week of life better than do those in cold climates. Cowan and Geist (1971) have reasoned—based on implication and circumstantial evidence from studies of other ruminants—that poor nutrition and energy drain on dams results in reduced nutrients for their young and reduces the lambs' chances for survival.

Population dynamics

Short-term rates of population increase can be approximated by applying certain assumptions, based on field observations of population characteristics to herds under average conditions. These assumptions are: (1) ewes give birth for the first time at age three, (2) one lamb per mature ewe per year, (3) ewes remain fertile throughout their lives, (4) equal ratio of rams to ewes, and (5) no mortality. Using these assumptions and the equation $N_t = N_0 e^{rt}$ (Odum 1959), the maximum rate of annual increase is 26 percent. A living example occurred on Wildhorse Island, Montana when 12 bighorns increased to about 100 from 1947–1954, and approximated the theoretical maximum rate of increase (Buechner 1960a). By adjusting the ratio of rams to ewes to 25:100, the theoretical rate of increase may appear to be an appropriate goal in managing bighorn populations. However, when adjusting sex ratios in this manner, managers should examine carefully the behavior and dynamics of rams. Their survival is based largely on learned traditions of following other sheep along safe routes to distant seasonal ranges. Continuity of distant movements among years should be assured. Rams older than two or three years generally occupy different ranges than do rams in nursery herds; thus the food resources are used from a greater

area. Young rams learn of distant ranges from older rams. Ewes may or may not use the ram ranges. Generally, ewes occupy nursery or winter ranges. By reducing the age of rams in a population to less than three years, the rams generally will remain on nursery ranges.

Behavior

Bighorns are highly social animals and characteristically are separated into nursery bands comprised of ewes, lambs and subadults, and ram bands. The two groups come together primarily during the rut and again in the spring as sprouting vegetation appears.

Young rams usually leave the nursery herds after two years of age to join ram bands and become part of a social hierarchy where their rank depends on strength and horn size. Horns are used as weapons and shields, and most encounters are among equal-sized rams. As rams mature, they frequently display their horns as symbols of dominance to lesser rams. A dominance battle between two large, well-matched rams is an unforgettable sight. After backing a short distance, they rise on their hind legs and rush forward, colliding with a crack that often can be heard more than 1.6 kilometers (1 mile) away. Encounters may last a few minutes or several hours until one of the rams finally is overpowered and behaves in a subordinate manner. Once dominant-subordinate relationships are formed, rams live in the same bands with a minimum of conflict (Geist 1971a).

Few animals are as well-adapted to extremes of elevation and temperature as are bighorn sheep. Bighorn range extends from snow fields of the Canadian Rockies to the edge of the palm tree stands of the Baja Peninsula, Mexico, and from high mountains in Colorado to the floor of Death Valley, California. The common feature throughout their distribution is rocky escape terrain in close proximity to open stands of grass and shrubs.

Food habits

A review of the literature on bighorn food habits lists a wide variety of plant species eaten. Grasses, sedges and forbs are the preferred foods. Browse species are important foods during fall and winter. In desert regions, where lack of moisture limits grass growth, shrubs and trees are the major foods (Todd 1972).

Bighorns are attracted to mineral and artificial salt licks, particularly during spring and early summer. Although mineral requirements for big game are not understood clearly, Cowan and Brink (1949) found a clue when they discovered that sodium was the element common to all natural licks sampled in national parks in the Rocky Mountains of Canada. Weeks and Kirkpatrick (1976) since have shown that the intense sodium drive of white-tailed deer in spring is correlated closely with peak obligatory intake of potassium and water in succulent forage. They postulated a mechanism whereby a high intake of potassium and water in new spring forage leads to excessive sodium loss and a temporary period of negative sodium balance. For several years, salt blocks were set out to accommodate the dietary needs of bighorns in Canada's national parks. However, this practice was stopped when bighorns developed severe cases of contagious ecthyma or "soremouth" (Samuel et al. 1975).

Competition with livestock for food along with their associated parasites and diseases, particularly scabies, have been implicated as the principal cause of the bighorn decline during the last 50 years of the Nineteenth Century (Buechner 1960a). Becklund and Senger (1967) reviewed the literature on the external and internal parasites of the Rocky Mountain bighorn and listed 51 species, 36 of which were known parasites of domestic sheep and 18 of cattle in North America. The significance of multiple parasitism as a limiting factor in bighorn populations largely is unappreciated since insufficient data are available to evaluate the problem.

The capability of range to support bighorn sheep is governed by the amount and quality of foods available during seasons of greatest scarcity. Bighorns are not well-adapted to deep and crusted snow and are forced to winter on the confines of southern exposures or wind-blown slopes next to escape terrain. Desert bighorns are restricted in distribution depending on available water supplies. In addition to physical limitations, harassment from human activities or predators may deny either food or water to bighorns on potential range.

MORTALITY FACTORS

Parasites and disease

During periods of stress, bighorns historically have suffered catastrophic die-offs, particularly in the Rocky Mountains. In recent decades, the principal cause of death invariably has been pneumonia with the nematode lungworm *Protostrongylus* strongly implicated.

The life cycle of the lungworm begins when the adult female lays numerous eggs in the lungs of the bighorn. These eggs hatch into first stage larvae, move up the trachea, are swallowed, and are voided by way of feces. The larvae leave feces pellets and penetrate the feet of terrestrial snails where they moult twice to produce the infective third stage. The life cycle is completed when snails are ingested incidentally by bighorns during the normal process of grazing (Forrester et al. 1966).

The fact that lungworm predisposes bighorns to pneumonia has been demonstrated in Colorado. During the early 1970s, the Pikes Peak herd suffered high mortality of lambs in early fall due to pneumonia and heavy lungworm infestations. Prior to birth, young were discovered heavily infected with lungworms as a result of transplacental migration of third stage larvae into their livers. After lambs are born, larvae migrate to the lungs, where they complete development into adult lungworms. Researchers believe that fetal infections of lungworms may be curtailed by treating gravid ewes with antihelminthic drugs. The logistics problem of chemotherapy for herds of wild bighorn was solved by placing the prescribed drug in baits of a highly palatable, fermenting apple mash. The result was a dramatic increase of lamb survival in treated herds compared to lamb survival rates in untreated herds (Schmidt et al. 1976). Bighorn managers recognized that they were treating the symptoms of a problem that had developed from overprotected and overcrowded ranges where sheep were being exposed continuously to lungworm infections. In 1976, an either-sex bighorn season was initiated to help reduce and disperse the sheep to population levels more compatible with their range capacities.

Competition and predation

The carrying capacity of bighorn range can be reduced as a result of competition for food among bighorn herds, or among bighorns and other populations of grazing ungulates such as elk, deer, horses, burros and domestic sheep and cattle. Aside from direct competition for food, other behavioral interactions among various species can occur that deny bighorns access to their unique habitat, such as their fear of and aversion to cattle (Trefethen 1975). Managing integrated grazing systems requires an awareness of potential disease problems plus a considerable knowledge of the food, time and space requirements of indigenous and potential animal populations. Finally, there is the most difficult problem of establishing species priorities before manipulating populations or habitats.

Wolves, coyotes, cougars, lynx, bobcats, wolverines and eagles all have been recorded as bighorn predators (Post 1971). However, bighorns are able to counter most predator threats with their exceptional eyesight, climbing ability and habits of feeding and resting in open areas adjacent to or within rugged terrain. Under most circum-

stances, predator control is not considered necessary to enhance bighorn populations.

Accidents

Mountain sheep are subject to a variety of accidental fatalities, including falling off cliffs, slipping on ice, being caught in avalanches, fighting and lightning strikes. However, accidental deaths are inevitable for any animal that frequents precipitous terrain, and must be considered a normal but relatively insignificant drain on the population.

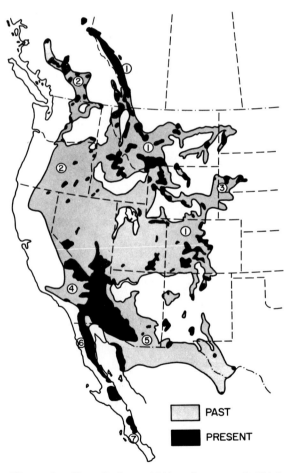

Figure 35. Past (before 1800) and present (1970s) distributions of bighorn sheep (after Cowan 1940, Buechner 1960, Trefethen 1975): 1. *Ovis canadensis canadensis;* 2. *O. c. californiana;* 3. *O. c. auduboni* (extinct); 4. *O. c. nelsoni;* 5. *O. c. mexicana;* 6. *O. c. cremnobates;* and 7. *O. c. weemsi.*

MANAGEMENT

Distribution and status

Bighorns were widely distributed in most mountain ranges and badlands of western North America prior to settlement, but estimates of bighorn numbers prior to that time are a matter of debate. However, by examining the present distribution and abundance of relatively undisturbed populations of thinhorn sheep and the bighorns (Figure 35), the latter probably never approached the 1.5–2 million individuals estimated by Seton (1929). Today, there are less than 45,000 bighorns in North America (Table 22). Bighorns declined drastically during the latter half of the Nineteenth Century. In addition to the bighorn disease problems, persistent and unregulated hunting contributed to their further decline. By 1916, the Badlands bighorn was extinct (Buechner 1960a).

Early management

Bighorn management programs began in the late 1800s and early 1900s with widespread hunting closures in the United States. During the same period, some states and provinces introduced fall hunting seasons with licenses, but with rather generous bag limits. For example, as many as six sheep of unspecified sex or age were allowed to be taken per hunter in Alberta. The establishment of sanctuaries, refuges and parks, plus intensive predator control, began about the turn of the century in order to help stem the decline of bighorns and other game species and populations. During the 1920s, bighorn trapping and transplanting programs were initiated. Since that time large numbers of bighorns have been reintroduced successfully to former ranges in Canada and the United States (Table 22).

Harvesting

In addition to establishment of management areas, hunting laws gradually changed to male-only seasons. As bighorn inventories improved during the 1950s, many areas formerly closed to hunting were reopened. Hunting permits were restricted in number and issued in conjunction with horn size. Requirements ranging from one-

Table 22. Bighorn sheep population estimates in North America, 1974.[a]

Province or state	Rocky Mountain bighorn	California bighorn	Desert bighorn
Alberta	7,100–7,900		
Arizona			2,100–2,600
Baja California			4,000–5,000
British Columbia	1,250–1,400	1,800–1,900	
California		175–200	3,540
Chihuahua			50
Colorado	2,250–2,550		
Idaho	2,200–2,700	275–300	
Montana	2,700–3,100		
Nevada		30	2,200
New Mexico	300–400[b]		300
North Dakota		250–300[b]	
Oregon	40–60[b]	320[b]	
Sonora			600
South Dakota	100–150[b]		
Texas			75–100
Utah	250–350		200–300
Washington	20[b]	400[b]	
Wyoming	4,200–4,800		
Totals	20,440–23,430	3,250–3,450	13,065–14,690

[a]Compiled from Trefethen (1975).

[b]From introduced populations.

A trophy-sized, "split-horned" Rocky Mountain bighorn ram. Photo by R. G. Petocz.

half curl to full curl varied among states and provinces. To be harvested, desert bighorn rams now must have a horn mass not less than a specified Boone and Crockett score, such as 144 points in Nevada and New Mexico (Trefethen 1975). An integral part of this trophy desert ram regulation system is the requirement that all tag holders attend an educational session on aging and scoring techniques prior to hunting. In conjunction with their trophy ram seasons, Alberta, Montana and Colorado manage bighorn numbers by allowing ewe hunting on a permit basis.

Estimating populations

Bighorn sheep populations have been estimated through the use of ground counts and time-lapse photography. Watercraft, fixed-wing aircraft and helicopter surveys also are used. The use of helicopters, although expensive, has proven to be more expedient and accurate than other methods used to estimate population sizes and sex-age compositions. Determining age classifications of ewes and yearlings under field conditions is difficult. However, lambs and the various horn classes of rams older than two years are identified readily. With northern bighorns, the most opportune time for surveys is during the rut in early winter when all sex and age classes are on winter ranges. For desert bighorns, the optimum place and time for ground censuses are at waterholes during hot periods of the summer.

Lamb-ewe ratios (in this case, ewes and yearlings are classified together) are of limited value when estimating annual increases of bighorn populations, since the highest losses generally occur during the first year of life. The net annual increase for both desert and northern bighorns, on the average, is 10–12 long yearlings per 100 sheep (60–70 adults). Assuming no difference in survival ratios among sexes during the first few years of life, the numbers of yearlings or two-year old rams can be used to estimate the numbers of ewes entering the breeding population. Cowan and Geist (1971) stated: "Once yearling age has been attained, the sheep embark upon a stage of life through which there is a relatively steady death rate of about 2.5 percent per year until the age of eight or nine years is reached when there is a sharp increase to about 30 percent per year." Therefore, 100 bighorns potentially can yield an average of four or five legal (three-quarter curl) rams annually. It takes approximately 25 sheep in the field (fall population of all ages and both sexes) to produce one trophy ram annually.

Managing habitat

In recent years, the emphasis of bighorn management has shifted from managing population numbers to managing habitat. Hunting seasons and closures have done nothing to prevent degradation and reduction of bighorn ranges due to livestock overgrazing and disturbances from recreational, urban and industrial developments. In addition, intensive forest protection through fire prevention and suppression has resulted in forest encroachment upon former fire-induced bighorn habitat.

The key to management of all races of bighorn sheep is habitat protection, maintenance and enhancement. Bighorn managers are faced with identifying and carefully mapping existing and potential bighorn habitats in order to integrate management strategies with other land-use interests. When negotiation fails and bighorn habitats are destroyed, then compensation for losses should be provided for by acquisition and management of alternative habitats.

There are a number of methods used to improve habitats for bighorn, keeping in mind that the most productive bighorn habitat is range that supports native plants. Lands that are essential for the survival of

Forest encroachment on former fire-induced grassland of bighorn sheep range. Photo by author.

bighorn populations need to be acquired through purchase or easements. Consequently, livestock already has been removed or reduced in some areas where lands have been acquired. In other areas, through coordination and multiple-use planning, new livestock-grazing systems are being placed in operation on publicly owned bighorn ranges. In 1975, the British Columbia Forest Service and the Fish and Wildlife Branch conducted the first of many planned prescribed burns on overgrown bighorn ranges (Demarchi 1976). Other range-improvement methods include chaining, slashing or logging in areas where trees have invaded grasslands. Fertilizing, planting and winter feeding also may be recommended in certain areas and situations. Waterhole improvement and development has been a useful technique in aiding bighorn survival on desert ranges (Trefethen 1975).

Chapter 12

DALL'S SHEEP

Lyman Nichols, Jr.
Wildlife Biologist
Alaska Department of Fish and Game
Cooper Landing, Alaska

The thinhorn group of North American sheep includes both the Dall's and Stone's sheep, found in Alaska and northwestern Canada. Both are wilderness animals residing for the most part in spectacular alpine and subalpine mountain habitat. They are considered among the best of North America's trophy species; their horns and meat are highly prized by hunters. Because these sheep are highly visible in their white coats against the treeless green of their summer alpine environment, Dall's sheep in particular are favored subjects of amateur and professional photographers alike. In some particularly accessible areas, Dall's sheep are valued above all else for viewing and photography.

TAXONOMY

There is some debate among taxonomists whether American thinhorn sheep actually are separate species or, in fact, are subspecies of Siberian snow sheep, which are very similar in size and appearance to Stone's sheep (Cherniavski 1962, Cowan 1940, Rausch 1961). Arguments tend to favor the American thinhorn sheep as a distinct species, *Ovis dalli.*

At present, two subspecies of American thinhorn sheep are recognized. One is the "true" Dall's sheep *(O.d. dalli),* also commonly referred to as the Alaskan Dall's sheep. It is found in Alaska, the Yukon and Northwest Territories, and the extreme northwestern part of British Columbia. The other is Stone's sheep *(O.d. stonei)* of northern British Columbia and the southern part of the Yukon Territory. Both subspecies were named after persons, W.H. Dall and A.J. Stone, respectively. Consequently, their common names should be capitalized and used in possessive forms rather than the frequently used but incorrect forms "Dall sheep" and "Stone sheep." To avoid confusion, further reference in this chapter to Dall's sheep will indicate the subspecies by that name and differentiate it from Stone's sheep. Readers should keep in mind, however, that both Dall's sheep and Stone's sheep subspecies are of the Dall's sheep species.

Two other subspecies formerly were recognized, the white sheep *(O.d. kenaiensis)* of the Kenai Peninsula, Alaska (Buechner 1960a), and the gray or saddleback Fannin's sheep *(O.d. fannini)* found between the main ranges of Dall's and Stone's sheep. The former now is considered identical to other Dall's sheep, and the latter is recognized as no more than a color gradation between the white Dall's and dark Stone's sheep.

DESCRIPTION

The pelage of Dall's sheep consists of pithy, crinkled guard hairs with an undercoat of fine wool. It may be more than 5.1 centimeters (2 inches) thick in winter. The coat is typically all-white in color, although a few black hairs on the tail are not uncommon. Some newborn lambs have a considerable amount of brown in their coats with a dark middorsal line and dark hairs on the brisket, tail surface and elsewhere. These neonatal coats are lost or overgrown shortly after birth. All lambs appear white within a week or two. Dall's sheep often appear yellowish or grayish due to staining of their white coats.

Stone's sheep are typically dark brown or black with lighter-colored heads and white muzzles. They have white rump patches, bellies and rear portions of the legs. However, they may vary greatly in color, from nearly white to black. In both the Mentasta Mountains and the mountains northeast of Eagle in eastern Alaska, occasional sheep are found with gray or brown markings. Such color variations are more common in the northwestern part of Canada between the ranges of the true Dall's and Stone's sheep. These are Stone's sheep, formerly called Fannin's sheep.

The amber-brown horns of both Dall's and Stone's sheep are lighter in constuction than those of the bighorn sheep. Both sexes have horns which continue to grow throughout the animals' lives (Figure 36). Horns of rams are massive at the bases and taper to relatively fine tips. They grow in a spiral form as

Young Dall's sheep ram (left) and mature ewe in winter pelage. Note black hairs in ram's tail and thickness of coat. Photo courtesy of the Alaska Department of Fish and Game.

Mature Stone's sheep ram in late summer pelage. Photo by Leonard Lee Rue III.

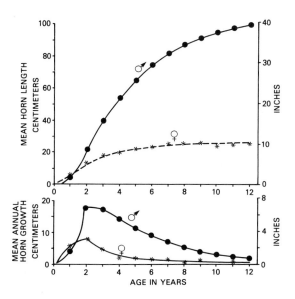

Figure 36. Dall's sheep horn growth by age and sex. Data courtesy of W. E. Heimer, Alaska Department of Fish and Game.

viewed from the side. Outside diameters of the curls of adult Dall's rams' horns average about 27 centimeters (10.5 inches), and basal circumferences average about 36 centimeters (14 inches). Exceptionally large horns may have bases more than 36 centimeters (14 inches) in circumference. The average length of a full-curl ram's horns in Alaska is about 90.1 centimeters (35.5 inches); the largest recorded horns from a Dall's ram measured 123.5 centimeters (48.6 inches) in length. Most Alaskan rams have horns of three-quarter curl by age six and reach full-curl by about eight to nine years of age. Most rams attain about 90 percent of their potential horn growth (by volume) by the time their horns are full curl. There is considerable variation in horn size among Alaskan Dall's sheep populations. This is believed to be related to "population quality" which, in turn, probably is dependent upon population density (Heimer and Smith 1975).

Mature Dall's sheep ram in summer pelage. Photo by Len Rue, Jr.

Similar data on horn curl and age are not available for Stone's sheep, but in a sample of six horns from eight-year old rams, the average length was 90.5 centimeters (35.6 inches) (Geist 1971a). Measurements of the 50 top-scoring horns (using only right horn measurements) for both subspecies as listed in the Boone and Crockett Club's record book show an average length of 111.3 centimeters (43.8 inches) for Dall's sheep and 111.5 centimeters (43.9 inches) for Stone's sheep (Nesbitt and Parker 1977). Basal circumferences averaged 36.3 centimeters (14.3 inches) and 37.1 centimeters (14.6 inches), respectively, suggesting almost identical horn growth. The largest recorded set of horns taken from a Stone's ram measured 131.6 centimeters (51.8 inches) in length.

Ewes' horns are much shorter, slimmer and less curved than rams'. In cross section, female horns form a rather narrow oval, whereas ram horns are roughly triangular. A sample of 52 horns from female Dall's sheep more than six years old averaged 24.5 centimeters (9.7 inches) long (Heimer 1972, Nichols 1971). Stone's sheep ewes probably have horns of about the same length.

Thinhorn sheep, like most northern ungulates, are heaviest and fattest in late fall and are lightest in spring after rigors of winter have taken their toll. A sample of 13 Dall's ewes weighed in the fall averaged about 56 kilograms (124 pounds) (Nichols, Unpublished), but exceptionally large ones may reach 63.6 kilograms (140 pounds) or more. By later winter and early spring, average weight in a sample of 45 ewes dropped to about 48 kilograms (105 pounds), a loss of 18 percent of average fall body weight (Nichols 1971). Data on fall weights of Dall's rams are scanty, but estimates place the average weight of adult rams from 82–100 kilograms (180–220 pounds) with some very large rams possibly exceeding 114 kilograms (250 pounds). A spring sample of nine adult Dall's rams in Alaska showed an average weight of 69.6 kilograms (153 pounds) (Heimer 1972). Average weight of adult Stone's rams is estimated to be somewhat heavier in the fall, from 100–104 kilograms (220–230 pounds). Exceptional individuals possibly exceed 114 kilograms (250 pounds). Whether or not a real weight-size difference exists among the subspecies has not yet been demonstrated.

Mean height at the shoulder for nine Dall's rams more than six years old was 93.3 centimeters (36.8 inches), and 84.4 centimeters (33.2 inches) for 62 ewes older than six years.

LIFE HISTORY

The life cycle of thinhorn sheep begins with the rut, which takes place in early winter, generally extending from mid-November to early December. For two successive years in Alaska's Kenai Mountains, the peak of rutting activity in one herd was found to be November 30 (Nichols, In press).

Lambing occurs during late May and early June, following a gestation period of about 171 days. Chronology of lambing appears to vary somewhat from year to year and among herds in Alaska. Whether it is a function of variation in the rutting season is not yet known. It may be merely an anomaly of data resulting from variable mortality at birth which, in turn, affects the numbers of living newborn lambs observed. Single births are the rule for both subspecies, although twinning occurs infrequently.

Lambs weigh about 3.2–4.1 kilograms (7–9 pounds) at birth and grow rapidly during their first summer, reaching an average weight of about 30.4 kilograms (67 pounds) by fall. Weaning usually takes place by October even though most lambs appear capable of fending for themselves by two to three months of age. Lambs remain with

their mothers during their first winter, and nursing occasionally may be observed during winter and even the following summer. There is some evidence on poor ranges in Alaska that many Dall's ewes nurse their lambs throughout the winter and only bear one lamb every other year (Heimer 1976). If these behaviors are general rules, they may function as adaptations to reduce the birth rate and increase survival of lambs born on depleted ranges. The sex ratio at birth is probably about equal, although the few data available suggest a preponderance of males (Geist 1971a, Nichols, In press).

Yearlings of both sexes may be sexually mature by 18 months of age, although some do not mature until the following fall. Maturity in domestic sheep is related to physical condition and weight rather than age alone, and this may apply to wild sheep as well. If so, well-fed, larger individuals tend to mature faster than smaller, less adequately nourished sheep. Male yearlings, even though physiologically capable of participating in reproductive activities, seldom do. Dominance order among males prevents most rams from breeding until they are about seven years of age (Geist 1971a).

Ewes and rams probably are capable of reproducing throughout their life-spans. In several seasons of observing Dall's sheep during the rut, I saw no old rams which were not active participants. I collected two pregnant Dall's ewes which, from horn annuli, were estimated to be more than 13 years old. I also found one 15-year old ewe that died after giving birth. Another ewe, 16 years old when captured and marked, was accompanied by a lamb. She was observed for three more years, but without lambs.

During a study of a Dall's sheep herd in Alaska believed to have reached or exceeded the carrying capacity of its range, all 18 adult ewes taken were found to be pregnant. Three of four yearling (18-months old) ewes collected also were pregnant (Nichols, In press). Thus, even under conditions of environmental stress, Dall's sheep can have a pregnancy rate of as high as 100 percent in adult ewes and, in this case, 75 percent in yearling females. The effective natality rate—the number of lambs that survive long enough to be observed—normally is much lower than this, however. A ratio of only 20 lambs to 100 ewes was observed in the above herd the following spring, reflecting an approximate 80 percent loss from potential reproductive gains. Average productivity of Dall's sheep in Alaska was about 37 lambs per 100 ewes over a number of years and within a number of herds (sample = 57; standard error of mean = 2.10). However, great variability among herds and years was noted—the range was 8–81 lambs per 100 ewes.

Life-span of a wild sheep is believed to be limited primarily by teeth condition and corresponding feeding ability. The oldest Dall's ram skull found in a large series of naturally occurring mortalities in an overcrowded population was 12 years old at death (Murie 1944). Ewes tend to live longer than rams. In addition to the aforementioned Dall's ewe that was captured and marked at age 16 and lived at least three more years, Geist (1971a) reported a Stone's ewe that reached 16 years of age.

MORTALITY AND LIMITING FACTORS

Nutrition

A number of factors can affect the productivity of thinhorn sheep which, in turn, is a major determinant of herd status. In a herd with adequate winter forage, pregnant ewes receive sufficient nutrition to maintain their own physical condition and allow growth of fetuses to optimum size. Healthy, well-nourished ewes give birth to well-developed lambs and are able to provide them with ample milk, thereby assuring maximum production and early survival of young. Furthermore, these young grow quickly during their first summer and have a better chance of surviving their first winter. Under these conditions, expected mortality of adults would be low and herd increase probably would occur. On the other hand, in a herd that has reached or exceeded its winter range's carrying capacity and thus faces a shortage of winter feed because of crowding and competition, pregnant females are unable to obtain sufficient nourishment to maintain their own physical conditions or enable optimum growth of fetuses. As a result, the pregnant ewe may experience fetal mortality through resorption or abortion to enhance her own chance of survival. Neonatal mortality, because of weakness and consequent hypothermia, and/or abandonment, also increases—sometimes drastically. Furthermore, surviving lambs may be small and grow slowly because of dams' inadequate milk supplies. They are poorly prepared to face their first winter, during which they may succumb in large numbers.

Density-dependent natality factors appear to be the most important limiting factors affecting thinhorn sheep. These sheep usually occur at near-maximum densities in relatively stable, climax habitats which are subject to harsh winters. The availability of food in these habitats may be limited severely by deep snow cover. Once a sheep herd reaches a certain density on its winter range, natural controls limit reproduction and survival, and its population becomes stable or begins to decline.

During normal winters and when snow remains soft, sheep are able to dig feeding craters down to good quality forage that is still green. Strong winds, prevalent in alpine winter ranges of thinhorn sheep, remove much of the snow from open ridges and slopes, exposing forage. By late winter, however, snow may be wind packed and impenetrable. Sheep then are forced to depend on limited amounts of poor quality feed on the few, windscoured ridges that remain snow free. At this time, sheep are in a potentially negative energy-balance situation; they may use more energy than they can take in feeding. From this time until spring, they depend heavily on stored body fat for nutritional needs. Body fat reserves

Three Dall's sheep ewes feeding in pawed-out snow craters in early winter. Photo courtesy of the Alaska Department of Fish and Game.

decline rapidly; the last to be catabolized are those stored in the bone marrow. Both lambs and yearlings, with limited fat reserves, suffer more than adults do (Figure 37).

Mortality among lambs surviving the initial rigors of birth normally is very low the first summer but high during the first winter, reaching about 40–50 percent or more in stable or declining herds. The winter of their second year is another critical period in the lives of northern sheep. Much of a yearling's summer nutrient intake supports growth rather than being stored as fat, and nutrition is not supported by mother's milk. Therefore, yearlings are more vulnerable to nutritional scarcity in winter than are adults. Few data are available on mortality rates of sheep in their second winters, but those rates appear to approach 15–20 percent.

After sheep are two years old, mortality rates decrease, presumably because their physiological growth rates decline and more nutrition is available for the production of fat reserves needed during winter. Geist (1971a) found that bighorn sheep mortality averaged about 4 percent per year from ages two to seven, then increased to 23 percent per year thereafter. Murie's (1944) data indicated a similar pattern for Dall's sheep.

179

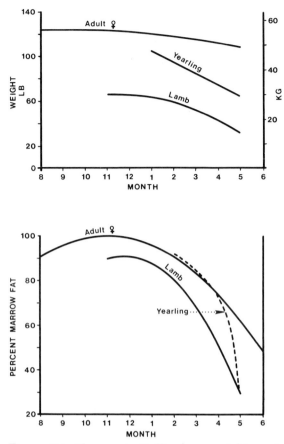

Figure 37. Changes in Dall's sheep weights and percentage fat in bone marrow by month and age classes. Least squares curves fitted to data from a series of sheep collected in the Kenai Mountains, Alaska (after Nichols, Unpublished).

Winter weather

At present, the main influence on thinhorn sheep numbers appears to be winter weather. Exceptionally severe winters may cause drastic "crashes" in sheep numbers regardless of population densities or range conditions. Successive severe winters occurred in Mount McKinley National Park, Alaska, between the late 1920s and the mid-1940s and probably elsewhere in the state. Unusually deep and crusted snow resulted in high mortality, and herds dropped to a fraction of their former abundance. Other, more localized declines have since been documented following

severe winters. These were not winters of exceptional cold, but of above-normal temperatures and more-than-usual precipitation. During normal winters, snow remains light and fluffy and is blown free of alpine feeding areas. Wet snows, or thaws and subsequent refreezing, fix snow in place with a hard crust, preventing removal by wind or digging by sheep. Snow depth and hardness, maximum winter winds and temperatures the previous winter are correlated inversely to lambing success (Murphy 1974, Nichols 1976). The inferences are that lambing success is depressed by deep and hard snow, above-freezing temperatures lead to crusting, and high winds along with thawing temperatures pack snow to rock hardness. Dall's sheep are adapted to continuing cold, high winds and normally light snowfall of winters in northern interior mountain ranges.

Disease and parasites

Disease, such as actinomycosis, and parasites including lungworms and gastrointestinal nematodes are present in northern sheep, but have not been shown to be main causes of any herd declines. Neilsen and Neiland (1974) suspected, however, that gastrointestinal nematodes in particular may contribute significantly to spring mortality because of the coincidental "spring rise" in internal parasite loads and weakened condition of sheep at that time. It is probable that parasite infestations and disease exert more influence on sheep survival during times of maximum population density and environmental stress than during other times.

Predation

Thinhorn sheep are capable mountaineers, able to negotiate rugged terrain with speed and grace. They depend on this terrain for protection from predators. Excellent eyesight and a well-developed sense of smell enable them to detect potential threats before most predators become dangers. The hearing of sheep appears to be very acute, but this sense may be heeded somewhat less than others because sheep environments often are disturbed by such natural sounds as falling rocks.

Although coyotes, wolverines, lynx, black bears, grizzly bears and golden eagles occasionally take adults and lambs, the only serious predator of thinhorn sheep is the wolf. Although wolves have been observed capturing sheep both in summer and winter, they do not appear to exert any major influence on sheep numbers except in times of population overabundance, when sheep may be weakened or forced by competition and food scarcity to feed far from escape terrain.

From 1947–1961, when wolves were protected and presumably abundant, the McKinley National Park sheep herd increased at an average annual rate of approximately 11 percent (Murphy 1974). Average annual increase rates of 11–14 percent were observed in three Kenai Peninsula herds where no wolves were present (Figure 38).

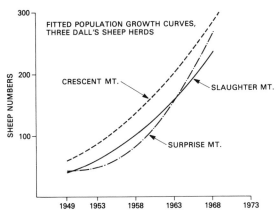

Figure 38. Increase patterns of three Dall's sheep herds in the Kenai Mountains, Alaska, two of which (Surprise Mountain and Crescent Mountain) were heavily hunted for rams, while the third (Slaughter Mountain) was closed to hunting (after Nichols 1976).

Accidents

Accidental falls take a small number of sheep, as do avalanches and other accidents. Nevertheless, it is winter weather which—by restricting both food supplies and movements—exerts the only known mortality of significance to thinhorn sheep populations at the present time.

BEHAVIOR

In general, sheep are diurnal, although some movement may occur at night. Summer daylight in the North is long, so sheep may be found moving or feeding at almost any time. Major feeding periods generally occur during early morning and late afternoon with occasional shorter periods of grazing activity about mid-day. Much of the time between feeding is spent resting and ruminating. Preferred resting sites, particularly at night, are on or very close to cliffs or large rock outcrops which serve as escape cover. Daily movements generally consist of moving out of rugged terrain to preferred feeding areas in the morning, then drifting back before dark. During the short winter days, morning and evening feeding periods are interrupted by a brief midday rest. Most rumination probably occurs at night when feeding and movement are relatively difficult.

During summer, thinhorn sheep may move considerable distances from winter home ranges to occupy nearly all suitable alpine habitat in an area. By late summer, they begin to drift back to wintering ranges, where they congregate before the rut begins. Winter range usually is a small part of the overall range and is limited by snow conditions to those areas where snow-free feeding sites and escape terrain lie in close proximity. In early spring, sheep usually move lower on slopes, often into the upper limits of subalpine timber. They seek the first emergent green vegetation when snow lines begin to recede. Sheep move upward with the receding snow line until they are free to leave their winter-spring ranges.

Mid-day rests between morning and evening feedings are common during short winter days. Photo by William E. Ruth.

Where summer and winter ranges are contiguous, annual movements can be characterized as dispersal over all suitable habitat during summer, and withdrawal to smaller areas that provide necessary winter habitat. Actual migrations may occur along traditional routes in spring and fall where summer and winter home ranges are separated by unsuitable habitat such as forests or wide river valleys. Visits to mineral licks are an important part of winter-to-summer range movements of Dall's sheep. Sheep, especially ewes with lambs, may linger in the vicinity of licks for days, weeks or even much of the summer. Heimer (1974) and Geist (1971a) reported high incidence of individual adults returning to their previously occupied seasonal ranges year after year.

Sheep society centers about two basic groupings: maternal ewe, lamb and yearling groups which often merge into larger herds; and ram groups. As parturition approaches,

pregnant ewes leave their past year's lambs and seek isolation in the most rugged terrain available, where births take place. They remain there for several days following parturition (Pitzman 1970). They then move away from lambing cliffs, which usually are merely part of the spring range, and join other ewes with new lambs. Meanwhile, abandoned yearlings frequently form small groups which follow one or more barren ewes. Frequently male yearlings begin to follow older rams.

Nursery groups, consisting of ewes with new lambs and occasional yearling females, persist for a few weeks after parturition, then gradually merge with groups of barren females and yearlings to form loose herd associations that occupy summer ranges. The basic unit of these groupings is a lactating ewe, her lamb and frequently her yearling female. However, some male yearlings remain with ewe-lamb combinations.

Dall's sheep ewe seeks solitude and rugged terrain just prior to parturition in the spring. Photo courtesy of the Alaska Department of Fish and Game.

After the rut, during which all ages and sexes are intermixed, older rams usually seek the company of other rams even though they may remain on the same winter range as the ewe groups. As soon as snow conditions permit in the spring, groups of rams which have begun congregating on spring range move toward summer range, frequently assembling in large groups en route. During these movements, smaller rams follow the largest ram in the group. At this time, many yearling rams and most two-year-old rams leave the association of ewes and follow older rams. Rams' summer range may overlap that of ewes' or may be geographically separate. Most rams remain separate from ewes even when occupying the same areas.

Social behavior, like that of other members of the genus *Ovis,* is well-developed in thinhorn sheep. Ram behavior revolves about the establishment and maintenance of a dominance hierarchy based on the size of horns. Interactions among rams, including horn displays and the well-known clashing, may become quite complicated and occur throughout the year except during stress conditions of late winter.

Sheep interactions are well-documented by Geist (1971a). Rams determine and maintain social orders with limited confusion and damage to individuals through visual recognition of each other's horn size-dominance status. Large-horned rams are socially dominant, treating all smaller individuals as "females," while small-horned rams are aggressive toward dominant rams. Ewes are largely ignored by rams since they react passively except during estrus periods. When in estrus, ewes behave somewhat like small males and encourage social and sexual behaviors by adult males. During the rut, the established dominance pattern between rams may be disrupted temporarily when a ewe comes into estrus, with all nearby classes of mature rams jostling and clashing for possession of the ewe. Possession is established quickly by the largest ram, who then remains with the ewe through her approximately one-day estrus, defending her against other rams and breeding her repeatedly.

Rams neither maintain territories nor gather harems. Instead, they seek out one ewe at a time and eventually leave her at the end of her one-day estrus for another. They travel widely among ewe groups just before and during the rut seeking receptive females. Although sexually mature at 1.5–2.5 years of age, rams generally do not become behaviorally mature and participate seriously in reproduction until the age of 7 (Geist 1971a). Where mature rams are removed from a herd through hunting, younger males become sexually active. In at least one Alaskan herd of Dall's sheep, all rams with horns of three-quarters curl (about six to seven years of age) and older were removed by hunting for a number of years (Nichols 1976). The remaining young rams in the four-to-six year age classes carried out all rutting activity, behavior in which they would not normally be allowed to participate. The rates of increase in this herd and another nearby herd subject to

Clashing or horn displays among rams may occur at slightest provocation during much of the year as well as during the rut. Ram on right provoked this short-lived clash to take over a hollowed out resting site. Photo by William E. Ruth.

similar hunting pressure and age structure were nearly the same as that of a third herd which was not hunted. The results infer little short-term effect on the rate of reproduction by the removal of large rams.

Serious formal clashes generally occur only among rams of nearly equal horn size and who are unable to identify each other's dominance status. Clashing and other breeding and social interactions appear to be less intense among Stone's rams than among bighorn rams, and even less intense among Dall's rams than among Stone's rams. This circumstance may be an adaptation to conserve energy resources of species facing long and severe winters in northern latitudes.

Ewe social behavior is much less apparent than that of rams. Except during the estrus period, it consists of little more than maternal treatment of lambs and occasional ag-

gressive behavior towards others for space or food, as well as banding together loosely for companionship. Lambs interact frequently in play, running and jumping, and in the learning process, they exhibit many of the behaviorisms of adults. On occasion, adults will run and leap in play for short periods.

HABITAT

Dall's sheep habitat is typically alpine: steep, open grasslands interspersed with broken cliffs and talus slopes on recently glaciated mountains. It usually lies almost entirely above timberline which, in Alaska, is variable in elevation but averages about 765 meters (2,500 feet) above sea level. Winter snowfall is comparatively light, averaging 31.9 centimeters (12.5 inches) over a five-year period on three Kenai Mountains sheep ranges (Nichols 1976). Temperatures normally remain below freezing during the winter, and high winds sweep many ridges and slopes free of snow.

Vegetation consists largely of sedges, bunchgrasses, low shrubs such as blueberry, crowberry, dwarf willow, mountain avens, and mosses and lichens. The lower portions of sheep habitat may have large stands of dwarf birch interspersed with larger willows and dense alder and alpine hemlock thickets. In some places where broken cliffs extend suitable habitat below timberlines, sheep utilize benches supporting stands of twisted cottonwood, aspen and occasional white spruce.

Stone's sheep habitat is somewhat more subalpine in nature, and in mountains less recently glaciated and with higher precipitation than Dall's sheep habitat. There are fewer open alpine grasslands, and much of the higher slopes are covered with thickets of dwarf birch and alpine fir. Aspen, Engelmann spruce and lodgepole pine are common.

Both subspecies are primarily grazing animals, although many forbs and browse plants are eaten as well. A study of three herds of Dall's sheep in Alaska found that sedges and bunchgrasses made up the bulk of their diet, followed by lesser amounts of browse (mainly dwarf willow), moss and lichens (Figure 39). During summer, forage of good nutritional quality and great diversity is available. Sheep eat a greater variety of plants in summer than in winter when the variety, quantity and quality of available forage are reduced greatly. As indicated by amounts of crude protein, gross energy and total available carbohydrates in their summer diets, Dall's sheep obtain more than adequate nutrition during that season— which allows them to accumulate fat. By late winter, however, diet quality, as indicated by the relative amounts of the same components, deteriorates to a level below that presumed necessary for physical maintenance.

In addition to suitable climate, terrain and food, mineral licks appear to be nec-

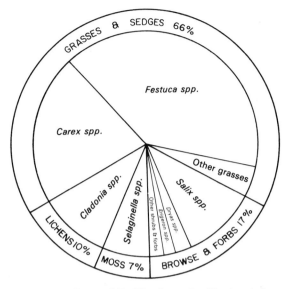

Figure 39. Diet of Dall's sheep in Alaska (after Nichols, Unpublished).

essary components of Dall's sheep habitat. Licks are found on most of Alaska's sheep ranges. Use is highest in late spring and early summer, and diminishes by late summer. Some licks are quite large; one serves a population of about 1,500 sheep that travels as much as 19.3 kilometers (12 miles) to the lick (Heimer 1974). Hebert (1967) found that sodium was the element most sought in natural licks by mountain goats. He suggested that lick use was the result of a high water intake on a low sodium diet (initiated by feeding on succulent forage in the spring) rather than a winter dietary deficiency. Geist (1971a) suggested that sheep use licks to replace skeletal minerals lost through catabolism during winter.

MANAGEMENT

Distribution and status

In Alaska, Dall's sheep occupy suitable habitat in the Brooks Range, the Alaska Range from the Canadian border to Lake Clark, the Wrangell Mountains, the Chugach Range, the Talkeetna Mountains and parts of the Kenai Mountains. Small isolated herds are found in the White Mountains and Tanana Hills north and east of Fairbanks (Figure 40). Estimates place the state's population from 30,000–50,000 sheep. Early market hunting and possibly hunting by natives depleted a few local herds which appeared to recover by the 1920s. In response to a series of severe winters, a major decline apparently occurred in the 1930s and early 1940s, leaving many of Alaska's sheep populations at very low levels. Since that time, herds have recovered and now appear to have stabilized in most areas while declining gradually in a few others (Nichols 1975).

Management in Alaska mainly has consisted of allowing only the harvest of rams with horns of three-quarter curl or larger in annual August-September hunting seasons. Nonresident hunters are required to have a licensed guide. One ram is allowed per hunter each year. Approximately 1,000–1,200 rams are harvested annually (Figure 41). Recently initiated management practices include establishment of restricted access areas and full-curl ram-only hunts as well as limited either-sex hunts.

In the Yukon Territory, Dall's sheep are found in all ranges between the Yukon River and the Alaska border to the west and the British Columbia border to the south. They occur north of the Yukon River in the

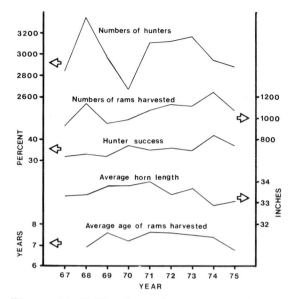

Figure 41. Dall's sheep harvest statistics in Alaska, 1967–1975.

British, Richardson, Warnecke, and Ogilvie mountains. An estimated 18,000 Dall's sheep occur in the Yukon Territory, and populations are believed to be generally stable. Stone's sheep are found in relict populations in the Cassiar, Pelly and Selwyn mountains, and the Salmon Range; a few occur in the Ogilvie Mountains. There are some 4,500 present, mostly in small and scattered bands. Populations are thought to be relatively stable (Hoefs 1975). Both subspecies are hunted under the three-quarter curl regulation, with one ram per hunter per year allowed. Guides are required for nonresident hunters, and natives are allowed unrestricted hunting of both sexes. The estimated annual harvest of thinhorn sheep in the Yukon Territory is about 250 rams.

From 3,000–8,000 Dall's sheep are estimated to inhabit the MacKenzie Mountains in the Northwest Territories (Stelfox 1975). Populations are stable. As elsewhere, nonresidents must hire a guide, and hunting by natives is unrestricted. Approximately 150 rams are taken annually under the three-quarter curl restriction, with one ram per non-native hunter allowed each year.

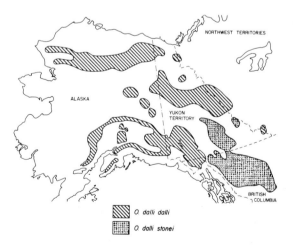

Figure 40. Current distribution of Dall's and Stone's sheep.

Small herds of Dall's sheep totaling about 200 animals are found in the northwest corner of British Columbia (Demarchi 1975). Stone's sheep occur on the Yukon and Stikine plateaus, and in the Skeena, Cassiar, Omineca and Rocky mountains north of the Peace River. From 9,000–15,000 Stone's sheep inhabit British Columbia. Market hunting reduced some populations in past years, but most herds are thought to have recovered and now are relatively stable or possibly declining slightly. Most herds are harvested on the basis of the three-quarter curl, ram-only regulation, but a seven-eighths curl law now applies to rams of Rocky Mountains populations. Relatively heavy harvests have decreased the male segment of some accessible herds. Also, predator control, primarily poisoning of wolves, has been undertaken in some Stone's sheep ranges.

In general, management of thinhorn sheep in both Alaska and Canada has had the primary objective of furnishing trophies to hunters. Harvesting only adult rams has not been shown to adversely influence thinhorn sheep populations' capacity to reproduce, nor is it effective to control or reduce herd numbers where desired. Intensive ram-only hunting reduces the number of available rams. Some individuals contend that if selective ram-only hunting is carried out over a long enough time, there may be a genetic effect in selecting for the survival of small-horned males. However, this has not yet been demonstrated. Accumulated evidence reported earlier in the chapter shows breeding by young rams and herd reproduction are not reduced.

Recent innovations of controlling access, limiting numbers of hunters harvesting from select herds, and increasing the minimum size of rams to be harvested should have even less impact on populations while increasing opportunities for enjoyment of recreational hunters. Controlled hunting of ewes will enable manipulation and management of sheep herds by making possible control or reduction of populations, alteration of sex ratios in favor of rams, and improvement of reproduction and survival rates in overcrowded herds. In addition, need has been recognized in both Canada and Alaska to set aside certain sheep herds for nonconsumptive uses, such as viewing, photography and scientific study.

Estimating populations

Because of the size and ruggedness of sheep habitats, aerial surveys are the most economical and efficient way to evaluate population status. Thinhorn sheep can be classified by sex and age classes on the basis of horn and body sizes and conformations. Aerial surveys are applicable especially to Dall's sheep, which reside in treeless alpine regions and usually are highly visible in the summer. Light, fixed-wing aircraft are relatively economical and can provide the means of determining distributions and population sizes with fairly high degrees of accuracy. Using fixed-wing aircraft to determine sex and age classes is possible also, but requires considerable flying and observing skills.

Use of helicopters allows for more accurate surveys, but generally is economically impractical except under special circumstances. Also, sheep react more to low-flying helicopters than to small airplanes—a harassment factor that must be considered, especially when young lambs are present.

Use of ground surveys to examine samples of a herd, combined with aerial surveys to estimate total herd size and distribution, generally is preferable to exclusive use of either aerial or ground surveys. Because rams usually are not with the ewe bands after lambing, detailed sex-age classifications are best conducted just prior to the lambing season. The objective is to obtain the best ram-ewe and yearling-ewe ratios and ram size class estimates before the ram portion of the herd becomes segregated. During aerial surveys conducted just after lambing, the proportion of new lambs (which are readily visible from the air) and total herd size may be estimated effectively. Population models then may be constructed mathematically by combining results of both surveys; and population parameters—such as reproduction, survival, and herd composition—may be estimated (Nichols 1970).

Up close, thinhorn rams may be aged accurately by their horn annuli (Geist 1966, Hemming 1969). These annuli, reflecting a cessation of horn growth each fall, are readily visible to the trained eye. They may be used to estimate age of carcasses or just horn specimens to within about one month if the date of death is known. Ages of ewes also may be estimated from horn annuli, but more careful examination is required because these annuli are closer together and difficult to distinguish in older-aged specimens.

THE FUTURE

At present, Dall's sheep in Alaska and Canada have no serious man-related habitat problems. They inhabit rugged and remote terrain, for the most part inhospitable to man. However, the future may bring several types of human activity that could cause habitat damage or reduction. The well-publicized trans-Alaska oil pipeline has already pushed a road through the heart of sheep habitat in the formerly remote Brooks Range. The road does no significant damage in itself, but undoubtedly will open the area to further mineral exploration and possible development. Harassment of sheep by helicopters during mineral exploration already is common in many ranges. Mineral development in sheep habitat may affect sheep populations adversely by severely disturbing habitat and forcing sheep to abandon vital ranges. One major mineral lick already has been staked out (but not developed) as a mineral claim. A planned hydroelectric project on Alaska's Susitna River, although probably doing no damage to sheep habitat in itself, will open heretofore remote sheep ranges to boat traffic and possible further development.

The greatest danger facing Dall's sheep in Alaska is a plan now being considered to open large tracts of sheep habitat to grazing by domestic livestock, including domestic sheep. Should this materialize, wild sheep populations may be depleted as a result of competition for forage and diseases brought in by livestock.

In Canada, Stone's sheep already are faced with loss of habitat to a large hydroelectric project as well as to mineral developments. A railroad has been constructed through the heart of sheep habitat and a highway is planned, both of which will open sheep ranges to further exploitation. A potential problem facing both Dall's and Stone's sheep in northern Canada is the increasing commercial value of their horns and capes. Since natives have no restrictions on the number of sheep they can kill, there is a potential for wholesale destruction of populations. A management approach is needed immediately to permit use of sheep populations only within biological limits.

Although not necessarily harmful to sheep, large tracts of land will be withdrawn soon from unrestricted public use under the Alaska Native Claims Settlement Act. Included will be large blocks of sheep habitat probably set aside as national parks on which all hunting will be restricted, and large areas to be under the control of private, native corporations, on which the future of sheep hunting is unknown as yet. These withdrawals not only will remove presently available sheep herds from public hunting, but will concentrate hunters on the remaining open lands. This undoubtedly will necessitate more intensive management and restrictive harvests.

The most important future need of thinhorn sheep will be habitat protection. This will require a herd-by-herd inventory of critical sites, including mineral licks, lambing and wintering areas, and migration routes. Once known, these sites and the sheep that use them will need protection from human development and undue harassment. Unless undertaken promptly, such habitat protection may come too late for many sheep populations.

Continuing and long-term research is vital to understanding of thinhorn sheep ecology and management needs. Research to date has been limited in scope, area and time. In particular, comparative studies of sheep occupying different habitats are needed. To make more efficient use of the thinhorn sheep resource, management policy makers will have to provide more money and manpower for sheep management and research, and managers will have to make better use of modern management techniques and research findings.

Chapter 13

COLLARED PECCARY

Lyle K. Sowls

Leader
Cooperative Wildlife Research Unit
University of Arizona
Tucson, Arizona

The collared peccary is an important game mammal in Arizona, New Mexico and Texas. In all three states, it has passed from unprotected to managed status and has increased in numbers. It is an important source of meat and hides in many parts of Mexico, and thus is hunted heavily in many parts of that country (Leopold 1959). Leopold found that, despite overhunting, peccaries persisted in small numbers where habitat was suitable. Basic knowledge needed for its proper management also has increased greatly. As recently as 30 years ago, very little was known about its basic biology, and the literature held little for the person who sought knowledge of the "javelina," as it is commonly known in the Southwest. Significant studies of nearly all ecological aspects of this species have been made during the past several decades.

TAXONOMY

Mearns (1907) recognized three separate collared peccary subspecies in the United States. Miller and Kellogg (1955) recognized 10 separate subspecies in North America, but only 2 in the United States. The two subspecies that Mearns, and Miller and Kellogg agreed were in the United States were classified as *Pecari tajacu sonoriensis* (Mearns) and *P. t. angulatus* (Cope). Southwestern New Mexico and northern Arizona were given as the northern extent of the former's range. The very eastern part of New Mexico and as far east as the Brazos River valley in Texas were given as the latter's northernmost range. Both subspecies ranged southward into Mexico. Differences among subspecies are essentially those of color and size. Northern animals tend to be lighter in color and heavier than those found in the tropics. The scientific name for collared peccary, at this writing, is *Dicotyles tajacu* L. (Woodburne 1968).

DESCRIPTION

Many hunters and many nonhunters refer to the collared peccary as a "wild hog" or talk about "pig hunting." Because the feral hog and wild boar also are considered game animals in some states, distinction should be made among the family Suidae, to which the latter animals belong, and the family Tayassuidae, to which peccaries are assigned.

Comparisons of pigs and peccaries provide a classic example of parallel evolution. Though only remotely related, these two distinct groups have evolved similar habits and physical characteristics, including general appearance, size, snout, small ears and cloven hooves. Superficially, peccaries look like pigs.

Most paleontologists who have studied the evolutionary histories of peccaries and true pigs of the family Suidae agree that the latter developed exclusively in the eastern hemisphere, and that peccaries of the family Tayassuidae evolved mostly in the western hemisphere. Both families began their separate developments from common stock during the Eocene geological epoch, 40–70 million years B.P.

The Tayassuidae had a relatively brief early history in the eastern hemisphere. Over the years, many peccary species evolved and became extinct. The most recent and best known of these was a large peccary known as *Platygonus* which lived during the Pleistocene epoch throughout much of what is now the United States. In time, peccaries moved southward to inhabit much of Central and South America. Today's species, as we know them, developed there. Besides collared peccary, the white-lipped peccary lives from southern Mexico through the dense tropical forests of Central and South America, and the newly discovered Chacoan peccary is found in parts of Argentina, Bolivia and Paraguay (Wetzel 1975).

Similarities between peccaries and swine are conspicuous; differences are more subtle. Animals often are classified by their teeth. Peccaries have 38 teeth and swine have 44. Large tusks or canine teeth are present in both groups, but peccaries' teeth are very sharp and pointed and are directed straight upwards and downwards. They fit closely together and upper canines sharpen lower ones. Canines grow until the animal is about four years old and remain sharp through wear. The edges of these teeth are as sharp as razor blades. Teeth of the "old world" swine are much longer and curve outward to the sides.

True pigs have gall bladders and simple stomachs; peccaries have more complex stomachs and no gall bladders (Tyson 1683). Pigs have well-separated metacarpals and

Tusks of a collared peccary. Photo by Steve Gallizioli; courtesy of the Arizona Game and Fish Department.

metatarsals. In the peccary, some of these bones are fused into a cannonbone, which usually is regarded as a more advanced structure (Alston 1879, Scott 1913).

The collared peccary is smaller than the true swine. An adult collared peccary from Arizona weighs 13.6–27.2 kilograms (30–60 pounds), is 45.7–55.9 centimeters (18–22 inches) high at the shoulders, and is 88.9–96.5 centimeters (35–38 inches) long. A wild European boar is much larger and may reach 181.4 kilograms (400 pounds), 91.4 centimeters (36 inches) in height and 177.8 centimeters (70 inches) in length. Adult warthogs and bush pigs, other old world Suidae, also can weigh more than 90.7 kilograms (200 pounds).

The hair of a collared peccary is very coarse and long. On the neck, "hackles" may measure 15.2 centimeters (6 inches) in length. The white collar is conspicuous. All three species of peccaries have scent glands located in the midline of their backs on the rump, and from which a powerful musk is emitted. This accounts for the occasional reference to peccaries as "musk hogs." Impressed with this, many early explorers spoke of the scent gland as the navel, which in this animal, they said, was not on the belly but on the back (Pfefferkorn 1795, Smith 1863). Many early English and Spanish explorers said that the meat would not be fit to eat unless the scent gland was removed. They also attributed this belief to many Indian tribes. In fact, there is no movement of scent into the meat unless the musk touches ,the meat, and it is unnecessary to cut the scent gland away from the rest of the hide. Some hunters still remove a large section of skin with the gland after a peccary is killed.

Numerous writers have given descriptions of the collared peccary, including Mearns (1907), Seton (1929), Bailey (1931), Knipe (1957), Neal (1959a) and Leopold (1959). Most have agreed that, in appearance, peccaries are piglike. Distinguishing characteristics include grayish-to-black color with bristles showing white annulations, and an erectile mane of longer bristles extending from the occiput to the scent gland on the back. The longest hairs or bristles in Arizona specimens reached 15.24 centimeters (6 inches) in length. The large scent gland is located about 12.7–15.2 centimeters (5–6 inches) forward of the base of an abortive tail. An incomplete whitish collar runs obliquely upward and backward from in front of the shoulder to the mane. Sides usually are a lighter color than the backs.

Young peccaries are reddish-to-gray and show the collar at birth. The ridge along the back is darker. As they grow older, they gradually turn gray. Adult coloration, a peppered black and gray with a lighter collar, is reached at about 10 weeks of age. At birth, young weigh about 0.45 kilograms (1 pound). On good diets, they gain approximately 0.45 kilograms (1 pound) per week and are mature in size at about 9–10 months of age.

DISTRIBUTION AND ABUNDANCE

The collared peccary is found in the southern parts of Texas, New Mexico and Arizona in the United States. This area constitutes, however, only the narrow northern fringe of this animal's total range, which extends southward across Mexico, Central and South America to northern Argentina. Few wild ungulate species have such an extensive and varied range (Figure 42).

ECOLOGY

Reproduction

The breeding season of the collared peccary in the United States has been identified by a number of writers. Knipe (1957), Neal (1959a) and Sowls (1966) reported that the principal parturition period for collared peccary in Arizona was July and August, when vegetation was most abundant following summer rains. The principal part of the breeding season is in February and March, determined by back-dating a gestation period of 142–148 days. Sowls (1966) found males to be in breeding condition throughout the year and that females in captivity went through an estrus cycle every

▨ PRESENTLY OCCUPIED COLLARED PECCARY RANGE

Figure 42. Collared peccary range in North America.

193

17–30 days. By back-dating parturition dates, Jennings and Harris (1953) found that breeding in Texas took place every month except February. However, the true gestation period of 142–146 days had not been determined when they published their work. Consequently, they actually found breeding in all months except January. Low (1970) found that the principal breeding season in Texas included January, February and March.

Sowls (1966) in Arizona and Low (1970) in Texas both reported that captive male peccaries became sexually active at about 11 months. Low found that the earliest age at which conception occurred among captive peccaries in Texas was 11.3 months. He also gave the most complete description of male reproductive organs and a good description of female reproduction. Sowls learned that captive females first became pregnant at 33–34 weeks of age. Normal litter size is two (Jennings and Harris 1953, Knipe 1957, Sowls 1966, Low 1970, Smith and Sowls 1975), but litters of three and four are not uncommon. An incidence of five fetuses was reported by Halloran (1945).

Smith and Sowls (1975) described fetal development of collared peccary, and Sowls et al. (1976) described hormone levels and ovarian characteristics during various stages of pregnancy. Sowls et al. (1961) described the chemical composition of the milk of collared peccary, and Brown et al. (1963) gave more detail on the chemical composition of the milk fat.

Peccaries come into heat and ovulate as soon as eight days after parturition (Sowls 1966), and males are sexually active throughout the year. The small number of pregnant females found during the February and March hunting season in Arizona and the large number of females without young during most of year, however, indicate that in wild situations they do not necessarily breed so readily. The ability of females to become pregnant again soon after abortions or losses of recently born young probably accounts for births during autumn and winter in the southwestern United States. It also contributes to the fact that peccaries have the highest reproductive potential among North American ungulates.

Studies indicate that more females than males are born. Of 147 young peccaries, including both fetuses and young observed a few hours after birth, 40 percent (59) were males (Sowls 1966). Of 55 fetuses from 34 sows in eastern Texas, 42 percent (23) were males and 58 percent (32) were females (Low 1970). The addition of data for 32 young born in captivity and one litter from western Texas brought his total male-female ratio of young to 47:53. Low also found that the sex ratio of a sample population in Texas became even closer as the animals grew older. I have found the same to be true in Arizona. From 1957–1971, sex information on 2,563 adult peccaries killed by hunters and examined by checking stations showed a 52:48 ratio in favor of males. Of 186 adults captured in the Tucson Mountains, Arizona from 1956–1968, 44 percent were males.

A differential mortality working against the females with young can occur due to poor nutrition during lactation. Even while the females had excellent food and obesity was common among males and some lactating females, two thriving young I witnessed caused their mothers to be thin and emaciated. In a dry year, both mother and young can die from starvation, thus causing an unbalanced sex ratio favoring males.

Behavior

Although they are highly social animals, there is no indication that harems exist among peccaries. In this respect, they differ from many ungulate populations in which large numbers of females are in heat within a few weeks and are controlled by a single male. Females seem to have many mates, but no prolonged male-female relationships develop. There is very little fighting in herds when females are in heat (Sowls 1974).

The daily activity pattern of the collared peccary has been described by several writers (Jennings and Harris 1953, Elder 1956, Knipe 1957, Neal 1959a, Ellisor and

Harwell 1969, Day 1969a, 1970, 1973, 1974, and Bissonette 1976). The collared peccary, being a social animal, moves about in herds which are loosely scattered during feeding. In the arid and warm Southwest, they usually feed early in the morning and late in the evening. They visit waterholes when water is available and bed down in the shelter of thickets during the hot part of the day. During the hottest days of summer, they feed at night. Their activities are correlated closely to temperature. During resting periods, they sleep in small groups in unlined depressions in the ground under low trees and shrubs.

Peccaries, except very old or sick animals, seldom are found alone. There is some exchange of animals among herds. Whereas herds of the collared peccary number 6–20 individuals with occasional herds of 30, white-lipped peccaries may travel in herds of more than 100. Unlike most large ungulates that form temporary seasonal groups or harems according to sex and age, peccaries do not have seasonal aggregations. The peccary herd is a permanent social unit that moves, feeds and rests together. The sex and age divisions of a herd represent a sample of the population as a whole, and are not a result of particular behavioral relationships.

Within a peccary herd there is a dominance order (Schweinsburg 1969, Schweinsburg and Sowls 1972, Sowls 1974, Bissonette 1976). Evidence of dominance can be detected when animals come together at waterholes or to feed. Schweinsburg and Sowls (1972) and Sowls (1974) described the behavioral postures that distinguish dominant and subordinate animals in social encounters. Sowls (1974) found that, among receptive peccaries, females were dominant over males in most situations. These conclusions were made from observations of the animals at feeding troughs and watering pans.

The scent gland plays a significant part in a peccary's existence. Experimental removal of scent glands from young captive animals revealed that their absences did not impair health or normal activity or influence reproductive capabilities (Sowls 1974). The

Collared peccaries bedded down under mesquite tree, in winter. The base of mesquite often is used in this manner throughout the year. Photo by Jerry Day; courtesy of the Arizona Game and Fish Department.

gland's value lies in the fact that the peccaries use scent to hold herds together, identify individuals and delineate herd territories. Friendly peccaries engage in reciprocal rubbing: two animals stand side-by-side but face in opposite directions, and each vigorously rubs its head against the other's hindquarters and scent gland. This rubbing is indulged in by both sexes.

Peccaries rub their scent glands against rocks, tree trunks and similar objects. They also sniff these "scent posts" and like dogs "remark" them. Apparently, home territories of herds are so marked, and there is evidence that individual animals have individual smells (Müller-Schwarze 1974, Eibl-Eibesfeldt 1967).

Peccaries' sense of smell is keen, and it might well be said that the animals live in a world of odors. Their sense of hearing also is good but their sense of sight is poor. It is possible for a careful observer to walk right into a herd and have them on all sides before being seen. When an intruder is detected, the excited peccaries often emit sharp, clicking sounds that sound like castanets. This sound can startle even the most experienced observer. However, few people have the opportunity to see peccaries closely and frequently enough to identify the causes of this clicking behavior. The only authenticated records of attacks on people I know of were by captive or pet animals—resulting in bites.

Mortality

Collared peccaries live as long as 18 years in captivity, but such longevity does not occur commonly in wild populations. In eastern Texas, Low (1970) found almost 15 percent of a population were more than seven years old, and that the annual mortality rate was 21.5 percent. In western Texas, he found no animals in a population sample more than nine years of age, and the mean mortality rate was 27.5 percent. Low emphasized a low mortality rate for peccaries of two to seven years of age and a higher rate among the animals of younger and older ages.

Unfortunately, most studies of peccaries have been done at the northern fringe of the species' range, in Texas and Arizona. The causes of death are difficult to determine because carcasses quickly decompose or are consumed by scavengers. I have found that respiratory diseases are a common cause of death during winter among captive animals. Five of 11 peccaries that died in captivity in Tucson, Arizona, died apparently from intestinal enteritis.

Dardiri, Yedloutschnig and Taylor (1969) determined that peccaries were susceptible to hog cholera, vesicular exanthema of swine, vesicular stomatitis, Rinderpest, and hoof and mouth disease. However, they did not find peccaries susceptible to African swine fever.

Knipe (1957), Neal (1959a) and Schweinsburg (1969) reported high juvenile mortality among peccary populations. Parasites of the peccary in Texas have been described by Samuel and Low (1970), and in Arizona by Neal (1959a).

HABITAT

In the American Southwest, collared peccary occupy a variety of habitats. Knipe (1957), Neal (1959a) and Eddy (1961) described the habitat types occupied by the peccary in Arizona. The vegetational pattern of this area is complex because of the wide range in altitudes and resulting differences in rainfall.

The oak-woodland, chaparral and lower fringes of pine forest are suitable summer habitats for peccaries but can be too cold in the winter. In Arizona, peccary populations may inhabit areas of low desert-scrub vegetation at elevations of 457 meters (1,500 feet) above sea level where the dominant plants are palo verde, saguaro, mesquite and various cacti. Desert environments at lower altitudes have extremely high summer temperatures and small amounts of annual precipitation. Peccaries are able to inhabit

Collared peccary in typical setting. Photo by author.

these environments because they make use of microclimates and, during hot periods of summer, move about only in evenings and at night. By consuming succulent foods, peccaries obtain both food and water.

Jennings and Harris (1953), Ellisor and Harwell (1969), and Low (1970) described habitat of the collared peccary in southern Texas. This part of the peccaries' range has an average annual rainfall of 63.5–76.2 centimeters (25–30 inches). The dominant vegetation is honey mesquite, several other acacias and a variety of other shrubs. Several species of cacti also are present, including prickly pear, which offers emergency food.

Low (1970) and Bissonette (1976) described the habitat of collared peccary in western Texas. The rainfall average is about 25.4–35.6 centimeters (10–14 inches), droughts are common and the vegetation consists of a large number of succulents such as century plants and cacti. In addition to these emergency foods, there are numerous shrubs which offer cover, such as creosote bush, catclaw and mesquite. Important to the diet of peccaries in desert areas is a large variety of ephemerals which occur only in wet years.

Jennings and Harris (1953) examined stomach contents of 17 peccaries collected in southern Texas. They concluded that cladophylls of prickly pear were the main staple of peccaries in that area. They concluded further that seasonal foods such as grass, mesquite beans, ebony bean and a great variety of other plants made up substantial parts of the diet. In two stomachs collected in the Trans-Pecos region of Texas, lechuguilla made up more than one-half of the contents. Jennings and Harris expressed belief that acorns were important in the diet of peccaries at certain times.

Also very important to the collared peccary's diet are roots, tubers, bulbs and rhizomes of a variety of plants. A number of writers noted that the animals obtain plants by digging (Alvarez 1952, Leopold 1959, Knipe 1957, Eddy 1959, Enders 1930). Consumption of underground plant parts is greatest in fall and winter when very little of the above-ground parts are green.

Leopold (1959) studied peccaries over a large part of Mexico and concluded: "A wide variety of fruits, roots, bulbs and greens contribute to the normal fare. Acorns, pine nuts and manzanita berries are favorite foods in the pine-oak upland. Cactus fruits and the beans of mesquite, catclaw and juniper are other common items of diet in the uplands."

Eddy (1959) gave detailed accounts of peccaries seeking out and eating five different underground tuberous or bulbous plants in the oak-woodland habitat of Arizona. His field observations and those of other researchers with the Arizona Cooperative Wildlife Research Unit indicated that peccaries are able to locate edible underground parts by smell. Apparently, it is not important that above-ground portions of the plants be present for peccaries to locate the underground plant parts. The plants described by Eddy were morning glory, thistle and gourds. He described densities of as many as 30 morning glory tubers per square meter (10.76 square feet). The animals usually leave small saucer-shaped excavations in places where the tubers or bulbs are taken. Eddy found 704 excavations in seven sites which had been rooted by peccaries where gourd bulbs were sought. He reported areas as large as 4.05 hectares (10 acres) which were completely rooted of thistles.

Eddy also gave the size and number of rootings per square meter (10.76 square feet) for three species in the lower desert areas in Arizona. He counted 753 rootings in an area of 125 square meters (1,346 square feet) where lily species grew, 508 diggings in 84 square meters (904 square feet) where the bulbs of wild onion were sought, and 103 diggings in 37 square meters (398 square feet) where peccaries rooted for Mariposa lily bulbs. These figures demonstrate the thorough search that peccaries undertake in their efforts to obtain the underground morsels. They also demonstrate the versatile nature of their feeding habits.

Practically everyone who has written about the foods eaten by peccaries has mentioned mast and berries. The amount of mast and berry species consumed by peccaries over their vast range is enormous. Most of the nuts, for example, are very nutritious and are eagerly sought when available to peccaries. Because of the large number of oak species, there is often a sequence of availability which prolongs the mast food supply in any one area. For the oak-woodland in Arizona, Eddy (1961) gave such a sequence for four oak subspecies that shed their fruit from June through December. Unlike the staple, less nutritious foods such as cacti, mast-bearing plants often are sporadic in their production of fruit. In this regard, certain years become known as "good" or "bad."

Several writers have commented on the ability of peccaries to consume large quantities of spiny cacti and suffer no apparent ill-effects. Eddy (1959) described how peccaries eat the soft centers of the barrel cactus or bisnage; and Knipe (1957) reported large numbers of spines in peccary excrement after the animals had consumed small pin-cushion cacti. These small and very spiny cacti are consumed freely by peccaries.

They eat out the center parts but swallow large numbers of spines in the process.

Eddy (1961) studied the foods eaten by peccaries in three different vegetative types, including: (1) the palo verde-bursage-cactus vegetative type; (2) the "semidesert" subtype where the dominant vegetation was cactus, burroweed and mimosa; and (3) a foothill subtype where the dominant vegetation was live-oak, manzanita and century plant. This latter area reaches altitudes of 1,524 meters (5,000 feet) above sea level. By study of stomach contents and droppings and systematic field observations where lengths of feeding periods of individual peccaries were recorded, the roles of various plant foods were determined. Although different plant communities grew in each of the areas studied, the number of plant species eaten by peccaries in each habitat type was nearly the same—15, 17 and 19, in the order that the areas were listed earlier.

Of all foods eaten by peccaries, prickly pear cactus was most common. It was eaten in 56.4 percent of the observed feedings in the desert study area where it was abundant, and in 52.3 percent of feedings observed in the intermediate area. Where prickly pear was uncommon in areas of higher altitude, it was eaten during less than 1 percent of the observations. In the study area of highest altitude, century plants and morning glories were consumed most frequently. These two plants comprised 70.7 percent of all observed feedings in the third area.

Knipe (1957) concluded that prickly pear was the preferred food of the peccary in Arizona, but listed tubers, bulbs and rhizomes as important, chiefly the roots of gourds, morning glories and dock. He also listed the root of sand-verbena as a favorite food.

Low (1970) examined 73 stomachs from peccaries in Texas and found they contained 63 percent prickly pear, 18 percent grasses, 7 percent forbs, and small parts of animal matter and unidentified plant fibers. He found great seasonal variation in composition of diets. Besides cladophylls of prickly

Collared peccary feeding on prickly pear. Photo by Jerry Day; courtesy of the Arizona Game and Fish Department.

pear, he found that flowers and fruit of prickly pear were consumed readily when available. Low found that a high percentage of peccaries' diets consisted of grass: 25 percent in spring, 14 percent in summer, and 10 percent in fall. He also found that forbs were taken in preference to other plants whenever they were available.

Numerous references to prickly pear cactus in the peccary's diet have given the impression that it is preferred, adequate and always plentiful. Knipe (1957) and Bissonette (1976) referred to it as the preferred food of peccary. Discussing the increase in the basal metabolic rate of the collared peccary in winter, Zervanos (1973, 1975) said, "However, this increased food requirement is not a real problem for the peccary where sufficient food supplies are available all year round."

The term "preferred food" originated with Leopold (1933), who used it to designate the palatability rank and the order in which available foods are consumed by a given species at a particular time and place. In the desert regions of the southwestern United States, where most studies have been done and where prickly pear is eaten in large quantities, it is the only food available during a large part of the year.

The value of prickly pear as a food for range livestock has long been known, especially when used as an emergency ration in times of drought. In experiments with captive peccaries on diets of only prickly pear, I found that they survived for about three months and that pregnant sows aborted their young. Morrison (1954) said of prickly pear cacti for livestock: "Since they are low in protein, all the cacti should be fed with a protein-rich concentrate or roughage. Cacti alone will not maintain livestock. Though desert cattle sometimes subsist on them for three months of the year, they become very emaciated. . . . The chief importance of cacti is to furnish emergency forage for stock in the semi-arid regions in case of drought, for these plants are able to utilize most efficiently small and irregular supplies of moisture."

From Eddy's (1961) work, it is apparent that in most areas only a few particular plants make up a substantial or staple part of the animals' diet. However, because peccary habitat covers a large area with varied topographic features, climatic conditions and vegetative communities, there are a great number and wide variety of plant species that are important in the animals' diet. Local availability of plant foods, however, appears to be the principal dietary factor.

Unlike grassland ruminants which largely forage on grasses, peccaries feed on a great variety of plants. The anatomy of their teeth, jaws and digestive systems reveals the types of food they eat. Like their remote relatives, the hogs, they have well-developed snouts which they use in rooting out bulbs, roots and tubers. Unlike hogs, peccaries cannot move their mandibles sideways and chew their food. A common characteristic of all three species of peccaries is the presence of long, interlocking canine teeth which greatly reduce the transverse movement of mandibles in chewing motions. Thus, the only extensive chewing of the food that can occur is the up-and-down movement, which crushes food (Herring 1972, Langer, In press). The incisors, however, are well-adapted to cropping vegetation which is swallowed after a minimum of chewing.

A characteristic of the digestive system in all three species of peccaries is the unusual stomach. It consists of a voluminous gastric pouch with two blindsacs and a glandular stomach. The stomach of the collared peccary was described by an English surgeon (Tyson 1683), 75 years before Linnaeus gave the species its first scientific name. The stomach has since been studied by Stewart (1964) and in great detail by Langer (1974, In press). The stomach of the other two species have not been studied thoroughly but, superficially, they show the same pouches as does the collared peccary.

The stomach, although not that of a ruminant, acts to some extent in a similar way. Peccaries are able to digest very coarse food which is not finely chewed. Although peccaries graze to some extent, they are not predominantly grazers as are warthogs which, in some places, primarily eat grass (Dorst and Dandelot 1970). The lateral movement of the warthog's mandibles allows freedom in chewing.

There are numerous questions regarding diets of the collared peccary that await further research. For example, what nutritional needs are lacking in diets of prickly pear and other coarse succulents? What levels of protein and other nutrients are necessary for a peccary to reproduce and remain in good health? What is the role of the microflora in breaking down cellulose in the digestive system? What is the effect of oxalic acid when cacti are a large part of peccaries' diet for long periods? And, what are the effects of drought on reproduction and survival of young?

MANAGEMENT

Hunting

The collared peccary is classified as a game animal in the three southwestern states in which it is found. Each of these states has an annual, regulated hunting season for peccary. Texas has the largest area of peccary habitat, the highest population and probably the largest annual harvest (Texas Parks and Wildlife Department 1973). Harvest data from Texas are available only from public hunts, and records from private lands are incomplete.

In New Mexico, peccaries are confined to a small southern part of the state. Legal hunts on a limited basis were held annually from 1963 through 1968 and have been held from 1971 to present. During the period 1963 through 1968, 1,215 permits were issued and 370 peccaries were taken (Johnson 1969). From 1971–1974, 506 hunters took 155 ± 16 animals (Johnson, personal communications 1975). Available data show that in the 1972–1973 season, 135 hunters harvested 74 animals. In 1975, 186 hunters bagged 49 animals (Johnson 1976).

Arizona has huntable populations of peccary in the southeastern one-quarter of the state. Data on the number of permits issued and estimated take from hunter reports were recorded by Knipe (1957). Data about numbers of hunters afield, annual harvests, total harvest and percentage of hunter success in Arizona have been recorded since 1957 (Arizona Game Management Survey 1974). Knipe reported 9,706 permits sold in 1950 and 31,208 in 1971. After 1971, the Arizona Game and Fish Department set peccary harvest quotas by areas and restricted the number of permits issued. In 1972, a total of 25,830 permits was sold. Arizona records showed a peak harvest of 6,602 in 1970, with a hunter success percentage of 20.6. The smallest harvest was 2,236 in 1957, with a hunter success percentage of 13.4. The popularity of the collared peccary as a game animal is reflected by these figures.

Day (1975) reported the effects of hunting on collared peccary populations. In 10 herds on his study area in Arizona, he recorded losses to hunting of 26 peccaries from a total population of 127. This 20 percent reduction was double the annual recruitment rate. Day found that most losses were from two herds that were reduced more than 65 percent. These data illustrate the difficulty encountered in setting hunting seasons on this species. Being herd animals, peccary populations can be seriously reduced by hunting that is not carefully regulated.

Most difficult in the management of the collared peccary is to obtain a good distribution of hunting pressure. For this reason, the range must be divided into units as small as feasible and a set number of hunting permits be assigned to each on a yearly basis. Even with this type of management, some herds may be overhunted.

Estimating population parameters

Increased interest in hunting collared peccary has led to research programs and the development of new inventory methods. Jennings and Harris (1953) reported on experimental aerial surveys, cruise censuses by ground vehicles and counts of peccary tracks along sandy roads and washes. They ruled out aerial surveys and cruise censuses by ground vehicles as unfeasible in brush country.

Extensive research to find methods to determine peccary populations in Arizona has been done by the Arizona Game and Fish Department (Day 1960, 1965, 1966, 1967, 1968). Methods tried have included counts of tracks, observations at waterholes and from helicopters, questioning hunters on animals seen and surveys by people on foot.

The Arizona Game and Fish Department found that counts from helicopters were too variable and too expensive. Track counts also were too variable to be of any value, and waterhole observations did not yield accurate population data.

Day found that sightings of peccaries reported by deer hunters immediately after they returned from the field were more accurate than sightings reported later in questionnaires. He also reported that the data obtained in the former manner compared closely to that obtained by wildlife managers on regular foot surveys.

Therefore, of methods devised for annual censuses of peccary populations, the most promising is questioning hunters who are on the range during hunting seasons for other species, such as deer. This method, combined with observations by wildlife managers on foot or horseback, gives a good indication of population numbers and trends. Road blocks and organized checking stations can also reveal important information on peccary populations, and by making age determinations at checking stations, data on productivity can be obtained.

Along with increased effort to obtain better inventory information during the past few years, many techniques for research of the peccary have been developed. Neal (1959b) reported on early efforts to trap animals for research and transplant to new areas. Ellisor and Harwell (1969) described methods for capturing peccaries in large traps that were built originally to capture

Trapped collared peccaries. Photo by Jerry Day; courtesy of the Arizona Game and Fish Department.

deer. They also used bells attached to collars around the necks of peccaries to study home range movements.

Peccaries have long, sharp teeth and are able to bite a person severely. For this reason, special precaution must be taken when handling peccaries for such activities as tagging, affixing radio collars and determining age. Various restraining mechanisms have been used to prevent the animals from biting handlers. Ellisor and Harwell (1969) used a snare made of cable and pipe with the restraining cable around an animal's neck. The most common snare

used by the Arizona Cooperative Wildlife Research Unit consists of a noose of plastic-covered cable through a 1.3-centimeter (0.5-inch) pipe. The noose is inserted over a peccary's upper jaws behind the canines (Neal 1959b).

By far the most satisfactory and widely used method of handling collared peccaries is to immobilize them with drugs (Day 1969b, 1969c). Day recommended the drug Sernylan (phencylidine hydrochloride). He gave 60–75 milligrams as a complete dose for a wild adult when a dart gun was used. The drug is available in concentrations of

Radio transmitter and antenna on a collar of a "javelina." Photo by Jerry Day; courtesy of the Arizona Game and Fish Department.

100 milligrams per cubic centimeter, which is ideal for such use. This drug is not to be used if the animal is to be eaten. Another technique that has shown promise is the use of alpha-chlorolose in bait to immobilize peccaries for research purposes and transplanting.

Intensive home range and population studies have been made in recent years by the use of radio telemetry. Schweinsburg (1969, 1971) and Day (1973) used radio transmitters fixed to collars to study home range, activity patterns and survival of the collared peccary. This animal has proven to be an ideal subject for such studies.

Kirkpatrick and Sowls (1962) described tooth-replacement and tooth-wear patterns as related to age (Table 23). Low (1970) described the use of cementum layers to determine ages of collared peccaries. These techniques are used to gather information on age ratios and reproductive successes in peccary populations.

Sowls (1961) used the tooth-replacement pattern to obtain ages of animals up to about two years and the tooth-wear pattern for

Table 23. Ages at which various teeth are present in collared peccaries (after Kirkpatrick and Sowls 1962).

Age	Teeth present
2–6 months	All temporary teeth
7–10 months	All temporary teeth plus first permanent molars
11–12 months	All temporary teeth plus first permanent molars and canines
13–18 months	All temporary teeth plus first and second permanent molars and canines
19–21.5 months	As above except third permanent molars just appearing
21.5 months +	All permanent teeth

animals with complete adult dentition. For peccaries with adult dentition, a quick appraisal can be made of the age composition of animals brought to checking stations. The five categories used by the Arizona Cooperative Wildlife Research Unit were: (1) slight wear on all teeth but no particular teeth show more wear, (2) wear conspicuous on first and second molars, (3) all teeth show wear, (4) very heavy wear but all teeth present, and (5) very heavy wear with some or all teeth missing.

Low (1970) correctly pointed out shortcomings in this system—the principal fault being that categories (4) and (5) overlap and both cover a wide span of years. He assigned approximate ages to the animals in various tooth-wear categories by counting cementum layers.

Nevertheless, tooth-replacement and tooth-wear patterns are valuable for obtaining age estimates of large samples of hunter-killed specimens. An increasing number of peccary hunters do not want or permit the removal of teeth from their kills. Therefore, large samples need to be obtained with methods whereby the animals merely are examined.

Richardson (1966) and Low (1970) experimented with eye-lens weights to determine peccary ages. Richardson did not find the technique reliable after the animals were 1.5 years old because of the great variation in lens weight among age classes. Peccaries below average weight for their ages had significantly lighter lenses. Low also found the technique unreliable. The best method to determine ages of animals to two years of age is by the tooth-replacement pattern. Beyond this age, the best method is counts of annual cementum layers.

Low (1970) found reliable correlation between the annular cementum layers in the lower first incisor in 13 specimens from Arizona and Texas. He then used this technique to construct life tables from 218 specimens collected in south Texas and another group of 102 older than 12 months of age from Black Gap of western Texas. There were higher mean mortality rates in animals less than two years old and those older than seven years. He found the mean mortality rate in eastern Texas to be 21.5 percent. In western Texas, it was 27.5 percent. In the humid area of eastern Texas, 85 percent of the peccary population was less than 7 years of age and only 0.05 percent more than 10 years old, with a few animals living to 15 years. In the drier Black Gap area of western Texas, Low found no animals more than nine years of age and only 10 percent of the population older than five years.

The best method to obtain age-composition information is to collect at random large numbers of peccaries including all age classes. This is seldom possible, however, because of low population numbers in most areas and resistance from sportsmen's and nature groups. Hence, the information collected during hunting seasons is, in most instances, the best that can be obtained. When animals in various age groups—as determined by annual cementum layers—are compared to the grouping of ages which Low (1970) assigned to the wear classes, similar percentages are found for younger and older segments of populations with more variation for age groups in between.

Future management

Inasmuch as the greatest threat to collared peccary populations is habitat loss, the first and most important management consideration is that as much suitable habitat be maintained as possible. The collared peccary has demonstrated remarkable adaptability and has a very high reproductive potential. Consequently, healthy and productive populations of collared peccary can be managed effectively throughout the extent and diversity of their range by well-regulated and monitored hunting. However, such populations can be assured only by maintenance of their habitat.

Chapter 14

MOUNTAIN LION

Kenneth R. Russell

Leader
Colorado Cooperative Wildlife Research Unit
Colorado State University
Fort Collins, Colorado

The mountain lion *(Felis concolor)* is among the most majestic yet persecuted big game animals in American history. Until about 1965, it was treated legally as a threat to the welfare of the ranching industry. Lately, it has been given legal protection in most states in response to public concern for its survival. Countless tales have been told, factual and otherwise, about the habits and deeds of the mountain lion, and untold miles traveled in pursuit of lions for purposes of recreation, eradication or both.

Compared with many other big game species, little scientific information has been gathered about mountain lions because of long-held popular feelings and official public policies declaring that lion populations should be reduced or eliminated. Until the late 1960s, much that was written about lions consisted of personal opinion and recollection of hunts and other incidents. Nonetheless, state and federal legislative bodies and agencies have made and will continue to make decisions that affect mountain lions, recreationists, livestock growers, preservationists and the general public.

Mountain lions are important economically because of actual or potential negative effects on livestock production in some situations and because of positive effects on the hunting recreation industry, particularly guides and outfitters. Lions are important from a social standpoint because of contradictory views held by different segments of the public as to whether the animals are good or bad. Lions are important from a political standpoint because politics is the process by which opposing values are resolved and molded into policies that constitute mountain lion management. Public attitudes toward mountain lions have changed significantly in recent years, from indifference or antagonism to concern for sound management.

The mountain lion lives in a variety of topographic and vegetative areas including mountainous areas. Its common names include cougar, puma, panther, painter and catamount. It is a member of the genus *Felis* in the family Felidae. Fourteen subspecies occur in the United States, Canada and Mexico (Hall and Kelson 1959).

ECOLOGY

The mountain lion is a highly adaptable animal with widely varying attributes. It lives within a broad spectrum of environmental conditions. Differences among lions and their habitats necessitate caution when making generalizations about any aspect of lion ecology or management.

Distribution and habitat

Probably no other native land mammal in the western hemisphere has a more extended range from north to south. At one time, mountain lions ranged from northern British Columbia to the Straits of Magellan in South America, and coast to coast from the northern United States or southern Canada southward. In the United States, mountain lions were restricted to mountainous areas of the West and certain swamps in Florida by the late 1920s, but there have been no major changes in their distribution during the last 50 years (Nowak 1976). Current distribution in the United States and Canada is shown in Figure 43. Mountain lions are found in favorable habitat in all of the Mexican states (Young and Goldman 1946).

Mountain lions prefer dense cover or rocky, rugged terrain, but occur ". . . from deserts to swamps, from tropical jungles to subalpine forests" (Hornocker 1976). In the Rocky Mountains, lion habitat commonly is associated with areas of pinyon pine, juniper, mountain mahogany, ponderosa pine, oak brush and other brushlands. Probably

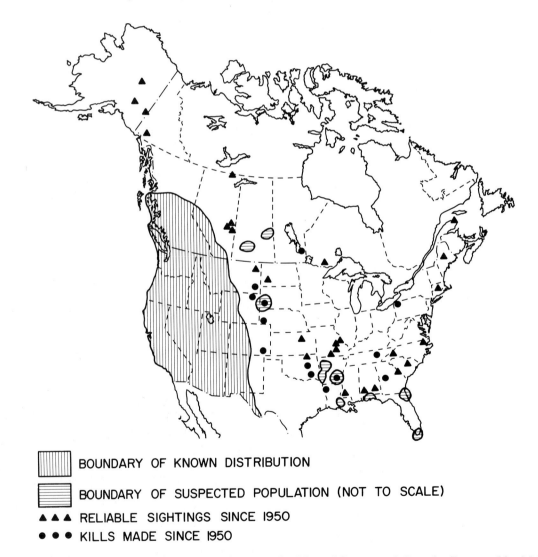

BOUNDARY OF KNOWN DISTRIBUTION

BOUNDARY OF SUSPECTED POPULATION (NOT TO SCALE)

▲ ▲ ▲ RELIABLE SIGHTINGS SINCE 1950

● ● ● KILLS MADE SINCE 1950

Figure 43. Recent distribution of mountain lions in the United States and Canada. Prepared by M.J.P. Currier (after Nowak 1976).

Mountain lion kitten with spotted markings that will disappear before adult age is reached. Photo by James D. Yoakum.

the most consistent feature found in mountain lion habitat of western North America today is the presence of mule deer.

Description

The color of adult mountain lions varies in solid but graded tones of yellow, brown, red and gray. Pelage colors do not appear to be related to season or locality, though there is some degree of consistency within subspecies. Kittens are spotted, but these markings gradually disappear before the adult stage is reached.

In western North America, adult males generally weigh from 63–73 kilograms (140–160 pounds) and adult females weigh 41–50 kilograms (90–110 pounds), but exceptions are to be expected. Lions on the coastal range of California weigh somewhat less than lions in other areas. Females grow to 213 centimeters (7 feet) in length and males to 244 centimeters (8 feet) or more. The only larger cat in the western hemisphere is the jaguar *(Felis onca)*.

Mountain lions are exceptionally strong in relation to their weights. They are especially powerful in the shoulders and

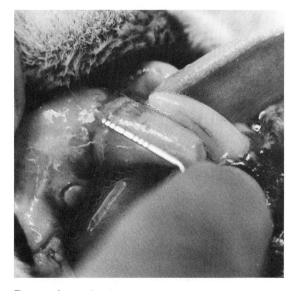

Researcher obtains canine measurement from gum line to cementoenamel junction. Courtesy of the Colorado Cooperative Wildlife Research Unit.

209

Paw print of drugged adult lion is recorded to compare measurements with other sex and age characteristics. Photo by E. G. Currier; courtesy of the Colorado Cooperative Wildlife Research Unit.

hindquarters. These characteristics enable lions to attack prey explosively and maintain tight grips with their forepaws, which are well-adapted to clasping and ripping. Claws are constructed so that the harder a victim struggles the more firmly they grip. The heavy-boned jaw has no backward or forward motion, enabling the lion to absorb the shock that accompanies an attack. Tooth arrangement is conducive to slashing and tearing. Paws are well-padded, with the back paws smaller than the front. When walking, the hind paws often are placed in imprints made by the front paws, enhancing silence during movement.

Food habits

Mountain lions eat almost any animal available, as well as some vegetation (Table 24). In western North America, however, mule deer are the staple food, probably constituting 60–80 percent of the total consumption over a year in most lion populations. A substantial number of deer taken are either fawns or in poor health, including the very old. Elk, porcupine, other small mammals and domestic sheep and cattle can be important food items in some locations.

Grass apparently is a standard part of a lion's diet. Semiconfined individuals have been observed grazing for as long as five minutes at a time, without regurgitating (Bogue and Ferrari 1974). One function of grass consumption may be to reduce the parasite load in the digestive tract.

Mountain lions seem to take cattle or sheep frequently only in Arizona, California, Nevada, New Mexico and Utah. One explanation is that stock there remains on open range and calves are dropped throughout the year.

The results of two food habits studies (Robinette et al. 1959, Spalding and Lesowski 1971) revealed that about 25 percent of the lions had empty stomachs (126 of 401 and 12 of 132, respectively). This can be interpreted to mean lions eat on only 75 percent of the

Table 24. Foods reported to be eaten by mountain lions in the United States and Canada.

Wild mammals	Other wildlife	Vegetable matter	Domestic animals
Mule deer	Insects	Grasses	Sheep
White-tailed deer	Grouse	Berries	Cattle
Porcupine	Fish		Horse
Bighorn sheep			Burro
Mountain goat			Goat
Pronghorn			Pig
Moose			Dog
Ground squirrels			Cat
Other squirrels			Chicken
Elk			Turkey
Beaver			Peacock
Marmot			
Mice			
Snowshoe hare			
Other rabbits			
Pika			
Armadillo			
Bobcat			
Coyote			
Skunk			
Raccoon			
Fox			
Cub bear			
Badger			
Feral pig			

days in a year. As such, the percentage represents a significant factor when speculating on annual rates of food consumed or prey killed by lions.

Movement

The usual area of activity for established residents is about 40–80 square kilometers (15–31 square miles) for females, and 65–90 square kilometers (25–35 square miles) for males. Areas may be smaller or larger depending on seasonal and environmental characteristics. One male lion in California and another in British Columbia have been recorded in areas of 450 square kilometers (174 square miles) and 650 square kilometers (250 square miles) (Christensen

Tagged adult female lion is weighed before release. Photo by E. G. Currier; courtesy of the Colorado Cooperative Wildlife Research Unit.

and Fischer 1976) respectively. Tagged juveniles in transient status have been recovered more than 161 kilometers (100 miles) from tag sites. Movement data are a composite from telemetry studies done in Arizona, California, Nevada, and Vancouver Island, British Columbia (Christensen and Fischer 1976), and Idaho (Hornocker 1970).

Reproduction

Female mountain lions have their first litter as early as 20–21 months of age (Eaton and Velander, Unpublished) and as late as after 36 months (Seidenstecker et al. 1973). Two and one-half years probably is a common age when female lions reach sexual maturity (Rabb 1959, Robinette et al. 1961).

Estrus duration is 4–12 days, averaging about 8 (Eaton and Velander, Unpublished). The interval between one estrus cycle and the next averages 14.4 days when conception does not occur (Rabb 1959). Females are capable of having an estrus cycle immediately following the loss of a litter (Rabb 1959, Eaton and Velander, Unpublished), but may not do so for nearly a year. The gestation period is 90–96 days.

Litter sizes may range from 1–6 kittens (females have three pairs of mammae), but 2 and 3 kittens apparently are most common, with an average of about 2.6. The few data available indicate substantially more male than female kittens are born, perhaps 120–130 males per 100 females.

Mountain lions can have litters in any month of the year. Robinette et al. (1961) reported parturition in June in Utah and Nevada, but reasoned it could occur from July–September. Eaton and Velander, (Unpublished) reported peak periods in April and August at the Olympic Game Farm in Washington. Weaning was reported at four to five weeks (Young and Goldman 1946) and about eight weeks in California (Bruce 1922). In Idaho, Hornocker (1969) found a litter of three still with the female at age 22 months and another of two (1970) evidently cast off at slightly more than one year of age.

A female can rear only four successful litters if she lives to be about 10 years old. Eaton and Velander, (Unpublished) reported a captive female bearing a litter at 12 years of age.

Mortality

There seems to be three periods during its life cycle when the mountain lion is most vulnerable to starvation. First, some postnatal mortality or retarded growth undoubtedly occur as a result of intralitter competition for nursing. The second period is during the weeks following independence when young lions have not yet become proficient in stalking and killing prey, and especially when there is a simultaneous absence of small mammals (Hornocker 1970). The third period occurs when lions reach advanced age. Badly worn teeth and arthritis can severely impair their abilities to take large prey (Hornocker 1970).

Accidental deaths occasionally occur when lions collide with natural obstacles while chasing prey or clinging to a fleeing victim. Death also may result from injuries inflicted directly by a lion's intended victim. Motor vehicles kill some mountain lions each year, and that inevitably will increase as more roads are built, more vehicles are in operation and lion numbers increase. Drownings (Macgregor 1974, Sitton and Wallen 1976) and deaths attributed to falls (Hornocker 1970) also have been reported.

Adult male lions will kill young males, and may at times kill other adult males (Sitton and Wallen 1976) or kittens (Hornocker 1970). These occurrences may arise from aggression, fear, hunger or self-defense. Other less common forms of natural mortality undoubtedly occur (such as lightning, avalanches, rockslides, poisoning by venomous reptiles, postpartum complications, choking and predation by birds of prey, bears and perhaps even wolves) and in aggregate, may have significant influence on a population size or structure. It is likely that deaths of nearly grown and older lions caused by man are the greatest single cause

of mortality in most lion populations. There is evidence of 15–18 year lifespans in the wild, but 8–12 years is considered old for mountain lions (Young and Goldman 1946).

Diseases and parasites

Trichinella larvae are fairly common in mountain lions and have been reported in animals of all age groups except kittens (Greer 1974). Tapeworms (Hornocker 1970, Sitton and Wallen 1976), ticks and fleas (Sitton and Wallen 1976) and mites (McLean 1954) sometimes infest lions, with little or no effect on populations. No doubt other organisms, as yet unreported, also parasitize lions.

Rabies was found in at least one mountain lion (Storer 1923). But if rabies presently occurs with significant frequence, it is virtually undetected.

Bittle (1970) described feline panleukopenia as an acute viral disease occurring in mountain lions, but did not distinguish among its effects on captive and wild hosts. Symptoms include vomiting, diarrhea, severe dehydration and often blood in the feces. For lions with the disease, estimated mortality is 60–90 percent. If present in wild populations, this disorder could be a substantial source of undetected mortality.

Certain normal habits of mountain lions minimize the possibility that diseases or parasites will limit the size of any lion population. Those habits include: (1) using dens for only short periods, (2) not using bedding in dens, (3) avoiding spoiled meat, (4) seeking isolation except in breeding and rearing situations, (5) remaining almost continuously mobile, and (6) occurring only in low densities.

Behavior

A female mountain lion's estrus behavior includes vocalization and normally is accompanied by several days of consorting until the visiting male leaves or is driven away by the female. A female usually will seek concealment in a rocky depression, uprooted tree or dense thicket as the site to have her litter, but no bedding is prepared.

When her kittens become mobile, a female will return for them after making a kill and lead them to the victim to feed. Afterward, she will lead her young to a subsequent kill site.

In addition to physical attributes of strength and keen eyesight, a number of highly developed behavioral patterns contribute to lions' prowess as hunters. These patterns include: (1) proper selection of hunting sites, (2) skillful stalking ability, (3) selection of a target (prey) individual, and (4) ability to disable or kill victims immediately. Mountain lions hunt (not necessarily remote from human habitation) during daylight as well as at night. The patterns of hunting behavior, therefore, are vitally necessary, particularly in habitat where opportunities for concealment by terrain and vegetation are minimal.

When hunting, lions stalk prey to within a distance of 15 meters (50 feet). The intended victim then is rushed and sometimes knocked down. Observers report the large victims are killed by a bite on the back of the neck or throat. Disemboweling as a kill method was reported by Bruce (1922), but questioned by Robinette et al. (1959).

Mountain lions kill and eat almost every kind of animal available, but selection by individual lions depends on experience, such as a dead specimen provided when the lion was young (Bogue and Ferrari 1974). Adult male deer are taken by lions in greater proportion than they occur in their populations. This may be because the preferred winter habitat of adult bucks, to a greater extent

Some lions kill porcupines by slipping a paw underneath the animal then flipping it in the air, disemboweling it in the process. Other mountain lions do not have that proficiency, as illustrated by this immobilized young lion with numerous porcupine quills embedded in its scalp. Photo by S. L. Sheriff; courtesy of the Colorado Cooperative Wildlife Research Unit.

than deer of other sex and age classes, closely coincides with that of mountain lions. The other, smaller deer are more abundant, however, and no doubt are taken in greater total numbers.

The frequency of kills by mountain lions varies considerably among individuals. It evidently depends on the individual lion's hunting skill, disposition, sex, presence of kittens, availability and type of prey, season of year and, correspondingly, the rate at which meat spoils. Some lions make kills on nearly a daily basis during certain periods of the year, and others occasionally make multiple kills (especially of domestic sheep) during a single night. Rapid spoilage of meat during hot weather is believed to be one possible reason for increased kill frequencies, as lions generally refuse to eat tainted meat. Estimates of lion-kill frequencies over a one-year period are as much as one deer per week to as few as one deer every three to four weeks, with interim feeding on smaller animals assumed (Robinette et al. 1959, Hornocker 1970, Shaw 1977).

A mountain lion usually will drag or carry its quarry to a hiding place before or after feeding on it. Robinette et al. (1959) measured 15 such distances of 4.9–335 meters (16–1,000 feet), and averaged 93 meters (305 feet). The lion usually first eats the liver, heart and lungs through an opening in the ribs. Intestines and the stomach frequently are removed and eaten only when the lion is extremely hungry. If a lion is hungry enough, its prey may be entirely consumed in a single feeding. Robinette et al. (1959) found lion stomach contents to weigh as much as 4.34 kilograms (9.56 pounds). Unless it eats all the edible portions of its prey, the lion likely will make some effort to cover the remainder of the carcass with debris. Then, after resting nearby for one or two days, the lion will return to feed. If meat is still available and unspoiled after the lion has eaten its fill for the second time, the carcass may be moved and covered again. Disembowelment of a prey and covering of the carcass may delay spoilage and serve to keep flies and carrion-

eating birds from reaching the meat. Although it is the exception, feeding lions have been observed to become aggressive toward humans.

Only one reference to lions' drinking habits (Young and Goldman 1946) was found in the literature. However, this does not infer that lions do not necessarily need fresh water, for they undoubtedly do. This need presumably is met by deliberate efforts to seek out and return to water sources.

On mountain lions' sleeping behavior, Dewar reported "they sought cover such as under a rock or in a hollow tree. . . . We observed a female that had found cover to sleep in, but the kittens slept out in the snow, under no cover at all" (Christensen and Fischer 1976). The apparent preference for snow may be a consequence of the fact that the body heat-retention benefits it affords are greater than those of the alternative, circulating air.

Mountain lions are solitary, with exceptions of: (1) brief periods of courtship, (2) fights among males to establish territorial rights or access to females in estrus, (3) females with dependent young, and (4) siblings for as long as two or three months after separation from the mother. Occurrence of lions in close proximity (within a few hundred meters) to other lions has been ascertained through telemetry studies. No social reason for a lion to tolerate the presence of another has been discovered, however. The fundamental behavior pattern is one of avoidance. Fighting among males, to the extent that mortalities result, has been observed in some lion populations but not in others. Hornocker (1969) interpreted the significance of avoidance behavior as follows: "Territoriality appears to be extremely important in regulating numbers of mountain lions in the Idaho Primitive Area. . . . A solitary predator must depend on its physical well-being to survive. . . . The mutual avoidance mechanism appears to have evolved as a much more economical means of spacing solitary individuals."

Communication between mountain lions occurs through smell, sound and sight. Hornocker (1969) found that: "The same areas were used by different individuals but never at the same time—lions were spaced in time as well as area. Scrape or scratch marks appear important in this spacing. Lions urinate and frequently defecate on top of these marks; a visual as well as olfactory mark is made. All lions, but particularly the males, make these marks in trails, or high ridges, and at crossings; some permanent stations occur in each territory." Scrapes made by a lion may vary in size depending on the type of substrate, and are spaced erratically from only one meter to several kilometers apart. It seems possible that this indirect means of identifying territories may have arisen as a consequence of evolved avoidance-behavior patterns.

Bogue and Ferrari (1974) stated that lions have a wide vocal range of cheeps, chirps, peeps and whistles, and that the researchers were able to induce consistent responses by imitating hunting and fear chirps. They also reported that, "Threat consists of the ears being halfway down against the head. Impending attack is signalled with the ears flat against the head, usually accompanied by a growl or hiss or both. If the ears indicate attack, a glance at the hindquarters is helpful: when the feet are suddenly moved directly under the body, an attack is imminent. Pleasure is signified with the ears peaked straight up and parallel to each other; confusion and/or frustration, by the ears wandering about in all directions and usually in conjunction with rapidly changing facial expression." In one instance, Sitton and Wallen (1976) also were able to induce vocal responses from lions for more than an hour using tape-recorded calls.

Tagged and collared, an adult male mountain lion is about to be released to await recovery from an immobilizing dose of phencyclidine hydrochloride (Sernylan). Even in a stuporous condition, the animal's ears are drawn back in a "threat" position. Photo by Steve Gallizioli; courtesy of the Arizona Game and Fish Department.

Lions sometimes travel distances of 32.2–40.2 kilometers (20–25 miles) in a single day, probably between kills. The route may cross itself at irregular intervals or may be circular. When traversing a plain or valley, a lion usually will follow a water course because of concealment provided by bank vegetation. A route may be used repeatedly, but irregularly, and may not be used for intervals of several months. Traveling is done during both night and day, and on occasion, may involve swimming across rivers or deliberate circumventing of snow patches. Instances of lions idly or curiously following humans are not uncommon.

Mountain lions may climb trees to obtain food that is in trees and to escape pursuing dogs. Sometimes they will swim when pursued, but their coats do not resist moisture, so lions usually avoid swimming.

Natural competitors

Grizzly bears and wolverines are likely competitors with mountain lions (Young and Goldman 1946) in the few locations where they coexist. Bobcats and coyotes seem to be more frequent competitors for small mammals and sometimes deer, and mountain lions are known to eat both bobcats (Robinnette et al. 1959) and coyotes (Christensen and Fischer 1976). Other animals undoubtedly feed on kills made by mountain lions whenever the opportunity arises and are not inhibited by the proximity of the lion. Feeding activity by coyotes, bobcats and bears around lion kills is not uncommon. Spoiled or abandoned carcasses may be utilized by scavengers, especially black bears.

A treed mountain lion. Photo by author.

Density and abundance

After canvassing 30 states and 10 provinces, Cahalane (1964) stated that, "No informant suggested cougars are increasing in numbers anywhere in the United States with the possible exception of Florida." After a similar survey, Nowak (1976) reported, "Although exploitation may be excessive in some local areas, many biologists and field personnel with first hand knowledge of the species suggest that within the last few years there have been moderate numerical increases in most western states." He estimated the total population of mountain lions in the United States and Canada to be 16,000. During the 12-year interim between surveys, a change in public attitude toward mountain lions resulted in a widespread shift away from uses of bounties, government hunting and other eradication pro-grams. The shift was toward legal classification of the mountain lion as a game animal with attendant restrictions on the manner and conditions of taking them.

Following the pioneer work by Hornocker and his associates in Idaho, several intensive mark and reobservation studies permitted a number of population density estimates that produced a higher degree of confidence than was previously justified. Most of these studies employed radio telemetry techniques. Densities were found to be as high as one lion per 25.9 square kilometers (10 square miles) to one per 259 square kilometers (100 square miles), and are summarized in Table 25. It is assumed that relatively high density populations were selected for study in most instances.

Hornocker (1969) and Seidenstecker et al. (1973) established that there is an upper, finite density limit for mountain lions at any given location and time. They provided

Mountain lion (upper left) bayed by hounds in typical, rugged terrain of Arizona, and about to be shot with tranquilizer gun. Photo courtesy of the Arizona Game and Fish Department.

Table 25. Estimates of mountain lion populations in certain areas of North America.[a]

Location	Study area size		Population estimate[b]	Average area per lion		Source
	Square kilometers	Square miles		Square kilometers	Square miles	
California	450	174	18	26	10.0	Sitton and Wallen 1976
Arizona	550	212	20	29	11.2	Shaw 1977
Idaho	520	201	14.6	36	13.9	Hornocker 1970
Colorado	1950	753	50	43	16.6	Currier 1976
Colorado	900	347	20	48	18.5	Currier 1976
Vancouver Island, British Columbia	518	200	8	65	25.1	Christensen and Fischer 1976
Nevada	390	151	7.5	52	20.1	Ashman 1975
Nevada	1800	695	11	165	63.7	
Nevada	1675	647	7	261	100.8	

[a]Modified from Currier (1976).
[b]Midpoint of the population estimate range shown in Currier (1976).

valuable insight into the factors that determine that limit. The following paragraph is a condensation of what they learned and what appear to be the fundamentals of mountain lion population regulation, in accord with the information available at the time. The conclusions from their studies

An identifying number is tattooed on the inside of an ear of an immobilized mountain lion. Photo by E. G. Currier; courtesy of the Colorado Cooperative Wildlife Research Unit.

may or may not hold true under other conditions or at other locations (for example, resident male ranges have been shown to overlap, and adult-sized males have been known to socialize elsewhere).

Mountain lion numbers were determined by factors other than food supply and lion predation was not controlling ultimate numbers of the prey animals. The amount of space a resident lion uses (requires) is a function of a vegetation-topography/prey-numbers-vulnerability complex. The resident males will not occupy the same range, but the ranges of females may overlap with those of males and other females. The primary factor limiting the density of resident males is the presence of adult resident males, and the presence of resident breeding females is what limits the female breeding population. When a male dies, its replacement in the population is also male. When a female dies, its replacement in the population is another female, although females may not be replaced as quickly as males. If a population is stable and no opportunity exists to occupy a vacated home area, delayed social maturation—which depends on site attachment—can occur and result in suppressed reproduction among lions that have reached reproductive maturity. Litter size among breeding females does not increase in response to deaths of proximate breeding females, indicating litters are as large, even in maximum density populations, as the availability and vulnerability of the principal food resource will support. Lion densities actually may increase, at least in the short run, as a result of killing territorial individuals. This may occur as a consequence of disruptions of the social stability of the local population, and result in a net increase in the number of reproductively active females, provided transients are available from adjacent populations (Hornocker 1976).

Breeding population density of a given unit of area apparently is fixed, presumably in accordance with (1) genetically dictated tolerances for interaction and space between individuals, and (2) existing environmental conditions. This density could not be exceeded permanently unless environmental conditions (cover, food and water) change in favor of lions. If the density dropped below saturation level, it would be so only until transients established residency and successfully reproduced. The amount of time required to do that would depend on the frequency with which transients traversed the area, and the frequency with which transients were killed by people.

MANAGEMENT

Managing a mountain lion population requires monetary resources and considerable time, energy and expertise. Identifying the desirable end result, in quantitative terms, is the most difficult of lion management tasks. It also is the first and most important task in order to insure that all resources and time are utilized in a manner that produces maximum and viable results.

Mountain lion management can be considered systematically, involving and defining six levels of organization from broadest to most specific:

1. Program. Only one or a combination of two or more species usually receive primary attention in a program. Mountain lions, as a single species, must be the focus in the program, but with the under-

standing that any program intended to affect lion populations also can influence other species, and vice versa.

2. Goals. The direction(s) of a program's efforts must be determined. They should not preclude the alternative of doing nothing. Priorities should be established among goals, and they may be quantified in broad terms.

3. Objectives. Within each goal, identify products or outputs and establish quantitative constraints on how many units of each product are to be produced (a measure of the resource yield), in what time frame and in what location. Concise objectives are the most critical feature of the entire program in that they determine which strategies and tactics are appropriate and relative to manpower and other resource needs. They also provide criteria by which a program can be evaluated. Priorities should be established among all program objectives.

4. Problems. Difficulties or obstacles that prevent objectives from being met must be identified. This is a key step that cues orientation of both management and research efforts.

5. Strategies. Identify how objectives are to be met. Strategies lead to selection of solutions and should be directed only at solving identified problems.

6. Tactics. Identify within each strategy what action will be taken to meet the objective(s). Tactics include all measures and actual wildlife management activities that may be undertaken to reach the objectives.

Manpower and other resources rarely, if ever, are available to satisfy all desired program objectives or to employ all beneficial tactics. Available resources, priorities among goals and program objectives determine which tactics must be used, and serve to guide decisions about which of the beneficial tactics must be sacrificed.

This systematic approach is illustrated in the mountain lion management option chart (Figure 44). Fundamental to its success is

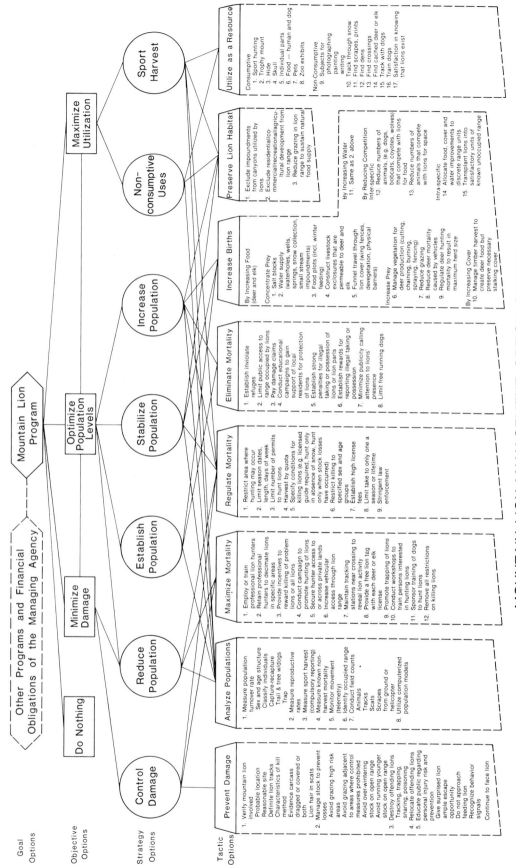

Figure 44. Mountain lion management chart.

the formal adoption of a specific set of goals and objectives at policy and executive levels of the management agency. Each level includes a finite set of choices, each offering a "go" or "no go" decision option, and progresses from the top level downward. A basic question that must be answered initially is: how many mountain lions are enough? The answer, along with whatever pertinent information is available, will provide an operational foundation for the entire management program.

Ideally, the management option chart includes a universal set of management options and activities that pertain to mountain lion management. Certainly some options have been omitted from this chart, and some of the tactics included would be practical only under very unusual circumstances or not under any conditions. Some are socially undesirable or even prohibited by law in some locations, and none should be construed as recommendations. The overriding objective of the management option chart is to show all possible alternatives.

Goals

The goal or goals of any mountain lion management program should be comprehensive because both negative and positive effects accrue from manipulation of lion populations. Major goal-related considerations about mountain lion management programs were expressed by a wildlife conservation officer: "While preservation and extermination advocates loudly voice their opinions, the Division of Wildlife recognizes that its management of all wildlife species, predator and prey alike, must be carried out in a manner that is consistent with maximum public benefit and minimum detriment, and at the same time compatible with the conservation of the species involved" (Lewis 1976).

Objectives

The mountain lion resource yield can be expressed in terms of: (1) number of damage complaints—a negative product; (2) number of lions harvested; (3) number of hunting days; (4) number of nonconsumptive recreation days; and (5) number of lions—the population size. When yield is quantified and referenced to a time period and a specific geographic area, a statement of attainable objective(s) can be formulated. Examples are:

1. Limit mountain lion damage complaints in the state to no more than 20 in 1979;
2. Provide at least 2,000 mountain lion hunting recreation days in the southern half of the state in 1980;
3. Harvest at least 25 lions in Management Unit 4 each year between 1978–1982; and,
4. Increase the lion population from 10 to 35 by 1984 in the Cougar Wilderness Area.

Results are measurable, and no additional resources need be allocated for management activities in areas where objectives already are being met. Each objective can be met through one or more strategies, usually employing a combination of tactics.

Strategies and tactics

Each strategy includes its own, and for the most part, exclusive set of tactics, and is referenced to one or more objectives. Important strategies and tactics for mountain lion management include:

1. Preventing damage. Lion damage management (preventing the killing of domestic animals) often is oriented toward individual cases rather than the more conventional approach of managing whole wildlife populations. Usually, some damage is experienced before steps are taken to prevent further damage. Damage prevention activities historically have been predicated on the assumption that livestock predation in a particular instance and place is caused by one lion that has deviated from the

normal habit of subsisting on wild animals. Hence, killing that individual was considered the reasonable solution. However, studies in Arizona using radio telemetry revealed that essentially all lions of an observed population apparently were taking livestock (Shaw 1977). To what extent that phenomenon occurs in other lion populations is uncertain.

When it has been confirmed that a particular lion is causing damage, quick remedial action is necessary. Of all the procedures employed for removing an offending lion (including federal, state or professional hunter, landowner self-help, trapping, etc.), the one used in Colorado seems to offer the most satisfactory results. When a complaint is made, Division of Wildlife officials select a hunter from a list maintained for out-of-season lion hunts. The hunter, in turn, contacts a professional guide (Sandfort and Tully 1971). Results are quick and effective, at

no cost to the landowner or the state. The hunter gets his quarry and the guide receives a fee from the hunter. This method has not been equally successful in all states where tried, however.

Although mountain lion predation has little impact on the entire livestock industry, ranchers in some areas can suffer considerable losses. Complaints about lions in the West usually are fewer than 10 or 15 per state per year. On the other hand, livestock losses to lions on two ranches under study in Arizona ranged from 21–97 head of cattle annually (Shaw 1977). Relocation of offending lions does not seem to be a viable solution because of the high cost and mobility of lions after release, the tendency of some to continue killing livestock after translocation, and difficulty in finding sites where the release of lions is politically acceptable.

Lion attacks on humans are infrequent but increasing, and inevitably will continue if more people establish homes and

The carcass of a steer killed and partly eaten by a mountain lion. As is typical, certain preferred organs were eaten through a hole in the side before the carcass was covered with litter and left until a later feeding. Photo by S. L. Sheriff; courtesy of the Colorado Cooperative Wildlife Research Unit.

take up recreation in mountain lion ranges, and if lion numbers increase. From 1917–1967, there were 14 reported attacks on humans in British Columbia (Christensen and Fischer 1976). During the next five years, there were 12 attacks, and 4 in a three-month period after that. Most attacks were made by juvenile female lions. The frequency of reported mountain lion incidents is substantially greater in British Columbia than elsewhere. This situation could be a consequence of changes in occurrence or behavior of people, lions or both in that province.

After an informal canvass of western states and provinces in 1977, L. Sanders (personal communication) learned that some lions that had attacked humans were found to be in poor physical condition. Others were females with kittens, and still others were young lions that evidently were on their own but not proficient enough in securing food to adhere to conventional habits. In some instances, no reason for an attack on a human was apparent. Children were involved in 13 of 39 such incidents.

Avoiding areas where lions occur certainly would prevent attacks. Making sufficient noise to warn lions of human presence and being accompanied by one or more dogs probably would deter attack.

If a confrontation should occur, watching the lion but avoiding direct eye contact could prevent an attack (G. Bogue, personal communication). Also, trying to maintain as neutral a manner as possible could help. This would involve refraining from any aggressive movements, as well as not turning and running away. Giving the lion sufficient time and room to escape is important. Loud noises, such as those made with a whistle or a pocket-sized compressed air horn, might serve as deterrents.

If an attack does occur, attempting to disorient the animal by screaming and waving one's arms might help, then covering the head and neck to protect them could prevent fatal injuries. It has been said that there is no more than one chance in 100,000 of a mountain lion attacking a human. Lions, however, cannot count.

2. Analyzing populations. Mountain lion population analyses are extremely complex because only a few lions permanently occupy home ranges that may cover several hundred square kilometers. Further complicating population analyses are the facts that lions are very mobile, are secretive in their behavior and produce litters only in alternate years but during any month. In addition, there are limited data available from samples of dead or (especially) living lions. Consequently, securing information that accurately reflects population characteristics through field surveys is difficult and time-consuming.

The alternative to repeated field counts is to compute sex, age and reproductive data on the basis of population-turnover rates. Computer models that calculate turnover rates and simulate population responses to any combinations of birth and death rates frequently offer the most practical means for evaluating potential effects of harvests or other management efforts. Lack of a dependable method for estimating ages of lions is a major limitation on population analyses, but efforts to find a reliable method are underway in several locations.

3. Maximizing mortality. In the past, bounty payments, federal and state lion hunters, and absence of restrictions on when and how lions can be killed have contributed to maximizing lion mortality. Collectively, these methods were effective in suppressing lion populations in many areas. It is doubtful that they will be employed again, but there exists a possibility if lion numbers radically increase in a particular area.

4. Regulating mortality. All available evidence indicates a population of lions that inhabit a large area can be manipulated by regulating the number killed, prin-

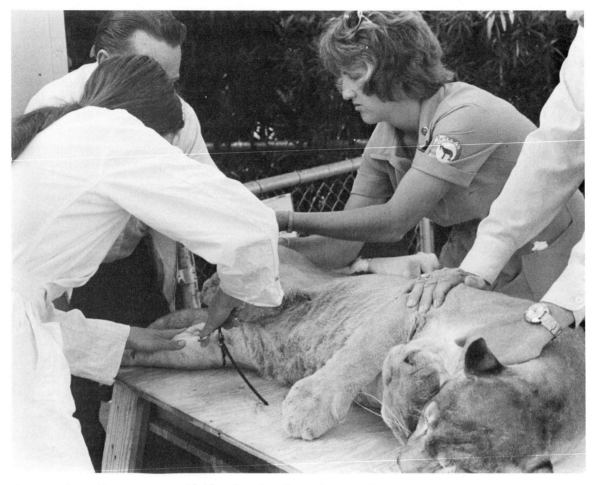

A captive lion of known age provides baseline data for evaluation of an aging technique. Photo by author.

cipally through recreational hunting, damage control or both. Further, Hornocker concluded that a local population can recover in a short time from moderate mortality losses if there are transients in the vicinity (Christensen and Fischer 1976). A thriving lion population possibly could be assured through a management system of checkerboard-like open and closed recreational hunting areas, or a multiyear open-closed area rotation or both. At present, however, neither recreational harvests nor damage control kills exceed or even equal the annual production of mountain lions in the western United States as a whole. However, in some local areas, yearly lion removals may exceed annual recruitment.

The fact that lion populations are stable or slightly increasing does not necessarily warrant liberalization of harvest restrictions. Rationale developed by Poelker (1974) in support of an April-through-July closure of lion hunting seasons in Washington warrants repeating. "Few pumas were taken during the April to July closure period in the past, thus, closing the season does not have a significant impact on the total harvest. Why close it then? Firstly, if an animal, in this case the puma, is to be given some intrinsic or esthetic value in the total scope of game management, a closed season is the first alternative available. By providing a time when the puma is not a hunted animal, but one protected from hunting by law, a value is placed on it that can be recognized by both the hunting and nonhunting public. The nonhunting public does have a right to its own assignment of values to game animals and a right to have the value recognized in existing management programs. Secondly, while the puma may have kittens at most any time of the year, the existing closure provides protection to the mother and her kittens during the period most commonly associated with the early rearing of her young."

5. Eliminating harvest mortality. Whenever a lion population is composed of only a few individuals and the management objective is to increase the population's size, the most effective strategy probably would be to eliminate harvest mortality. Such a situation could arise when effort is being made to extend the range of a healthy population or to reintroduce lions to former ranges. Total harvest restriction also may be employed to protect a low-density but stable population in marginal or poor habitat.

6. Providing for increased natality. This objective probably would be warranted only under extreme conditions, such as where it was ascertained that inadequate food supply was jeopardizing the existence of a lion population, and where the political-social climate strongly supported recovery of that population. Even if the probability was high for increasing births or survival of young, a tenuous assumption at best, this strategy likely would be discounted in favor of less expensive options (such as eliminating mortality and deer harvest).

7. Maintaining lion habitat. Not much lion habitat can be termed "critical" because of lions' adaptability and wide distribution. Continuous encroachment of man into habitat that supports the mountain lion and many of its prey species gradually reduces viable opportunities for enhancing lion populations.

Land-use planning that accounts for wildlife as well as human spacial needs, and corresponding mitigation policies may be the only practical means of arresting the rate at which mountain lion habitat is being lost.

8. Utilizing the resource. A number of western states report annual harvests of 100 or more lions. Mountain lions provide recreational and sometimes economic benefits to the hunters who pursue them. Of significance to a greater number of people are nonconsumptive values of the lion resource, including economic, recreational, ecological and educational values. The change of mountain lions' status in recent years from unprotected varmint to managed big game is testimony to growing public awareness of the animals' numerous values.

THE FUTURE

Mountain lion populations currently are secure in North America. Whether lion populations should be reestablished or fortified in uninhabited, viable areas can be decided only by increased public understanding of the importance of the lion resource and by adoption of responsible land-management policies. Total protection of lion populations east of the Rocky Mountain states may be warranted, except to remove verified troublesome individuals. Mountain lion populations are responsive to harvests and can be consistent with local, state or province wildlife management objectives. The future of mountain lions hinges on habitat maintenance, additional facts from research, whatever additional management investments the research and public policy dictate, and public appreciation for their invaluable ecological roles.

Chapter 15

BLACK, BROWN (GRIZZLY), AND POLAR BEARS

Charles Jonkel

Professor of Research
School of Forestry
University of Montana
Missoula, Montana

Bears are large, wide-ranging animals with low reproductive rates and low population densities. They are highly evolved, intelligent animals with both genetic and "culturally inherited" or learned abilities to utilize the resources in their environments, adapt to new ranges, or cope with environmental changes. Their ways of surviving, locating foods and other needs, and reacting to the activities of man have evolved differently among and within the various species in different habitats. This gives the family remarkable capabilities to cope with habitat changes brought about by man. This is generally more true of omnivorous bears such as American black bear (*Ursus americanus* Pallas) and Asian black bears (*Selenarctos thibetanus* Cuvier), and less true of the highly carnivorous polar bear (*U. maritimus* Phipps), the mostly herbivorous giant panda *(Ailuropoda melanoleuca),* and the spectacled bear (*Tremarctos ornatus* Cuvier).

In prehistoric times, man and bears apparently competed for food resources but were not important prey of one another. During historic times in North America, bear populations were systemically eradicated in many areas. Because of their domi-

nance in the hierarchy of wildlife, physical stature, and generally omnivorous food habits, bears competed with the settlers of this continent for space as well as for food. And because of their unpredictable nature, bears posed real and imagined threats to the settlers. To counter such threats and potential conflicts, settlers and their descendants for many generations wantonly killed bears by shooting, trapping, and poisoning.

Today, with improved public understanding only within the past few decades, most bear populations have been accorded the statuses of big game or threatened species, and are managed as such. Bear hunts, for the most part, are associated with regulated recreational hunting of trophy individuals. Widely publicized attacks of bears on humans demonstrate that bears need all the respect, attention, and most of all, space that management of truly wild animals can provide. It would be in error, however, to omit reporting the fact that bears are not, and perhaps never have been, as aggressive toward man as is commonly believed.

Also, in the mythology of people in the northern hemisphere, bears have long been held in high esteem. This status was born, perhaps, out of the mutually competitive relationship of men and bears. In many areas, the age-old status of bears in mythology still prevails, and evokes forces and unusual considerations in management of the species.

TAXONOMY AND DISTRIBUTION

Even among individuals of the same subspecies, bears commonly have widely variant skeletal characteristics, a circumstance which has led to considerable taxonomic confusion in the past.

With regard to brown or "grizzly" bears in North America, Rausch (1963) determined that only *U. arctos horribilis,* which range over a large portion of the continent, and *U. a. middendorffi,* which exist only on Kodiak, Afognak, and Shuyak islands, have certain subspecific status (Figure 45). Earlier,

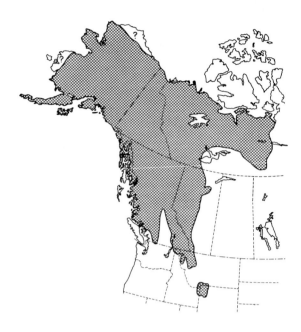

Figure 45. Grizzly bear range in North America.

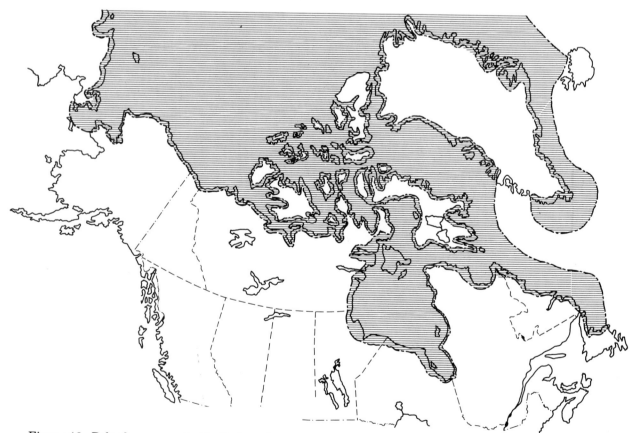

Figure 46. Polar bear range in North America.

Figure 47. Black bear range in North America.

Rausch and others held that three other North American subspecies were valid, including *U. a. gyas* Merriam, *U. a. richardsoni* Swainson and *U. a. californicus* Merriam (Rausch 1953, Storer and Tevis 1955, Banfield 1958, Murie 1959, Cowan and Guiguet 1960).

The polar bear recently has been reclassified as *U. maritimus,* dropping the generic name *Thalarctos.* Despite their

white coats and generally more water-adapted body forms, polar bears have serological (blood serum) and chromosomal similarities to brown bears. Also, recent records of fertile offspring from brown-polar bear crosses in several zoos indicate that the two species are related closely. Manning (1971) concluded that, for the present, the "extant circumpolar race therefore stands as *U. m. maritimus.*" He added that evidence is strong for an unnamed subspecies in the Bering Strait-Chukchi Sea area, and if it is so named, then another subspecies in the area from East Greenland to the northern Alaskan coast is implied (Figure 46).

The type locality for the American black bear includes all of central North America, extending from the arctic coast at the mouth of the Mackenzie River, southward to northern Mexico (Figure 47). Banfield (1974a) listed 10 subspecies in Canada alone, and Hall and Kelson (1959) suggested 18 viable subspecies for the entire continent. Both of these taxonomic treatments probably are too liberal, but there can be no doubt from color phases alone that several gene pools are involved. The greatest variability occurs along the Pacific coast and inland, with 8–10 subspecies identified by most authors. This region includes color variations ranging from pure black to pure white. The pure white coloration is unique to the Kermodes black bear of the central British Columbia coast. In between is the bluish glacier bear of the Northwest coast, and reddish-brown to blond color phases which are found from northern California inland through eastern Washington, Idaho, Montana, Alberta, and into Saskatchewan.

ECOLOGY

Reproduction

All three bear species breed in spring. The polar bear breeding season starts in April and continues through May. Black and grizzly bear breeding is concentrated during May and June, with a peak in early June. There is, of course, variation among individuals of the three species. All species have delayed implantation—a six to seven month arrest in growth of the blastocysts. Implantation apparently occurs about the time pregnant females enter or build maternity dens in late October through November, perhaps triggered by shortened periods of daylight.

Young bears are born from late November through February. Polar bear young usually are born earlier than black and brown bear cubs. Black bear young usually are born in January or February.

All bears are very small when born. Grizzly cubs weigh about 400 grams (14 ounces) or less, polar bear cubs about 680 grams (24 ounces) and black bear cubs 225–280 grams (8–10 ounces). Except for polar bear young, cubs have little insulating fur when born. Young of all bears require a great amount of care from their mothers.

Family groups are closely associated during the cubs' first year. Black and grizzly bear cubs den with their mothers the following winter, while polar bear young hunt with their mothers on the pack ice during winter, denning only during severe storms. Family groups of black bears commonly break up when young reach about 1.5 years of age, but some black bear families and most grizzly and polar bear families persist for 2.5 years or longer. The survival rate of young is high during the time spent with their mothers (Figure 48), essentially equaling that of adult females. This apparently is not true where bear populations are crowded

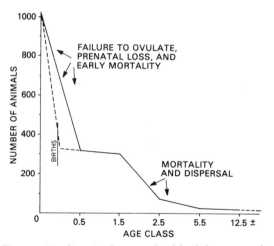

Figure 48. Survival curve for black bears on the Big Creek, Montana study area based on estimated and measured mortality (after Jonkel and Cowan 1971). Loss before birth is based on a potential of 50 percent pregnancy rate for adult females. An unknown level of dispersal is included in the 1.5–2.5 age classes. The broken line may be a more realistic representative of the true curve for birth to 0.5 years.

(Craighead et al. 1974). Lactation may occur for 18–20 months, but young usually are weaned from July through September of their first year. The bond of family groups apparently is broken finally when adult females come into estrus because of reduced family contact, and allow adult males to approach. Young bears—especially immature males—then must leave to avoid encounters with adult males.

Breakup of family units subjects subadults to precarious circumstances for a few years. The combination of youth (inexperience), relatively small size (high rates of heat loss and limited physical ability to secure food), growth (need to secure large quantities of food to accommodate increasing body size and to store energy), movement (dispersal to new and unfamiliar range), and large adult bears (competition and conflict) complicates survival of independent subadults. Therefore, it is among animals of this age group where the strongest population control occurs.

Another important consideration in bear biology is their generally low rate of reproduction in the wild, which apparently results from:

1. Genetically determined small litter sizes;
2. The two- to three-year intervals between litters, and extended family relationships;
3. The slow subadult growth rate and subsequent delay in reaching sexual maturity—up to five to seven years of age; and,
4. Climatic upsets (food shortages) and stress (high bear density or disturbances) which affect bear reproductive physiology.

Black bear reproductive potential may be slightly higher than that of polar and brown bears, probably because black bear family groups endure for shorter periods between litters. This advantage for black bears probably occurs because of the more productive ranges they inhabit and because, as a

A confrontation between male grizzly bear and female with cub. A Wildlife Management Institute photo.

species, they tend to congregate less and experience fewer population stresses. Black bear litters vary from 1.7–2.6 in various portions of their range. Litter sizes of brown bears average 2.24 in the Yellowstone area of Wyoming and Montana, and 1.7 in the Yukon (Stirling et al. 1976). Polar bear litters average 1.7–1.8, with a high of 2.4 reported on the Ontario coast (Jonkel et al. 1976).

Great variability in bear reproductive rates occurs under optimal and minimal conditions. In Pennsylvania, for example, black bears are three times more productive than brown bears of the Alaskan north slope. Cub sex ratios of 1:1 are common for all three bear species, but wide local variations have been noted.

The Craigheads (1971), in a study of the grizzlies congregated in Yellowstone National Park, determined that annual produc-

tivity per female was only 0.658, with maximum female productivity extending only to about 22 years of age. Given that annual productivity rate per female and the average life span of bears in that population, females produce an average of 6.6 cubs in their lifetimes (Craighead et al. 1974). These figures probably approximate guidelines for other bear populations and bear species, but are considered minimal by many persons because of artificial feeding stresses then operating on the Yellowstone population.

Mortality

Natural mortality in bear populations varies among age classes for all three species; subadults are the most vulnerable, especially after families break up. Cub

Black bear "sow" and two cubs in Allegheny National Forest, Pennsylvania. Photo by B. D. Nehr; courtesy of the U.S. Forest Service.

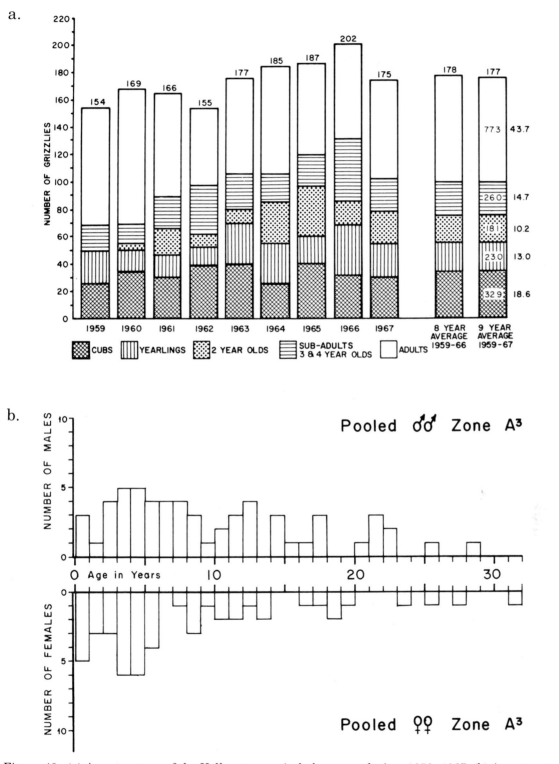

Figure 49. (a) Age structure of the Yellowstone grizzly bear population, 1959–1967. (b) Age structure of James Bay-Belcher Islands polar bears. Both figures show the predominance of young animals in the populations (after Craighead et al. 1974, Jonkel et al. 1976).

mortality is low. Jonkel and Cowan (1971) found that annual cub mortality in black bear populations was only 5 percent, and annual adult mortality was 14 percent. Average annual mortality for all age classes was found to be 17.7 percent. Kemp (1972) found a similar annual rate of adult mortality of 12.5 percent in Alberta. In the Yellowstone area, grizzly mortalities averaged 18.9 percent per year (Craighead et al. 1974). Polar bear adult mortality from all causes has been calculated at 18 percent per year (Stirling et al. 1975). In far northern regions, both polar and grizzly bear cub mortality apparently is high in certain years. Low nutritional levels (Figure 49) and the killing of young by adult males constitute the main mortality factors (Stirling et al. 1976). Hunting, of course, increases the population losses at various levels but cannot be considered natural mortality.

Age ratios

Age ratios of given bear populations favor the young-age classes (Figure 50). Black bear cubs and yearlings comprised 31 percent of the total population in Virginia, 46 percent in Michigan, and 11 percent in Montana (Jonkel and Cowan 1971). In the Montana studies, the percentage of subadults in the population varied considerably from year to year because of changes in

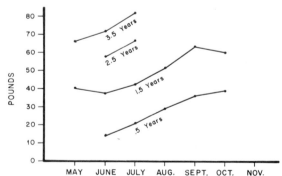

Figure 50. Seasonal levels in the average weights of known-age, subadult black bears in Big Creek, Montana, 1959–1965, illustrating the low levels of nutrition (after Jonkel and Cowan 1971).

recruitment, but the number of adults on the study area remained relatively constant. Also, the young-age classes of females are the most important segment of the population because they have the greatest potential for recruitment.

Behavior

Under natural conditions, brown bears are the most social of North American bears. They tend to congregate at food sources such as salmon streams, and often form family foraging groups with more than one age class of young. Black bears usually are solitary except for family groups, breeding pairs, and congregations in garbage dumps. Polar bears normally are spread widely over their range except for family groups and breeding pairs. Polar bears do congregate, however, at food sources in restricted feeding areas such as ice-bound fiords and floe edges, and in denning areas and areas of summer sanctuary when the sea ice melts. Social hierarchies develop within populations of all three species during periods of close association, but the social interactions apparently are highly developed only among brown bears (Figure 51).

For all three species, however, family behavioral relationships are highly evolved. The mothers are very strict disciplinarians who teach the young feeding habits, hunting techniques, locations of denning areas, orientation, and fear of man and other bears. Adult females have many sounds and movements used to communicate. At present, these sounds, movements, and warning signals as given during encounters with people are not fully understood.

If bears are territorial, the phenomenon exists primarily at important feeding sites, and probably is influenced by former and existing family relationships, long-term family and local relationships, or the degree of crowding in restricted areas, such as polar bears on small islands. Jonkel and Cowan (1971) described the tolerance of black bears familiar with one another, and the exclusion of invading bears.

Figure 51. (Top) Bear "confronting" an opponent off the picture to the left. Note lowered head and stiff position. (Bottom) Subordinate bear on left "facing away." Dominant bear on right showing "frontal" orientation (after Stonorov and Stokes 1972).

Daily movements of black and brown bears are influenced greatly by temperature. They move and feed primarily during the cool of evening and morning hours. Direct sunlight strongly deters both blacks and grizzlies from feeding in open areas, probably because of heat absorption more than lack of cover. Daily movements of polar bears during hunting are influenced greatly by seal activity and storms. In southern portions of their range, polar bears make concerted efforts to keep cool by entering water frequently, sliding along on snow, and in summer, by digging caves and pits in snow drifts and deep earth dens down to permafrost (Jonkel et al. 1976).

Seasonal movements are made primarily to food sources such as salmon streams, mast crops, areas of high berry production, or to spring ranges at low elevations. Polar bears move great distances to areas where ice floes persist into summer and they can continue to hunt seals, to areas of summer sanctuary (when the sea ice of Hudson Bay melts, they must go to isolated coasts or islands), to capes where the sea ice reforms earliest in the autumn, such as Cape Churchill, Manitoba, to denning areas, and when accidental drifting on ice floes extends any of their normal movements. Some polar bears in the High Arctic apparently move very little, but bears traveling with the drift ice of the Davis Strait and the Labrador Sea probably make normal winter-spring movements of 483–644 kilometers (300–400 miles).

Food habits

Although the diets of black and brown bears vary greatly in different habitat types and portions of their range, vegetation is the mainstay. Common horsetail, grasses, sedges, and the bulbs and aerial portions of glacier lily and spring beauty comprise the earliest spring foods (Figure 52). However, in some areas, clover and dandelion or other plants and carrion—particularly those of the Artiodactyla family—are very important. In late spring, succulent, perennial forbs such as cow-parsnip, angelica, and sweet cicely are especially important.

During summer and early autumn, berries become essential for blacks and grizzlies, and even some polar bears. Huckleberry, blueberry, soapberry, red oiser dogwood, and kinnikinick are some of the most noteworthy berry-producing plant foods. Succulent forbs used widely in spring diets include painted-cup, hawkweed, and others.

During early autumn, berries continue to be important, as do some of the succulent forbs. Bulbs and tubers also are important in early autumn, especially those of the glacier lily, spring beauty, yampa, and biscuit root. In the West, pine nuts are important to both black and grizzly bears. In mid- and eastern North America, oak and ash mast are very important to black bears. In late autumn, important foods are mountain ash at higher elevations, kinnikinick, the aforementioned bulbs, hunter-killed carrion of hoofed mammals, and stream algae at lower elevations such as flood plains. Fish during salmon runs and various plants and berries are locally important foods, more so in some years than in others. Bears are very opportunistic in their food habits and readily make use of any abundant foods.

Throughout their range, polar bears depend primarily on the ringed seal for food, but feed abundantly on invertebrates such as clams, vegetation (dock, blueberry, black crowberry, grasses, and marine algae), and waterfowl at times, especially in the southern portions of that bear's range (Russell 1975).

In all of their food habits, bears seek food items high in protein or sugars, and are able to extract protein from plant sources with almost the same efficiency as do herbivores (Mealey 1975, Best 1976). Brown and polar bears apparently are capable of consuming as much as 40 kilograms (90 pounds) per day, and all three bear species can gain weight at the rate of several pounds per day when nutritious food is in good supply. Polar bears often select only the high energy fat.

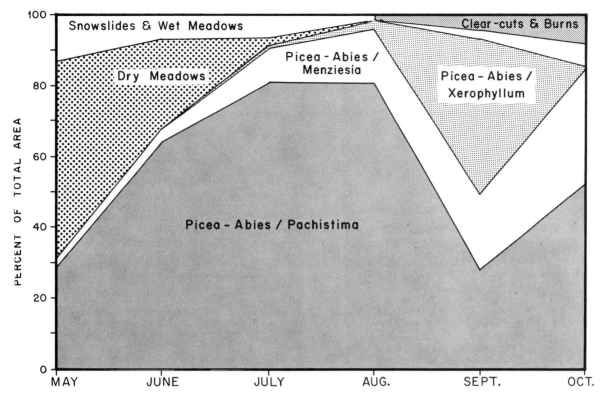

Figure 52. Dry meadows comprised only about 1 percent of the total area of Big Creek, Montana, but during May, 55 percent of the bear observations were made in this vegetative community (after Jonkel and Cowan 1971). The spruce-fir habitat type, on the other hand, comprised 40 percent of the drainage, but only 8 percent of the captures and observations were made in it.

Cover

Black bears seek and use dense cover, and apparently utilize trees to escape from grizzly bears and larger black bears. Rugged terrain and dense shrubs provide excellent escape cover and bedding sites for black and brown bears. Even polar bears will utilize shrubs and trees for cover, although they normally escape into the sea or onto rough ice. Travel corridors of cover along streams or across inhabited valleys are important for black and grizzly bear dispersal and movement to food sources.

Denning

Black bears commonly make dens under windfalls, in hollow trees or caves, and in previously occupied dens. The brown bear

A brown bear den in natural cave on Unimak Island, Alaska. A U.S. Bureau of Biological Survey photo; courtesy of the National Archives.

usually digs a den at the base of a large tree, often on a densely vegetated north-facing slope. In the Yellowstone area, dens usually occur above 2,133 meters (7,000 feet). In the Yukon and other areas, brown bears are less selective. Polar bears seek the lee side of icebergs, "old year" (thicker) ice, steep hillside slopes where snowdrifts persist through summer, or the lee side of lake and stream banks where deep snow drifts accumulate (Figure 53).

Space

Areas of summer sanctuary are the most pressing need of polar bears, especially in southern portions of their range and where human developments are taking place in the Arctic. Wherever they are hunted, polar bears fear man and seek isolated capes, coasts, and islands. Human invasion and developments, as well as increased conflict among highly concentrated bear populations, undoubtedly are limiting factors in some areas. In general, however, space needed by bears is related to food types, availability, and abundance. Where many kinds of foods are available, bears can live on relatively small home ranges. Home ranges for black bears can be as small as 2.6 square kilometers (1 square mile), and for brown bears, as small as 26 square kilometers (10 square miles). In relatively dry, open areas, such as the Yellowstone area, brown bear home ranges may be as large as 437 square kilometers (168 square miles).

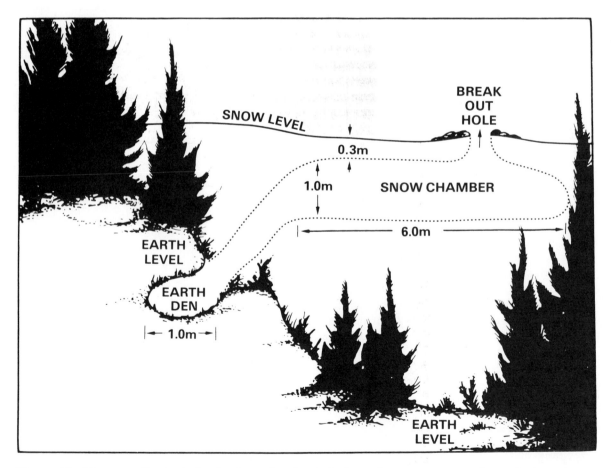

Figure 53. Diagram of a typical polar bear den located where deep snow accumulates during winter (after Jonkel et al. 1972).

MANAGEMENT

The management of bears as a means to maintain each species and delineated populations is desirable, but difficult. Long-term data are vital to proper management of most bear populations. However, little information is available because extensive and intensive studies were not possible until the invention of dart guns and quick-acting, wide-tolerance drugs made the capture of large numbers of live bears possible. Also, because bear populations are influenced by the economics of other resources, such as timber and grazing lands, more than biological considerations must be assessed and used in making bear management decisions. In fact, the value of other natural resources and abundant populations of less-threatening big game species placed bears in low regard until the past few decades. In many areas, bears were considered neither desirable nor game species. Conflicts between

Biologist prepares to shoot an immobilizing drug from a dart gun at a black bear. Photo by Lee Perry; courtesy of the Maine Department of Inland Fisheries and Wildlife, Wildlife Division.

bears and people did not improve the situation. Aside from lost space for ranching or farming where bears were abundant, conflicts often resulted in bears threatening, injuring, and sometimes killing people or damaging property. Both the cultural relationship of man to bear and people-bear conflicts have introduced emotional considerations in the already complex ecological aspects of bear management. Conflict among bears and people has given rise to (1) public misconceptions of bear behavior, (2) political interference in management, and (3) widely variant views on the need for and methods of bear population maintenance.

Bears are disliked and feared by many people. The poorly understood behavior of bears triggers some of these attitudes. But, it must be made clear that all three bear species are adaptable and, as noted earlier, easily acquire unnatural behavioral traits when associated with artificial stresses. The various behavioral responses of bears to people have been studied incidently by Herrero (1970), but most studies have centered on the behavior of individual animals and interactions among certain bears instead of among bear populations and people.

Because of the formidable size and sometimes aggressive behavior of bears, and the opposing concerns for their welfare, it often is a precarious duty to manage bear populations at healthy and productive, yet harmless levels. With ever-increasing numbers of people, and ever-decreasing bear habitat, more intensified research and management of bear populations throughout North America are urgently required. Three primary objectives of bear management programs are: (1) habitat conservation, (2) minimization of people-bear conflicts, and (3) improved understanding and balance of consumptive and nonconsumptive values and uses of bear resources.

Disregard and exploitation of wildlife in the past by development-oriented government and private interests have been displaced by strong public concern for the welfare of wild species and habitats. Also, it generally has become recognized that the ecological, physiological, and behavioral relationships of big game species and populations interact in many ways, thereby requiring simultaneous consideration of all three parameters for sufficient understanding of their biologies and habitats in order to manage them effectively. All of these considerations have created a tenuous balance between protective management of bears and control of various bear populations in which individuals tend to be predators, competitors, or dangerous marauders. As a result of increased public interest, improvement of management techniques, and greater awareness of bears' biological and habitat circumstances, bear management has improved greatly during the past two decades. Bounty programs for bears have all but ceased in North America, and most states and provinces now have adequate management programs or protective legislation for their bear populations.

In addition to wildlife programs of government agencies, there is growing concern for the population status and habitat of bears by private interests and professional organizations. The failure of various state and provincial programs to accommodate changing environmental conditions and growing public concern for ecological values unfortunately has generated public distrust of certain agencies. This distrust, and the need of large management areas by the wide-ranging bears have resulted in national and international acts and conventions. Several international groups (the International Union for Conservation of Nature and Natural Resources [IUCN] Polar Bear Specialists Group and the Border Grizzly Committee) and cooperative programs (the Convention on International Trade in Endangered Species of Wild Fauna and Flora—effective in 1975, and the Agreement on the Conservation of Polar Bears—effective May 1976) now oversee national management programs of several bear species.

Long-term population data and many of the habitat evaluation techniques which normally are used in the management of deer, elk, and other big game herbivores have not been tailored to the management of bears except in certain situations. As a result, some bear management programs in North America are barely adequate while others are excellent. Because management agencies are reluctant to extrapolate data from the few completed studies, most jurisdictions have their own research programs. This should rapidly improve the quality of information on which to base bear management.

Unlike wildlife species managed almost totally as game animals, bear populations must be managed carefully regardless of their status. Even in areas where only nonconsumptive uses are permitted, such as national parks and closed areas or in areas of low human density, bears that are marauders, predators, or competitors may be of concern to people. Therefore, it is important to consider first the management of bears in protected areas and, second, to discuss management of the three North American bear species separately as game and predatory animals in nonprotected areas.

Management in protected areas

Bears are "protected" in most parks, in certain states and provinces where their numbers are considered low, in other states and provinces during certain portions of each year, in remote areas where no hunters travel and, in the case of polar bears, in areas outside national jurisdictions. For most species, protection is an uncomplicated and effective method of preservation. When bears are totally protected, however, some individual bears can become aggressive toward people or cause damage to livestock and property, which make imperative a different form of management. Bear-people conflicts are common in national parks of both Canada and the United States. Less well-known are similar problems in Manitoba where polar bears are protected, and in the Mackenzie Mountains of the Northwest Territories, and along the Alaskan pipeline

Snared polar bear is about to be drugged and translocated from vicinity of Cape Churchill, Manitoba. Photo courtesy of the Canadian Wildlife Service.

where brown bears are protected. During calendar year 1976 alone, a total of five persons were killed in North America by black, grizzly, or polar bears, all in areas where bears are protected.

Needs are obvious for bear control through relocation and killing, planning which considers bear habitat needs, bear behavioral-modification programs, clean camps, hiker and camper limits, etc. It is not always clear, however, how to carry out the various programs. Management problems only can become more complicated with ever-increasing public use of bear habitat in backcountry areas (Table 26). The pressing need is to guide human activities to avoid people-bear encounters and conflicts. This may involve prohibiting public use of designated bear feeding and breeding areas at certain specified times.

Table 26. Visitors to Yellowstone National Park, 1959–1970 and the correlation between numbers of people and bear-people conflicts (after Craighead and Craighead 1971)

| Year | Park visitors[a] | Personal injuries | Grizzly control measures | | |
			Killed	Sent to zoos	Total
1959	1,408,667	0	6	1	7
1960	1,443,288	0	4	0	4
1961	1,528,088	1	1	2	3
1962	1,925,227	2	4	0	4
1963	1,872,417	6	2	4	6
1964	1,929,316	1	2	1	3
1965	2,062,476	4	2	0	2
1966	1,130,313	1	3	0	3
1967	2,210,023	0	3	2	5
1968	2,229,657	1	5	0	5
1969	2,193,814	6	10	0	10
1970	2,200,000[b]	3	14	8	22
Total	22,133,286	25	56	18	74

[a]Data obtained from Yellowstone Park records, 1959–1969.
[b]Visitor numbers estimated for 1970.

The main problems of bear population management in protected areas are:

1. The construction of townsites, campgrounds, trails, oil camps, etc. on heavily used seasonal home ranges and natural travel routes of bears. These detrimental actions are particularly commonplace in national parks.

2. Careless storage of food or bait, and garbage disposal which create atypical bear behavior, including increased boldness or aggression toward people. Undesirable traits may be learned by cubs from their mothers in these areas.

3. Careless behavior by people, such as approaching bears too closely, feeding them to take photographs, pestering them in garbage dumps, and chasing them with vehicles, helicopters, or horses. The nuisance behavior by people creates stress conditions for bears that may be manifested in the bears' increased aggressiveness.

4. Inviting (or allowing) too many people into prime bear habitat for a multitude of activities, such as hiking, fishing, hunting, and camping, thereby forcing the bears to move elsewhere or increasing the likelihood of serious bear-people conflicts.

5. The failure to act quickly and decisively to remove (by relocation or killing) bears which are aggressive toward people in all but the three "normal" circumstances:
   a. a female protecting her young;
   b. any bear protecting its food; and
   c. any bear protecting itself when a person approaches too closely.

6. The insensitivity of people to threats or warning behavior from bears, and the lack of appreciation by people of the extensive efforts bears make to avoid confrontations.

7. The failure of people to reroute, postpone, or cancel their trips if bears are noted on the trail ahead, if visibility is poor and/or the trail leads into the wind, if aggressive bears have been reported in the area, or if the area is administratively closed because of bears.

8. Careless livestock management, such as allowing the depletion of succulent bear foods by the livestock, or leaving sick, dead, injured, or newly born livestock easily accessible to bears.

9. Inadequate methods of decision making for equitable allocation of space, forage, and other resources in areas heavily used by both bears and humans.

Solutions to normal problems that occur where bears are protected are rather obvious and direct. However, in complex situations, it is well to note several general guidelines:

1. Use of handguns is not desirable because people who carry them tend not to take

The daily movements of the collared black bear are monitored by telemetry. Photo courtesy of the Maine Department of Inland Fisheries and Wildlife, Wildlife Division.

normal precautions to avoid confrontations, and do not as readily acknowledge the warning signals bears give when confronted. The sidearm is not adequate protection against bears. Sidearms, cameras, and bears are an especially dangerous combination.

2. Training sessions for people on bear behavior, habits, and ecology would be appropriate in certain areas, just as behavioral modification programs for bears might be in some places. Bear behavior is highly ritualized; they give warnings that seldom are recognized by people possibly because bears are somewhat doglike in appearance but give different warning signals than do dogs.

3. Areas of bear concentrations, such as feeding sites and travel routes, should be avoided in the planning of campsites, trails, townsites, etc. However, the location of developments in areas less attractive to bears may increase costs greatly and be unpopular decisions. Nevertheless, such relocations are essential actions in a sound bear management program.

4. Valued equipment at unattended field stations or camps should be fenced or enclosed to prevent destruction by the bears. No simple chemical, electrical, or acoustical deterrents to bears yet exist, but elaborate electrical fence arrangements have been successful in some parks and field camps. A dog in camp can provide effective warning, but unless trained, it will not provide significant protection. Also, dogs should be inoculated for rabies.

5. Warning devices such as bells, and scaring devices such as bird bombs, teleshots, and thunderflashes can prevent many potential confrontations. Throwing an article of clothing or pack to an aggressive bear may give a person extra time to act in an emergency. "Playing dead" sometimes halts an attack but, under many circumstances, a counter-attack with a gun, clubs, axes, or chemicals may be the only alternative.

6. The economic and social values of bears and their habitats should be determined on an area-to-area basis in decision making.

Management in nonprotected areas

The black bear has adapted very well to human settlement in North America and, therefore, has not evoked much public concern for its welfare throughout most of its range.

The polar bear, however, has been considered an endangered species by Canada since 1960, primarily to expedite research and better management. The species was protected from recreational hunting by the United States under the Marine Mammal Protection Act of 1972. The Agreement for the Conservation of Polar Bears was signed in 1973 by all five arctic nations with polar bear populations and presently is in effect.

South of Canada the brown bear was listed officially as a threatened species in 1975 under the United States Endangered Species Act, and proposed as endangered in Mexico under the 1973 Convention on International Trade in Endangered Species of Wild Fauna and Flora.

1. **Black bears.** Management problems with black bear populations vary from place to place. In some areas, the populations are overabundant, and in others, populations are at critically low levels. In the eastern United States, increasing human populations, reduced tolerance of people toward large carnivores, and habitat destruction primarily from agriculture and residential sprawl are affecting black bear numbers and suitable habitat. In the past, large, swampy areas with dense cover and the rugged mountainous areas provided adequate sanctuary for black bears despite adjacent, high density urban areas. Recently, however, the clearing of the swamps or "bays" by large mechanized farming operations and the proliferation of second and "com-

243

muter" homes in the mountains rapidly are eliminating these formerly secluded black bear areas. In Mexico, intensive land use by peasants relocated to formerly large ranches likewise is reducing black bear habitat and population numbers at an increasing rate.

On the other hand, high black bear densities continue to be a problem in the Pacific Northwest where hunting pressure is inadequate to control population numbers (Poelker et al. 1973). These black bears destroy trees by girdling them to feed on cambium and sap (Figure 54). As a result, black bear management programs range from total protection to year-round open seasons with supplemental control programs. In the State of Washington, hunting and control programs in recent years have resulted in annual kills of 3,500–10,000 black

bears without a detrimental effect on the population. The annual kill of black bears for North America may total about 30,000 (Cowan 1972).

2. **Brown bears.** The grizzly bear populations of the central Rocky Mountains undoubtedly are in a precarious management situation. In western Canada, grizzlies are hunted in the spring for their hides, and in the autumn during big game seasons, but the kill does not appear to be excessive. South of Canada they are hunted as a game animal only in part of Montana where the kill is strictly regulated under an annual quota system. Illegal and control kills are considered in the establishment of annual quotas. The main management goals in Montana are: (1) to remove surplus young animals before they disperse into developed areas, causing problems and a

A drugged black bear is tagged and fitted with a collar transmitting device. Photo courtesy of the Maine Department of Inland Fisheries and Wildlife, Wildlife Division.

backlash of public sentiment; and (2) to help prevent people-bear conflicts by encouraging bears to be wary of people as a result of hunting pressure.

There has been considerable concern in recent years that the grizzly bear cannot withstand both hunting pressure and habitat destruction. But, in fact, the grizzly can cope rather well with disturbances by man, even garbage dumps in national parks—"the ugliest of human pollution" (Pearson 1975). Whether the habitat is disturbed or not, excessive killing is the crucial consideration. Management programs must be designed to consider carefully and on annual bases the reproductive potential of grizzly bear populations, the important role of young

Figure 54. Bears strip the bark from many conifers throughout the West, inflicting serious damage to closely managed, high-yield forest tracts.

females in the population, and the survival of young whenever human population pressures, habitat disturbances, climatic fluctuations, and food shortages coincide. Brown bear populations are secure in Alaska and the Yukon; but on the fringes of good habitat, such as the range of the barren-ground grizzly or in areas where remnant populations exist in relative isolation, management must be improved greatly.

Relocation of grizzlies that cause minor problems such as breaking into cabins and preying on cattle, and reintroduction of orphaned cubs to the wild are major management objectives in areas with low bear numbers, especially south of Canada where the species is listed as threatened. Reintroduction of cubs to the wild has been accomplished successfully by saturation feeding of the animals until such time as they accumulate sufficient fat reserves, and then placing them in artificial dens in good habitat (Jonkel et al. 1977). Many relocation efforts have been successful, but agencies must be prepared for serious public reaction when the attempts fail. Induced adoptions of orphaned cubs by females with cubs of the same year is under experimentation (Jonkel et al. 1977).

Greatest assurances of the species viability and high recreation potential appear to occur in grizzly bear populations maintained at natural levels in undisturbed range (Pearson 1975) and, where possible, restored to natural levels in disturbed range. Habitat maintenance and restoration is possible through identification of grizzly bear population requirements, predetermination of consequences of land-use impacts on habitat, application of land uses that have positive or neutral effects, and avoidance of habitat alterations with negative effects. An example of a land-management practice with potentially positive effects for brown bears is prescribed or managed burning. Such fire can stimulate new vegetative growth and, thereby, increase cover and nutritious foods. Another example is timber-harvesting practices that result in openings that are the vegetative equivalents of prescribed burns (Mealey et al. 1975). An example of a negative practice is domestic livestock grazing that removes important herbaceous forage. Another is unrestricted human access to areas of high grizzly bear use, resulting in increased potential conflicts of people and grizzlies.

3. **Polar bears.** The Inuit, or Eskimos, always have killed polar bears for food, clothing, and dog feed. The native peoples of northern Alaska, Canada, and Greenland still survive to varying degrees on a hunting economy. A single hide has brought as much as $3,500 in past years, but the price fell to $600–$1,000 during 1976. More important, many of the Inuit cultural values are based on hunting or a close spiritual relationship with wildlife. The hunting of polar bears is the single most important annual event in the life of many people (Jonkel 1970). This fact must be recognized by polar bear management authorities.

In Alaska, the hunting of polar bears is done strictly by native peoples, and the hides cannot be sold. A minor craft industry exists, based on items manufactured from bear hides by Eskimos. Since the polar bear was removed from state jurisdiction by the Marine Mammal Protection Act, there are no "bag limits" for the native hunters. In fear of losing their present unlimited hunting privilege, some of these hunters are resisting the state's petition for the return of management authority.

At present, North American polar bear populations appear to be very secure, despite an annual kill of 500–700. Their range is much larger than formerly understood; it extends from Newfoundland and southern James Bay northward for 3,200 kilometers (2,000 miles) as well as laterally across the Arctic about 4,300 kilometers (2,700 miles), not counting Greenland.

In Canada, the polar bear kill is controlled on an annual basis through settlement quotas, with the quota in each area based on bear numbers, the extent of the area hunted, the numbers of settlements hunting a given subpopulation, and the age and sex composition of each bear population (Figure 55). Females and cubs are protected, and most hunting seasons extend from October 1 through May 31. A small number of permits (±10–20 per year) from the settlement quotas are sold annually to nonresident hunters who must hunt with an Inuk guide and by dog team. In Manitoba and certain oil-drilling camps, protected polar bears become a threat to people and 10–25 bears must be killed each year through control programs.

A sharp decline in polar bear numbers in the western Arctic during recent years has been attributed to a decline in ringed seal numbers (Stirling et al. 1976). Climatic fluctuations and resultant changes in sea ice patterns and snow depths on the ice appear to be the ultimate causes, largely because of the delicately balanced recruitment rates of polar bear populations.

Bear mortality and management

Jonkel and Cowan (1971) and Stirling et al. (1976) showed that food shortages arrest both black bear and polar bear recruitment. Consequently, careful attention must be paid to reproductive females during food shortages in areas of sustained, light hunting pressure. In models, removal of even 5 percent of the population, in addition to natural mortality, may be critical (Figure 56). Models are limited in their applicability, of course, and the saving phenomenon for most hunted populations is that as bear population numbers decline, hunting successes and efforts usually decline concurrently.

Cowan (1972) gave rule-of-thumb estimates for management removal at about

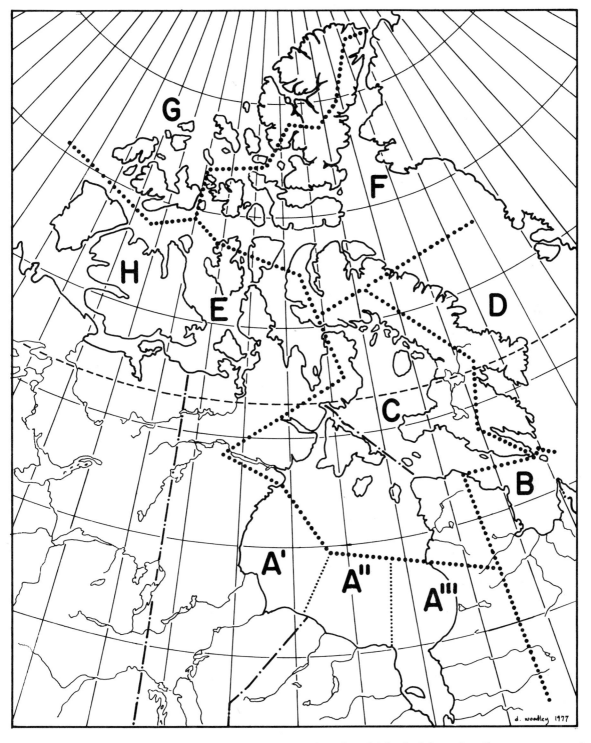

Figure 55. Polar bear management zones in Canada based on biological data, hunting pressure, and physiographic features.

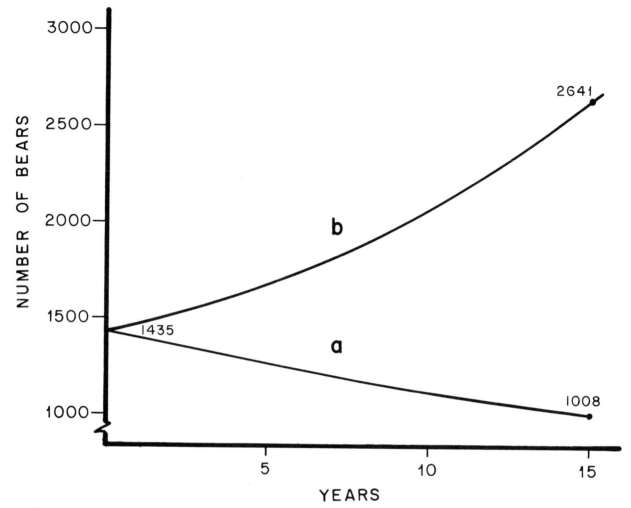

Figure 56. Computer projected polar bear populations. Line "a" shows that without partial protection of females and young from hunting, a polar bear population would decline. Line "b" indicates an increase when females and young are protected year-round (after Stirling et al. 1976).

1:17–20 for grizzly and polar bears, and 1:12–18 for black bears, with higher removal only under unusually high recruitment rates. When bear population declines are confronted with increased hunting pressure for such purposes as food, trophies, rising hide values, and collection of rare specimens, extirpation may occur rather quickly. Herein lies the main responsibility of the bear management agency. Annually set and regulated quotas are the most effective management tool at present, provided they have biologically and ecologically sound bases.

Chapter 16

EXOTICS

Eugene Decker

Associate Professor
Department of Fishery and Wildlife Biology
Colorado State University
Fort Collins, Colorado

Few subjects can generate as much heated discussion among hunters, fishermen and wildlife ecologists as "exotic wildlife." Some shudder at the term, recalling horror stories resulting from introductions of the starling, English sparrow and carp in America, the rabbit in Australia, or the red deer and opossum in New Zealand. Others anticipate success, such as introductions of ring-necked pheasant, chukar partridge and brown trout in the United States. Regardless of one's views, the introduction of nonnative wildlife has been, and will be, a continuing problem for wildlife managers throughout North America.

POSITIVE AND NEGATIVE ASPECTS

There have been a number of reasons both supporting and opposing the introduction of big game mammals in North America. The following is a summary of the major arguments of both perspectives.

Reasons proposed for introducing exotic big game in North America

1. Exotics can provide a new "game" animal to occupy ecological niches unoccupied by native game species. Such habitats may never have been occupied by big game populations (some arid brush lands and deserts of the Southwest), or man's activities (grazing, forestry, crop farming, outdoor recreation disturbances, etc.) have so changed habitat conditions that native wildlife no longer is able to be maintained. Supporters of this reason believe that some exotic Asian or African species may be adapted to these conditions and could offer new opportunities for recreational hunting in areas where few or none now exist.

2. The introduction of suitable exotic species may provide an additional source of income to landowners from recreational hunting and sales of meat and/or live animals. This reason has great appeal inasmuch as traditions and present legal restrictions in most areas of North America prevent landowners from managing native big game populations to maximize economic benefits. Selection of suitable exotic animals also could allow for better utilization of forage resources through combinations of various browsers, grazers and mixed feeders, or through the use of exotic browsing mammals with grazing livestock. This philosophy has been demonstrated successfully in Texas with the establishment of a number of wildlife ranches for exotic animals. In 1974, 316 ranches comprising about 1,821,862 hectares (approximately 4.5 million acres) reported having exotic mammals (Harmel 1975).

3. Species facing extinction from various causes in other parts of the world possibly could be introduced to suitable habitat in North America. Such wild or semiwild populations on refuges would be good insurance for saving some threatened species.

4. The introduction of exotic mammal species would present a more varied fauna for people to view, photograph and hunt. Since most of North America is inhabited by deer species, supporters of this view see no reason why there also should not be exotic deer species or other ungulates in the same habitat.

Reasons for opposing the introduction of exotic big game in North America

Craighead and Dasmann (1966) listed the following reasons:

1. Exotics can create further land-use conflicts in areas already fully stocked by livestock or native big game animals.

2. Exotics may displace native wildlife species or populations from habitats where they still exist.

3. Exotics can disturb the ecological balance of natural communities that people want to maintain in a pristine or representative natural state.

4. Management efforts should concentrate on preserving native biota in North America and not on accelerating a worldwide trend toward biotic uniformity.

5. Funds spent on programs to introduce exotics would do more good if used to improve and maintain habitats for native species.

6. Exotic ungulate populations can be difficult or impossible to control where circumstances favor their rapid spread or increase.

Other arguments for opposing introductions of exotic big game include:

7. Exotics may introduce new diseases or parasites to domestic livestock or native wildlife species. However, present United States Department of Agriculture quarantine procedures greatly reduce the chance of such occurrences.

8. Some exotics may breed with native wildlife, presenting the possibility of

destroying gene pools of some North American species.

9. Some exotics have the potential for causing serious depredations to crops and forests.

There are a number of exotic wild ungulates that undoubtedly would be successful in America if introduced into suitable habitats in adequate numbers. However, it is obvious that such introduction should be considered with great caution for the reasons stated above. Most federal land management agencies have policies either forbidding introduction of exotics or discouraging such programs when and where there is potential competition with native species. Most state wildlife agencies also discourage introductions. The few exceptions are programs of introducing exotic animals on private lands.

A thorough study of potential impacts of introduced exotics on native wildlife populations and their habitats must be undertaken prior to initiation of any exotic mammal program. In addition, information should be obtained concerning the life history of the candidate exotic in its native habitat. Such factors as food habits, reproductive potential, disease resistance, competition with wild and domestic animals, mortality, movements and behavior (does it jump fences, etc.) should be known in advance of an introduction. Little of this information is known at present about most Asian and African wildlife species proposed for introduction in North America.

PRESENT SITUATION

Exotic big game animals presently are free roaming in varying numbers in many localities of North America. The sources of these introductions have been one or more of the following: (1) escaped domestic animals; (2) escapes from private zoos, game reserves, parks, etc.; (3) intentional releases by wildlife agencies; and (4) releases by well-intentioned individuals or groups with or without approval of wildlife agencies.

A survey of the 50 state wildlife agencies of the United States and of the Canadian Wildlife Service was made to determine the presence of exotic big game mammals in their areas. Information was requested about nonnative big game mammals which are free roaming. Excluded from this survey were animals in parks, outdoor zoos, or within fenced game preserves or ranches.

The most successful exotic big game species in North America north of Mexico is the feral hog (*Sus scrofa*). This animal is found in the southeastern and Gulf Coast states and California. It is available for recreational hunting in most of these states, but harvest information was difficult to obtain since the hogs are considered "domestic livestock," and hunting generally is controlled by private landowners. However, some states do require a hunting license for hunting on state wildlife management areas or in counties where the jurisdiction on the animal has been delegated to the state.

Hunter-kill reports reveal that the feral hog is the number two big game animal in California, with a reported kill exceeding 18,000 in 1975, and in Florida, with a reported kill in some parts of the state exceeding 36,000. When one realizes that there also is hunting on private land not under control of the state, the extent of the feral hog contribution to recreational hunting becomes more evident.

It is the opinion of state officials in the southeastern United States that feral hog populations have been reduced during the last several decades to minimize their depredations to forest reproduction and agricultural crops. Populations in California appear to be increasing and, within the near future, the harvest of hogs may equal or surpass the deer kill.

Other exotics existing in considerable numbers in North America are barbary sheep (*Ammotragus lervia*), fallow deer, (*Dama dama*) Axis deer (*Axis axis*) and sika deer (*Cervus nippon*).

A program dealing with the introduction of exotic big game was conducted by the New Mexico Game and Fish Department during the past two decades. This program has resulted in successful establishment of two species which now provide hunting opportunities. These are the gemsbok or Kalahari oryx (*Oryx gazella*) on the White Sands Missile Range and the Iranian ibex (*Capra aegagrus*) in the Florida Mountains. Both areas are in southern New Mexico.

Information on exotics in North America north of Mexico was obtained primarily from wildlife agency personnel during late 1976 and early 1977. It includes only free-roaming animals. Not included are: (1) introductions or reintroductions of North American species (deer, bison, elk, etc.); (2) feral horses, burros, sheep or cattle; (3) reindeer; and (4) animals within "game-proof" fences on private land.

Accurate population estimates, in many cases, have not been made by the wildlife agencies because the numbers of animals are small in relationship to native big game populations, or because the exotics are dispersed in habitats where surveys are difficult to make. The following is a list of free-roaming exotic big game mammals in North America.

Feral hog (*Sus scrofa*)
1. California
   A. Coastal mountains, Mendocino to Santa Barbara counties; also foothills of central valley, mostly on private land
   Population estimate: 30,000
   Harvest estimate: 16,728 (1976) from hunter survey
   Remarks: Considered big game, license required, year-round season; population appears to be increasing.
   B. Catalina Island, southern California, private ownership
   Population estimate: 500
   Harvest estimate: Annual average 200± (1976)
   Remarks: Hunting controlled by landowners.

2. Florida—statewide
   Harvest estimate: 36,000± (1975)
   Remarks: License required in some counties and on state wildlife management areas.
3. South Carolina—coastal areas
   Remarks: Hunted on wildlife management areas during deer season, and deer licenses required.
4. Georgia—coastal areas
   Remarks: Considered domestic livestock; license required when hunted on state wildlife management areas with deer.
5. Alabama, Arkansas, Louisiana, Mississippi and Texas
   Remarks: Considered domestic livestock; no population or harvest estimates available.
6. Oklahoma
   Remarks: Few found on eastern wildlife management areas.
7. Arizona—Colorado River-Toprock Marsh on Havusu National Wildlife Refuge
   Population estimate: 200–400
   Remarks: Not presently hunted.
8. Hawaii—found on Hawaii, Maui, Molokai, Oahu and Kauai islands
   Harvest estimate: 457 on public hunting areas (1975)
   Remarks: No population or harvest estimates on private lands.

European boar-feral hog hybrids (*Sus* sp.)—retain European boar characteristics
1. Tennessee—eastern counties, mostly Cherokee National Forest and Great Smoky National Park and some state and private lands
   Population estimate: 1,500± on United States Forest Service and private lands plus 800± in Great Smoky National Park
   Harvest estimate: 100–120 annually, outside of National Park
   Remarks: Regulated hunts on wildlife management areas with deer and bear; license required.
2. North Carolina—six westernmost counties, mainly in Graham and Cherokee counties (contiguous population with Tennessee)

Gemsbok (Kalahari oryx) have been introduced on the White Sands Missile Range in New Mexico and now provide limited hunting. Photo courtesy of the New Mexico Game and Fish Department.

Population estimates: 700–900
Harvest estimate: 100 (1975–1976)
Remarks: License required.
3. Kentucky—Appalachian Chain and Cumberland Plateau, mostly in Cherokee National Forest and Great Smoky National Park
Population estimate: 300±
Harvest estimate: 200–300 annually
Remarks: License required.
4. West Virginia—state wildlife agency recently released European boar into western counties on large private land (timber or mining) holdings

Fallow deer *(Dama dama)*
1. Georgia—mainly on coastal islands; Little Saint Simons (private) and small number on Jekyll Island
Population estimate: 400–500
Remarks: Hunted on private land as deer under state regulation; no harvest estimate.
2. Kentucky—"Land Between the Lakes" management unit; 17,000-acre wooded peninsula in western Kentucky
Population estimate: 600
Harvest estimate: 172 (1974); 115 (1975)
Remarks: Hunted in regular season as deer.
3. Alabama—central portion, mostly in Wilcox County, some in Dallas County, mainly on private land
Population estimate: 1,000±
Harvest estimate: 100±
Remarks: Considered deer in regular season.

4. Nebraska—northcentral portion in Boone and Wheeler counties
Population estimate: Two small herds, 35–40 animals
Remarks: Not hunted.

5. Maryland—Eastern Shore in Cecil County
Population estimate: 10±
Remarks: Not protected; considered a deer in regular season.

6. Oklahoma—small herd on McAester Army Ammunition Depot

7. California
A. North coastal-Mendocino County
Population estimate: 55± (1976)
Remarks: Hunted as deer in regular season.
B. Central coastal peninsula—Point Reyes National Sea Shore
Population estimate: 500± (1975)
Remarks: No recreational hunting.

8. Texas—Edwards Plateau, Real County
Population estimate: 60±
Remarks: Protected.

9. British Columbia, Canada—James and Sidney (coastal) islands, private
Population estimate: James Island, 100–500; Sidney Island, 200–250
Harvest estimate: 12–18 annually on James Island
Remarks: Controlled by private landowners.

Barbary sheep *(Ammotragus lervia)*

1. New Mexico
A. Northeast—Canadian River Canyon, mainly Harding County, private land
Population estimate: 800±
Harvest estimate: 34 (1976)
B. Southeast—Hondo Canyon, Chavez and Lincoln counties, private land
Population estimate: 525±
Harvest estimate: 140 (1976)
C. Southeast—Otero County, west side of Guadalupe Mountains
Population estimate: 200±
Harvest estimate: 8 (1976)
D. Northwest—Largo Canyon, San Juan County, private land
Population estimate: 200±
Harvest estimate: 21 (1976)
Remarks: Hunted on all areas by permits issued by New Mexico Game and Fish Department.

2. Texas
A. North ("Panhandle")—in Palo Duro Canyon of Amarillo area
Population estimate: 1,200–1,400
Harvest estimate: 62 (1973); 72 (1974); 100 (1975); 135 (1976)
Remarks: Hunted by permits issued by Texas Wildlife Department; herd increasing.
B. Northcentral—Palo Pinto and Stephens counties, private land
Population estimate: 200±
Remarks: Controlled by landowner.
C. Southwest—Brewster County, private land
Population estimate: 180±
Remarks: Controlled by landowner.

3. California—coastal mountains, San Luis Obispo County, on Hearst Ranch
Population estimate: 400±
Harvest estimate: 6–10 annually
Remarks: Controlled by landowner.

Axis deer *(Axis axis)*

1. Texas—southcentral around San Antonio in Bexar County
Population estimate: 6,000
Harvest estimate: 200–300± annually
Remarks: Hunted as deer in regular season.

2. California—central coastal peninsula, Point Reyes National Sea Shore, Marin County
Population estimate: 460± (1976)
Remarks: Herd increasing; insignificant recreational hunting.

3. Hawaii—Molokai, Lanai, Oahu and Maui islands
Harvest estimate: 169 from public hunting areas in 1975
Remarks: No population or harvest estimates from private lands.

Sika deer *(Cervus nippon)*
1. Maryland—Eastern Shore, mainly in Dorchester County; marsh habitat; a few on Assateaque Island
   Population estimates: 5,000±
   Harvest estimate: 300–500 annually
   Remarks: Special season, 3 deer per hunter in 1976; herd increasing.
2. Virginia—coastal islands, Chincoteaque Island National Wildlife Refuge; adjacent island and marsh habitat
   Population estimate: 700±
   Harvest estimate: 25–30 annually
   Remarks: Special hunts, archery and rifle.
3. Wisconsin—southeast
   Population estimate: 25–30
   Harvest estimate: 5–6 annually
   Remarks: Considered a deer in regular season.

Sambar deer *(Cervus unicolor, Rusa unicolor)*
1. Florida—Saint Vincent National Wildlife Refuge (Gulf Coast island)
   Population estimate: 50–90
   Remarks: Not hunted.
2. California—coastal mountains, San Luis Obispo County, on Hearst Ranch
   Population estimate: 100±
   Remarks: Not presently hunted, controlled by landowner.

Mouflon-Barbados sheep hybrids *(Ovis musimon* x *O. aries)*—southwest Texas, on private land in Jeff Davis and Brewster counties
   Population estimate: 800±
   Remarks: Controlled by landowners.

Aoudad (Barbary sheep) have been successfully established in Texas, New Mexico and California. Photo by James D. Yoakum.

Feral sheep (*Ovis aries*)—Hawaii and Kahoolawe islands

Harvest estimate: 392 from public hunting areas in 1976

Remarks: No population or harvest estimates from private lands.

Mouflon sheep and Mouflon-domestic sheep hybrids—Hawaii and Lanai islands

Harvest estimate: 82 on public hunting areas in 1976

Remarks: No population or harvest estimates on private lands.

Feral goats (*Capra hircus*)
1. California
   A. Santa Catalina (southern coastal island)
   Population estimate: 5,000±
   Harvest estimate: 800± annually
   Remarks: Controlled by private landowner.
   B. San Clemente (southern coastal island)
   Population estimates: 5,000±
   Remarks: A military reservation; herd recently reduced.
   C. Additional small herds scattered around state
2. Hawaii—Hawaii, Maui, Kahoolawe, Lanai, Molokai, Oahu and Kauai islands

Harvest estimate: 295 from public hunting areas in 1975

Remarks: No estimate of harvest on populations on private lands.

Persian ibex (Iranian) (*Capra aegagrus*)—New Mexico, southwest in Florida Mountains, Luna County

Population estimate: 200±

Harvest estimate: 3 (1975); 3 (1976); 9 (1977)

Remarks: Hunted by special permit.

Gemsbok-Kalahari oryx (*Oryx gazella*)—White Sands Missile Range, southcentral New Mexico

Population estimate: 250±

Harvest estimate: 5 (1974); 6 (1975); 11 (1976)

Remarks: Hunted by permit.

Siberian ibex (*Capra siberica*)—northeastern New Mexico, in Canadian River Canyon, Harding County, on private land

Remarks: 40 animals released in 1976.

Tahr (*Hemitragus jemlahicus*)—central coastal mountains, San Luis Obispo County, California, on Hearst Ranch

Population estimate: 150±

Harvest estimate: 6–10 annually

Remarks: Controlled by landowner.

Chapter 17

EARLY MANAGEMENT: INTENTIONAL AND OTHERWISE

John L. Schmidt

Assistant Dean,
College of Forestry and Natural Resources
and Associate Professor,
Department of Fishery and Wildlife Biology
Colorado State University
Fort Collins, Colorado

When Europeans arrived and began settling on the North American continent, they found a wealth of big game resources. Deer, elk, moose, caribou, bison and others were so numerous that discussions of conservation seldom occurred. Thousands of years before this, early Asian pioneers (the first human discoverers of North America) presumably also found a virtually unlimited supply of large mammals and an even greater variety.

We can only speculate what the consequences of these early Asian settlers were to big game resources since neither the magnitude of the populations before or several thousand years after their arrival can ever be known. We do, however, have better documentation, albeit not ideal, on the impacts on big game since the arrival of European pioneers. The intent of this chapter is to summarize briefly what is known and/or

Bison herds "as far as the eye could see," were witnessed by pioneer settlers for the first time in valleys of the Allegheny Mountains. Such herds spawned the erroneous and reckless notion of unlimited wildlife resources. Courtesy of the Denver Public Library, Western History Department.

speculated to have been the effects of man on big game resources prior to 1935 in North America north of Mexico. Why 1935? Prior to that time, most of man's impacts on big game resources, whether beneficial or harmful, were incidental to management, as we think of it today. Few efforts were made for the express purpose of benefiting (or hurting) a given big game species. Some of man's activities, whether intentional or not, did have some tremendous repercussions on big game populations. Early forestry practices, for example, created tremendous impacts on big game species. Yet, because of the lack of intent, this could hardly be called "big game management." Laws, regulations and practices enacted with big game management in mind generally were the result of emergency, emotionalism, or trial-and-error management, rather than sound planning and management.

The land left barren, riverbanks eroded and wildlife without suitable or sufficient habitat were of little concern to those engaged in the commercial exploitation of North America's pristine forest. Courtesy of the National Archives.

In the 1930s, a number of events occurred which served as catalysts for change. The first Cooperative Wildlife Research Units were established in 1935 to train biologists and accomplish much needed technical research. In 1937, the United States Congress passed the Federal Aid in Wildlife Restoration Act, creating funds from an excise tax on sporting arms and ammunition to be used for wildlife research, and habitat acquisition and development. Several colleges and universities began offering courses and curricula in the new field of wildlife management. Also, valuable insight had been gained while experiencing the near extinction of some big game populations through exploitation in the latter decades of the Nineteenth Century, followed by a period of over protection in the 1920s and 1930s. Recent trends in big game management, from 1935 to present, are well-covered in other chapters. To avoid repetition, no effort will be made here to review this period.

Two basic types of man's impact on big game will be reviewed: (1) exploitation, and (2) land-use changes that indirectly affected most big game species.

EXTINCTION OF PREHISTORIC LARGE MAMMAL SPECIES

It is interesting to speculate what big game might be available today had not so many species become extinct about 12,000 years B.P. Before that time, in the late Pleistocene epoch, North America was home to a much greater variety of animal life than exists now. Large numbers of camels, mammoths, mastodons, ground sloths, giant armadillos and other large mammal species roamed the continent. Then, with relative

The "take" of an organized hunting party in 1885, led by Cooke Rhea of Pearl, Colorado. Rhea (lower right next to the mountain lion) was one of very few hunters in the Nineteenth Century who differentiated harvesting from indiscriminate killing of big game. Photo by Rudolph Eickemeyer; courtesy of the Colorado Division of Wildlife.

259

suddenness, many species became extinct. Some scientists have theorized that catastropic climatic changes eliminated these species. Others believe that this high incidence of extinction coincided with and was caused by the arrival of Stone Age Man.

Martin (1973) speculated that Paleolithic pioneers who crossed the Bering Strait land bridge from Asia found a productive and unexploited ecosystem. They increased rapidly and continually pushed southward, perhaps exterminating 31 genera of large mammals in the process. Martin suggested that this was possible because of a lack of fear by these large mammals, hence little defensive behavior toward man, their new predator.

Whether or not early man or other factors were responsible for the extinction of these many species is purely academic. We will never have the opportunity to hunt or photograph them, or to keep them out of a rancher's haystack for that matter.

EARLY HISTORY

There is no indication that pre-Columbian Indians had any serious adverse effect on large mammal populations. There are several reasons or factors why this is true. Their numbers were never great by current standards. Their level of technology for hunting weapons and for equipment to destroy habitat was low. Finally, they had a belief in and respect for the spiritual powers of plants and animals, including big game.

Apparently, Indians efficiently utilized what was available for their food, clothing and shelter. The exceptions may be worthy of note. One was a method used by Indians to kill bison. They frequently were successful in stampeding herds over cliffs high enough to kill them. These "jumps" were effective enough, but not too efficient inasmuch as there was little control over how many ani-

Bison bone deposit at the base of a "jump" along the bluffs of the Grand River in South Dakota. Photo by Olaus J. Murie; courtesy of the National Archives.

mals were killed. In some cases, many more were killed than could be utilized. A second exception involved the Indians of the far North and caribou. Kelsall (1968) reported many accounts of wasteful killing of barren-ground caribou by Indians. According to these reports, thousands of caribou were killed annually for their tongues, hides and/or fetuses, leaving the rest of the meat to rot. While most of these accounts were late enough in history that the Indians could have been using guns, it is assumed these same practices occurred, though perhaps to a lesser degree, when more primitive weapons were used. In both of these cases, though, there were no serious repercussions to big game populations since the low human population and high big game population permitted these wasteful practices.

We do know of more subtle influences that Indians had on big game populations. They were quite familiar with and adept at the use of fire as both process and tool (Stewart 1956, Mutch 1976). Stewart (1951) found "more than 200 references to Indians setting fire to vegetation in aboriginal times, and these references cover all major geographic and cultural areas." Allen (1970) observed "wherever plant cover would burn, it was burned repeatedly as part of the cultural way of life. Some of the beneficial effects probably were evident. Fires opened up thick growth where game might be hunted more easily." American Indians knew that bison and elk were drawn to plant growths of burned-over areas and, therefore, were "handily" hunted (Allen 1967). Other grazing species also were attracted to prairies where fire maintained an early successional stage of vegetative growth. In other environments, such as forested regions, some Indian cultures used fire to discourage mosquitoes and to encourage production of shrubs that were attractive to browsing animals (Allen 1970).

Farming practices of Indians, particularly in the eastern United States, played a somewhat similar role with regard to big game. Many thousands of acres either were cut or burned to clear areas for farming. On a canoe trip down the Shiawassee River in southern Michigan in 1837, Hubbard (1887) observed that "many of the Indian clearings stretched for several continuous miles, and many acres bordering the river were covered with luxurient maize—the chief cultural food of the natives." When Indians were gone from these areas, the invading vegetation no doubt was very attractive and conducive to a number of big game species. It is likely that the clearing of forested areas east of the prairies largely accounted for the presence of bison as far east and south as Pennsylvania and Georgia, respectively. This also favored deer and elk. Predator populations, namely those of the wolf and mountain lion, likewise prospered (Allen 1970).

In addition to serving as food, clothing and a medium of exchange, big game animals dichotomously were an obstacle to settlers "taming" the North American wilderness. Courtesy of the U.S. Forest Service.

When European immigrants began settling North America, two important trends became evident. First, habitat of big game species changed rapidly as settlers invaded and cleared the land. This was to the advantage of some species and the disadvantage of others. Second, big game was used intensively as an increasing human population depended on it as a primary source of meat. Related to this is the culture and religion that the colonists brought with them. Trefethen (1975) stated "the European colonist, poised on the shores of a wild continent, recognized no value in wilderness, which he faced with feelings of dread. He and his companions had left behind geometrically patterned landscapes of farms, pastures, woodlots, and villages, neatly compartmented by fences and hedgerows. His dream and, as he saw it, his God-given duty, was to tame the wilderness and change the new land to conform to the old. He realized this dream sooner than anyone at the time could have thought possible."

When the United States became independent of England in 1776, its human population was little more than 1.5 million. More than 95 percent of the people lived by tilling the soil. Shipbuilding was the principal industry, and wood and charcoal were the dominant fuels. Demand for wood products coupled with repeated burning of uncultivated land to produce grassy vegetation for thousands of livestock modified much big game habitat. Furthermore, big game was eliminated from some settled areas through excessive killing. However, very little of North America had been settled at that time. The continent was still largely an unspoiled wilderness (Trefethen 1975).

Even during the latter part of the Eighteenth Century and first decades of the Nineteenth Century, many of our big game populations and their habitats remained intact. Lewis and Clark made their historic exploration of the Louisiana Territory from 1804–1806. For approximately 40 years thereafter, fur trappers and traders, missionaries and government explorers were the only white visitors to the interior of the continent. These early adventurers truly lived "off the land," and although their numbers were not large enough to deplete big game resources, they did exterminate the beaver over large areas. In the East, vast forests between the Mississippi River Valley and the Appalachian Mountains were log-

Clearing a homestead. Photo by Fritz Sethe; courtesy of the National Archives.

ged and the land converted to farms soon after the War of 1812 (Trefethen 1976). East of the Mississippi River, bison nearly were exterminated by 1830 (Rorabacher 1970), as were elk by 1830 (Murie 1951). Throughout most of the East, white-tailed deer remained common though not abundant beyond this time.

About the mid-1800s, several events occurred which were to have dramatic effects on many big game resources. The discovery of gold in California in 1848 increased the human population there from a few thousand to several million in just three years. While this was the most dramatic mining "boom," many of lesser extent occurred throughout the West. The Homestead Act of 1862 caused thousands of easterners to move westward in search of free land on the prairies. Virtually millions of hectares of big game habitat were converted to farmland. In 1869, the first transcontinental railroad was

Visions of an agricultural utopia and reduced threat of Indian attacks brought thousands to the Great Plains in the late 1800s. From 1880–1889, in the Dakotas alone, homesteaders claimed 16,772,800 hectares (41,321,472 acres). Courtesy of the Denver Public Library, Western History Department.

The combination of cattle, sheep, barbed wire fences and the transcontinental railroad was an insurmountable burden on the habitat of many big game populations in the western United States. In a single decade, the 1870s, Texas raised, grazed and trailed out more than 3 million cows. Courtesy of the Denver Public Library, Western History Department.

completed—an event that produced a number of significant repercussions. For the sake of brevity, it may be summarized that transcontinental railroads accelerated mining, homesteading, ranching, logging, agriculture and other human endeavors in the West.

Bison were nearly extinct by the 1880s, victims of mindless killing and market hunting. In their stead came cattle and sheep. Domestic livestock often competed with the remaining populations of big game herbivores and, in some cases, transmitted diseases. But there were benefits as well. Invasions of various shrubs on grasslands overgrazed and then abandoned by livestock proved beneficial to some browsing wildlife species, especially mule deer.

The lure of gold and free land in the West and the competitive advantage of western farms caused many people to abandon their farmlands in the East. Shrubs and young trees which invaded these abandoned farms and clearcut forests eventually would play an important role in restoration of white-tailed deer. In 1876, the United States had approximately 45 million people, and the geographic center of human population in the United States had moved 500 miles westward from near Baltimore in 1776 to a point near Cincinnati, Ohio (Trefethen 1976).

COMMERCIALIZATION AND EXPLOITATION

Since the beginning of colonial times in the United States, settlers utilized wildlife as food and clothing much as the Indian did. In addition, deerskins and other hides or furs served as mediums of exchange during colonial and early frontier days when money was scarce. For example, in the "State of Franklin" (an attempt in 1784 to establish a sovereign state including most of Tennessee), the salaries of the civil officers were to be as follows: governor—1,000 deerskins per annum; chief justice—500 deerskins per annum; minor state officials—specified numbers of beaver, otter and raccoon skins (Young 1956).

Historical records for market hunters document the extent of exploitation of big game. The first marketing of deer in the United States started shortly after the establishment of the first white settlements. Indians were the source of this supply. Many deer hides were shipped overseas. For example, between 1755 and 1773, 1,170,518 kilograms (2,601,152 pounds) of deerskins (from about 600,000 deer) were shipped from Savannah, Georgia to England, and in 1786, Quebec exported 132,271 deerskins (Young 1956). In 1763, deerskins "in the hair" were valued by the traders at 18 pence a pound (Young 1956).

In Randolph County, West Virginia, "in 1861, three men named Mace, Harper, and Stalnaker living in the upper end of Randolph County, entered into a partnership to hunt to raise money to pay for land. In one season they killed 169 deer and 49 bears and carried the meat to Clover Lick where they sold it at three cents a pound" (Young 1956).

Swanson (1940) documented several examples of market hunting in Minnesota in the 1870s. St. Paul housewives could purchase venison in liberal quantities at 18–22 cents per kilogram (8–10 cents per pound). In December 1872, 5,445 kilograms (6 tons) of venison were loaded at Litchfield for the Boston market.

At Leadville, Colorado, a mining boom town in 1878, prices for big game were 22 cents per kilogram: (10 cents per pound) for elk, deer and antelope, 27.5 cents per kilogram (12.5 cents per pound) for bighorn sheep, and 33 cents per kilogram (15 cents per pound) for bears. Frank Mayer of Leadville marketed 15,875 kilograms (35,000 pounds) of elk meat in less than three months (Madson 1966). These prices were in the same price range as beef, pork and mutton at that time.

By far the most dramatic example of big game exploitation during this era was that of bison. While no one knows precisely the magnitude of the bison population prior to

Market hunting for big game meat, hides and other parts was a lucrative and acceptable profession in the 1800s. Courtesy of the U.S. Forest Service.

Boon to the market hunter were the repeating rifle and the railroad. This wagonload of elk, worth hundreds of dollars even at a few cents per kilogram, was shipped to insatiable eastern markets. A Wildlife Management Institute photo.

arrival of white men, most authorities have estimated the number at about 60 million. By 1894, roughly 300 were left in the United States (Rorabacher 1970). This incredible loss was accomplished in about 60 years, with the most intensive killing in the 1860s to early 1880s.

In the case of the bison, factors other than the demand for meat and hides contributed to the species' near extinction. Bison presented an obstacle to crop and livestock ventures on the plains, so many were killed to rid the plains of a "pest." Also, there was a demand for the animal's meat by the railroad crews, United States Army troops and settlers. Many bison were killed for hides which, for a time, brought a price of up to $4.00 apiece. Some bison were shot merely for "sport" from passing railroad trains. The waste involved was almost unimaginable. It is estimated that 99 percent of the meat of bison killed by hide hunters was not utilized. Because of poor marksmanship, skinning techniques and wanton killing, an estimated five bison were killed for every hide that reached market (Rorabacher 1970). Because of improper curing, probably less than one-half of the hides taken reached the marketplace.

Efforts by some to halt the bison massacre were ineffective. Several territories passed legislation against the killing of bison between 1864 and 1883, but these laws largely were ignored or unknown to the hide hunters. Bills designed to protect the bison were introduced in Congress between 1871 and the early 1890s, but repeatedly were defeated or vetoed. An important factor in decisions not to protect bison was the belief that bison extermination would remove the last obstacle to "Manifest Destiny"— namely, the Plains Indians. The United States Army undertook an exhaustive and successful bison eradication program.

Forty thousand bison hides await shipment by rail from Dodge City, Kansas in 1874. Used for carriage robes, shoe leather and sold as winter coats to foreign armies, 1,500 hides were shipped daily from Dodge City. From 1872–1874, 459,453 bison hides were transported from this single depot. Courtesy of the Denver Public Library, Western History Department.

After the bison herds were depleted, some of the hide hunters moved to arctic North America and concentrated their efforts on the musk-ox. Musk-ox numbers were greatly reduced in response to heavy harvest by explorers, whalers, trappers and native peoples using firearms, in addition to the market hunters taking hides. Musk-oxen actually were eradicated from Alaska and greatly reduced in Canada. This decline occurred in the Nineteenth Century and first two decades of the Twentieth Century (Hone 1934, Tener 1965).

Caribou in northern North America also were exploited commercially during this same time period. Caribou provided virtually the only source of fresh meat at many remote trading posts, missions and other establishments. However, it was not until the middle of the Twentieth Century that the decline became critical (Kelsall 1968).

Nixon (1970) reported that white-tailed deer in the Midwest increased in much of the region as logging and pioneer settlement temporarily improved deer habitat and populations when virgin forests were opened. However, growing human populations, unrestricted hunting and removal of forest cover eliminated deer from all of Ohio, Indiana, Illinois, Iowa and southern Michigan by the early Twentieth Century. Only small scattered populations remained in southern Wisconsin, Minnesota and the Ozark Mountains of Missouri. In 1910, the Midwest deer population, excluding captive herds, probably totaled fewer than 2,000 (Nixon 1970).

Elk presented a unique example of exploitation. Unlike other members of the deer family in North America, elk possess a pair of ivorylike canine teeth in the upper jaw. These are the prized "elk teeth" or "buglers" or "tusks." In the early 1900s, countless elk were shot just for their teeth (Madson 1966). These teeth were especially cherished as fobs for pocket watches and by members of

Market hunters on the trail near Seward Creek Camp, Alaska. The pack horse is laden with caribou meat and antlers. Photo by W. H. Osgood; courtesy of the National Archives.

Benevolent Protective Order of the Elk. They sold for as much as $75.00 a pair. Illegal traffic was so persistent and profitable that poachers around Jackson Hole, Wyoming resorted to fastening elk hooves to the soles of their boots to disguise their movements and avoid apprehension by game wardens.

Although market hunting accounted for the kill of an incredible number of big game animals, and its effects on many big game populations undoubtedly were harmful, it is generally agreed that market hunting was not the greatest cause of decline of many big game populations. Of greater influence was the kill of big game for direct consumption by increasing numbers of miners, farmers, loggers and others who settled this continent. Swanson (1940) stated, "While the amount sent to market was large, it was small compared to that taken by hungry settlers who were often dependent upon game for food." Also, the unrelenting wave of human occupation of pristine lands restricted the normal movements of some big game species and populations, and drastically reduced attractive habitats.

LEGAL PROTECTION

Laws for the protection of big game were common in colonial times. In 1646, Rhode Island became the first colony to establish a closed season on deer. By the end of the colonial period, all colonies except Georgia had enacted closed seasons on deer (Young 1956).

During the period of intense big game exploitation, 1850 to the first decades of the Twentieth Century, game laws became increasingly restrictive as wildlife resources were depleted. The trend of local protection for big game during this period is represented by legislative action in the State of Minnesota (Moyle 1965):

1858—Closed deer and elk seasons from February 1–September 1.
1864—Closed deer and elk seasons from January 1–August 1.

1871—Exportation of carcasses to another state for purposes of sale or trade became illegal.
1874—Closed deer and elk seasons except from October 1–December 15; and sale of carcasses or green skins was allowed only during the months of October and November through the first day of January.
1891—Hunting of moose, deer, elk and pronghorn was allowed only during November, and sale of big game animals was prohibited except during this period.
1893—Hunting and possession of any fawn was prohibited; elk, moose, caribou and pronghorn seasons were closed entirely for five years, until January 1, 1898; deer season was November 1–November 20; and use of artificial light was prohibited in the taking of big game.
1895—Bag limit of five deer declared.
1899—The first resident license to hunt big game was required, at a cost of 25 cents; the nonresident license was $25.00.
1901—Deer season was open from November 10–November 30 with a season limit of three deer, and it became unlawful to offer for sale or to sell big game animals (thus ending market hunting).
1905—Caribou were given full protection (the last open caribou season was 1904); and the season bag limit on deer was reduced to two.
1915—Only one deer or one antlered moose could be taken during open seasons.
1917—It became unlawful to shoot or kill game birds or animals from a motor vehicle.
1923—Moose season closed, and deer seasons closed in odd-numbered years.

Restrictive laws across much of the continent were regarded as a minor nuisance to the market hunter in the 1880s and a major nuisance in the 1890s. With passage of the federal Lacey Act in 1900, which restricted interstate (and foreign) commerce of game, the era of the market hunter was essentially over.

Other federal legislation was important to big game habitat. In 1905, during Theodore Roosevelt's administration, the United States Forest Service was created. By 1908, approximately 59.9 million hectares (148 million acres) had been reserved. Much of this land was important to the maintenance of big game herds. The Taylor Grazing Act of 1935 promulgated control of livestock grazing on public lands. Probably the most important single piece of federal legislation with respect to wildlife, including big game, was the Pittman-Robertson Act of 1937. It levied an excise tax on sporting arms and ammunition with the revenues used for wildlife research and management. To date, the Act has raised more than $687 million.

OVERPROTECTION

Extreme and zealous protection afforded big game in the late 1800s and early Twentieth Century was needed at that time. However, the concept of total protection was difficult to adjust to when big game populations later recovered.

Three factors—better habitat, legal protection, and predator control—combined not only to increase deer herds but to create many areas where overpopulation occurred. As mentioned earlier, shrubs and young trees invaded abandoned farms and clearcut forest areas over much of eastern North America. This vegetative situation proved to be a boon to white-tailed deer populations. A similar situation occurred in the West where livestock grazing and logging created vast areas of shrubland preferred by mule deer. Although habitat conditions were favorable to abundant and productive populations of deer, efforts backfired in the attempt to rejuvenate herds by eliminating natural predators. Mountain lions and wolves nearly were eliminated in the East, and wolves and grizzly bears began to disappear in the West.

These situations, coupled with restrictive hunting seasons, created numerous problems.

Pennsylvania provides a good example. By 1900, white-tailed deer had been extirpated. In 1906, a stocking program was initiated and, in 1907, a buck-only law was passed giving deer populations protection from nonselective harvests. A lush food base from logged forests and overprotection caused a deer population irruption. By 1925, deer exceeded the carrying capacity of their habitat. By 1935, the population was believed to be four times more than carrying capacity allowed. Ranges were overbrowsed, tree production was reduced, farm crop damage increased, and quality of the deer declined. The public continued to balk at the idea of more liberal hunting harvests. In the winter of 1935, an estimated 100,000 deer died from malnutrition or associated problems (Lindzey et al. 1975). Finally, in 1938, a statewide antlerless deer season was declared. Pennsylvania was not alone with its deer crises. Aldo Leopold reported that 30 of 48 states faced similar deer problems (Lindzey et al. 1975).

Devotion of the public to the buck-only law was so entrenched that when deer populations did rebound to healthy and productive levels, it was difficult to enact more liberal seasons or harvests. Many states in the East and Midwest experienced long and bitter controversies before their publics were willing to accept harvests of antlerless deer or elk. Western states generally were spared such controversy although, in California, conservative attitudes prevailed and some deer populations still are excessive for their ranges (Swanson 1970).

REFUGES AND TRANSPLANTING

Other efforts to bring big game herds back from low levels at the turn of the century included establishing refuges and transplanting. In many states where only remnant populations of a big game species existed, their ranges were declared refuges. Refuges were created for pronghorn, deer, elk, sheep, bison and other animals by various states and the federal government. Two such federal refuges are the National Bison Range in Montana, established in 1908, and the National Elk Refuge established in 1913 at Jackson Hole, Wyoming.

Big game herds prospered on these refuges as a result of habitat and harvest management. As populations reached or exceeded carrying capacity, excess animals were transplanted to areas where the species had been extirpated. Elk provide an excellent example. Yellowstone National Park was one of the earliest refuges for elk. From 1892–1939, 5,210 elk from the Yellowstone Park population were shipped to 36 states, the District of Columbia, Canada and Argentina. From a herd at Gardiner, Montana, five carloads of elk were translocated in 1912, and 90 more elk in 1916 (Murie 1951).

While considerable efforts were made to replenish vacant ranges with ungulates, no documented evidence has been found of similar attention given to large carnivores prior to recent decades. Certainly, the grizzly bear, wolf and eastern mountain lion populations were in as equally bad predicaments as were a number of the ungulate populations, but apparently there was little interest in their behalf.

SUMMARY

Most of man's effects on big game were incidental or, if intentional, showed little forethought. Stone Age hunters who may have exterminated 31 genera of large mammals likely assumed that the supply of animals was limitless. Likewise, there was little indication that European settlers in North America were aware of ramifications of their various actions on wildlife resources until big game population declines nearly were irreversible.

Fortunately, we have learned much from the past that can benefit management programs of the future. It also is fortunate that we still have all of the big game species that were here when European man arrived. It is hoped that in centuries to come, our descendants will be able to say the same.

Moose *(Alces alces)*. Photo by William Ruth.

Collared peccary *(Dicotyles tajacu).* Photo by Walter Elling.

Grizzly bear *(Ursus arctos).* Photo by William Ruth.

Rocky Mountain bighorn sheep *(Ovis canadensis canadensis)*. Photo by James Yoakum.

Pronghorn *(Antilocapra americana)*. Photo by James Yoakum.

White-tailed deer *(Odocoileus virginianus)*. Photo by Luther Goldman.

Roosevelt elk *(Cervus canadensis roosevelti)*. Photo by James Yoakum.

Dall's sheep *(Ovis dalli dalli)*. Photo by William Ruth.

Mountain goat *(Oreamnos americanus)*. Photo by Steve Wakeland.

Mountain lion *(Felis concolor)*. Photo by Maurice Hornocker.

Caribou *(Rangifer tarandus).* Photo by William Ruth.

Chapter 18

BIG GAME VALUES

Harold W. Steinhoff
Regional Administrator
Colorado State University
Durango, Colorado

Value, like beauty, is in the eye of the beholder. No objective natural law of value exists independent of man. Each person individually decides the amount that any item is worth to him. People are similar enough to one another that they want approximately the same things, and seldom is there enough of any commodity to go around. Scarcity increases man's desire and, consequently, the value of the scarce resource to him. The objective of this chapter is to present an introduction to understanding the values of big game for mankind. These

are not wholly economic, but involve instead the application of social sciences to man's quest to satisfy his wants and needs. The reader is encouraged to study further basic principles of economics, psychology, sociology and philosophy, which together make up the understanding of values, including those of big game animals.

MEANINGS OF VALUE

The value of big game is whatever someone is willing to pay for it. Value is an exchange ratio. For example, the cartoon character "B. C." may exchange one mating club for five clams. Therefore, the value of the club is five clams. To possess big game, one may be willing to exchange money or some commodity such as gasoline, or some other resource such as time. The payment may be direct—a deer hunter who buys all the equipment and the gasoline necessary for his hunt. Or it may be indirect and inadvertent—the tourist in Alaska who is thrilled by the sight of a moose on the Kenai Moose Range but who scarcely realizes the cost of that experience in terms of money, gasoline and time.

Methods of measuring and expressing the values of big game and in using those values properly in analyses of comparability, efficiency and accountability are the purpose of this discussion. Values which can be measured in dollars can be dealt with by economic methods. Some think all values can be expressed in terms of money. This is not yet true. Many values to be discussed here cannot yet be equated to money in a satisfactory way. The emotional thrill of unexpectedly seeing a brown bear at close range while fishing in the wilderness may be assigned a dollar value once we learn how to do it. For purposes of comparison, it would be very desirable to express all big game values in dollars. However, some are satisfied with only intangible emotions as measures of value. Comparison of dollars and emotions is very difficult. Value decisions, based on these two greatly different measures of value rather than on just one measure, is correspondingly difficult.

Although other philosophical views of value are possible, we shall consider value as a human-oriented term. If a person does not exist to visualize and quantify a value and the exchanges it implies, the value does not exist. Therefore, a value cannot just "be." We must specify whose value. Every value is an exchange ratio in the mind of at least one person. Each value can be thought of either as a "cost" or a "benefit" to a given person in a given situation. Accordingly, big game can have both positive and negative values. For example, an elk eating a rancher's haystack is a cost (negative value) to the rancher who can measure the exchange ratio quite easily in dollars. The same elk may be a benefit (positive value) to a hunter.

Value to one individual may have both cost and benefit components. The elk hunter may benefit from the experience, but it may cost him time and money for a license, rifle, etc. His "net value" would equal all benefits minus all costs.

It is obvious that there is no single value of a big game animal, population or species. Rather, to a great variety of people, there is a whole set of values, both positive and negative. The user of an expression of value must determine the correct one for the purpose or circumstance at hand. He may want to determine how much money could be invested wisely in bighorn sheep management, to give elk their proper value in a multiple-use management plan on a national forest, to show the importance of big game to a legislative body or to assess cost of deer loss due to construction of a reservoir. The following discussion should clarify the various values and indicate the proper ones to use in a given situation.

Wildlife values are classified as recreational, aesthetic, educational, biological, social or commercial. This list is an adaptation of one originally proposed by King (1947). Recreational values have been very important in the United States, so their discussion will serve as an example. Other values will be described and quantified to the extent possible.

Sometimes we speak of "market values" which have a price, usually in money, set in the market place. "Extra-market values" are those which are not fixed in a conventional market, because none exists. Most big game values are extra-market values.

RECREATIONAL VALUES

Measurement and expression

The unit of value, or the thing that is purchased or exchanged, is very important in expressing big game values. One might think that the animal itself, such as a caribou or a musk-ox, would be a logical unit. But, in that case, no values exist if a tourist does not see an animal he expects to see, or a hunter does not kill or see the animal hunted. Even if the expected big game does not even occur in the area, the value exists if the tourist or hunter thinks that it occurs. This leads one to the conclusion that the recreational user of big game is purchasing an experience as the unit for which he is exchanging money and time.

Recreational values of wildlife are those related to sports and hobbies (King 1947). The recreational experience is made up of components, such as the deer (whether seen or not), beauty of nature and companionship. When big game is available for viewing or hunting experiences, we provide the essential component. But, it is the experience as a whole that has the value. We should be able to assign portions of the value to each component. But, at present, the best that can be done is to assume most of the value accrues because of the anticipated presence of big game. The value for the total experience consequently is assigned to the essential component—big game.

Benefits and costs are an important concern in expressing big game values. "Who gets the benefits and who pays the costs?" This is the basic question in resource conflict, land-use and other environmental problems. Many natural resource decisions and, in fact, human decisions of all kinds should be based on what the benefits and costs are to all concerned. This is especially important when dealing with the value of "collective goods," such as a scenic piece of landscape in which many have an interest, as compared to single goods which may be owned by just one person.

Benefit-cost ratio is a measure of the percentage return on an investment. If the elk hunter's benefit is $110 and the cost is $100, the ratio is 1.1:1, or a 10-percent return. In simple exchange of a loaf of bread for 54 cents, the benefit-cost relationship may be 1:1 if the market is in equilibrium.

But, in complex systems where direct exchange is not involved, such as environmental impacts, we need to reduce benefits and costs to some common denominator, usually dollars. We assume that the described benefit at least equals the recognized cost, and maybe more. Often, the minimum value may be measured best by cost, because the benefits are more difficult to measure directly.

If we were operating in a normal economic system, the cost and therefore the value of recreational use of big game could be calculated by assessing the conventional elements of production: land, capital, labor and enterprise. Costs result from net income which is due each of these elements. The income components are rent (income from land), interest (income from capital), wages and salaries (income from labor), and profit (income from enterprise). "Land" is the element furnished by nature, usually without human labor. A deer, in most cases, is a land component. "Capital" is a material thing or condition which owes its usefulness to human labor. The rifle one uses to hunt deer is capital. "Labor" is an exertion of mind or body undergone partly or wholly for some good (some economists add "other than the pleasure derived"). The effort of the hunter and the big game manager are examples of labor. "Enterprise" is boldness, energy and invention in practical affairs. Enterprise results in either normal profit (usually expected from the enterprise of organizing the elements of production), or excess profit (due to innovation rewards, windfalls, abnormal risk or monopoly power). The hunter or wildlife viewer exerts enterprise and realizes a profit which is related to his experience, skill and luck. Elements of production are illustrated in Figure 57.

A secondary cycle of production may start with an item such as wheat, a log or a hunting experience, and proceed without need for the land element, to include capital, labor and enterprise in a new product (flour, board or vicarious experience) which has a still greater value (Table 27). This is the "value

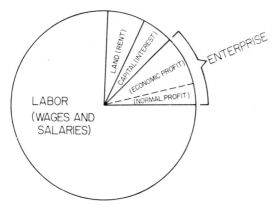

Figure 57. Elements of production and associated income.

added" concept. The comparability of the elements of production, of costs relating to each element, and the resulting values of the products are shown in Table 27 for two common market commodities (bread and a house) and for one recreational big game commodity (vicarious experience). Notice that the outdoor writer adds a value to the latter by describing a hunting experience, which is salable to the reader sitting in his living room.

But we have difficulty using the "elements of production" for estimating a recreational experience value because the labor and enterprise components are difficult to evaluate. The deer, as well as the entire recreational experience, often do not have a market price in the usual sense. There is no single selling price, so we use

alternative methods of measuring recreational wildlife values. This involves measuring components of the value of an experience, both costs and benefits. By combining the proper components, we can estimate total costs and total benefits to the individual and to any group in society. By subtracting total costs from total benefits, we get net benefits or net values.

The components to be considered in such a value system are: (1) expenditures, (2) consumer surplus, (3) opportunity cost, (4) diseconomies, and (5) management cost. These components and their proper measurement and use are described below.

1. Expenditures component. Cost components of a log may include soil, tree, axe, logger's lunch, logger's trailer, log truck, gasoline and logging permit. Comparable value components of a deer hunting experience may include soil, deer, rifle, hunter's lunch, hunter's trailer, vehicle, gasoline and hunting license. We use the term expenditures as a substitute for costs. The license fee is assumed to pay cost of management. The deer may be given free to the hunter; the tree seldom is free to the logger. Also, in the hunting experience, the deer may not be harvested and may serve the experiences of many hunters, perhaps in the course of several years. The consumer of a log (the sawmill operator) pays one agreed

Table 27. Comparable elements of production for bread, a house and the big game recreational experience.

Elements of production	Land	+	Capital	+	Labor	+	Enterprise	=	Product
Income from the elements	Rent		Interest		Wages		Profit		Market value
Primary cycle	Soil		Tractor		Farmer		Farm management		Wheat
Secondary cycle 1			Wheat		Miller		Management		Flour
Secondary cycle 2			Flour		Baker		Management		Bread
Primary cycle	Tree		Axe		Logger		Forest management		Log
Secondary cycle 1			Log		Sawyer		Management		Board
Secondary cycle 2			Board		Carpenter		Contractor		House
Primary cycle	Deer		Rifle, etc.		Manager and hunter		Hunter		Hunting experience
Secondary cycle			Hunting experience		Writer		Publisher		Vicarious experience

market price to the producer (logger). The deer hunter is both a producer, to a great degree, and a consumer of the experience. He is the producer because his previous knowledge, current thoughts and efforts play the major role in creation of the hunting experience. A person who hunts on a preserve transfers some of the production cost to the preserve owner. We can total all expenditures of the hunter for his experience as an estimate of the expenditures component.

2. Consumer surplus component. If one hunter pays $5 per day for a deer hunting experience and another hunter pays $35 per day for an exactly comparable experience, then the first hunter receives a consumer surplus of $30 per day. The difference between what a consumer would be willing to pay and what he does pay (which is related to costs of production and the profit as limited by competition) is the "consumer surplus." This normally is considered to be near zero for most commodities because supply and price have been adjusted to demand. This depends, however, on the elasticity of the demand. A demand is considered "elastic" if consumers quickly stop purchasing when the price increases. If demand is very elastic for normal market commodities, there is a minimum consumer surplus. If demand is very inelastic, there may be a considerable consumer surplus when the supply is adequate and easily obtained. Sugar and coffee are good examples. They formerly yielded consumer surpluses, because we found when prices rose that we were willing to pay considerably more than previously.

Geographic position has much to do with consumer surplus. Someone close to the supply usually pays less for the item. Big game hunting or viewing experiences, of Dall's sheep for example, must be done at particular sites in Alaska, the Yukon Territory, the Northwest Territories and British Columbia. For most commodities, we solve the distance problem by transporting them close to

wherever we live and preserving them there if that is necessary. But, for many recreational experiences, such as viewing Dall's sheep, the consumer moves to the area where the experience is available. In some cases, we pay extra, thus reducing consumer surplus in subtle ways. Nonresident tuition, higher food and living costs in Alaska, and lower salaries in some desirable areas, such as Colorado, may be examples.

Consumer surplus is calculated by a very ingenious method used by Clawson (1959). A simplification of his method is as follows:

Step A. Choose a specific area, such as a big game refuge, count the number of people coming to the area from various distance zones, and measures the expenditure cost to each person for each visit (Figure 58 and Table 28).

Step B. Construct a demand curve which plots the number of visitors per 100,000 population in a given distance zone against total monetary cost per visit from that zone (Figure 59).

Step C. Estimate from Step B the number of visitors to be expected from each zone under a series of hypothetical additional fees. In Table 28, for example, an added fee

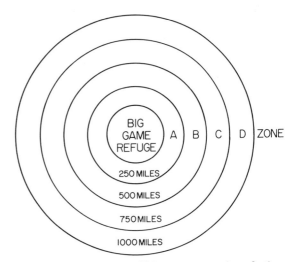

Figure 58. Diagram of big game area in relation to travel distance zones.

Table 28. Hypothetical relationships among number of visitors and costs of visits to a big game area.

Zone	Population in zone (in 100,000's)	Number of visitors from zone	Visitors per 100,000 population	Expenditure cost per visitor	If the added fee was		
					$1	$2	$3
					Expected number of visitors from zone	Expected visitors	Expected visitors
A	3	120	40	$1	90	60	30
B	4	120	30	2	80	40	0
C	5	100	20	3	50	0	0
D	6	60	10	4	0	0	0
Totals		400			220	100	30

of $1 would mean a cost of $2 for visitors from Zone A. From Figure 59, we could expect 30 visitors per 100,000 population when the cost is $2. There is 300,000 population (3 × 100,000) in Zone A, so 90 visitors could be expected from Zone A if we added a $1 fee.

Step D. Construct a second demand curve to show number of visitors expected who will pay each additional fee (Figure 60). These data are derived from Table 28 by plotting the total number of visitors expected (400, 220, 100 and 30) against the additional fees ($0, $1, $2 and $3).

Step E. Add all visitors from all zones under the second demand curve, by segments, to show additional fee income available to a discriminating monopolist—one who would charge each person what that person would be willing to pay as a fee (Table 29). A nondiscriminating monopolist would use the more practical procedure of charging one set additional fee to all (*cf.* Clawson 1959).

The total of $550 is the consumer surplus available from the big game refuge for a given period of time. It represents the value which visitors received from the refuge, but for which they did not pay. An example of an actual demand curve for the Kenai National Moose Range, Alaska, is in Figure 61. Many variations of the Clawson method have been devised to meet inadequacies some

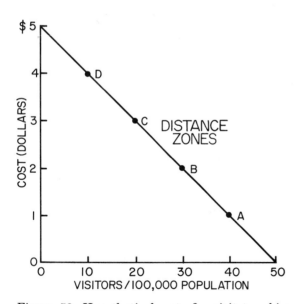

Figure 59. Hypothetical cost of a visit to a big game area as related to distance travelled, and resultant number of visitors from each distance zone.

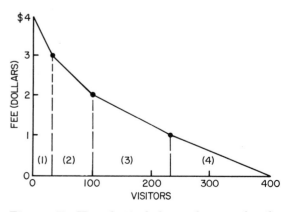

Figure 60. Hypothetical demand curve for the number of visitors expected at a big game area if various additional fees were charged.

Table 29. Estimate of consumer surplus from each segment of the demand curve (see Figure 60).

Segment	Visitors	Average fee	Consumer surplus
(1)	30	$3.50	$105.00
(2)	70	2.50	175.00
(3)	120	1.50	180.00
(4)	180	.50	90.00
Total	400		$550.00

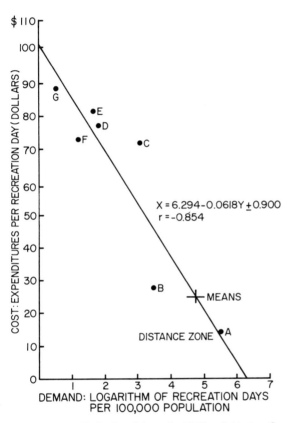

Figure 61. Relationship of 1968 visit to the Kenai National Moose Range to number of visitors from various distances. Zones include: A = Anchorage (0–483 kilometers: 0–300 miles); B = central Alaska (483–1,207 kilometers: 300–750 miles); C = southeast Alaska and Canada (1,207–3,540 kilometers: 750–2,200 miles); D = northwest United States (3,540–4,827 kilometers: 2,200–3,000 miles); E = western United States and Lake States (4,827–6,436 kilometers: 3,000–4,000 miles); F = rest of United States except Southeast (6,436–8,045 kilometers: 4,000–5,000 miles); and G = southeast United States, mostly Florida (8,045–9,654 kilometers: 5,000–6,000 miles).

have seen in the method. Some of these are described by Lerner (1963).

3. Opportunity cost component. The opportunity cost of a recreational experience is the loss of opportunity to earn income during time of travel, on-site participation in the experience and/or the value of products that could have been bought instead of the recreational experience.

The opportunity cost of time is most obvious for a self-employed wage earner who actually gives up hourly wages he could have earned during the period of recreation. It is least apparent for a salaried worker on official vacation. One could argue that there is a maximum number of hours per day, days per week and weeks per year in which one can exert productive work that will yield income. Other time is necessary for sleeping, eating, personal care, rest and, perhaps, recreation.

Historically, man seems to have been able to work up to 12 hours per day, six days per week, all year long, year in and year out. Therefore, the maximum work period (MWP) per week would be 72 hours. If so, then a portion of that time is chargeable to whatever alternative non-income activity is chosen. The leisure time of each individual in today's society has an opportunity cost. If leisure time, including vacations and recreational experiences, contributes to efficiency and effectiveness in normal working time so that productivity rate is increased, then there must be an optimum work period (OWP) which will yield maximum income, with the rest of the maximum work period devoted to leisure. The OWP might be 40 hours per week. Let us call the difference in time between the optimum and the maximum, "productive leisure time," or PLT. MWP (72 hours) = OWP (40 hours) + PLT (32 hours). The PLT then has a value equal to income that could have been earned in that time under conditions of maximum work. Because the PLT increases OWP and income, it would be a benefit rather than a cost of the recreational experience. However, any of the optimum work period time which is expended on travel and participation in the recreational experience should be accounted in the value of the experience as the opportunity cost of time. The amount people are willing to spend for a recreational experience, including the opportunity cost of time and, thus, its value for them, depends on their individual incomes. We would expect that among observed visitors, most of those from nearby zones would be of low income, making short visits. As the distance of travel increases, observed incomes will rise and the proportion of self-employed, professional and independent-income receivers will rise (Johnson 1966).

The extra cost of living in a given location—to the extent that this is purposely borne in order to be closer to the site of the recreational experience and, thus, to save travel and time costs—should be counted as a part of the cost of the experience. This might be measured by higher living costs or lower income costs. For example, an avid moose hunter may willingly bear the extra cost of living in Alaska in order to be near his hunting experience. If there is no extra cost of living in the desired area, then the savings in travel constitutes a consumer surplus. To isolate this component would be extremely difficult, and I do not think it has ever been attempted.

4. Diseconomy component. Diseconomies are unreimbursed costs to an individual or group as a result of activities of another individual or group. For example, providing the moose-viewing experience and maintaining related aesthetic quality on the Kenai Moose Range, Alaska cost oil companies an estimated $173,200 per year to protect the environment during the exploration phase in 1968 (Steinhoff 1971). Extra costs accrued because of narrow seismic trails, less heavy equipment, seismic

operation only with snow cover and on frozen ground, careful containment and disposal of wastes, and restoration of areas by leveling, reseeding grass and replanting trees. At the same time, the area occupied by oil operations caused habitat losses estimated at $18,000 per year in potential profit from wildlife. Diseconomies always have existed, but they have not always been recognized. Recently, they have become important because of environmental problems and the increasing complexity of our society, which result in increasing conflicts among segments of society that want different things from the same resource.

Some people feel that diseconomy costs should be charged to the individual or group that benefits from the action that resulted in the unreimbursed cost in the first place. This is known as "internalizing" the cost. For example, if a landowner is given a portion of the big game license fee, or if he receives payment for permitting others to hunt on his land, these might be thought of as compensations for his costs (diseconomies) of supporting wildlife and related recreational activities.

An important consideration is whether a diseconomy should be considered as an expected expense for the privilege of conflicting with a group that has vested interest in the area. For example, the Kenai National Moose Range might be considered as allocated to wildlife protection and related public recreation by the citizens of the United States who, in fact, own the area. In this case, a diseconomy to the oil industry is the expected cost of the privilege of extracting another resource, oil. Should the oil companies be charged in addition for their diseconomy to wildlife resources of the Range? The answer to this question depends on the collective will of the people as reflected in public policy and legislation, which results in the allocation of public lands for various but specified uses. Also included in unreimbursed costs or diseconomies to citizens in general would be wildlife damage costs, including those resulting from automobile accidents. The previously noted reasoning for allocation of and payment for diseconomies applies to damage costs as well.

5. Management component. Included here are the costs of managing a resource to provide recreational experiences. These are the more traditional production costs of any economic system. For example:

Land (lease payment)
+
Capital (trucks and buildings)
+
Labor (monthly wages)
+
Enterprise (skill of manager)

= Management cost.

Efficiency and accountability

By combining value components as costs and benefits in proper combinations as they apply to specified individuals and groups, expressions of the economic efficiency of a recreational experience system can be derived. Accountability for the management of that system can be achieved. For example, some 1968 data for the Kenai National Moose Range can be used to see how they apply to an individual who used the Range for a recreational experience, and to the United States as a whole (Steinhoff 1969). These data are incomplete but will provide some insight to the analytic process.

I. Value of the Moose Range to individuals who used it
   A. Gross benefits
      Expenditures of users $ 7.5 million
      Opportunity cost of time of users   6.3 million
      Consumer surplus of users   2.7 million
      Total individual benefits $16.5 million

B. Costs
   Expenditure of users   7.5 million
   Opportunity cost of time of users   6.3 million
   Total individual costs $13.8 million
C. Net benefits
   1. Gross benefits ($16.5 million) minus costs ($13.8 million) equal net benefit ($2.7 million) for 360,000 recreational days; or an average net benefit to the individual user of $7.50 per recreational day.
   2. Benefit-cost ratio $= \dfrac{\$16.5 \text{ million}}{\$13.8 \text{ million}}$
      = 1.2:1, or a 20 percent return to the group of individuals who benefitted.

II. Value of the Moose Range to the nation as a whole. (Based on the premise that the sum of all benefits and all costs to all individuals in the United States is equal to total benefits and costs to the nation as a whole. This is true because the nation as a whole simply is the sum of all individuals in the nation. And, any value to the nation simply is the sum of all values to its individuals.)
   A. Gross benefits
      Expenditures of users $ 7.5 million
      Opportunity cost of time of users   6.3 million
      Consumer surplus of users   2.7 million
      Total benefit to people of the United States $16.5 million
   B. Costs
      Expenditures of users $ 7.5 million
      Opportunity cost of time of users   6.3 million
      1968 federal budget for the Range   0.15 million
      Capital equipment and wildlife damages   0.15 million
      Total cost to people of the United States $14.1 million

C. Net benefits

1. Gross benefits ($16.5 million) minus costs ($14.1 million) equal net benefits ($2.4 million)

2. Benefit-cost ratio $= \dfrac{\$16.5 \text{ million}}{\$14.1 \text{ million}}$
   = 1.17:1, or 17-percent return

The 17-percent return represents profit from recreational use of the Range alone. It includes an element that might be thought of as rent, plus payment for enterprise in managing the range. But, the net benefit of $2.4 million did not flow into the public bank account. It remained in the pockets of the users of the Range, in the form of their consumer surplus.

The rent element in the analysis deserves special attention. If a fair rental value could be determined from a similar area of private land nearby, and if that value was less than the $2.4 million net benefits from the Range, then the difference would be considered a profit or payment for the enterprise of management. If a fair rental rate was more than $2.4 million, then costs would exceed gross benefits, and it would be uneconomical to manage the area for wildlife values alone. However, rents often are taken as the difference between gross benefits and costs (capital, labor and other costs) of managing the land area for its most profitable use. In this case, the rent would be $2.4 million. It might be recovered by charging $6.67 per recreational day for recreational use of the Range ($2.4 million rent divided by 360,000 recreational days) if the consumer surplus assumptions were correct.

The preceding analyses could be used to determine: (1) how much more investment could be made wisely in the Range to produce additional recreational experiences; (2) how much to charge for an entrance fee; and (3) the relative importance of recreational use compared to other uses of the Range in a multiple-use management system.

AESTHETIC VALUES

Although our society is considered quite materialistic, we still place a high value on aesthetic aspects of big game. Such values relate to wildlife objects and associated environments possessing beauty, evoking inspiration and contributing to the arts. The average recreational user of big game scarcely distinguishes the recreation of mind, spirit and body from the beauty of wildlife and the environment which stimulates pleasure and satisfies artistic urge. Part of the recreational value should be assigned as aesthetic value, but we do not know how to do it.

Much of the environmental movement is aimed at aesthetic values. Environmental impact statements contain narrative descriptions of effects on aesthetic values, but these rarely are quantified in dollars. However, they do affect decisions, and society sometimes seems willing to bear the extra costs of environmental protection in order to preserve valued aesthetics. One way of looking at aesthetic values in dollar terms is to assume they are worth at least as much as society is willing to pay to forgo having them.

EDUCATIONAL VALUES

Educational values are those which add to human knowledge, either collectively through research, or individually through personal learning. Big game animals are a part of natural communities from which we can learn about the functioning of individual organisms and the operation of natural ecosystems. These principles then can be applied in mankind's efforts to live in greater harmony with his environment and to increase the benefits therefrom.

BIOLOGICAL VALUES

The worth of services rendered by wild animals is classifed as biological value. Big game animals play an integral role in the ecosystem; they contribute to its function. So, when we speak of the worth of big game as individual animals or groups of animals, we really are talking about ecological values. For example, all the ecology of a moose is integrated into one fact, namely, the presence of the moose. Similarly, the economics of much of the ecology of the Kenai National Moose Range is integrated into one value—the wildlife experience. The worth of a nematode that makes organic material available for moose food shows up in the expenditures of moose hunters.

The ultimately expressed value of dollars in the pocket or of gleams in the eye are affected just as much or more by changes in biological complexes as they are by immediate manipulation of moose herds. A change in biological values inherent in the moose-wolf relationship will change the recreational and other big game values of the area significantly. Thus, any economic system must take into account the operative biological system. We must recognize a bioeconomic system. Variations in value are a result of both biological change and difference in human value systems.

SOCIAL VALUES

Social values are nonmonetary values that accrue to society as a result of the presence of wild animals. These values are demonstrated by what people do, say and commemorate. They add the "big game flavor" to a society or community. In a 1968 study of the Kenai National Moose Range, it was estimated that one-third of the human population of 7,500 that lived close to the Range was dependent wholly on wildlife and related recreation for a livelihood (Steinhoff 1971). These dependencies were in the form of commercial fishing, food and businesses providing goods and services for hunters, fishermen and other recreationists. This gave both a figurative and literal flavor to that area and its society's regard for and relationship to wildlife. In addition, 50 percent of those families used the Range for

recreation. Their entire social structure and individual lifestyles were related closely to the presence and prevalence of big game. In some unspecified way, this may be a "quality of life" indicator.

Wildlife and recreation rivaled weather as a topic of social conversation on the Kenai Peninsula. Approximately 13 percent of the column inches of news in the Cheechako News was conservation-related and about 5 percent directly concerned the Kenai National Moose Range.

Names of local features, such as lakes and streams, may indicate a social value of big game. The terms Elk Meadows, Deer Creek, and Wolf Creek Pass all contribute to characteristics of nearby communities. This could be measured by counting the number of such names per 259 square kilometers (100 square miles). For example, on the Kenai Moose Range, they averaged 3.4 per 259 square kilometers (100 square miles).

COMMERCIAL VALUES

Commercial values are those derived from direct sale in the market place. A big game item, such as meat or a hide, may be sold or it may substitute for a market item (game meat consumed instead of commercial meat). Values may accrue from reexpenditure of funds originally spent for the big game experience (the multiplier effect). For example, some of the money spent by the recreationist for gasoline is paid by the filling station owner to his employees, who in turn spend it for food, and so on. Rohdy and Lovegrove (1970) estimated that the multiplier for hunting and fishing in Grand County, Colorado was 2.0 times the original recreational expenditures. Others have found that 1.5–1.7 is a more usual economic multiplier for recreational expenditures in local areas.

We have dealt mainly with primary values to the users and consumers of the big game resource. But there are secondary benefits to those who sell big game goods and services. Expenditures by the big game user not only indicate value of the resource to the user, but they represent a secondary and indirect value to the merchant. In addition, one could compute the multiplier effect in the community and to society as a whole for big game expenditures. These could also be considered commercial values. They may exceed by several times the initial value of the big game recreational experience. These commercial values may be very important to a local economy and, therefore, constitute a significant local value. However, from the perspective of the individual who harvests the big game experience, and to the nation as a whole, multiplier money does not create new income from the big game resource in the same way that noncommercial values do. "New" income is created only when man converts a resource from nature to his own use. When a person has an outdoor recreational experience he is doing this. Multiplier money simply is redistributed within the economic system, without creation of any new money.

EMPIRICAL MEASURES OF VALUE

The following tabulation gives sources of information on big game values that have been measured in various studies. Actual dollar values are not given because methods of expression and interpretation of them are too lengthy for this chapter. Interested individuals may examine these references for more specific measures of wildlife values.

1. Expenditures
   A. General—Bolle and Taber (1962), Buckley (1957), Crutchfield (1965), Davis (1967, 1972), Gilbert and Nobe (1969), Krug (1965), Lerner (1963), Nobe and Gilbert (1970), Pearse (1967, 1968), Shoever (1965), U.S. Department of the Interior (1955, 1960, 1966, 1972b), Wallace (1956)
   B. White-tailed deer—Gamble and Bartoo (1963), Hahn (1951), Pasto and Thomas (1955), Thomas and Pasto (1956), Williamson and Doster (1977)
   C. Mule deer—Garrett et al. (1970), Ramsey (1965), Rohdy and Lovegrove (1970), Wallace (1956)
   D. Elk—Rohdy and Lovegrove (1970), Seckler (1966)
   E. Moose—Steinhoff (1971, 1973)
2. Consumer surplus
   A. General—Clawson (1959), Lerner (1963), Pearse (1967)
   B. Mule deer—Garrett et al. (1970)
   C. Moose—Steinhoff (1971, 1973)
3. Opportunity cost
   A. General—Lerner (1963)
   B. Moose—Steinhoff (1971, 1973)
4. Diseconomies
   A. Moose—Steinhoff (1971)
5. Other resource use
   A. White-tailed deer—Clarke (Unpublished), Gamble and Bartoo (1963), Hahn (1951), Pasto and Thomas (1955), Thomas and Pasto (1956)
   B. Mule deer—Biehn (1951), Garrett et al. (1970), Ramsey (1965)
   C. Moose—Clarke (Unpublished)
   D. Grizzly bear—Gard (1971), Shuman (1950)
6. Efficiency
   A. Moose—Steinhoff (1975)
7. Business
   A. General—Stubblefield et al. (1972)
   B. Mule deer—Ramsey (1965), Rohdy and Lovegrove (1970)
   C. Elk—Rohdy and Lovegrove (1970)
8. The six values
   A. General—Berryman (1962), Bevins et al. (1968), Bolle and Taber (1962), Boulding (1956), Buckley (1957), Davis (1962, 1967), King (1947), Lerner (1963)
   B. Moose—Steinhoff (1971)
9. Overview—Berryman (1962), Lobdell and Coulter (1969), Schick et al. (1976)

Chapter 19

BEHAVIOR

Valerius Geist

Professor
Faculty of Environmental Design
The University of Calgary
Calgary, Alberta

This chapter deals with the question: What should game managers know about animal behavior in order to accomplish management objectives? Ultimate objectives may be (1) to maximize the number of animals available for harvest, (2) to maximize the number of trophy animals, (3) to provide a high quality hunting experience irrespective of harvest, or (4) to maintain populations in a near-natural state for viewing or study. Most commonly, the manager's concern will be to maximize the amount of

game that can be harvested annually. In North America, such harvesting will be performed largely through recreational hunting. Primarily it is this objective that the chapter addresses, but with full recognition that managing for preservation is an increasingly important task, and that management for trophy animals is likely to affect a significant portion of our wildlife in designated areas as well.

This account does not focus on academic aspects of animal behavior but on a few aspects important to management. There are two reasons for this. First, there are a great number of good textbooks available on animal behavior, and those who desire a closer acquaintance with academic aspects are referred to those sources. Second, management deals with problems that usually are not solved by recourse to a single field of knowledge or discipline—an interdisciplinary approach is required. Therefore, the chapter includes only those aspects of animal behavior that aid the big game manager in reaching his or her goals. Moreover, a comprehensive account is not envisioned, but only a sketch sufficiently detailed for the interested to pursue the matters further. There simply are too many problems and goals that could be discussed. Only one topic, harassment of big game, is singled out for somewhat more detailed treatment, since it is of urgent concern today.

Man has managed big game animals for a long time, as stock held under domestication to wild populations maintained for the pleasure of royalty. One can recognize in the herding technique of herders from diverse cultures a sophisticated understanding of the principles of animal learning and conditioning, as illustrated by the study of Baskin (1974), or as can be read in parts of Zhigunov's (1961) book on reindeer husbandry.

A sophisticated knowledge of animal behavior was part of the trade of the medieval hunter who earned his keep in the service of nobility (Linke 1957, Knaus and Schroder 1975). Given the primitive hunting weapons of those days, detailed knowledge of the quarry probably was essential. The traditions of hunters from various cultures may strike us as odd, since traditions may contain real or apparent irrationalities. Still, it is important to remember that traditions contain the experience of generations, and some of them are as valuable today as ever before. Traditional herding, hunting and management practices offer no theoretical justification for associated actions and lessons, but these often can be provided

by science. Note, for instance, the accent on calm quiet grazing, or on disturbing game as little as possible, as stressed by herders or managers of game preserves in central Europe (von Raesfeld 1952). Today, these practices of paramount importance can be explained.

In recent times, the maturation of animal behavior as a scientific discipline has focused attention on its relevance to wildlife management. Behavioral considerations have entered wildlife management through: bioenergetics, since the actions of animals cost calories of energy and grams of nutrients (Moen 1973); game ranching (Bigalke 1974, Parker and Graham 1971); concern about the impacts of industrial and recreational activities on wildlife (Geist 1971a, Klein 1971, Child 1974); danger to humans from large carnivores in National Parks (Herrero 1970); and efforts by individuals to provide an overview of the significance of animal behavior to wildlife (Leuthold 1969, Cowan 1974). But, more often than not, they have appeared as comments or papers which arose out of the study of some single species or population in which certain idiosyncracies of the study animals had obvious management implications. Here we may point to Bergerud's (1974c) conception of the responses of caribou to disturbances; Owen-Smith's (1974) idea of localities to be kept free of game in order to receive the surplus expelled by territory holders; Laws et al.'s (1975) concept of cropping family units in elephants to reduce sampling bias, harassment and population distortion; Buechner's (1974) assessment of management of Uganda kob; or Geist's (1975b, 1967a) views on the relation of mountain sheep behavior to various management goals and practices. It is difficult to do justice to this category of papers, since a good many authors writing about behavior of given species have made references to management and vice versa. Various contributions are found in volumes edited by Geist and Walther (1974) on the behavior of ungulates and its relation to management, by Herrero (1972) on bears and their management, and by Bedard et al. (1975) on the ecology of moose, and in monographs on single species such as those of Mech (1970) on wolves, Knaus and Schroder (1974) on chamois, Kurt (1970) on roe deer or Butzler (1972) on red deer. A great diversity of views on how animal behavior benefits management is expressed in the works cited. Each should be read and assessed on its own merits.

Big game management deals with problems, and understanding the behavior of a given species or population is essential to dealing successfully with them. The literature on behavior of different species and populations within a species invariably reveals unforeseen surprises. The conclusions are, therefore, that: (1) knowledge of the behavior and biology of local populations is necessary, (2) generalizations are warranted only when and where great care is exercised, and (3) verification of assumptions is most desirable. To appreciate how detailed behavioral considerations can be utilized in management plans, readers should refer to the management guidelines proposed for different forms of American mountain sheep by Lanny O. Wilson, Raymon Demarchi, William Wishart and Lyman Nichols as reporters of workshop groups dealing with the management of desert, California and Rocky Mountain bighorns and northern thinhorn sheep, respectively (Trefethen 1975). The information collected in these writings makes evident that, despite valid generalizations, management ultimately must be based on the knowledge of local populations and their behaviors.

CHRONOLOGY OF EVENTS, HABITAT PREFERENCES AND ECOLOGY

Although, in a general manner, the chronology of events in any game population is known today, such information ought to be identified with precision and have annual variations recorded. This includes the dates and duration of such events as season of birth, juvenile seclusion periods, rutting periods broken down into their subcategories, occupation of seasonal home ranges, and dates of migrations and antler shedding. Precise data are imperative.

The same is to be said of local, seasonal food habits. Here attention must be paid to deviations from assumed generalizations by direct observation of individuals in the field. The notion of "winter home range" is very crude and must give way to a detailed understanding of what foods are taken at what time of the winter in which locality. There is no substitute for direct observations, a point which cannot be emphasized enough. For instance, following severe frost and the autumn fall of leaves, mule deer may feed on natural soilage and the fallen leaves of cottonwoods. No indirect manner of assessing food habits will identify these food sources nor a good many others, such as the terminal twigs of Douglas firs felled by wind, berries picked off bushes or fescue grasses pulled from their clumps. Unfortunately, accurate information on food habits is very difficult to obtain and no effort must be spared, not only to know this subject well, but to monitor it over time. Food habits change with seasons, within seasons due to weather and snow conditions, and among different sex and age classes (Harper et al. 1967, Dzieciolowski 1969).

In a similar manner, it is important to know where individuals of a given population go and for what reason. It is essential to identify and safeguard "ecological hotspots," such as areas for foraging, mineral licks, escape cover or terrain, or areas with unusually favorable microclimates such as thickets or caves offering a radiation shield, cover from convective heat losses in areas with regular strong winds, areas of shade where heat is a problem, inversion layers in the mountains where ambient temperatures are higher than elsewhere, and solar bowls which concentrate solar radiation. Again, emphasis is on a detailed understanding of localities favored, based on direct field observation. The end product of this type of research is detailed overlay maps—similar to those pioneered by Ian McHarg (1969)—showing seasonal-use patterns of a managed population.

No matter how meticulous the data gathered on chronologic events and their geographic occurrence, they remain less than useful unless one knows the reasons why individual animals act as they do. One can put some order into data by searching for adaptive strategies of the wildlife population concerned. For instance, differences in maternal behaviors of moose and mountain sheep are puzzling unless one conceives them as necessary and logical differences generated by different strategies of maximizing dispersion over the available habitat (Geist 1967a, 1971b). Sheep exploit small patches of stable climate plant communities and adapt by passing on the tradition for occupying home ranges having these habitat types; thus, exploration by individuals is minimized. Moose adapt by maximizing reproduction and dispersal of juveniles which chance upon newly created early seral stages of plant successions. Thus, sheep society is "designed" to conserve juveniles, and that of moose to disperse its young with concomitant differences in mother-young behavior.

The advantage of organizing data and knowledge about species into adaptive strategies is that it permits species-specific management and avoids the consequences of faulty generalizations. Sheep ought not to be managed like moose or deer, and vice versa. Also, one can explain and act on the crucial elements in a population's biology by identifying actions of that population. For instance, sheep cannot be expected to colonize a landscape as readily as do deer or moose because of sheeps' limited ability to explore new landscapes. Transplants of sheep can be used to accelerate distribution of the animals, but even these have to be fitted to the sheeps' biology. Bergerud (1974c) took these concerns into account in his successful relocations of caribou populations.

In addition, one can develop very sound explanations for a given management plan having researched an adaptive strategy and identified its crucial elements. For instance, it is poor biology to justify the manipulation of some vegetative cover solely on the basis that it has been done before. It is better to be able to explain in detail what the costs are to deer, for example, if the cover is removed. The vegetation in question may be the only thicket close to a given feeding area that provides a radiation shield and protection from convective heat loss during winter. Loss of that vegetation would preclude deer from utilizing the available forage, leading to reduction of the population.

Some species are K-strategists and some are r-strategists, and the biology of the two differs fundamentally (Wilson 1975). They cannot be subjected to the same type of management (Miller and Botkin 1974). K-strategists exploit climax communities, and r-strategists exploit ecotones and early seral stages of plant succession. K-strategists retain their population size through individual longevity, low reproduction coupled with great parental investment, complex social behavior which permits gregariousness, and a precise strategy for exploiting patches of habitat in space and time. The r-strategists are diametrically opposed in these characteristics. They are more robust, highly productive, easily dispersed, and comprise most of our game species. It is K-strategists that mainly grace lists of endangered species (Geist 1971b).

During periods of population growth, each species conceivably can act as an r-strategist; and during periods of population stress or decline, each species may become a K-strategist. The concept of K- and r-strategists is useful, but must not be adhered to too closely.

Each species, and probably each population, uses its own manner to maximize homeostasis as well as the uptake and use of nutrients. By so doing, each posesses: (1) strategies to minimize contact with predators, diseases and parasites; (2) means of maintaining body surfaces in a highly functional state; and (3) efficient means of procuring and using food so that a maximum amount of energy is spared from maintenance for reproduction. However, these homeostatic functions are only beginning to be understood. Strategies which maximize income, minimize expenditures and contact with dangers, as well as the compromises reached among different strategies, provide a promising way of studying the biologies of big game animals. They promise to be of utility in planning and managing research. An attempt to relate adaptive strategies to mountain sheep management was reported by Geist (1975b).

HARASSMENT OF WILDLIFE

In order to maximize productivity of a big game population, the manager must maximize the amount of energy and nutrients individuals can spare from maintenance towards reproduction and growth. The manager's goal must be, therefore, not only to ensure the largest possible food supply of high quality, but also to ensure full utilization and efficient conversion of nutrients to animal tissues. He must be aware of and able to reduce inefficiences in the utilization-conversion process, such as excessive energy and nutrient expenditures due to various causes. A very significant cause is harassment. This is not only topical, as papers such as that of Heath (1974) or public hearings on the effects of oil and gas pipelines in arctic environments indicate, but also embodies several principles of animal behavior which should be known and used by wildlife managers.

A big game population's ecology is the product of both habitat and food preferences. The ecology also can be a product of learned experiences that humans have taught the animals or to which humans have exposed them. Frequently, these experiments are reflected in where individual animals go at what time and what they are forced to eat. Food habits, too, may be a product of learning—a tradition transmitted from female to young (Kiley 1974).

The topic of harassment also illustrates the importance of a basic grounding in bio-

energetics, a subject long neglected but being reviewed again in wildlife management, as exemplified by Moen's (1973) approach. To maximize productivity, harassment of the managed population must be reduced severely.

Harassment is a term applied to actions which may only cause arousal in one situation, but may lead to panic, exertion or death of the individual in another situation. A harassing stimulus precipitates excitement, a physiological state that is not always detectable in the behavior of an individual because the animal may rigidly control its skeletal muscles while its organ system remains prepared for instant exertion. This state was termed "active inhibition" by Pavlov (Moore 1968). Frequent harassment, repeatedly preparing the individual for exertion, imposes a burden on the energy and nutrient supply of the animal and can lead to the "alarm reaction," the first of the three phases of stress (Selye 1950). If prolonged, an alarm reaction can be expected to result in organ damage, reduced viability and early death.

Harassment of wildlife has a number of consequences. The following is a list of three primary results. Secondary consequences are identified within each.

1. Harassment elevates metabolism at the cost of energy resources and reserves needed for the animal's normal growth and reproductive potential. Energy expenditure caused by excitation can temporarily double the expenditure for maintenance. As a rule, excitement increases an animal's metabolism about 25 percent more than that required for maintenance for long periods. What few measurements there are on energy costs of excitation were gathered, for the most part, incidentally to other metabolic measurements (Webster and Blaxter 1966, Blaxter 1962).

Since excited animals tend to leave the site of harassment, they incur cost of locomotion. This cost varies with distance, type of locomotion and amount of climbing done in the process. Hard running can exceed by 20 times the cost of basal metabolism, as indicated in the work reviewed by Brody (1945) and confirmed for white-tailed deer by Mattfeld (1974). Climbing requires about 12 times as much energy expenditure as locomotion on level surfaces. For many large mammals, the cost of horizontal movement is about 0.5 calories per kilogram of body weight per meter; and the cost of vertical upward movement is about 6.5 calories per kilogram of body weight per meter. The cost of harassment depends, therefore, on the distance traveled and elevation ascended, cost of excitation before and after locomotion, and food-intake opportunities lost as a consequence.

The above figures are cause for concern since daily intake of food (energy) by ruminants is relatively low. In addition, if fat stores of an individual animal are used to pay the cost of undue excitement, harassment is exceedingly expensive. For every calory of energy stored in fat, about one calory is lost in the process of storing it (Blaxter 1962, Kleiber 1961). Moreover, energy is converted to work at an efficiency rate of only 20–25 percent (Brody 1945, Kleiber 1961). The inefficiency of converting food to body tissues is demonstrated by the work of Bobek et al. (1974)—it amounted to 1.3 percent of the food calories consumed. This finding is similar to those of Davis and Golley (1963), Petrides and Swank (1965) and DuPlessis (1972).

The low intake of energy by a ruminant is well-illustrated by the findings of Drozdz and Osieki (1973) working with roe deer. In summer, the intake was 197 ± 0.53 kilocalories per kilogram $^{0.75}$ of digestible energy. In winter, it was only 70–102 kilocalories per kilogram $^{0.75}$ when deer had to rely on stored fat, since their daily intake fell much below that required for maintenance. These findings compare favorably with those from studies of domestic ruminants and North American deer. Maintenance energy cost

for sheep on good and poor pastures ranged from 1.1–2.0 times basal cost (Lambourn 1961, Young and Corbett 1968). Maintenance values for two-year old calves averaged 114 kilocalories per kilogram $^{0.75}$ (Young 1971). For white-tailed deer, Moen (1973) reported energy expenditures of 1.24–1.7 times basal cost. Thus, energy costs of locomotion and excitation are very high compared to observed food (energy) intake and normal energy expenditures.

The same conclusion has been reached by those engaged in the husbandry of large mammals. Elsewhere, Russian findings on reindeer are reviewed and their insistence on calm, undisturbed grazing, because a high level of unrest among reindeer leads to increased abortion and reabsorption of fetuses, excessive weight loss in adults and increased frequency of disease (Geist 1971a). Kiley (1974) pointed out that unrest may interfere with normal grazing not only through reduced food intake but also by an increased uptake of poisonous plants.

The sensitivity of ungulates to disturbance is reflected by the following. An observer can detect, on the basis of the external appearance of the animals, which herd of domestic ungulates temporarily escaped the attention of herders. Those that did are in noticeably superior physical condition (Gauthier-Pilters 1974, Baskin 1974). This is because herding depends on keeping the animals in a state of chronic low-level alarm (Baskin 1970, 1974).

2. Harassment can cause death, illness or reduced reproduction due to secondary effects from physical exertion and temporary confusion. Disturbance can lead to high rates of energy expenditure on maintenance and the functioning or repair of organs. Saiga antelope chased by cars (Bannikov et al. 1961) and reindeer exerted in cold weather (Zhigunov 1961) seriously damaged their lungs. African antelope developed fatal "overstrain disease" as a result of intense

chasing (Young and Bronkhorst 1971). In reindeer, harassment increases susceptibility to disease (Zhigunov 1961).

Psychological stress tends to lead to toxemia in pregnant female sheep (Reid and Miles 1962). If stress is experienced frequently and the level of the adrenocorticotrophic hormone is raised to abnormal levels in pregnant females, young may be damaged before parturition or act abnormally after birth (Thompson 1957, Ward 1972, Dennenberg and Rosenberg 1967).

When animals panic, accidents of various kinds may take their toll. Hard running through crusted snow can cause female reindeer to hit their bellies against the crust or hidden obstacles and lead to abortion. Also, exertion alone can produce the same result (Zhigunov 1961), and it is true for horses as well (Nishikawa and Hafez 1968). Panic among reindeer at calving time can lead to displacement of unborn young and, therefore, to difficult and slow delivery, particularly in females giving birth for the first time (Baskin 1970). Much the same is known from extensive experimental work with sheep and goats, as reviewed by Moore (1968). Trampling or desertion of newborn calves are other panic-induced causes for mortality (Zhigunov 1961). The most critical times of disturbance tend to be during cold weather, late pregnancy when the fetus is most sensitive to maternal nutrition, the fly season in the Arctic or cold temperate areas, and whenever else animals are in a state of negative energy balance.

Another poorly known consequence of harassment is the displacement of individuals into unfamiliar habitat, and in social contact with unfamiliar conspecific animals that often are territorial. Present theoretical understanding of this phenomenon suggests an increase in aggressive encounters as a result, plus reduction of available nutrients to all and, therefore, energy for reproduction. Rats introduced into already dense rat populations in Baltimore, Maryland created social havoc among the animals and, consequently, increased emigration and mortality of resident rats (Calhoun 1948). The resident population of rats dropped much below the preexperiment level.

3. Harassment can lead to avoidance or abandonment of areas and to reduction in a population's range and, ultimately, to reduction of the population due to loss of access to resources, increased predation or increased energy cost for existence.

Using theoretical understanding of animal behavior, biologists have predicted that animals associate unpleasant experiences with the localities and times in which they experienced the unpleasantness and avoid the places thereafter. This hypothesis was applied successfully for control of red deer and chamois in New Zealand (Batcheler 1968). In areas where deer found the best habitat and caused damage, heavy hunting and harassment were instituted purposefully. Areas of poor habitat were kept undisturbed. In the former areas, deer responded with reduced reproductive performance and lowered levels of fat deposition. In one population, barren females became evident. Several years after the experiment was initiated, females were of reduced body size. By then, the animals had moved into unfavorable escape terrain and become nocturnal. They did not return readily to the areas of good habitat after termination of heavy hunting pressure and harassment.

Caribou and wild reindeer abandon large areas and suffer reductions in population sizes as a result of disturbances. This was documented for wild reindeer south of Trondjheim, Norway (Klein 1971). The effect of disturbance is difficult to evaluate for these deer, since significant shifts by caribou occur over decades (Kelsall 1960, Skoog 1968, Parker 1972a, Bergerud 1974c). Nevertheless, in Scandinavia, range shifts caused by disturbance do occur. Moreover, once migratory traditions are disrupted, reindeer do not regain them spontaneously; it takes years to develop new migratory patterns (Espmark 1970, Klein 1971). This is very much in agreement with Bergerud's (1974c) methods of reintroducing caribou to potential habitat by teaching liberated animals their routes of movement.

In addition to range abandonment by reindeer, there is some similar information for mountain sheep (Geist 1971a, Light 1971). White-tailed deer responded with increased roaming and avoided areas where they experienced snowmobile traffic (Dorrance et al. 1975).

However, animals also can adjust to some disturbances or link them to some positive aspects. Identified by Heath (1974), an unpublished study reported that deer which approached the noise of chain saws as a prelude to feeding on browse cut by loggers did not respond noticeably to the noise of snowmobiles. In general, highly gregarious ungulates suffer most seriously from disturbances. They also suffer greatest range reductions and fail to recover spontaneously from low population levels (Geist 1971a). There are a few exceptions to the latter characteristic as shown by Saiga antelope (Bannikov et al. 1961) and pronghorn in some areas (Einarsen 1948). Another exception is Dall's sheep on open continuous mountain ranges, such as the Ogilvie Mountains, Yukon Territory, and in the Alaska Range where the sheep once were decimated by market hunters (Murie 1944).

It must be pointed out that displacement of populations from critical areas, such as caribou from calving grounds, can lead to heavy predation (Miller 1972). It also can lead to foraging in unfavorable areas, as Batcheler's (1968) experiments on red deer showed.

In the preceding list of harassment consequences, the major principle considered was that of the conditioned response. In the following list and discussion of three types of harassment stimuli, a number of principles are identified.

1. Stimuli that yield other than predicted or familiar physical and social behavior of individual animals. This type concerns a widely recognized principle: discrepancy between the expected and the experienced causes arousal. Arousal may lead to exploration or to flight and, in any event, to an attempt by the individual to restore familiarity. This principle is very important to understand and predict animal behavior, or human behavior for that matter.

2. Stimuli based on "stimulus contrast," including sudden changes in the animal's perceivable vicinity, such as quick movements, loud or sudden noises, pungent odors and other sudden tactile stimuli. This type actually is a subcategory of the principle noted under Type 1.

3. Stimuli to which an animal responds innately with alarm. Although we do include here stimuli based on stimulus contrast, or "looming" (the sudden increase in apparent size of an object denoting a rapid approach by the object), this category ought to be reserved for the innately recognized complex stimuli. For instance, Müller-Schwarze (1972) showed that black-tailed deer fawns respond not only to predator odors with which they had no previous experience, but are most affected by the scent of predators normally preying on deer, the coyote and mountain lion.

From these points, one can see at once that an *a priori* prediction of what constitutes a harassing stimulus for any given species is likely to be false or incomplete. Species differ in learning ability, may or may not have innate responses to specific stimuli and have different thresholds to various stimuli which contrast with their immediate surroundings. For example, in pest control, one method of harassment for one bird species does not work at all for a second species. Loud noises produced by acetylene exploders are effective in scaring away starlings, but are useless for robins

(Brown 1974). Nevertheless, three types of stimuli do explain a good many aspects of behavior that otherwise would remain puzzling.

Caribou arriving at seismic lines or graveled roads may mill about, run along the road and cross it only hesitantly, if at all. Migrating elk at river crossings act in much the same manner. Their reluctance or hesitation can be explained as follows: a caribou moving over tundra suddenly experiences a very different sensation when stepping on a hard-surfaced road. The discrepancy in the proprioceptive stimuli between the tundra and the gravel road is great and can be alarming. In Scandinavia, this phenomenon is recognized by reindeer herders. Bridges constructed for reindeer are covered with soil, inasmuch as reindeer otherwise would refuse to cross freely (Klein 1971).

The "discrepancy principle" also explains why a reindeer trotting along a dark path may shy from a white rock on the trail (Baskin 1970). It also predicts correctly that caribou confronted by a "dummy" pipeline ought to become alarmed, as was amply demonstrated in a study by Child (1974). Also, animals are expected to investigate and seek ways around a blockage rather than cross it (Miller et al. 1972, Child and Lent 1973, Child 1974).

Harassment may be precipitated by stimuli too inconspicuous or subtle for the uninitiated observer to detect or understand. Again, reindeer are an example. Wild reindeer may be alarmed severely by unfamiliar behavior of domestic reindeer. The latter, for instance, may continue grazing while wild reindeer assume alarm behavior in response to the same signal, such as the presence of human (Baskin 1970). Thus, wild reindeer on the move may give domestic reindeer a wide berth since they act incongruently. Thomson (1972) emphasized that loud sounds do not necessarily alarm reindeer, although they can. Relatively subtle sounds frequently cause alarm, such as the crunching of snow under a human foot, human voices, whistles, the click of a camera or the call of a raven. Klein (1971)

reported that humming of telephone wires apparently upsets reindeer and contributes to difficulties in herding. I have run across a number of instances in which animals panicked at unpredictable stimuli. A most impressive one occurred when three mule deer bucks panicked when a large bull moose suddenly appeared about 100 paces away on open prairie and trotted past; moose were common to the park but only exceptionally appeared in the area where I studied deer. I also have seen moose in a hunted population completely ignore the power saw and axe noises of two men cutting a trail. In fact, the moose bedded down as close as about 46 meters (50 yards) from the men.

On the other hand, mountain sheep and mountain goats tend to respond to very loud noises by fleeing to the sanctuary of cliffs. This appears to be an innate response to avalanches and rockfalls. Bighorn sheep also panicked at strange antics of conspecifics, such as individuals jumping around and about with a paper bag stuck between their teeth. I am not aware of any study that systematically explored harassing stimuli in large mammals.

Classical learning theory explains some puzzles in responses of big game to motor noises. The animals may take flight, remain indifferent or even be attracted to such noises, as has been observed for caribou (Klein 1971, Thomson 1972, Bergerud 1974c) and for deer (Heath 1974). Naive animals initially may spook from an unusual sound, but subsequent behavior depends on experiences associated with that sound. If the sound persists and remains localized, and the animals can approach or withdraw of their own volition, it can be expected that they soon will ignore it. If the sound becomes associated with alarming events—such as being pursued by a snowmobile—the animals subsequently will respond to the sound with excitation and flight. If the sound, upon investigation, becomes associated with something favorable, such as an abundance of food, the individuals will search out the source. Thus, big game animals become con-

If motor noise is persistent, localized and not associated with alarming events, some big game can become conditioned to tolerate or ignore it. Photo by Cecil W. Stoughton; courtesy of the National Park Service.

ditioned to and accept noisy highways and airports, crowds of harmless tourists, and the presence of loud, dusty, smelly, industrial activities—all of which tend to be localized and, therefore, highly predictable activities.

The astonishingly high degree to which large mammals are willing to associate with humans can be seen primarily in national parks, but not only there. Outside Banff National Park, Alberta, a population of bighorn sheep regularly frequents a limestone quarry, the adjacent cement factory area and town. In Alaska, a Dall's sheep population lives in an active strip mine (Heimer, personal communication). A number of authors have pointed out that large mammals

will habituate to what appears to be, at first glance, noxious stimuli (Kelsall 1968, Geist 1971b, Ericson 1972, Bergerud 1974). Moreover, large mammals also will search out human activities in order to benefit from them. The most impressive of these examples is caribou following the sound of chain saws of logging operations in order to feed on the lichens of downed trees. This has been observed in Newfoundland (Bergerud 1974c), Scandinavia (Klein 1971) and British Columbia (Ritcey, personal communication). The same was reported for white-tailed deer in Wisconsin (Heath 1974). Also, it is quite easy to tame ungulates because I have done so in the course of my investigations.

Bighorn sheep habituate readily to humans and artificial situations where there is no hunting. A Wildlife Management Institute photo; taken by N. P. Sorensen.

To the question—What is the effect of noise on big game?—there is no simple answer. The question, in fact, is scientifically unacceptable because it ignores the significant parameters of habituation and learning. Thus, to discover in an area with heavy logging where deer have learned to associate the sound of chain saws with food, that they are not upset by the similar noise of all-terrain vehicles is neither surprising nor a very important discovery. It is unimportant because it does not permit generalizations to other areas, as Heath (1974) correctly indicated; at least not to areas without chain saw logging and, so, with deer not conditioned to follow chain saw sounds.

Not all species adapt uniformly to the same stimuli. While mule deer may accept humans and their activities very readily, as is well-illustrated in Waterton Lakes, Banff and Jasper national parks in Canada, white-tailed deer in the very same areas remain shy and flighty. Although it is easy to habituate bighorn sheep to humans provided there is no hunting, and even tag them without restraints, mountain goats tend to remain flighty and are far less readily approached. In Lapland, reindeer have not become accustomed to herding by snow vehicles; and careless use of these vehicles can lead to losses of females and calves. (Klein 1971).

LEARNING

It is important that wildlife managers be familiar with the principles of learning for several reasons, the most important of which is to develop guidelines for human activities that prevent and minimize adverse impacts on big game animals. How does one ensure the continuing existence of grizzly bears in national parks when the policy is to permit extensive backcountry travel? How does one make oil or mineral exploration and production compatible with ecological requirements of wildlife? How should roads be constructed to minimize hazards to big game? For instance, in order to reduce contact between grizzly bears and people, removal of all garbage and edible matter from places accessible to grizzly bears is necessary but not sufficient. As long as people and grizzlies meet, and such meetings are not reinforced negatively for bears, then bears will not only learn to ignore people, but they will go the next behavioral stage. They will explore people ultimately to the point of total familiarity. The prelude to total exploration is attack.

Bighorn sheep initiate total exploration of a human by sniffing, licking, chewing and pulling on various parts of the person. Once thoroughly familiar with that human, a few are inclined to become aggressive. Mule deer act quite similarly. In short, if people are to mix in wilderness areas with large mam-

Neck-banded mule deer doe exits from highway underpass in Colorado. Photo by D. F. Reed; courtesy of the Colorado Division of Wildlife.

mals, it is important that the large mammals habituate to humans, but that they are taught not to go further. This requires teaching them to ignore human beings, but not permitting them to approach too closely or, in turn, to be approached too closely. This conception is warranted particularly for big game animals that evolved in cold or temperate regions, for a large part of these animals' adaptations are thought to be based on learning. The reverse is to acclimatize big game animals systematically to some inevitable industrial activity so that a population can be retained and expanded once the industry is gone and the land rehabilitated. Teaching game animals, thus, can become a management tool, and wildlife managers ought to accept its implications. Normally, game animals are taught inadvertently, often through harassment. Such "lessons" are not to the animals' benefit or to the benefit of people.

Where major traffic arteries cut migration trails of big game, passage opportunities can be designed and provided to ensure use by at least a few individuals. Once they have passed, more and more will follow over time and normal movements can continue. Pioneering efforts in this area by the states of Colorado (Reed et al. 1975) and Utah deserve praise. In short, wildlife management can assist wildlife to adapt and cope with change by making use of the principles of learning behavior.

As large mammals can be expected to generalize from hunters to other human beings, it follows that hikers can be as much a source of harassment as hunters. This is an important principle of learning to consider in management if a large crop of wildlife for harvest is a primary goal. Hunting and hiking may not be compatible activities, and it behooves wildlife managers to consider how these activities can be separated and regu-

Mule deer "follow" fence adjacent to highway east of Vail, Colorado. Photo by D. F. Reed; courtesy of the Colorado Division of Wildlife.

lated carefully. Is it possible to plan trails in wilderness areas in such a way as to minimize contact with big game? The answer probably is yes. Also, wildlife-viewing opportunities should be encouraged in areas where the animals are totally protected, such as in wildlife preserves and national parks. Recreational activities should be minimized in regions designated for wildlife production and recreational hunting.

SUMMARY

In order to fulfill the conventional goals of big game management, wildlife managers should make use of knowledge of animal behavior in combination with other information. This discipline has entered the realm of wildlife management comparatively recently and a fair number of papers, often written from divergent viewpoints, are available. The discipline of animal behavior can be pursued profitably in a number of good textbooks. In this chapter, I have presented only some of the basic knowledge from which big game managers can benefit.

In order to maximize efficiency in big game management, additional knowledge of behavioral attributes of local wildlife populations is needed. Accurate information is required on the chronology and time of events, local differences in food habits and localities frequented. These must be put in the context of adaptive strategies to explain why animals are doing what is observed. To achieve a precise knowledge of local populations and their requirements, an unrelenting and ongoing effort is required. Such knowledge ought to prevent unwarranted generalizations and simplistic theoretical extrapolations from dominating management decisions, policies and actions. A basic lesson of animal behavioral studies is that the animals themselves teach us best about their requirements, and that armchair biology is not nearly as effective or accurate.

In order to illustrate the kind of behavioral principles which big game managers need to consider, the topic of harassment was discussed in some detail. In order to maximize productivity, management must reduce the cost of existence to big game and ensure efficient utilization of available food resources. This requires minimizing harassment of the animals, not only because it usurps energy needed for reproduction and growth or inflicts damage on individuals, but also because it teaches inefficient foraging patterns. Individual animals strive to live in the most predictable physical and social environment they can find to reduce the costs of living. This is a most important principle to apply in big game management.

Classical learning theory explains how certain problems can be anticipated and solved so that big game can be made as compatible as possible with diverse human activities. The wildlife manager must not shy away from the thought of teaching the wildlife he manages, as such teaching is done inadvertently anyway and often is of no benefit to the populations managed. Learning theory also indicates that some activities, such as hunting and hiking, may not be compatible, and both must be regulated carefully if the goal is to produce a large crop of wildlife in a given area. Hiking and game viewing ought to be promoted in areas closed to hunting.

Chapter 20

ESTIMATING POPULATION CHARACTERISTICS

James R. Gilbert

Assistant Professor
School of Forest Resources
University of Maine
Orono, Maine

Management of a population of any big game species requires knowledge of the parameters of productivity, mortality and numbers or density. Almost without exception, exact knowledge of these population parameters is not attainable, even with unlimited manpower and finances. Therefore, the values of these parameters are estimated.

Estimates vary widely in their reliability, cost and usefulness. They should be judged as good or bad only in the context of their application. An intuitive guess may be sufficient for management planning for one population while a precise and accurate estimate may be necessary for the management plan of another. While it is recognized that each big game species and population presents unique problems in estimation, there are certain general rules and methods that can be adapted and applied in many situations.

This chapter will address some practical and statistical considerations in estimating population parameters of big game species. To accomplish this, sources of information will be identified, some sampling procedures will be outlined, and procedures will be described for estimating population numbers and productivity and mortality rates. The chapter will conclude with some cautions in interpretation.

The reader is presumed to have some basic knowledge of statistical concepts which would be contained in a first course in biometrics. Specifically, understanding the concepts of random sampling, mean, variance, precision and accuracy would be helpful to interpreting the following material.

SOURCES OF DATA

Information used in estimating population parameters is of several types and can be obtained in a variety of ways. The general types of available information are: (1) field observations of animal sign, (2) field observations of the animals themselves, (3) data from marking and recapturing or resighting, and (4) data from biological examination of individual animals.

Types of sign often used for estimates of some population parameters include pellet groups, tracks, range conditions, browse utilization and special signs such as scrapings. Often, these indirect data sources are used as indices of one of the parameters and no attempt is made to derive an actual estimate. Sometimes, if members of a population are secretive or rare, so that observation of the animals themselves is difficult, the only readily available information may be from indirect sources.

Field observation of the animals probably is the most common method of obtaining information for estimating one or more population parameters. The information obtained can be counts of animals to use in estimating population size or counts of several classes of animals, such as male and female or young and adult, in some ratio estimate of mortality or production.

Fixed-wing aircraft or helicopters often are used as platforms of observation because large areas that may be inaccessible on foot can be observed in a relatively brief time span. However, there are several problems with observing from aircraft. For example, animals are less likely to be observed and boundaries of sample areas can be difficult to locate during aerial surveys.

Some direct counting is accomplished from the ground, either from observation points along a transect route or in a drive count. Direct counting from the ground requires more manpower and time than does aircraft survey of the same area.

In some situations, marking animals and recording information from recaptures or resightings is a feasible method to obtain data for estimating certain population parameters. Marking or tagging projects usually are expensive and generally are conducted over a relatively long time. But, estimates from marking or tagging programs can be quite reliable. Procedures for capturing and marking are generally species-specific, but efficient techniques have been developed for most big game species.

Much information from which to estimate population parameters can be obtained if the animals can be examined. Ages can be estimated from morphological measurements, tooth wear and/or cementum layers in teeth. These data then can be used to construct a population age structure and, along with information on changes in population size, to develop a survival curve from which mortality rates can be calculated. Fecundity rates can be estimated from counts of fetuses or by rectal palpations. The most common source of animals for an "in-hand" examination is hunter-killed animals. Personnel at check stations also gather some of the data necessary to determine the age structure of the dead animals. Sometimes, other samples are desired because the age structure of the harvest is not representative of the age structure of the population. Sources of these other samples include animals killed by automobiles and those collected specifically for the purpose of estimating these parameters.

Information obtained at hunter check stations can be a valuable source of data. Data from hunter-killed animals often is analyzed in combination with other information to determine various population parameters. Photo by Don Domenick; courtesy of the Colorado Division of Wildlife.

An animal does not need to be dead for an investigator to palpate for pregnancy determination or to extract a tooth to identify age.

DESIGNING THE SAMPLING SCHEME

In estimating any population parameter, it is desirable to have an estimate that is unbiased and adequately precise. Both accuracy and precision can be insured with a proper plan of procedure for obtaining samples. To be accurate, an estimate should be based on a representative sample and calculated according to some unbiased procedure. Since most calculation procedures generally result in unbiased estimates if the sample is representative, the big game researcher should attempt to gain a representative sample. Often, the best way to do this is by random sampling, because the sample not

only is likely to be representative but variance of the estimate can be calculated by standard formulas. In many situations, systematic sampling is a reasonable alternative to random sampling. Systematic sampling will result in a representative sample if there is no pattern or periodicity in the population which is in phase with the interval between samples. A variance then can be calculated from subdivision of the sample into sections and computing among sections, or by replicating the systematic sample with different starting points and calculating of variance among replicates. One caution: a systematic sample does not mean that the observer goes wherever he chooses in a systematic manner, rather, that the samples are spaced in some regular pattern, generally equidistant from each other.

Estimates from biological populations generally are imprecise. One reason is because of inherent variability within any population being sampled. Animals are not distributed randomly, and these "contagious distributions" naturally inflate estimates of variance. Another reason is that sample sizes often are small and limited by the practical considerations of expense and availability. As is evident from the formula for calculating the variance of the estimated mean $\bar{y}$,

$$s_{\bar{y}}^2 = [\Sigma\, y^2 - (\Sigma\, y)^2/n]/(n(n - 1)),$$

one way of reducing the variance is to increase the sample size (n).

Another way to decrease the variance is to stratify the sampling procedure. This can be done if some previous knowledge of distribution of the subject population or species is known. For example, it might be known that approximately two-thirds of a caribou herd is distributed on one-third of a given area. From this, two strata (high density versus low density) can be devised and the total number of samples (n) can be allocated between these two strata, so that n_1 samples are obtained from stratum 1, and n_2 samples are obtained from stratum 2. Therefore, $n_1 + n_2 = n$.

There are two allocation procedures which insure enhanced precision (Cochran 1963). The easiest is "proportional allocation," where the number of samples in the stratum i (n_i) is calculated as

$$n_i = n \cdot N_i/N,$$

where N_i is the number of possible samples in the stratum i, and N is the total number of possible samples ($N = \Sigma\, N_i$).

In the example with the caribou, if there were 30 samples to allocate over a possible 300 samples (100 in stratum one and 200 in stratum two),

$$n_1 = 30 \cdot 100/300 = 10 \text{ samples,}$$
$$n_2 = 30 \cdot 200/300 = 20 \text{ samples.}$$

The second allocation procedure is "optimum allocation." This procedure results in the least variable estimate of any allocation

procedure. The number of samples in stratum i is calculated as

$$n_i = n\,\sigma_i\, N_i / (\Sigma\sigma_i N_i),$$

where σ_i is the standard deviation in stratum i. Unfortunately, standard deviations in the strata generally are not known. The only exception might be where some presampling investigation has been conducted. However, there is a reasonable way to approximate this optimum allocation. Because the variance (σ_i^2) in a stratum is generally proportional to its mean (μ), the relative density in each stratum (Z_i) can be used to calculate sample size in each stratum as

$$n_i = n \cdot \sqrt{Z_i}\, N_i / \Sigma(\sqrt{Z_i}N_i).$$

In the caribou example, relative density in stratum one is four times that in stratum two, therefore

$$n_i = 30 \cdot \sqrt{4} \cdot 100/(\sqrt{4}(100) + \sqrt{1}(200))$$
$$= 15,$$
$$n_2 = 30 \cdot \sqrt{1} \cdot 200/(\sqrt{4}(100) + \sqrt{1}(200))$$
$$= 15.$$

Whether proportional or optimum allocation, the mean number per sample units over all areas is

$$\bar{x} = \left[\textstyle\sum_i N_i \left(\textstyle\sum_h x_{hi}/n_i \right) \right]/N,$$

and the variance of this mean number per sample unit is

$$s_{\bar{x}}^2 = [\Sigma(N_i^2 s_i^2/n_i) - \Sigma N_i s_i]/N^2$$

Stratification, then, is a procedure that allows use of previous information. It can be applied in a variety of situations, whether the estimation employs direct counting (Siniff and Skoog 1964) or mark-recapture (Chapman and Johnson 1968) procedures. Even if the previous knowledge is not exact, some gain in precision can be made if the basis for stratification is reasonably correct.

INDICES OF ABUNDANCE

Population size can be estimated, or some index to relative abundance can be derived, from one or more sources of information. At the least-refined level is a simple determination of presence or absence from casual observation of animals and their sign. For big game, these determinations often are extended to indices of abundance which are compared over years to determine trends.

Pellet group and track counts, browse conditions, roadside kills, hunter kills and casual observations can be used as indices and trends. In certain situations, these data have been extended to population estimates. Pellet group counts, for example, have been extended to population estimates by calculating pellet group numbers on an area, the daily defecation rate, and the number of days deer were on the area. Track counts have been extended to population estimates by calculating the length of track an animal would make in a particular period of time. With both pellet group counts and track counts, population estimates are no more reliable than are estimates of the auxiliary variables.

In certain cases, the number of animals killed by automobiles may be an index to population size. The usefulness of road kills as an indicator depends on whether the number of animals on the road is a function of population size or of local movement in response to seasonal or abnormal habitat conditions.

The number of animals killed in a legal season may be an indicator of population size, and its age structure an indicator of survival, but estimates of population number or survival rate seldom can be made from hunting kill alone. There are too many other factors which influence numbers harvested to extend kill figures reliably to estimates of population parameters. For example, hunting season regulations or weather conditions during a hunting season may influence numbers killed.

ESTIMATES FROM DIRECT OBSERVATIONS

Direct observations of animals are the most common methods of obtaining information from which to estimate population density, mortality rates and productivity. With direct observation, the sample unit can be a quadrat or strip of area on which animals are counted. It also can be the animals themselves, with the information collected being the distance from the observer. In the first instance, counts of animals are used to make estimates of numbers directly and, therefore, are called "direct" estimates. The second type of estimate of population numbers is an "indirect" estimate because it is not the population number being estimated but the sample area.

Line transect estimate

A line transect estimate is an indirect estimate originally developed for such wildlife species as ruffed grouse. The line transect should not be confused with a strip sample. In a strip sample, all animals within a certain distance of a line are counted; whereas, in a line transect, all animals observed are included in the sample, no matter how far from the line they are. Either the distance from the observer to the animals and perhaps the angle away from the line of travel is measured, or the right-angle distance from the line of travel to the animal is measured. From either measurement of distance, a sample area is calculated and a population estimate is made.

In procedures for estimating populations from line transect data, one must assume that the probability of detecting an animal along the line of travel is one. As distance from the line of travel to an animal increases, probability drops in some smooth manner. With many of the estimates, a particular mathematical probability distribution is presumed while a few are nonparametric in that one need assume only probability of detection decreases with distance. There are a variety of estimators from which to choose, but several have been shown to be better than others (Eberhardt 1968, Gates 1969).

The applicability of line transect estimates to big game population has yet to be verified. If the highest probability of sighting is not along the line of travel, such as counting from a fixed-wing aircraft where observations directly underneath are more difficult, there is no line transect estimating procedure which can be applied. However, the future theoretical development of line transect estimates provides some promise for this method.

Direct estimates

The most common method of estimating population density, which involves actual observations of animals, is the use of direct estimates. In this procedure, (1) the total study area is divided into potential sampling areas or units, (2) a sample of these is selected, (3) the numbers of animals on these sample units are counted, and (4) the counts are entered into a formula from which an estimate is made. As discussed previously, selection of the sample units can be random, stratified random or systematic.

Generally, sampling units are all the same size and shape and have the same probability of being included in the sample. The size and shape of sampling units depend on the methods to be employed to count animals and on the terrain in the area. Quadrats or square sampling units may be appropriate for counting from either the ground or aircraft if boundaries can be designated without appreciable error. There is a trade-off in the selected size of the quadrat in that, if too small, determination of which animals are to be included in the count becomes difficult. If the quadrat is too large, animals may be counted twice or not counted at all.

An alternative to the quadrat is the strip or belt sample unit. When counting in a strip sample unit, the observer moves along a straight, predetermined path, counting animals within a certain distance on one or both sides of the path. The primary problem with strip samples is choosing a realistic strip width. If the strip is too wide, many animals may be missed, especially near its outer edges. If the strip is too narrow, few animals may be encountered and observations of many outside the strip will be useless. Strip width should be such that all or nearly all animals within the strip are observable from the predetermined path.

Counting individuals of any population of big game species can be difficult, especially from the air. In situations where the animals are in large concentrations or groups, photography can be used to obtain accurate counts. Also, there is evidence that counts from aircraft generally are low because some animals are not easily observed. The fraction not observed can be significant. If an absolute population estimate is desired, some correction factor must be calculated from comparisons of simultaneous ground and aerial counts over the same areas.

Counts for ratios

Often, a direct count will not be used to estimate the number of animals in a population but will be used to determine the relative frequency of two or more subclasses within the population. For example, the relative frequency of young-of-the-year or of males might be the objective. Relative frequencies, with proper interpretation and other information, can lead to estimates of productivity or mortality rates. For these counts of ratios, it is necessary to be able to identify individual animals as belonging to a particular class. Age ratios and sex ratios are commonly used statistics in big game management planning. Estimation of ratios by direct counting requires little preparation in addition to that for counts to estimate total numbers. However, many populations of big game segregate over an area by sex and/or age classes. Therefore, knowledge of the segregation patterns of a subject species is required so that the sampling procedure can be designed to account for them.

Change-in-ratio estimate

A population estimate sometimes can be calculated using direct counts in a ratio of two population classes before and after a hunting season. There must be a differential mortality rate as a result of the hunting season; and actual numbers of each class killed during the hunting season must be known. Then, a change-in-ratio estimate of the population size can be made as follows:

Let N_1 = population size before the hunting season,

N_2 = population size after the hunting season,

R = total number of animals killed in the hunting season,

R_x = total number of animals of type x killed in the hunting season,

x_1 = total number of animals of type x in sample prior to the season,

n_1 = total number of animals (including type x) in the sample prior to the season, and

x_2, n_2 = same counts in samples after the hunting season,

then the population size prior to the season is

$$N_1 = [R_x - R\,(x_2/n_2)]/[(x_1/n_1) - (x_2/n_2)],$$

and the population size after the season is

$$N_2 = N_1 - R.$$

If there is little difference in mortality between the two classes, the denominator is close to zero and the population estimate will be quite variable. This procedure can be used when one age class is more susceptible to hunting pressure, or when one sex or age class is hunted more heavily than others.

MARK-RECAPTURE ESTIMATES

Depending on the design and effort in a marking-and-recapturing or resighting program, the information derived can be used to estimate not only population size, but mortality and production rates as well. There are a variety of designs and estimation procedures used in analyzing marked animal data which require varying amounts of effort and information (Seber 1973). The more complex designs require increased sample sizes and fewer assumptions. Every mark-recapture estimate requires that marked and unmarked animals are equally susceptible to recapture, and that no marks are lost from individuals.

The most simple mark-recapture estimate is the Lincoln-Peterson index. This method utilizes data from one marking period and one recapture period to estimate population size. One also assumes that no production, mortality immigration or emigration occur between the two periods.

Often, the number of animals captured at any one time is so small that the resulting estimate from a single mark and recapture is quite variable. This is particularly true of big game populations. In such a situation, information from multiple marking and recapturing periods can be used to estimate population size. There are a number of models for estimating population size which use multiple markings and recaptures of a population in which no new individuals are introduced into the population during the course of study. Among the most common is the Schnabel estimate. A Seber-Jolly estimate can be used if both the number of marked animals and the period when they were last captured are known. With this procedure, it is not necessary that the population remain static, since estimates of production, immigration and survival rate can be made.

One problem with many mark-recapture programs is that marks often are lost. Although the rate of such losses can be estimated if there is double marking, population estimates are more difficult. A serious

A polar bear drugged from a helicopter will be tagged, examined and released. If and when the bear is recaptured, similar data will provide comparative information concerning its movements, growth and reproductive status. Photo by R. Russell; courtesy of the Canadian Wildlife Service.

problem with many big game species is that marked and unmarked animals may remain segregated between sampling periods, and some sex and age classes may be more vulnerable to capture. In such situations, separate estimates might be made for each class.

SUMMARY

There are a variety of sources from which to obtain procedures for estimating big game population size, and productivity and mortality rates (Cochran 1963, Seber 1963, Schultz et al. 1976). Only a few survey opportunities and procedures have been identified in this chapter. Anyone contemplating actual field work is encouraged to investigate these and other methods more thoroughly, and to plan the effort with the help of someone familiar with statistical techniques and big game population dynamics. Caution should be exercised in interpreting estimates, because some seemingly obvious assumptions may not necessarily apply to the particular population model used or the big game population under study. For example, an age structure by itself is not sufficient basis from which to estimate survival rate except in most unusual circumstances. Sometimes, the resources available for gathering data will not be adequate to obtain an answer of required precision. Serious consideration should be given to forgo or abandon any effort in which results may be significantly biased or imprecise.

Chapter 21

POPULATION MODELING

Walt Conley

Assistant Professor
Department of Fishery and Wildlife Sciences
New Mexico State University
Las Cruces, New Mexico

In recent years, modeling of big game populations has developed into a major management and research tool. In this chapter, I will explain how to conduct a demographic analysis and construct a basic model to provide big game population projections. The concepts presented are common to all wildlife populations. To make the task of suitable length, a generalized big game species is used. Such use of a "theoretical ideal" has both advantages and disadvantages.

On the positive side, the approach emphasizes the similarity of all big game populations. The interrelationships among various population processes are similar; the numerical values associated with such processes are species-specific. Thus, while each big game species is ecologically distinct in specifics, general patterns apply to all. The material in this chapter emphasizes these general patterns.

The disadvantage of this approach involves difficulties in transferring concepts learned about an "ideal" but nonexistent population into an actual species-specific management problem. Concentration on general patterns presented will facilitate understanding. There is no shortcut; and while an attempt has been made to simplify this material, too much simplification can result in a presentation that is misleading or incorrect in identifying essential elements of population dynamics.

Demography, the study of vital statistics of a population, is a subject less complex than it may appear at first. However, a considerable amount of arithmetic is involved, and data needed for demographic analyses can be difficult to obtain. Demographic analyses deal with patterns of population productivity and mortality and, in the form of a model, can be used to project future trends and characteristics of a particular population.

Models are abstractions of reality, and because they invariably omit some significant population or environmental characteristics or conditions, no model is perfect.

Space restricts this discussion to a skeleton model. A theory that applies to all populations is presented at the beginning, followed by some procedures for adding demographic reality specific to a particular site and species.

PATTERNS OF MORTALITY AND FERTILITY

Populations may be divided into two major patterns of mortality and fertility: (1) seasonal breeders that do not contain overlapping generations, and (2) seasonal or periodic breeders that contain overlapping generations. The simplest demographic situation is found in populations of seasonal breeders without overlapping generations. All big game species are iteroparous, or repeat breeders. Therefore, big game populations contain several generations at any given point in time. In this respect, they require relatively complex models for adequate description.

An important characteristic of populations is growth rate. I first consider a basic growth rate, then separate that rate into demographic components and, finally, return to growth rates in the projection model.

Assuming that some initial population size at $t = 0$ (that is, the time a new group of age zero animals enters the population) is N_0, and that these N_0 individuals will mature to breed and promptly die, then the population contains only one generation at any given point in time. If each of the N_0 individuals has been replaced on the average by λ offspring, then at $t = 1$, the population size after one season will be $N_1 = \lambda N_0$. Repeating for a second breeding period gives

$$N_2 = \lambda N_1 = \lambda (\lambda N_0) = \lambda^2 N_0,$$

and a third breeding period gives

$$N_3 = \lambda N_2 = \lambda (\lambda^2 N_0) = \lambda^3 N_0.$$

In general, for t breeding periods,

$$N_t = \lambda^t N_0, \qquad [1]$$

where N_t is the population size in the tth season, and λ is the per capita rate of increase per season. This form of population increase is called geometric growth because of the geometric series $1, \lambda, \lambda^2, \lambda^3, \ldots, \lambda^t$.

This population contains only a single generation, and equation [1] requires only two parameters—initial population size (N_0) and the finite rate of population increase (λ)—for projection to any given tth breeding period.

More difficult to project are populations containing seasonal or periodic breeders that breed more than once or survive past reproductive age. The procedures and model discussed here utilize discrete time intervals and, therefore, are presented as difference equations. Such structures are wholly satisfactory since most wild populations are comprised of seasonal or periodic breeders. Continuous breeding in wild populations is quite uncommon.

When discussing patterns of mortality and fertility, it is standard to concentrate on the female portion of a population. This is no problem when the ratio of males to females is 1:1 (total population size is simply doubled at any given time t). More will be said about sex-specific survival rates. For now, I assume a sex ratio of 1:1 for all age classes, and will consider only the female portion of the population.

BASIC LIFE TABLES

Strictly speaking, a life table is a schedule of survivors over time. Other useful information may be derived from a survivorship schedule and, altogether, such data comprise an "expanded" life table. Most columns in an expanded life table are not sex-specific and may be computed for males and females alike. Several additional columns that require birth schedules are specific to females.

Life tables express much of the basic demographic data that are important for population models. Good life table data are difficult to obtain and highly subject to misinterpretation. The basic assumptions involved in life table construction will emerge from this discussion. However, the procedures for obtaining such data in the first place are beyond the scope of this chapter and, for purposes of discussion, I will assume that adequate data have been collected.

A cohort of animals is a group of individuals of the same age in a population. Starting with an initial cohort of 100 age-zero females ($n_0 = 100$) at $t = 0$, and applying a constant survival of 60 percent per year, the cohort will decrease in size so that at $t = 1$, $n_1 = 60.0$; at $t = 2$, $n_2 = 36.0$; at $t = 3$, $n_3 = 21.6$; and so on. Note that as time increases by one-year intervals, the individuals get one year older, but that there are always 40 percent fewer individuals one year later. These results can be seen in the first three columns of Table 30. Note that the age column, x, begins at zero. This is done to avoid ambiguities that will become apparent shortly. The n_x column contains the number of individuals that are alive at the beginning of the age interval x to $x + 1$, and D_x is the number of individuals that die during the age interval x to $x + 1$. Columns of n_x and D_x express information in terms of numbers of individuals in the original cohort. A more general procedure is to convert this information to proportions (probabilities), thus allowing comparisons among cohorts of different initial sizes.

The n_x column is converted to survivorship probabilities by

$$l_x = n_x/n_0. \qquad [2]$$

The result is a survivorship curve (l_x) with the values of l_x representing the probability that an individual of age zero will survive to enter the xth age class. In this manner, for

Table 30. Expanded life table with six columns. Hypothetical data show an initial cohort of 100 females, 60 percent per year survival, and expected production of female offspring. See text for specific definitions of each column. All numbers are truncated at accuracy level shown to avoid "rounding rules."

x	n_x	D_x	l_x	m_x	$l_x m_x$
0	100.00	40.00	1.000	0.0	
1	60.00	24.00	0.600	0.75	0.450
2	36.00	14.40	0.360	0.75	0.270
3	21.60	8.64	0.216	0.75	0.162
4	12.96	5.19	0.129	0.75	0.096
5	7.77	3.11	0.077	0.75	0.057
6	4.66	4.66	0.046	0.75	0.034
Total				4.5[a]	1.069[b]

[a]Data in the m_x column are obtainable only from research; these values are hypothetical. The sum of the m_x column is the Gross Reproductive Rate (GRR). This is a per female rate for female offspring.
[b]The sum of the $l_x m_x$ column is the Net Reproductive Rate (R_0). This is a per female rate of female offspring as shown. R_0 is best indicated as such a per capita rate (multiply by 10^3 to change from per capita to per thousand).

any initial size cohort, standardized curves are produced for comparison with other populations or species. It is a common practice in wildlife management (although by no means necessary) to express survival information as numbers surviving per thousand. This is readily accomplished by multiplying the l_x values as obtained above by 10^3. Base cohorts to any power of 10 are obtained in a similar fashion. Several columns in the expanded life table are best understood when cohorts are treated on a base of 1000 (etc.) individuals rather than as probabilities.

Fertility information typically is presented as an age-specific column representing the expected number of females born to a female of age x to $x + 1$. These values (m_x) are the expected per capita production of female offspring by females of a given age interval.

As is the case with survival data, m_x values are difficult to obtain. Researchers frequently will count embryos, placental scars or similar indicators if autopsy is feasible. Another procedure is to count the number of offspring observed in a population and, by knowing sex ratio and density, estimate the number of young produced by the average female in the population.

For our purposes, this definition of m_x is less satisfactory than it should be, because it confounds two very distinct biological processes affecting the demographic character of the population. First, the question of whether or not a given female will produce young must be considered. Second, given that a female will produce young, it is necessary to know how many she is expected to produce. The number of young produced by any given female ultimately is determined by evolutionary history and is fixed genetically within certain limits. These ideal values are modified by nutrition and a number of proximate ecological factors. The proportion of females in a population that actually breed is determined by rather different conditions among which sex ratio, density and behavior may play an important role.

It is necessary for modeling purposes (and for clear thinking as well) to define m_x somewhat differently than usual. Let n'_{ix} be the number of young produced by the ith female of age x to $x + 1$, with $i = 1, 2, \ldots, a$ (that is, there are "a" total females who produced young). In this way, the fertility function becomes

$$m_x = \frac{1}{2} \left(\frac{1}{a} \sum_{i=1}^{a} n'_{ix} \right), \qquad [3]$$

under an assumption of a sex ratio of 1:1 at birth. This definition of m_x is more restrictive than that generally used where the number of female offspring produced is considered across all females in a given age class. Either definition is valid; the one used depends on available data and the intended purpose. The portion of the equation inside parentheses is simply the average number of young per female in an x to $x + 1$ age class. The portion outside parentheses may be modified appropriately if the sex ratio at birth is skewed to males or females. In general, there are compelling theoretical arguments for assuming a sex ratio of 1:1 at birth unless there is specific evidence to the contrary.

This definition of m_x leads to several considerations. First, all m_x values will be ≥ 0.5 (with a sex ratio of 1:1) since only females actually producing offspring are included. Also, because these values are averages, distributional properties within age classes become a worthy subject for analysis. Second, the proportion of any given x to $x + 1$ age class that actually breeds becomes an important variable in population-growth studies, and has considerable value in studies simulating potential population responses to environmental constraints. In the section on modeling, I will show how to incorporate these two notions into a projection model.

Given schedules of l_x and m_x, a variety of useful columns may be generated to form a complex "expanded" life table. Most of these columns may be calculated by starting with the m_x or l_x schedules discussed above. One should recognize that there is no new information in these columns, but only a different way of expressing the original survival data to facilitate various interpretations.

As mentioned, l_x expresses the probability that an individual of age zero will survive to enter the xth age class.

The death schedule, the probability at $x = 0$ of dying during the age interval x to $x + 1$, is obtained by

$$d_x = l_x - l_{x+1}. \qquad [4]$$

Age-specific death rate, q_x, is the probability that an individual that enters the xth age class will die before entering the $x + 1$ age class. Age-specific death rate is obtained by

$$q_x = d_x/l_x. \qquad [5]$$

In contrast to the q_x schedule, age-specific survival, the probability than an individual that enters the xth age class will survive to enter the $x + 1$ age class, is

$$p_x = 1 - q_x. \qquad [6]$$

Values of p_x will be particularly important in the population projection model.

The number of animal time units to be lived in the x to $x + 1$ age class is obtained by integrating the l_x curve as

$$L_x = \int_x^{x+1} l_x dx. \qquad [7]$$

Values of L_x generally are approximated by

$$L_x = \frac{l_x + l_{x+1}}{2}, \qquad [8]$$

under the assumption that l_x is linear between x and $x + 1$.

The estimated total number of animal time units remaining to be lived from age x is

$$T_x = \int_x^{\omega} l_x dx. \qquad [9]$$

The lower case omega (ω) indicates the last age class that contains individuals. Contrasting to L_x, the values of T_x are the area under the l_x curve from age x until no animals remain from the initial cohort. T_x may be approximated by summing the values of L_x:

$$T_x = \sum_{x=x}^{\omega} L_x. \qquad [10]$$

The total life expectancy, or the mean length of life remaining to an individual alive at age x is:

$$e_x = \frac{\int_x^{\omega} l_x dx}{l_x}. \qquad [11]$$

Values of e_x may be approximated by dividing T_x by l_x,

$$e_x = T_x/l_x. \qquad [12]$$

The $l_x m_x$ column is an age-specific, expected-reproduction column, with expectations based on an individual of age zero. If all females were to live to the maximum age, and breed at the expected rate throughout, the Gross Reproductive Rate (GRR) would be achieved. This does not happen in big game populations, where the average individual dies somewhere between age zero and the maximum age. Summing the $l_x m_x$ column produces the Net Reproductive Rate (R_0), and reflects the average number of female offspring that will be produced by the average female in the population.

A complete equation structure for an expanded life table is shown in Table 31. Two numerical examples of expanded life tables are shown in Table 32. Each of these columns has useful information, subject to some restrictions concerning the validity of the data involved. Assumptions involved in life table use will be understood more readily after the projection model has been discussed.

Table 31. Equation structure for the columns making up an expanded life table.

x	n_x	D_x	l_x	d_x	q_x	P_x	L_x	T_x	e_x	m_x[a]	$l_x m_x$
0	n_0	n_0-n_1	n_0/n_0	l_0-l_1	d_0/l_0	$1-q_0$	$(l_0+l_1)/2$	$L_0+L_1+\cdots+L\omega$	T_0/l_0	0.0	$l_0 m_0$
1	n_1	n_1-n_2	n_1/n_0	l_1-l_2	d_1/l_1	$1-q_1$	$(l_1+l_2)/2$	$L_1+L_2+\cdots+L\omega$	T_1/l_1		$l_1 m_1$
2	n_2	n_2-n_3	n_2/n_0	l_2-l_3	d_2/l_2	$1-q_2$	$(l_2+l_3)/2$	$L_2+L_3+\cdots+L\omega$	T_2/l_2		$l_2 m_2$
.	.	.	.	.	.	.	.	.	.		.
.	.	.	.	.	.	.	.	.	.		.
.	.	.	.	.	.	.	.	.	.		.
x	n_x	n_x-n_{x+1}	n_x/n_0	l_x-l_{x+1}	d_x/l_x	$1-q_x$	$(l_x+l_{x+1})/2$	$\displaystyle\sum_{x=x}^{\omega} L_x$	T_x/l_x		$l_x m_x$

$$\text{GRR} = \sum_{x=0}^{\omega} m_x \qquad R_0 = \sum_{x=0}^{\omega} l_x m_x$$

[a]See text

BASIC POPULATION PROJECTIONS

Assuming that new individuals in the population are born at the same moment each year or time interval, the number of new females that enter the population at time t is obtained by multiplying the number of females in each age class by the respective expected production of female offspring and, then, summing across all ages.

For example, in Table 33A, the top entry in Year 3 is obtained by summing the products of the number of females in a given age class and their expected production.

Table 32. Expanded life tables from data presented in Table 34C. All numbers are truncated at accuracy level shown.

A. A time-specific analysis taken from Year 9.

x	n_x	D_x	l_x[a]	d_x	q_x	p_x	L_x	T_x	e_x	m_x	$l_x m_x$
0	475.82	235.94	1.000	0.495	0.495	0.504	752.0	1500.0	1.500	0.0	0
1	239.88	118.95	0.504	0.249	0.495	0.504	379.1	747.9	1.483	1.0	0.504
2	120.93	59.96	0.254	0.126	0.495	0.504	191.1	368.8	1.451	1.0	0.254
3	60.97	30.24	0.128	0.063	0.495	0.504	96.3	177.6	1.386	1.0	0.128
4	30.73	15.24	0.064	0.032	0.495	0.504	48.5	81.3	1.258	1.0	0.064
5	15.49	7.68	0.032	0.016	0.495	0.504	24.4	32.7	1.004	1.0	0.032
6	7.81	7.81	0.016	0.016	1.000	0.0	8.2	8.2	0.500	1.0	0.016
7	0.0	0.0									
Total										6.0	0.999

B. A true cohort analysis that starts in Year 3 and ends in Year 9.

x	n_x	D_x	l_x[a]	d_x	q_x	p_x	L_x	T_x	e_x	m_x	$l_x m_x$
0	167.40	66.96	1.000	0.400	0.400	0.600	800.0	1929.9	1.929	0.0	0
1	100.44	40.18	0.600	0.240	0.400	0.599	479.9	1129.9	1.883	1.0	0.600
2	60.26	24.11	0.359	0.144	0.400	0.599	287.9	649.9	1.805	1.0	0.359
3	36.15	14.46	0.215	0.086	0.400	0.600	172.7	361.9	1.675	1.0	0.215
4	21.69	8.68	0.129	0.051	0.400	0.599	103.6	189.2	1.459	1.0	0.129
5	13.01	5.20	0.077	0.031	0.399	0.600	62.1	85.5	1.100	1.0	0.077
6	7.81	7.81	0.046	0.046	1.000	0.0	23.3	23.3	0.500	1.0	0.046
7	0.0	0.0									
Total										6.0	1.4298

[a] l_x is sometimes easier to understand if converted to per thousand. To do this, multiply by 10^3.

This is

$$n_{0,3} = n_{1,3}m_1 + n_{2,3}m_2 + n_{3,3}m_3$$

$$86.40 = 43.20(1.0) + 21.60(1.0) + 21.60(1.0)$$

More generally, the number of new age-zero individuals entering the tth year is expressed as:

$$n_{0,t} = \sum_{x=x}^{\omega} n_{x,t}m_x. \qquad [13]$$

Although portions of individuals typically do not survive in real populations, several decimal places should be carried in these constructions to avoid accumulating excessive rounding errors.

Individuals in any given age class at time t that survive until time $t + 1$ will appear in the next age class. These diagonal transitions in the table are obtained by multiplying the number of individuals in an age class at time t by the probability of survival for that age class.

Table 33. Life history projections showing effects of varying initial age composition. For these tables, all p_x values are 0.6, m_o is 0.0, and all other m_x entries are 1.0. Additional information about this population structure is contained in Tables 32A, 34C, 35B, 36 and 37. Population in 33A was started with 100 age zero individuals; 33B was started with 100 age one individuals; and 33C was started with 100 age four individuals. All numbers have been truncated at accuracy level shown.

A.

Age	Year 0	Year 1	Year 2	Year 3	Year 4	Year 5	Year 6	Year 7	Year 8	Year 9
0	100.00	60.00	72.00	86.40	103.68	124.42	149.30	176.36	209.95	249.93
1		60.00	36.00	43.20	51.84	62.20	74.64	89.57	105.82	125.97
2			36.00	21.60	25.92	31.10	37.32	44.79	53.74	63.48
3				21.60	12.96	15.55	18.66	22.39	26.87	32.24
4					12.96	7.77	9.33	11.19	13.43	16.12
5						7.77	4.66	5.59	6.71	8.06
6							4.66	2.79	3.35	4.03
$\sum n_x$	100.00	120.00	144.00	172.80	207.36	248.83	298.52	352.71	419.90	499.85

B.

Age	Year 0	Year 1	Year 2	Year 3	Year 4	Year 5	Year 6	Year 7	Year 8	Year 9
0	100.00	120.00	144.00	172.80	207.36	248.83	293.93	349.92	416.54	495.82
1	100.00	60.00	72.00	86.40	103.68	124.42	149.28	176.36	209.95	249.93
2		60.00	36.00	43.20	51.84	62.20	74.64	89.57	105.82	125.97
3			36.00	21.60	25.92	31.10	37.32	44.79	53.74	63.48
4				21.60	12.96	15.55	18.66	22.39	26.87	32.24
5					12.96	7.77	9.33	11.19	13.43	16.12
6						7.77	4.66	5.59	6.71	8.06
$\sum n_x$	200.00	240.00	288.00	345.60	414.71	497.60	587.86	699.83	833.08	991.64

C.

Age	Year 0	Year 1	Year 2	Year 3	Year 4	Year 5	Year 6	Year 7	Year 8	Year 9
0	100.00	120.00	144.00	151.20	181.44	217.73	261.27	310.73	369.51	439.39
1		60.00	72.00	86.40	90.72	108.86	130.64	156.76	186.44	221.71
2			36.00	43.20	51.84	54.43	65.31	78.38	94.05	111.86
3				21.60	25.92	31.10	32.65	39.19	47.02	56.43
4	100.00				12.96	15.55	18.66	19.59	23.51	28.21
5		60.00				7.77	9.33	11.19	11.75	14.10
6			36.00				4.66	5.59	6.71	7.05
$\sum n_x$	200.00	240.00	288.00	302.39	362.87	435.45	522.54	621.45	739.02	878.77

Again, in Table 33A, individuals in the Year 3 column move to Year 4 as shown in this sequence.

Age	Year 3		Year 4	Age
0	86.40(0.6)	=	51.84	1
1	43.20(0.6)	=	25.92	2
2	21.60(0.6)	=	12.96	3
3	21.60(0.6)	=	12.96	4

In this general this equation is

$$n_{x,t}p_x = n_{x+1,t+1}. \qquad [14]$$

Work with the life history projections shown in Tables 33 and 34, and become convinced that the equations actually provide a projection of the population into future time periods. These examples were contrived to emphasize specific points. However, doing more complex survival and fertility schedules is no different.

In Table 34, the effects of varying annual survival probabilities for all ages from 0.4 (Table 34A) to 0.6 (Table 34C) are shown. Table 34B is nearly stationary, although it declines gradually. Substitute m_x values of 1.0159 for an example of a stationary popu-

Table 34. Life history projections showing effects of varying probabilities of survival across age classes. All populations are shown at stable age distribution at Year 9. All numbers have been truncated at accuracy level shown.

A. Age-specific survival 40 percent for all age classes. Production of one female offspring per year beginning at age one. Finite rate of increase, $\lambda = 0.79343$.

Age	Year 0	Year 1	Year 2	Year 3	Year 4	Year 5	Year 6	Year 7	Year 8	Year 9
0	100.00	78.75	62.50	49.60	39.36	31.23	24.78	19.66	15.60	12.37
1	50.00	40.00	31.50	25.00	19.84	15.74	12.49	9.91	7.86	6.23
2	25.00	20.00	16.00	12.60	10.00	7.93	6.29	4.99	3.96	3.14
3	12.50	10.00	8.00	6.40	5.04	4.00	3.17	2.51	1.99	1.58
4	6.25	5.00	4.00	3.20	2.56	2.01	1.60	1.26	1.00	0.79
5	3.12	2.50	2.00	1.60	1.28	1.02	0.80	0.64	0.50	0.40
6	1.56	1.25	1.00	0.80	0.64	0.51	0.40	0.32	0.25	0.20
$\sum n_x$	198.43	157.50	125.00	99.20	78.72	62.46	49.53	39.39	31.26	24.71

B. Age-specific survival 50 percent for all age classes. Production of one female offspring per year beginning at age one. Finite rate of increase, $\lambda = 0.99179$.

Age	Year 0	Year 1	Year 2	Year 3	Year 4	Year 5	Year 6	Year 7	Year 8	Year 9
0	100.00	98.43	97.65	96.87	96.09	95.31	94.53	93.75	92.98	92.21
1	50.00	50.00	49.21	48.82	48.43	48.04	47.65	47.26	46.87	46.49
2	25.00	25.00	25.00	24.60	24.41	24.21	24.02	23.82	23.63	23.43
3	12.50	12.50	12.50	12.50	12.30	12.20	12.10	12.01	11.91	11.81
4	6.25	6.25	6.25	6.25	6.25	6.15	6.10	6.05	6.00	5.95
5	3.12	3.12	3.12	3.12	3.12	3.12	3.07	3.05	3.02	3.00
6	1.56	1.56	1.56	1.56	1.56	1.56	1.56	1.53	1.52	1.51
$\sum n_x$	198.43	196.76	195.29	193.72	192.16	190.59	189.03	187.47	185.93	184.40

C. Age-specific survival 60 percent for all age classes. Production of one female offspring per year beginning at age one. Finite rate of increase, $\lambda = 1.19014$.

Age	Year 0	Year 1	Year 2	Year 3	Year 4	Year 5	Year 6	Year 7	Year 8	Year 9
0	100.00	118.12	140.62	167.40	199.26	237.17	282.27	335.92	399.80	475.82
1	50.00	60.00	70.87	84.37	100.44	119.56	142.30	169.36	201.55	239.88
2	25.00	30.00	36.00	42.52	50.62	60.26	71.73	85.38	101.62	120.93
3	12.50	15.00	18.00	21.60	25.51	30.37	36.15	43.04	51.22	60.97
4	6.25	7.50	9.00	10.80	12.96	15.30	18.22	21.69	25.82	30.73
5	3.12	3.75	4.50	5.40	6.48	7.77	9.18	10.93	13.01	15.49
6	1.56	1.87	2.25	2.70	3.24	3.88	4.66	5.51	6.56	7.81
$\sum n_x$	198.43	236.24	281.24	334.79	398.51	474.31	564.51	671.83	799.58	951.63

lation (among other things, a population that is not changing density from year to year). In contrast to the decreasing-stationary-increasing populations shown in Table 34, effects of differing age structure in the initial population are given in Table 33.

The proportion of the total population contained in an x to $x + 1$ age class in year t is obtained by dividing the total number of individuals in a given age class $(n_{x,t})$ by the total number of individuals in the population (N_t). In Table 34C, Year 9, for example, the proportions in the age classes are:

Age			Proportion
0	475.82/951.65	=	0.500
1	239.88/951.65	=	0.252
2	120.93/951.65	=	0.127
3	60.97/951.65	=	0.064
4	30.73/951.65	=	0.032
5	15.49/951.65	=	0.016
6	7.81/951.65	=	0.008

A column of such proportions indicates the age structure of the population at any given time. Understanding age structure patterns is a fundamental problem in big game management. Often, the biologist has only age structure data with which to work, and must estimate the various population parameters discussed here from such data.

More generally, let $C_{x,t}$ be the proportion of the population at time t in the x to $x + 1$ age class. Successive values are given by

$$C_{x,t} = \frac{n_{x,t}}{\sum_{y=0}^{\omega} n_{y,t}}. \qquad [15]$$

A fundamental law of demographics is that although populations may have shifting age distributions at certain stages of growth, given constancy of survival and reproduction, they tend toward an ultimately unchanging age distribution. An unchanging age distribution of this sort is called a "stable age distribution." While stable age distributions probably are never found in wild populations, the concept is of major importance. All populations at Year 9 in Tables 33 and 34 are at stable age. Compute

several age distributions in early years from these two tables for comparison. Populations may be increasing, not changing or decreasing and still be at stable age distribution. A special case of stable age, called "stationary age distribution," exists when the population density as well as age structure is unchanging (that is, the finite rate of increase, λ, is 1.0). Note that the stable age distribution is determined by the relative values of l_x and m_x, not by the initial age structure. Table 33 illustrates three populations started with different age structures. Even though ultimate population size may be different, the final proportions of individuals in each age class are the same.

RATES OF INCREASE

Given fixed schedules of l_x and m_x and sufficient time, populations tend toward and finally reach a stable age distribution. Once the stable age distribution is reached, population growth with respect to time is

$$\frac{dN_t}{dt} = rN_t. \qquad [16]$$

In integrated form this is

$$N_t = N_0 e^{rt}. \qquad [17]$$

Taking natural logs of both sides, equation [17] becomes

$$log_e N_t = log_e N_0 + rt.$$

From this equation, a graph of population size against time is a straight line of slope r.

Replacing t with 1 in equation [17] defines the finite rate of increase, λ, as

$$N_1 = N_0 e^r = N_0 \lambda. \qquad [18]$$

Thus, $log_e \lambda = r$ and $\lambda = e^r$.

Given a population that has achieved a stable age distribution and increases at the finite rate λ per unit time, the ratio of total population size at $t - 1$ divided into the population size at t is the rate of increase. This fact is expressed as

$$\lambda = N_t/N_{t-1}. \qquad [19]$$

Solving for N_t gives

$$N_t = \lambda N_{t-1},$$

continuing backward in time,

$$N_{t-1} = \lambda N_{t-2},$$

for k time periods

$$N_t = \lambda^k N_{t-k}. \qquad [20]$$

Here again is the geometric growth series, with the difference that equation [20] is reaching back into time for values of N_{t-k}, and computing successive steps results in population size for time t.

Given a sequence where it may be assumed that all members entered the population at age n_0 (for example, starting about Year 6 in Table 34C), then the number of individuals in any given age x to $x + 1$ at t is

$$n_{x,t} = n_{0,t-x} l_x. \qquad [21]$$

In equation [21], the number of individuals in the x to $x + 1$ age class at time t is the total number that began that cohort at $t - x$, (that is, $n_{0,t-x}$) multiplied by the probability of survival, l_x, from age 0 to age x.

As discussed above, the number of new n_0 individuals entering the population at t are produced by the number of reproducing females in the various age classes at time t. This relationship was

$$n_{x,t} = \sum_{x=1}^{\omega} n_{x,t} m_x,$$

as given in equation [13]. Then, utilizing equation [13] to express the number of age zero individuals entering the population, but substituting $n_{0,t-x} l_x$ from equation [21] for $n_{x,t}$ in the right hand side, gives

$$n_{0,t} = \sum_{x=1}^{\omega} n_{0,t-x} l_x m_x.$$

Dividing both sides by $n_{0,t}$ gives

$$1 = \sum_{x=1}^{\omega} \frac{n_{0,t-x} l_x m_x}{n_{0,t}}. \qquad [22]$$

As discussed, the rate of increase of total population size once stable age has been attained is, from equation [20], for k seasons of population growth

$$N_t/N_{t-k} = \lambda^k$$

Since the proportion of any given age class does not change in a stable age distribution, this result will hold for any age class. Thus, the number of age zero individuals entering the population at time t (that is $n_{0,t}$) has a similar relationship to the number of new individuals at $t - 1$. The rate of increase of the zero age class is obtained by

$$n_{0,t}/n_{0,t-x} = \lambda^x$$

Taking reciprocals this becomes

$$n_{0,t-x}/n_{0,t} = \lambda^{-x}$$

(remembering that $\lambda^{-x} = 1/\lambda^x$). Substituting this result in equation [22], we obtain

$$1 = \sum_{x=1}^{\omega} \lambda^{-x} l_x m_x. \qquad [23]$$

This is an equation for the solution of the finite rate of increase, λ, in a seasonally breeding population with overlapping generations. It is a discrete version of

$$1 = \int_{x=0}^{\omega} e^{-rx} l_x m_x dx, \qquad [24]$$

which should be used for continuously breeding populations.

Equation [23] is a polynomial in lambda and, given constancy in l_x and m_x, can be solved by inserting trial-and-error values of

λ. A simple first approximation of λ can be obtained by applying equation [19] to total population sizes from projections such as those in Table 33 and 34. Thus, the finite rate of increase can be obtained for any set of l_x and m_x schedules in two ways: (1) iterate through a life history projection as in Tables 33 and 34, and (2) solve equation [23] by inserting trial-and-error values of λ.

An instantaneous rate of increase, r, is obtained by taking the natural log of λ (see equation [18]). Considerable confusion exists as to what this rate of increase really implies. Space limits this discussion; however, one should be aware that various instantaneous rates of increase exist according to the restrictions, or assumptions, placed on the $l_x m_x$ schedule in equations [23] or [24]. If environmental conditions are optimal in all respects for the growth of a population, the rate of increase is appropriately called "biotic potential," and can be denoted by r_p. Under specified conditions of temperature, humidity and other abiotic factors, and with biotic factors (such as competitors, predators, etc.) being optimal for growth, the intrinsic rate of increase, r_m, is obtained. If one specifies the abiotic and biotic environments—both of which would be suboptimal for population growth—then a rate of increase denoted by r_s is obtained.

Each of these three rates of increase are computed in identical ways. The only difference between them is the assumptions placed on the l_x and m_x schedules involved. Each of these three rates of increase assumes that the population is at stable age distribution; thus, each is to be considered as a constant under specified conditions.

A fourth rate of increase, r, can be obtained (see equation [17]). Here only density estimates over time are required. By regressing log_e of population size against time, a straight line of slope r is obtained. This rate of increase, r, under conditions specified above, can estimate any of the three rates of increase: r_p, r_m or r_s. Conversely, r may not be an estimate of any of these three, because the restrictions are not met.

All of these instantaneous rates of increase may be either negative, zero or positive. Finite rates of increase (for example, λ) may be either zero or positive.

STABLE AGE DISTRIBUTION

It may be seen, from Tables 33 and 34, that an iterative solution for the stable age distribution is obtained from the life history projections. By having an estimate of λ for a population, several additional demographic parameters become available.

The equation for stable age distribution may be obtained by starting with equation [15]. In equation [15], C was used to denote simple age distribution. A small c will be used to denote elements of a stable age distribution. By utilizing concepts developed in the derivation of λ, equation [15], which was written as (substituting c for C)

$$c_{x,t} = \frac{n_{x,t}}{\sum\limits_{y=0}^{\omega} n_{y,t}},$$

can be modified by using the relationship

$$n_{x,t} = n_{0,t-x} l_x, \text{ and}$$

$$n_{y,t} = n_{0,t-y} l_y$$

to obtain

$$c_{x,t} = \frac{n_{0,t-x} l_x}{\sum\limits_{y=0}^{\omega} n_{0,t-y} l_y}.$$

Dividing the numerator and denominator of the right hand side by $n_{0,t}$ gives

$$c_{x,t} = \frac{n_{0,t-x} l_x / n_{0,t}}{\sum\limits_{y=0}^{\omega} n_{0,t-y} l_y / n_{0,t}},$$

and by applying the fact that $\lambda^{-x} = n_{0,t-x}/n_{0,t}$, the result is

$$c_{x,t} = \frac{\lambda^{-x} l_x}{\sum\limits_{y=0}^{\omega} \lambda^{-y} l_y}. \qquad [25]$$

Using equation [25], stable age distribution can be obtained as shown in Table 35. The stable age distribution obtained in Table 35B is the same as the age distribution in Table 34C for Year 9. This shows that stable age distributions also may be obtained by iterating through a life history projection, or by utilizing equation [25] if an estimate of λ is available.

GENERATION TIME

It has been shown previously that Net Reproductive Rate (R_0) of a population starting with an n_0 cohort at stable age distribution is the sum of the products of the expected age-specific production of females and the respective age-specific probabilities of survival. This value (R_0) is the net reproductive rate of the population over the time an average female is expected to remain in the population, and is expressed as

$$R_0 = \int_{x=0}^{\omega} l_x m_x dx, \qquad [26]$$

or approximately as

$$R_0 = \sum_{x=0}^{\omega} l_x m_x. \qquad [27]$$

If, in its lifetime, a female is expected to produce R_0 female offspring, and generation time is defined as the time it takes a population at a stable age distribution to grow by the factor R_0, one notion of generation time may be derived as follows. Given that a population is growing according to

$$N_t = N_0 e^{rt},$$

let T be the generation time discussed above, and substitute T for t as

$$N_T = N_0 e^{rT}.$$

Table 35. Calculation of stable age distribution. Data were taken from population projected in Table 34C.
A. Calculated stable age distribution from time-specific analysis shown in Table 32A. Value of λ used is 0.999988.

x	n_x	l_x	m_x	λ^{-x}	$\lambda^{-x}l_x$	c_x
0	475.82	1.000	0.0	1.000000	1.000000	0.500002
1	239.88	0.504	1.0	1.000012	0.504146	0.252974
2	120.93	0.254	1.0	1.000024	0.254156	0.127078
3	60.97	0.128	1.0	1.000036	0.128145	0.064073
4	30.73	0.064	1.0	1.000048	0.064583	0.032036
5	15.49	0.032	1.0	1.000060	0.032552	0.016276
6	7.81	0.016	1.0	1.000072	0.016411	0.008206
Total					1.999993	0.999745

B. Calculated stable age distribution from cohort (time-dynamic) analysis shown in Table 32B. Value of λ used is 1.190149.

x	n_x	l_x	m_x	λ^{-x}	$\lambda^{-x}l_x$	c_x
0	167.40	1.000	0.0	1.000000	1.000000	0.499999
1	100.44	0.600	1.0	0.840231	0.504139	0.252069
2	60.26	0.360	1.0	0.705988	0.254156	0.127078
3	36.15	0.215	1.0	0.593193	0.128130	0.064065
4	21.69	0.129	1.0	0.498419	0.064595	0.032297
5	13.01	0.077	1.0	0.418787	0.032565	0.016282
6	7.81	0.046	1.0	0.351878	0.016419	0.008209
Total					2.000104	0.99999

Dividing both sides by N_0 gives

$$\frac{N_T}{N^0} = e^{rT},$$

but since N_T/N_0 is the rate that the population will grow during the time T, then

$$\frac{N_T}{N^0} = R_0 = e^{rT}.$$

Taking

$$log_e R_0 = log_e e^{rT} = rT,$$

and dividing both sides by r, an expression is obtained for generation time, T, as

$$T = log_e R_0 / r. \qquad [28]$$

While this expression may seem to make sense in some situations, it is undefined for the case of a stationary age distribution where $r = 0$, thus making the solution unsatisfactory as a general property of populations.

Other derivations for generation time follow from the notion that equations of the form

$$E(x) = \sum_{x=0}^{\omega} x f(x)$$

are a general solution for the first moment of $f(x)$, that is, the mean of the discrete probability density function $f(x)$. One such measure is "cohort generation time," T_c, which is expressed as

$$T_c = 1/R_0 \int_0^{\omega} x l_x m_x dx, \qquad [29]$$

or approximately

$$T_c = 1/R_0 \sum_{x=0}^{\omega} x l_x m_x. \qquad [30]$$

Here we have the mean of the $l_x m_x$ schedule divided by the net reproductive rate. This equation for T_c represents the mean age of

mature females at the birth of all of their female offspring. It is scaled externally (outside the integral sign) by the fact that the population may not be at a stationary age distribution ($R_0 \neq 1$).

A slightly different interpretation of generation time can be obtained as

$$\overline{T} = \int_0^{\omega} x e^{-rx} l_x m_x dx, \qquad [31]$$

or approximately as

$$\overline{T} = \sum_{x=0}^{\omega} x \lambda^{-x} l_x m_x. \qquad [32]$$

In this case, $\overline{T}$ represents the mean age of mature females at the birth of their first female offspring. Thus, $\overline{T}$ is the expected value (mean) of the probability density function $e^{-rx} l_x m_x$. Only in the case where the population is at a stationary age distribution ($\lambda = 1$, $R_0 = 1$, $r = 0$) will T_c and $\overline{T}$ provide a common result. The value $\overline{T}$ "corrects" for the fact that the population may not be at a stationary age distribution. However, these corrections appear within the integral sign; that is, $l_x m_x$ for each x is being scaled by e^{-rx} while T_c scales the summed products of the $l_x m_x$ schedule.

Thus, T_c and $\overline{T}$ reflect rather different biological concepts, T_c being mean age of mature females at the birth of all offspring and $\overline{T}$ being mean age of mature females at birth of first offspring. In a growing population, $r > 0$, where younger age classes might be proportionally larger, $\overline{T}$ will be smaller than T_c, since the probability that any given age zero young will survive to reproduce is less than the converse situation of a declining population, where the probability that any given age zero individual will survive to reproduce is proportionally high. In a declining population, $r < 0$, the reverse is true, and $\overline{T}$ will be greater than T_c. The important point to recognize is that neither of these values, $\overline{T}$ or T_c, is necessarily preferable, but that both reflect different interpretations. Taken together, they provide a better understanding of the population than either presented alone. A sample computation of these two generation times is shown in Table 36.

REPRODUCTIVE VALUE

If a female is removed from a population, its yet-to-be-born offspring (and their offspring, etc.) also are removed. Some females have the potential to contribute more future offspring than others. Thus, a female past reproductive age can be removed without any depressant effect on population growth rate, while a female just entering breeding age might have quite a strong effect, particularly in a small population. This concept can be observed in Table 33.

Each population of Table 33 starts with 100 individuals and, once stable age distribution is reached, will grow at the same rate, because the $l_x m_x$ schedules are the same. It can be seen, however, that the population in Table 33B contains roughly twice as many individuals in Year 9 as does the population in Table 33A. Since both of these populations were started with the same number of females, one might guess that a

one-year old female is worth about 991.42/499.64 = 1.98 times as much as a zero-year old female.

One procedure for estimating reproductive value is to set the value of a zero year old at 1. Then, for seasonal breeders, reproductive values for the remainder of the age classes are relative to 1, and are given by

$$v_x = \frac{\lambda^x}{l_x} \sum_{y=x}^{\omega} \lambda^{-y} l_y m_y, \qquad [33]$$

where v_x is the reproductive value of an x year old, relative to $v_0 = 1$. The procedure for calculating reproductive values is shown in Table 37. Subject to some rounding errors, the v_x column in Table 37 shows a reproductive value of about 1 for the zero age group, 1.98 for the one year olds and so on.

Knowledge of reproductive value can have important management applications. If a goal is to control overpopulation, females of higher reproductive values might be removed. Conversely, one should leave such females if goals involve optimizing or maximizing production. In restocking or in-

Table 36. Calculation of two different generation times. Data taken from cohort schedule in Table 32B. The value of λ used is 1.19014.

x	l_x	m_x	λ^{-x}	$x l_x m_x$	$\lambda^{-x} x l_x m_x$
0	1.0000	0.0	1.0000	0.0	0.0
1	0.6000	1.0	0.8402	0.6000	0.5041
2	0.3600	1.0	0.7059	0.7200	0.5083
3	0.2160	1.0	0.5932	0.6300	0.3737
4	0.1296	1.0	0.4984	0.5184	0.2583
5	0.0777	1.0	0.4188	0.3885	0.1627
6	0.0466	1.0	0.3518	0.2796	0.0983
Total				3.1365	1.9056

$$R_0 = \sum_{x=0}^{\omega} l_x m_x = 1.4299 \qquad T_c = 1/R_0 \sum_{x=0}^{\omega} x l_x m_x \qquad \overline{T} = \sum_{x=0}^{\omega} x \lambda^{-x} l_x m_x$$

$$\sum_{x=0}^{\omega} x l_x m_x = 3.1365 \qquad T_{\underline{c}} = 0.6993\,(3.1365) \qquad \overline{T} = 1.90$$

$$\sum_{x=0}^{\omega} x \lambda^{-x} l_x m'_x = 1.9056 \qquad T_c = 2.19$$

Table 37. Calculation of Fisher's Reproductive Value. Data taken from cohort schedule in Table 32B. The value of λ used is 1.19014. All numbers were truncated at accuracy level shown.

x or y	l_x	m_x	λ^x	λ^x/l_x	λ^{-y}	$\lambda^{-y}l_y m_y$	$\sum_{x=y}^{\omega} \lambda^{-y}l_y m_y$	v_x
0	1.000	0.0	1.000000	1.000000	1.000000	0.0	0.998574	0.998574
1	0.600	1.0	1.190140	1.983567	0.840237	0.504142	0.998574	1.980738
2	0.360	1.0	1.416433	3.934537	0.705999	0.254160	0.494432	1.945361
3	0.215	1.0	1.685754	7.840715	0.593206	0.127539	0.240272	1.883904
4	0.129	1.0	2.006283	15.552582	0.498434	0.064298	0.112733	1.753289
5	0.077	1.0	2.387758	31.009841	0.418803	0.032248	0.048435	1.501962
6	0.046	1.0	2.841766	61.77721	0.351894	0.016187	0.016187	0.999993

troduction programs where population success is the goal, females of high reproductive value should be well-represented in the translocated population.

A POPULATION MODEL

The basic population projections shown in Tables 33 and 34 were obtained from equations [13] and [14]. Although these projections are real enough for some purposes, several critical assumptions make them unsuitable for many desirable applications. Three of these assumptions are:

1. The inclusion of only females implies a sex ratio of 1:1 in all age classes (there must be no difference in survival between males and females);
2. Survival and reproductive rates must be constant over time, and independent of density and the environment; and
3. All females produce young according to the m_x schedule at each time interval.

While additional assumptions are involved, these three are presented to indicate: (1) some inherent weaknesses of simple models, and (2) some procedures for incorporating various algebraic structures that provide additional realism.

If a model is to have some realistic applications, it must account for some realistic biological phenomena. Therefore, models are constructed by listing sets of assumptions and writing mathematical structures that provide for the inclusion of information that such assumptions avoid.

For example, expanding the model to include different survival schedules for males and females is very important for treating big game populations because of differential hunting mortality. If the sex ratio is 1:1 at birth, the number of age zero males entering the population at time t will be the same as the number of females entering at that time. Thus, the main concern is survival projections.

To produce a model that includes age- and sex-specific survival, we need two life history projections instead of one as in Tables 33 and 34; one for females and one for males. Algebraically, the model is identical, except that there must be a separate equation [14] for females and one for males. To accomplish this, write

$$\mathrm{n}_{x+1,t+1,i} = p_{x,i}\mathrm{n}_{x,t,i}$$

$$i = \begin{cases} 1 \text{ for females} \\ 2 \text{ for males} \end{cases} \qquad [34]$$

where total population age structure is obtained by adding the columns for males and females across ages.

If one has reason to believe that all females do not produce young at each time interval, then the model can be modified to include a "proportion breeding" column. This column includes elements that indicate the proportion of any given age class that will breed at any given time t. To accomplish this, let $\beta_{x,t}$ be the proportion of females of age x to $x + 1$ that will breed at time t, and modify equation [13] so that

$$n_{0,t} = \sum_{x=1}^{\omega} n_{x,t}\beta_{x,t}m_x. \qquad [35]$$

This structure also allows incorporation of seasonality (when no breeding occurs) as well as periods of reduced breeding. The aspects of season-specific breeding require one breeding proportion column for each season involved. Such seasonal columns would "recycle" on an annual basis, for example, or could be set to change by inclusion of breeding components as functions of environmental variables that are believed to affect the population's breeding structure.

In this manner, realism may be added step-by-step. Each addition requires more information about the population. Some may not be at hand, so the researcher must go back to the field population for more data.

This model has the potential to reflect many important biological changes in a population. It can incorporate those demographic parameters that are of major importance if sufficient data are available. If it is known, for example, that survival is affected by density in an algebraically describable way, then the survival values, p_x, may be set as functions of density, and this function may be substituted into equation [34].

This section on advanced concepts is, of course, too brief. It has been included to show how additional complexities are added. Models that are realistic are likely to be complex; simple models will leave out potentially important factors. Either way can be beneficial provided one avoids asking questions of the model that it was not designed to address.

ASSUMPTIONS IN LIFE TABLE CONSTRUCTION

To this point, I have presumed to deal with appropriate data in the life table constructions and the population projections. By now, one should have noticed the considerable differences between the expanded life tables shown in Table 32. The true picture of what occurs in the population projection (Table 34C) is reflected by the life table in Table 32B. Thus, an important point is made: only when the population is at stationary age distribution will a time-specific (Table 32A) and a time-dynamic or cohort (Table 32B) life table be identical.

In a growing population (for example, Tables 33 and 34C) a time-specific analysis will underestimate true survival. In a declining population (for example, Table 34A), a time-specific analysis will overestimate true survival. The fact that populations are almost never at a stationary age distribution should not deter attempts to analyze demographic properties of a population. Taken in conjunction with a population projection model, as described here, demographic analyses and population projections can tell the big game manager much about the potential for response in a population. No model of this sort will indicate what will happen; constructed and used properly, it will indicate what can happen.

Modeling has much to contribute to understanding how wildlife populations respond to changing environments. Given such understanding, managers responsible for big game populations will be able to apply knowledge based on performance measures (in this case, demographic response potentials) rather than intuition. Misuse of models, such as using them for purposes not intended, will delay the ultimate future of modeling as an integral part of big game management.

Chapter 22

NUTRITION AND CARRYING CAPACITY

William W. Mautz

Associate Professor
Institute of Natural and Environmental Resources
University of New Hampshire
Durham, New Hampshire

The inclusion of a chapter dealing with nutrition and carrying capacity in a book on big game management represents, in itself, a positive and significant step in the developing science and art of wildlife management. The usefulness and acceptance of nutrition and physiology as tools in wildlife management slowly are gaining recognition among wildlife professionals. Consideration of nutritional factors will become more commonplace as the field of wildlife management matures and as information accumulates on the multitude of variables in the lives and ecological relationships of the many different avian and mammalian wildlife species. It is not practical to cover, in depth, the entire subject of big game nutrition in a single chapter. This chapter briefly summarizes basic nutritional fundamentals and the methodologies frequently used in big game nutritional investigations. Reference is made to existing big game nutritional information found in the literature. A discussion of the practical use of such information in carrying capacity considerations is included. For additional information the reader is referred to excellent overviews on this subject by Dietz (1965), Short (1966), Paulsen et al. (1970) and Verme and Ullrey (1972). After reading this chapter, the reader should have at least a rudimentary understanding of how nutritional information relates to big game management and why, in many cases, it should be an essential component of any wildlife management program.

It is possible to liken knowledge—the accumulation of information needed to manage—to a chain with each link representing a different major category of information. As understanding of one link for a species increases, emphasis of study moves to a weaker link or less understood parameter. Eventually, in the study of wildlife, a link is reached that deals with nutrition.

The "managing capacity" of a biologist is directly related to the strength of his knowledge chain which, in turn, is related to the strength of each of its links. Based on this, we might formulate two new, although perhaps not revolutionary, management laws. These "laws" could be thought of as corollaries to Liebig's law of the minimum.

1. Law of wildlife management. The ability of a biologist to manage a species is directly related to the strength of the managing chain or his understanding of that species. In most cases, the manager deals with a population or group of individuals of the same species. The term "species," as used henceforth in this chapter, might also be interpreted in most cases as "population."

2. Law of the limiting link. The strength of the managing chain is only as great as that of the weakest link. Successful management of a species or population can be no greater than that allowed by the least-understood vital factor. A vital factor is one for which an understanding is essential to the successful management of the species. Understanding of a given factor may be vital to the management of one species and nonessential to another. How we decide what is and what is not vital generally is a slowly evolving process. Also, what may be essential at one point in time for a given species may not necessarily be so at a later time.

For the sake of illustration, let us assume there are five vital factors which need to be understood to manage a particular species (Figure 62A). If we have little or no knowledge of one link of this chain, the continued study of better understood factors, at the expense of the weak link, does little to increase our management ability (Figure 62B).

To clarify and substantiate this idea, food-related information will be used as an example. Theoretically, food factors might be considered a single link in a rudimentary management chain. Such a chain might include as links major categories such as food, cover and population dynamics. Each of these major categories may be broken into a number of more specific components. There also can be a good deal of overlap among categories and components. The complexity of the management chain tends to increase with our level of understanding. An expansion of food-related parameters is depicted in Figure 63. In the case of research dealing with food, the general procedure with most wildlife species has been to document food habits first. This is, of course, a vital consideration. As information accumulates in this area, a point is reached at which this link of the management chain becomes stronger than other equally vital links. At this stage, further research in this particular area does little to bolster management capability for the species under consideration. Thus, research efforts should move on to other less understood links. They generally do, but too often through the very slow system of interest and educational shifts.

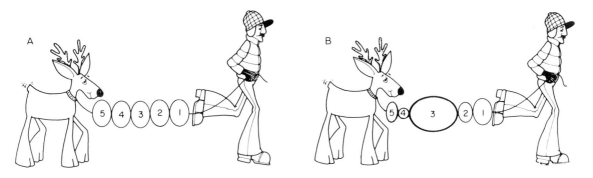

Figure 62. The "law of wildlife management" and the "law of the limiting link." The wildlife biologist manages a species through his understanding of vital characteristics.
A. Management of a wildlife species may be visualized as "towing" that species with a management chain made up of several links. Each link of this management "chain" represents a characteristic of the species for which an understanding is essential for sound management.
B. The management chain is only as strong as its weakest link. In this example, link number 4 represents the least understood vital factor.

Expansion of research into nutritional and other physiological aspects already has occurred for some big game species, notably several cervid species. Deer are a prime example. Among the literature dealing with deer food, the proportion reporting research on specific nutritional aspects has risen steadily in the 40-year history of the *Journal of Wildlife Management*. During the *Journal's* first 10 years, less than 5 percent of the papers dealing with deer food were directed toward digestibility information and no papers were printed that dealt with the food requirements of deer based on nu-

trition-oriented studies. The shift in these areas of research has evolved slowly to the point where, during the period of 1970–1977, more than 20 percent of the deer food-related papers dealt with digestion while another 20 percent dealt with food and/or nutritional requirements. Our nutritional understanding of many of the other big game herbivores and the big game carnivores stops essentially at the "food habits" link, a stage we were at with deer 30 years ago!

As the demand placed upon big game populations becomes greater and greater in

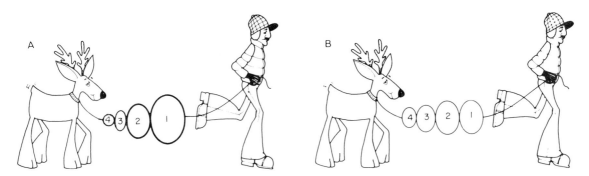

Figure 63. A specific example of the "law of wildlife management" using just food-related research with deer (representative of papers published in the *Journal of Wildlife Management*). The relative size of the links indicates the relative degree of understanding of each of these parameters.
A. Prior to 1950: (1) food habits, (2) food availability, (3) food digestibility, (4) food requirement.
B. 1970–1977: (1) food habits, (2) food availability, (3) food digestibility, (4) food requirement.

terms of hunter pressure and/or habitat destruction, management efforts must increasingly intensify, requiring greater understanding. It is in this light that consideration of nutritional and physiological factors is of growing importance. What once could be accomplished by "seat-of-the-pants" management and rudimentary understanding is no longer adequate for most wildlife populations, and particularly big game species.

NUTRITION FUNDAMENTALS

Nutrition may be defined as the sum of the processes by which an animal takes in and utilizes food substances. These processes include not only ingestion and digestion, but also subsequent metabolism of food. The study of nutrition involves quantification of the various nutrients required by an animal. Nutrition deals with a vast spectrum of variables, including (1) how well natural foods are utilized—efficiencies and rates of digestion and metabolism, and (2) how much food an organism requires to meet the seemingly infinite dimensions of life processes.

Nutrients

A nutrient generally is considered a chemical compound or element essential to the total life process of an organism and which is obtained through feeding. There are approximately 40 nutrients or required components which most animals must obtain from their food. The exact number of nutrients varies not only among major groupings of animals but often among species within a major grouping as well.

The following annotated list will delineate the major classifications of food components. For a detailed description, the reader is referred to Maynard and Loosli (1962), Church (1972) or one of many other books presently available on domestic animal nutrition.

1. Carbohydrates. Carbohydrates are a class of compounds which make up the largest portion of food consumed by herbivorous big game mammals. Roughly 75 percent of the dry matter ingested by herbivorous animals is carbohydrate. Animals whose diet consists primarily of meat consume very little carbohydrate. Sugar, starch, cellulose and many other organic compounds are carbohydrates. While there are no essential carbohydrates per se, this group of compounds provides energy and derivatives needed for the synthesis of other nutrients.

2. Proteins. Proteins are nitrogenous compounds made up of amino acids. Ten of the 20 classified amino acids are essential to the diet of most nonruminant animals. Ruminant organisms have the ability—through microbial action—to synthesize all required amino acids, provided an adequate source of energy, nitrogen and other components is available in the food. Amino acids are synthesized by bacteria growing within the rumen, and subsequent digestion of these microbes by the ruminant releases the amino acids, many of which are then absorbed by the host animal. Dietary protein provides several other essential nutrients for some animals and is a major source of energy for carnivorous animals.

3. Lipids. Lipids, commonly referred to as fats, are a group of compounds physiologically important to the life function of all organisms. In general, carbohydrates are converted readily to lipids, thus eliminating most lipids from the nutrient list. There are, however, three essential "fatty acids" which cannot be synthesized in the body and, thus, must be provided in the diet. Lipids are a significant energy source for both herbivores and carnivores.

4. Vitamins. Vitamins represent a group of chemically unrelated compounds which have been found to be essential to life. Most animals need to acquire approximately 15 vitamins from their food.

5. Inorganic elements. There are approximately 13 inorganic elements believed to be essential to life. About 30 others are found in the animal body and, in the future, some of these likely will be found to be essential.

Two other essential dietary factors are energy and water. Energy is present in all organic compounds and, therefore, generally is not considered a separate food component. Dietary energy is supplied by a number of the above-listed food components. There are major differences among the quality of various foods as suppliers of energy, particularly in diets of big game herbivores (Figure 64A and 64B, Table 38). Winter deer browse species frequently are less than 50 percent digestible and may have digestibility coeffi-

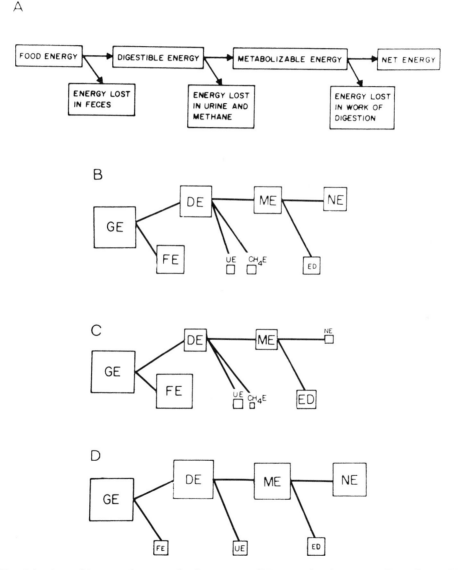

Figure 64. Partitioning of ingested gross (food) energy (GE) into fecal energy (FE), digestible energy (DE), urine energy (UE), methane energy (CH₄E), metabolizable energy (ME), work of digestion (ED) and net energy (NE). Partitioning of ingested gross energy on a proportional basis for big game herbivores ingesting high quality summer food (B), big game herbivores ingesting poor quality winter food (C) and carnivores ingesting animal tissue (D).

cients as low as 30 percent. The digestibility of summer foods, on the other hand, may exceed 60 or 70 percent in some cases. The diet of carnivorous animals is typically much more highly digested, often exceeding 80 percent (Figure 64C, Table 38).

Requirements

A nutritional need or requirement is the amount or quantity of a nutrient which is necessary for an organism to fulfill optimally its total life process. Nutritional

Table 38. Digestibility and related information of several North American big game foods as determined from total collection digestion trials (some figures recalculated from reported values).

Species	Food	Digestible dry matter (percent)	Digestible energy Percent	Digestible energy kcal/gDMI[a]	Digestible protein Percent	Digestible protein g/gDMI[a]	Source
White-tailed deer	Acorns	37	39	3.4	[b]		Forbes et al. 1941
	Dogwood	28	26	1.8	[b]		
	Willow	29	27	1.5	[b]		
	Hemlock	56	55	1.5	32	1.4	Silver and Colovos 1957
	Hazelnut	62	49	3.8	9	0.3	
	Balsam	53			28	1.4	
	Mountain maple	54			38	1.5	
	Apple	65			25	1.0	
	White cedar	44	41	2.1	− 10	− 0.5	Ullrey et al. 1964
	White cedar	41	36	1.85	9	0.6	Ullrey et al. 1967
	Jack pine	41	44	2.35	− 14	− 1.1	
	White cedar	44	39	2.0	14	1.0	Ullrey et al. 1968
	White cedar	60	59	3.2	31	2.4	Ullrey et al. 1972
	Aspen	49	52	2.7	24	2.7	
	Hemlock	49	48	2.4	− 5	− 0.3	Mautz et al. 1976
	Balsam	48	50	2.6	11	1.0	
	Red maple	31	30	1.4	1	0.1	
	Striped maple	40	32	1.5	46	3.1	
	Mountain maple	37	38	1.8	51	5.0	
	Hobblebush	55	54	2.5	47	3.2	
	Hazelnut	32	33	1.5	44	1.0	
	Alfalfa	55	54		64	10.0	Robbins et al. 1975
	Brome	54	53		61	8.0	
Mule deer	Sagebrush				67	7.4	Smith 1950
	Mountain mahogany				54	5.7	Smith 1952
	Juniper				10	0.6	
	Bitterbrush				36	2.6	
	Alfalfa				77	14.4	
	Live oak		37	1.8	33	5.0	Bissell et al. 1955
	Chamise: live oak		55	3.0	20	1.5	
	Big sage		36	2.0	56	6.4	
	Bitterbrush		53	3.0	57	5.2	
	Alfalfa				71	10.7	
	Jojoba	48					Urness et al. 1977
	Filaree	67					
	Mesquite (fruit)	60					
	False mesquite	51					
	Desert ceanothus	55					
	Artemisia	47					
	Alfalfa	66	67				Milchunas 1977
	Blueberry: alfalfa	30	31				
	Fireweed: alfalfa	43	41				
	Blueberry wheatgrass: alfalfa	43	44				
Peccary	Prickly pear		81				Zervanos and Hadley 1973
Caribou/ reindeer	Lichen	75			− 6		Jacobsen and Skjenneberg 1975
Polar bear	Seal		92	5.2	83	32.4	Best 1975

[a]Dry matter intake.

[b]Authors did not calculate due to negative values.

needs vary among species and also among individuals of the same species. As examples, a young animal has a greater requirement for protein to meet its rapid growth process than does an adult animal, and a lactating female has greater requirements for calcium and other nutrients than does a nonlactating female. All individuals within a population may require more or less of a particular nutrient at some season of the year than at others.

It is a practical certainty that we will never understand fully the myriad of nutritional needs of all wildlife species. It is almost as certain that we will never understand the needs for even a single species. When one considers that there are more than 40 nutrients, with the requirements for any one of these within just a single species varying with sex, age, season of the year and perhaps other environmental factors, it is easy to understand the above statements. Although the statements appear to paint a bleak picture for the future of managing wildlife on the basis of their nutritional dimensions, this is not and need not be the case. Most organisms living in the wild are meeting their nutritional needs. Whether or not they are meeting all of their needs at an optimal level is debatable; but where a species has existed for a number of years, it is unquestionable that it is obtaining at least the minimal levels of various nutrients required for survival.

In most cases, energy is the nutritional factor to which most attention has been directed, although this does not necessarily imply that energy is more important than the other nutrients. In a sense, no nutrient is more or less important than any other nutrient since all are required for life. At present, however, it generally is agreed that if a wild animal is able to meet its energy needs, it consequently meets other nutrient needs. Exceptions include possible mineral and/or protein deficiencies in some big game populations during one or more seasons of the year. The relative magnitude of these deficiencies, as related to energy, is not well understood. In some areas, a nutrient or nutrients other than energy quite possibly could be the limiting factor from the nutrition standpoint.

NUTRITIONAL CARRYING CAPACITY

Carrying capacity can be defined as the number of healthy animals that can be maintained by habitat on a given unit of land. If a population is to survive and remain healthy, it cannot be at such a level as to destroy its habitat. Carrying capacity often is thought to be governed by the season of the year which is most limiting to a population in question. The previously discussed "law of the limiting link" can be altered to fit this phenomenon. For most big game populations, winter food is generally thought to be the limiting link; the food resources on a given unit of land during spring, summer and fall usually are able to support substantially greater numbers of animals than can foods available during winter. However, those familiar with recent work in wildlife energetics will realize that this oversimplified statement is somewhat misleading. White-tailed deer, and very likely many other big game species, have a number of mechanisms that tend to reduce the importance of winter food as the sole factor influencing winter survival. The build-up of body fat from summer and fall foods, subsequent catabolism of this fat during winter, lowered metabolic rate, development of a highly insulative coat and changes in behavior all tend to complicate the simplistic notion of a single "limiting" season.

Some factors relate and contribute to carrying capacity beyond nutritional aspects. Certain habitat needs have little to do with nutrition per se. Behavioral characteristics of an organism influence carrying capacity regardless of food availability. For example, white-tailed deer in northern areas typically seek out mature softwood cover during winter. These areas normally provide far less food than do adjacent hardwood or younger softwood areas (Barnes 1976). They do, however, modify winter conditions by decreasing snow depth, as well as wind, thus affording the animal greater mobility at a lower energy cost than possible elsewhere. Often, different factors are interwoven, some of which have a direct bearing on requirements for another factor. Thus, while the remainder of this chapter will deal with the relationship of nutrition and carrying capacity, it must be cautioned that this is not the only or final link of understanding for nutrition-related management of wildlife.

Nutritional carrying capacity might be defined as the size of a healthy and productive population that the food resources of a unit of land can maintain. Even here, caution needs to be stressed, for the true "food resource" of a particular habitat is represented by the amount and quality of foods actually available to animals, which may not be the total amount of food present. Unlimited winter forage is of little value to a deer population if it is located where the deer cannot make use of it. Thus, behavioral, physical and perhaps other characteristics of an animal population come into play in assessing a habitat's nutritional carrying capacity.

Nutritional factors

As discussed initially, there are several specific components that need to be considered when dealing with the nutritional carrying capacity of an area, including food habits, food availability, digestive efficiency and food requirements.

1. Food habits

Study of the food habits of a species is an essential first step to understanding nutritional carrying capacity. Before one can learn how efficiently an animal digests and metabolizes its food and how much food is available and required, the food resource first must be identified. Early nutrition-related studies of many big game species dealt almost exclusively with food habits, and this continues to be a major area of study.

The food habits of most species vary considerably according to location, season of the year, habitat conditions, weather, competition, population density, and sexes and ages of animals. Determining what foods are ingested by a particular animal and when they are ingested is a difficult task. A number of techniques have been developed and employed over the years for the study of food habits of herbivorous big game species, including stomach content analysis, (Anthony and Smith 1974, Harlow et al. 1975, Short 1977, Wilson et al. 1977), scat analyses (Zyznar and Urness 1969, Todd and Hansen 1973, Peden et al. 1974, Dearden et al. 1975, Hansen et al. 1977), and field measurements of browsed forage (Hjeljord 1973, Crete and Bedard 1975, Joyal 1976). Food habits of big game carnivores have been less widely studied, although data have been reported for mountain lion (Robinette et al. 1959, Hornocker 1970, Spalding and Lesowski 1971 and Toweill and Meslow 1977), grizzly bear (Craighead and Craighead 1972), black bear (Spencer 1955, Beeman and Pelton 1977) and wolf (Stenlund 1955, Mech 1966, 1970, Mech and Frenzel 1971b, Van Ballenberghe et al. 1975a).

One example of the intensity and sophistication of modern food habits studies is the "lead deer" technique. In this procedure, animals are trained to "work" with a handler and allow a researcher to remain close and observe what and, in some cases, how much (number of bites) food it consumes. This may involve training an animal to accept a harness and leash, as well as to enter and leave a truck or trailer for purposes of transportation to a particular study site. This technique has been employed with pronghorn (Schwartz and Nagy 1976), deer (Wallmo and Neff 1970, Crawford and Whelan 1973, Wallmo et al. 1973, Gill and Wallmo 1973, Neff 1974), elk (Gill 1978) and moose (H. Crawford and W. Regelin, personal communications). Obvious biases can arise with this procedure, the most apparent of which are the possible influence of the handler and, perhaps more important, the previous feeding history of the "lead" animal. Care must be taken to insure that the animal has consumed a diet representative of that consumed by animals of the same species in a wild population. Allowing experimental animals to forage in a study area for a period of time prior to the actual study often is used to reduce possible bias.

2. Food availability

The quantity of food available to a big game population is as important as the quality of this food. Numerous sampling schemes have been devised and used for the quantitative measurement of food and will not be dealt with in detail here. Readers are referred to one of many articles including Ehrenreich and Murphy (1962), Shafer (1963), Jordan et al. (1965), Shaw and Ripley (1965), Stiteler and Shaw (1966), Stearns et al. (1968), Barrett and Guthrie (1969), Wallmo et al. (1972), Carpenter (1972), Bobek and Dzieciolowski (1972), Wolters and Schmidtling (1975), Pearson and Sterniske (1976), and Barnes (1976).

3. Food evaluation

Once the specific food habits of an animal are understood, it is possible to set up experiments to determine how well that animal is able to digest and utilize foods. Obviously, an animal's body is not able to utilize fully all ingested energy. To do so would constitute an exception to the second law of thermodynamics which states that no transfer or transformation of energy is 100 percent efficient. Actually, much of the energy in food is discharged as fecal matter, urine and methane or expended in the work of digestion (Figure 65). As discussed previously, evaluation of the nutritive values of wildlife foods is an area of research which only recently has become fairly commonplace. There are several levels of precision in food evaluation studies.

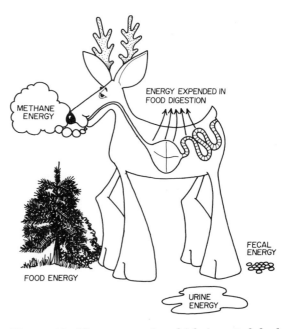

Figure 65. The manner in which ingested food energy is "lost" in the digestion process.

A. Chemical analysis

Chemical analysis of a food can yield data on a variety of constituents and components which make up that food (Dietz and Currow 1966). The traditional and perhaps most common food analysis procedure is the proximate analysis. This procedure separates food into the following components: crude protein, crude fiber, ether extract (fat), nitrogen-free extract (NFE), and ash. There are several shortcomings in this method of analysis, notably its lack of precision, specifically within the crude fiber and NFE components. The technique originally was designed to break the carbohydrate faction into digestible (NFE) and nondigestible (crude fiber) components, but this breakdown is not realistic because the crude fiber component is partially digestible. Newer techniques allow the separation of the traditional crude fiber component into a better approximation of digestible and nondigestible portions (Van Soest 1964, Van Soest and Wine 1967).

329

All chemical analyses have a basic short-coming. While they identify the different components in foods or diets, they do not specify how well animals are able to digest the various components. The measurement of energy is a prime example. Nearly all ecological substances have an energy content in the range of four to seven kilocalories per gram of dry matter. (The greatest possible span in biological materials would be from 4.0 kilocalories per gram for pure carbohydrate to 9.5 kilocalories per gram for pure fat.) The energy content per gram of an oak table is similar to that of most herbivorous big game foods, although the substances obviously differ tremendously in their level of digestibility and, thus, value to animals. Chemical analyses, however, do allow at least an initial comparison among foods. With new and more sensitive techniques, chemical analyses will become increasingly useful to wildlife managers. Also, data generated through such analyses can be used to predict digestibility mathematically.

B. Feeding trial

The most direct way to determine how well an animal is able to digest a particular food is to feed the animal the food in question. There are several food evaluation procedures which involve feeding animals.

1) Total collection

The traditional feeding trial, referred to as the total collection method, has been used to evaluate natural foods of white-tailed deer (Forbes et al. 1941, Silver and Colovos 1957, Ullrey et al. 1964, 1968, 1971, 1972, Ullrey, Youatt, Johnson, Fay and Brent, 1967, Mautz 1969, Mautz et al. 1976, Robbins et al. 1975), mule deer (Smith 1950, 1952, Hagon 1953, Bissell et al. 1955, Urness et al. 1977, Milchunas 1977), caribou and reindeer (Jacobsen and Skjenneberg 1975) and peccary (Zervanos and Hadley 1973). To the author's knowledge, no feeding trials have been conducted on mountain lion or any of the bear species with the exception of the work on polar bear by Best (1975).

The total collection method involves measuring the food eaten and waste material eliminated over a given period of time. Combined with a chemical analysis of food and wastes, this allows calculation of the degree to which an animal is able to utilize (digest and metabolize) the food in question. There are several different levels in the digestion/metabolism process at which energy can be lost (Figure 64A). Not all feeding trials attempt to measure all the parameters shown. The degree of difficulty and the expense involved increases with the level of evaluation.

a. Digestible dry matter

Digestible dry matter can be calculated knowing only the amount of food consumed and feces excreted over a given period of time (Equation 1). Thus, it is the amount or proportion of food which is absorbed that is measured. Theoretically digestible might be better termed absorbable, although this term is rarely used.

Separation and collection of urine and feces are integral parts of feeding trials. Photo by author.

Deer are placed in digestion crates for browse evaluation trials. Photo by author.

Equation 1.

$$\text{Digestible dry matter (grams) per gram of food ingested} = 1 - \left[\frac{\text{dry matter feces excreted per unit time}}{\text{dry matter food ingested per unit time}} \right]$$

The prefix "apparent" sometimes is used in combination with the term digestion. Fecal matter contains metabolic waste and sloughed cells from the gastro-intestinal tract which do not actually arise directly from the food item being studied. Thus "apparent digestion" is always somewhat lower (generally by just a few percent) than true digestibility.

Digestible dry matter is of value primarily in comparing different foods. It represents a relative measure of a food's nutritive worth.

b. Digestible energy

Digestible energy is the energy (in kilocalories) or percent of gross energy of an ingested food which is absorbed from the gastro-intestinal tract. Its calculation, as that of digestible dry matter, takes into consideration only fecal losses. For determining digestible energy, however, measurements are required of the energy content (kilocalories per gram) of food and feces as well as the actual amounts of dry matter ingested and excreted over a period of time (Equation 2).

Equation 2.

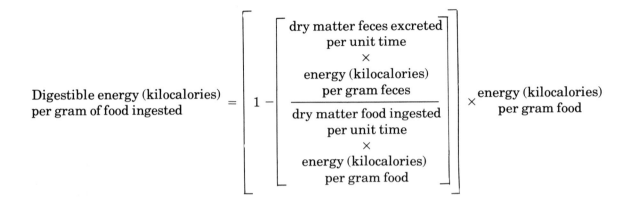

$$\text{Digestible energy (kilocalories) per gram of food ingested} = \left[1 - \frac{\left[\begin{array}{c}\text{dry matter feces excreted per unit time} \\ \times \\ \text{energy (kilocalories) per gram feces}\end{array}\right]}{\begin{array}{c}\text{dry matter food ingested per unit time} \\ \times \\ \text{energy (kilocalories) per gram food}\end{array}}\right] \times \text{energy (kilocalories) per gram food}$$

The determination of digestible energy is slightly more complicated than that of digestible dry matter. However, this parameter still deals solely with the digestive process and requires only a measure of food and fecal matter. Actually, digestible energy is generally very similar (within a few percent) to dry matter digestibility. This is due to the fact that there is only a small difference in the energy concentration (kilocalories per gram) of food and feces.

c. Metabolizable energy

Metabolizable energy is that food energy left after losses in the form of urine and methane as well as feces (Figure 64A). Urine represents another form of nutritive loss (primarily energy and nitrogen) associated with the feeding process; and although not as significant as fecal energy, it nonetheless represents a substantial food energy loss (Figure 64B, C, D). Thus by taking urine into consideration, it is possible to obtain a more accurate measure of a food's nutritive value. In most feeding trials, urine as well as feces is separated and collected.

In the case of herbivores, particularly the big game herbivores, another "loss" or by-product of digestion is methane gas. Methane is a by-product of the fermentation process which occurs primarily in the rumen of herbivorous animals. Therefore, one would not expect carnivores to lose energy in this form. Studies with fisher and coyote detected only negligible methane production from these animals when fed natural foods (Mautz, personal files). Metabolizable energy can be calculated with Equation 3.

Equation 3.

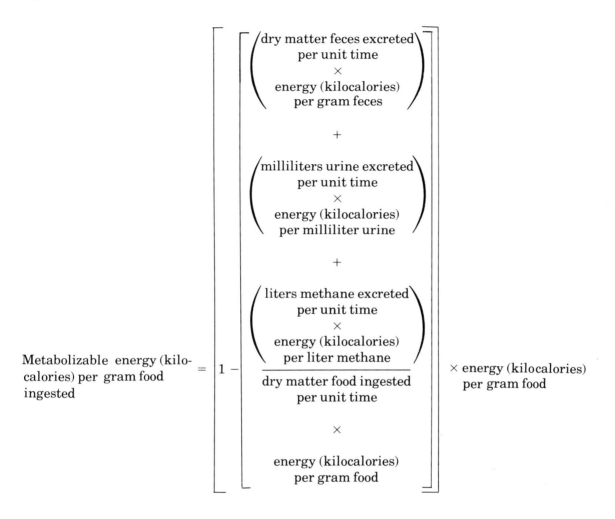

$$\text{Metabolizable energy (kilocalories) per gram food ingested} = \left[1 - \frac{\left(\begin{array}{c}\text{dry matter feces excreted} \\ \text{per unit time} \\ \times \\ \text{energy (kilocalories)} \\ \text{per gram feces}\end{array}\right) + \left(\begin{array}{c}\text{milliliters urine excreted} \\ \text{per unit time} \\ \times \\ \text{energy (kilocalories)} \\ \text{per milliliter urine}\end{array}\right) + \left(\begin{array}{c}\text{liters methane excreted} \\ \text{per unit time} \\ \times \\ \text{energy (kilocalories)} \\ \text{per liter methane}\end{array}\right)}{\begin{array}{c}\text{dry matter food ingested} \\ \text{per unit time} \\ \times \\ \text{energy (kilocalories)} \\ \text{per gram food}\end{array}}\right] \times \begin{array}{c}\text{energy (kilocalories)} \\ \text{per gram food}\end{array}$$

d. Net energy

A final "loss" of food energy centers around the fact that a certain amount of energy is required for the digestive process (Figure 64A). This utilization of energy has been given various names, including work of digestion, calorigenic effect, heat increment, and specific dynamic action. It is not as clear-cut as the previously discussed energy losses, but can represent a significant loss, particularly with regard to foods of herbivorous big game (Figure 64C). One reason why understanding net energy is confusing is that energy expended in the digestion process eventually is "degraded" to the form of heat. If an animal is in a situation where this heat is used to help maintain body temperature, then the "work of digestion" does not represent a loss. More specifically, if an organism is in a harsh environmental situation and "burns" fat and/or other materials to maintain its body temperature, and thus its life process, any heat produced from the feeding process would serve to lessen or take the place of other heat production mechanisms within its body. The calorigenic effect and, thus, net energy vary directly with external temperatures. For that reason care must be taken to control and report the temperature at which the calorigenic effect is measured. The apparent calorigenic effect decreases with decreasing temperature to a point beyond which there is no measurable heat loss associated with the digestive process (Kleiber 1961).

The calorigenic effect of a food is measured by subtracting the metabolic rate of a feeding animal from that of the "fasting" animal. Theoretically, the test animal behaves metabolically exactly the same in the two periods of measurement in all other respects. This represents a significant and certainly recognized problem with wildlife species where it is highly unlikely that any animal behaves the same over any two 24-hour periods.

It is likely that the true value of a food in terms of usable energy during the winter months lies somewhere between metabolizable and net energy. In most circumstances net energy would be theoretically the best measure of a food's energy worth during the summer months. Net energy can be calculated with Equation 4.

Equation 4.

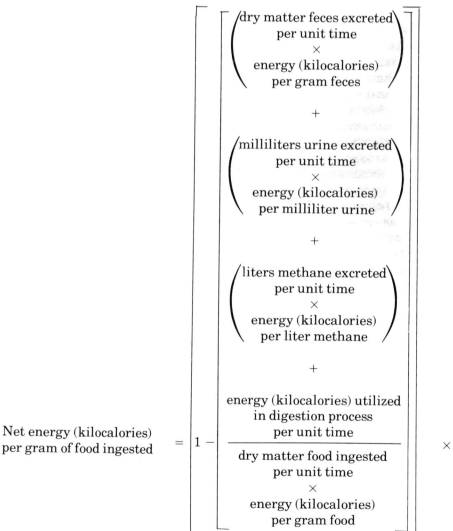

$$
\begin{aligned}
&\text{Net energy (kilocalories)} \\
&\text{per gram of food ingested}
\end{aligned}
= 1 -
\left[
\frac{
\left(\begin{array}{c}\text{dry matter feces excreted per unit time}\\ \times\\ \text{energy (kilocalories) per gram feces}\end{array}\right)
+
\left(\begin{array}{c}\text{milliliters urine excreted per unit time}\\ \times\\ \text{energy (kilocalories) per milliliter urine}\end{array}\right)
+
\left(\begin{array}{c}\text{liters methane excreted per unit time}\\ \times\\ \text{energy (kilocalories) per liter methane}\end{array}\right)
+
\dfrac{\begin{array}{c}\text{energy (kilocalories) utilized in digestion process per unit time}\end{array}}{\begin{array}{c}\text{dry matter food ingested per unit time}\\ \times\\ \text{energy (kilocalories) per gram food}\end{array}}
}{}
\right]
\times \begin{array}{c}\text{energy (kilocalories)}\\ \text{per gram food}\end{array}
$$

There are several problems inherent in techniques that involve the feeding trial approach to food evaluation. The problems arising from keeping any wild animal captive, and big game animals in particular, cannot be overstressed. Perhaps more fundamental is the question of the degree of "truth"—relative to natural conditions—in what is measured using captive animals. There is little reason to believe that a captive animal, conditioned to captivity and a particular diet, would digest this diet to a lesser or greater degree than a wild animal eating the same diet. Studies with white-tailed deer suggest that this is a valid assumption (Mautz 1971b).

The actual amount of food ingested, however, might not be the same for captive and free-ranging wild animals. Some captive animals, particularly those confined to digestion crates, tend to reduce food consumption while others increase consumption. What causes these changes is not clear, but it undoubtedly is related to a number of factors involving either increased or decreased energy expenditures and the relative level of "frustration" of the confined animal.

A feeding trial by the total collection technique involves collection of a large quantity of the particular food material to be evaluated. There is no set length of time firmly established for feeding trials of this type. Any feeding trial requires a "conditioning" period during which time the animal is allowed to become digestively adjusted to the particular food(s) under study. The length of this period needs to be such that the animal is in a "steady state" condition (that is, digesting the new diet at a stable level). For a large ruminant being changed over to a new, dissimilar diet, a period of approximately two weeks is required. A less radical dietary change would require a shorter preliminary or conditioning period. The animal also needs to be conditioned to the collection crate or other ap-

Collection of natural foods used in feeding trials is an expensive and time-consuming job. Photo by author.

paratus used for the collection of feces. Usually this can be done at the same time that the "new" diet conditioning is taking place. It should be borne in mind that not all individual animals make good subjects for feeding trials. Different animals exhibit different degrees of adaptability to confinement.

A five- to seven-day collection period (time during which all food consumed and feces and urine excreted are measured) generally is considered minimum for a moderate-sized ruminant, such as sheep or deer. In general, food, feces and urine values are calculated on a per-day basis and need to be measured over several days to ensure a representative mean (*cf.* Golley and Buechner 1968).

A feeding trial thus requires a fairly substantial length of time for each food or diet to be evaluated, as well as a major effort for collecting sufficient samples of the food to be studied. Because of the time and expense involved, a number of shortcut methods or variations have been proposed and evaluated. These are too numerous to cover comprehensively here, but a few will be listed for illustrative purposes.

2) Ratio method

This technique involves the use of an inert, nondigestible food marker. Chromic oxide, lignin, stained straw, radioactive chromic chloride and rubber particles are a few of the many inert substances that have been used in the ratio procedure. Since the food marker is not absorbed, its concentration per gram of digesta increases as food absorption occurs along the gastro-intestinal tract. The amount of dry matter absorbed from a ration can be determined by comparing the concentrations of the marker in the food and in the feces. Use of the ratio or "indicator" technique provides flexibility not possible with the total collection procedure. It has the advantage of not requiring the quantitative measurement of all food and fecal material, and it also allows a shorter trial period. Since all fecal material need not be collected, a trial can be conducted without strict confinement of the test animal. Inert markers perhaps have been used more frequently in passage rate studies. Interest in passage rate stems from the relationship and influence of food passage on digestion and vice versa. Radioactive chromic chloride has been used with white-tailed deer in both digestion and passage rate trials (Mautz 1971a, Mautz and Petrides 1971).

3) Substitute animal species

A limited amount of study has been directed toward use of substitute animals in big game food-evaluation research. It is possible that a domestic or easily maintained wild animal could be used to evaluate or predict the relative worth of big game foods. Some work has been done in this area with a variety of species, including domestic rabbit (Forbes et al. 1941), snowshoe hares (Mautz, Unpublished), and voles (Mautz, personal files).

Impetus for the search for a substitute species to be used in big game nutritional studies is the previously mentioned investment of expense and effort required with traditional feeding trials. A smaller, easily held animal requiring less space and food has obvious advantages for research. In general, the use of substitute animals has met with only limited success. While substitute animals may provide an approximation of the degree to which a big game mammal digests its food, the level of accuracy realized at this time does not favor this procedure over other shortcut food evaluation methods discussed below.

C. Microdigestion techniques

In addition to actual feeding trials there are several other shortcut food evaluation procedures, generally referred to as microdigestion techniques. Most of these techniques are carried out *in vitro,* which means outside the living body or in an artificial environment. However, another microdigestion method involves a small nylon bag containing a food sample placed directly in the rumen via a fistula. This technique has been used with goats to evaluate deer foods (Short and Epps 1976).

In vitro techniques generally involve removal of a portion of rumen fluid from either the big game species being studied or a substitute animal. Artificial rumens then are created, in which foods being studied are subjected, under carefully controlled conditions, to digestion by a small amount of collected rumen fluid. Digestion is measured by the reduction in the food's dry matter. There are numerous advantages to this technique, including the large number of artificial rumens (small tubes or vials) that can be set up and analyzed at one time and the small amount of food required per sample.

Several *in vitro* techniques currently are being assessed for their applicability to big game food evaluation. Compounding the problem of evaluation of these techniques is the fact that a specific *in vitro* technique may give accurate results for one category of food, but not for another. Nonetheless, there are several *in vitro* techniques which currently offer strong evidence of being useful in big game food evaluation. Among these are methods proposed by Tilley and Terry (1963), Van Soest et al. (1966) and Pearson (1970). Direct comparisons of the *in vivo* (total collection) and *in vitro* technique recently have been evaluated for white-tailed deer (Robbins et al. 1975, Ruggiero and Whelan 1976) and mule deer (Milchunas 1977, Urness et al. 1977).

D. Predictive techniques

Perhaps the most logical form of big game food evaluation involves prediction of digestibility by some readily measured parameter, such as the previously discussed chemical variables in predictive equations. Preliminary predictive equations based on studies of white-tailed deer and northern browse species have been developed by Mautz et al. (1976). Using the traditional proximal analyses, equations were developed which allowed prediction of approximate digestible and/or metabolizable energy content of browse species. It is likely that these equations can and will be improved and expanded by the use of more precise chemical analyses.

One or more of these "short-cut" techniques likely holds the key to widespread evaluation of the many diets of herbivorous big game. It does not take long to become overwhelmed by the task of evaluating big game foods using conventional techniques. Not only are we talking about many different species of food, but also numerous plant parts and stages of growth for each species. In addition, there may also be variations within species and plant parts between different growing sites. When these considerations are coupled with the fact that most big game animals normally ingest more than one food item in any given day, the complexity of the problem is fully realized.

For example, let us assume that a deer ingests five different food species at a given location in a given season of the year. Let us further assume that there are only two categories or components of each plant species that we need to consider: current annual growth and one other. This leaves us essentially with 10 different dietary components. If we assume these plants and components may be eaten either singly or in combination, we find that the total number of possible "diets" the deer may ingest in any one day is 3,628,800 (10!)! The 10! is just the number of possible combinations assuming equal proportions of each component. If we consider that the relative proportion of the different constituents of each combination may and likely would vary, we are faced with an infinite number of possible diets. While, in reality, it is not necessary to look at all dietary possibilities, some rapid and relatively inexpensive food evaluation technique is needed nonetheless. Feeding trials will continue to be important to confirm the reliability of various shortcut methods. It is hoped that the traditional trials with captive wild animals eventually will not be required beyond this function.

4. Food requirement

Food or nutrient requirements of big game have received only limited study. Big game ecologists presently have greater knowledge of energy requirements than of other nutrient requirements even though with energy there is still much to be learned. Energy expenditure or requirement has been studied for white-tailed deer (Silver et al. 1959, 1969, 1971, Ullrey et al. 1970, Thompson et al. 1973, Mattfeld 1974, Holter et al. 1977, Holter and Hayes 1977, Fair 1978), mule deer (Robinette et al. 1973, Kautz 1978), black-tailed deer (Nordan et al. 1970), caribou and reindeer (Hammel et al. 1961, McEwan 1970, McEwan and Whitehead 1970), mountain goat (Krog and Monson 1954), elk (Thorne et al. 1976), pronghorn (Wesley et al. 1973), and polar bear (Best 1976) (Table 39). Other nutrient requirements of big game which have received at least some attention include protein (Ullrey et al. 1967b, Robbins et al. 1974,

Smith et al. 1975, Holter, Urban and Hayes, Unpublished, Holter, Hayes and Smith, Unpublished), and minerals (French et al. 1956, Whelan et al. 1967, Ullrey et al. 1973, Ullrey, Youatt, Johnson, Cowan, Fay, Covert, Magee and Keahey 1975, and Ullrey, Youatt, Johnson, Fay, Covert and Magee 1975). Studies of the energetics of

black bears have been undertaken by Cowan et al. (1957), Maxwell and Thorkelson (1975), and Rogers (personal files).

There is a broad spectrum of techniques for measuring energy requirements in big game animals. One procedure involves feeding a captive animal or group of animals at a known and controlled rate and measur-

Table 39. Energy expenditure and related information for several North American big game species (some figures recalculated from reported data).

Species	Kcal/kg body weight$^{0.75}$/day	Age	Season	Condition[a] measured	Method of measurement	Source
White-tailed deer	71	Adult	Winter and summer	Fasted-resting	Chamber[b]	Silver et al. 1959
	97	Adult	Winter	Fasted-resting	Chamber[b]	Silver et al. 1969[c]
	144	Adult	Summer	Fasted-resting	Chamber[b]	Silver et al. 1969[c]
	90	Fawn	Winter	Fasted-resting	Chamber[b]	Silver et al. 1969[c]
	131	Fawn	Summer	Fasted-resting	Chamber[b]	Silver et al. 1969[c]
	131[d]	Adult[d]	Winter	Fed	Feeding trial–estimated[e]	Ullrey et al. 1970
	173	Fawn	Growth period	Fed-resting	Feeding trial–estimated[e]	Thompson et al. 1973
	125	Fawn	Winter	Fed-resting	Feeding trial–estimated[e]	Thompson et al. 1973
	197	Fawn	Winter	Fed-bedding	Face mask[b]	Mattfeld 1974, 128
	318	Fawn	Winter	Fed-standing	Face mask[b]	Mattfeld 1974, 128
	651	Fawn	Winter	Fed-walking	Face mask[b]	Mattfeld 1974, 128
	1469	Fawn	Winter	Fed-running	Face mask[b]	Mattfeld 1974, 128
	82	Adult	Summer	Fed-bedding	Tracheotomy[b]	Fair 1978
	140	Adult	Summer	Fed-walking	Tracheotomy[b]	Fair 1978
	209	Adult	Summer	Fed-bounding	Tracheotomy[b]	Fair 1978
Mule deer	121	Fawn	Winter	Fed-bedding	Face mask[b]	Kautz 1978
	193	Fawn	Winter	Fed-standing	Face mask[b]	Kautz 1978
	305	Fawn	Winter	Fed-walking	Face mask[b]	Kautz 1978
Black-tailed deer	149	Fawn[f]	Winter	Fed-resting	Chamber[b]	Nordan et al. 1970
	80	Fawn[g]	Winter	Fed-resting	Chamber[b]	Nordan et al. 1970
Reindeer/caribou	98	Adult	Winter	Fed-standing	Face mask[b]	Hammel et al. 1962
	387	Adult	Winter	Fed-pulling load	Face mask[b]	Hammel et al. 1962
	97	Adult	Winter	Fasted-resting	Chamber[b]	McEwan 1969
	116	Adult	Winter	Fed-resting	Chamber[b]	McEwan 1969
	144	Adult	Winter	Fed-standing	Face mask[b]	Young and McEwan 1975
	200	Adult	Winter	Fed-winter maintenance	Feeding trial–estimated[e]	McEwan and Whitehead 1970
Pronghorn	119	Adult	Year	Fed-resting	Chamber[b]	Wesley et al. 1973
	76	Adult	Year	Fasted-resting	Chamber[b]	Wesley et al. 1973
Peccary	88	Adult	Summer	Fed	Feeding trial–estimated	Zervanos and Day 1977
	95	Adult	Winter	Fed	Feeding trial–estimated	Zervanos and Day 1977
Mountain goat	76	Adult	Winter	Fed-resting	Chamber[b]	Krog and Monson 1954

[a]Most trials conducted at the average temperature of the season during which measured.

[b]Indirect respiration calorimetry.

[c]Silver et al. (1971) evaluated the effect of falling temperature on the metabolic rate of deer.

[d]Pregnant.

[e]Metabolizable energy required for maintenance.

[f]Female.

[g]Male.

ing performance (generally body weight changes). If several groups of animals are used, all fed at different rates, it is possible to determine the level of intake required to maintain body weight, to gain weight at a desired rate or to produce viable young. This "feed lot" procedure has not received much attention in the wildlife field, probably due to its inherent lack of precision. With this approach, the final measure is expressed as pounds of food per day required for the level of performance desired. The amount of ingested food required to maintain body weight varies, of course, with food quality. If the study is conceived properly and conducted with natural foods, there is no reason why such a technique could not provide pertinent information. An advantage of this method is that no elaborate laboratory facilities are required. When expanded to include a feeding trial, this procedure can yield specific information on digestible or metabolizable energy and/or nitrogen requirements.

A more accurate means of measuring energy requirements for big game animals involves determination of metabolic rates. Metabolic rate is the rate at which an animal's body uses energy (calories) and produces heat. This rate represents a requirement in that, to maintain itself over any length of time, an animal must take in and digest at least as many calories as it burns up.

A. Direct calorimetry

All energy burned within an animal's body eventually is released as heat. Metabolic rate can be determined by measuring the amount of heat given off by an animal over a given period of time. This type of measurement frequently is referred to as "direct calorimetry." Heat measurement is possible with animals as large as big game species. Measurement of body heat, however, requires highly sophisticated and expensive heat-sensing equipment. Since there are other less cumbersome methods of accurately measuring energy expenditure,

direct calorimetry—to the author's knowledge—has not been attempted with big game animals.

B. Indirect calorimetry

Metabolic rate generally is measured by indirect means referred to collectively as "indirect calorimetry." Theoretically, this includes all determinations of metabolic rate (heat production) through measurement of parameters other than heat loss.

Indirect respiration calorimetry involves determination of metabolic rate through the measurement of gases exchanged in the respiration process. Combustion or burning of substances (catabolism) within the body results in the consumption of oxygen and the production of carbon dioxide. The ratio of carbon dioxide produced to oxygen consumed is termed the respiratory quotient (RQ). Through a knowledge of the RQ, it is possible to determine how many calories of heat are produced for each liter of oxygen consumed. This caloric equivalent, multiplied by the liters of oxygen consumed per unit of time, yields the metabolic rate or energy requirement (in calories) per unit of time. Respiratory quotient and, thus, caloric equivalent vary depending on what substance is being burned (catabolized) by the body. For example, if an animal is burning carbohydrates, a liter of consumed oxygen represents 5,000 calories; a liter of oxygen consumed in protein catabolism represents 4,500 calories. For a thorough discussion of these principles the reader is referred to Kleiber (1961).

Measurements of gas exchange generally involve use of indirect respiration calorimeters or chambers. This technique has been used to a limited extent with big game animals. Working with a mountain goat, Krog and Monson (1954) were the first to use indirect respiration calorimetry with a big game species. Silver et al. (1959) initiated intensive studies of the metabolic rate of white-tailed deer using such a system. Since that time, several other respiration chambers have been employed in

Big game energy metabolism studies were pioneered in 1959 by Helenette Silver using this indirect respiration calorimeter (chamber) for white-tailed deer. Photo by Haven Hayes.

studies of energy metabolism with caribou (McEwan 1970), black-tailed deer (Nordan et al. 1970), pronghorn (Wesley et al. 1973), polar bear (Best 1976, Oritsland et al. 1976), and black bear (Rogers, personal files). A limitation of the traditional respiration chamber is the close confinement to which the test animal is subjected. Also, there is a limit to the types of environmental conditions to which the animal can be exposed while in the chamber. Nonetheless, respiration chambers do provide valuable baseline information.

Indirect respiration calorimetry can be conducted on an animal not confined to a chamber, provided there is a way to collect and measure expired air. Face masks have been used to a limited extent in an attempt to measure energy expenditure (and thus requirement) for different activities of white-tailed deer (Mattfeld 1974), mule deer (Kautz 1978), and reindeer and caribou (Hammell et al. 1961, Young and McEwan 1975). Tracheotomies also have been performed on deer, to measure and sample expired air and thus allow calculation of energy expenditure (Fair 1978). These indirect respiration calorimetry techniques allow measurements of energy expenditure for different activity levels and environmental conditions. However, at the present time, use of tracheotomies as well as face masks requires that test animals not be totally free roaming. A handler must be close by and be able to collect gas samples and take readings.

Other indirect methods of measuring metabolic rate in big game are desirable and currently are being sought. As with the evaluation of wildlife foods, measurement of energy expenditure currently is being subjected to a number of shortcut methods. Use great asset to big game management. Another indirect calorimetry technique, designed to measure CO_2 entry rate by an isotope dilution procedure, has been evaluated with caribou/reindeer (Young and McEwan 1975).

A more likely answer to the question of how to determine free-roaming animals' energy expenditure involves the use of "time-budgets" in which the length of time spent in different activities is measured for a representative segment of a wild population. Total energy expenditure over a longer period (day, month or season) could be calculated by multiplying the energy cost for each activity (as determined with captive

The measurement of metabolic rate by respiration calorimetry using tracheal fistula in a semifree-roaming white-tailed deer. Photo by author.

of heart rate as a predictor of energy expenditure now is being evaluated for white-tailed deer (Holter et al. 1976, Fair 1978) and mule deer (Kautz 1978). There is some question whether or not this parameter will provide a tool for measuring metabolic rate. Further evaluations are needed, but it is unlikely that a single factor such as heart rate, controlled as it is by many different variables, will give precise measurements of energy expenditure, at least over short time periods. Perhaps long-term (daily) measures of heart rate calibrated to individual research animals will provide more accurate estimates of energy expenditures. There can be no question that energy expenditure and heart rate are correlated to at least some degree, and because of this and the tremendous potential payoff, this particular area is receiving increased attention. The ability to measure and telemeter heart rates, and thus predict energy expenditures in free-roaming animals in their natural habitats would be a

The measurement of a mule deer's metabolic rate by respiration calorimetry using a face mask. Photo by William Seitz.

animals by indirect respiration calorimetry with face masks or tracheotomies) by length of time spent in each activity.

OTHER NUTRITION-RELATED PHENOMENA OF CONSEQUENCE TO BIG GAME MANAGEMENT

Winter survival

White-tailed deer and several if not most other big game species have numerous nutritionally related adaptations that enable them to survive winter seasons. During winter, food availability as well as quality is greatly reduced in most areas. Also, numerous energy costs are imposed on animals by weather and other environmental conditions that are not so extreme during other seasons.

How, then, are deer able to survive the winter months? We still do not fully understand all the adaptations which fit together in an amazingly integrated physiological puzzle. Some of the phenomena which we now know to be very important to winter

In many areas, big game animals are faced with decreased mobility as well as decreased quantity and quality of food during the winter. Photo by Karl Strong.

survival of deer include: (1) highly insulative winter fur coat, (2) reduced metabolic rate (reduction of nearly one-third in the energy required to meet basal life functions), (3) behavioral adaptations (deer remain bedded for long periods—several days—during severe weather), (4) high level of reliance on a supply of stored body fat (20–30 percent of the energy requirement throughout a wintering period can be met through catabolism of body fat).

The fact that more natural deaths of adult deer normally occur during the winter rather than other seasons has stimulated intensive studies of food and winter feeding habits of big game populations. However, perhaps equally important to winter food and feeding habits is the supply of body fat each animal accrues prior to the winter season. Consequently, late summer and fall foods are receiving increased attention because it is these foods that provide the energy stored as fat reserves, which ultimately are of major importance to survival through winter of a big game population. The energetics of a 12-month period for deer can be likened to sledding on a brushy hillside (Figure 66). In this analogy (Mautz 1978), summer represents the uphill climb (deposition of body fat) and winter represents the downhill slide (catabolism of body fat). Death occurs if the bottom of the hill is reached prior to spring. Brush (food) on the downhill slide slows but does not stop the sled ride. The uphill climb is hindered by energy demands, such as lactation, the rut and growth. Thus, there are many factors which enter into and influence winter survival in addition to simply the climatic conditions and food supply of that season.

Productivity as related to nutrition

The relationship of productivity and nutrition is readily apparent and has been studied to a limited extent with big game. In this relationship, a number of factors related to breeding physiology are of particular interest and significance, including the nu-

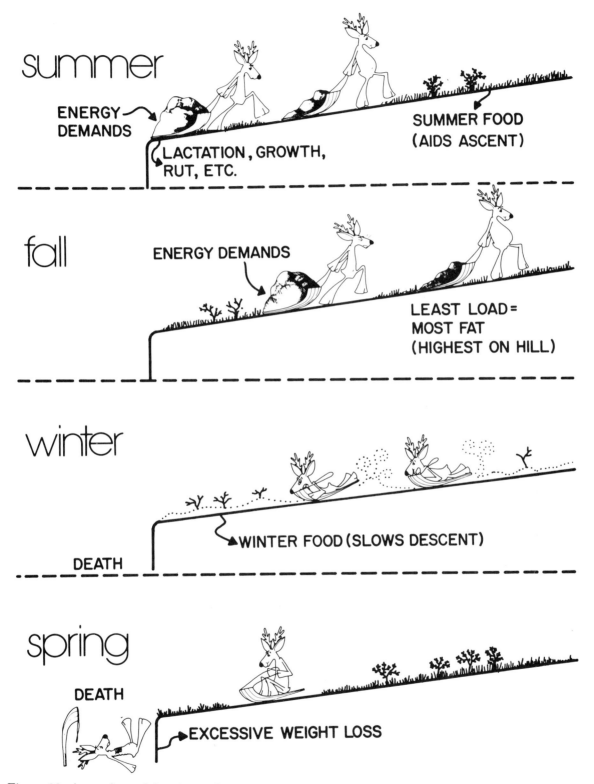

Figure 66. An analogy of the 12-month energetics of many deer and other big game species.

tritional status of the female during gestation and subsequent lactation, and the plane of nutrition the animal experienced prior to ovulation.

Several studies with white-tailed deer have related condition of the habitat and, thus, presumed nutritional plane to incidence of fawn pregnancies, ovulations per doe, fawns per doe and body size (Morton and Cheatum 1946, Cheatum and Severinghaus 1950, Severinghaus and Tanck 1964). Verme (1965a, 1969) evaluated reproductive patterns of captive white-tailed does fed at different nutritional levels. Taber (1956), Taber and Dasmann (1957), Julander et al. (1961) and Klein (1964) conducted range condition versus productivity studies for mule deer and black-tailed deer. These studies all reported a general decrease in productivity (40–50 percent reduction in fawns born) and/or growth with decreased nutritional plane. Rogers (1976) reported reductions in survival, growth and reproductive success of black bear with decreased nutritional plane caused by mast and berry crop failures. Verme's work (1965a, 1969) further suggests an increasing proportion of male fawns with decreasing nutritional plane (for example, approximately 42 versus 69 percent male fawns born to does on a high nutrition versus low nutrition diet). Several extensive reviews of the relationship between range forage quality and animal nutrition are presented by Paulsen et al. (1968).

Starvation

It is difficult to avoid the topic of starvation when dealing with big game nutrition. Animals die because of lack of nutrients. If we define starvation as death caused by lack of anything to eat, then starvation rarely occurs in the wild. Death generally results from malnutrition rather than starvation. Emaciated dead deer frequently are found with material in their rumens during the winter months. This kind of rumen content really cannot be considered food because it is highly indigestible and of little or no value

to deer. When the more palatable and, frequently, the more highly digestible foods are removed from an area, big game animals are forced to consume increasingly less digestible materials. This is of no immediate consequence during early winter because most animals have fat reserves upon which to draw. As the energy supply (nutritious food plus fat reserve) dwindles the animals slowly become increasingly susceptible to stress, whether it be from predators or climatic conditions. With northern white-tailed deer the last one-third of the wintering period (March) is an especially critical time. Late winter storms, which occasionally "lock" deer into winter concentration areas for a longer than normal period of time, often result in significant mortality. If late storms coincide with the inherent increase in metabolic rate first reported by Silver et al. (1969) the problem is compounded. Eventually, for some animals, the fat reserve is depleted and a significant catabolism (burning) of protein begins. If this continues for any length of time, death occurs.

Winter feeding

Winter feeding of big game populations seems to run through various cycles of public and political controversy. It generally is considered by wildlife ecologists to be a poor practice. All too frequently animals are "rescued" by providing them with artificial foods (corn, hay or other) midway through or late in the winter, after they have exhibited signs of severe malnutrition. If the new food is radically different than that to which the animals and their rumen microflora are accustomed, the result often is death, with rumens impacted with high quality food. In the sled ride analogy this form of abrupt winter feeding may be likened to creating a narrow, heavily sanded strip near the bottom of the hill. The downhill slide (weight loss) may be arrested for a few animals but death is a frequent result.

This is not to say, however, that winter feeding could not be made to work from the nutritional standpoint. Many areas could

Late winter storms severely stress many big game animals already under conditions of malnutrition. Photo by Gardiner Bump.

sustain larger wild ungulate populations in winter than otherwise possible if they were either: (1) gradually introduced to new food(s), although gradually introducing new foods to a wild big game population is extremely difficult when there is no control of individual animals within the population; (2) fed throughout winter (which could be represented in the sled analogy by sprinkling sand over the entire hillside); or (3) fed foods nutritionally similar to their natural diets. A prime example of a successful winter feeding program is the National Elk Refuge in Wyoming where 6,000–8,000 elk are maintained during winter by supplemental feeding. This is done on an area where natural winter forage can support only a much smaller population. Nutritional

aspects of protein-energy blocks for winter feed supplements for deer have been evaluated by Ullrey, Youatt, Johnson, Fay, Covert and Magee (1975) and Anderson et al. (1975).

In most cases, arguments against winter feeding do not or should not stem from nutritional considerations, but instead from economic, sociological and perhaps ecological factors. Supplemental winter feeding does not necessarily reduce the pressure on natural food resources. Wild ungulates rarely feed only on that which is provided by man. They continue to utilize natural foods to the extent possible. Therefore, if supplemental feed causes animals to congregate in an area, even greater than normal damage may occur to the natural food plants of the

Winter feeding of elk has been successful on management areas in Wyoming. Through careful monitoring and strictly controlled harvest, the elk do not increase in number beyond the limits of viability afforded by supplemental feeding programs. Photo courtesy of U.S. Fish and Wildlife Service, National Elk Refuge.

area. Moreover, artificial maintenance of a big game population during winter will result in its increased production the following spring. Consequently, there may be more animals to feed the following fall. If harvests can be set to take advantage of production surpluses, then winter feeding probably can be viewed in a different light. As ever-increasing demands are placed on

our big game resources for hunting and other human uses, perhaps winter feeding holds the key to increasing or maintaining some big game populations and providing a harvestable surplus in the face of increased destruction of natural habitat. The major argument against winter feeding is the artificiality which it creates, but the magnitude and implications of this are debatable.

APPLICATION OF NUTRITIONAL INFORMATION TO ESTIMATE CARRYING CAPACITY

Just how do different factors of nutrition fit together? More specifically, how can information such as this be put to a practical management use? Carefully tied together, the information discussed in this chapter will approximate the number of organisms that a particular area of land can support. A simplified formula for calculating this is:

$$A = \frac{B \times C}{D}$$

A = number of animal days which an area can support

B = food resource (grams of available food per area)

C = amount of metabolizable energy contained in this food (kilocalories per gram)

D = amount of metabolizable food energy required by an individual animal per day (total energy requirement minus energy provided by catabolism of body tissue).

If population size is known, this information will indicate how many animals should be harvested from the unit of land in question. It will also allow a precise evaluation of habitat management efforts in terms of their potential for increasing or maintaining carrying capacity.

For example, let us assume we have conducted studies with a big game population which show that:

1. X, Y and Z are the principle food species ingested during the winter;

2. There are 6, 4 and 2 kilograms per hectare (33, 22 and 11 pounds per acre) respectively, of these three food species available to the animal during the period of time with which we are concerned;

3. The metabolizable energy of species X, Y and Z is 2.2, 1.5 and 3.0 kilocalories per gram, respectively;

4. The energy requirement based on an average daily activity is 150 kilocalories per kilogram $^{0.75}$ body weight per day;

5. The average body weight of animals in the population at the beginning of the winter season is 45 kilograms (99 pounds);

6. The average body weight loss is 20 percent or 9 kilograms (20 pounds);

7. Each gram of body weight loss provides the animal with 6.0 kilocalories of energy; and

8. The wintering period is 100 days (time during which the population is restricted to intake of food species X, Y, Z).

Applying these data to the previous equation allows the calculation (below) of the number of animal days the food resource on this land would support (13.4 days per hectare; 5.4 days per acre).

Animal days per hectare =

$$\frac{(6000 \text{ g/ha} \times 2.2 \text{ kcal/g}) + (4000 \text{ g/ha} \times 1.5 \text{ kcal/g}) + (2000 \text{ g/ha} \times 3.0 \text{ kcal/g})}{(16.1 \text{ kg}^{0.75a} \times 150 \text{ kcal/kg}^{0.75}/\text{d}) - (90 \text{ g/d} \times 6 \text{ kcal/g})^b}$$

$$= 13.4 \text{ days/ha } (5.4 \text{ days/acre})$$

[a] Average metabolic body weight during 100-day weight loss period.
$$\frac{45 \text{ kg} + (45 \text{ kg} - 45 \text{ kg} \times 20 \text{ percent})}{2} = 40.5 \text{ kg} = 16.1 \text{ kg}^{0.75}$$

[b] Energy supplied by catabolism of fat, weight loss/day $= \dfrac{0.20 \times 45 \text{ kg}}{100} = 90 \text{ g}$

The number of hectares or acres of this type of habitat needed to sustain one animal through a hypothetical 100-day winter period can be calculated (7.4 hectares per animal; 18.4 acres per animal).

Hectares needed per wintering animal =

$$\frac{100 \text{ days}}{13.4 \text{ days/ha}} =$$

7.5 ha/animal (18.4 acres/animal)

While this is a gross oversimplification, it does emphasize the point that such information can be tied together in a manner which will allow for increased scientific management of our big game resources. As discussed previously under "Winter survival," there are many other nutritionally related factors in big game carrying capacity. Ullrey et al. (1970), Mautz et al. (1976), Wallmo et al. (1977) and Whelan et al. (1976) attempted to tie together several different nutritionally related factors in big game carrying capacity estimates. Also, Moen (1973) presented a detailed mathematical approach to many carrying capacity factors.

There are many assumptions and generalities in any existing formula for calculating carrying capacity. With continued research, it will be possible to strengthen further this link of our big game management chain. For instance, rather than assuming a single identical metabolic rate for all segments of a wildlife population, with further research we could include different energy requirements (per kilogram 0.75 body weight) for each component of the population deemed necessary (adult or young, male or female, etc.). On the other hand, as illustrated earlier with the "law of the limiting link," nothing will be gained from additional research in this or any other area, with regard to our present management capabilities unless this area is, in fact, the limiting link.

Chapter 23

HABITAT CHANGES AND MANAGEMENT

Michael L. Wolfe

Associate Professor
Department of Wildlife Sciences
Utah State University
Logan, Utah

The purpose of this chapter is two-fold. First, I will sketch the nature of land-use changes in North America that have occurred since 1935 and some of their implications for big game resources. The second half of the chapter will present a brief overview of the current state of the arts of habitat management practices for big game animals.

LAND-USE CHANGES: 1935–PRESENT

Sweeping alterations of the North American landscape during the first four centuries of European man's habitation of the continent were described in Chapter 17. The Twentieth Century also witnessed striking changes in major human uses of the land, virtually all of which affected big game habitat. Some merely were continuations or reversals of trends in plant-successional trends resulting from earlier disturbances of the pristine habitat and involved logging, livestock grazing, fire suppression and agricultural practices.

However, the Twentieth Century involved a new dimension, namely the multiplicity of environmental disturbances in the wake of the rapid growth of human population and its increasing mechanization. This genre of land-use changes—including urban sprawl, development of transportation systems, mineral exploration and energy development—differed in that the impacts of these changes on the landscape generally are indelible. In many cases, the consequence of Twentieth Century land use has been the permanent or long-term loss of big game habitat.

Thus, for purposes of discussion, I will distinguish between successional changes and technological and sociological influences. These two categories obviously are not mutually exclusive, since improved technology enables us to increase both the extent and intensity of a particular disturbance and, hence, its impact on big game habitat.

Successional changes

1. Forestry practices. Modern forest science in North America emerged in the present century. It predicated a shift in consumptive emphasis from mere exploitation to management. Timber harvest still remains the most visible aspect of forest management. However, numerous practices now associated with intensive forestry, such as fire control, prescribed burning, reforestation, timber stand improvement and road construction, have considerable effect on wildlife resources.

With respect to big game habitat, perhaps the most ubiquitous of these trends has been the progressive exclusion of wildfire as a result of sophisticated fire detection and suppression techniques. The elimination of fire as a major ecological disturbance has not been limited to forested areas, but also has occurred on vast acreages of western brushlands and grasslands as well. The statistics in Table 40 illustrate this trend clearly. The figures for the latter half of the 1960s show an approximate eight-fold decrease in the total acres burned and a five-fold decline in average fire size in contrast to figures from a period three decades earlier.

Impacts of fire suppression on big game habitat have varied with respect to both the plant communities and animal populations involved. In many forest ecosystems, the effect has been maturation of plant communities toward climax conditions, often with attendant declines in forage productivity and nutrient quality. This succession has resulted in reduced quantity and quality of habitat for some big game populations, including those of deer and moose, which thrive best on ranges dominated by early and/or mid-successional vegetation. Longhurst et al. (1976) considered the decreased amount of acreage subject to wildfires and prescribed burns in California as a major factor contributing to recent deer declines in that state.

Table 40. Average annual wildfire statistics for the United States[a].

Period	Number of fires (thousands)	Area burned		Average size of burn	
		Hectares (millions)	Acres (millions)	Hectares	Acres
1936–1940[b]	211	12.6	31.2	59.9	148.0
1965–1969	120	1.5	3.8	12.7	31.5

[a]From annual wildfire statistics compiled by the United States Forest Service (1969) for federal, state and private lands.
[b]Figures for this period do not include those of Alaska.

In certain plant communities, however, the influence of fire exclusion on big game habitat has been somewhat positive. This was the case for extensive acreages of shrub-grass communities, such as sagebrush, pinyon-juniper and the desert grasslands of the Southwest. In these communities, the effect of continued fire suppression, in concert with excessive livestock grazing, has favored the shrub component at the expense of competing grasses, thereby creating improved habitat for mule deer.

Generalization about the net effects of timber removal during the Twentieth Century on big game habitats and populations is difficult. Farming, settlement and timber exploitation of forest lands in eastern North America partially replaced the natural role of wildfire in terms of rejuvenating pristine forest ecosystems. In the Northeast, many vast, once-cultivated areas were abandoned by settlers in search of more productive land. In time, some areas reverted to second-

growth forests of benefit to white-tailed deer and, to some extent, moose populations. However, maturation of these second-growth woodlands during the past several decades has resulted in the deterioration of big game habitat. In the eastern United States, timber growth now exceeds timber cut.

By the 1930s, most of the original southern hardwood forest had been removed as a result of agricultural development and logging. Subsequent decades have seen the emergence of this region as the most important timber-producing area of the United States. Contemporary silviculture in much of the South is based largely on even-aged management of several rapidly growing pine species. Prescribed burning is employed extensively to reduce fuel accumulations and control the encroachment of competing understory hardwoods. Periodic burning induces low sprout growth that is within reach of browsing deer (Lay 1956, 1957, Lewis and Harshbager 1976). In some

Cut-over areas and stump farms, following settlement of eastern North America, temporarily set back forest succession in some areas to the benefit of big game. Photo by C. H. Park; courtesy of the National Archives.

areas, however, the excessive application of this technique has led to degradation of deer habitat by the virtual exclusion of mast- and browse-producing hardwoods in pine monocultures with "clean" understories.

Although logging activities in forests of the West date back to the late 1800s, large scale timber harvest on public lands commenced in the 1930s and did not increase substantially until after World War II. In comparison to successional changes caused by early wildfires and livestock grazing, logging per se probably was not a major factor in the mule deer population "booms" experienced by several western states in the 1950s and early 1960s. However, in dense coastal forests of the Northwest, increased levels of palatable forage on recently logged areas temporarily improved black-tailed deer habitat.

Modern logging practices and public attitudes toward timber harvesting have changed. Some earlier logging operations were linked to the railroads. A common practice was to clearcut progressively all timber adjacent to rail lines (Hooven 1973). The advent of heavy-duty logging trucks and crawler-type tractors made practicable the harvest of timber on smaller units. In the interim, land managers were forced to accept the fact that very large clearcuts are of limited value to most wildlife species, since such practices merely substitute one monoculture for another. Increased public awareness of the unsightliness of large clearcut tracts also influenced timber interests to harvest smaller units, with resultant benefits for some big game species and populations.

Other practices associated with intensive silviculture for production of conifers on a monocultural basis frequently are inimical to big game populations. The increasing application of reforestation techniques to shorten the cutting cycle may limit regrowth of desirable forage species following logging, thus reducing

the usefulness of the "disturbed" area for big game (Hines 1973). In some forests on the west coast, timber stand improvement practices include removal of competing hardwoods, especially oaks, to favor conifers. This practice can be harmful to deer, for which acorns are a nutritious food source. Another interesting consequence of intensive forestry was noted in the Appalachians by Beeman et al. (1977), namely the removal of large decadent trees that provide den sites for black bears.

Road construction, a by-product of both timber harvest and fire control, has both positive and negative implications for big game. Forest road systems provide access to forest areas by conventional as well as off-road vehicles and, thus, increase the vulnerability of big game populations to human disturbance, particularly during hunting seasons. Logging roads, however, are not always detrimental to big game. Secondary and lower-level roads within logging areas may facilitate movements of big game to foraging areas created by logging. Seasonal closures of these roads following logging have minimized human disturbances and enhanced use of logged areas by big game, particularly elk.

2. Livestock grazing. The dust bowl era of the 1930s focused attention on abuses of public lands in the West. The year 1934 marked passage of the Taylor Grazing Act, which was intended to regulate grazing on these lands. This law established the predecessor of the Bureau of Land Management, curtailed grazing on severely overgrazed areas and brought some control to grazing on other areas. The forerunner of the Soil Conservation Service was established in 1935 to control soil erosion on public lands and provide private landowners with financial and technical assistance for the proper management of their lands.

Wagner (1977) analyzed records of the United States Department of Agriculture's Statistical Reporting Service to ascertain historical changes in the number of domestic livestock grazed on public lands of the 11 westernmost states (Figure 67). From 1935–1975, sheep numbers declined significantly. However, this decline was offset by a gradual but continuous increase in cattle numbers. Thus, Wagner concluded that the potential forage demand of domestic livestock on western rangelands was at an all-time high in 1975. However, increased use of supplemental feeding and implementation of modern range-management practices, such as fencing, water development and measures to distribute grazing pressures, partially compensated for the effects of increased numbers of domestic livestock on public lands.

Certain facets of this scenario have produced changes in big game habitat. The excessive grazing pressures of the late Nineteenth and early Twentieth centuries occasioned the invasion or increase of woody plants on grassland areas of the West, thereby creating favorable forage and cover conditions for deer. Throughout much of the West during the first half of this century, deer populations increased to unprecedented levels.

In some areas of the Mountain and Intermountain West, where grazing has been eliminated or drastically curtailed in recent years, there appears to be a reversion of brushy foothill ranges to the original bunchgrass vegetation (Smith 1949, Wagner 1969). While such changes probably have improved the quality of habitat for elk, they have worked to the detriment of mule deer.

Other livestock-oriented activities such as range-improvement programs, predator control and fencing also have affected big game habitat. Vegetation type conversions and water developments will

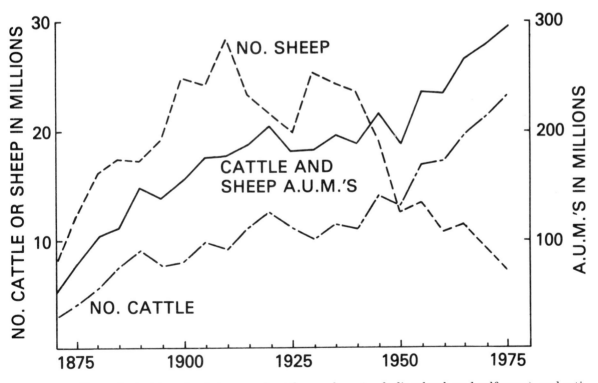

Figure 67. Chronological trends of sheep and cattle numbers (excluding lamb and calf crops), and estimated total livestock forage need (Animal Unit Months) in the 11 westernmost states (after Wagner 1977).

be treated later in this chapter, and the impact of predator control efforts is covered in other chapters.

Fencing is an integral aspect of livestock production. Certain economic factors have resulted in a substantial increase in fencing of both public and private rangelands in the West. In the past, herders tended sheep on both winter and summer ranges, without need for fences. In areas where sheep remain, the cost of hiring capable herders has led to fencing of some sheep ranges.

The general transition from sheep to cattle ranching throughout much of the West also has necessitated extensive fencing. This trend promises to continue as federal land management agencies implement rest-rotation systems for grazing lands. These systems involve systematic rotation of grazing on different subunits ("pastures") of a given grazing allotment at monthly, seasonal or yearly intervals.

Within a given rotation cycle, each pasture is "rested" during at least one interval to allow its vegetation to recover. The use of such systems requires fencing of the component pastures within each allotment.

While most big game animals can clear livestock fences easily, occasional mortalities occur when animals become entangled in the wire. Pronghorn are affected most severely by fences. They do not leap fences readily, but can pass through or under barbed wire fences used to confine cattle. However, woven-wire fences represent virtually impenetrable barriers to pronghorn movements. Where such fences confine pronghorn during severe winters, many may die of starvation.

In recent years, feral horses and burros have become a significant ecological factor in western North America. The forerunners of the modern horse evolved

The effects of livestock grazing on big game ranges are striking when contrasted to "rested" or ungrazed land. The soils of heavily grazed areas can be compacted and, thereby, contribute to rapid erosion and topsoil loss. Rest-rotation systems have shown that multiple uses of rangeland can be compatible. Photo courtesy of the U.S. Bureau of Land Management.

in North America and spread to Asia via the Bering Strait land bridge, after which other modern equid forms such as asses and zebras arose (Clabby 1976, Stirton 1959). Horses suffered the same mysterious demise as many other large prehistoric land mammals, becoming extinct on this continent some 12,000 years B.P.

Spanish exploration and settlement occasioned the reintroduction of horses and burros to the American West in the Sixteenth Century. Subsequently, many of the animals escaped from captivity and proliferated in the wild. By the mid-Eighteenth Century, virtually all Indian tribes of the West had horses, and their warriors were skilled horsemen. Estimates of the number of free-roaming horses in North America at that time range from 2–5 million (McKnight 1959). During the Nineteenth Century, most horse populations occurred west of the Rocky Mountains. Wild herds were augmented by animals released or lost by ranchers and the U.S. Army during the late 1800s and into the present century. By 1935, an estimated 150,000 feral horses existed on public lands in the 11 western states (Zarn et al. 1977). Subsequently, these numbers were reduced severely by commercial exploitation and removal to reduce competition with domestic livestock.

Public concern about the demise of feral horses prompted passage of protective federal legislation—most recently the Wild Horse and Burro Act (Public Law 92–195) in 1971. Under the protection afforded by this law and in the absence of effective natural predator populations, feral horse and burro populations have increased dramatically, some by as much as 20 percent per year. In 1975, there were more than 50,000 horses and 5,500 burros on public lands in the West.

At present, ecologists know very little of the impact of these animals on the desert and mountain ecosystems they occupy (primarily shrub-dominated habitats). Potential competition for food exists among feral equids and several big game ungulate populations of mule deer, elk, pronghorn and bighorn sheep. Of particular concern is the possibility that burros may exclude desert bighorns, whose future is already precarious, from vital water sources. The question of competition and conflict among feral equids and native big game animals has not yet received adequate study. One thing is clear, however: lacking some form of control, the continued increase of horses and burros will intensify whatever competition does exist. Very probably, this will result in the degradation of habitat of all species involved.

Technological and sociological influences

An in-depth treatment of the many influences of our growing technological society on big game resources is beyond the scope of this chapter's brief overview. However, a few major influences must be considered.

1. Urban sprawl. The continuing flux of an increasing human population into urban centers and the attendant urban sprawl of large and small cities alike in recent years have resulted in significant and permanent losses of big game habitat. This trend is particularly acute in the mountainous areas of the West, where suburban subdivisions often are located in foothill areas that formerly provided crucial wintering ranges. Excessive snow depths prevent the animals from wintering at higher elevations. Uncontrolled dogs comprise another problem associated with the encroachment of suburbia on big game habitat. Where these animals are allowed to roam freely, they may inflict losses on local deer populations.

2. Transportation systems and vehicles. A serious consequence of technological progress during the Twentieth Century has been the proliferation of vehicular

transportation systems. Highways in particular have had substantial direct and indirect impacts on many big game populations. While highways and highway construction result in some losses of big game habitat, more important are their effects on migration routes, the separation and isolation of otherwise contiguous habitats, and more ready access to remote natural areas by recreationists. The construction of the interstate and other multilaned highway systems in recent decades has aggravated these conflicts.

Not to be overlooked is the loss of big game in collisions with vehicles. Puglisi et al. (1974) reported that deer-vehicle collisions in Pennsylvania increased by 218 percent from 1960–1967. They noted that this increase was due in part to the construction of an interstate highway across the state. Longhurst et al. (1976) noted that at least 20,000 deer are killed annually on California highways. This represents approximately 60 percent of the average number of deer harvested annually on a statewide basis for the period 1970–1975. In recent years, some efforts have been made to reduce deer-vehicle collisions by the construction of high fences along segments of rights-of-way that intersect known summer or winter range areas or traditional migration routes. These fences force the animals to use special underpass structures to cross the highways.

The phenomenal increase in the popularity and number of off-road recreational vehicles (ORVs) during the past 15 years represents yet another manifestation of advanced technology, affluence and increased leisure time. Prior to the mid-1950s, production of four-wheel-drive vehicles, motorcycles, snowmobiles, and most recently, all-terrain vehicles was insignificant. A report of the United States Department of Interior (1972b) estimated the total number of all types of these vehicles in the United States at more than 5 million. These

figures represented a trend, and at least with regard to snowmobiles, the trend undoubtedly applies to Canada as well.

At present, the impact of ORVs on big game animals is not well-documented. However, at least two major impacts are obvious. One is the increased disturbance and possible displacement of animals from areas subject to heavy ORV traffic (Dorrance et al. 1975). These effects are most critical during seasons when young are born and during winter. In the latter case, forced movements of animals deplete energy reserves at a time when they already are under environmental stress. Such disturbance also can displace animals from areas of vital shelter and food resources. In terms of habitat degradation, the long-term effects of ORVs represent an even greater liability. Soil

Gullies and rills initiated by ORV traffic precludes restoration of the area to big game habitat for many years, once the traffic is banned. Photo courtesy of the United States Geological Survey.

Sheep graze along a hillside on public land in California where ORV hill-climbing contests took place the weekend before. Livestock grazing, in some places, can accelerate erosion and reduce vegetative growth. When land, almost anywhere, is exposed to persistent livestock grazing plus recreational use, its viability as big game habitat is seriously diminished or lost. Photo courtesy of the U.S. Bureau of Land Management.

or snow compaction, erosion, destruction of vegetation, and change of species composition all are potential impacts of ORV traffic on big game habitat. Such habitat damages vary in terms of duration, but all are of serious consequence.

3. Water developments. Large-scale water impoundments, developed largely since the 1930s, have inundated millions of hectares of big game habitat. A compilation by Martin and Hanson (1966) revealed more than 1,500 large reservoirs in the United States with a total impoundment acreage of almost 6 million hectares (15 million acres). As with highway construction, the detrimental effects of these impoundments are not limited to the areas actually flooded. Large reservoirs often disrupt big game migration patterns and may result in the isolation of otherwise suitable habitat. Indeed, where critical winter ranges of migratory populations are inundated, the total effective loss of habitat may involve a much larger area.

4. Mineral exploration and energy development. Looking to the future, mineral exploration and energy development hold considerable potential for the destruction of big game habitat. According to Platts (1974), surface mining currently accounts for approximately 80 percent of the ore and solid fuels produced. By 1971, in the United States alone, some 1.6 million hectares (4 million acres) of land had been disturbed by surface mining and related activities. Wildlife habitat accounted for approximately one-half of the disturbed land. While in the past mining was centered in the Appalachian and midwestern states, the West will bear the brunt of future mineral extraction activities. For example, 42 percent of the United States' known phosphate

reserves are located in the West. Also, a study by the National Academy of Sciences (Box 1973) indicated that 0.6 million hectares (1.5 million acres) of the 51 million hectares (126 million acres) of coal underlying the western United States could be surface mined using current methods. This same study projected a total surface disturbance of about 780 square kilometers (300 square miles) by the year 2000. While the magnitude of this disturbance may seem small in relation to the total area impacted by forest, range and agricultural activities as well as urban sprawl, it represents only a fraction of the total disturbance for all mineral and energy reserves in North America. Oil shale and tar sands also underlie vast areas in the western United States and Canada.

Surface mining is one of the more potentially devastating environmental disturbances on big game habitat, since it involves not only the removal of vegetation but disruption of the soil profile and local topography as well. In many cases, however, properly executed reclamation of disturbed sites can create habitat that actually is more attractive to big game than that which existed prior to mining activities. These effects are particularly important where mineral reserves underlie extensive tracts of presently marginal habitat.

Site disturbance represents only one of many factors involved in the impact of mineral and energy development on big game habitats and populations. Other consequential factors include increased harassment and adverse effects associated with support facilities such as roads, construction camps and pipelines. For example, studies (Klein and Hemming 1976) confirmed initial fears that the construction of large diameter pipelines for transfer of crude oil and natural gas over arctic habitats can impede movements of caribou and to a lesser degree, other ungulates. Where pipelines intersect traditional migration

corridors specific modifications are necessary to minimize their impact.

HABITAT IMPROVEMENT PRACTICES

As human populations and land uses continue to impinge upon big game habitat, we can no longer rely merely on the largess of the land for big game production. Future big game populations will require deliberate and effective habitat management strategies.

The following discussion is predicated on the assumption of continued emphasis on consumptive use of big game resources. Should hunting no longer be a viable big game population management option or opportunity in coming decades, habitat management concerns likely will change. Wildlife habitat still will be important, but not in terms of optimizing big game production as is now the case.

A cautionary note at the outset of this discussion must be interjected. The limited scope of this chapter precludes enumeration of the specific effects of various habitat manipulation practices in all the numerous climatic and vegetative regimes of North America. At the same time, the response to a particular treatment is largely site specific, thus rendering generalizations difficult at best. The reader should bear in mind that beneficial effects obtained by a given practice in one area may not be duplicated on another site where plant composition and growth conditions differ markedly.

The essence of habitat management for any big game population is to provide optimum interspersion of those vegetation types required by the animals for food and cover. This usually entails manipulation of existing vegetation either to maintain or alter its successional stage. In terms of effects on vegetation, different manipulative methods may be employed to achieve similar results. For example, given a closed pinyon-juniper stand with a sterile understory, a manager may use either fire or mechanical

When juniper—a low quality forage—is browsed to this extent by deer on winter range, the habitat is not adequate to maintain a healthy and productive herd. A Wildlife Management Institute photo; taken by Seth Gordon.

means to rehabilitate the stand for use by deer or elk. The choice will be determined by economic and aesthetic constraints as well as biological considerations.

Where the weight of such constraints does not dictate an alternative course of action, "natural" methods of vegetation manipulation such as prescribed burning, controlled grazing and silvicultural practices should receive higher priority than artificial manipulations, including mechanical and chemical methods. Unexpected side effects, which many plant communities cannot readily absorb, more frequently are incurred with artificial techniques than with natural methods or phenomena.

The wildlife literature contains the results of numerous studies that purportedly document beneficial effects for big game populations of various habitat manipulation practices. Most studies report marked in-

creases in animal utilization of treated areas, but few show conclusive population responses such as increased birth rates and/or survival and population growth. Such responses might simply reflect redistributions of static populations with no increases in numbers. A notable exception is the work of Biswell et al. (1952) in which the investigators documented substantial increases in both the density and reproductive rate of a black-tailed deer population in response to opening up dense stands of chamise brush in northern California. While differential attractiveness of treated areas to big game cannot be rejected summarily, the utility of future habitat improvement measures must be evaluated in terms of definitive population responses, not just circumstantial evidence.

Most habitat improvement practices are aimed at increasing forage supplies. These practices often are based on the sometimes erroneous assumption that food resources in a given area are a limiting factor to the big game population(s) of that area, in terms of either nutritional quality or available quantity. Such an assumption can lead to manipulations of vegetation that produce foods that are neither needed nor used. In the process, the actual limiting factor may be ignored to the further detriment of the population(s).

It is imperative that managers not overlook the fact that residual, untreated areas of vegetation usually provide animals with essential cover as refuge from human activity and natural predators as well as protection from adverse weather conditions. To a certain extent, the nutritional status mediates the dependency of an animal on protective cover for thermoregulation. However, microclimatic attributes of some cover types are virtually indispensable to the survival of big game animals during periods of climatic extremes. This is the case with winter "yarding" areas in northern portions of white-tailed deer range. Numerous investigators, including Verme (1965b) and Ozoga (1968), showed that the dense, usually coniferous cover of preferred yarding areas has less snow accumulation, warmer ambient temperatures, and lower wind velocities than do surrounding uplands. In addition, Moen (1968b) demonstrated that a dense canopy of swamp conifers markedly reduced radiation heat losses from deer, particularly on clear and cold nights when, without overhead cover, emissions would have been excessive.

Cover may be equally important in providing animals with protection from heat stress. Linsdale and Tomich (1953) noted that California deer sought out chamise brush and closed woods for protection from summer heat. Similar behavior was reported for peccaries by Bissonette (1976). Edgerton and McConnell (1976) attributed higher summer elk use of dense, unlogged conifer stands to the more stable thermal environment found there than in adjacent partial-cut and clearcut stands. Also, al-

though moose are not affected adversely by extreme cold, they are not well-adapted to high temperatures. In the southern limits of moose range, the shade of forest stands provides moose with a vital refuge from extreme summer temperatures (Kelsall and Telfer 1974).

The point of this discussion is that the size and spatial distribution of openings will determine their utility to big game animals regardless of the method of treatment employed to create openings in forested stands. Depending on the species, the animals generally will venture only a limited distance into open areas to feed. Openings whose dimensions exceed this distance will be utilized only at their periphery.

Recommended sizes for forest openings prescribed by several authors for various big game species are summarized in Table 41. Although the figures relate primarily to logging practices, they also should serve as guidelines for other methods of vegetation conversion. Of the statistics given, those for maximum width (or diameter) of a treatment unit are most critical. Treatment units exceeding the recommended maximum area may be acceptable, provided widths are not appreciably greater than prescribed maximums. Aside from the maximum areas and widths specified, individual treatment units should be well-dispersed within a larger management block to provide a balanced mosaic of food and cover tracts.

Controlled grazing

Since at least the turn of the century, sportsmen, scientists and conservationists have debated whether domestic livestock grazing is detrimental to big game habitat. The subject of grazing is inherently too complex to permit pat generalizations or conclusions. For any given situation, the impact of livestock grazing on wildlife habitat is determined by feeding behavior of the species involved, stocking rates, the plant community and the season in which the grazing occurs.

Table 41. Recommended maximum sizes of openings in forest or woodland cover for various big game populations.

| Species and source | Location and/or vegetation type | Allowable maxima | | | |
| | | Area | | Width | |
		Hectares	Acres	Meters	Feet
White-tailed deer (McCaffery and Creed 1969)	Northern Wisconsin, mixed hardwood and conifers	2	5	100	330
Mule deer and elk (Reynolds 1966a, Patton 1974)	Arizona, Ponderosa pine	18	46	490	1,600
Mule deer and elk (Reynolds 1966b)	Arizona, spruce-fir	8	20	320	1,060
Mule deer (Terrel 1973)	Utah, pinyon-juniper	10–30	25–75	320–640	1,060–2,120
Deer and elk (Leopold and Barrett 1972)	California	8	20	200	660
Deer and elk (Hooven 1973)	Oregon, Douglas fir	12–24	30–60		
Moose (Telfer 1974)	Canada, boreal forest	130	320	500	1,640
Moose (Peek et al. 1976)	Minnesota, spruce fir	80	198		

Excessive grazing sometimes causes irreparable habitat damage and often is detrimental—at least in the short term—to some big game populations. Extreme grazing pressures of the late Nineteenth and early Twentieth centuries resulted in loss of habitat for bighorn sheep, elk and pronghorn populations in the West. While successional changes caused by grazing ultimately proved beneficial to some deer and elk populations, these same changes appear to have eliminated bighorns and pronghorns permanently from much of the animals' former ranges.

Given this somewhat pessimistic introduction, the positive aspect of grazing should be emphasized, namely its potential as a tool for manipulation of wildlife habitats. The practice of grazing, regulated with respect to timing and intensity, to maintain a specific plant community or produce desired successional changes represents a relatively new and viable management strategy.

Prescribed grazing involves deliberate application of forage consumption by one species of domestic herbivore on a plant community to modify competition among the plants of that community, thereby enhancing production of forage species preferred by wild herbivores. Successful use of this method requires that: (1) stocking rates are such that the domestic grazers forage on their preferred food, and (2) timing and duration of grazing be applied at the appropriate stage of plant growth to effect desired changes in the plant community. Failure to observe these constraints spells the difference between desired optimum utilization and unwanted direct competition.

In most cases, populations of two or more herbivore species can utilize primary production of a given plant community more effectively than can a population of a single herbivore species. Conversely, total animal biomass that a unit of habitat can support on a sustained basis usually is greater with multiple-species use than with single-species use. An example is the relationship of big game and livestock populations in the Intermountain West. In recent studies, Smith and Doell (1968) and Jensen et al. (1972) investigated the compatibility of spring grazing by cattle and sheep on deer-elk winter ranges, where the primary browse species was bitterbrush. These investigators found that spring livestock grazing caused little competition with big game for forage provided that grazing was restricted to the early growing season before rapid growth of shrubs. In fact, removal of herbaceous vegetation around the bitterbrush plants by grazing livestock increased moisture available to bitterbrush. This significantly increased browse production for winter use by deer and elk.

Similar results in vegetation manipulation can be obtained by the use of an appropriate combination of big game animals. In fact, in natural grazing communities, the feeding niches of wild herbivores show considerable diversification that minimizes direct competition for food and allows effective utilization of available forage in a given habitat. An interesting example of such interactions among native ungulates was found at Elk Island National Park in Canada, described by Holsworth (1960) and more recently by Wagner (1969). In this ecosystem, browsing by elk and moose was largely responsible for maintenance of grassy openings utilized by bison. In the absence of browsing pressure by elk and moose, openings would have been invaded by shrubs and trees, ultimately resulting in the exclusion of bison.

Use of the grazing animal to manipulate habitat for big game represents an effective and ecologically sound management tool. In terms of cost effectiveness, this approach usually is less expensive than use of mechanical methods that would produce comparable results because the tool itself represents a marketable product.

Forest management

Virtually all silvicultural practices have been shown to affect forest-dwelling big game animals in one way or another. These practices include timber harvest and slash disposal, site preparation and regeneration efforts, rotation lengths and timber stand improvement measures. Of these, timber-cutting programs have by far the greatest impact. Indeed, Shaw (1970) suggested that 90 percent of habitat manipulations required by forest wildlife can be achieved by properly planned cutting programs. Given this premise, the following discussion is framed primarily in the context of enhancing big game habitat through timber-harvest procedures.

Most forest-dwelling big game animals, in either deciduous or coniferous forest habitats, thrive best where a diversity of age and composition classes of plants occur in relatively small stands interspersed with small openings (Telfer 1974). There is even some evidence that woodland caribou, inhabitants of extensive stands of boreal forest, also may benefit from a diversity of cover types (Bergerud 1971c). Fire was the major primeval agent that maintained this diversity. With progressive exclusion of wildfire from managed forest ecosystems, timber harvest constitutes the most practicable means of creating or restoring the necessary variety of cover types.

A major ecological consequence of forest maturation and closure of the forest canopy is a decrease in diversity and production of shade-intolerant shrubs and herbaceous plants in the understory. This generally results in a reduction of palatable forage for big game. Conversely, the primary benefit of opening up a dense forest stand is to allow light to reach the forest floor, thereby stimulating the production of understory forage plants.

The wildlife literature contains numerous references documenting increased diversity, productivity and nutrient content of forage plants following logging, as well as increased big game utilization of cutover tracts. In this respect, moderate-sized clearcuts or patch cuts generally are more beneficial than selective-cutting or thinning operations (Murphy and Ehrenreich 1965). For example, the great increase in Scandinavian moose populations during the present century has been attributed largely to the shift from selective-cutting systems to clear cutting (Lykke and Cowan 1968). There probably exists for each combination of forest cover type and site potential some threshold below which residual canopy cover or basal area must be reduced to stimulate an appreciable increase in forage production. With respect to the transition zone between coniferous and deciduous forests in

Canada's Maritime provinces, Telfer (1973) stated that the residual basal area of a logged stand must be reduced below 17.2 square meters per hectare (75 square feet per acre) before increased browse production results.

Increased light penetration represents only one cause for increased forage production often observed following logging. Other factors include: (1) increased availability of soil moisture, and (2) the release of nutrients previously tied up in tree biomass. Of course, some nutrients are removed permanently from the site when it is logged, but Horwitz (1974) estimated that two-thirds of the nutrients in trees are left on the logging site in the form of roots, branches and other unharvested material. Hence, the method of "slash," or logging debris, disposal becomes an important consideration for the release of nutrients for future forage production and the utility of a cut for big game. In areas of high precipitation, such as eastern North America, organic decomposition of slash will result in relatively rapid return of the nutrients to the soil. However, in the drier climate of the mountainous West, slash may remain largely intact for many years. Under these circumstances, slash disposal by prescribed burning will insure more rapid nutrient release.

These facts do not imply that all logging operations are inherently beneficial to big game animals. Pengelly (1972) identified some detrimental aspects of large clearcuts, including increased snow accumulations and wind velocities, barriers created by logging debris, and losses of vegetative diversity. Pengelly also pointed out that success in rehabilitating big game ranges by logging often varies along a moisture gradient. Moderate-sized clearcuts may improve habitat for deer and elk in dense, coastal forests where forage supplies are limiting. However, a cut of the same size in the sparser and moisture-limited forest stands of the eastern Rocky Mountains likely will be less beneficial, since browse regeneration often is poor on drier sites. The moisture variable also will determine, to some degree, the relative longevity of those benefits to big game that might result from logging. In areas with lower rates of annual precipitation, the seral stages that follow the disturbance of timber harvest generally persist longer.

Whether silvicultural practices are beneficial or detrimental to big game is determined by many factors, the most important of which are the size and pattern of the treatment units and the site potential for both plants and animals. Cutting schemes and the ensuing practices of slash disposal, site preparation, reforestation and timber stand improvement should be planned and executed with purposeful, not incidental, benefits in mind.

Prescribed burning

Some biologists have long recognized the role of fire to maintain or rejuvenate habitat quality for certain big game populations. Indeed, as we have seen, species like deer and moose benefited fortuitously from early wildfires and from some fires prescribed for timber management. Only recently, however, has the planned use of fire gained some measure of acceptance as a valuable tool to enhance and improve big game habitat.

The objective of prescribed burning is periodic application of controlled fire to produce the ecological benefits of a natural state, while minimizing the negative effects of wildfire.

Fire may be used to alter plant species composition and increase production of selected species. The response of the vegetation to a given burn is determined by an assortment of factors too numerous to consider in detail here. Some of the more important variables include existing plant community composition, season, weather, intensity of the burn (heat) and fire frequency.

Impressive and sometimes spectacular increases of herbaceous and browse plant species have been observed following fire. Such responses can occur for a number of reasons, including increased availability of nutrients released in the ash and decreased competition among new-growth plants for available light and soil moisture. Frequently, increased levels of protein and other nutrients in plants on burned-over areas accompany the quantitative increases in forage production. The duration of elevated nutrient levels depends on local site and climatic conditions as well as the nature of vegetative cover prior to burning, but it seldom exceeds three to five years.

Where browse has grown out of reach of big game animals, fire damage to the aerial portions of the plants often induces prolific sprouting from root stocks. As a result, stem densities frequently increase dramatically over preburn levels, thereby producing an abundant browse supply that remains available to big game animals for several years.

A prime example of the use of fire to improve big game habitat can be drawn from recent studies in northern Idaho and Montana by Leege and Hickey (1971) and Gordon (1976), respectively. In these areas, extensive wildfires of the early 1900s created seral brush fields that were important winter ranges for elk, moose and deer. The principal browse species in these areas include redstem ceanothus, willow, red osier dogwood, serviceberry, mountain

maple, chokecherry and aspen. In the absence of recurring fire, browse production in many of these areas decreased because of invading conifers, and the remaining palatable shrub species grew too tall to be utilized effectively. During the past decade, prescribed spring and fall burning has been used effectively to curb conifer growth and rejuvenate production of preferred accessible browse species.

When contemplating the use of prescribed burning for big game habitat, the manager should heed Komarek's (1966) advice that wildlife needs may not be met by application of burning techniques developed for other purposes. The forester and range manager seek clean burns and maximum coverage, whereas burning appropriate for big game usually is less intensive and thorough. Timing, frequency and size of burns for wildlife purposes do not necessarily coincide with other land-use interests, but vary according to the species, habitat and region. The challenge to the land manager is to optimize beneficial effects of prescribed burning for big game in conjunction with other recognized land-use objectives.

Mechanical and chemical methods

Since World War II, numerous mechanical and some chemical methods for vegetation

An experimental area in Florida before the last of a series of prescribed burns.

Same area as in previous photo, soon after the last prescribed burn.

conversion have been developed. These include bulldozing, cabling, chaining, railing, root plowing, and aerial or ground-based application of herbicides. Such treatments have been used extensively on western rangelands in projects variously termed as "brush control," or "range rehabilitation." The shrub types involved are varied and in-

Same area as in previous two photos, eight years after last prescribed burn. This sequence demonstrates the powerful influence fire has in regulating the composition and physical structure of vegetation. In the hands of an experienced wildlife manager, fire can be used to develop or maintain the diversity of flora on nearly any landscape. When, where, and at what frequency and intensity fire is employed can provide suitable forage and shelter for one or more species of wildlife including big game animals. Photos by Roy Komarek; courtesy of the Tall Timbers Research Station.

clude mesquite, pinyon-juniper, sagebrush and chaparral. As the result of overgrazing and fire suppression, many of these brush communities developed into "closed stands" with little or no herbaceous understory.

The treatment regimen is fairly standard; namely, removal of the brushy cover followed by seeding to a mixture of grasses and forbs (and sometimes browse). Early conversion programs were conducted with increasing forage production for livestock as the primary objective. Wildlife and watershed considerations were of secondary importance, and what enhancement of big game habitat did occur was largely accidental. Uniform conversion of large tracts to homogeneous grasslands often nullified the potential benefits of such "improvement" practices to big game populations of deer, pronghorn, elk and bighorn sheep. For example, between 1950 and 1964, 1,200 projects converted some 1.2 million hectares (3 million acres) of pinyon-juniper woodland in the United States. This translates to an average treatment unit of 1,000 hectares (2,500 acres). Admittedly, not all of the treatment units were this size; the point is that many far exceed the recommended maximum sizes shown in Table 41.

The "Big Mac" is the ultimate weapon among mechanical methods of vegetation type conversions. Photo courtesy of the U.S. Forest Service.

In some areas, juniper eradication by chaining can enable regeneration of nutritious understory vegetation. Photo by Don Domenick; courtesy of the Colorado Division of Wildlife.

Vale (1974) estimated that approximately 10–12 percent of the total area (40 million hectares: 99 million acres) of sagebrush vegetation in the western United States has been subjected to some form of control. Despite the relatively slight impact of these treatments on the total extent of this vegetation type, projects involving winter ranges represent a potential threat to big game habitat. Specifically, sagebrush is a staple, nutritious winter food for many mule deer populations. Its large-scale removal can appreciably decrease a habitat's winter carrying capacity.

Vale (1974) stated: "If designed, however, to achieve a heterogenous vegetation of small grassy regions, local areas of dense brush, and expanses of open shrubs with abundant herbaceous growth, sagebrush control should help both wildlife and domestic livestock. Control projects already completed have been planned to produce not this type of vegetation, but pure homogenous grasslands. Rangeland environments with little brush are beneficial only for livestock, not wildlife."

As suggested, such programs need not be detrimental to big game. In fact, where properly designed, substantial enhancement of big game habitat can be achieved. The specifics of a properly planned and executed project will differ according to the vegetation type and primary animal population(s) involved, but some generalizations can be made.

Individual treatment units should be small and well-interspersed throughout a larger complex of residual cover. This means abandonment of the massive area approach. Terrel (1973) considered that the proper concept for pinyon-juniper management on deer winter ranges was to "punch" strategically spaced holes in the forest stands rather than leaving islands of woody vegetation in units cleared by chaining. Treatment should not be done on sites where terrain, soil type or average annual precipitation is inadequate to insure the desired conversion (Plummer et al. 1968). Likewise, treatment should be avoided on ridgetops that provide important cover tracts. Where reseeding of disturbed brushfields is part of the treatment, palatable browse species should comprise a substantial component of the seed mixtures used. Since establishment of browse-producing shrubs may take several years, livestock grazing on treated areas should be deferred initially. Some reduction in densities of big game populations through liberal harvests also may be necessary to insure establishment of seeded species.

Lyon and Mueggler (1968) described the results of efforts to increase browse production by herbicide treatment of several shrub species in northern Idaho. They found some lag in the mortality of competing, undesirable shrub species. Desired browse plants showed relatively quick recovery from crown dieback and poor persistence of sprouting, but the most desirable browse species, redstem ceanothus, was killed by all treatments. The investigators concluded that herbicide spray projects for browse improvement should be based on consideration of the plant composition of the shrub community and careful weighing of the positive and negative effects of spraying at different times of the year.

Other habitat improvement practices

1. Water developments. Water represents the third vital element of the habitat trilogy for any wildlife population. Water requirements differ seasonally, among species and populations, and even among sex and age classes within a given population. For example, lactating does have greater water demands than do bucks. In arid areas where the distribution of surface water sources is a limiting factor, the carrying capacity of habitat for some big game animals may be improved by adding water areas. This may entail modification of existing springs or, more frequently, construction of "guzzlers." Basically, these devices consist of large and impervious rain-collecting aprons that drain water into permanent storage tanks for later use. Guzzlers originally were developed for desert game birds, but may be of particular benefit to desert bighorns, deer and pronghorns. Big game animals will also use simple dugouts installed for livestock as a part of range-improvement programs. To a large degree, optimum distribution of such water sources depends on the cruising radius of the target animal(s).

2. Browse rejuvenation. Many hardwood browse species sprout vigorously following moderate mechanical injury. This phenomenon may be employed advantageously to stimulate browse production, especially where browse plants are excessively tall, dense or decayed. In the East, hand cutting has been used in some hardwood stands to improve browse production for white-tailed deer. Similar results may be obtained through properly conducted thinning or "cleaning" operations during timber stand improvement (Della-Bianca and Johnson 1965). Mechanical treatment is most beneficial when conducted immediately prior to or

during winter, because the downed material yields a browse supply that otherwise may be unavailable.

Numerous other methods of browse rejuvenation have been employed, particularly in shrub-dominated communities in the western United States. Ferguson and Basile (1966) found that "topping" of old-age bitterbrush plants resulted in a nine-fold increase in twig growth the following year. The magnitude of response declined substantially in subsequent growing seasons but, even after four years, production of the treated plants was twice as great as that of untreated plants. In California chaparral, brushfields have been treated by crushing, mowing, rolling and chopping to encourage new growth in the form of crown sprouts or seedlings (Dasmann et al. 1967).

3. Supplemental feeding. Artificial feeding of wild ungulates to carry them through stress periods long has been championed by sportsmen as a panacea, but generally decried by biologists as impractical. Specifics of winter feeding are covered in the chapter on nutrition. The following brief discussion focuses primarily on the rationale involved.

Artificial feeding is rarely, if ever, justified as an alternative (1) to improve natural food supplies through habitat manipulation, or (2) to implement adequate harvest regulations to maintain a big game population within carrying capacity limits. Certain special circumstances, however, may dictate its use. In some cases, the economic returns to be gained by supporting overwinter population levels of big game in excess of natural carrying capacity may justify the expense of supplemental feeding. Such situations do exist on commercial hunting reserves or on intensively managed areas. One example of the latter situation is provided by the forest areas of middle Europe where winter feeding of big game has been practiced for centuries. Other considerations may dictate judicious and usually local use of winter feeding, such as: (1) to keep deer and elk out of commercial orchards, (2) to supplement temporary habitat losses on winter range due to highway construction, suburban development, etc., and (3) to help bring an ungulate population through an unusually severe winter as an emergency measure.

The success of an artificial feeding program depends both on the foods used and the species involved. In the past, alfalfa hay was used widely but, in recent years, pelleted foods for deer and even pronghorn have become increasingly popular. Being broad-spectrum feeders, elk generally fare reasonably well in winter-feeding operations. With deer, however, unless feeding—especially of hay—is commenced early in the winter before the animals experience nutritional stress, their rumen microorganisms will not be able to cope with abrupt change in diet. Under these conditions, mortality may be as great or greater than it would be without supplemental feeding. This problem may virtually negate the use of short-term, spontaneous, artificial-feeding programs as an emergency measure for deer in severe winters. For white-tailed deer, a browse-cutting program as described earlier may represent a more effective emergency measure.

Regardless of the food materials used or the big game species involved, overutilization of and damage to vegetation from concentration of animals on feeding grounds represents a deleterious side effect of artificial feeding. There is also an ethical consideration that should be mentioned, namely the obligation to wild animals to allow them the opportunity to remain wild (Leopold 1933). Habitat management provides that opportunity.

Chapter 24

PREDATORS AND PREDATOR CONTROL

Guy E. Connolly
Wildlife Research Biologist
U.S. Fish and Wildlife Service
Denver Wildlife Research Center
Denver, Colorado

Wherever carnivores and ungulates live together, the former usually eat some of the latter. Man also preys on ungulates and, from earliest times, he has harassed and killed other animals that compete with him for food. Certain cultural groups have revered, worshipped or been too afraid of predators to molest them, but the predominant attitude up to the present century was that predators were vermin to be destroyed by any available means.

Even William T. Hornaday (1914), the noted crusader for wildlife preservation, considered the large North American carnivores so destructive to valuable property that they ought to be eradicated. Heading his list of undesirables was the timber wolf, ". . . strong of limb and jaw, insatiable in appetite, a master of cunning and the acme of cruelty . . . wherever found, the proper course with a wolf is to kill it as quickly as possible." Similar sentiments were extended to the coyote and the mountain lion.

European settlement in North America was accompanied by destruction of the large carnivores for the protection of livestock. Governmental predator control programs eventually were established for the benefit of agriculture and animal husbandry, and large scale eradication of predators was thought to benefit the more desirable species of wildlife.

Early in the Twentieth Century, the United States government adopted a lead role in the protection of agriculture from predators and other vertebrate pests. Wildlife management activities of the individual states, meanwhile, were directed toward the major game species. A dichotomous system of managing wild animals was soon in effect; states managed the resident game species while the United States Bureau of Biological Survey and its successor agencies dealt with migratory, undesirable and problem animals. This arrangement kept most wildlife biologists in the United States from direct contact with animal damage control problems.

Before the advent of college-trained wildlife biologists, predator control was an accepted wildlife restoration tool along with closed hunting seasons, law enforcement, refuges and restocking. State wildlife agencies paid bounties and employed predatory animal hunters to augment the work of federal trappers. But, research in the 1930s and 1940s began to show predator control as ineffective and unnecessary in game

Grizzly feeding on cow moose it killed earlier. Only recently have wildlife researchers begun to understand fully the complex predator-prey relationship and selection pressures among large carnivores and big game ungulate populations. Photo by William E. Ruth.

management. Wildlife management instructors in colleges and universities adopted ecosystem concepts and taught that predator control for the prevention of damage to other wildlife had no place in contemporary wildlife management. Ecologists came to regard predators as a valuable and desirable component of natural ecosystems.

By 1950, the predominant big game management problem in the United States was too many deer, and wildlife managers desired more predation to relieve ungulate overpopulations. Many began to oppose the federal animal damage control program, which continued the wholesale destruction of predators to protect livestock. Such opposition, aimed especially at indiscriminant poisoning of predators, eventually led to various modifications and restrictions in the federal predator control program. In 1972, the United States government banned the use of toxicants in predator control. Subsequent publicity and political action resulted in a large increase in predator research activities by governmental agencies, colleges and universities, and private groups. At about this same time, a general decline of mule deer in the western United States stimulated some state wildlife management agencies to reexamine the factors that were limiting deer numbers. Predation by coyotes, wolves and mountain lions is under investigation in several states. At this time, there is a resurgence of interest in predator control as a big game management tool in the western United States.

A sufficiently selective review of the literature can reinforce any desired view on the subject of predation. Thus, one may read that coyotes play a measurable part in regulating deer numbers but do not control rodent or rabbit populations (Horn 1941), or that coyotes alone cannot regulate deer populations but can efficiently reduce rodent populations (Craighead 1951). One also is told that there are few instances of intensive predator control leading to substantial increases in deer (Dasmann 1971) or,

conversely, that it is hard to find a single instance in which effective predator control has not produced good wildlife increases (McCann 1972). These and other contradictory statements demonstrate the need for careful review to elucidate the facts regarding predator-prey relationships.

Public opinion on the predator issue is remarkably polarized: interested persons tend to be either for or against predator control. In this atmosphere, many will find fault with some of the statements expressed here. However, the intent of this review is not to antagonize but to stimulate reassessment of traditional views in light of the very considerable literature on this subject.

Some large carnivores are classified as big game animals in many states and provinces, and some of these animals may kill other carnivores or conspecifics. However, this review is limited to predation by carnivores on ungulates in North America. In particular, it concerns predation on deer, elk, moose, caribou, pronghorn and wild sheep by coyote, wolf, dog, mountain lion, bobcat, lynx and bears. The golden eagle, as a predator, also is considered briefly.

In this chapter, I summarize the organizational structure, policies and methods of governmental predator control programs in the United States and Canada. The role of predator control in ungulate irruptions is reviewed along with studies of predation as a limiting factor of ungulate populations. Finally, the issues are organized into a framework of political, biological and economic considerations against which predator control proposals for specific ungulate populations can be judged.

PREDATOR CONTROL: POLICY AND PRACTICE

The largest organized predator control effort in the United States is the Animal Damage Control (ADC) Program administered by the Fish and Wildlife Service within the United States Department of the Interior. The history of this program is given by Young (1944) and Cain et al. (1972). Program funding arrangements vary from state to state, but in general, the federal government provides funds for administration and supervision while states, local governments, livestock associations and individuals finance most of the actual control and damage prevention work. The major emphasis of the program, since its inception in 1915, has been the protection of livestock, rangelands and crops from predators and other vertebrate pests.

Predator control is the major activity of the ADC program in the western states, but elsewhere, other nuisance animals such as birds and rodents receive more attention. In Fiscal Year 1976 (July 1, 1975–June 30, 1976), the total ADC operations budget was approximately $11 million (Johnson 1976), including cooperative funds but excluding research. About 50 percent of the funds were spent for livestock protection and only about 0.2 percent for wildlife protection. In current ADC program guidelines, predator control for wildlife protection is defined as control effort directed toward less desirable species which are depressing populations of more desirable species.

Current emphasis of the ADC program on livestock protection results from the fact that livestock interests in the United States believe predator control is essential to their enterprise. Therefore, they provide funds and political support for this purpose. State wildlife agencies, in contrast, generally have not found predator control necessary to achieve their goals and, therefore, have been reluctant to participate in the program. Several states, including Oregon, Idaho, Arizona, Utah, Montana, Wyoming and Nevada, have contributed wildlife funds to the ADC program in recent years, but these funds were not necessarily spent for wildlife protection.

In the United States, the management of resident wildlife, including big game, is a prerogative of individual states. Therefore, the federal ADC program takes no formal position regarding the desirability of predator control for the benefit of big game popu-lations, even though it does provide wildlife protection services when they are requested and financed by the responsible state agencies. The justification for predator control to protect wildlife must be provided by the states that request it.

As noted earlier, states generally have been reluctant to request predator control in behalf of big game. In the mid-1970s, however, some states reexamined their positions on this issue. Coyote control on winter ranges currently is an important part of mule deer management in Oregon (Ebert 1976). In recent years, Idaho, Nevada, Arizona, New Mexico and Wyoming also have requested predator control assistance from the ADC program to protect big game animals. In most of the western states, studies of the effects of predators on big game are in progress.

While the federal ADC program is by far the largest single organization conducting predator control in the United States, it actually operates on only 10–25 percent of the land area in the western states (Balser 1974). An indication of the relative impact of the ADC program on predators, in comparison with removals through other efforts, is given by recent statistics on the number of coyotes killed. In Fiscal Year 1974, the ADC program took 71,777 coyotes, while state and local control programs, fur trappers and hunters in the 17 western states took at least 223,000 more (Pearson 1978). Thus, the ADC program is responsible for less than 25 percent of the recorded, man-caused coyote mortality.

Since 1974, the United States government has been negotiating to transfer predator control operations to each of the states in which they are located. As of early 1977, two state governments (South Dakota and Washington) had accepted such transfers. Alaska and Colorado conduct their own programs. In a few states with federal programs, some counties also conduct independent programs. Thus, the administrative structure of governmental predator control operations in the United States is complex and subject to change.

Similar complexity exists in Canada, where the provinces exercise wildlife management responsibilities analogous to those of state governments within the United States. But, unlike the United States, Canada does not have a national predator control program. Each province has its own policies and programs to deal with predator problems. The federal government has no jurisdiction over terrestrial wildlife except in national parks.

Public and governmental attitudes regarding predators do not differ greatly between Canada and the United States. In British Columbia, predators at one time commonly were regarded as detrimental to game animals, livestock interests and human welfare (McKay and Demarchi 1972). The predator control program of British Columbia accordingly attempted to reduce predator populations throughout the province. More recently it has been recognized that predators have positive as well as negative values, and the Predator Control Division of the Fish and Wildlife Branch was disbanded in 1967, concurrently with a decision to manage wolves, mountain lions and coyotes as game animals. Where wildlife is the prey involved, predator control normally is not practiced. Similar policies prevail in most other provinces.

In Alberta, maintenance of healthy predator populations to prevent high prey population densities is an integral part of wildlife management. Predator control for the protection of other wildlife would be recommended only if predators were suppressing game numbers over a large area. In both Alberta and Saskatchewan, predator control for the protection of livestock uses the most selective and local control methods (Gurba and Neave 1973, Ewart et al. 1975).

Predator control for the benefit of big game may be implemented in Ontario if wildlife managers immediately responsible for management of a local population or herd believe that predation is excessive. Currently, a limited amount of wolf control is exercised in the vicinity of certain white-tailed deer wintering yards. The total take

for this purpose would not exceed 25 wolves annually (Kolenosky 1977). In Quebec, predators also are removed around wintering yards. Wolves, coyotes and feral dogs are taken primarily with traps and snares. Toxicants, such as strychnine, are used only in extreme cases (Banville, personal communication).

A wide variety of methods has been used to kill predators in North America (Young 1944, Young and Goldman 1946, Young and Jackson 1951, Cain et al. 1972). Space in this chapter does not permit a full description of these, but it is necessary to discuss the legal status, effectiveness and efficiency of certain methods.

The most efficient and effective way to reduce coyotes and wolves over broad geographic areas is with the use of toxicants. From the late 1940s through the 1960s, cyanide guns, or "coyote getters" (Robinson

The sodium cyanide spring-loaded ejector mechanism, or M-44 (lower left), ejects sodium cyanide powder when it is pulled. A scent attractant stimulates coyotes to bite and pull on the device. The M-44 is more or less selective for coyotes, depending on where it is placed and what scent is used. Under current (1978) regulations of the U.S. Environmental Protection Agency, the M-44 can be used in the United States to protect livestock but not wildlife. Photo by author.

1943), and lethal bait stations (Robinson 1948) were used extensively for this purpose in the western United States and Canada. The principal toxicants were sodium cyanide in the "getters" and sodium monofluoroacetate (Compound 1080), thallium sulfate, and strychnine in baits. The use of toxic baits declined in the 1960s as control became increasingly limited to livestock depredation problem areas. Increased recreation and other human activities on many ranges also stimulated reductions in the use of toxicants to avoid hazards to humans and their pets. In 1972, the United States government ceased legal uses of toxicants in predator control on federal lands or in federal programs, and banned interstate shipment of toxicants for predator control purposes. This ban was relaxed in 1975 to permit use of the M-44, or spring-loaded sodium cyanide ejector mechanism, with certain restrictions. As of early 1977, the M-44 could be used in the United States (by ADC employees and other trained persons) to protect livestock but not wildlife. Toxicants continue to be used to control predators under some conditions in Canadian provinces, but these uses are declining.

Since the use of toxicants on federal lands in the United States was restricted in 1972, aerial shooting of coyotes has increased in much of the western United States (Wade 1976). Both helicopters and fixed-wing aircraft are used. In addition, the steel trap continues to be the most effective and widely used technique in many areas. Den hunting, the M-44 and shooting from the ground are locally important as well.

The policy of governmental programs in both Canada and the United States is to deal as selectively as possible with individuals or local predator populations that cause damage. The trend away from wholesale predator reduction with toxicants is in accordance with this policy. Predator control research by the United States government is oriented toward more selective lethal and even nonlethal methods, and geared to the reduction of coyote predation on domestic sheep.

The steel trap has long been the standard predator control device in the western United States. As used in the federal Animal Damage Control (ADC) program, the 3N Victor Trap is an effective and selective technique for removing coyotes from local depredation areas. Photo by author.

At this point, it is relevant to note that predator control to protect wildlife must differ in some respects from predator control to protect livestock. Skilled trappers may take individual coyotes that are raiding a sheep flock, but such selective approaches are not applicable to the control of predation on wild ungulates. Livestock sometimes can be penned at night or removed from the damage area; wild ungulates cannot. The only remedy for excessive predation on big game animals is wholesale reduction of predator populations in the problem area. Given the present restrictions on toxicants, aerial shooting presently is the most practical way of accomplishing this. However, aerial shooting is effective only on ranges with sparse vegetative cover and, as a technique for the reduction of coyote populations, probably is more expensive than the use of toxicant bait stations.

It has not been determined whether aerial shooting is an economically feasible means

Aerial shooting, from either helicopters or fixed-wing aircraft, has become an increasingly important predator control technique in the western United States since toxicants were banned in 1972. When coyotes or wolves are to be reduced for the benefit of wild ungulates, aerial shooting usually is the technique of choice. Photo by Eric Peacock; courtesy of the U.S. Fish and Wildlife Service.

of reducing coyote predation on deer and pronghorn herds. In the western Arctic, however, the current wolf control program is based on limited issuance of aerial shooting permits to the public. Permit holders are motivated by high prices they can receive for wolf pelts, and the expense to the State of Alaska is limited to the costs of administering the permit system (McKnight, personal communication).

PREDATORS AND UNGULATE IRRUPTIONS

There is widespread belief that the numbers of ungulates in pristine North America were limited by predators, especially wolves and mountain lions. This is an attractive

field for speculation since there is little risk of being proved wrong by new data. The most prevalent argument is that ungulate numbers must have been controlled by predators because nearly all documented instances of dramatic ungulate increases in North America were preceded by removals of large predators. Leopold et al. (1947) reviewed approximately 100 instances of deer irruptions in North America and found that all irruptions in the western United States followed—and none preceded—the initiation of federal predator control on public lands about 1910. In the eastern United States, both deer irruptions and the removal of effective deer predators occurred earlier. Irruptions had not occurred in Canada or Mexico where large predators were still numerous. Leopold et al. concluded that predator control was a predisposing cause because irruptions coincided in time and space with greatly reduced predation by wolves and mountain lions, and because irruptions were not known to have occurred in the presence of these predators. (These workers believed that the coyote was not an effective deer predator.) Numerous other observers have also attributed ungulate increases or overpopulations to the control or absence of large predators.

Despite a general opinion that deer irruptions in the first half of the Twentieth Century resulted from predator control, some authors have taken issue with this view. They have pointed out that most irruptions occurred in habitats altered by man, and that influences such as grazing, logging, burning and farming increased the carrying capacities of deer, elk and moose ranges. These changes were concomitant with predator control, making it impossible to separate the effects of predator control from other influences. Caughley (1970) reviewed a number of irruptions in New Zealand and elsewhere where predators never were present. He suggested that ungulate irruptions in North America and New Zealand resulted not from reduction of predators but from changes in habitat or food conditions. Actually, one could just as well use

Caughley's examples to hypothesize that ungulates were regulated by predation during most of their evolutionary histories. In North America, predators were removed from ungulate ranges, while in New Zealand, ungulates were placed on predator-free ranges. The common denominator was the absence or scarcity of effective predators at the time of irruptions.

The most widely publicized North American deer irruption occurred on the Kaibab plateau in Arizona, where an increase in mule deer in the early 1900s was followed by a catastrophic die-off about 1924–1925. The deer population reportedly blossomed from 3,000–4,000 to about 100,000 between 1907 and 1923, which also was the period when the greatest removal of mountain lions, coyotes, bobcats and wolves occurred (Russo 1964). The subsequent deer die-off was blamed on overuse and destruction of browse by deer. This example was cited by Leopold et al. (1947) and others (see Burk 1973) as overpopulation resulting from removal of predators. However, Caughley (1970) challenged this interpretation, pointing out that the data are inconsistent and unreliable, and that the factors responsible for the increase are hopelessly confounded. He argued that the deer increase probably was due to habitat changes. Caughley's views, in turn, were criticized by Keith (1974), who agreed that the data were poor but did not believe that the lack of good data was ample grounds to discount predation as a significant regulator of natural ungulate populations.

Another argument in support of the idea that large predators regulated ungulate numbers in pristine times is the absence of intrinsic mechanisms to prevent deer populations from increasing beyond the sustaining level of their food supplies. Allee et al. (1949) suggested that deer, moose and other ungulates have had very efficient predators until quite recently, so that forces of selection kept ungulates busy evolving ways and means not of limiting their own numbers but of keeping abreast of mortality factors. This view was reiterated by Pimlott (1967),

who also proposed that ungulate-predator relationships may have evolved in relatively stable forest environments that could not support high-density prey populations. Pimlott observed that wolf populations were self-regulating at maximum densities of about one wolf per 26 square kilometers (10 square miles) and, therefore, that they might be capable of regulating moose and deer populations in pristine forests but not in habitats where human activities have increased the carrying capacity for ungulates. [The idea that wolves limit themselves to population densities of about one wolf per 26 square kilometers needs reexamination in light of the fact that wolf density on Isle Royale recently increased to one per 12 square kilometers (4.6 square miles) (Peterson 1976).] These speculations were endorsed by Mech (1970) and Keith (1974), both of whom believed that wolf predation could have been the main limiting factor on most, if not all, big game before man so greatly disturbed the habitat.

Here it may be in order to point out that ungulate irruptions do not invariably accompany the extirpation or absence of large predators. The overpopulations mapped by Leopold et al. (1947) may have been preceded by predator control and/or habitat modifications, but other deer herds that were subjected to these same influences did not irrupt. One is left with the impression that it is overly simplistic and pointless to try to account for all ungulate irruptions in terms of any single cause.

Regarding the influence of predators in modern times, Huffaker (1970) pointed out that, because large predators have been reduced or eliminated on many North American big game ranges, they cannot exercise their predatory roles as in times past. Robinette (1956) also acknowledged that, in most states with mule deer, modern predator control methods were rapidly relegating predators to a secondary role. If predators did control big game populations in pristine North America, it is conceivable that they might do so in present or future times as well, given sufficient relaxation of control pressures currently directed at them. The impact of uncontrolled predator populations could be especially significant on ungulate herds that also receive heavy hunting pressure from humans.

PREDATION AS A COMPENSATORY VERSUS NONCOMPENSATORY CAUSE OF MORTALITY

Predation can be regarded as either a compensatory or noncompensatory form of ungulate mortality, depending on whether it supplants or is additive to other causes of loss. A coyote may kill a fawn that otherwise would have survived to maturity, or an adult deer which might have lived for several more years. In my view, such losses would be noncompensatory if the available deer habitat was understocked. But the killing of a sick or weak deer about to succumb from the rigors of winter is compensatory because the death of that animal was inevitable. Some wildlife biologists also regard

predation as compensatory if it stimulates a higher rate of reproduction in the prey than would otherwise occur, but others question whether predation can induce increased reproduction among ungulates.

One example of increased ungulate reproduction associated with wolf predation was reported by Mech (1966, 1970). Before wolves arrived on Isle Royale, only 6 percent of the cow moose there produced twin calves. After the moose herd had been cropped by wolves for 10 years, the twinning rate was as high as 38 percent in some years. In the early 1960s, this increased reproduction appeared to be either a direct or indirect response to predation; that is, the wolves either selectively removed the least productive females or raised the general level of nutrition by removing enough moose to reduce intraspecific competition for forage. In the late 1960s and early 1970s, however, the rate of wolf predation increased as moose became more vulnerable due to habitat changes and severe winters. The moose population declined approximately 40 per-

"If a moose stands its ground upon attack, it is usually able to fend off the wolves" (Mech 1970). Photo by Durward L. Allen.

cent between 1969 and 1976, but twinning and calf survival rates were low throughout this period (Peterson 1976). The apparent compensatory increases in reproduction noted in the early 1960s vanished in the early 1970s at the very time when wolf predation was at its peak.

Studies of white-tailed deer in northern Minnesota during the same series of winters showed wolf predation there to reduce the breeding population and fawn survival rate simultaneously. In this case, it appeared that female fawns in particular were vulnerable to predation, and no compensatory increase in reproduction was noted (Mech and Karns 1977).

These and other observations lead one to believe that reproductive rates in ungulates are related to nutritional conditions that can and do vary independently of predation rates. Poor range conditions could accentuate the depressive effects of predation by impairing the reproductive capability of ungulate populations to replace the animals killed.

The outstanding advocate of predation as a compensatory form of mortality was Paul Errington (1946, 1967), whose studies of muskrats and quail convinced him that the effects of various mortality factors were strongly compensatory. Errington proposed that severe loss rates from different causes could, in effect, substitute for each other without becoming excessive in total; and that extraordinarily high losses from one cause may automatically protect from losses by other causes. The death of one individual may mean little more than improving the chances of survival for another one. Thus, he visualized each prey population to have surplus individuals whose death was assured, regardless of the immediate cause of death.

These ideas found immediate acceptance in wildlife management circles, possibly because they provided a theoretical rationale to support recreational harvesting (Errington 1967). The notion of a harvestable biological surplus is basic to the justification of recreational hunting in contemporary society. Advocates of this concept saw no need

for predator control as long as underharvest, or failure to utilize the harvestable surplus, was the predominant big game management problem (Leopold et al. 1947, Longhurst 1957, Petrides 1961). The very existence of ungulate overpopulations was regarded as proof that predator control was not needed. In fact, predator control frequently was indicted as a contributory cause of deer overpopulations (Leopold et al. 1947, Longhurst et al. 1952). In retrospect, the latter argument seems tantamount to recognition that predation was at least partly noncompensatory. If predation was compensatory, deer populations should not have increased because of the reduction of predator populations.

Although Errington's views dominated the thinking of wildlife biologists on the effects (or lack thereof) of predation for at least 20 years, they generally were not accepted by those in closest contact with predators, including livestock ranchers and predator-control workers. In the 1970s, some biologists reexamined their views on the subject. Huffaker (1970) challenged the view that predators do not control their prey but take only surpluses, pointing out that the term "surplus" can be interpreted in more than one way. He criticized the circularity of Errington's logic which defined "thresholds of vulnerability" and "doomed surplus" only after the number of "surplus" animals dying was known. Thus, it seems that the "threshold of vulnerability" may have been somewhat below the potential carrying capacity of the habitat in the absence of predation.

Keith (1974) pointed out that Errington's theory depended on the assumption that prey populations largely are self-limiting (self-regulating), and that the prey species studied by Errington, indeed, may be quite self-limiting. Keith suggested that Errington's ideas might have been different had Errington worked instead with ungulates or, perhaps, lagomorphs. But Errington (1946) recognized that: "Intercompensations in rates of gain and loss are evidently less complete in the life equations of the ungulates than in the muskrats. There is vastly more reason that I can see for believing that predation can have a truly significant influence on population levels of at least some wild ungulates."

He also suggested that predation losses inflicted by canids seem less marked by intercompensations than losses from general predation, and he obviously believed that some ungulate populations at times could be limited by canid predators.

The distinction among compensatory and noncompensatory mortality due to predation, as far as big game management is concerned, may be more a matter of degree than a choice between the two alternatives. Most ungulate populations endure some predation or hunting without ill effect, but there is a limit to the amount of predation any population can tolerate. The higher the rate of predation (or hunting kill)–in percentage of the prey population removed annually–the more likely it is to be noncompensatory. It seems reasonable to propose that wherever predators are found to control big game populations, the predation is at least partly noncompensatory. As a corollary, predation may be of concern to management only when it is noncompensatory. In such cases, one would expect to find that game populations are underutilizing forage or other habitat resources available to them. Pimlott (1970) suggested that intercompensations may be of importance in areas where the habitat is in poor condition or where big game is not hunted, but not in good habitat where the game is cropped adequately by hunting.

THE FACTS OF PREDATION

Predator food studies

Efforts to determine the impact of a particular predator on a particular prey often begin with examination of predator stomachs or scats to determine how frequently that prey is eaten and how much is consumed (Cain et al. 1972). Such studies

This pronghorn buck carcass was partly covered by a bobcat before it was found by a biologist near Lakeview, Oregon. Even though the fresh carcass had been fed on, an autopsy revealed that predation was not the cause of death, illustrating the need for careful examination to distinguish between predation and scavenging. Photo by Rodney P. Canutt; courtesy of the Oregon Cooperative Wildlife Research Unit.

are not reviewed at length here because they reveal almost nothing about the influence of a predator on a prey population. Frequently, they fail to distinguish killed prey from carrion, and rarely is the consumption of various prey items compared with the relative availability of those items. But, regardless of the dietary findings, such studies indicate only the fact of predation or scavenging and not the effect.

Ungulate mortality studies

Recent advances in electronics have made it possible to monitor the habits of radio-collared animals and, when they die, to locate their remains while the evidence of cause of death is fresh. Such studies often provide impressive evidence of predation, but leave unresolved the question of whether the prey population actually is controlled by predation or by other environmental factors.

Newborn fawns may vanish quickly after they have been killed by predators. On Steens Mountain, Oregon, the radio collar led biologists to the remains of this mule deer fawn killed by a coyote no more than 48 hours before the picture was taken. In other instances, only some hair and a blood spot have been found with the transmitters. Photo by Walt Van Dyke; courtesy of the Oregon Department of Fish and Wildlife.

Identification of predator kills

There is no definitive guide to the diagnosis of causes of death in wild ungulates. However, the publications of Rowley (1970) and Roy and Dorrance (1976) on domestic livestock are useful. Several investigators have cited the presence of subcutaneous hemorrhage on ungulate carcasses as evidence of predation, since animals dying of other causes do not bleed extensively when scavengers feed on them. Color photographs

Coyotes kill domestic sheep by clamping their jaws on the underside of the victim's throat and waiting for the prey to succumb. Death appears to result primarily from suffocation. Large deer often are killed by a similar technique, while small fawns more often are bitten through the skull. Photo by author.

of mule deer killed by coyotes showed fang (canine tooth) holes and tissue damage in the neck, particularly in the nasopharynx region (Nielsen 1975, Bowns 1976). On mature deer, wounds also were found on the hindquarters. Nielsen believed that coyotes usually kill deer by collapsing the trachea and smothering the animal. A similar technique is used by coyotes to kill domestic sheep (Connolly et al. 1976, Timm and Connolly 1977).

In Washington, Ogle (1971) found that all white-tailed deer carcasses fed upon in winter by coyotes had the ribs, vertebrae and shoulder blades chewed, and the limbs widely scattered. The characteristics of coyote kills, as opposed to carrion, were large patches of hide as much as 37 meters (40 yards) away from the carcass, separation of the vertebral column in the thoracolumbar region of adults and at the atlas of fawns, and nasal and maxillary bones chewed away. White (1973) presented photographs of the remains of very young whitetail fawns killed by coyotes, and noted that such fawns often were almost entirely devoured.

Most studies of wolf predation on North American ungulates have been made during winter when the presence of snow enhanced the visibility of carcasses and often permitted the circumstances of death to be reconstructed from tracks. In southcentral Alaska, moose killed by wolves were distinguished from starved moose on the basis of location, fat reserves in marrow of long bones, presence of blood on heel bones (calcanei), and body position (Stephenson and Johnson 1973).

Selective predation on vulnerable prey individuals

The proposition that certain individuals within prey populations are more likely than others to be killed by predators causes many heated arguments. Some aspects of this subject remain unresolved, but much acrimony could be avoided if the differing

parties would distinguish the facts from the overlying amalgam of opinion, overgeneralization and misinterpretation.

Perhaps the most controversial contention is that predators selectively remove sick, weak and malnourished prey individuals. This idea is contested by many predator control specialists whose experience with domestic livestock indicates that predators willfully and deliberately select the healthiest, choicest and fattest animals from livestock herds (Young 1944). Despite the prevalence of this view, its actual documentation is weak. Statistical evidence from one study shows that the sheep killed by coyotes are neither more nor less healthy than other members of the flock (Henne 1977). Predation on domestic animals, in any event, cannot be equated with predation on natural wild prey. In terms of alertness, defense and escape ability, domestic animals are inferior to all but the most debilitated members of wild ungulate populations.

Most of the detailed studies of predation on wild ungulates have shown that the prey differs in some way from the prey population as a whole. Many studies have shown that predators selectively remove sick, diseased or malnourished individuals. Such findings have been reported for predation by wolves on Dall's sheep (Murie 1944), moose (Mech 1966, Peterson 1976), caribou (Miller 1975) and white-tailed deer (Mech and Frenzel 1971a), and by coyotes on mule deer (Murie 1940) and white-tailed deer (Ozoga and Harger 1966). One of the earliest studies that found diseased ungulates to be especially vulnerable to predation was that of Murie (1944). Murie concluded that diseases infecting the jawbones of Dall's sheep predisposed middle-aged sheep to wolf predation. However, many of the bone specimens were gathered long after the animals died, and it may be questioned whether all of the deaths resulted from wolf predation.

Parasites, such as tapeworms (Mech 1970) and cerebrospinal nematodes (Peek et al. 1976), also have been found to increase the vulnerability of infested moose to wolf predation. Other parasites harbored by carnivores may be directly fatal to ungulates. *Sarcocystis hemionilatranis,* which infests the coyote as the definitive host and mule deer as the intermediate host, killed 9 of 11 infested fawns within 63 days after inoculation. The fawns appeared to be healthy at the time of infestation (Hudkins and Kistner 1977). This parasite, and many others, could not exist on ungulate ranges if carnivores were absent. It seems possible that the perpetuation and transfer of such parasites by carnivores could sometimes be quite detrimental to ungulate populations, but this aspect of predator-prey relationships has received little attention.

Contrary to the traditional view that predators selectively remove sick and weak individuals, a number of wildlife biologists have suggested that the average state of health of predation victims does not differ from that of the prey population as a whole or, in other words, that malnutrition is not a factor in the vulnerability of prey. Such conclusions have been offered in connection with predation on moose by wolves (Stephenson and Johnson 1973, Franzmann and Arneson 1976), on elk calves and mule deer fawns by mountain lions (Hornocker 1970), on pronghorn fawns by bobcats (Beale and Smith 1973), and on pronghorn (Bruns 1970) and mule deer (Nielsen 1975) by coyotes.

Given conflicting evidence and opinions as to the selection or lack of selection of sick or malnourished prey by predators, neither concept can be endorsed as universally correct. However, it is interesting to note that many of the studies that found predators to take disproportionate numbers of sick or malnourished individuals also found the predators to test many animals for each one that they were able to kill. Conversely, some of the studies that found malnutrition not to be a factor in prey vulnerability also mentioned that predators could select and kill prey with relative ease. The obvious hypothesis is that the importance of malnutrition and debilitation in prey vulnerability is related inversely to the vulnerability of healthy prey individuals.

While there are conflicting views regarding debilitation as a predisposing factor to predation, most published evidence supports the notion that predation is selective, for sick and malnourished individuals. A comprehensive review of prey selection by wolves was given by Mech (1970), who concluded that wolves generally kill the young, old, sick, weak, injured and diseased members of prey populations. However, one must avoid thinking that wolves perform such services deliberately or purposely. Predators kill whatever prey they can, and the young, sick or weak individuals simply are easiest to catch and, therefore, most likely to be killed.

Although many students of prey selection have concluded that the most vulnerable animals are killed, the vulnerable individuals are not necessarily sick, inferior or surplus animals. Mountain lions, for example, have been found to take more adult mule deer than would be expected in random selection (Robinette et al. 1959, Hornocker 1970, Spalding and Lesowski 1971, Shaw 1977). This may result from the tendency of bucks to frequent higher elevations or broken terrain that also is the preferred habitat of mountain lions. Behavioral differences between male and female caribou calves apparently render the males more vulnerable than females to lynx predation (Bergerud 1971a). Wolves, on the other hand, have been shown to take more female than male white-tailed deer fawns (Mech and Frenzel 1971a). Many other forms of selective prey vulnerability also have been reported.

A very frequent finding in studies of ungulates is that young animals bear the brunt of predation. Whenever very young animals are the prey, it seems unlikely that weak and unfit individuals would be taken selectively, as any newborn ungulate discovered by a predator would be vulnerable. (Witness the popularity of studies in which new-born ungulates are captured for marking.) Excessive losses of young individuals, whether from predation or other causes, obviously can be detrimental to prey populations.

In most parts of its range, the mountain lion feeds primarily on deer. Adult bucks are the largest and strongest members of mule deer populations, and yet, lion predation is somewhat selective for bucks. This may be because the bucks are more likely than does or fawns to frequent broken, ledgy terrain that is the preferred hunting ground of mountain lions. Photo by Maurice Hornocker; courtesy of the Idaho Cooperative Wildlife Research Unit.

THE EFFECTS OF PREDATION

The central issue in this chapter is whether various carnivores cause ungulates to be either more or less abundant than they would be without predation. Three possible answers to this question are considered here.

Predators control some ungulate populations

There are numerous accounts of specific ungulate populations whose numbers or growth rates were thought to be limited by predation (Table 42). This compilation is intended to include as many North American examples as possible. Documentation, of course, is better in some cases than in others. The main criterion for inclusion of each example is the original author's conclusion that predation was an important or limiting influence on ungulate numbers. These conclusions are qualified in various ways, and readers should consult the original reports for details.

A number of general points can be made about the studies summarized in Table 42.

1. Rarely have predators been implicated as the sole direct cause of widespread decline of ungulate populations, except when man was one of the predators.
2. In one case (Mech and Karns 1977), a predator (wolf) was found to extirpate its major prey (white-tailed deer) from a sizable study area.
3. Predators sometimes appear to be the agent by which ungulate numbers are adjusted to the carrying capacity of the

habitat, rather than a direct limiting factor.

4. Predators may amplify mortality in prey populations during severe winters and prevent or retard the recovery of ungulate herds reduced by other factors.

5. Predators can accelerate ungulate declines due to other causes, such as habitat deterioration.

6. The most commonly offered evidence of predation as a limiting factor was low survival of calves or fawns. But low fawn survival can result from a variety of causes, and some of the studies cited in Table 42 fail to show unequivocally that the poor survival was due to predation. Nevertheless, it is clear that predation, at times, can be the primary cause of mortality for young ungulates.

7. Habitat frequently was mentioned as the ultimate limiting factor. At times, predation may depress or maintain the number of ungulates below that which the habitat could support.

Table 42. Reports of predation as a limiting or regulating influence on ungulate populations in North America.

Prey	Predator	Location of study area	Notes	References[a]
White-tailed deer	Coyote	Texas	Coyotes caused 53–80 percent of the fawn mortality and played a major role in stabilizing deer with their food supply.	(1)
White-tailed deer	Coyote, Bobcat	Texas	Following removal of predators, fawn-doe ratios were 300–400 percent higher than in the check area (no control).	(2)
White-tailed deer	Coyote	Texas	Deer were declining due to habitat modification by man. Coyotes caused 10–60 percent of fawn losses in various years. Predator control was recommended to slow the rate of decline.	(3)
White-tailed deer	Wolf	Ontario	Wolves were believed to be capable of controlling deer if there was more than 1 wolf per 100–150 deer. Wolf predation was a major deer mortality factor.	(4)
White-tailed deer	Wolf	Minnesota	Deer decline due to other causes was accelerated by wolf predation. A combination of deteriorating habitat, severe winters and use of alternate prey enabled wolves literally to kill off the deer in part of the Superior National Forest.	(5)
Deer	Wolf, Cougar	North America	Removal of predators was implicated as a cause of deer irruptions.	(6)
Mule deer	Coyote, Bobcat	Oregon	Predators, mostly coyotes, killed at least 31 of 48 instrumented fawns that died. Coyote control on winter deer range appeared to increase winter survival of fawns.	(7)
Mule deer	Coyote	Arizona	The number of fawns per 100 does was 16 percent higher where 1080 was used against coyotes than on areas where toxicants had not been used for two years.	(8)
Mule deer	Coyote	Utah	After reduction of coyotes with 1080, the number of fawns per 100 does increased 17 percent on one range and 7 percent on another.	(9)
Mule deer	Coyote	Utah	Postwinter numbers of fawns per 100 adults averaged 29 on a range with light predator control and 59 on a nearby range with more intensive control. Prewinter fawn-adult ratios did not differ.	(10)
Black-tailed deer	Coyote	California	Fawn survival reportedly increased following removal of coyotes.	(11)
Black-tailed deer	Coyote	Washington	Fawn-doe ratios improved on 32,400 hectares (80,000 acres) treated with 1080, but remained low on a no-control area. Density of poison bait stations was one per 2.6 square kilometers (1 square mile).	(12)

Table 42.

Prey	Predator	Location of study area	Notes	References[a]
Black-tailed deer	Cougar	California	Following removal of cougars, deer increased and eventually were reduced by disease.	(13)
Sitka deer	Wolf	Coronation Island, Alaska	Introduced wolves increased, reduced deer drastically and then declined to extinction.	(14)
Sitka deer	Wolf	Alaska	Wolves appeared to hold deer in balance with habitat during study of Klein and Olson (1960), but later the deer were virtually extirpated by predation and starvation losses during three severe winters. As of 1977, wolf populations also were depressed.	(15)
Elk	Black bear	Idaho	Bears were the main cause of a 68 percent calf loss from calving through October.	(16)
Moose	Wolf	Isle Royale, Michigan	In early 1960s, wolves and moose appeared stable with wolves holding moose within range carrying capacity. In early 1970s, moose vulnerability to wolf predation increased due to severe weather and habitat changes. From 1969–1976, wolf numbers increased 250 percent while moose declined 40 percent.	(17)
Moose	Wolf	Alaska	Moose declined primarily because of severe winters; wolves appeared to be preventing recovery. Approximately 86 percent of calves died in their first 2–3 months of life.	(18)
Caribou	Lynx	Newfoundland	Lynx predation was the primary mortality factor. Following lynx trapping, improved survival of calves to two years of age was documented (by comparison with noncontrol area).	(19)
Caribou	Wolf, Man	North America	The general decline of caribou in the 1800s and early 1900s was due to predation by humans and wolves.	(20)
Caribou	Wolf	Northwest Territories	High calf mortality, due primarily to wolf predation, prevented the herd from increasing. Caribou population was well below range capacity.	(21)
Caribou	Wolf, Man	Alaska	Western Arctic herd declined from 242,000 to 50,000 caribou between 1970 and 1976 due to predation by humans and wolves. Even without human harvest, wolf predation could continue the decline.	(22)
Pronghorn	Coyote	Texas	Coyote predation on fawns prevented pronghorn from increasing. Coyote control with cyanide guns, strychnine drop baits and steel traps failed to reduce coyote numbers significantly and, therefore, did not reduce the level of predation.	(23)
Pronghorn	Coyote	Arizona	Predator control caused pronghorn population to increase enough to be hunted. The 1080 program cost $0.12 per square kilometer ($0.31 per square mile).	(24)
Pronghorn	Coyote	Oregon	Pronghorn herds recovered from about 1,000 in 1920 to 10,000 by 1935 due to protection and elimination of 7,500 predators.	(25)
Pronghorn	Coyote	Utah	Removal of coyotes increased fawn-doe ratios in small (remnant) herds. Other limiting factors including illegal killings, severe winters and overgrazing by livestock.	(26)
Pronghorn	Coyote	Texas	Compared to a range without predator control, the number of fawns per 100 does was 142 and 129 percent higher (in successive years) where coyotes had been removed.	(27)
Pronghorn	Coyote	Oregon	Seventeen pronghorn transplanted to the Umatilla Ordnance Depot in 1969 failed to increase. Following the removal of 135 coyotes (2.1 per square	(28)

Table 42.

Prey	Predator	Location of study area	Notes	References[a]
Pronghorn	Bobcat	Utah	kilometer; 5.4 per square mile) during winter of 1970–1971, 9 does produced 13 fawns in 1971. Coyote control was continued and the herd increased to about 100 by July, 1976. Of 44 instrumented pronghorn fawns recovered after death, 29 had been killed by bobcats. Bobcat predation was the greatest single decimating factor. Only a few individual bobcats were involved.	(29)
Desert bighorn sheep	Coyote, Bobcat	Arizona	Predator control helped raise the lamb-yearling ratio from 100:16 to 100:71.	(30)
Dall's sheep	Wolf	Alaska	Wolves held sheep numbers in check even though caribou were their main prey.	(31)

[a]References:
(1) Knowlton (1968), Cook et al. (1971).
(2) Beasom (1974a,b).
(3) Daniel (1976).
(4) Pimlott (1967), Pimlott et al. (1969).
(5) Van Ballenberghe et al. (1975b), Mech and Karns (1977)
(6) Leopold et al. (1947).
(7) Trainer (1975), Ebert (1976).
(8) McMichael (1970).
(9) Robinette et al. (1977).
(10) Austin et al. (1977).
(11) Horn (1941), Young and Jackson (1951), Longhurst et al. (1952), Robinette et al. (1977).
(12) Brown (1961).
(13) McLean (1954).
(14) Merriam (1964), Klein (1959), Rausch (1972).
(15) Klein and Olson (1960), McKnight (personal communication).
(16) Schlegel (1976).
(17) Mech (1966, 1970), Peterson (1976)
(18) Coady (1976).
(19) Bergerud (1971a)
(20) Bergerud (1974b)
(21) Miller and Broughton (1974).
(22) Alaska Department of Fish and Game (1976).
(23) Jones (1949)
(24) Arrington and Edwards (1951).
(25) Young and Jackson (1951).
(26) Udy (1953).
(27) Knowlton et al. (1971).
(28) Oregon State Game Commission (1972), Oregon Dept. Fish and Wildlife (Unpublished records).
(29) Beale and Smith (1973).
(30) Halloran (1949).
(31) Murie (1944).

Predators do not control some ungulate populations

Although a substantial number of studies have implicated predators as a limiting or regulating influence on ungulate populations (Table 42), many others have reached the contrary conclusion (Table 43). A number of these citations are from general big game ecology or management studies which gave only superficial consideration to predation as one of many possible causes of mortality. Ungulate populations often were found to be regulated by habitat conditions, such as forage or deep snow, with predators exerting a relatively minor influence.

Several of the studies cited in Table 43 showed predators to take substantial numbers of deer, especially fawns, but concluded that predation was not limiting to deer numbers. Some authors, who studied lightly hunted herds on overpopulated ranges, considered predator control to be more of a hindrance than a help in deer management.

Although Table 43 contains data mainly about predation by native North American carnivores, two studies of feral dogs are cited as well. Harassment of big game by dogs is a frequent cause of concern to sportsmen and wildlife managers, but the effects of such harassment are not well-documented. In Quebec, feral dogs are controlled around winter deer yards along with wolves and coyotes: 123 dogs were killed for this reason in 1975 (Bouchard and Gauthier 1976). The killing of feral dogs is a relatively uncontroversial aspect of predator control because dog predation on native North American wildlife generally is perceived as unnatural and undesirable.

The golden eagle is widely reported to prey occasionally on ungulates, especially upon young fawns. Pronghorn apparently are much more wary of golden eagles than of coyotes (Bruns 1970), but no study has shown eagle predation to be a serious cause of loss to wild ungulate populations. It has been found, however, that some nesting pairs of eagles feed heavily on black-tailed deer fawns (Carnie 1954).

Predation increases the numbers of ungulates

In contrast to the previously discussed concepts that predators limit (Table 42) or have little effect (Table 43) on ungulate numbers, the idea that predators stimulate big game populations to maintain higher densities than would exist without predators is largely theoretical and undocumented.

Howard (1974) proposed that "somehow vertebrate predators under the natural scheme of things seem to enable prey species to sustain a higher density than occurs in the absence of such natural predation, even though prey populations temporarily increase whenever predators are abruptly removed." He argued that predators have

The harassment and killing of big game animals by feral dogs is of increasing concern to sportsmen and biologists. This problem exists throughout North American big game range, and needs more attention than it has received to date. A Wildlife Management Institute photo; taken by Francis Dickie.

Table 43. Studies where predators have been found not to control or limit the size of ungulate populations in North America.

Prey	Predator	Location of study area	Notes	References[a]
White-tailed deer	Coyote	Washington	More deer died from other natural causes than from predation.	(1)
White-tailed deer	Coyote	Michigan	Deer carrion was the primary winter food of coyotes. Few deer were actually killed.	(2)
White-tailed deer	Dog	Missouri	Dogs harassed deer but were negligible as a direct cause of mortality.	(3)
White-tailed deer	Dog	Alabama	Transplanted deer increased greatly in the presence of feral and free-ranging dogs.	(4)
White-tailed deer	Wolf	Wisconsin	An overpopulation of deer developed in spite of the presence of wolves. Wolf density was 1 per 90 square kilometers (35 square miles).	(5)
White-tailed deer	Wolf	Ontario	During winter wolves removed 9–11 percent of the deer present in late fall.	(6)
White-tailed deer	Several species	Ontario	Deep snow was the limiting factor for deer over much of Ontario.	(7)
Mule deer	Coyote	California	Deer declined in spite of intensive coyote reduction with 1080.	(8)
Mule deer	Coyote	Arizona	Despite heavy predation, fawn survival was correlated with rainfall and winter forb yield.	(9)
Mule deer	Coyote	Nevada	Coyote control with 1080 failed to reverse poor fawn crops due to habitat deterioration. Any possible effects of predation were masked by the influence of declining range.	(10)

Table 43.

Prey	Predator	Location of study area	Notes	References[a]
Mule deer	Coyote, Black bear	California	Predators took many deer, yet range remained overpopulated with deer.	(11)
Mule deer	Cougar, Coyote	Utah	Predation was the major natural mortality factor, but was considered to be beneficial.	(12)
Mule deer	Cougar	Arizona	Deer were below range capacity and lions killed more deer than did hunters. Yet it appeared that lion predation would not keep deer from increasing if other losses could be reduced.	(13)
Mule deer	Several species	Arizona	On most Arizona deer ranges, food was the primary limiting factor.	(14)
Mule deer	Several species	Nevada	Cougars, coyotes and golden eagles had no notable impact. The effect of bobcat predation was uncertain.	(15)
Black-tailed deer	Coyote, Bobcat	California	Predators killed a few deer, mostly fawns, but were not an important deer mortality factor.	(16)
Mule deer, Elk	Cougar	Idaho	The density of lions remained constant while deer and elk increased.	(17)
Elk	Cougar	North America	Lion predation normally was not a problem in elk management.	(18)
Elk	Kodiak bear	Afognak Island, Alaska	Transplanted elk increased in spite of abundance of bears.	(19)
Elk	Grizzly bear	Yellowstone Park, Wyoming	Predation assisted other natural processes that regulated elk numbers.	(20)
Caribou	Wolf	Canada	After intensive wolf control for 11 years, it remained uncertain whether predator control benefited the caribou. Overhunting was the main problem; wolves took 5 percent or less of caribou each year.	(21)
Pronghorn	Golden eagle	Utah	Range condition, not predation, was identified as the key to pronghorn survival. Actual impact of eagle predation was not determined.	(22)
Bighorn sheep	Coyote	Wyoming	Predation caused few lamb losses, although coyotes ate most of the sheep that died. Coyotes were reduced 75 percent by trapping but lamb survival did not improve.	(23)
Bighorn sheep	Several species	United States	Wolves and cougars might have depressant effects if they were present on bighorn ranges. Coyotes and eagles had no significant effect.	(24)
Bighorn sheep	Several species	Colorado	A high rate of lamb mortality was due to disease.	(25)
Several species	Coyotes	Yellowstone Park, Wyoming	Ungulate populations were limited by range conditions. Coyotes took only weak and sick animals.	(26)
Six species	Wolf	Rocky Mountain Parks, Canada	Wolves did not control big game; 300–400 ungulates were present for each wolf.	(27)

[a]References:
 (1) Ogle (1971).
 (2) Ozoga and Harger (1966).
 (3) Progulske and Baskett (1958).
 (4) Scott and Causey (1973).
 (5) Thompson (1952).
 (6) Kolenosky (1972).
 (7) Cumming and Walden (1970).
 (8) Longhurst et al. (1952).
 (9) Smith and LeCount (1976).
(10) Robinette et al. (1977).
(11) Leopold et al. (1951).
(12) Richens (1967).
(13) Shaw (1977).
(14) Swank (1958).
(15) Papez (1976).
(16) Taber and Dasmann (1958).
(17) Hornocker (1970).
(18) Murie (1951).
(19) Troyer (1960).
(20) Cole (1972).
(21) Kelsall (1968).
(22) Hinman (1961).
(23) Honess and Frost (1942).
(24) Beuchner (1960a).
(25) Woodard et al. (1974).
(26) Murie (1940).
(27) Cowan (1947).

evolved under natural selection, so predation in some way must favor keeping the predator food supply (prey species) at the maximum density inherently permissible under self-limitation. Howard also argued that predators, such as coyotes, may increase the vigor and reproductive success of prey sufficiently to more than replace the individuals destroyed.

A related proposition—that wolves selectively remove inefficient and nonreproductive individuals and thereby give advantage to more productive individuals—already has been discussed in connection with compensatory mortality. Several workers have suggested that large predators force redistribution of elk and deer on limited winter range, thus achieving wider and less intense utilization of forage (Leopold 1933, Hunter and Yeager 1956, Hornocker 1970).

While it may be true that predators helped maintain ungulate populations at an "ecologically optimum density" (Howard 1974) under pristine conditions, this concept has limited application to management of big game populations currently hunted by man. It remains to be shown that ungulate populations can thrive under high rates of hunter harvest in addition to predation by unchecked numbers of carnivores.

THE IMPORTANCE OF PREDATOR-GAME RATIOS

Scrutiny of many reports on the impact (or lack thereof) of predators on ungulate numbers reveals one interesting generalization: the likelihood that predators control big game numbers seems to increase with the relative numbers of predators to prey. This concept, first put forward in general terms by Leopold (1933), recently has been presented convincingly for wolf predation on ungulates. Pimlott (1967) suggested that wolves may not be capable of exercising complete control of white-tailed deer wherever the number of deer per wolf exceed about 100–150.

Mech (1970) reviewed a number of cases of wolf predation on ungulates and considered the prey-predator ratios in pounds of prey per wolf. His tentative conclusion was that wolf predation is the major controlling mortality factor where prey-predator ratios are 11,000 kilograms (24,000 pounds) or less of prey per wolf. At higher ratios, wolf predation cannot keep up with annual reproduction. It becomes only one of several contributing mortality factors and cannot be considered the primary controlling influence.

The predator-prey ratio at which mountain lion predation may become limiting has not been determined. Ratios of lions to deer in northern Idaho, on a numerical basis, declined from 1:135 in 1964–1965 to 1:201 in 1967–1968 during Hornocker's (1970) study. Deer increased while lion numbers remained stable; thus, it appears that lions were not limiting the deer population at those ratios.

Apparently no attempt has been made to analyze coyote predation in terms of predator-ungulate ratios. The ubiquitous food habits of coyotes may make such analysis unrealistic; ungulates usually are not their principal food. Udy (1953) reported that the numbers of coyotes taken in some years were nearly equal to the numbers of pronghorn present. Therefore, the predators must have outnumbered the pronghorn. In another case, 135 coyotes were removed to enhance the prospects for increase of 13 pronghorn (Oregon State Game Commission 1972). At such high predator-prey ratios, it is not surprising that the coyotes exerted a substantial limiting influence.

Since the numbers of both predators and prey are dynamic, predator-prey ratios change over time. On Isle Royale, Michigan, for example, the ratio of wolves to moose increased from 1:80 in 1969 to 1:20 in 1976; moose numbers decreased as wolves increased (Peterson 1976). It may be uncertain whether the predator-prey ratio observed at a specific time and place reflects the cause or the effect of observed population changes. As a rule of thumb in big game management, however, it may be appropriate to give special consideration to herd units where observed predator-ungulate ratios are unusually high, or where sudden changes in predator-prey ratios are seen.

THE IMPORTANCE OF ALTERNATE PREY

Most researchers conducting studies of predation on ungulate populations have not considered the possible role of alternate prey in either ameliorating or accentuating the effects of predation. However, several studies found the utilization of alternate prey to enhance the ability of predators to affect ungulate populations adversely. During recent declines of moose (Peterson 1976) and white-tailed deer (Mech and Karns 1977), increased predation on beavers by wolves was noted. The change to alternate prey, coupled with increased vulnerability of ungulates due to severe winters, enabled wolf populations to increase and intensify the level of predation on the declining ungulate populations.

In a study of mountain lion predation in Arizona, Shaw (1977a, 1977b) hypothesized that alternate prey in the form of livestock calves enabled the lions to maintain a higher density than would have been possible on native prey alone and, thereby, to increase their impact on the mule deer population. In this situation, the availability of calves each year was greatest in late spring when deer numbers were lowest.

Coyotes seem to rely primarily on rodents and rabbits for food. This permits the maintenance of a higher coyote-ungulate ratio than could exist if ungulates were the sole or primary coyote food. When coyotes are numerous, they might inflict serious losses to ungulate populations in a short period of time whenever weather or other conditions temporarily increase the vulnerability of the ungulates. On the other hand, an abundance of alternate prey conceivably could reduce or postpone coyote predation on ungulates. Because the number of alternate prey species may be substantial, studies of their role in predation on ungulates pose a tremendous challenge to research workers.

PREDATOR CONTROL AS A BIG GAME MANAGEMENT PRACTICE

In big game management, it is not enough to study and theorize about predator-prey relationships. One must know whether the control of predators offers any prospect for increasing big game numbers. The only way to determine this is by direct trials, a number of which are summarized in Tables 42 and 43. Some of these efforts were found to be effective and others were not. In at least one case (Horn 1941), the original conclusion of effectiveness was disputed by later workers.

The predator control efforts cited in Tables 42 and 43 illustrate a number of important principles.

1. Predator control to increase ungulate numbers is only justifiable when the ungulate population is below the carrying capacity of its habitat.

2. Several studies that revealed increased fawn survival following the removal of predators failed to indicate whether the fawns saved from predators survived to adulthood or succumbed to other causes. Perhaps the best demonstrations of genuine population gains due to predator control are those reported by Arrington and Edwards (1951) and Bergerud (1971). In Utah, Robinette et al. (1977) showed that some of the mule deer fawns saved from coyotes were taken by hunters. For unhunted populations near the carrying capacity of their habitat, it seems probable that decreased predation would be compensated, in time, by increased mortality from other causes.

3. Big game population declines due to habitat deterioration or overuse cannot be reversed by predator control. This seemingly straightforward principle may be difficult to apply in practice because it

is not always easy to determine trends in habitat quality.

4. Predator control costs money. Arrington and Edwards (1951) concluded that a 1080 poisoning program that cost $0.12 per square kilometer ($0.31 per square mile) per year produced justifiable gains in pronghorn numbers. However, Jones (1949) found control with traps, cyanide guns and poison drop baits too expensive at $1.16 per square kilometer ($3.00 per square mile), especially when coyote populations were not reduced substantially by this effort. He suggested that large scale use of 1080 bait stations covering thousands of square kilometers might be a practical solution. Udy (1953) also advocated the practice of control over large areas to prevent an influx of predators from areas not being controlled. He recommended the use of 1080 poison stations, "denning" in pronghorn fawning areas, and long lines of traps and coyote "getters."

As noted earlier in this chapter, the recent history of predator control in North America has been away from broad scale population reductions toward more selective, local control. Given the deemphasis or withdrawal of toxicants such as 1080, one may question whether predator control to benefit big game populations is now economically feasible. However, Beasom (1974a) suggested that control could be justified economically in south Texas if the increased production of deer and turkeys was used by hunters.

5. When the numbers of ungulates failed to increase following predator control, the usual conclusion was that predators were not a major cause of mortality. However, ineffectiveness also may have resulted from failure to remove a sufficient number of predators.

Jones (1949) found that four months of intensive predator control failed to reduce coyote populations on two pronghorn ranges of 30,800 and 37,600 hectares (76,000 and 93,000 acres) due to almost immediate influx of predators

from adjoining untreated areas. But even where such immigration does not occur, large numbers of predators may be taken without significantly reducing predator populations. Based on results of simulation modeling experiments, Connolly and Longhurst (1975) suggested that coyote populations can withstand annual removals of up to 70 percent by means of compensatory adjustments in birth and natural death rates (without recruitment of animals from elsewhere). In order to control wolf numbers, it appears to be necessary each year to kill at least 50 percent of the animals aged 5–10 months or older (Mech 1970).

The studies cited in Tables 42 and 43 apply to predator-ungulate relationships under open range conditions. But, when ungulates are maintained in fenced enclosures for special research or management purposes, predator control may be essential to protect the captive animals. Few such cases appear in the literature, but a single coyote in a 202-hectare (500-acre) enclosure in Utah reportedly took about one-half of an expected crop of 45 mule deer fawns (Robinette and Olsen 1944).

From the collective experience of predator-ungulate studies in North America, it is possible to propose a general rationale for the use of predator control in big game management (Figure 68). This framework incorporates both subjective and objective elements, in keeping with reality. The rationale begins with a choice among management objectives, since much controversy over the exercise of predator control stems from disagreement as to which animal species should receive preference, and for what purpose. Thus, specification of the management objective should precede consideration of the facts and issues. The fundamental questions are: (1) whether man should attempt to increase ungulate numbers, and (2) whether man or natural predators should receive priority in utilizing the production of big game

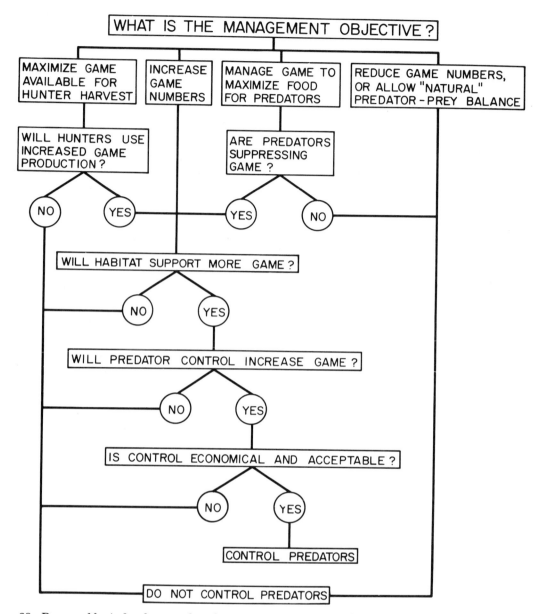

Figure 68. Proposed logic for the use of predator control in ungulate management.

populations. In Figure 68, these choices are arbitrarily shown in four alternative management objectives. Many more objectives could be specified, but these probably encompass most of the current possibilities for North American ungulates.

Once an objective has been selected, one may proceed to more factual aspects of the decision-making process. Control of

predators generally would be considered only when an increase in game numbers is desired. Whenever the objective is to increase the amount of game available to hunters, economic justification of predator control will require that the resulting game increases will be used by hunters. This idea may seem self-evident, but it is worth reiterating that underharvest was a major deer management problem in the

United States for many years (Longhurst 1957, Petrides 1961).

There is little doubt that the public interest in large predators, such as wolves and mountain lions, will increase. Therefore, it is likely that, in certain areas, these predators will receive primary consideration in the management of ungulate populations which support them. In such areas, the killing of predators probably will be prohibited or strictly regulated, but predator control may be needed occasionally to prevent declines in predator populations due to depletion of their prey. On Coronation Island, Alaska, for example, introduced wolves nearly exterminated the black-tailed deer population and then declined to extinction (Klein 1969, Rausch 1972).

In a portion of the Superior National Forest in Minnesota, wolf numbers declined approximately 55 percent as the wolves extirpated their major prey, the white-tailed deer. Mech and Karns (1977) believed that if wolf numbers had been 25 percent lower each year, beginning in 1968, the deer population would have begun to recover by 1973. In actuality, the deer were gone by late 1972 or early 1973.

The studies summarized in Tables 42 and 43 permit some generalizations as to the conditions under which predator control will be useful in big game management. Control is most likely to produce substantial increases where the ratio of predators to prey is high, and where the ungulates are not fully using available forage resources. In no case will predator control be of demonstrable value unless it is intensive enough to reduce predator populations significantly, and any comprehensive study must monitor the effectiveness of control in this regard. The feasibility of predator control as a management practice will require that substantial predator reductions be achieved at reasonable cost and that such reductions are followed by genuine increases in the adult or harvestable segment of the game population. In addition, the control must not unduly damage other wildlife or environmental values.

More than 20 years ago, Cowan (1956b) pointed out the urgent need for controlled experiments to determine the impact of different levels of predator control. The need for such research is even more urgent today. The justification of predator control as a big game management technique presents a growing challenge to biologists. The desire of hunters for larger game populations must be balanced against the interests of others who may prefer that the game animals be harvested by native predators. Aside from social and political considerations, rising costs due to inflation and restrictions on methods present ever-greater obstacles to the economic justification of predator control.

SUMMARY

Carnivores eat ungulates on most ranges where the two coexist. Predation can limit ungulate numbers and is most likely to do so when the ratio of predator to prey numbers is high. Predator food studies reveal little about the impact of predators on prey populations. Mortality studies of big game populations may show predation to be a major cause of loss, but such findings do not necessarily prove that predation actually limits prey numbers. Predators frequently kill young, old, diseased or other classes of prey individuals at disproportionate rates, relative to their incidence in the population. However, predation is not restricted to "surplus" or sick individuals whose death is imminent; healthy animals are taken as well. Carnivores perpetuate a number of parasites which may cause debilitation or death in ungulates, but the role of such parasites in ungulate population dynamics has received little study.

Ungulate populations in pristine North America probably were limited in many areas by predators, particularly wolves and mountain lions. Because ungulate irruptions typically followed supression of large predators concurrently with human modification of habitats, the relative roles of predator control and habitat modification in promoting ungulate irruptions cannot now be assessed.

A number of studies have shown predators to limit ungulate numbers, but others have found predators to have litte effect. The theory that predators stimulate ungulates to maintain higher densities than would be possible without predation is not well-documented.

The federal government is the chief predator control agency in the United States; provincial agencies fulfill that role in Canada. The emphasis of present governmental control programs is on livestock protection, and both policy and restrictions on methods prohibit wholesale reduction of predators over broad geographic areas. Compared with the amount of time and resources expended to protect livestock, little predator control work has been done expressly for the benefit of big game or other wildlife. In 1976,

however, coyote control on big game winter ranges was practiced in Oregon, Wyoming and Quebec, and limited wolf control was exerted on certain moose ranges in Alaska.

Predation by humans and wolves appears to be limiting certain caribou and moose populations in Canada and Alaska. Several studies have documented temporary increases in deer and pronghorn fawn survival following predator control, but it is not known whether the fawns saved from predators survived to a huntable age.

Because of conflicting public attitudes over ungulate and predator management objectives, as well as the increasing costs of predator control, careful biologic and economic justification is required for the exercise of predator control. In general, predator control is justified in big game management only when it will produce substantial ungulate increases at reasonable cost without undue damage to other environmental values and when the increased production will be used. In some cases, control may produce long-range benefits for the predator itself.

Chapter 25

MANAGING THE HARVEST

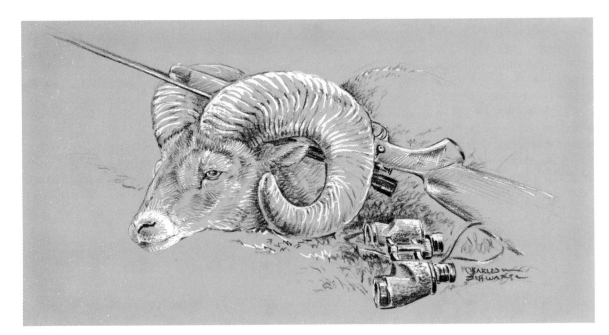

Richard N. Denney
Big Game Manager
Colorado Division of Wildlife
Denver, Colorado

No longer is hunting a matter of subsistence in the United States. In fact, in North America, except for certain indigenous people who still hunt for primary sustenance, the fruits of the hunt may be considered secondary in importance to the activity of the hunt by an individual, though the harvest may supplement the contemporary hunter's diet. Nevertheless, the harvest is the necessary result of the application of an essential tool in modern big game management—the licensed sportsman.

Harvest, in the sense used in this chapter, refers to the removal of big game animals deemed surplus to achieve a specified management objective for a given population. While this chapter will identify (1) reasons for hunting seasons, (2) their objectives, and (3) action options available to attain objectives from the wildlife management standpoint, moral and ethical considerations of hunting will not be addressed. Likewise, while the term "quality" will be used in reference to a special season, the philosophies and criteria relating to individual definitions of quality are not discussed.

ESTABLISHING HUNTING SEASON OBJECTIVES

Big game management and, for that matter, all wildlife management deals primarily with wildlife populations and their habitats, and with people. The basic resource necessary for big game species and populations is habitat, and people are the tool—utilized through hunting seasons—to obtain desired harvests.

The amount and kind of harvest is determined by population or herd management objectives which, in turn, are mandated by carrying capacities, densities, sex and age compositions of populations, and other ecological parameters. During the first

one-quarter to one-third of the Twentieth Century, big game managers were concerned primarily with protection of declining big game populations, as well as with translocations and reintroductions. During the 1940s and into the 1960s, mule deer populations throughout the western United States experienced a population high probably never reached previously. The pattern of Colorado mule deer populations and hunting data from 1940 through 1975 is illustrated in Figure 69. In terms of population trend, this pattern was fairly representative of the general situation throughout the West.

During years when seasonal conditions are relatively similar, the size of harvests may reflect population trends (Geis 1971). When a big game population is high, resulting in severe utilization of key forage plants on critical winter home ranges, it is obvious

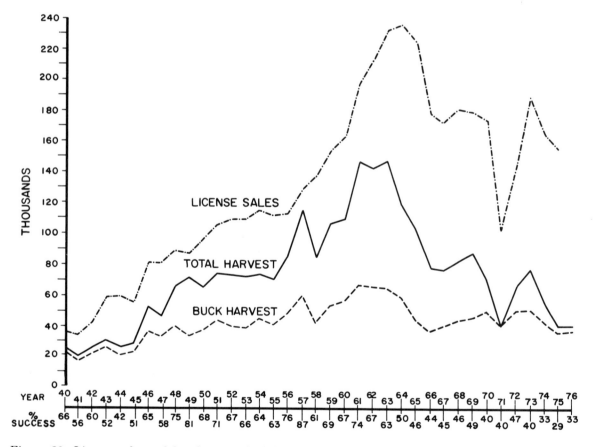

Figure 69. License sales and deer harvests in Colorado, 1940–1976.

Controlled harvest of designated big game populations by licensed hunters can prevent excessive and accelerated losses of the animals from starvation, disease and other unnecessary mortality factors. A Wildlife Management Institute photo.

that the population should be reduced to or below carrying capacity of the range to ensure maintenance of that winter range and the population. The basic tool available to the wildlife manager to affect a population reduction is a liberal hunting season, before malnutrition or other natural mortalities remove a significant portion of the population. It is more logical and practical to allow licensed hunters the opportunity to remove surplus animals and utilize them than it is to have a big game population continue to damage its winter range and suffer starvation and wasteful death.

Aside from attempting to keep big game populations within the carrying capacities of their ranges, properly conceived and implemented hunting seasons can achieve population objectives designed to alter sex and age compositions. In addition, there are types of hunting seasons which have a minimal management impact on a big game population. The objectives of such a season are to provide opportunities for special outdoor groups, such as archers, to combine the possibility of harvest with their aesthetic and recreational values. Therefore, the primary objective of some hunting seasons is to provide outdoor recreational opportunities, not to control wildlife populations or their adverse impacts on their habitats. As is usual in archery hunting seasons, hunter success is low, relatively few big game animals are harvested and there is insignificant impact on big game populations.

Another objective of some types of hunting seasons is the dispersal of a concentrated wildlife population. This was the case with Colorado's first bighorn sheep hunting season in 1953, after 66 years of closed seasons. The rationale for this season, even though preceded by an exceptionally heavy mortality of bighorns from the lungworm-pneumonia complex, was that hunters would break up the concentrations of sheep on traditional bedding grounds so that the infective larvae-intermediate host's (snail) life cycle could be broken. The sheep might be forced to move to new ranges with a lower rate of infection. The result was generally satisfactory, with a harvest of 58 rams and the dispersal of larger herds into smaller groups, thus breaking up unhealthy concentrations.

Ancillary benefits from hunting seasons include the opportunity to obtain valuable samples such as stomach contents, blood and tissue, and physical weights and measurements. In addition, biological data on harvested animals can be collected, such as sex, age and weights from specific management units or populations. Hunting seasons can be the source of other types of information, too, by polling hunters at check stations or through mail surveys and questionnaires to determine areas hunted, days hunted, animals observed by sex and age, banded or marked individuals, dead and abandoned or wounded animals by species, amount of time and money spent, etc.

From the preceding discussion, it can be seen that the basic objective of a hunting season per se is a controlled harvest, but that various degrees of control, described later, can be utilized to obtain specific management unit or population objectives.

ACCOMPLISHING HUNTING SEASON OBJECTIVES

Managers generally think of hunting seasons in terms of a controlled harvest. This control can range from a very loose framework of unlimited hunters pursuing animals of species of the individual hunter's choice for an indefinite period of time, to very strict regulations for limited numbers of hunters pursuing a specific population of a single species for a short period of time and only within designated management units.

The most liberal type of hunting season may be allowed under conditions of high population levels of primary species approaching or exceeding home range carrying capacity. If a population is nearing the carrying capacity of its critical range, the management objective must be to remove or harvest the same number of animals as the annual recruitment. The objective may be to

reduce the population if it exceeds carrying capacity; that is, harvest more animals than the number added to the population through annual production. To attain the latter degree of harvesting, an unrestricted number of hunters must be attracted to the population's area and given opportunity to harvest either sex, and perhaps more than the usual bag limit.

To use mule deer in Colorado as an example, relatively high populations existed in the late 1940s and early 1950s, in relation to rather limited hunter numbers and pressure. This necessitated increasing the bag limit by offering a free, second-deer tag for herds or game management units with winter ranges which were overutilized, in a downward trend and in poor condition. In certain herds or units, one of the two deer had to be an antlerless animal; that is, an animal from the producing portion of the herd. This meant that a hunter could take one buck (antlered) and one doe or fawn, or two antlerless animals (does and/or fawns), but not two antlered bucks. During high deer populations in the 1950s and into the early 1960s, the number of deer hunters more than doubled. Early in this period, when demand for licenses increased, it was decided that a second-deer or additional license could be purchased by hunters at a cost less than the first license. These additional licenses were called "multiple licenses," and replaced the free second-deer tag. In critically overstocked deer herd areas, more than one multiple license could be issued. For several years, the number of multiple licenses that could be purchased for specific management units was unlimited. During the period of two-deer and multiple license areas (approximately 17 years) hunter success—based on the number of licenses sold—varied from 63–89 percent (Denney 1977). In 1963, the mule deer populations in Colorado began to show the effects of liberalized seasons and bag limits. Subsequent decreases in license sales, total harvest and hunter success rates dictated a change in management philosophy and strategy (Figure 69).

During periods of overstocked deer ranges and high populations, the primary objective is simply to remove as many deer as possible without regard to sex or age. This attempts to bring the herd or population to within the carrying capacity of its winter range. Once a population balance has been achieved, it must be maintained by the judicious selection of the type of hunting season which will best achieve the size and composition of the herd desired in relation to its habitat. A slightly restrictive hunting season, such as antlered-only deer, may be necessary if the objective is to hold a population at a given level. Depending on the big game species involved—as well as habitat factors other than critical range, hunter demand, access and success—an either-sex or even a male-only-type season may be required to modify sex ratios to keep the population in a vigorous condition and within the carrying capacity of its habitat.

A males-only or antlered-only hunting season to keep herds at their carrying capacities is not the panacea of deer management it was once thought to be. For many years, big game managers generally have accepted the concept that ungulate populations can not be affected adversely by the harvest of males only. This generalization is not acceptable today because recent investigations of various species, the same species in different environments, and more intensive sociological and behavioral studies have demonstrated that wide sex ratios produced through selective hunting of males-only may significantly reduce production or the availability of huntable males (Lewis Nelson, Jr., personal communication).

Moose researchers in Scandinavia and northern Europe have reported that bull-only harvests have affected moose productivity adversely because of the animals' social structure, density and generally solitary nature (Lykke 1975, Markgren 1974). The desired result is a relatively narrow sex ratio required for optimal annual production and recruitment. Similarly, in the Cooperative Interstate Deer Study in California and Oregon, Salwasser (1975)

reported that states that have been liberal in setting seasons and either-sex harvests of mule deer have healthier deer populations with more optimal sex ratios than do states that have permitted bucks-only hunting. This has been particularly true in California where bucks-only is statutory with certain exceptions. In California, mule deer sex ratios have become progressively wider under antlered-only hunting, accompanied by decreased numbers of legal-sized bucks and decreased hunter success rates (Lewis Nelson, Jr., personal communication).

To maintain a vigorous big game population with a balanced sex ratio, the manager must be guided in his objectives by such criteria as sex ratio and age class determinations in harvests. The manager, therefore, must be prepared to set some "hunter's-choice" or limited either-sex seasons intermittently with male-only-type seasons. Some managers believe that when given the choice between an antlered-only season with limited either-sex or hunter's-choice licenses for deer, or an antlered-only season with limited antlerless licenses, the latter is preferable for two reasons. First, the wildlife manager can estimate the number of antlered animals that most likely will be killed, based on relatively constant hunter pressure and demonstrated success rate with a given population and sex ratio. Second, the manager has a greater chance for achieving removal of a certain number of the producing portion of the herd. Therefore, a limited number of antlerless-only licenses gives a more precise prediction of the number of females and young-of-the-year that will be removed. An equal number of limited either sex licenses most probably would result in an unpredictable number of antlered animals removed by the either-sex license holders, in addition to the normal antlered-only harvest by hunters holding regular licenses. Also, there would be fewer antlerless deer harvested and sex ratios further imbalanced. In reference to this latter point, if some data on the selectivity of sexes by hunters during previous hunter's-choice either-sex seasons exist, then the

Habitat condition and carrying capacity are two primary criteria used to identify harvest goals. The age and sex ratio of a big game population helps dictate whether hunting in a particular area will allow for the harvest of either sex. Photo by Don Domenick; courtesy of the Colorado Division of Wildlife.

probable number of bucks taken by either-sex license holders could be estimated more accurately.

In the preceding discussions, hunter numbers were presumed to be within normally accepted levels of hunter pressure or density. There are occasions when certain areas—because of increased popularity due to high hunter-success rates or because of increased or easy access—become overcrowded with too many hunters. This can result in undesirable impacts on a local big game population and/or a lessening of the quality of the recreational experience. When this occurs, it may be necessary to limit the total number of hunters involved. Limited numbers of licenses for use in a given management unit can enable the wildlife manager to control and direct hunter pressure toward the wildlife population segments needed to be harvested to accommodate herd management objectives.

Sale of limited licenses is a practice adopted by many states and provinces to control the number of people hunting big game species with relatively low populations, such as pronghorn, bighorn sheep, mountain lions, mountain goats, moose, grizzly bears and caribou. Besides limiting the total sales of licenses, these limited licenses can specify the sex or size of the animals to be taken.

Limiting the number of hunters in selected areas is a harvest-management technique used in Colorado for elk, even though elk are in abundance. The intent has been to control totally the number of hunters and to obtain population management through selective harvesting of predetermined numbers of antlered and antlerless animals. Also, management unit-specific licenses have been used in pronghorn management to manipulate sex ratios in given populations.

A Conservation Officer checks unit-specific licenses of successful elk hunters, and records data which will be used in determining future season lengths, licensing structure and herd management objectives. Photo by Don Domenick; courtesy of the Colorado Division of Wildlife.

Other hunting season options available to benefit management of a big game population, from the most liberal to the most restrictive, include:

1. Unlimited license sales for any animal (any age or sex) of a given species and population, with an unlimited or a multiple bag limit. This is the type of season adopted by several western states for varying periods of time when mule deer populations have been at peak levels, and when hunting pressure has been less than necessary to reduce the herds to range carrying capacity.

2. Unlimited licenses for any animal of the hunter's choice. This means unlimited license sales, with a limit of one license per hunter per season or year. Many states have used this option at one time or another or are still using it for bear, elk and/or deer management.

3. Unlimited license sales for any male or antlered animal, with limited either-sex licenses. This is one of the primary management options in many states where wild ungulate populations are at or near optimal levels. Increased either-sex license sales may be authorized for species with populations to be reduced slightly, or sales of these licenses may be lowered to allow a population buildup in accordance with management objectives.

4. Unlimited license sales for any male or antlered animal, with limited licenses for females or antlerless only. This is aimed more specifically at removal of a specific number of producing animals than is the sale of either-sex limited licenses identified in option 3. It is used for intensive management of deer and elk in units or herds that are at or approaching population objectives.

5. Unlimited license sales for males or antlered-only animals with minimum specifications (for example, branched antlers, four points or better, horns at least 15.2 centimeters (6 inches) long or three-quarter curl), with limited either-sex licenses. Corresponding seasons have been set for elk, deer and bighorn sheep in specific areas or management units.

6. Unlimited licenses for males or antlered-only animals with minimum requirements, and limited female or antlerless-only licenses. Similar to option 5, but more restrictive on the female requirement, and used much less for deer and elk.

7. Unlimited licenses for any male or antlered-only animals. This is one of the most commonly used types of seasons for deer, elk and sometimes pronghorn, to afford the opportunity to harvest a segment of a population or herd without age restriction. It has been commonly accepted that a big game population can

not be hurt irreparably in a hunting season with these restrictions. However, in a heavily hunted population, this type of season should not be used indefinitely without periodic monitoring of sex and age compositions.

8. Unlimited licenses for males or antlered-only animals with minimum specifications. This type of season has been set for limited early hunts, or "quality" or trophy hunts, which give recreational hunters the opportunity to hunt areas that may not be accessible during the regular season. It also has been used to harvest animals that are not readily available or as high quality as those harvestable during the regular season. These hunts generally are in specified areas of limited or restricted access.

9. Totally limited either-sex licenses. This option is utilized to control pressure on limited or concentrated populations which must be restricted in total numbers but, otherwise, are in good condition. The number of licenses sold is determined on a year-to-year basis, consistent with population trends and objectives.

10. Totally limited license sales, each license specifying which sex or age class animal a license holder can harvest. This system has been used in selected populations of deer, elk and pronghorn, where hunter pressure must be limited. The harvest of desired numbers usually is directed toward a specific sex in order to manipulate the sex ratio.

11. Totally limited license sales for males or antlered-only animals. This type of season commonly is employed in areas with limited pronghorn populations, but with bucks in excess of the number required for optimal breeding.

12. Totally limited license sales for male or antlered animals of minimum requirements. This is similar to option 8, but is directed more specifically toward animals of trophy value. Both this and option 8 have little impact on big game populations from a management standpoint, but offer limited opportunities for quality, highly valued hunting experiences.

This list of season types may have raised several questions or points which should be clarified. Unlimited licenses usually are sold over the counter at license agencies and conservation department offices. Limited licenses, in most cases, require written application on official forms sent to a central office by a specified date. The number of licenses authorized then are drawn randomly by lottery system or randomly selected by computer. Some areas operated on a limited license basis are oversubscribed, while others may be undersubscribed. For this reason, applicants often are allowed to list a second-choice area. If unsuccessful in obtaining a license for their first-choice area, they will be eligible for selection for the second-choice area if that area is undersubscribed. On occasion, licenses still may be offered for use in undersubscribed areas after selections have been made, in which case the remaining licenses may be offered over the counter at selected offices on a first-come-first-served basis.

The various types of licenses are established and authorized by the individual state legislatures with differential license fees for resident and nonresident hunters. Legislatures in some states have not established nonresident licenses for certain game species; and a few legislatures have limited the total number of nonresident licenses that can be sold, either in general or on a species-specific basis. Some state conservation or wildlife management agencies prorate the number of nonresident limited licenses available in designated areas for certain species. Each state appears to have varying philosophies and different attitudes toward nonresident hunters as reflected in the licensing structures and fees enacted by the legislatures. There is a great need for uniformity in state statutes pertaining to nonresident fees.

A single licensing option seldom is employed statewide by the wildlife management agencies. Usually, one or two options are set for broad areas of combined management units with common or comparable big game population characteristics. Other options may be applied to specific areas to attain management objectives for a particular wildlife population.

In addition to various licensing options, modification of hunting season dates is an essential tool for managing big game populations and harvests. Such modification—as dictated by varying conditions of weather, habitat and the hunted population—usually is made annually (but may be done more frequently). As a rule, hunting season dates are set in accordance with the biological timetable of the game species. In establishing hunting dates, managers must take into consideration the probable weather conditions that affect hunter access, tracking ability, visibility, and spoilage of meat on harvested carcasses. Also, the dates and classes of livestock permits on public land grazing allotments may influence the establishment of hunting dates and management areas, as well as recreational uses by people other than hunters. Likewise, biologically critical life history periods of primary populations must be taken into account. These include periods of breeding, parturition, nursing and rearing of young, the age of self-sufficiency, and the times of body condition peaks and nadirs.

The length, or number of days, of the season may influence harvest efficiency and the effectiveness of harvesting as a management tool. For example, a nine-day season may be more effective if it includes two weekends than a similar season length including only one weekend, assuming the objective is a substantial harvest within that period of time.

Data reveal that, in areas where hunting is permitted on the basis of unlimited-type licenses and/or unlimited hunting pressure, 75–90 percent of the pressure and total harvest occurs during the first 3–5 days of that particular season regardless of season

length up to 21 days (Colorado Division of Wildlife harvest records, E. Reade Brown, personal communication, Coggins and Magera 1973).

Many wildlife managers believe that a hunting season is most popular and successful from a sportsman's viewpoint when "opening" day occurs on a weekend. This undoubtedly is most convenient for local hunters since it does not require taking time off from jobs. Analysis of day-of-the week openings in Washington indicated no appreciable disenchantment of hunters, or difference in harvest, with a Monday opening. Therefore, the day of the week that hunting season begins depends on a number of variables of which geography, climatic conditions, hunter participation numbers and game population densities are most important.

Under the limited license option, season length may be the most critical factor in terms of obtaining the desired harvest. A season should be long enough to allow hunters opportunity to harvest the limited number of animals authorized. Usually, hunts of this type are for animals of a specific species and population, such as three-quarter curl or more bighorn rams which may be in limited supply and difficult to find or shoot. They may involve specific animals, such as old male bison which need to be culled from a particular population. Inasmuch as the number of licenses is limited and set on the basis of calculated harvest or removal goals, the season should be of sufficient duration to permit ample hunting time and opportunity. Within harvest goals, a relatively long season cannot impact the herd adversely. However, various aspects of stress and harassment should be considered if relatively long seasons are necessary.

In general, long seasons require increased law enforcement effort, but in the context of this limited license season with relatively few and generally high quality hunters, the effort may be less than would be necessary for a shorter season with many hunters. Under the limited license option discussed here, shooting hours are not a particularly critical factor, at least during daylight, because the manager usually desires the highest harvest affordable.

The types of big game hunting seasons generally have been considered in respect to traditional hunts with high-powered rifles because these rifles are most significant in terms of management and hunter impact on a big game population. However, other methods of taking a species within an authorized seasonal framework can influence harvest objectives and hunter success and/or satisfaction. Archery hunting, for example, is relatively inefficient from a species or population management standpoint, but is permitted and often encouraged because of associated recreational and economic benefits. Big game archery hunting during late summer and early fall has received some criticism because of hunter harassment of wildlife in the late young-rearing period, during the rut or breeding season for elk, and when elk are forced off public land ranges onto private lands. The significance of wildlife harassment by archery hunters has yet to be well-documented.

There is strong sentiment about special hunts for muzzle-loading firearms. Some believe muzzle-loaders are a primitive weapon, little more effective than bows and arrows. Others believe they are equally as effective as high-powered rifles. The truth appears to fall somewhere between these two extremes, as indicated by analysis of muzzle-loading firearm seasons in Colorado, where the number of muzzle-loading firearm licenses was limited to 2,000 during a special season in September in 1976 and 1977. The season also was limited to antlered-only deer and elk. Comparative elk hunter-success percentages were: archers, 9.1 percent over nine years; muzzle-loaders, 11.5 percent over four years; and breech-loading rifle hunters, 19.5 percent over nine years (Denney 1977). Some wildlife management personnel are apprehensive that muzzle-loading firearm hunting may become too popular, and that a ceiling on the number of participants must be maintained by limited license sales.

Another consideration, in relation to the type of season or licensing option, is whether certain big game hunting seasons should be separated or allowed to run concurrently. This primarily concerns deer and elk seasons, and the problem of excessive hunter pressure which may occur with unlimited license sales. Public welfare, hunter safety, crowded hunting conditions on opening days, and animal stress because of hunter harassment are factors to be considered in setting single or simultaneous hunting seasons for different big game species.

Efforts to distribute hunter pressure throughout a hunting season, or for definite periods within a season, were attempted in Minnesota during 1972 through 1974. The "choose-your-own" season consisted of having a license good for a number of consecutive days, increasing as the blocks of days progressed into the 30-day season. Because of law enforcement problems related to party hunting, staggered consecutive days were permitted in the same block of days hunted by a particular party. This type of season was limited to only the forested portion (upper one-half) of the state in 1975, and dropped entirely before the 1976 season (Tom Isley, personal communication). However, in New Mexico, a "stratified" deer hunting season was successful in 1975 and 1976, as was such an elk season in 1976. From a number of time options, each hunter was allowed to select a single period during which to hunt (Johnson 1977). In Colorado, approximately one-half of the deer hunters also hunt elk and would prefer to hunt both species at the same time (Colorado Division of Wildlife 1976). Therefore, managers in Colorado designed a seasonal framework, initiated in 1977, whereby deer are hunted exclusively for up to five days starting October 15, followed by a minimum two-day closure. Then, a separate elk-only season of a maximum of 12 days is held beginning October 22, followed by a minimum 2-day closure. Finally, a combined deer and elk season is begun November 5, for a maximum of 11 days. The deer and elk seasons during the concurrent hunting period do not have to be of equal length. It is felt that the concurrent season will appeal to nonresident hunters who wish to hunt both deer and elk but do not wish to make separate trips to hunt both species. It is anticipated that approximately one-half of the hunters who wish to hunt both deer and elk, one-half of whom desire to do so at the same time, will hunt during the concurrent season. This hunting season framework should have the effect of reducing by about 50 percent the usual hunting pressure exerted on the two species during any one season.

Bows and arrows, muzzle-loaders and, in some states, certain handguns are considered legal weapons for taking big game and can be used during regular rifle seasons. However, use of archery equipment during special firearm (muzzle-loading rifles and/or handguns) seasons has been a matter of controversy. The potential conflict, possibly less real than imagined, involves the concern of archers—who usually dress in camouflaged clothing—that they may be mistaken for big game animals by special firearm hunters and be shot. They also are concerned that the shooting noise of guns disturbs their mode of hunting. In Colorado, archery hunters have enjoyed an average of more than 35 days of deer and elk hunting in a special statewide season during the attractive time of late summer and early fall. But, there is a feeling of jealousy in regard to the nine-day muzzle-loading firearm season during the second and third weeks of September, even though muzzle-loader hunters are limited in number and restricted to a limited number of open areas and to harvesting antlered-only deer and elk.

Another modification with potentially significant impacts on seasonal harvests and hunting pressure during the regular season is the "one-and-only hunt." This means that a hunter may purchase only one type of license and participate in only one type of season for a given species, unless specifically excepted. For example, a hunter who chooses to hunt deer during the archery season will not be permitted to hunt during the muzzle-loading season or rifle season for deer, even if unsuccessful during the archery hunt.

Species in limited supply or harvested under very restricted licenses, and for which there is considerable hunter demand for those limited licenses, may be classified as a "once-in-a-lifetime" trophy, with a literal corresponding bag limit per licensed hunter. This may apply to such species as the bighorn sheep, mountain goat and other selected species in various states.

The preceding discussions have identified the variety of options available for setting the type of license and/or seasonal system which will most likely help attain the harvest and other management objectives for a given big game population. Undoubtedly, there will be other options, modifications and innovations that will be developed as management techniques become more refined. Not discussed is the experienced judgment necessary to (1) interpret properly the available data on any population or management unit, and (2) predict the effects of a management action. The complexities of these management parameters are compounded by vagaries of weather and human behavior.

THE MECHANICS OF SETTING A HUNTING SEASON

People outside the wildlife profession often are surprised to learn of the amount and kinds of data collected, data interpretation and planning that must be devoted, at least annually, to setting reasonable big game hunting seasons and regulations. Data considerations include: population structure and composition; population trend; range utilization, condition and trend; the effectiveness of past harvests as a management tool; harvest success during past seasons; and, the various considerations discussed previously relative to license and season options most likely to help attain current management objectives.

Aside from law enforcement activities, the most time-consuming and difficult job facing

Deer are trapped in a baited box, then ear-tagged, weighed, measured and released. When deer are killed later by hunters or retrapped, data again are recorded and compared, giving information on migration patterns and growth. Photo by George D. Andrews; courtesy of the Colorado Division of Wildlife.

wildlife management agency fieldmen is assessing big game populations and range parameters within given management units or areas. A population status usually is estimated by modified census counts, and compared with previous counts to learn if the current population is decreasing, stable or increasing. The technique generally used is to count big game animals, such as deer and elk, when they are concentrated on customary or traditional winter home ranges, and under conditions as comparable as possible from year to year from the standpoint of snow coverage, quality and depth. If all other factors are constant or comparable, variations in such counts from year to year and compared with a previous five-year average serve as an index or trend of the population. While most trend counts

are based on enumeration of the animals during given periods or in particular areas, other indices of population trend also are employed where and when applicable. Examples of these are: meadow counts—when animals are drawn to greening vegetation on fields and meadows in the spring, track counts on suitable migration routes, and pellet group counts in high-use areas or along transects. Most trend counts on open winter concentration areas, particularly in the West, are made from the air. Aerial surveys usually are conducted from fixed-wing aircraft, but helicopters may be utilized depending on ground cover, visibility of the animals and economic constraints.

Population-structure determinations are based on sex- and age-classification counts, often secured during surveys from heli-copters. These consist of prehunting and posthunting season enumerations of sample sizes determined statistically from previous data. Certain conditions must be met in making sex- and age-ratio counts, such as, within definite time periods before and after hunting seasons, and classifying every animal in a herd or group. If some animals in the group being counted reach cover in trees or brush before the entire group is classified, the incomplete data for that group are discarded as being unrepresentative. Sex and age ratios are expressed as the number of males per 100 females, and the number of young of the year per 100 fe-males, respectively. The difference between preseason data and postseason ratios is assumed to be a function of the removal of animals by hunters. Sex and young-per-fe-male ratios can be used in various formulas calculated to determine a total population.

The number of animals that can be main-tained in a viable population is dependent on the carrying capacity of the popula-tion's habitat. Monitoring big game ranges usually involves collection of data on tran-sects of key forage species production and utilization, and determination of critical range conditions and trends. Fecal pellet group transects often are employed on winter ranges to obtain an index of relative deer or elk use per acre from year to year. In many states, range transects are run cooperatively with federal land-use agency personnel, since most big game range in western states is public land. A primary ancillary benefit of such cooperative activities is the opportunity for fieldmen representing different agencies to get together in the field, examine the same physical evidence, and discuss the rela-tionships among habitat data and big game populations.

Research check stations are of considera-ble value in big game management for ob-taining sex and age data from harvests in given management units. Check stations also serve to assess levels and rates of harvest and hunter success. They provide other management opportunities, such as, a place to conduct hunter opinion surveys, and to collect biological specimens and banded or marked animal observation data. Also, they have certain public relations value, but are of limited importance in terms of law enforcement. This check station to gather biological data or hunter opinions is not to be confused with a roadblock or law enforce-ment check station. Law enforcement may be conducted at check stations established for gathering research data, but the effec-tiveness of their use for law enforcement purposes is limited because such stations generally are in the same location year after year. As such, they can be avoided by inten-tional violators. Practically all hunters who voluntarily stop at these check stations are in compliance with the laws. Law enforce-ment check stations, per se, are geared specifically to apprehend violators and, be-cause of citizens' band radios, must operate only a short time in one location. The public

Research check stations can provide vital informa-tion not only on the number, age and sex of ani-mals harvested, but also on the attitudes, opinions and demographic characteristics of the hunters. Photo by Don Domenick; courtesy of the Colorado Division of Wildlife.

relations value of research check stations pertains to opportunities for familiarizing large numbers of hunters with current or proposed laws, programs and other information.

Harvest surveys vary from hunter-report cards, supplied with every big game license, to random samples of mail questionnaires. Many states project big game harvest statistics from survey responses of small, stratified samples of licensed hunters. Relatively accurate age estimates of a harvest are obtained through cooperation of hunters who submit, in special envelopes, one or two incisor teeth from their deer or elk kill. These teeth are encased in plastic, thin-sectioned, stained, and the dental cementum annuli counted under a microscope for age estimation. The percentage of yearlings in a harvest is used as a measure or index of annual survival or recruitment to the base population.

Fieldmen keep records on natural mortalities, particularly winter losses, and those due to diseases, parasites, predation and accidents. Wounding losses, in conjunction with harvests, are considered in determining harvest regulations and the various types of season and licensing options. Definitive data on these and poaching losses are lacking at this time. Preliminary studies in some states have indicated that the wounding loss is considerably higher than previously estimated.

As much of the foregoing data as are available or can be determined is used in formulating population or management unit objectives. These data are the foundation on which subsequent years' big game hunting season regulations are based. Admittedly, definitive quantification of each segment of this biologically sound management matrix remains to be refined. Major efforts are being directed toward this goal.

Computer technology recently has begun to assist in wildlife management. The development of simulated modeling through computers has added a new tool whereby a given big game population can be structured mathematically. By programming known attributes of a population, certain unknown factors can be tested at different levels and intensities to simulate the probable value or range of values of that parameter. The impacts of selected factors can be evaluated with respect to the modeled population and in relation to actual quantified data, without subjecting the real population to the hazards of chase and harassment. Undoubtedly, the primary benefit of computer modeling, at this stage, is pinpointing specific areas in which managers lack "real" data, or in which the quality of data must be increased.

FUTURE CONSIDERATIONS

There is no doubt that the future of big game management will depend more on improved data gathering and refined techniques than it has during the past era of plentiful populations when the primary concern was to obtain an adequate harvest. Totally limited license sales probably will be representative of public hunting sometime within the next 20 years because of increased demand and decreased big game populations due to decreased quantity and quality of big game habitats. To manage big game populations best, both now and in the future, new levels of refinement must be attained which will define more precisely the characteristics of populations and quantify the management objectives by management units.

The various types and degrees of regulations imposed on big game hunters are for the purposes of (1) regulating the size, composition and/or density of hunted big game populations in accordance with the ability of each population to maintain itself at a healthy, optimal level within the carrying capacity of its habitat; and (2) enhancing recreational opportunities. Emphasis on one or the other purpose can differ from one management unit or area to another. But no matter which emphasis is foremost, or for whatever reasons, the harvest objective must be a management decision based on scientific information.

Chapter 26

SOCIOLOGICAL CONSIDERATIONS IN MANAGEMENT

Douglas L. Gilbert
Colorado State University
Fort Collins, Colorado

In recent years, problems associated with human activities and attitudes have become a primary concern of wildlife managers, including those responsible for big game populations. At present, many wildlife biologists and managers are ill-prepared to deal with sociological problems such as economics, public involvement, communications, politics, access, legal difficulties, nonconsumptive uses and users, and antiharvest or antiharvester sentiment. All of these problems have one common denominator—people. All, too, can be included under the encompassing umbrella of public relations. Gilbert's text, *Natural Resources and Public Relations* (1975), is suggested to readers. Much of the material in this chapter is presented in greater detail in that book.

Many wildlife professionals are rank amateurs when it comes to working with people. They entered the profession because of a love of the out-of-doors and an affinity for hunting and fishing. Some are introverted to the point of being shy, wanting to avoid crowds and preferring not to work with people.

Part of the blame for these idiosyncracies must be placed on the colleges and universities where these individuals are educated. Curricula for students in wildlife science programs have included very few, if any, courses in sociology, psychology, communications, public relations or similar academic disciplines. Most graduates are capable managers or biologists but neophytes in convincing, placating, administering or otherwise working with people. Only recently have curricula included any of the above courses, partly as a result of the anti-harvest attitudes that are rampant and increasing, and partly because of ecological awareness and interests brought about by the energy crisis and expanding human populations. Scheffer (1976) also voiced these two basic concerns as the primary effects in shaping the destiny of wildlife management.

Research in wildlife management received a tremendous boost from the Pittman-Robertson Act in 1937. Manufacturers' excise tax dollars, provided for in that Act, have been spent wisely and undoubtedly have caused the profession of wildlife management to be far ahead of what it would have been without federal aid. But, how about research on the sociological or humanistic problems related to wildlife management? As of this writing, they are barely starting to be considered. Natural resource agencies have few sociologically oriented research projects under consideration. And, most researchers of such agencies are biologists.

Some economics-oriented research projects are being "farmed out" to universities. Other similar projects on "anti-" sentiment also are done by students or through contracts. The dollars spent for this research are but an infinitesimal part of the average research budget of a typical conservation agency (Gilbert 1975). I advocate that as much money should be spent on people-oriented research as on biologically oriented studies. Hendee and Potter (1971) agreed with this statement when they suggested that more research is needed in such social science areas as causes for satisfaction or success, opportunities desired, and motivation of nonconsumptive users.

THE PUBLICS INVOLVED

One of the primary areas of research necessary to solve a public relations problem is delineation of the publics. A public is composed of two or more people with a common interest. Before working with a public, it is necessary to understand that specific public. Information such as reasons for the common interest, strength of purpose and identification of leaders can be of great importance in influencing a public.

Each public is different with different interests and purposes. Each has certain characteristics and interests that must be known before positive action can result. Basically, there are two kinds of publics: (1) those within the organization (internal publics), and (2) those not part of the organization (external publics). Within each broad group, there are many subpublics. For example, internal publics of a state conservation agency would include administrators, biologists, managers, law enforcement personnel and office workers, among others. The manager public includes subpublics of wildlife managers and fish managers. The subpublic of wildlife managers may include further subpublics of big game managers, waterfowl managers, etc.

Each of these publics and subpublics must be delineated and understood before effective public relations efforts can be fruitful. Certainly, administrators would view a big game season differently than would big game managers. To the administrator, it means dollars in the budget, added personnel and increased office hours. To the big game manager, the season means many hours of preparation, check stations and endless field duty.

External publics also are extremely important and diversified. A few of the most important are rural landowners, local communities and businesses, protectionist groups, youth groups, and the media. It is easy to see that each of these large publics also contains many subpublics.

Some publics really can be included in either the internal or external category. Examples are other land-use or natural resource management agencies and advisory boards or commissions. My suggestion is to consider them as internal publics insofar as possible. In this way, they will have the advantage of being informed at the outset, and can have early input.

IMPORTANT PUBLIC RELATIONS TECHNIQUES

In "selling" or promoting a solution to a natural resource issue, the internal publics must be convinced first. This is a cardinal rule of public relations. If the internal publics cannot agree, it may be difficult, if not impossible, to convince the external publics. Once a solution has been accepted as organization policy, internal publics that disagree should be encouraged to avoid making public statements in the capacity of organizational representatives.

Empathy means to view the issue from another's viewpoint. For example, by viewing an issue from the landowner's perspective, others can understand the landowner's concerns. A common ground of understanding often can be arrived at as a starting point, and future efforts will be positive and gain an ally instead of an adversary.

Natural resource agencies tend to react to an issue instead of act. They wait until they are being criticized for something they are doing or plan to do, and they then try to defend their actions or proposals. Effort to explain the situation during the preliminary planning stages, so the publics understand the situation and reasons for the activity, can offset the need for reaction.

Working with leaders, sometimes referred to as the "domino effect" or "elitism," can save much time and effort. Research may be necessary to detect the informal leaders. The formal leaders usually are known by position or responsibility. These leaders, in turn, can influence the lesser leaders and the followers.

An idea is not accepted in one move. The adoption (or rejection) process is a sequence of definite steps. These steps—awareness, interest, attitude, opinion and belief—are characterized by increased solidarity and definiteness as the process goes from awareness to belief. Research is necessary to determine the stage in the sequence where the particular public is. It is much harder to influence thinking at the belief stage than in the earlier stages. Mass media are most effective in the earlier stages. The later stages require a face-to-face effort to promote acceptance or change.

Most natural resource professionals tend to formulate opinions and positions by processes of scientific reasoning. In debates on natural resources issues, they rely primarily on facts. People who do not have scientific training often argue points primarily on the basis of emotional reactions. Although emotions are important considerations for the identification and expression of viewpoints about a particular problem relating to natural resource consumption and management, the professional must use scientifically sound judgment when making decisions. Such judgment then can be presented effectively to others with proper emotional expressions, so long as these expressions do not ignore the facts as they relate to the inductive or deductive process of scientific reasoning.

COMMON PUBLIC RELATIONS PROBLEMS AND THEIR SOLUTIONS

Public involvement

With increased interest in natural resource efforts, including big game management, public involvement has become a by-word with most natural resource agencies. Public hearings and presentations are held concerning important legislation. For example, the United States Forest Service recently conducted many public meetings to get the opinions of people and to inform them of forest management plans. The Colorado Division of Wildlife used the public-meeting approach throughout the state to inform people when it planned to alter drastically the deer and elk season format that had been used for years. But a public meeting is not by itself public involvement. Many agencies shudder at the thought of true public involvement because of traumatic experiences at public meetings.

To have public involvement, it is necessary to know the specific publics. Leadership must be provided. One way this can be done is to establish semiofficial adviser groups. These groups can be formed throughout the state or area and should contain representatives from a broad range of interests. Included should be positive thinkers who are knowledgeable and can attend the meetings. These groups should not be confused with game and fish commissions or advisory boards that are formally established for agencies, such as the United States Forest Service and the Bureau of Land Management. Definite goals should be set for each group, and each group should understand the agency's legal responsibilities and limitations. The agency must supply the needed data base to the groups. Agency personnel also should give professional evaluations of alternatives.

For efficiency in operation, the groups can be broken down into small working clusters or teams of five or six persons. Each team then can attack a phase of the larger problem. Also, it is important that each team contain a mix of interests. Team reports are compiled into the group report. The group reports, collectively, should give the most popular solution to the larger problems.

It is necessary to report back to the groups after the ultimate agency decision is made. If the involvement groups have been structured correctly, their suggestions should be nearly identical to the proposed, earlier suggestions arrived at by the professionals. Through this process, good communications may be established with leaders of the publics involved. Also, it is entirely possible that the professionals will obtain some new, viable ideas and solutions.

The last step may be to hold a public meeting. The involvement group members will be allies, and the meeting should go well.

People are interested in big game, other wildlife and all natural resource management. They have ideas. They want to be involved. It is up to the professional to see to it that this involvement is positive.

Communications

Frequently a lack of communication is the basic deterrent to success. Things that are clear and simple to professionals may not be understood by others. Communication implies understanding, not necessarily agreement. However, if the professional is working for the good of both the resource in question and the publics involved, and if the situation is understood, agreement is automatic.

For communications to be effective, interest is required on the parts of both sender (communicator) and receiver (person being communicated with). If either party is uninterested, it just will not happen. If questions can be asked and answered, the chances of achieving understanding are greater. This is referred to as "two-way" communication. Thus, a very complicated controversy may require face-to-face effort to change people's minds instead of a large group or mass media approach.

An aid to effective communication is the use of as many sensory experiences as possible. A multisense effort has more chance of succeeding than a single-sense effort. For example, participation in a field situation would be much more effective in selling a deer season than would a written message. For lectures, visual aids that are simple, interesting and colorful necessitate use of the sense of sight as well as hearing.

A resource manager shows a group of landowners how rangelands are classified, inventoried and mapped to provide compatible uses for both domestic livestock and wildlife. Such "on the ground" communications are essential to assure public understanding of needs for resource husbandry, as well as to advance intensive management on a cooperative basis. Photo courtesy of the Bureau of Land Management.

Barriers to effective communication are many. From the standpoint of the communicator, several important potential barriers are: (1) improper identification of the publics concerned and their leaders; (2) improper timing (communicating only after an issue has become a controversy); (3) inadequate coverage of the subject matter; (4) improper choice of medium to present the message; (5) ineffective use of proper medium; (6) too simple or too complex presentation of facts, opinions, alternatives, etc.; and (7) failure to provide mechanisms for feedback. From the standpoint of the receiver, potential barriers include: (1) apathy; (2) reservations about the communicator's credibility; (3) emo-

tionalism without factual basis; (4) tangential or irrelevant interests; and (5) preconceived beliefs based on faulty or incomplete information. These constraints to effective communication can be minimized, if not eliminated, by detailed analyses of the problem, the publics, the appropriate message(s), the medium to be used, methods of retrieval (feedback), and alternative responses.

Special publics

Three important specific publics cause special problems and deserve special attention. These are legislators, commissions or advisory groups, and media.

Legislators, our elected or politically appointed officials, generally are responsible for final approval of budgets. They also are responsible for making or revising laws and, in many instances, for establishing licenses and license fees. They should be informed and convinced. All effort possible must be used in communicating with legislators.

Commissions or advisory groups set or recommend policy under which the agency must operate. Under this umbrella of policy are seasons and limits for harvesting animals, budgetary matters and procedural guidelines. As with legislators, this public must understand completely the reasons and rationale behind every effort. It should be involved in the organization's operation as much as possible, but it must not be involved directly in administration. When commissioners start issuing orders to agency personnel, confusion and/or dissension result.

Reporters and other media representatives can be adversaries or important allies. They welcome information regarding natural resources management, including big game management, because it interests their audiences. However, media representatives operate under rules and regulations, some formal and others informal. The wildlife professional should search out these rules and abide by them. Deadlines, techniques and responsibilities, if known and followed, can pave the way toward a positive and profitable alliance for both the organization and the medium.

Antihunting and antihunter sentiment

This problem recently has received much attention. Books, such as *The Politics of Extinction* by Regenstein (1975), have stimulated much concern among wildlife professionals. A similar book, *Man Kind* by Cleveland Amory (1975), really set the stage for the "anti-" movement. It is suggested that wildlife professionals and students read

these two books to familiarize themselves with ideologies and expressions of the authors and those they represent.

Many people, mainly natural resource managers, have written in favor of hunting. Many of these articles give results of surveys (Applegate 1973, 1975, Peterle 1967, Schole et al. 1973, Wright and Lancaster 1972). Most surveys show that rural habitation and prohunting views have decreased in recent years in favor of urban dwelling and antihunting attitudes. This trend may be the number one problem facing the wildlife manager today.

Shaw and Gilbert (1974) pointed out that the hunting-antihunting controversy may be less a philosophical issue than a pragmatic question relative to hunter behavior. Philosophical aspects of the controversy relate to ethics, morals and religion. Often-debated philosophical concepts include whether hunting is a sport, whether killing of wild creatures is morally or ethically right, should man hunt for pleasure, does hunting promote violence, and whether natural things should be preserved. Pragmatic arguments include areas of game law violations, property destruction and accidental shooting of people.

The question of hunter behavior may be attacked best by a combination of required education and more severe penalties for misbehavior. At least 23 states now require hunter safety-training programs of one type or another. However, hunter safety is but a small part of the issue. Hunter ethics, including all rules of conduct and knowledge of laws, should be included. Basic wildlife ecology and identification of wildlife also should be required before a hunting license can be purchased. It would be well if people in the United States would consider adopting the European system of very difficult and complete programs of hunter education as a prototype, with perhaps a lesser degree of severity or control.

Many states have tried various hunter-landowner cooperative programs with varying degrees of success. One of the best known and most successful is New York's

Fish and Wildlife Management Act that is operative today. It first was described by Bromley (1945). The plan provides for financial remuneration to landowners by the state for hunting and fishing access rights for long periods of time. Leased areas are posted and managed by the Department of Environmental Conservation. Swanson and Waldbauer (1967) described the continued success of the program.

Other states have different programs. Chalk et al. (1940) described a rancher-sportsmen council in Utah that helped resolve differences relating to big game management, specifically elk damage control. For years, the Izaak Walton League has sponsored an informational program—Hunt America Time. Colorado's "Operation Respect" has been mildly successful. With this program, a card system is used to identify the hunter. The cards are left with the landowner when the hunter is on his property. The chances for misbehavior are reduced and hunter numbers on a given property are controlled.

Wildlife laws are frequently ridiculed. Violators often brag about their ability to "beat the system." As game law violators, "them good old boys" are often held in high esteem by many. Perhaps if jail sentences were mandatory and fines more severe, hunter misbehavior would decrease.

The problem of antihunting and antihunter attitudes certainly is not decreasing. The ironic part is that both sides of the controversy think they are correct! The antihunting groups are as sincere in their convictions as are those that make up the prohunting faction.

One approach that certainly will not work is name calling. "Bloodthirsty killers" and "little old ladies in tennis shoes" are terms often used by one side to describe the other. The obvious solution to the problem is education. Neither faction wishes to destroy wildlife. Thus, in reality, both groups are working toward the same goal and have a common ground. Empathy and understanding resulting from good communication and education can reduce controversy and its adverse impact on wildlife management efforts.

MISCELLANEOUS PUBLIC RELATIONS PROBLEMS

Problems of access and trespass constantly are plaguing the wildlife manager. In the West, especially, large tracts of public lands are blocked by private landowners controlling access. One solution is for the federal agencies, such as the Forest Service and the Bureau of Land Management, to use their powers of condemnation. Perhaps this should be done.

Another solution to the problem is face-to-face contact by a state official with the landowner. If the state conservation agency would aid the landowner by imposing and enforcing hunting regulations, posting lands or even securing a long-term lease, the problem might be reduced. The landowner has the right to control access, but an approach with understanding often will be successful to gain public access to recreational opportunities on privately owned land or public land blocked by private ownership.

It is extremely difficult to establish dollars and cents values on some phases of natural resources. Pearse and Bowden (1969) stated that relevance of economic theory to natural resources has increased. Quantification of recreational values, such as an experience or aesthetics, is difficult in the absence of market prices. Prediction of natural resource use allied to recreation is inadequate in determining values. Expenditures can serve as an index to some resource values, while other values are beyond dollar expression. Cooperation between natural and social scientists is essential in dealing with conflicting demands on natural resources.

Budgets are a never-ending cause of concern and frustration. Public agencies must defend budgets to commissions and to legislative groups at state or federal levels. Budget presentations should be clear, simple and straightforward. Visual aids should be used, but used correctly. Legislators and commissioners tend to be busy people. They are defensive and protective of tax or public dollars, as they should be. It is logical that presentations be well-prepared and made by the most capable, knowledgeable individuals. It is hoped that good communications and understanding will result in an adequate budget.

SUMMARY

Natural resource managers should be aware of the power of good public relations. They should prepare themselves, either through formal education or through personal dedication, to do the job that needs to be done. The days of "railroading" issues, such as big game seasons and regulations, are finished. People are interested in natural resources in general, and especially in wildlife. This interest can be a tremendous asset if wildlife professionals will communicate factual information in a clear and concise way.

At present, sociological issues may be more important than biological problems to most natural resource management agencies. It seems logical that, in the immediate future, increased research and communications be directed toward solving people-oriented problems in wildlife management.

Chapter 27

THE FUTURE

Wildlife Management Institute Staff
Washington, D.C.

The future of big animals in North America always has been a matter of considerable doubt. Speculations have ranged from outright pessimism to guarded optimism, with the former more prevalent than the latter.

About 1810, Daniel Boone reportedly told John James Audubon, ". . . when I was left to myself on the banks of the Green River [in Kentucky], I daresay for the last time in my life, a few signs only of deer were to be seen, and, as to a deer itself, I saw none" (Matthiessen 1959).

In 1827, James Fennimore Cooper wrote, "The vast herds which had been grazing among the wild pastures of the prairies gradually disappeared. . . ."

On August 5, 1843, Audubon recorded, "Even now there is a perceptible difference in the size of the herds, and before many years, the Buffalo, like the Great Auk, will have disappeared; surely this should not be permitted."

In 1872, historian Francis Parkman wrote, "A time would come when those plains would be a grazing country, the buffalo give place to tame cattle, farmhouses be scattered along the water courses, and wolves, bears and Indians be numbered among the things that were."

Twenty years later, Parkman eulogized, "The buffalo is gone, nothing is left but bones . . . The mountain lion shrinks from the face of man, and even grim 'Old Ephriam,' the grizzly bear, seeks the seclusion of his dens and caverns."

Scientist, conservation spokesman and a founder of what now is the National Audubon Society, George Bird Grinnell wrote in 1897, "On the great plains is still found the buffalo skull half buried in the soil and crumbling to decay. The deep trails once trodden by the marching hosts are grass-grown now and fast filling up. When these most enduring relics of a vanished race have passed away, there will be found, in all the limitless domain once darkened by their feeding herds, not one trace of the American buffalo."

In 1904, conservation activist and organizer Madison Grant predicted, "It may be confidently asserted that twenty-five years hence, the rinderpest [a virus disease] and repeating rifle will have destroyed most, if not all the larger African fauna . . . and game in India and North America in a wild state will almost have ceased to exist."

The same year, author and sportsman Dwight Huntington reported, "The antelope are no longer to be seen in many places they were formerly abundant, and the naturalists predict that they soon will be exterminated." He also noted that, "The zoologists, like the ornithologists, are inclined to be pessimistic when discussing the decrease of game."

Ernest Thompson Seton wrote in *Life Histories of Northern Animals* (1909), "In 1882, when first I visited the Province [Manitoba], there were plenty of old [elk] antlers on the Carberry Sandhills. In the three years which followed, I saw tracks three times, but once only did I see a Wapiti . . . At that time the Wapiti was practically exterminated." Seton also reported, ". . . all the 'old-timers' agreed that there were no Antelope in the country now." And, "The Buffalo of the wild Plains is gone forever; and we who see those times in the glamour of romance can only bow the head and sadly

say, 'It had to be. He served his time but now his time is past.' "

Ex-bear hunter William Wright (1928) noted, ". . . the first chapter of the history of the grizzly is the beginning of the story's end. When my grandson was born, the grizzly had never been heard of. If my grandson ever sees one, it will likely be in the bear pit of a zoological garden."

In the early 1900s, wildlife preservationist William T. Hornaday predicted that it would not be long until many of North America's big game species would be extinct. His fervent admonitions against hunting and other causes of wildlife's demise lost none of their force by 1931 when he observed: "Now, just visualize this enormous increase in guns, hunters, and other perils of game today, savagely operating against about ONE-TWENTIETH of the number of game birds and beasts that were here in 1900." He also wrote, "It seems as if all the killable game of North America, except rabbits, is now being crushed to death between the upper millstone of industries and trade, and the conglomerate lower millstone made up by the killers of wildlife. We are certain that not one percent of the people of the United States realize this, and that not one-tenth of one percent is doing anything to reform and stabilize this deadly condition."

Eight years later, E. M. Dahlberg reported in his book, *Conservation of Renewable Resources,* that bighorn sheep, moose, pronghorn and elk were facing "serious emergencies," and some "are already on the verge of extinction as wild species."

"The grizzly," Dahlberg wrote, "and in many places also the black and brown bears are being crowded toward extinction. Here and there an individual or a society protests the extermination of these animals. But for the most part, the persecution of bears goes on with the general public approval."

These are but a few of the sentiments and forecasts expressed before scientific management was applied to big game resources. Given the changes of landscape, diminution of habitat quality, unregulated shooting and lack of concern for big game, it is not surprising that "the black cloud of extermination hung low over the big game ranges of North America" (Trefethen 1961).

There is no denying that North America's big game were less plentiful in the late 1800s and early 1900s than at any time in recorded history. In the words of Seton (1909), "The dwindling process . . . was the low ebb in many parts of America for many kinds of game. . . ." But, as often is the case in times of cataclysm and crisis, there also was a tendency of chroniclers to overstate the case. Then, as today, the status of wildlife was commonly evaluated in terms of relative abundance.

It may be hypothesized that, following the Exploitation Era, the North American public was less alarmed about the disappearance of big game populations than they were flabbergasted that the loss actually could have occurred. "Not until the time of [George Perkins] Marsh and [Carl] Schurz and [John Wesley] Powell did we begin to understand that our resources were not inexhaustible," wrote John F. Kennedy in his introduction to *The Quiet Crisis* (Udall 1963). Superabundance and Manifest Destiny were erroneous notions that faltered with the advent of plowed prairies, denuded forests, accelerated soil erosion, abuses of streams and rivers, and then died with the disappearance of wild animals that once numbered in incomprehensible millions.

"When the pioneer hewed a path for progress through the American wilderness, there was bred into the American people the idea that civilization and forests were two mutually exclusive propositions. Development and forest destruction went hand in hand; we therefore adopted the fallacy that they were synonymous. A stump was the symbol of our progress" (Leopold 1918).

A few observant individuals such as Powell, Schurz, Marsh, John Muir, Henry David Thoreau and others had realized that wild animals and wild places were being mindlessly exploited. But not until those had been excessively exploited did others pay heed. When the "low ebb" was reached in the 1890s and "the lesson of the vanished Buffalo had sunk deep in men's minds" (Seton 1909), the shattered myth of limitless resources spurred castigations and exaggerated laments by antihunting proponents such as William Hornaday. The public, seeking ready reason and excuse, listened to the words and sentiments of Hornaday and others who popularized their appeals for change by overstating the case of relative abundance.

In 1914, Hornaday conjured historic images of a land once "teeming" with wildlife when he wrote, "Abundance is the only word with which to describe the original supply of animal life that stocked our country a short half century ago. Throughout every state, on every shoreline, in all the millions of fresh-water lakes, ponds and rivers, on every mountain range, in every forest,—aye, even in every desert—the wild flocks held sway. It was impossible to go beyond the haunts of civilized man and escape them." Such statements served Hornaday well, for his audience had only an erroneous notion of greater wildlife abundance on which to reflect.

However, at the very time to which Hornaday referred, George Perkins Marsh (1864) reported: "The elk, moose, muskox, caribou and smaller quadrupeds popularly embraced under the general name of deer, though sufficient for the wants of a sparse savage population, were never numerically very abundant, and the carnivora which fed upon them were still less so. The Rocky Mountain sheep and goat must always have been rare. It is evident that the wild quadrupeds, even when most numerous, were few compared to their domestic successors, that they required much less supply of vegetable food, and were far less important as geographical elements than the millions of hoofed and horned cattle now fed by civilized man on this continent."

Even earlier, 1804–1806, members of the famed Lewis and Clark expedition—

through what is now a significant portion of the continent's big game range—fared well when and where game was abundant, thanks in no small measure to the expert marksmanship of several in the party. But there were repeated occasions when large wild mammals were not to be found in number or at all. During these periods, the expedition subsisted on horsemeat, dog-meat, flour, roots, berries or pounded fish (DeVoto 1953). As Lewis and Clark discovered, and so did those who followed into the unsettled Louisiana Purchase tract, it was a land of plenty, but by no means everywhere at all times.

Settlers to the lake states of the "Old Northwest Territory" in the 1830s were attracted by reports of plentiful resources. And although deer, bear, elk, moose and caribou did exist there in isolated pockets, most settlers found it necessary to rely on food sources other than big game. In fact, the Territory was opened to settlement following the defeat in southcentral Wisconsin of Indians led by the Sak chief Black Hawk. Before the final battle, Black Hawk and his band of about 1,200 followers traversed Iowa, Illinois and Wisconsin during spring and early summer of 1832. The ill-fated Indians were caught by forces of militia and Army regulars in part because fish and game were not to be found and the band was weakened severely by starvation.

Wildlife throughout the continent undoubtedly were "teeming," at least relative to what early pioneers had experienced in other homelands of the world. Bison, passenger pigeons and a few other species excepted, Marsh's assessment of wildlife populations in pristine North America undoubtedly was more accurate than that of Hornaday 50 years later. But Hornaday's proclamation was opportunistic, made at a time when lament overshadowed reason. To Hornaday's credit, his antihunting ministrations served to stimulate protective legislation and enforcement. In addition, his impassioned objections to hunting actually helped bring sportsmen together in coalitions that eventually became the founda-

tions of state conservation agencies and private organizations still of considerable influence in wildlife-related issues.

Significant to this or any other discussion of the future of big game is the fact that, with few exceptions, large mammals never were as abundant nor as widely distributed prior to this century as is popularly believed. It also is true that, today, most of North America's big game populations are more secure from waste and abuse than ever before in historic time. Although some of the species are less numerous now than when first sighted in North America, most have increased in abundance and distribution in the last four decades. These developments have not been accidental. They are the direct results of scientific management and of legislation based on scientific data. Only three subspecies of large terrestrial mammals (Eastern elk, Merriam elk, Badlands bighorn) became extinct in North America since occupation of the continent by nonnative peoples. All three were eliminated before wildlife management became a scientific reality (U.S. Fish and Wildlife Service 1973). The record testifies to the value of the science and the effectiveness of its practitioners (Williamson 1973).

Regardless of the reported abundance of big game when North America was discovered, explored and settled, the fact remains that some populations were at critically low levels in the score of years before and after 1900.

As noted and implied in Schmidt's chapter (17) on early management, this condition was brought about by ignorance or indifference on the part of those who reaped enormous but short-lived harvests from virgin forests, wetlands and prairies. Had it been otherwise and had the people somehow realized the inevitable consequences of their rampant exploitation, wildlife might have been spared its critical circumstance. But that seems improbable, for the untapped wealth of the land sparked a pioneering spirit that was both unbridled and universal. Until almost too late, there was little evidence or reason to believe that the bounties of the land were limited. Exploitation took place without concern for or knowledge of realistic mechanisms to salvage and restore big game populations when the need suddenly came.

Fortunately, not all the voices for wildlife then were of the Henny Penny variety, advocating abolition of hunting or other drastic steps. Separate from the handwringing and self-righteous reproaches, some individuals—including Theodore Roosevelt, Gifford Pinchot, Stephen Mather, John F. Lacey, Clinton Hart Merriam and Charles Van Hise—saw the urgent need for scientific and legislative efforts to preserve remnant big game populations and protect habitat resources vital to the animals' recovery. These far-sighted people marshalled scientific talent, progressive ideas and public support to frame protective legislation and the basic precepts of natural resource conservation.

The constructive leadership of such key people was a turning point toward a better future for big game in North America. Their positive outlook is mirrored in the words of Theodore Roosevelt (Boone and Crockett Club 1978), "In order to preserve the wildlife of the wilderness at all, middle ground must be found between brutal and senseless slaughter and the unhealthy sentimentalism which could just as surely defeat its own end by bringing about the eventual total extinction of the game. It is impossible to preserve the larger wild animals in regions thoroughly fit for agriculture; and it is perhaps too much to hope that the larger carnivores can be preserved merely for aesthetic reasons. But throughout our country there are large regions entirely unsuited for agriculture, where if people only have foresight, they can, through the power of the state, keep game in perpetuity."

Conservation catalysts Colonel Henry S. Graves and Aldo Leopold represented the enlightened tenor of a new era for wildlife. Graves, successor to Pinchot as chief U.S. forester, noted in 1916, "As long as wild life administration consists only of protection, state game preserves on national forests are all right, especially in the absence of Federal authority. In a number of instances such action has saved a bad game situation. But we have certainly now reached a point where we can begin to handle game in an intelligent and constructive way with a view toward using them and enjoying the increase, just as is the case of any other natural resource." Leopold, considered by many the "Father of modern wildlife management," elaborated further in the preface of his classic treatise, *Game Management* (1933): "The central thesis of game management is this: game can be restored by the creative use of the same tools which have heretofore destroyed it—axe, plow, cow, fire, and gun." Leopold envisioned and practiced management as "the purposeful and continuing alignment, or control, of these forces" (Flader 1974).

Considering that scientific management of big game has evolved in only the past four decades, its national application has produced substantial accomplishments. The limits of its potential are unknown. But if one objectively reviews the accomplishments in light of bleak forecasts of the century past, the changes are impressive.

In the early 1920s, for example, authorities estimated 13,000 pronghorn in the United States, most of which were in Wyoming and Montana. One-half century later, as pointed out by Yoakum (Chapter 7), at least 425,000 pronghorn are to be found in all western states and in Canada. In 1907, an estimated 41,000 elk existed south of Canada, mainly in and around Yellowstone National Park. Today, about 1 million elk are present in at least 16 states (Wildlife Management Institute 1974). In 1895, white-tailed deer had been extirpated from more than one-half of the United States, and the total number south of Canada was about 350,000. Eighty years later, more than 12 million whitetails exist in at least 48 states (Wilcox 1976). The wild sheep and goats of North America, thought to be facing "serious emergencies" and "on the verge of extinction" not 50 years ago, are stable or increasing in areas where habitat is suitable. Even the bison, reduced to remnant herds totaling about 800 survivors in 1895, and whose chance for survival was thought to be nil, now number about 6,000 in the United States and are limited only by the amount of available range. These and other improvements have paralleled the evolution of scientific wildlife management.

As the authors of this book make clear, examples of big game's current abundance in North America are not to be considered as laurels, but as indicators of further opportunities for increasing their distributions and numbers. In the writings of these authors and the minds of other professional wildlifers, today's expressions of future goals for big game populations are as optimistic as were those of Theodore Roosevelt and others who, approximately eight decades ago, saw hope but certainly not the degree of progress that scientific management was to achieve.

Echoed throughout the chapters of this volume is the theme that big game management is, in essence, habitat management. Accordingly, the future of big game depends on the availability and quality of habitat resources: space, food, water and shelter. It also depends on how much of the available but currently unoccupied habitat can be made accessible to big game, and on the extent to which quality and quantity of big game ranges will be compromised by other land uses.

A most important variable of the future is public acknowledgment of big game values as an integral cultural entity. Application of improved management efforts will depend mainly on public understanding and acceptance. To get public confidence and cooperation the wildlife profession must demonstrate that it can "replace unplanned events and uncertain results with planned actions and known results" (Foreword).

There are at least two certainties that must preface examination of future habitat for big game. First, human population will continue to grow. Second, society's demands for uses of natural resources will increase. Both certainties have potential for affecting big game habitats and populations adversely. However, adverse impacts can be countered by improved resource management.

Based on increased enrollments in wildlife programs at North American colleges and universities despite "intense competition for available positions" (The Wildlife Society 1977), improved wildlife management is a strong likelihood. Less than 50 years ago, wildlife ecology was not a major field of study, much less a scientific discipline. In 1976, nearly 3,000 students graduated with degrees in wildlife science from about 90 colleges and universities. The 1976 graduate number reflects an 18.5 percent increase from 1973, and a 61.7 percent increase since 1971 (The Wildlife Society 1973, 1975). Total enrollments in wildlife curricula presently exceed 12,000 students annually, and the trend is toward increased academic participation. As general and career interest in the science of wildlife continues to grow, so too will the knowledge standards for those who graduate and find employment in the field. Concepts that now are fundamental to wildlife and habitat management—such as carrying capacity, sustained yield, density dependence, population dynamics and compensatory mortality—were little understood and seldom applied one-half century ago. But wildlife management is a rapidly evolving science: none of its concepts and methodologies are sacred; all are subjected to continuous evaluation.

In recent decades, this dynamic process has resulted in substantial refinement of many policies and practices, including those for predator control, single-sex harvests, winter feeding, translocations and fire management. Furthermore, advances in related sciences—plant ecology, silviculture, agronomy, agriculture, climatology, soils science, limnology, etc.—are a boon to increased understanding of what must be done to maintain and enhance big game. As is characteristic of a young and dynamic science, new information continues to provide more effective means of managing big game resources.

Improved management includes better law enforcement. This is as true today as during the Exploitation Era when big game had little protection. Law enforcement's role in management was expressed by Leopold (1917) in no uncertain terms. "Why is the big game of the West disappearing today? Principally for the reason that game laws are not enforced. And why are they not enforced? Politics. Paper game laws and political game wardens are one and inseparable." The wardens to whom Leopold referred were poorly trained, ill-equipped, few in number and subject to political whim and expedience. Despite their dedication, the impossibility of their task placed "woods cops" in low public esteem.

In 1930, there were 24 federal game protectors in the United States to enforce a growing myriad of wildlife laws. Today, the U.S. Fish and Wildlife Service has an enforcement staff of approximately 165 special agents. In addition, the states field a force of more than 6,800 conservation officers (Morse 1976), many of whom are well-trained in resource management as well as police science. These wildlife agents and conservation officers monitor and enforce regulations that pertain to all aspects of maintaining wildlife resources. Their effectiveness can improve with greater public assistance.

Enlightened public attitudes about game values are evidenced by a growing body of conservation legislation, more sensitive uses of all public lands, a flurry of legal actions to maintain resource values, more environmental education programs, and increased participation and voice in conservation organizations. Not least of all is the election of conservation-minded citizens to public office. Public appreciation of big game values has led to successful wildlife restoration and maintenance programs, establishment of management units, acquisition of key wintering areas, improved recreational access laws, better law enforcement and other actions that encourage wise use of big game resources.

Undoubtedly the most important support for big game has been legislation at both the state and federal levels. Authority to regulate harvest numbers, seasons, licensing options, etc. has had considerable positive influence on the conservation of big game, but many other laws have been equally as significant. Recent federal legislation—such as the Multiple Use-Sustained Yield Act of 1960, the Forest and Rangeland Renewable Resources Planning Act of 1974, the Federal Land Policy and Management Act of 1976 and the National Forest Management Act of 1976—directs resource officials to consider equitably the impacts on and needs of wildlife resources in land-use plans. These laws and others sure to follow can provide opportunities to perpetuate wildlife.

Human developments create serious management problems for big game in some areas. However, space is available on which to maintain or increase big game. To do so, of course, requires that wildlife and the land be managed intelligently. Space is not yet a limiting factor in the United States because approximately one-third of all lands are publicly owned (305.5 million hectares: 755 million acres), primarily under the jurisdiction of federal agencies including the Forest Service, Bureau of Land Management, Fish and Wildlife Service, National Park Service, and the Department of Defense. Other public lands (approximately 30.3 million hectares: 75 million acres) are owned or otherwise maintained by state conservation, forest and park agencies. And of about 566 million hectares (1.4 billion acres) of privately owned lands in the country, nearly 80 percent are actual or potential fish and wildlife habitat (Wildlife Management Institute 1977). In Canada and Mexico, vast acreages are suitable for big game or have potential to be improved and managed to include big game populations.

Space for most big game populations, therefore, is not an immediate problem. Provision and maintenance of habitat to satisfy the animal's seasonal needs is the crucial matter. At some times and in some areas, people's activities, such as off-road vehicle traffic, hiking and backpacking, disturb big game resources. In other situations, overuses—such as public recreation on parklands and forests—and abuses—such as livestock overgrazing—limit the presence and abundance of big game. But, it must be remembered that the potential for intensive management does exist.

In the same regard, manpower and funds for managing big game are far short of what are required. Most state and federal wildlife programs regularly seek to increase investments in personnel, land acquisition, research and other management purposes. However, allocations have not kept pace with needs or opportunities. In addition, new responsibilities placed on fish and wildlife agencies have increased substantially. Few have been accompanied by sufficient funds and personnel to do the job. Authorities and guidelines for managing the resource base continue to overlap, often in competitive and contradictory ways. Communications among and within federal and state resources agencies tend to be slow and imprecise. And, vested-interest groups have the political leverage to advance their special uses of large tracts of public lands, sometimes in ways harmful to wildlife.

The solution to these and other problems facing big game in North America seems clear. Increased knowledge of the resource's needs and potentials, in relation to the public's needs and demands, is one part. More and better-trained personnel at all levels of wildlife management—from research to field operations to administration—is another part. More funds to generate scientific data and to attract and keep expertise where most useful is no small item. Clearly defined and communicated goals and responsibilities among resource personnel, agencies and the public are yet another element. Public understanding and cooperation must not be overlooked. When combined, these various elements can produce programs for improving wildlife resources. The resource base, the scientific information, the management skills, and the public interest all exist. And with unlimited opportunities for enhancement of each, the viability of big game in North America's future can be assured.

The future track is not entirely clear, nor will it ever be. But it is not as dismal a future as predicted at the turn of the century. There now is substantial reason to hope. Scientific wildlife management has achieved professional status. Its practice has been accompanied by the strong resurgence of many of North America's splendid large mammals. The time is at hand to manage these resources more intensively and aggressively.

PATHOLOGY AND NECROPSY TECHNIQUES

Alan Woolf

Research Director
Rachelwood Wildlife Research Preserve
New Florence, Pennsylvania

Why did that big game animal die? What significance does this animal's death have on the rest of the population? Are the people who handled the dead animal in danger from a contagious disease? Do big game populations harbor diseases of potential danger to man and domestic animals? These questions and others need to be answered.

For years, wildlife diseases had been studied in relation to the effects on man and domestic animals. Since Leopold's (1933) classic work on game management, wildlife diseases have been viewed more in terms of one of the factors that limits population productivity. Both are valid reasons for seeking to understand the cause and nature of wildlife diseases.

Biologists with the professional responsibility for the health and welfare of big game wildlife populations often are posed with questions relating to diseases. Too often, he or she is inadequately prepared to answer or to seek the answers to these questions. While the biologist should recognize that pathology is a highly specialized field and that final determination of causes of deaths should remain in the province of a trained pathologist, the biologist often is the prime source of information on which an accurate diagnosis can be based.

The purpose of this appendix is to introduce basic concepts of pathology so that the biologist and interested layman can better judge the significance of disease problems. Emphasis will be on broad classifications of disease rather than specific disease problems associated with a species or population.

The standard necropsy procedure outlined here will allow a biologist to examine a carcass in a thorough manner. Systematic examination of organs and tissues will provide a means to detect and describe any lesions present. This procedure, combined with properly preserved specimens, is one of the most important steps in determining the nature and significance of a disease.

PATHOLOGY

Pathology is the study of cause and effects—both structural and functional—produced by disease. Wildlife biologists most often are concerned with the functional effects produced by disease. The study of diseases may be aimed at any level of function, ranging from the molecular to the population. While an individual organism usually is the focus of attention, we seek answers to the nature of its illness so as to assess the significance of disease at the population level.

Disease may be defined in many ways, but perhaps the best concept is that of a departure from health, or a state of imbalance. An organism and its environment are constantly in a state of flux and shifting balance. When exposed to a deleterious force or environmental stimulus, there is a reaction that produces some immediate effect on an organism. The reaction may be at the molecular, cellular, tissue or organ level de-

pending on the nature of the stress. The type of reaction produced is determined, in great part, by the nature of the injury (causative or etiological agent), time or duration of injury, location, quantity or extent of the injury, and the animal's natural or acquired resistance.

Causes of disease

Etiology is the study of cause of disease. Many things cause disease, and there are several ways to classify etiologic agents broadly and, thus, the diseases they produce. One classification is simply that of either infectious or noninfectious diseases. Infectious diseases are those caused by the presence of living organisms that exercise a deleterious functional effect on the host's system. Noninfectious diseases are those caused by other factors. This type of classification fails to define the nature of disease adequately. Another classification used by Hopps (1964) broadly depicts etiologic agents under the category of intrinsic or extrinsic causes (Table 44).

Another grouping characterizes diseases by the nature of the environmental influence-producing disease. This grouping of causes of disease (modified from Smith et al. 1972) is the outline used in this discussion of wildlife diseases:

1. Intrinsic flaw
2. Deficiency diseases
3. Exogenous poisons
4. Trauma
5. Tumors
6. Living organisms

Table 44. Causes of disease (after Hopps 1964).

| Intrinsic | Extrinsic | |
	Inanimate	Animals
Genetic influences	Force	Viruses
Metabolic	Temperature	Rickettsiae
Nervous	Humidity	Bacteria
	Radiant energy	Fungi
	Electricity	Protozoa
	Chemicals	Worms
		Insects

a. Metazoan parasites
b. Protozoan parasites
c. Bacteria and fungi
d. Viruses
e. Mycoplasma, rickettsia, etc.

"Any disease involves the effects of some detrimental situation in the environment and the reactive activities by which the body tissues more or less successfully protect themselves from those effects" (Smith et al. 1972). Cells, tissues and organs are rather limited in the nature of response to insult by an etiologic agent. However, specific agents or groups of agents do tend to produce an expected bodily response.

1. Intrinsic flaw. This group of diseases usually is of little concern to the big game biologist. It includes diseases often classified as hereditary or congenital. Hereditary diseases are those passed genetically from parent to offspring. Congenital defects are those conditions existing at birth. A congenital defect may well have an hereditary basis, but generally results from injury to the germ plasm or developing embryo.

   Many hereditary defects are of little consequence to the individual. Polydactylism (having more than the normal number of toes), which is known to affect white-tailed deer and other ruminants, is an example. Hereditary defects in big game, if of a nature that interferes with normal function, usually are self-limiting. The individual has a reduced chance of survival and, therefore, reduced opportunity to pass the undesirable defect on to future generations.

2. Deficiency diseases. Deficiency diseases basically are disorders of a metabolism, and are one of the major mortality factors affecting big game. As a wildlife decimating factor, they are too often thought of as distinct from disease. Since a chapter of this book is devoted to wildlife nutrition, this appendix will say little other than to emphasize that metabolic disorders rank high among etiologic agents causing wildlife diseases.

In their introduction to deficiency diseases, Smith et al. (1972) list the major causes:

a. Lack of specific nutrient(s) in the diet.
b. A poor quality diet.
c. Interference with intake from anorexia, mechanical obstruction, etc., having the same effect as inadequate supply.
d. Interference with absorption of nutrients.
e. Interference with storage or utilization of nutrients.
f. Increased excretion.
g. Increased requirements associated with pregnancy, lactation, etc.
h. Inhibition of nutrients by specific inhibitors or analogs.

It probably is safe to say that the biggest deficiency problem in big game is lack of adequate food intake, or malnutrition. In addition to being a problem in itself, there is an important interrelationship of malnutrition and infectious diseases. A malnourished animal usually is less resistant to the deleterious effects of infectious diseases. These diseases can lead to death of an animal weakened by malnutrition, but which may have recovered if not for secondary complications.

3. Exogenous poisons. Some poisons exert their effect by producing local injury to tissues they contact when present in concentrated amounts. When diluted, these same poisons may not have immediate effects but cause destruction of epithelial cells in organs such as the liver or kidneys after poisons are absorbed. Still other poisons act on an organism by upsetting metabolic and functional activities because of associated chemical processes.

   Poisons are a difficult etiologic agent to identify because diagnostic lesions often are lacking. Smith et al. (1972) grouped poisons on the basis of expected pathological effects. Such a grouping can provide useful diagnostic clues. However, in a poisoning problem, one should attempt to obtain chemical identification of the suspected poison and/or clearly demonstrate its absorption into the body.

Plant poisons are a potential wildlife hazard. Under certain conditions, even plants not normally poisonous, such as oak or wild cherry, can cause mortality.

Environmental pollutants have affected big game and should be considered when mortality is encountered. A factor often overlooked is that excesses of certain essential nutrients, such as vitamins A or D, can act as exogenous poisons and cause disease.

4. Trauma. Accidents, one of the decimating factors cited by Leopold (1933), take a considerable toll of wildlife. Traditionally, accidents and predation have been thought of as mortality factors independent of disease. In reality, they should be thought of as trauma, a major cause of disease. For example, in 1976, at least 24,183 white-tailed deer were killed by vehicles in Pennsylvania, more than the number of deer harvested in approximately 35 other states that year.

A classical example of a major disease problem with a traumatic origin was reported by Bergerud (1971a). Caribou calf mortality was extensive and each year dead and moribund calves were found with cervical abscesses. The cause of death was a septicemia resulting from infection with *Pasteurella multocida*. Dr. John M. King and Dr. Lars Karstad investigated the problem and discovered the mortalities resulted from secondary infection following the bite of lynx.

Bodily reaction to initially sublethal traumatic insult commonly is inflammatory. If an organism survives the initial injury, risk of secondary infection remains high until tissue repair is complete. An initial traumatic insult may be difficult for an investigator to find, as was the case with caribou, but the investigator should never discount the possibility of trauma as the etiologic agent when a secondary infection is apparent.

Big game struck and killed by vehicles is a prevalent problem in some states. Photo by D. F. Reed; courtesy of the Colorado Division of Wildlife.

5. Tumors. Neoplasms are uncommon in wildlife, perhaps because they occur most frequently in older animals, and free-ranging wildlife rarely reach physiological longevity. One commonly encountered tumor of big game animals is fibromas. While neoplastic in appearance and character, viral etiology clearly has been demonstrated. So, in reality, fibromas should be included among viral diseases.

Any known tumor can occur in big game, but none is encountered frequently. Since they affect only the individual, tumors are not an important etiologic agent as far as species or population disease problems are concerned.

6. Living organisms. This disease etiology is that with which the big game biologist most often is concerned. The list of organisms and specific diseases is large

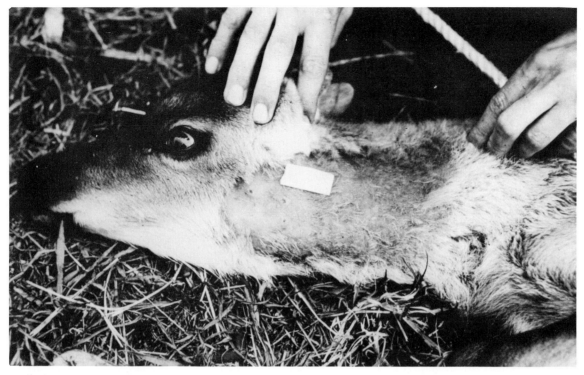

Lesions produced by lynx bite on neck of caribou calf. Photo courtesy of J. M. King.

Fibromas on face and neck of white-tailed deer.

and, to varying degrees, big game animals are susceptible to many. This classification includes those diseases that are most important to population management because of their potential for being contagious.

Metazoan, or multicellular, parasites frequently have been cited as big game mortality factors and, indeed, can and do cause death. However, if a generalization can be made, they most frequently are present in a host animal without causing undo harm. If the effects of parasitism are noted at postmortem, they usually are secondary problems resulting from initial insults caused by a primary etiologic agent or agents. For example, the effects of chronic and severe gastrointestinal parasitism may cause an animal's death, but the parasitism may have become severe because of weakened condition caused by the subtle effects of a deficiency disease.

Bodily responses to metazoan parasites range from little discernible reaction to locally severe lesions caused by migratory movements or encapsulations of the parasites. An unnatural parasite may produce a severe degenerative and inflammatory response and death. More commonly, these parasites further weaken a host by usurping essential nutrients or producing anemia combined with local irritation and/or infection caused by mechanical injury at the site of attachment or activity.

Pathogenic protozoa can produce serious or fatal injuries without inciting obvious inflammatory reactions (Smith et al. 1972). These single-celled parasites can be seen only by microscopic examination and their effects on a host frequently are difficult to see at postmortem. As with other parasites, pathogenic protozoa often are found in a host without causing apparent harm.

Some examples of pathogenic protozoan organisms that have been incriminated frequently in big game diseases are: coccidia, usually affecting the intestinal tract; anaplasma found in the blood stream; and toxoplasma, usually affecting nerve tissue but occasionally producing systemic lesions.

Bacteria, fungi, viruses, etc., are the microorganisms most often associated with infectious diseases. Many of the organisms can be or are present in a host without producing disease. However, under certain conditions, the same organisms become pathogens and produce disease. The organisms causing these diseases are not always, but may be passed from one animal to another and then are considered to be contagious. It is against the bacteria, viruses, etc., that the animal's body reacts most vigorously (Smith et al. 1972). The most intense inflammatory and/or antibody-producing responses are found when these organisms cause disease.

Based on time, diseases produced by these organisms may be peracute, acute, subacute or chronic. With peracute and acute diseases, animals are sick for so short a period of time that sickness often is not observed. With chronic diseases, illness may last for months. If the disease organism is highly virulent, an infected animal may die in a matter of hours from toxins produced by the organism, and little visible evidence may be found at postmortem. Some organisms lack a high degree of virulence or, by nature of the disease they produce, gradually exert their effects on an animal and prominent lesions usually are evident at postmortem. In many cases, diagnostic lesions may not be found at postmortem and supporting laboratory studies such as histopathology, microbiology, virology, etc., are needed to define the nature of the disease.

IMPLICATIONS OF PATHOLOGIC PROBLEMS TO MANAGEMENT

Pathologic problems in big game management can be placed in three broad categories:

1. Diagnostic procedures to obtain information on cause of death or to detect presence of high levels of potentially harmful substances or agents useful for biological knowledge or ecological monitoring.
2. Epizootiologic studies to define disease problems that potentially threaten the welfare of big game populations.
3. Understanding of the ecology of diseases that are zoonotic, or transmittable to man or domestic animals, in nature.

A sick wild animal usually dies unnoticed and the carcass quickly decomposes. Even in cold weather, repeated freezing and thawing of the remains may make it difficult, if not impossible, to obtain an accurate diagnosis of cause of death. Thus, a sick animal that can be observed or studied before death or a fresh carcass are valuable specimens. That animal can indicate potential problems or provide valuable information on the nature of disease affecting big game. Often overlooked, but extremely important, are public relations values to be gained by obtaining a diagnosis for the benefit of the concerned citizen who may have submitted the case. For example, the conservation officer or wildlife manager frequently represents the public image of the natural resource agency. If the officer or manager can determine or find out the cause of death of a wildlife specimen, and then report the cause to the individual who submitted it, the stature of the agency and its professionalism can only be enhanced.

There is growing awareness of the value of wildlife as ecological indicators, in terms of both environmental quality and frequency of zoonotic diseases. Johnson (1970) discussed the value of wildlife in an ecological approach to the study of zoonotic diseases. Trainer (1970) pointed out that wild animals usually are considered to be vectors, reservoirs or primary targets of disease. He stressed the importance of wildlife as sentinels for detecting and monitoring zoonotic diseases. White-tailed deer were cited as an excellent warning and gauge of California encephalitis. Bigler and McLean (1973) pointed out the value of deer for monitoring Venezuelan equine encephalitis activity. Deer and other big game species are valuable sentinels because of their widespread distributions and the availability of specimens in conjunction with already established harvest goals. Trainer (1970) noted that the potential for early warning and monitoring systems is unlimited in regard to a variety of infectious diseases and problems such as environmental pollutants. Management goals to add these warning and monitoring values to wildlife harvests would provide benefits in addition to recreational pleasures enjoyed by a segment of the public.

Big game populations that are relatively stable and occupy habitats that provide for their needs rarely are in danger of disease epizootics. The manager who maintains optimum densities of animals on good quality habitat usually does not have to be concerned with disease problems. However, when wildlife populations are faced with poor quality habitat, conditions producing insufficient habitat or high population densities, the danger of disease becomes real. Disease then could become the major decimating factor of a population, and may even endanger survival of a species. Perhaps the best example would be Rocky Mountain bighorn sheep. A lung-worm-pneumonia complex long associated with these big game animals may be the single greatest danger to the species' survival. Management goals to provide adequate habitat have to be supplemented by efforts to protect remnant herds living in marginal habitats. Only comprehensive understanding of the epizootiology of the disease complex will provide the knowledge needed for a wildlife manager to protect remaining Rocky Mountain bighorn herds.

While it is unrealistic to expect a wildlife manager to be able to treat an outbreak of disease in big game populations, the manager should understand the nature of the disease problem and potential dangers well enough to avoid the problem, or at least minimize the risk. The effects of meningeal worms, *Parelaphostrongylus tenuis,* that infect "unnatural" hosts such as moose, caribou or elk are an excellent example. These species run a high risk of disease when they share habitats with white-tailed deer harboring these parasites, but in which the meningeal worms are relatively non-pathogenic. Imaginative habitat manipulation to restrict contact among deer and species potentially in danger of the parasite would reduce problems. Habitat manipulation or treatment to break the parasite's life cycle and, hence, reduce infections is another alternative; but only when the disease process is understood fully will solutions be available.

Sometimes the well-meaning attempts of managers to help big game introduces unforeseen disease problems. Samuel et al. (1975) reported on the occurrence of a viral disease, Contagious Ecthyma, affecting bighorns and mountain goats in several western Canadian national parks. All infected herds had artificially prolonged contact in areas where salt was provided to concentrate animals for tourist viewing.

Maintaining animal densities in excess of available habitat carrying capacity can lead to disease problems in addition to those related to deficiency diseases. Without question, high densities can contribute to the spread of disease by increasing risk of infection and enhancing opportunity for spread among wildlife population(s). Also, Wobeser and Runge (1975) pointed out the potential risk of supplemental feeding programs using carbohydrate-rich foods. They diagnosed rumenitis in 30 of 108 deer found dead during a severe winter in Saskatchewan. Rumenitis, or rumen overload, caused by grain was considered either the cause of death or a contributor in 9 of the 30 cases.

Zoonotic diseases are important to the big game biologist because of the potential dangers to human health or economic losses that may be involved. Understanding these diseases is essential both to protect man or to preclude wildlife being accused unjustly of causing a problem, particularly to live-stock. Wildlife often are thought of as reservoirs of disease and, in fact, do suffer from many diseases that are zoonotic. Many times, however, wildlife species are not the cause of the problem. Prestwood et al. (1976) reported on parasitism among deer and domestic sheep populations sharing ranges in the southern Appalachian region. They found it unlikely that white-tailed deer are reservoirs of common parasites infecting domestic sheep.

Brucellosis in the Yellowstone National Park bison herd demonstrates the necessity to understand diseases in wildlife so that effective management can be undertaken. The disease has been known to occur in the bison herd since 1917, and evidence indicates that it has little effect on the herd. However, the disease is economically important to the cattle industry and of potential public health concern (Meagher 1973). Most bison herds in the United States are maintained in a brucellosis-free condition as part of a United States Department of Agriculture control program. However, this poses management problems for the National Park Service. Yellowstone Park personnel have cooperated in the program by vaccinating calves and culling reactors, but this is in conflict with management objectives to maintain wild populations under natural conditions. Present management goals are to prevent contact among park bison and domestic livestock. However, the epizootiology of brucellosis and the actual role of the bison, either as a reservoir for disease or as a transmitter, must be understood clearly before management plans can be designed, implemented and defended.

NECROPSY PROCEDURES

The purpose of the necropsy procedure outlined here is to enable the wildlife biologist to make a thorough and detailed gross examination and obtain information that can be passed on to a pathologist for final diagnosis. There are many ways to perform a necropsy. Cowan and Karstad

(1969) described a very acceptable technique. The most important consideration is that the operator follow a systematic procedure that will insure that all organs and tissues are examined. This procedure not only minimizes the chance of missing lesions, but facilitates recording data and describing lesions. Lesions are any discontinuity of tissue or loss of function of a part. If present, lesions will be apparent to the experienced observer because of differences in color, texture, size, etc., from surrounding normal tissue or in contrast to normal tissue from other animals of the same species.

The method described here is modified from King (1961) and is a proven systematic examination procedure. If followed carefully, few lesions will be missed. Special studies may require modification to a small degree, but any changes should be designed to supplement the general examination procedure—not to eliminate steps or drastically change the sequence.

Equipment required

Very few items really are needed to perform a postmortem examination. The operator should wear medium-weight rubber gloves and coveralls for personal protection. The entire necropsy can be done with a sharp, strong-bladed knife, a hack-saw or brush cutters, several leak-proof containers and plastic bags for specimens, and a 10-percent formalin preservative. In addition, it is desirable but not essential to have forceps, scissors, glass slides, blood tubes (several with anticoagulant) and suitable syringes, metric rule and scales, and culture media or tubes.

Preliminary observations

1. If the animal is living, collect blood samples from the jugular vein or other suitable location. Save samples in appropriate tubes and make smears.
2. Note clinical signs if present (labored breathing, staggering, etc.) and determine history to the greatest extent pos-

sible. Check the surrounding area for any clues that may help arrive at an accurate diagnosis.
3. Make an external examination, noting conditions of body orifices, limbs, pelage, parasites and general appearance. Take appropriate measurements and sex-age data. Examine carefully for signs of trauma, and skin the carcass if necessary to detect puncture wounds or other trauma-induced lesions.

Opening the carcass

1. Lay the carcass on its left side and:
A. Incise skin at armpit (axilla) and, from the inside outward, extend cut to ramus of mandible; dissect skin to expose the neck, separate leg and scapula from the thoracic wall.
B. Extend the cut down the ventral midline, going above udder or prepuce.
C. Lay the right hind leg back by cutting free at the hip (coxo-femoral) joint. Dissect skin dorsally and ventrally from the midline cut to expose the entire right side.
D. Examine the mammary glands or testes, prepuce and penis.
E. Make an incision through the abdominal wall behind and parallel to the last rib, extending from the vertebrae to the midline. Continue the cut from the vertebrae caudally to the pelvis and lay the muscle wall downward to expose the abdominal cavity.
F. Cut the diaphragm along its costal attachments.
G. Sever ribs at their sternal and vertebral ends to expose the thoracic cavity.
H. Cut the pubis and ischium on both right and left sides and remove the symphysis. The carcass now is exposed completely and prepared for organ and tissue examination.

Organ and tissue examination

1. General. Note general appearances of organs and tissues. Also note statuses of body and visceral fat, muscle color and

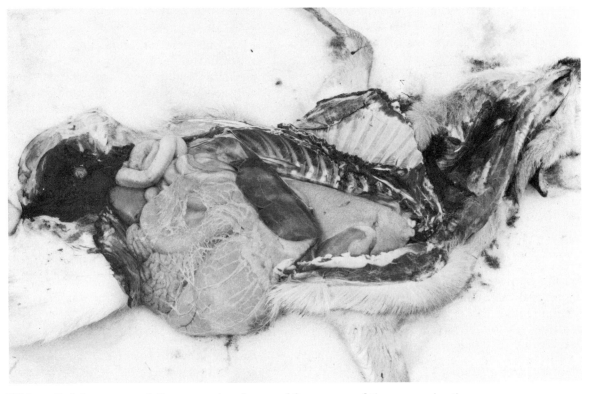

White-tailed deer carcass fully prepared and exposed for organ and tissue examination.

texture, appearance of blood or blood clots, and quantity and color of any fluid that may be present in the thoracic or abdominal cavities. Check for presence, size and condition of lymph nodes. As each major system is examined, take desired sections and specimens for laboratory studies. Formalin-fixed sections of lung, liver, kidney and any lesions should be taken for histopathology studies. A 10-percent formalin solution should be used, and sections not more than 0.5 centimeters (0.2 inches) thick should be taken and placed in at least 10 times the volume of formalin as tissue saved. Note size (normal, enlarged or shrunken), color, texture and general appearance of organs and tissues as the systems are examined. If possible, take photographs (preferably color) of suspected lesions for future reference and descriptive value. Always include a size reference in pho-

tographs. Known-size knives, pens, etc., may be used if metric rules are not available.

2. Examination sequence.

A. Remove gastrointestinal tract from abdominal cavity and place aside to examine last (to avoid contamination of instruments and other tissues.)

   i. Note type, amount and condition of stomach contents.

   ii. Examine stomach lining for lesions and parasites.

   iii. Note condition of intestinal contents and fecal material.

   iv. Examine intestinal lining for lesions and parasites.

   v. Examine mesenteries for lymph node development and parasite cysts.

B. Remove and examine spleen.

   i. Examine surfaces for lesions.

   ii. Make parallel slices to examine parenchyma for lesions.

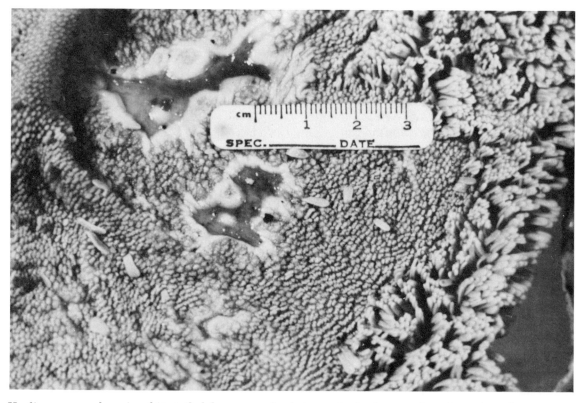

Healing rumen ulcers in white-tailed deer, properly photographed using metric scale as size reference.

C. Remove and examine liver.

    i. Check gallbladder for obstructions, lesions or parasites.

    ii. Check hilus of liver (area of attachment) for lymph node development, and examine surface and parenchyma of entire organ for lesions.

D. Examine adrenal glands. Cut in cross-section and note cortical-medullary ratio.

E. Examine kidneys.

    i. Strip capsule and check surface.

    ii. Cut each kidney in half longitudinally from the convex surface to the hilus.

    iii. Strip ureters to check for obstructions and lesions.

F. Examine bladder.

    i. Note quantity and appearance of urine.

    ii. Check for obstructions.

    iii. Check for lesions.

    iv. If female, check reproductive tract at this time.

    v. Examine uterine horns for embryo counts or signs.

    vi. Examine ovaries for evidence of reproductive history.

G. Skin back neck to point of lower jaw. Remove tongue, trachea and esophagus together. Continue into thoracic cavity and free the lungs and heart intact.

    i. Examine tongue surface and section.

    ii. Strip and examine esophagus.

    iii. Examine surface of lungs and pleura.

    iv. Open trachea, continuing into major bronchi and bronchioles to examine lung parenchyma. Note presence and type of fluid, parasites, etc.

    v. Open heart sac (pericardium) and

examine for quantity and type of fluid present.

vi. Open heart and examine walls, valves and vessels for lesions.

H. Examine joints and bones. Hip, hock, knee and shoulder joints always should be examined plus others that appear swollen or otherwise abnormal. Femur bone can be broken to evaluate condition of marrow.

I. Remove head from carcass at the first joint (atlanto-occipital joint) and examine joint.

i. Remove lower jaw and examine dentition for condition and wear.

ii. Look for bots in retropharyngeal pouch and in turbinates.

iii. Expose brain by making a transverse cut across frontal bones and connect with sagittal cuts to either side of occipital.

iv. Remove brain and examine surface and skull for lesions and parasites.

v. Make cross-sectional cuts in brain to examine for lesions.

J. Return to gastrointestinal tract previously removed and examine as described.

3. Culture, toxicology and parasitology.

A. Bacterial-viral agents. Usually, only relatively fresh specimens are suitable for culture attempts. If possible, bring the entire carcass to a laboratory where fresh culture material can be obtained under sterile conditions. If this is not possible, take tissue from the following organs: lung, liver, kidney and any organs or tissues where lesions are found. Methods of preservation vary, so if possible determine the method preferred from the person who will be examining the materials for you. Fresh specimens are preferable. Refrigerate materials if there will be a short delay. Freeze if the delay will exceed one day. Avoid freezing and thawing during storage and transport.

B. Special handling for rabies suspects. Remove entire head, place in water-tight container, and seal. Refrigerate, but do not freeze or use chemical preservatives. Ship or transport specimen in double containers with dry ice on the outside to insure arrival in good condition for examination at designated laboratories.

C. Toxicology. Save fresh or frozen portions of liver, kidney and stomach contents for analysis. Possible sources of toxic materials (plants, chemicals, etc.) should be identified and submitted also.

D. Parasitology. Parasites can be preserved in 70 percent alcohol or 10 percent formalin for identification. Fecal samples, either dried or formalin-preserved, and blood smears should be taken if parasitism is suspected as a cause of death.

CARE AND USE OF THE HARVESTED ANIMAL

John L. Schmidt
Colorado State University
Fort Collins, Colorado

Big game hunting, in addition to providing many days of outdoor recreation, can be a source of top quality meat, leather, fur, trophies and other valuable products. To maximize benefits of these products requires careful planning and preparation by the hunter, as well as some knowledge of the animal's physiology and anatomy.

According to Ross et al. (1975), each resident deer and elk hunter in Colorado spent on the average $273 and $325 in pursuit of his respective recreation. Given an average boneless meat yield of 22.5 kilograms (50 pounds) per deer and 90 kilograms (200 pounds) per elk, and a harvest success of 46 percent for deer hunters and 19 percent for elk hunters, the average cost of meat harvested was $26.17 per kilogram ($11.87 per pound) for deer and $18.85 per kilogram ($8.55 per pound) for elk. Costs, hunter success and carcass weights vary considerably among geographic areas and species of big game. In any case, there is certain economic justification for proper care of the carcass, in addition to a moral obligation.

Most of the techniques covered in this chapter should be considered a matter of art rather than science. Only a limited number of scientifically collected facts are available to document many of the statements made, although decades of practical experience have been incorporated.

Since most of this appendix will be devoted to meat values, a few introductory comments are in order. It is my contention that virtually all of the wild or so-called "gamey" taste in meat is due to the hunter, not the animal. Poor hunting practices, field and camp care, transportation and butchering, and cooking are responsible for nearly all poor quality big game meat. If a fattened hereford steer were shot through the rumen, chased around the pasture for a few hours, killed but not eviscerated and skinned immediately in spite of 22-degree Centigrade (70-degree Fahrenheit) temperature, thrown on the top of a station wagon and hauled for hundreds of kilometers before finally being processed, it too probably would have a "gamey" taste.

FIELD CARE

While processing big game in the field, it is impossible to duplicate exactly the procedure used by commercial slaughter houses. However, enough poor practices can be eliminated to make the difference negligible. The following recommended procedures should apply to all hooved big game species in North America.

Equipment

A knife with a 12–15 centimeter (5–6 inch) blade, approximately 5 meters (15 feet)

of nylon rope for dragging or hanging the animal, a plastic bag for the heart and liver, and about 60 centimeters (2 feet) of string (for tying the dead animal's anus and esophagus) should be carried by each hunter in the field.

If the animal is to be skinned in the field, one should carry enough cheesecloth or old sheets to cover the carcass. A meat saw or hatchet is desirable for splitting the breastbone in larger animals, such as elk or moose.

Making the kill

The animal should be killed instantly. The best locations for bullet placements are the head and neck (Figure 70). If the head is to be saved for mounting or if the head-neck region is hidden, the shot should be placed in the heart-lung area just behind the front shoulder. It is wise to aim close to the shoulder. Placing the shot in the paunch region will allow the animal to escape and die, perhaps days later.

A third choice is the middle of the shoulder. This shot position is just as deadly as the second area although more meat will be ruined by the projectile. If these areas cannot be hit with reasonable assurance, one should not shoot. Hunters should practice before the beginning of each big game season to make sure their weapons and ammunition function properly. Sights and scopes are easily jarred out of alignment and, therefore, should be checked before each hunt.

Hunters should not take long or difficult shots. The most successful hunters try to get within easy range of their quarry and kill it instantly with one shot.

Every shot should be followed up. Unless the target animal "drops in his tracks," a hunter seldom is sure whether or not a hit is made. Frequently, there may be no obvious sign of a hit; the animal may not jump, fall or even slow down, yet may be mortally wounded and die out of sight within minutes. If no effort is made to follow up

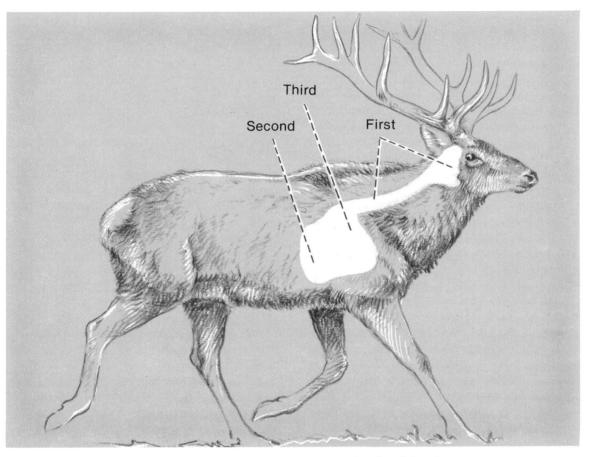

Figure 70. Recommended bullet placement for big game animals (after Schmidt 1974a).

such shots, the animal will be wasted as far as the hunter is concerned.

If the animal did not appear to be hit, it is normally best to wait several minutes before beginning the search, and then to do so very quietly. A wounded animal normally will run for some distance, but then may lie down if it feels secure. If severely wounded, it may bleed to death at the location. By contrast, if a hunter immediately begins moving in the direction of a wounded animal, it will sense danger and continue to run, perhaps for miles, before dying—making recovery of the carcass very unlikely.

While waiting for the animal to lie down, the hunter should recall the reaction of the animal to each shot and in which direction the animal was headed when the shot(s) was fired. When beginning the search, the hunter should go immediately to the spot where the animal was when shot at. The path of the animal should be followed from that location onward. The only evidence of a hit may be bloodspots, and these can be extremely difficult to see on certain ground covers, such as brown pine needles.

Some fatal wounds will not cause much external bleeding. Therefore, if no blood is found, the hunter should walk slowly and quietly in increasingly larger circles from the point of last visual contact with the animal and constantly look for blood and the animal.

Once the animal is found, it should be approached carefully from the rear until the hunter is certain it is dead. If there is any sign the animal is alive, it should be killed immediately with a shot in a vital organ.

Bleeding

If an animal has been hit in the heart or lung region by a modern rifle bullet, it normally will bleed internally. Opening and eviscerating the carcass will get rid of the blood. If the shot hit in the head or neck, the animal's main arteries and veins at the base of the neck should be cut. If in doubt whether to bleed the animal, the hunter should. If the head is to be mounted, the animal can be bled by entering through the diaphragm and severing the large veins and arteries connected to the heart.

Scent glands

Most big game animals have several scent glands in various locations. One pair is located on the inside of the hind legs at the hock (tarsal glands) and another is low on the outside of the hind legs. These scent glands are made conspicuous by long tufts of hair surrounding their openings. They excrete a penetrating odor of musk. Males frequently urinate on these glands during the breeding season.

Some hunters believe that an animal's scent glands should be removed soon after death because musk may taint the meat. An effort should be made to avoid touching these areas and then the exposed meat. However, the best way to accomplish this is to leave the glands on until the entire carcass is skinned. Then, the glands can simply be removed with the rest of the skin. There is no danger of contaminating the meat by leaving the scent glands on because they are contained completely in the skin and have only one opening, and it is external.

Field et al. (1973a) studied the effects of removing the scent glands from mule deer immediately after killing versus leaving them on until the carcass had cooled. They reported no difference in flavor. To confirm this finding, they saved the metatarsal glands from deer and placed them on top of beef roasts during cooking. They reported,

"although a distinct odor was present during cooking, no difference between flavor of beef roasts cooked with metatarsal glands and control beef roasts cooked in separate ovens was noted."

Eviscerating

Evisceration, or gutting, should take place as soon after the kill as possible. Gas resulting from microbial action will begin to accumulate in the rumen immediately after death. The longer the wait, the more difficult and unpleasant the animal is to "gut," and the less desirable it is for human consumption.

To eviscerate the animal, one should make the first cut through the hide over the abdomen and chest from the anus to the upper neck region or jaw. The next cut should be between the legs, down through the leg muscles to the pelvic bone. The knive can be turned over, and the skin over the abdomen should be cut using two fingers from the other hand to hold the intestines and stomach (viscera) away from the tip of the knife (Figure 71).

The cut should be continued through the breastbone and up the neck as far as possible. If the head is to be mounted, one should stop the cut between the front legs at the base of the brisket. If using a knife, one will find it easier, especially on larger animals such as elk, to cut on either side of the breastbone or brisket (through the joints) rather than up the middle (Figure 72). If a hatchet or saw is available, it is relatively easy to cut the breastbone down the middle, even on larger animals. To comply with laws in many states, it may be necessary to leave evidence of the animal's sex—either half of the mammary gland or a testicle—attached to the carcass.

The windpipe and esophagus should be severed as close to the head as possible. A string should be tied tightly around the esophagus to prevent contents from contaminating the meat. The next cut should be around the anus, and it must be tied with a string for the same reason. The thin

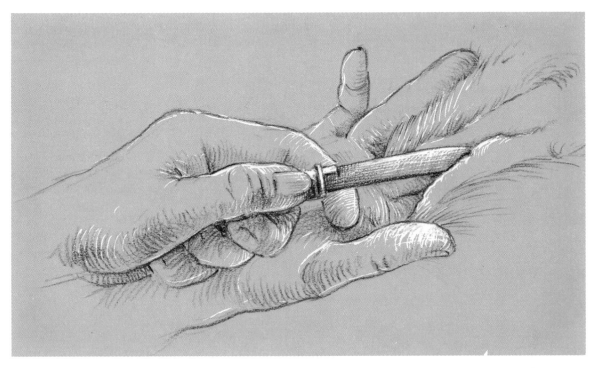

Figure 71. Recommended position of hands for making initial incision for evisceration of big game animal.

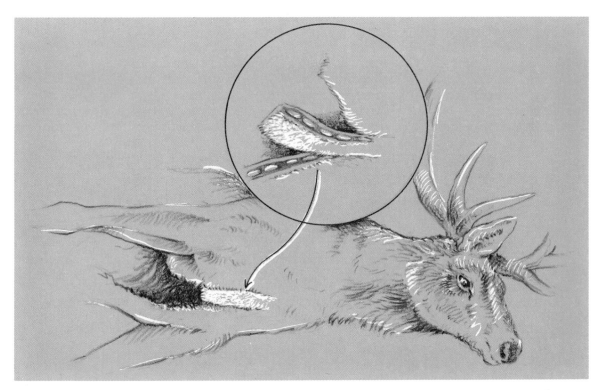

Figure 72. Recommended cutting diagram for removing the breastbone of larger big game animals.

diaphragm muscle that separates the heart-lung compartment from the main digestive tract can be severed away from the ribs, as shown in Figure 73.

Now is a good time to remove the heart and liver. If packed out of the area immediately, they should be put in a plastic bag until camp or vehicle is reached. The plastic bag then should be removed for cooling. If the heart and liver are to be left with the carcass for several hours, they should be placed in a clean, shady location.

Next, the animal is laid on its side. The viscera should either fall out or be pulled out easily. A few cuts close to the backbone may be necessary to separate organs that remain attached.

The carcass then should be hung in the shade to allow blood to drain from the body cavity and air to circulate around the body to cool it. It can be hung with either head or hind legs up. In the absence of a tree, fence or other object on which to hang the carcass, logs or stones can be placed under the carcass to keep it off the ground and, thus, allow heat to escape more easily. In either case, the body cavity should be propped open with a stick or two and wiped clean. If the body cavity accidentally is soiled from digestive tract contents, it should be washed with clean water. However, water should not be used to wash the body cavity after the cavity has been dried and "sealed."

Skinning

In most cases, when a big game carcass is dragged to a camp or vehicle, it is desirable to leave the skin on to keep the meat clean. Also, leaving the hide attached will prevent the outer layer of meat from becoming dry during the aging process. Field et al. (1973a, 1973b) compared temperature of meat on skinned and unskinned deer and elk carcasses. They found both deer and elk carcasses cool at a faster rate with the hide removed. The internal temperature of the thickest portion of the leg from the skinned side of a mule deer dropped to the temperature of the refrigerator, 3 degrees Centigrade (38 degrees Fahrenheit), within 10 hours. The hide side did not reach the same temperature for 14 hours. It took the skinned side of elk 25 hours to reach 3 degrees Centigrade (38 degrees Fahrenheit), while the hide side cooled to only 7 degrees Centigrade (45 degrees Fahrenheit) after the same period of time. However, they recommended leaving the skin on both elk and mule deer carcasses if the nighttime temperature was expected to be below freezing. These recommendations were based on consideration for the meat's cleanliness, moisture and flavor.

Obviously, a carcass will remain cleaner if the hide is left on, especially during transportation. Interestingly enough, even if the

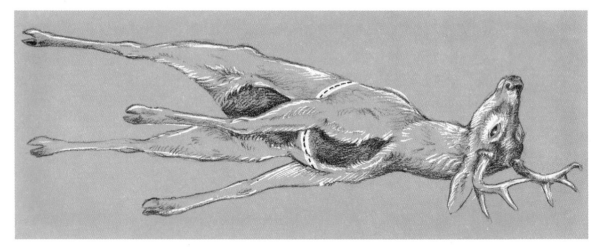

Figure 73. Diagram showing location of diaphragm.

hide is left on for several days of aging, there appears to be little loss of flavor. This assumes that the carcass was chilled and aged at the proper temperature. Field et al. (1973a) compared flavor differences of roasts from skinned and unskinned deer carcasses after two weeks of aging. A panel of trained tasters found no differences in taste. In addition, no significant differences were noted in flavor among meat from bucks and does.

In their work with elk carcasses, Field et al. (1973b) reported sides of elk aged with the hides on lost 2.8 kilograms (6.2 pounds) of moisture in a two-week period. Skinned sides of elk lost 3.6 kilograms (8 pounds) of moisture in the same period. In addition, they noted "the hide prevented some mold and bacterial growth on the outside surface of the carcass and prevented the lean from becoming dark and dry. Therefore, waste from trimming dried and darkened lean should have been lower from the hide side."

In warm weather, it is desirable that the carcass be taken to a refrigerator or cooler the day of the kill. If this is not possible, the carcass should be taken to camp or home. If the nighttime temperature is expected to

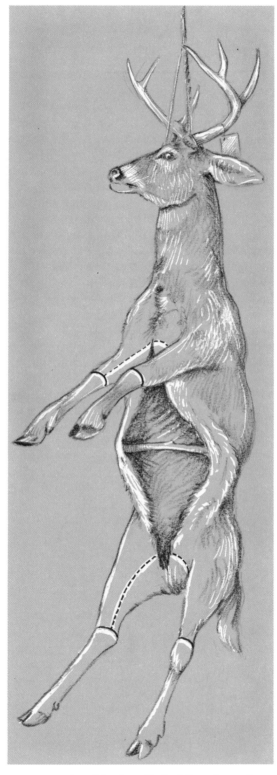

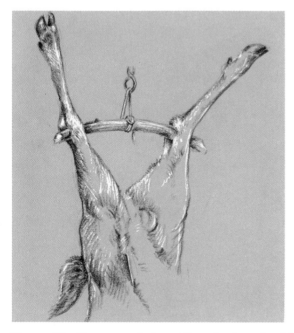

Figure 74. Recommended positions for hanging big game carcass for skinning. Dotted line shows location for cuts through the skin.

be above freezing, the carcass should be skinned.

If skinning is necessary, the carcass should be hung either by the hocks or head for ease and cleanliness during the skinning process. The skin is cut around the neck just below the head (assuming the head is not to be mounted) and around each leg above the hock, then up the inside of each leg to the center cut, as shown in Figure 74. Then, it is possible to work from top to bottom, and separate the hide from the carcass. One should leave as much fat, connective tissue and muscle fibers on the carcass as possible. It is best to avoid getting hair and dirt on the carcass and cutting holes in the hide. The skinned carcass then should be covered with an old sheet or cheesecloth to protect it from insects and dirt. Sprinkling black pepper on exposed meat will help keep flies away.

Transportation

Getting a big game carcass from the kill site to a camp or vehicle frequently is the most difficult task a hunter must face. Often, an eviscerated carcass can be dragged to a road and then loaded into or onto a vehicle. Many times, however, the animal is simply too big to drag or carry even for a short distance. This necessitates field skinning and quartering.

If the carcass cannot be hung, it can be skinned on the ground with a minimum amount of dirt getting on the meat. The carcass should be positioned so that it is lying on one side. The two upper legs are raised and held back so they may be skinned; it may be necessary to tie these legs to a tree to hold them in an elevated position. The upper half of the carcass is skinned leaving the hide attached along the vertebral column. The hide can be stretched back from the carcass. This will serve as a ground cloth for rolling the animal over on its other side and skinning the other half.

The carcass then should be halved or quartered for packing out. Normally, this is accomplished using a pack frame or with the

For big game hunting in many areas, the use of horses with pack frames is necessary for packing-out harvested animals. Photo courtesy of the Wyoming Game and Fish Department.

aid of horses equipped with a pack saddle and panniers.

Transporting a big game carcass in a vehicle for a few hours is seldom a problem. The carcass should be kept as clean and cool as possible. For long trips or in warm weather, it is advisable to place bags of dry ice in and around the carcass to keep it cool. For trips of several hundred kilometers, or in temperatures consistently above 21 degrees Centigrade (70 degrees Fahrenheit), the carcass should be butchered, frozen, packed in dry ice, and driven or flown to its destination.

Aging

The purpose of aging a carcass is to make the meat more tender (Table 45). If the entire carcass is to be processed into ground or stewing meats, there is no need to age it. It is advisable not to age the carcass longer than necessary, however, to minimize excessive carcass shrinkage and bacterial growth. The following aging recommendations are for temperatures at 4 degrees Centigrade (40 degrees Fahrenheit): pronghorn, 3 days; deer and cow elk, 7 days; bull elk, 14 days (Field et al. 1972, 1973a, 1973b). No research data are available to make specific recommendations for other big game species, although it seems logical that periods of one to two weeks would be acceptable.

It is possible to age a carcass too long. Meat will become too tender if aged for an excessive period. Steaks or roasts with a "liverlike" consistency are to be avoided just as are overly tough steaks and roasts.

Table 45. Tenderness differences for aged elk meat (after Field et al. 1973b).

Aging time	Warner-Bratzler shear values in kilograms[a]	
	Bulls (N = 6)	Cows (N = 6)
1 day	3.75	4.01
14 days	2.99	2.22

[a]Lower values mean more tender meat. Values are in kilograms of force to shear 1.3-centimeter (0.5-inch) diameter cores of rib eye muscle roasted to an internal temperature of 71 degrees Centigrade (160 degrees Fahrenheit).

Temperatures warmer than 4 degrees Centigrade (40 degrees Fahrenheit) will shorten the recommended aging period. If the carcass is exposed to 15–21 degree Centigrade (60–70 degree Fahrenheit) temperatures during the day, it should be butchered and frozen within a few days. A carcass always should be aged in the shade. If the hide has been removed, aging time should be reduced to prevent the carcass from drying out. After aging, the carcass is ready for butchering and freezing.

BUTCHERING

Deciding whether to cut up a big game animal or to pay a professional butcher for that service can be a difficult decision, especially for the novice. Locker plants have the advantage of cold storage facilities for cooling and aging the carcass. Rates in most sections of the country range from $25–$45 to have a deer, pronghorn or similar-sized animal skinned, butchered, wrapped and frozen, and $75–$100 for an animal the size of an elk.

An unheated garage, porch or shed, where the carcass can hang in cool weather (near freezing or below at night), is required for home-aging. Aging is not a necessary process, but if not done, the meat may be less tender than desired, depending on the species and age of the animal.

Advantages in butchering a big game carcass by the hunter include: (1) saving money; (2) cutting, wrapping and labeling exactly as desired; and (3) learning more about the anatomy and condition of the animal which, in turn, may make the hunter a more knowledgeable marksman and teach him the need for proper care of his kill. Furthermore, there may be no other options. Because of more stringent federal legislation regarding the commercial processing of wild game, many meat-processing facilities have closed their doors to hunters who want big game carcasses butchered. A person should expect to spend one or two evenings completing the job of skinning, cutting and wrapping a carcass.

Equipment

Required equipment for butchering meat includes a sharp knife, a sharpening stone and steel to keep the knife sharp, freezer wrapping paper, freezer tape and a marking pen. Desirable equipment includes a large cutting board, two containers—one for bones and meat scraps and one for burger and stew meats—(plastic pails, roasters, or cardboard boxes lined with freezer wrapping paper work well), and a butcher saw.

Trimming

The head of a carcass can be removed by cutting through the muscles at the base of the head between the skull and the first neck vertebra, then twisting it off.

The meatless lower legs can be removed with a saw or by cutting through the ligaments and cartilage at joints with a knife and twisting them off.

Cutting

Cutting can be made simple or difficult, depending on the types and size of meat cuts the person wishes to produce. Many hunters simply cut all the meat off the skeleton and have it ground for use as "hamburger,"

sausage, salami, etc. Others use the boneless meat for jerky or stew meat. Still others cut up a big game carcass as one would cut up beef, making several kinds of steaks and roasts as well as ribs and hamburger.

The decision on how to cut up a big game carcass should be based on the individual's preferences for meats and, to some extent, on the size of the carcass. For example, if it is a small pronghorn or deer and the family uses ground meat frequently, grinding most of the meat for this use would be a wise suggestion. On the other hand, a large elk or moose could be processed into many cuts to add variety to the larder.

Estimates of expected yields and losses from some typical big game animals are given in Table 46. Yields and losses will vary, depending primarily on the size of the animal and shot placement. An animal shot in the head will have a higher-than-average yield, while an animal with a single wound or multiple wounds in the legs, shoulders or loin will have a lower yield. Also, a carcass butchered without aging or with less than two weeks of aging will have proportionately higher yields because less moisture is lost and shrinkage is reduced.

The following procedures will provide a variety of cuts, including steaks, roasts and ground meat. As mentioned earlier, this can

Table 46. Average yields and weight losses from various harvested big game animals (after Field et al. 1972, 1973a, 1973b).[a]

| Big game animal | Field-dressed weight[b] | Losses | | | | Packaged cuts with bones left in leg, loin, rib and shoulder cuts | Packaged cuts without bones | Percent of field-dressed weight of packaged cuts without bone |
		Head	Skin	Aging	Cutting and trimming			
Pronghorn male	34.7(76.7)	2.8(7.1)	2.7(5.9)	3.2(7.0)	5.7(12.5)	20.0(44.2)	16.3(36.0)	47.0
Pronghorn female	31.0(68.5)	2.4(5.3)	2.3(5.1)	3.0(6.7)	5.7(12.6)	17.6(38.8)	14.3(31.6)	46.0
Mule deer male	51.5(113.7)	3.8(8.4)	4.2(9.3)	2.3(5.1)	11.3(25.0)	29.9(65.9)	24.7(54.6)	48.0
Mule deer female	41.9(92.6)	2.6(5.7)	3.6(8.0)	2.6(5.7)	9.4(20.7)	23.8(52.5)	20.1(44.4)	48.0
Elk male	197.9(437.0)	17.7(39.0)	15.4(34.0)	6.3(14.0)	51.6(114.0)	106.9(236.0)	85.2(188.0)	43.0
Elk female	153.6(339.0)	8.6(19.0)	11.8(26.0)	5.4(12.0)	39.4(87.0)	88.3(195.0)	66.1(146.0)	43.0

[a]Weight in kilograms; pounds in parenthesis.
[b]Eviscerated carcass with only the legs cut off, at lower knees and hocks.

Cutting meat is most efficient when done section by section. This procedure also allows uncut portions of the carcass to continue to cool and age. Photo by Don Domenick; courtesy of the Colorado Division of Wildlife.

be varied to personal preference. With this procedure, it is assumed that the carcass is hanging by its hocks, the most standard position. If the carcass is hanging by its head or lying on a table, however, the method can be changed accordingly. It is easiest to work with one part at a time while leaving the rest of the carcass hanging in a cool location. Figure 75 may be useful for determining location of various cuts.

One of the front legs and shoulders is removed from the rib cage. No saw is necessary. The muscles of the shoulder can be separated and made into steaks or roasts. The shank should be cut for stew or ground meat. The other front leg and shoulder can be removed and treated in a similar fash-

ion. As much meat as possible should be trimmed from the neck; it makes excellent mincemeat, stew or ground meat.

Boneless flanks are removed by cutting along the last rib down to the loin, along the loin to the leg, then down the leg. This section can be used for ground meat or jerky. On larger animals, flanks may be thick enough to be used as steak.

Next, each loin is removed at the backbone. The entire length of the loin can be cut next to the dorsal spines. The next cut is along the lateral spines of the backbone. The loin is severed where attached at the small of the back. Loosely attached meat near the neck end of the loin is good for stews, ground meat or other uses, but does not have the

447

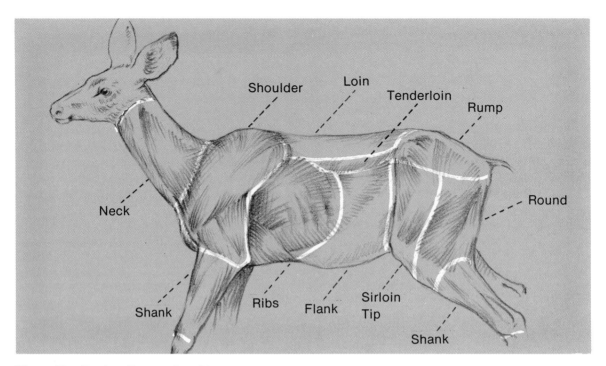

Figure 75. Cutting diagram for a big game carcass.

tenderness of steaks and should not be used as such. The loin is most suitable for steaks. Steaks should be cut crossways, 2.0–2.5 centimeters (0.75–1.0 inch) thick.

From loins of smaller big game animals, such as deer, it is recommended that butterfly steaks be made by cutting sections about 5 centimeters (2 inches) thick and cutting them almost in half, but leaving enough connective tissue to hold both halves together, as shown in Figure 76.

The meat on and between ribs can be cut off with a knife and used as ground meat or jerky. To prepare ribs for barbecuing, the ribs are sawed into 13–18 centimeter (5–7 inch) pieces. They then can be cut into desired widths, but usually are two to four ribs wide, depending on the size of the animal. Ribs also can be cut into shorter pieces and used in a stew.

The tenderloin is a small muscle connected to the underside of the backbone just in front of the pelvic area. It should be cut from the backbone. It, along with the loin, is one of the most tender pieces of meat and is

most suitable for steaks. Tenderloin from deer-sized big game can be cooked whole. Larger tenderloins may be made into butterfly steaks as previously described. To avoid excessive drying, many hunters remove the tenderloins before aging their big game carcasses.

The backbone is removed just in front of the hind legs. The two hind legs are separated by sawing through the middle of the backbone. The rump roast is removed by cutting off the upper end of the leg. This cut should go through the ball and socket joint.

The sirloin tip is the football-shaped muscle at the front of the hind leg. It is removed next. It makes an excellent roast. The large muscles of the round (upper part) of the leg can be cooked whole as roasts or cut into steaks.

The shank of the hind leg, like that of the foreleg, contains considerable connective tissue and probably is best for ground or stew meat. The remaining bones also can be used. The backbone can be cut into sections and used in making soup.

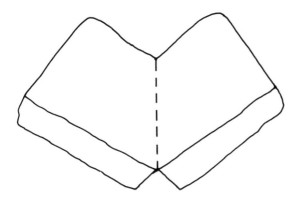

Figure 76. Diagram of a butterfly steak.

Ground meat and jerky

If a meat grinder is not available, many commercial locker plants will grind meat at a nominal cost. Big game meat does not contain nearly as much fat as does beef and, for ground meats, most people find it desirable to add about 20 percent beef suet. For making breakfast sausage, 30–35 percent pork fat can be added.

In addition to breakfast sausage and hamburger, there are several other delicacies one can make with the ground meat. Many locker plants make excellent salami and Polish, Italian and German sausage or bratwurst from big game meat. Jerky is another taste treat. Some locker plants will prepare it, although the process is very simple and can be done easily at home.

Many jerky recipes are available, but all involve cutting the meat into slices approximately 0.6 centimeters (0.25 inches) thick by whatever length and width is preferred. This is most easily done by chilling the meat until it is nearly frozen before slicing; this makes it much easier to cut thin strips. Then the meat must be seasoned and dried. The simplest method is to salt to taste and dry on oven racks, either with or without heat, depending on how quickly one wants to finish the job, utility rates, or both. Other seasonings called for by more complex recipes include: seasoned salt, popcorn salt, pepper, seasoned pepper, garlic powder, onion powder, Worcestershire sauce, soy sauce, sugar cure and liquid smoke. Meat strips frequently are marinated overnight in a solution of these seasonings before drying. The jerky may be dried in a smokehouse as well, in which case the liquid smoke could be omitted.

Wrapping, labeling and freezing

As much fat as possible should be trimmed off meat before wrapping. Meat should be wrapped in freezer paper designed especially for that purpose. It can be purchased at most grocery stores. Double wrapping is recommended if meat is to be frozen for several months. Steaks in a single package can be divided by two pieces of freezer paper to allow easy separation prior to thawing.

All packages should be labeled precisely as to contents and date. Loin steaks, for example, should be labeled differently than round steaks. Dating is particularly important if there is more than one carcass in the same storage unit or if meat is stored for a long period of time.

After wrapping, packages should be quick frozen at minus 18 degrees Centigrade (0 degrees Fahrenheit) or colder. Packages should be spread out on freezer shelves until frozen solid, after which time they may be stacked or placed in freezer drawers. Ideally, meat should be eaten within six months.

TROPHY CARE

If a hunter wishes to have a head-and-shoulder or full body mount or a "fur on" rug made, certain precautions need to be taken. Anytime the fur is to be preserved on the hide, it is critical that the skin be removed and salted soon after the animal's death, especially in warmer climates. To delay may cause "slipping," a condition in which the hair falls off the hide after the tanning process and ruins the hide for its intended use.

As indicated earlier, proper shot placement is essential. An improperly placed shot may create so much damage to the hide that it will be impossible for a taxidermist to repair.

Head-and-shoulder mounts of hooved mammals tend to be more popular than other trophy mounts. Therefore, these will be discussed in some detail. The initial cuts should be made as shown in Figure 77. Starting at the shoulder, the skin should be peeled forward until the base of the ears and antlers are reached. It is necessary to cut carefully around the base of the antlers or horns, if present, and to make sure all the flesh and hair remain with the cape. The ear should be skinned on its back side nearly to the tip. The ear cartilage should be cut as close to the skull as possible. When the cape is removed, a liberal quantity of salt should be applied to the ear and cartilage. The ear then is pushed back to its original shape.

Skinning should be continued toward the muzzle. One must be especially careful around the eyes. Eyelashes and the entire

Table 47. Quantities of salt required for adequate drying and tanning of big game hides (after Rockwell 1971)

Species	Hide part	Salt Kilograms	Pounds
Pronghorn	Cape	0.9	2.0
Bison	Cape	2.7	6.0
Caribou	Cape	1.8	4.0
Deer	Cape	1.4	3.1
Elk	Cape	2.3	5.1
Moose	Cape	2.7	6.0
Mountain goat	Cape	1.8	4.0
Musk-ox	Cape	2.7	6.0
Mountain sheep	Cape	1.8	4.0
Pronghorn	Whole	1.4	3.1
Bison	Whole	8.1	17.9
Caribou	Whole	3.6	8.0
Deer	Whole	2.3	5.1
Elk	Whole	5.4	11.9
Moose	Whole	8.1	17.9
Mountain goat	Whole	3.1	7.0
Musk-ox	Whole	5.4	11.9
Mountain sheep	Whole	3.2	7.1
Alaskan brown bear	Whole	8.1	17.9
Black bear	Whole	2.2	4.9
Grizzly bear	Whole	5.4	11.9
Polar bear	Whole	6.7	14.8
Mountain lion	Whole	2.7	6.0

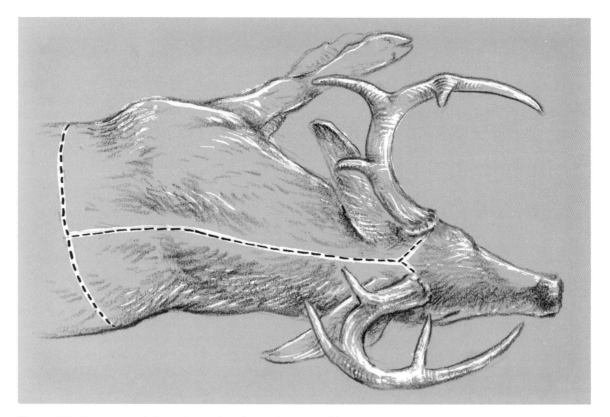

Figure 77. Recommended cutting points for caping-out a big game carcass.

eye gland, if present, should remain with the cape. The nose and mouth area also require extra attention. It is necessary to include the skin extending into the nostrils and into the mouth. After the cape is removed, the underside of the lips is split with a knife and salted liberally. The lips have the thickest skin on the cape and salt cannot penetrate to the middle without splitting them.

The cape is laid fur-side down and salt applied freely and rubbed into the entire fleshy side. The cape then can be folded (flesh to flesh) and rolled up. After approximately 12 hours, it should be unrolled and resalted. It is then rolled up again and kept cool until taken to a taxidermist for tanning. The cape should never be exposed to the sun or excess heat, such as a fire. Amounts of salt normally required for thorough drying are shown in Table 47.

For an antler or horn mount, the entire skull does not need to be saved, only the top of the skull with the horns or antlers attached. This "cap" should be removed with a saw.

Hunters wishing to make leather from a hide should follow the procedures described under "Skinning," and the entire hide should be salted as described above. Since fur will be removed anyway, it is not essential that the carcass be skinned soon after death. Skinning can wait until the animal has aged two weeks, if desired.

ALPHABETICAL LIST OF PLANTS MENTIONED IN TEXT [a]

Alder	*Alnus* sp.
Alfalfa	*Medicago sativa*
Angelica	*Angelica dawsoni*
Apple	*Pyrus malus*
Arctic poppy	*Papaver radicatum*
Ash	*Fraxinus* sp.
Aspen	*Populus* spp.
Aspen, quaking	*P. tremuloides*
Basswood	*Tilia* sp.
Bearberry or Kinnikinick	*Arctostaphylos uva-ursi*
Beard tongue	*Penstemon* sp.
Beargrass	*Xerophyllum tenax*
Beech, American	*Fagus grandifolia*
Birch, dwarf	*Betula nana*
Birch, dwarf (shrub)	*B. glandulosa*
Birch, white (paper)	*B. papyrifera*
Biscuit-root	*Lomatium cous* (simplex)
Bisnoga	*Ferocactus wizlizenii*
Bitterbrush	*Purshia tridentata*
Blackberry	*Rubus* sp.
Bladder campion	*Melandrium triflorum*
Blueberry	*Vaccinum* spp.
Blueberry, western	*V. occidentale*
Bluegrass	*Poa* spp.
Bluejoint or reed bentgrass	*Calamagrostis canadensis*
Burroweed	*Haplopappus tenuisectus*
Bursage	*Franseria* sp.
Catclaw	*Acacia* sp.
Cedar, white	*Thuga occidentalis*
Century plants	*Agave* spp.
Chamise	*Adenostemma faciculatum*
Cherry	*Prunus* spp.
Chokecherry	*Prunus virginiana*
Clover, white	*Trifolium repens*
Cottongrass	*Eriophorum* spp.
Cottongrass, narrow-leafed	*E. angustifolium*
Cottonwood	*Populus* sp.
Covina	*Brodiaea pulshellum*
Cow-parsnip	*Heraculeum lanatum*
Creosote bush	*Larrea tridentata*
Crowberry, black	*Empetrum nigrum*

[a]Primary source of information from Fernald, ed. (1950). Scientific names also reviewed by Stanwyn G. Shetler, Department of Botany, Smithsonian Institution, Washington, D.C.

Currant	*Ribes* sp.
Dandelion	*Taraxacum officinale*
Desert mariposa	*Calochortus kennedyi*
Dock	*Rumex* sp.
Dogwood	*Cornus* spp.
Dogwood, red osier	*C. stolonifera*
Dwarf cornel	*Cornus europea*
Ebony	*Pithecellobium flexicaule*
Englemann spruce	*Picea engelmannii*
Fescue	*Festuca* spp.
Filaree	*Erodium cicutarium*
Fir	*Abies* spp.
Fir, alpine	*Abies lasiocarpa*
Fir, balsam	*A. balsiferma*
Fireweed	*Epilobium angustifolium*
Fireweed, dwarf	*E. latifolium*
Foxtail, alpine	*Alopecurus alpinus*
Glacier-lily	*Erythronium grandiflorum*
Grouseberry	*Vaccinum scoparium*
Grass, alkali	*Puccinellia* sp.
Grass, beach rye	*Elymus arenarius*
Grass, brome	*Bromus* sp.
Gum, black	*Nyssa sylvatica*
Hairgrass	*Deschampsia brevifolia*
Hawkweed	*Hieracium* sp.
Hawthorn	*Crataegus* sp.
Hazelnut	*Corylus* spp.
Hazelnut, beaked	*C. cornuta*
Hemlock	*Tsuga* spp.
Hemlock, alpine	*T. mertensiana*
Hobblebush or witch-hobble	*Viburnum alnifolium*
Honeysuckle	*Lonicera* sp.
Horsetail, common	*Equisetum arvense*
Huckleberry	*Gaylusacia* sp.
Jojoba	*Simmondsia chinensis*
Juniper	*Juniperus* spp.
Juniper, western	*J. deppeana*
Labrador tea	*Ledum* sp.
Larch	*Larix* sp.
Lechuguilla	*Agave lecheguilla*
Lichen	*Cladonia* spp.
Lovage	*Ligusticum multenoides*
Manzanita	*Arctostaphylos* sp.
Maple	*Acer* spp.
Maple, mountain	*A. glabrum*
Maple, red	*A. rubra*
Maple, striped	*A. pensylvanicum*
Maple, sugar	*A. saccharum*
Mesquite	*Prosopis* spp.
Mesquite, honey	*P. juliflora*
Milk-vetch	*Astragalus* sp.
Missouri gourd or Buffalo gourd	*Cucurbita foetidissima*
Mountain-ash	*Sorbus* sp.
Mountain-avens or dryad	*Dryas* sp.
Mountain-cranberry	*Vaccinium vitis-idaca*
Mountain-heather	*Cassiope tetragona*
Mountainmahogany	*Cercocarpus* sp.
Mountain-sorrel	*Oxyria digyna*
Nagoon-berry	*Rubus arcticus*
Oak	*Quercus* spp.

Oak, black	*Q. kelloggii*
Oak, water	*Q. lobata*
Oak, white	*Q. alba*
Oak, willow	*Q. phellos*
Oregon tea-tree	*Ceanothus sanguineas*
Painted-cup or Indian paintbrush	*Castilleja* sp.
Paloverde	*Cercidium* sp.
Pea or Peavine	*Lathyrus* sp.
Pendant-grass	*Arctophila fulva*
Pin-cherry	*Prunus pensylvanica*
Pine	*Pinus* spp.
Pine, jack	*P. banksiana*
Pine, lodgepole	*P. contorta*
Pine, pinyon	*P. edulis*
Pine, ponderosa	*P. ponderosa*
Pine, whitebark	*P. albicaulis*
Prairie-mimosa	*Desmanthus* sp.
Prickly pear	*Opuntia phaeacantha*
Purple moonflower	*Ipomocea muricata*
Sagebrush	*Artemisia* spp.
Sagebrush, big	*A. tridentata*
Saguaro	*Carnegiea gigantea*
Saltbush	*Atriplex argentea*
Sand-verbena	*Abronia* sp.
Sassafras	*Sassafras albidum*
Saxifrages	*Saxifraga* spp.
Saxifrage, purple mountain	*S. oppositifolia*
Sedges	*Carex* spp.
Serviceberry	*Amelanchier alnifolia*
Snowberry	*Symphoricarpus albus*
Soapberry	*Shepherdia canadensis*
Solomon's seal	*Smilacina* spp.
Spring beauty	*Claytonia lanceolata*
Spruce	*Picea* spp.
Spruce, Englemann	*P. engelmannii*
Spruce, white	*P. glauca*
Sumac, staghorn	*Rhus glabra*
Sweet cicely	*Osmorhiza* sp.
Sweet clover	*Melilotus* sp.
Sweetgale	*Myrica gale*
Sweet gum	*Liquidambar stryraciflua*
Thistle, Canada	*Cirsium arvense*
Twisted cottonwood	*Populus balsamifera*
Vetch	*Vicia* sp.
Wheatgrass	*Agropyron* spp.
Wheatgrass, crested	*A. cristatum*
Wild grape	*Vitis* sp.
Wild onion	*Allium* sp.
Willow	*Salix* spp.
Willow, diamond-leafed	*S. pulchra*
Willow, polar	*S. polaris*
Woodrush, snow	*Luzula nivalis*
Yampah	*Perideridia gairdneri*

ALPHABETICAL LIST OF ANIMALS MENTIONED IN TEXT [a]

Armadillo	*Dasypus novemcinctus*
Armadillo, giant	*Priodontes giganteus*
Antelope, Saiga	*Saiga tatarica*
Badger	*Taxidea taxus*
Bear, Asian black	*Selenarctos thibetanus*
Bear, American black	*Ursus americanus*
Bear, brown (grizzly)	*U. arctos*
Bear, Kodiac	*U. a. middendorfi*
Bear, polar	*U. maritimus*
Bear, spectacled	*Tremarctos ornatus*
Beaver	*Castor canadensis*
Bison, plains	*Bison bison bison*
Bison, wood	*B. b. athabascae*
Bobcat	*Lynx rufus*
Caribou, Dawson	*Rangifer tarandus dawsoni*
Caribou, Grant's	*R. t. granti*
Caribou, Greenland (East)	*R. t. eogroenlandicus*
Caribou, Greenland (West)	*R. t. groenlandicus*
Caribou, Peary's	*R. t. pearyi*
Caribou, woodland	*R. t. caribou*
Carp	*Cyprinus carpio*
Chamois	*Rupricapra rupricapra*
Coyote	*Canis latrans*
Deer, axis	*Axis axis*
Deer, black-tailed, Columbian	*Odocoileus hemionus columbianus*
Deer, black-tailed, Sitka	*O. h. sitkensis*
Deer, fallow	*Dama dama*
Deer, mule, burro	*Odocoileus hemionus eremicus*
Deer, mule, California	*O. h. californicus*
Deer, mule, Cedros Island	*O. h. cerrosensis*
Deer, mule, desert	*O. h. crooki*
Deer, mule, Inyo	*O. h. inyoensis*
Deer, mule, peninsula	*O. h. peninsulae*
Deer, mule, Rocky Mountain	*O. h. hemionus*
Deer, mule, southern	*O. h. fuliginatus*
Deer, mule, Tiburon Island	*O. h. sheldoni*
Deer, red	*Cervus elaphus*
Deer, roe	*Capreolus capreolus*
Deer, sambar	*Cervus unicolor*
Deer, sika	*Cervus nippon*
Deer, white-tailed, Acapulco	*Odocoileus virginianus acapulcensis*

[a]Primary sources of names for mammals from Hall and Kelson (1959) and Walker and Paradiso (1968). Scientific names also reviewed by Richard C. Banks, National Fish and Wildlife Laboratory, U.S. Fish and Wildlife Service, Washington, D.C.

Deer, white-tailed, Avery Island	*O. v. mcilhennyi*
Deer, white-tailed, Blackbeard Island	*O. v. nigribarbis*
Deer, white-tailed, Bulls Island	*O. v. taurinsulae*
Deer, white-tailed, Carmen Mountains	*O. v. carminis*
Deer, white-tailed, Chiapas	*O. v. nelsoni*
Deer, white-tailed, Chiriqui	*O. v. chiriquensis*
Deer, white-tailed, Coiba Island	*O. v. rothschildi*
Deer, white-tailed, Columbian	*O. v. leucurus*
Deer, white-tailed, Coues	*O. v. couesi*
Deer, white-tailed, Dakota	*O. v. dacotensis*
Deer, white-tailed, Florida	*O. v. seminolus*
Deer, white-tailed, Florida coastal	*O. v. osceola*
Deer, white-tailed, Florida Key	*O. v. clavium*
Deer, white-tailed, Hilton Head Island	*O. v. hiltonensis*
Deer, white-tailed, Hunting Island	*O. v. venatorious*
Deer, white-tailed, Kansas	*O. v. macrourus*
Deer, white-tailed, Mexican lowland	*O. v. thomasi*
Deer, white-tailed, Mexican tableland	*O. v. mexicanus*
Deer, white-tailed, Miquihuana	*O. v. miquihuanensis*
Deer, white-tailed, Nicaragua	*O. v. truei*
Deer, white-tailed, northern Veracruz	*O. v. veraecrucis*
Deer, white-tailed, northern woodland	*O. v. borealis*
Deer, white-tailed, northwest	*O. v. ochrourus*
Deer, white-tailed, Oaxaca	*O. v. oaxacensis*
Deer, white-tailed, rain forest	*O. v. toltecus*
Deer, white-tailed, Sinaloa	*O. v. sinaloae*
Deer, white-tailed, Texas	*O. v. texanus*
Deer, white-tailed, Virginia	*O. v. virginianus*
Deer, white-tailed, Yucatan	*O. v. yucatanensis*
Eagle, golden	*Aquila chrysaetos*
Elk, eastern	*Cervus canadensis canadensis*
Elk, Manitoba	*C. c. manitobensis*
Elk, Merriam	*C. c. merriami*
Elk, Rocky Mountain	*C. c. nelsoni*
Elk, Roosevelt	*C. c. roosevelti*
Elk, Tule	*C. c. nannodes*
Fisher	*Martes pennanti*
Fly, nostril	*Gasterophilus haemorrhoidalis*
Fly, warble	*Hypoderma* sp.
Fox, gray	*Urocyon cinereoargenteus*
Fox, red	*Vulpes fulva*
Gemsbok (Kalahari oryx)	*Oryx gazella*
Goat	*Capra hircus*
Grouse, ruffed	*Bonasa umbellus*
Grouse, sage	*Centrocercus urophasianus*
Grouse, spruce	*Canachites canadensis*
Hare, showshoe	*Lepus americanus*
Hog	*Sus scrofa*
Ibex, Persian (Iranian)	*Capra aegagrus*
Ibex, Siberian	*C. siberica*
Jaguar	*Felis onca*
Lion, mountain	*Felis concolor*
Lynx, Canadian	*Lynx canadensis*
Magpies	*Pica* sp.
Marmot	*Marmota* sp.
Moose, Alaskan	*Alces alces gigas*
Moose, eastern	*A. a. americana*
Moose, northwestern	*A. a. andersoni*
Moose, Shira's	*A. a. shirasi*
Mountain goat, Alaskan	*Oreamnos americanus kennedyi*

Mountain goat, Columbian	*O. a. columbiae*
Mountain goat, rock (white)	*O. a. missoulae*
Mountain goat, Rocky Mountain	*O. a. americanus*
Musk-ox, barren-ground	*Ovibos moschatus moschatus*
Musk-ox, Hudson Bay	*O. m. niphoecus*
Musk-ox, white-fronted	*O. m. wardi*
Muskrat	*Ondatra zibethica*
Partridge, chukar	*Alectoris chukar*
Panda, giant	*Ailuropoda melanoleuca*
Peccary, Chacoan	*Catagonus wagneri*
Peccary, collared	*Dicotyles tajacu*
Peccary, white-lipped	*Tayassu peccari*
Pheasant, ring-necked	*Phasianus colchicus*
Pika	*Ochotona princeps*
Porcupine	*Erethizon* sp.
Pronghorn, American	*Antilocapra americana americana*
Pronghorn, Mexican	*A. a. mexicana*
Pronghorn, Oregon	*A. a. oregona*
Pronghorn, peninsular	*A. a. peninsularis*
Pronghorn, Sonoran	*A. a. sonoriensis*
Quail, bobwhite	*Colinus virginianus*
Raccoon	*Procyon lotor*
Raven	*Corvus* sp.
Reindeer	*Rangifer tarandus*
Robin	*Turdus migratorius*
Seal, ringed	*Phoca hispida*
Sheep, Barbary (Aoudad)	*Ammotragus lervia*
Sheep, Badlands bighorn (extinct)	*Ovis canadensis auduboni*
Sheep, California (Lava-bed) bighorn	*O. c. californiana*
Sheep, Lower California (Desert) bighorn	*O. c. cremnobates*
Sheep, Mexican (Desert) bighorn	*O. c. mexicana*
Sheep, Nelson's (Desert) bighorn	*O. c. nelsoni*
Sheep, Rocky Mountain bighorn	*O. c. canadensis*
Sheep, Weem's (Desert) bighorn	*O. c. weemsi*
Sheep, Dall's	*O. dalli dalli*
Sheep	*O. aries*
Sheep, Mouflon	*O. musimon*
Sheep, Siberian snow	*O. canadensis*
Sheep, Stone's	*O. dalli stonei*
Skunk, spotted	*Spilogale putorius*
Skunk, striped	*Mephitus mephitus*
Sparrow, English	*Passer domesticus*
Squirrel, ground	*Citellus* sp.
Starling	*Sturnus vulgaris*
Tahr	*Hemitragus jemlahicus*
Tick, cattle fever	*Boophilus annulatus*
Tick, moose	*Dermacenter albipictus*
Tick, wood	*Dermacentor andersoni*
Trout, brown	*Salmo trutta*
Turkey	*Meleagris gallopavo*
Warthog	*Phacochoerus aethiopicus*
Wolf	*Canis lupus*
Wolverine	*Gulo luscus*

REFERENCES CITED

Ahti, T. Unpubl. Preliminary survey of the range of woodland caribou in Ontario. Unpubl. Rep. On file at Wildl. Sect. Ontario Dep. of Lands and For., Maple. 7 pp.

———, and R. L. Hepburn. 1967. Preliminary studies of woodland caribou range, especially lichen stands in Ontario. Ontario Dep. of Lands and For., Res. Rep. (Wildl.) No. 74. 135 pp.

Alaska Department of Fish and Game. 1976. Status of the western Arctic caribou herd. Alaska Dep. Fish and Game, Wildl. Info. Leaf. No. 3. 4 pp.

Alendal, E. 1976. The muskox population (*Ovibos moschatus*) in Svalvard. Norsk Polarinst. Årbok 1974:159–174.

Allee, W. C., H. E. Emerson, O. Park, T. Park, and K. P. Schmidt. 1949. Principles of animal ecology. W. B. Saunders Co., Philadelphia, Pa. 837 pp.

Allen, D. L. 1967. The life of prairies and plains. Our Living World of Nature series. McGraw-Hill Book Company, New York. 232 pp.

———. 1970. Historical perspective. Pages 1–28 *in* National Research Council, Land Use and Wildlife Resources. National Academy of Sciences, Washington, D.C.

Allen, J. A. 1913. Ontogenetic and other variations in muskoxen, with a systematic review of the muskox group, recent and extinct. Mem. Amer. Mus. Nat. Hist. Vol. I, Part IV, pp. 103–226.

Allen, R. E., and D. R. McCullough. 1976. Deer-car accidents in southern Michigan. J. Wildl. Manage. 40(2):317–325.

Allred, W. J. 1943. Wyoming antelope—history and wartime management. Trans. N. Amer. Wildl. Conf. 8:117–122.

Alston, E. R. 1879. Biologia Centrali-American. Taylor and Francis, London. 220 pp.

Altmann, M. 1958. Social integration of the moose calf. Anim. Behav. 6:155–159.

———. 1959. Group dynamics of Wyoming moose during the rutting season. J. Mammal. 40(3):420–424.

Alvarez del Toro, M. 1952. Los animales silvestres de Chiapas. Ediciones del Gobierna del Estado, Tuxtla, Gutierrez, Chiapas. 247 pp.

Amory, C. 1975. Man kind? Our incredible war on wildlife. Dell Publishing Co., New York. 367 pp.

Anderson, A. E., and D. E. Medin. 1967. The breeding season in migratory mule deer. Colorado Div. Game, Fish and Parks Info. Leaf. 60. 4 pp.

———, and D. C. Bowden. 1972. Indices of carcass fat in a Colorado mule deer herd. J. Wildl. Manage. 36(2):579–594.

———. 1974. Growth and morphometry of the carcass, selected bones, organs and glands of mule deer. Wildl. Monogr. 39. 122 pp.

Anderson, A. E., W. A. Snyder, and G. W. Brown. 1965. Stomach content analyses related to condition in mule deer, Guadalupe Mountains, New Mexico. J. Wildl. Manage. 29(2):352–366.

Anderson, N. A. 1940. Mountain goat study. Bull. Wash. Dep. Game Biol. 2:1–21.

Anderson, R. C. 1964. Motor ataxia and paralysis in moose calves infected experimentally with *Pneumostrongylus tenuis* from a white-tailed deer. Path. Bet. 2:360–376.

———. 1972. The ecological relationships of meningeal worm and native cervids in North America. J. Wildl. Dis. 8:304–310.

———, and M. W. Lankester. 1974. Infectious and parasitic diseases and arthropod pests of moose in North America. Can. Nat. 101(1 and 2):23–50.

Anderson, R. H., W. G. Youatt, and D. E. Ullrey. A winter field test of food supplement blocks for deer. J. Wildl. Manage. 39(4):813–814.

Anderson, S. 1966. Re-establishing the musk-ox in West Greenland. Int. Zoo Yearbook. 6:229–230.

Andrewartha, H. G., and L. C. Birch. 1954. The distribution and abundance of animals. Univ. Chicago Press, Chicago, Ill. 782 pp.

Anthony, R. G., and A. A. Smith. 1974. Comparison of rumen and fecal analysis to describe deer diets. J. Wildl. Manage. 38(3):535–540.

Applegate, J. E. 1973. Some factors associated with attitudes toward deer hunting in New Jersey residents. Trans. N. Amer. Wildl. and Nat. Resour. Conf. 38:267–273.

———. 1975. Attitudes toward deer hunting in New Jersey: A second look. Wildl. Soc. Bull. 3(1):3–6.

Arizona Game and Fish Department. 1974. Arizona game management data summary. Arizona Game and Fish Dep., Phoenix. 92 pp.

Armstrong, G. A. 1965. An examination of the cementum of the teeth of Bovidae with special reference to its use in age determination. M.S. Thesis. Univ. Alberta, Edmonton. 72 pp.

Arrington, N., and A. E. Edwards. 1951. Predator control as a factor in antelope management. Trans. N. Amer. Wildl. and Nat. Resour. Conf. 16:179–193.

Asdell, S. A. 1964. Patterns of mammalian reproduction. Cornell Univ. Press, Ithaca, New York. viii and 670 pp.

Ashman, D. 1975. Mountain lion investigation. Nevada Dep. Fish and Game Performance Rep., Proj. W-48-6, Job No. 5. 18 pp.

Austin, D. D., P. J. Urness, and M. L. Wolfe. 1977. The influence of predator control on two adjacent wintering deer herds. Great Basin Nat. 37(1):101–102.

Bailey, V. 1926. A biological survey of North Dakota. N. Amer. Fauna No. 49. U.S. Dep. of Agriculture, Washington, D.C. 226 pp.

———. 1931. Mammals of New Mexico. N. Amer. Fauna No. 53. U.S. Dep. of Agriculture, Washington, D.C. 412 pp.

———. 1932. The Oregon antelope. Proc. Biol. Soc. 45:45–46.

Baker, R. H. 1956. Mammals of Coahuila, Mexico. Univ. Kansas Mus. Nat. Hist. 9:125–335.

———. 1958. The future of wildlife of northern Mexico—a problem in conservation education. Trans. N. Amer. Wildl. and Nat. Resour. Conf. 23:567–575.

———. In press. Origin, classification and distribution of the white-tailed deer. In L. K. Halls, ed. White-tailed deer: ecology and management. The Stackpole Co., Harrisburg, Pa.

Balser, D. S. 1974. An overview of predator-livestock problems with emphasis on livestock losses. Trans. N. Amer. Wildl. and Nat. Resour. Conf. 39:292–300.

Banasiak, C. F. 1961. Deer in Maine. Maine Dep. of Inland Fisheries and Game Bull. 6. 159 pp.

Bandy, P. J., I. McT. Cowan, and A. J. Wood. 1970. Comparative growth in four races of black-tailed deer (*Odocoileus hemionus*) Part 1. Growth. Can. J. Zoo. 48:1401–1410.

Banfield, A. W. F. 1958. Distribution of barren-ground grizzly bear in northern Canada. Nat. Mus. Can. Bull. 166:47–59.

———. 1961. A revision of the reindeer and caribou genus *Rangifer*. Nat. Mus. Can. Bull. 277. 137 pp.

———. 1974a. The mammals of Canada. Univ. Toronto Press, Toronto, Ont. 438 pp.

———. 1974b. The relationship of caribou migration behavior to pipeline construction. Pages 797–804. In V. Geist and F. Walther, eds. The behavior of ungulates and its relation to management. Vol. 2. IUCN New Ser. Publ. 24, Morges, Switzerland.

Bannikov, A. G., L. V. Zhirnov, L. S. Lebedeau, and A. A. Fandeev. 1961. Biology of the saiga. (Transl. from Russian.) U.S. Dep. of Commerce, Springfield, Va.

Barker, E. S. 1948. Antelope comeback. Field and Stream 53(4):26–27, 121–123.

Barnes, R. B. 1976. A quantitative evaluation of winter deer browse in southern New Hampshire forests. M.S. Thesis. Univ. of New Hampshire, Durham. 96 pp.

Barrett, J. P., and W. A. Guthrie. 1969. Optimum plot sampling in estimating browse. J. Wildl. Manage. 33(2):394–403.

Barrier, M. J., J. K. Reed, and L. G. Webb. 1971. Pesticide residues in selected tissues of the white-tailed deer, *Odocoileus virginianus*, in Calhoun County, South Carolina. Proc. S.E. Assoc. Game and Fish Commissioners 24th Annu. Conf., 1970. 24:31–45.

Barron, J. C., and W. F. Harwell. 1973. Fertilization rates of south Texas deer. J. Wildl. Manage. 37(2):179–182.

Baskin, L. M. 1970. Reindeer ecology and behaviour. (Transl. from Russian.) Navka, Moscow. Can. Wildl. Serv., Ottawa.

———. 1974. Management of ungulate herds in relation to domestication. Pages 530–541 in V. Geist and F. Walther, eds. The behavior of ungulates and its relation to management. Vol. 2. IUCN New Ser. Publ. 24, Morges, Switzerland.

Batcheler, C. L. 1968. Compensatory responses of artificially controlled mammal populations. Proc. N.Z. Ecol. Soc. 15:25–30.

Beale, D. M., and A. D. Smith. 1973. Mortality of pronghorn antelope fawns in western Utah. J. Wildl. Manage. 37(3):343–352.

Beasom, S. L. 1974a. Intensive short term predator removal as a game management tool. Trans. N. Amer. Wildl. and Nat. Resour. Conf. 39:230–240.

———. 1974b. Relationships between predator removal and white-tailed deer net productivity. J. Wildl. Manage. 38(4):854–859.

Becklund, W. W., and C. M. Senger. 1967. Parasites of *Ovis canadensis* in Montana with a checklist of the internal and external parasites of the Rocky Mountain bighorn sheep in North America. J. Parasitol. 53:157–165.

Beckwith, S. L., and L. G. Smith. 1968. Deer damage to citrus groves in south Florida. Proc. S.E. Assoc. Game and Fish Commissioners 21st Annu. Conf., 1967. 21:32–38.

Bedard, J., E. S. Telfer, J. Peek, P. C. Lent, M. C. Wolfe, D. W. Simkin, and R. W. Ritcey, eds. 1975. Alces: ecologie de l'original/moose ecology. Presses Université Laval, Quebec.

Beeman, L. E., and M. R. Pelton. 1977. Seasonal foods and feeding ecology of black bear in the Smoky Mountains. Paper read at the 4th International Conference on Bear Research and Management, 1977, Kalispell, Montana.

Beeman, L. E., J. J. Pelton, and D. C. Eager. 1977. Den selection of black bears in the Great Smoky Mountains National Park. Paper read at the 4th International Conference on Bear Research and Management, 1977, Kalispell, Montana.

Beer, J. 1944. Distribution and status of pronghorn antelope in Montana. J. Mammal. 25(1):43–46.

Behrend, D. F., and J. F. Witter. 1968. *Pneumostrongylus tenuis* in white-tailed deer in Maine. J. Wildl. Manage. 32(4):963–966.

Benson, W. A. 1956. A general view of the antelope in Saskatchewan. Proc. Fed.-Prov. Wildl. Conf. 20:23–34.

Bergerud, A. T. 1961. Sex determination of caribou calves. J. Wildl. Manage. 25(2):205.

———. 1963. Aerial winter census of caribou. J. Wildl. Manage. 27(3):438–449.

———. 1964. A field method to determine annual parturition rates for Newfoundland caribou. J. Wildl. Manage. 28(3):477–480.

———. 1967. Management of Labrador caribou. J. Wildl. Manage. 31(4):621–642.

———. 1971a. The population dynamics of Newfoundland caribou. Wildl. Monogr. 25. 55 pp.

———. 1971b. Hunting of stag caribou in Newfoundland. J. Wildl. Manage. 35(1):71–75.

———. 1971c. Abundance of forage on the winter range of Newfoundland caribou. Can. Field Nat. 85(1):39–52.

———. 1972. Food habits of Newfoundland caribou. J. Wildl. Manage. 36(3):913–923.

———. 1973. Movement and rutting behavior of caribou (*Rangifer tarandus*) at Mount Albert, Quebec. Can. Field Nat. 87(4):357–369.

———. 1974a. Rutting behavior of Newfoundland caribou. Pages 395–435 *in* V. Geist and F. Walther, eds. The behavior of ungulates and its relation to management. Vol. 1. IUCN New Ser. Publ. 24, Morges, Switzerland.

———. 1974b. The decline of caribou in North America following settlement. J. Wildl. Manage. 38(4):757–770.

———. 1974c. The role of the environment in the aggregation, movement and disturbance behavior of caribou. Pages 552–584 *in* V. Geist and F. Walther, eds. The behavior of ungulates and its relation to management. Vol. 2. IUCN New Ser. Publ. 24, Morges, Switzerland.

———. 1974d. Relative abundance of food in winter for Newfoundland caribou. Oikos 25:379–387.

———. 1977. Diets of caribou. Pages 243–266 *in* M. Recheigl Jr., ed. Diets for mammals. Vol. I. CRC Press, Cleveland, Oh. 645 pp.

———. In Press. The annual antler cycle in Newfoundland caribou. Can. Field. Nat.

Berryman, J. H. 1962. Wildlife: A community resource. Utah Sci. 23(1):16–17, 30.

Best, R. D. 1975. Ecological aspects of polar bear nutrition. Pages 203–211 *in* R. L. Phillips and C. Jonkel, eds. Proceedings of the 1975 Predator Symposium. Forest and Cons. Exp. Sta., Univ. of Montana, Missoula.

———. 1976. Ecological energetics of the polar bear (*Ursus maritimus* Phipps 1774). M.S. Thesis. Univ. Guelph, Ontario. 136 pp.

Betz, R. F. 1977. What is a prairie? The Nature Conservancy News 27(2):9–13.

Bevins, M. I., R. S. Bond, J. J. Corcoran, K. D. McIntosh, and R. J. McNeil. 1968. Characteristics of hunters and fishermen in six northeastern states. Univ. Vermont Agr. Exp. Sta. Bull. 565. 76 pp.

Biehn, E. R. 1951. Crop damage by wildlife in California. California Fish and Game Dep. Bull. No. 5. 71 pp.

Bigalke, R. C. 1974. Ungulate behavior and management, with special reference to husbandry of wild ungulates on South African ranches. Pages 830–852 *in* V. Geist and F.

Walther, eds. The behavior of ungulates and its relation to management. Vol. 2. IUCN New Ser. Publ. 24, Morges, Switzerland.

Bigler, W. J., and R. G. McLean. 1973. The potential of wildlife as sentinels for Venezuelan equine encephalitis activity. Wildl. Dis. Conf. Abstr. 1973:2.

Bindernagel, J. A., and R. C. Anderson. 1972. Distribution of meningeal worm (*Pneumostrongylus tenuis*) in white-tailed deer in Canada. J. Wildl. Manage. 36(4):1349–1353.

Bischoff, A. I. 1957. The breeding season of some California deer herds. Calif. Fish and Game 43(1):91–96.

Bishop, R. H., and R. A. Rausch. 1974. Moose population fluctuations in Alaska. Can. Nat. 101(1 and 2):559–593.

Bissonette, J. A. 1976. The relationship of resource quality to social behavior and organization in the collared peccary. Ph.D. Thesis. Univ. Michigan, Ann Arbor. 137 pp.

Biswell, H. H., R. D. Taber, D. W. Hedrick, and A. M. Schultze. 1952. Management of chamise brushlands in the north coast region of California. Calif. Fish and Game 38(4):453–484.

Bissell, H. D., B. Hams, H. Strong, and F. James. 1955. The digestibility of certain natural and artificial foods eaten by deer in California. Calif. Fish and Game 41(1):57–78.

Bittle, J. L. 1970. Feline panleukopenia. Pages 85–89 in J. W. Davis, L. H. Karstad, and D. O. Trainer, eds. Infectious diseases of wild animals. Iowa State Univ. Press, Ames.

Blaxter, K. L. 1962. The fasting metabolism of adult Wether sheep. Brit. J. Nutr. 16:615–626.

Blood, D. A. and A. L. Lovass. 1966. Measurement and weight relationships in Manitoba elk. J. Wildl. Manage. 30(1):135–140.

Blood, D. A., J. R. McGillis, and A. Lovass. 1967. Weights and measurements of moose in Elk Island National Park, Alberta. Can. Field Nat. 81(3):263–269.

Blood, D. A., D. R. Flook, and W. D. Wishart. 1970. Weights and growth of Rocky Mountain bighorn sheep in western Alberta. J. Wildl. Manage. 34(2):451–455.

Bobek, B., and R. Dzieciolowski. 1972. Method of browse estimation in different types of forests. Acta Ther. 17:171–186.

Bobek, B., A. Drozdz, W. Grodzinski, and J. Weiner. 1974. Studies on productivity of the roe deer population in Poland. Proc. XI Int. Cong. Game Biologists 11:115–123.

Boddicker, M. L., E. J. Hugghins, and A. H. Richardson. 1971. Parasites and pesticide residues of mountain goats in South Dakota. J. Wild. Manage. 35(1):94–103.

Boeker, I. L., V. E. Scott, H. G. Reynolds, and B. A. Donaldson. 1972. Seasonal food habits of mule deer in Southwestern New Mexico. J. Wildl. Manage. 36(1):56–63.

Bogue, G. L., and M. Ferrari. 1974. The predatory "training" of captive reared pumas. Pages 36–45 in R. L. Eaton ed. The world's cats. Vol. III, No. 1. Proceedings of the Third International Symposium on the World's Cats. Univ. of Washington, Seattle. 95 pp.

Bolle, A. W., and R. D. Taber. 1962. Economic aspects of wildlife abundance on private lands. Trans. N. Amer. Wildl. and Nat. Resour. Conf. 27:255–267.

Boone and Crockett Club. 1978. Quoted on foreword pages of booklet listing officers, by-laws and members, 1978. Boone and Crockett Club, Alexandria, Va. 25 pp.

Bormann, F. H. 1976. An inseparable linkage: conservation of natural ecosystems and the conservation of fossil energy. Bioscience 26(12):754–760.

Bos, G. N. 1967. Range types and their utilization by muskox on Nunivak Island, Alaska. M.S. Thesis. Univ. of Alaska, College. 113 pp.

———. 1975. A partial analysis of the current population status of the Nelchina caribou herd. Pages 170–180 in J. R. Luick, P. C. Lent, D. R. Klein, and R. B. White, eds. Proceedings, 1st International Reindeer/Caribou Symposium. Occ. Pap. No. 2, Inst. of Arctic Biology, Univ. of Alaska, College. 551 pp.

Bouchard, R. and C. Gauthier. 1976. Gros gibier au Quebec en 1975. Quebec Dep. Tourism, Fauna Quebec Spec. Rep. No. 6. 61 pp.

Boulding, K. E. 1956. Some contributions of economics to the general theory of value. Philos. Sci. 23(1):1–14.

Bowns, J. E. 1976. Field criteria for predator damage assessment. Utah Sci. 37(1):26–30.

Box, T. W., ed. 1973. Rehabilitation potential of western coal lands. Nat. Acad. Sci. Rep., Washington, D.C. 205 pp.

Boyd, R. J. 1958. Comparison of air and ground deer and elk counts. Quart. Progress Rep., Colorado Dep. Game and Fish, Oct.:145–146.

———. 1966. Rio Grande elk studies—physical characteristics. Colorado Game, Fish and Parks Dep. Game Res. Rep., July, Part 2:285–296.

———. 1967. Rio Grande elk studies—physical characteristics. Colorado Game, Fish and Parks Dep. Game Res. Rep. July, Part 2:247–249.

————. 1970. Elk of the White River Plateau, Colorado. Colorado Game, Fish and Parks Dep. Tech. Publ. No. 25. 126 pp.

————, and E. E. Ryland. 1971. Breeding dates of Colorado elk as estimated by fetal growth curves. Colorado Div. of Wildl. Info. Leaf. No. 88. 2 pp.

Boyd, R. J., T. M. Pojar, and B. D. Baker. 1975. Deer and elk management study. Colorado Div. of Wildl. Game Res. Rep. July, Part 2:365–412.

Brandborg, S. M. 1955. Life history and management of the mountain goat in Idaho. Idaho Dep. Fish and Game Wildl. Bull. 2. Pp. 1–142.

Brody, S. 1945. Bioenergetics and growth. Reinhold Co., New York. xiii and 1023 pp.

Brokx, P. A. In Press. White-tailed deer in South America. *In* L. K. Halls, ed. White-tailed deer: ecology and management. The Stackpole Co., Harrisburg, Pa.

Bromley, A. 1945. Evaluation of the New York State experimental cooperative landowner sportsmen controlled public hunting grounds program. Trans. N. Amer. Wildl. Conf. 10:9–29.

Bromley, P. T., and D. W. Kitchen. 1974. Courtship in the pronghorn (*Antilocapra americana*). Pages 356–364 *in* V. Geist and F. Walther, eds. The behavior of ungulates and its relation to management. Vol. I. IUCN New Ser. Publ. 24, Morges, Switzerland.

Brown, E. R. 1961. The black-tailed deer of western Washington. Washington State Game Dep. Biol. Bull. No. 13. 124 pp.

Brown, R. G. B. 1974. Bird damage to fruit crops in the Niagara peninsula. Can. Wildl. Serv. Rep. Ser. 26, Information Canada, Ottawa.

Brown, William H., J. W. Stull, and L. K. Sowls. 1963. Chemical composition of the milk fat of the collared peccary. J. Mammal. 44(1):112–113.

Brownlee, S. 1971. Composition and usage of plants by desert mule deer through rumen samples. Texas Parks and Wildl. Dep. Final Rep. Fed. Aid Proj. No. W-48-D-21, Job 3, Plan II. 45 pp.

Bruce, J. 1922. The why and how of mountain lion hunting in California. Calif. Fish and Game. 8(2):108–114.

Bruns, E. H. 1970. Winter predation of golden eagles and coyotes on pronghorn antelopes. Can. Field Nat. 84(4):301–304.

Bubenik, A. B. 1973. Hypothesis concerning the morphogenesis of moose antlers. Proc. 9th N. Amer. Moose Conf. and Workshop 9:195–321.

Buckley, J. L. 1957. Wildlife in the economy of Alaska. Univ. of Alaska Biol. Pap. No. 1, Fairbanks. 33 pp.

Buckley, J., D. Spencer, and P. Adams. 1954. Muskox (*Ovibos moschatus*) longevity. J. Mammal. 35(3):456.

Buechner, H. K. 1960a. The bighorn sheep in the United States, its past, present and future. Wildl. Monogr. 4. 174 pp.

————. 1960b. Regulation of numbers of pronghorn antelope in relation to land use. Int. Antelope Conf. Trans. 11:105–129.

————. 1974. Implications of social behavior in the management of Uganda kob. Pages 853–870 *in* V. Geist and F. Walther, eds. The behavior of ungulates and its relation to management. Vol 2. IUCN New Ser. Publ. 24, Morges, Switzerland.

Bunnell, F., D. C. Dauphine, R. Hilborn, D. R. Miller, F. L. Miller, E. H. McEwan, G. R. Parker, R. Peterman, G. W. Scotter, and J. C. Walters. 1975. Preliminary report on computer simulation of barren ground caribou management. Pages 189–193 *in* J. R. Luick, P. C. Lent, D. R. Klein, and K. B. White, eds. Proceedings, 1st International Reindeer/Caribou Symposium. Occ. Pap. No. 2. Inst. of Arctic Biology, Univ. of Alaska, College. 551 pp.

Burk, C. J. 1973. The Kaibab deer incident: a long persisting myth. Bioscience 23(2):113–114.

Burris, O. E., and D. E. McKnight. 1973. Game transplants in Alaska. Alaska Dep. Fish and Game Tech. Bull. 4. 57 pp.

Butzler, W. 1972. Rotwild. Bayerischer Land wirtschafts Verlag, Jagdbiologie, Munich. 165 pp.

Byford, J. L. 1971. Telemetrically determined movements of two white-tailed deer fawns in southwestern Alabama. Proc. S.E. Assoc. Game and Fish Commissioners 24th Annu. Conf., 1970. 24:57–63.

Cahalane, V. H. 1964. A preliminary study of distribution and numbers of cougars, grizzly and wolf in North America. New York Zoological Society, New York. 12 pp.

Cain, S. A., J. A. Kadlec, D. L. Allen, R. A. Cooley, M. G. Hornocker, A. S. Leopold, and F. H. Wagner. 1972. Predator control—1971. Report to the Council on Environmental Quality and the Department of the Interior by the Advisory Committee on Predator Control. Univ. Michigan Press, Ann Arbor. 207 pp.

Calef, G. W. 1974. The predicted effect of the Canadian Arctic gas pipeline project on the

Porcupine herd. Pages 101–120 *in* Research reports. Vol. IV of Environmental impact assessment of the portion the Mackenzie gas pipeline from Alaska to Alberta. Environment Protection Board, Winnipeg, Manitoba.

———. 1977. Status of the caribou in the Northwest Territories. Paper read at Symposium on Parameters of Caribou Population Ecology in Alaska, November 17–19, Fairbanks, Alaska.

Calhoun, J. B. 1948. Mortality and movement of brown rats *Rattus norwegicus* in artificially supersaturated populations. J. Wildl. Manage. 12(2):167–172.

Calhoun, J., and F. Loomis. 1974. Prairie whitetails. Illinois Dep. Cons., Springfield. 49 pp.

Carnie, S. K. 1954. Food habits of nesting golden eagles in the coast ranges of California. Condor 56(1):3–12.

Carpenter, L. H. 1972. Middle Park deer study-range fertilization. Pages 211–251 *in* Game Research Report, July 1972, Part Two. Colorado Div. Wildl., Denver.

———. 1976. Nitrogen-herbicide effects on sagebrush deer range. Ph.D. Thesis. Colorado State Univ., Fort Collins. xv and 159 pp.

Carroll, W. M. 1963. Deer economics and public policy. Pages 3–4 *in* Deer management in Pennsylvania. Pennsylvania State Univ. Coll. of Agr., Ext. Serv., University Park. 20 pp.

Casebeer, F. L. 1948. A study of the food habits of the mountain goat (*Oreamnos americanus missoulae*) in western Montana. M.S. Thesis. Univ. Montana, Missoula. 84 pp.

———, M. J. Rognrud, and S. Brandborg. 1950. Rocky Mountain goats in Montana. Montana Fish and Game Comm. Bull. 5:1–107.

Caton, J. D. 1877. The antelope and deer of America. Hurd Houghton, New York. 426 pp.

Caughley, G. 1970. Eruption of ungulate populations with emphasis on Himalayan thar in New Zealand. Ecology 51(1):53–72.

———. 1971. The season of birth for northern-hemisphere ungulates in New Zealand. Mammalia 35(2):204–219.

Chadwick, D. H. 1973. Mountain goat ecology—logging relationships in Bunker Creek drainage of western Montana. Montana Fish and Game Dep. Proj. W-120-R-3, 4. 262 pp.

Chalk, J. D., D. I. Rasmussen, F. C. Edminster, C. M. Reed, A. Nicholson, and J. P. Miller. 1940. Is the farmer-sportsman council the answer? Trans. N. Amer. Wildl. Conf. 5:54–72.

Chapman, D. G., and A. M. Johnson. 1968. Estimation of fur seal pup populations by ran-

domized sampling. Trans. Amer. Fish Soc. 97:264–270.

Chatelain, E. F. 1950. Bear-moose relationships on the Kenai Peninsula. Trans. N. Amer. Wildl. Conf. 15:224–234.

Cheatum, E. L., and C. W. Severinghaus. 1950. Variations in fertility of white-tailed deer related to range conditions. Trans. N. Amer. Wildl. Conf. 15:170–190.

Cherniavski, F. B. 1962. On the systematic relationships and history of the snow sheep of the Old and New Worlds [in Russian]. Bull. Moscow Soc. Nat. Biol. Sect. 68:17–26.

Chiavetta, K. J. 1958. Harvest antlerless deer! N.C. Wildl. 22(7):16–19.

Child, K. N. 1974. Reaction of caribou to various types of simulated pipelines at Prudhoe Bay, Alaska. Pages 805–812 *in* V. Geist and F. Walther, eds. The behavior of ungulates and its relation to management, Vol. 2. IUCN New Ser. Publ. 24, Morges, Switzerland.

———, and P. C. Lent. 1973. The reaction of reindeer to a pipeline simulation at Penny River, Alaska, interim report. Alaska Coop. Wildl. Res. Unit, Univ. of Alaska, College.

Church, D. C. 1972. Digestive physiology and nutrition of ruminants. Vol. 1 and 2. Oregon State Univ., Corvallis.

Clabby, J. 1976. The natural history of the horse. Taplinger Publishing Co. New York. 116 pp.

Clarke, C. H. D. 1940. Mammals of the Thelon Game Sanctuary. Nat. Mus. Can. Bull. 96. 135 pp.

———. Unpubl. Wildlife values in forestry in Ontario. Unpubl. On file at Colorado State University Library, Fort Collins, Colo. 14 pp. Multilith.

Clary, W. P., M. P. Baker, Jr., P. F. O'Connell, T. N. Johnsen, Jr., and R. E. Campbell. 1974. Effects of pinyon-juniper removal on natural resources products and uses in Arizona. USDA For. Serv. Res. Pap. RM-128. 28 pp.

Clawson, M. 1959. Methods of measuring the demand for and value of outdoor recreation. Repr. No. 10, Resources for the Future, Washington, D.C.

Coady, J. W. 1974. Influence of snow on behavior of moose. Can. Nat. 101(1 and 2):417–436.

———. 1976. Interior moose and moose disease studies. Vol. III, Prog. Rep. Fed. Aid in Wildl. Restoration. Alaska Dep. Fish and Game, Juneau. 26 pp.

Cochran, W. G. 1963. Sampling techniques, second edition. John Wiley Sons, New York. 413 pp.

Coggins, V. L., and G. G. Magera. 1973. Vehicle

restrictions, elk harvest and hunter behavior in the Chesnimnus Unit. Oregon Dep. of Fish and Wildl. Spec. Rep. 25 pp.

Cole, G. F. 1972. Grizzly bear-elk relationships in Yellowstone National Park. J. Wildl. Manage. 36(2):556–561.

———, and B. T. Wilkins. 1958. The pronghorn antelope, its range use and food habits in central Montana with special reference to wheat. Montana Fish and Game Dep. Tech. Bull. No. 2., Bozeman. 39 pp.

Colorado Division of Wildlife. 1975. 1975 Colorado big game harvest. Colorado Div. of Wildl., Denver. 198 pp.

———. 1976. Report of the special committee on recommendations for a regular deer and elk hunting season structure, 1977–1979. Colorado Div. of Wildl., Denver. 44 pp.

Colorado State University. 1969. Fish and wildlife resources on public lands. Colorado State Univ., Fort Collins. 326 pp.

Conaway, C. 1952. The age of sexual maturity in male elk (*Cervus canadensis*). J. Wildl. Manage. 16(3):313–315.

Connolly, G. E., and W. M. Longhurst. 1975. The effects of control on coyote populations. Univ. California-Davis, Div. Agr. Sci. Bull. 1872. 37 pp.

Connolly, G. E., R. M. Timm, W. E. Howard, and W. M. Longhurst. 1976. Sheep killing behavior of captive coyotes. J. Wildl. Manage. 40(3):400–407.

Cook, R. S., M. White, D. O. Trainer, and W. C. Glazener. 1971. Mortality of young white-tailed deer fawns in south Texas. J. Wildl. Manage. 35(1):47–56.

Cotton, D., and J. Herring. 1971. A preliminary survey of pesticide residues in white-tail deer (*Odocoileus virginianus*). Proc. S.E. Assoc. Game and Fish Commissioners 24th Annu. Conf., 1970. 24:23–30.

Cowan, I. McT. 1940. Distribution and variation in the native sheep of North America. Amer. Midl. Natur. 24:505–580.

———. 1944. Report of wildlife studies in Jasper, Banff and Yoho National Parks in 1944 and parasites, diseases and injuries of game animals in the Rocky Mountain National Parks, 1942–1944. Wildl. Serv., Dep. Mines and Resour., Ottawa. 83 pp.

———. 1947. The timber wolf in the Rocky Mountain National Parks of Canada. Can. J. Res. 25:139–174.

———. 1951. The diseases and parasites of big game mammals of western Canada. Proc. Annu. Game Conf. 5:37–64.

———. 1956a. What and where are the mule and black-tailed deer? Pages 334–339 *in* W. P. Taylor, ed. The deer of North America. The Stackpole Co., Harrisburg, Pa. 668 pp.

———. 1956b. Life and times of the coast black-tail deer. Pages 523–617 *in* W. P. Taylor, ed. The deer of North America. The Stackpole Co., Harrisburg, Pa. 668 pp.

———. 1972. The status and conservation of bears (Ursidae) of the world-1970. Pages 343–367 *in* S. Herrero, ed. Bears—their biology and conservation. IUCN New Ser. Publ. 23, Morges, Switzerland.

———. 1974. Management implications of behavior in the large herbivorous mammals. Pages 921–934 *in* V. Geist and F. Walther, eds. The behavior of ungulates and its relation to management. Vol. 2. IUCN New Ser. Publ. 24, Morges, Switzerland.

———, and V. C. Brink. 1949. Natural game licks in the Rocky Mountain National Parks of Canada. J. Mammal. 30(4):379–387.

Cowan, I. McT., and A. J. Wood. 1955. The growth rate of the black-tailed deer (*Odocoileus hemionous columbianus*). J. Wildl. Manage. 19(3):331–336.

———, and W. D. Kitts. 1957. Food requirements of deer, beaver, bear and mink for growth and maintenance. Trans. N. Amer. Wildl. Conf. 22:174–186.

Cowan, I. McT., and C. J. Guiguet. 1960. The mammals of British Columbia. B.C. Prov. Mus. Handbook II, Victoria. 414 pp.

Cowan, I. McT., and C. W. Holloway. 1978. Geographical location and current conservation status of the threatened deer of the world. Pages 11–22 *in* Threatened deer, proceedings of a working meeting of the Deer Specialist Group of the Survival Service Commission. IUCN, Morges, Switzerland. 434 pp.

Cowan, I. McT., and L. Karstad. 1969. Postmortem examinations. Pages 251–258 *in* Giles, R. H., ed. Wildlife management techniques. 3rd ed. The Wildlife Society, Washington, D.C.

Cowan, I. McT., and W. McCrory. 1970. Variation in the mountain goat, *Oreamnos americanus* (Blainville). J. Mammal. 51(1):60–73.

Cowan, I. McT., and V. Geist. 1971. The North American wild sheep. Pages 58–83 *in* R. C. Alberts, ed. North American big game. The Boone and Crockett Club. Pittsburgh, Pa.

Craighead, F. C. 1951. A biological and economic evaluation of coyote predation. N.Y. Zoological Society and the Conservation Foundation, N.Y. 23 pp.

———, and R. J. Dasmann. 1966. Exotic big

game on public lands. U.S. Dep. Interior, Bur. of Land Manage., Washington, D.C.

Craighead, F. C., Jr., and J. J. Craighead. 1972. Grizzly bear prehibernation and denning activities as determined by radio tracking. Wildl. Monogr. 32. 35 pp.

Craighead, J. J., and F. C. Craighead. 1971. Grizzly bear-man relationships in Yellowstone National Park. Bioscience 21(6):845–857.

Craighead, J. J., J. R. Varney, and F. C. Craighead. 1974. A population analysis of the Yellowstone grizzly bears. Montana For. and Cons. Exp. Sta. Bull. No. 40, Missoula. 20 pp.

Crawford, H. S., and J. B. Whelan. 1973. Estimating food intake by observing mastications by tractable deer. J. Range Manage. 26(5):372–375.

Crete, M. and J. Bedard. 1975. Daily browse consumption by moose in the Gaspé Peninsula, Quebec. J. Wildl. Manage. 39(2):368–373.

Christensen, G. C. and R. J. Fischer, eds. 1976. Transactions of the mountain lion workshop, January 13 and 14, 1976, Sparks, Nevada. U.S. Fish and Wildl. Serv., Portland, Ore. 213 pp.

Cringan, A. T. 1957. History, food habits and range requirements of the woodland caribou of continental North America. Trans. N. Amer. Wildl. Conf. 22:485–500.

Crutchfield, J. 1965. Can we put an economic value on fish and wildlife? Colo. Outdoors 14(2):1–5.

Cumming, H. G. 1974. Annual yield, sex, and age of moose in Ontario as indices to the effects of hunting. Can. Nat. 101(1 and 2):539–558.

———, and F. A. Walden. 1970. The white-tailed deer in Ontario. Ontario Dep. Lands and For., Fish and Wildl. Branch, Toronto. 25 pp.

Currier, M. J. P. 1976. Characteristics of the mountain lion population near Canon City, Colorado. M.S. Thesis. Colorado State Univ., Fort Collins. 81 pp.

Dahlberg, E. M. 1939. Conservation of renewable resources. C. C. Nelson Publishing Company, Appleton, Wis. 208 pp.

Dalquest, W. W. 1953. Mammals of the Mexican State of San Luis Potosi. Louisiana State Univ. Studios Biol. Ser. No. L:1–299.

Daniel, W. S. 1976. Investigation of factors contributing to sub-normal fawn production and herd growth patterns. Final Rep. Fed. Aid Proj. No. W-82-R-18, Job No. 10. Texas Parks and Wildl. Dep., Austin. 45 pp.

Dardiri, A. H., R. J. Yedloutshnig, and W. D. Taylor. 1969. Clinical and serologic response of American white-collared peccaries to African swine fever, hoof and mouth disease, vesicular stomatitis, vesicular exanthema of swine, hog cholera and Rinderpest viruses. Proc. Animal Health Assoc. 73:437–452.

Dary, D. A. 1974. The buffalo book. Swallow Press, Inc., Chicago. 374 pp.

Dasmann, W. 1971. If deer are to survive. The Stackpole Co., Harrisburg, Pa. 128 pp.

———, R. Hubbard, W. G. McGregor, and A. E. Smith. 1967. Evaluation of the wildlife results from fuel breaks, browseways and type conversions. Proc. Annu. Tall Timbers Fire Ecol. Conf. 7:179–194.

Dauphine, T. C. 1976. Growth, reproduction, and energy reserves. Pt. 4. Biology of the Kaminuriak population of barren-ground caribou. Can. Wildl. Serv. Rep. Ser. No. 38. 71 pp.

Davis, D. E., and F. B. Golley. 1963. Principles of mammalogy. Reinhold, New York.

Davis, F. D. 1973. Racks, rations and heredity. La. Conservationist 25(5 and 6):10–15.

Davis, J. 1977. Status of Alaskan caribou herd. Paper read at Symposium on Parameters of Caribou Population Ecology in Alaska, November 16–19, Fairbanks, Alaska.

Davis, L. S. 1967. Dynamic programming for deer management planning. J. Wildl. Manage. 31(4):667–679.

Davis, W. C. 1962. Values of hunting and fishing in Arizona, 1960. Spec. Stud. 21, Bur. Bus. and Pub. Res., Univ. of Arizona, Tucson. 61 pp.

———. 1967. Values of hunting and fishing in Arizona in 1965. Univ. of Arizona, Tucson. 91 pp.

Day, B. W. Jr. 1964. The white-tailed deer in Vermont, 1964. Vermont Fish and Game Dep. Wildl. Bull. 64-1. 25 pp.

Day, G. I. 1960. Javelina population trend techniques. Job Completion Rep. W-78-R-4, WP-1, J-7. Arizona Game and Fish Dep., Phoenix. 3 pp.

———. 1965. Javelina population trend techniques. Job Completion Rep. W-78-R-9, WP-1, J-7. Arizona Game and Fish Dep., Phoenix. 9 pp.

———. 1966. Javelina population trend techniques. Job Completion Rep. W-78-R-10, WP-1, J-7. Arizona Game and Fish Dep., Phoenix. 10 pp.

———. 1967. Javelina population trend techniques. Job Completion Rep. W-78-R-10, WP-1, J-7. Arizona Game and Fish Dep., Phoenix. 7 pp.

———. 1968. Javelina population trend techniques. Job Completion Rep. W-78-R-12,

WP-1, J-7. Arizona Game and Fish Dep., Phoenix. 1 p.

————. 1969a. Javelina activity patterns. Job Completion Rep. W-78-R-13, WP-2, J-9. Arizona Game and Fish Dep., Phoenix. 4 pp.

————. 1969b. Cap-chur problems and remedies. Abstr. 2. Arizona Game and Fish Dep., Phoenix. 4 pp.

————. 1969c. Drug use for capturing and restraining animals. Abstr. 4. Arizona Game and Fish Dep., Phoenix. 7 pp.

————. 1970. Javelina activity patterns. Job Completion Rep. W-78-R-14, WP-2, J-9. Arizona Game and Fish Dep., Phoenix. 7 pp.

————. 1971. Javelina activity patterns. Job Completion Report. W-78-15, WP-2, J-9. Arizona Game and Fish Dep., Phoenix. 9 pp.

————. 1972. Javelina activity patterns. Job Completion Rep. W-78-16, WP-2, J-9. Arizona Game and Fish Dep., Phoenix. 3 pp.

————. 1973. Javelina activity patterns. Job Completion Rep. W-78-R-17, WP-2, J-9. Arizona Game and Fish Dep., Phoenix. 5 pp.

————. 1974. Javelina activity patterns. Job Completion Rep. W-78-R-18, WP-2, J-7. Arizona Game and Fish Dep., Phoenix. 2 pp.

————. 1975. The effect of hunting on a javelina population. Job Completion Rep. W-78-R-19, WP-2, J-7. Arizona Game and Fish Dep., Phoenix. 16 pp.

Dearden, B. L., R. E. Pegau, and R. M. Hansen. 1975. Precision of microhistological estimates of ruminant food habits. J. Wildl. Manage. 39(2):402–407.

DeBock, E. A. 1970. On the behavior of the mountain goat, (*Oreamnos americanus*) in Kootenay National Park. M.S. Thesis. Univ. of Alberta, Edmonton. vii and 173 pp.

Dechert, J. A. 1968. The effects of overpopulation and hunting on the Fort Knox deer herd. Proc. S.E. Assoc. Game and Fish Commissioners 21st Annu. Conf., 1967. 21:15–23.

Della-Bianca, L., and F. M. Johnson. 1965. Effect of an intensive clearing on deer-browse production in the southern Appalachians. J. Wildl. Manage. 29(4):729–733.

Demarchi, R. A. 1976. Our mountain sheep, their present status and future prospects. B.C. Outdoors 32(6):36–39.

Denenberg, V. H., and K. M. Rosenberg. 1967. Non genetic transmission of information. Nature 216:549–550.

Denny, R. N. 1977. 1976 Colorado big game harvest. Colorado Div. of Wildl., Denver. 209 pp.

DeVoto, B., ed. 1953. The journals of Lewis and Clark. Houghton, Mifflin and Co., Boston. xix and 538 pp.

Dietz, D. R. 1965. Deer nutrition research in range management. Trans. N. Amer. Wildl. and Nat. Resources. Conf. 30:274–285.

————, and R. D. Curnow. 1966. How reliable is a forage chemical analysis? J. Range Manage. 19(6):374–376.

Dorg, D. A. 1974. The buffalo book. Swallow Press, Inc. Chicago. 374 pp.

Dorrance, M. J., P. J. Savage, and D. E. Huff. 1975. Effects of snowmobiles on white-tailed deer. J. Wildl. Manage. 39(3):563–569.

Dorst, J., and P. Dandelot. 1970. A field guide to the larger mammals of Africa. Collins, London. 287 pp.

Dow, S. A. 1952. Antelope aging studies in Montana. Proc. West. Assoc. Fish and Game Commissioners 32:220–224.

————, and P. L. Wright. 1962. Changes in mandibular dentition associated with age in pronghorn antelope. J. Wildl. Manage. 26(1):1–18.

Downing, R. L. In Press. Vital statistics of animal populations. *In* S. Schemnitz, ed. Wildlife management techniques, 4th ed. The Wildlife Society, Washington, D.C.

Drozdz, A., and A. Osiecki. 1973. Intake and digestibility of natural feeds by roe deer. Acta Ther. 18:80–91.

Dudak, D., G. W. Cornwell, R. B. Holliman, and B. S. McGinnes. 1966. The incidence and degree of infection of *Pneumostrongylus tenuis* in the white-tailed deer of western Virginia. Proc. S.E. Assoc. Game and Fish Commissioners 19th Annu. Conf., 1965. 19:128–141.

DuPlessis, S. S. 1972. Ecology of blesbok with special reference to productivity. Wildl. Monogr. 30. 30 pp.

Dzieciolowski, R. 1969. The quantity, quality and seasonal variation of food resources available to red deer in various environmental conditions of forest management. Polish Acad. Sci., For. Res. Inst., Warsaw. 295 pp.

Eaton, R. L., ed. 1976. The world's cats. Vol. 3, No. 1. Contributions to status, management and conservation. Dep. of Zoology, Univ. of Washington, Seattle. 95 pp.

————, and K. A. Velander. Unpubl. Reproduction in the puma: biology, behavior and ontogeny. Unpubl. On file at Colorado Cooperative Wildlife Research Unit, Colorado State Univ., Fort Collins.

Eberhart, L. L. 1968. A preliminary appraisal of line transects. J. Wildl. Manage. 32(1):82–88.

Ebert, P. N. 1976. Recent changes in Oregon's mule deer population and management. Proc. West. Assoc. Fish and Game Commissioners 56:408–414.

Eddy, T. A. 1959. Foods of the collared peccary, *Pecari tajacu sonoriensis* (Mearns) in southern Arizona. M.S. Thesis. Univ. of Arizona, Tucson. 102 pp.

———. 1961. Food and feeding patterns of the collared peccary in southern Arizona. J. Wildl. Manage. 25(3):248–257.

Edgerton, P. J. 1972. Big game use and habitat changes in a recently logged mixed conifer forest in northeastern Oregon. Proc. West. Assoc. Fish and Game Commissioners 52:239–246.

———, and B. E. McConnell. 1976. Diurnal temperature regimes of logged and unlogged mixed conifer stands on elk summer range. USDA For. Serv. Res. Note PNW-277. July 1976. 6 pp.

Edwards, R. Y. 1954. Fire and the decline of a mountain caribou herd. J. Wildl. Manage. 18(4):521–526.

———, and R. W. Ritcey. 1958. Reproduction in a moose population. J. Wildl. Manage. 22(3):261–268.

Ehrenreich, J. H., and D. A. Murphy. 1962. A method of evaluating habitat for forest wildlife. Trans. N. Amer. Wildl. Conf. 27:376–384.

Einarsen, A. S. 1948. The pronghorn antelope and its management. The Stackpole Co., Harrisburg, Pa. 235 pp.

Elder, J. B. 1956. Watering patterns of some desert game animals. J. Wildl. Manage. 20(4):368–378.

Ellisor, J. E. 1969. Mobility of white-tailed deer in south Texas. J. Wildl. Manage. 33(1):220–222.

———, and W. F. Harwell. 1969. Mobility and home range of collared peccary in southern Texas. J. Wildl. Manage. 33(2):425–427.

Ericson, C. A. 1972. Some preliminary observations on the acoustic behavior of semi-domestic reindeer (*Rangifer tarandus tarandus*) with emphasis on intraspecific communication and the mother-calf relationship. M.S. Thesis. Univ. of Alaska, College.

Errington, P. L. 1946. Predation and vertebrate populations. Quart. Rev. Biol. 21:144–177, 221–245.

———. 1967. Of predation and life. Iowa State Univ. Press, Ames. 277 pp.

Espmar, K.Y. 1970. Abnormal migratory behavior in Swedish reindeer. Arctic 23:199–200.

Evans, C. D., W. A. Troyer, and C. J. Lensink. 1966. Aerial census of moose by quadrat sampling units. J. Wildl. Manage. 30(4):767–776.

Ewart, D. A., J. R. Messer, and R. G. Dalgliesh. 1975. Saskatchewan coyote control policy, April 1, 1975–March 31, 1976. Animal Industry Branch, Saskatchewan Dep. Agr., Regina. 3 pp.

Fair, J. S. 1978. An analysis of the relationship between energy expenditure and heart rate of unrestrained white-tailed deer. M.S. Thesis. Univ. of New Hampshire, Durham. 61 pp.

Ferguson, R. B., and J. V. Basile. 1966. Topping stimulates bitterbrush twig growth. J. Wildl. Manage. 39(4):839–841.

Fernald, M. L., ed. 1970. Gray's manual of botany. 8th ed. D. Van Nostrand Co., New York. 1,362 pp.

Field, R. A., F. C. Smith, and W. G. Hepworth. 1972. The pronghorn antelope carcass. Univ. of Wyoming, Agr. Exp. Sta. Bull. 575. 6 pp.

———. 1973a. The mule deer carcass. Univ. of Wyoming Agr. Exp. Sta. Bull. 589. 6 pp.

———. 1973b. The elk carcass. Univ. of Wyoming Agr. Exp. Sta. Bull. 594. 8 pp.

Flader, S. 1974. Thinking like a mountain. University of Missouri Press, Columbia, Mo. 284 pp.

Forbes, E. B., L. F. Marcy, A. L. Voris, and C. E. French. 1941. The digestive capacities of the white-tailed deer. J. Wildl. Manage. 5(1):108–114.

Forbes, S. E. 1963. Deer biology, populations and effects of hunting. Pages 11–14 *in* Deer management in Pennsylvania. Pennsylvania State Univ. Coll. of Agr. Ext. Serv., University Park. 20 pp.

———, L. M. Lang, S. A. Liscinsky, and H. A. Roberts. 1971. The white-tailed deer in Pennsylvania. Pennsylvania Game Comm., Harrisburg. 41 pp.

Forrester, D. J., G. M. Forrester, and C. M. Senger. 1966. A contribution toward a bibliography of the lung nematodes of mammals. J. Helminth. 40: Supplement 1.

Forsyth, E. S. 1942. Our stocking experience in the Province of Saskatchewan. Trans. N. Amer. Wildl. Conf. 7:152–161.

Foss, A., and M. Rognrud. 1971. Rocky Mountain goat. Pages 106–113 *in* T. W. Mussehl and F. W. Howell, eds. Game management in Montana. Montana Fish and Game Dep., Missoula. xi and 238 pp.

Foster, B. R. 1976. Exploitation and management of the mountain goat in British Columbia.

B.S. Thesis. Univ. British Columbia, Vancouver. xiv and 273 pp.

Franzmann, A. W., and P. D. Arneson. 1973. P-R job progress report W-17-5. Alaska Dep. Fish and Game, Juneau. 117 pp.

———. 1976. Marrow fat in Alaskan moose femurs in relation to mortality factors. J. Wildl. Manage. 40(2):336–339.

Franzmann, A. W., A. Flynn, and P. D. Arneson. 1975. Levels of some mineral elements in Alaskan moose hair. J. Wildl. Manage. 39(2):374–378.

Franzmann, A. W., R. E. LeResche, P. D. Arneson, and J. L. Davis. 1976. Moose productivity and physiology. Alaska Dep. Fish and Game. P-R Proj. Final Rep. W-17-R. 81 pp. Multilith.

Franzmann, A. W., R. E. LeResche, R. A. Rausch and J. L. Oldemeyer. 1978. Alaskan moose measurements and weights and measurement-weight relationships. Can. J. Zool. 56(2):298–306.

Freddy, D. J. 1974. Status and management of the Selkirk caribou herd, 1973. M.S. Thesis. Univ. of Idaho, Moscow. 132 pp.

Freeland, W. J., and D. H. Janzen. 1974. Strategies in herbivory by mammals: the role of plant secondary compounds. Amer. Nat. 108(961):268–289.

Freeman, M. M. R. 1971. Population characteristics of musk-oxen in the Jones Sound region of the Northwest Territories. J. Wildl. Manage. 35(1):103–108.

French, C. E., L. C. McEwen, N. D. Magruder, R. H. Ingram, and R. W. Swift. 1956. Nutrient requirements for growth and antler development in the white-tailed deer. J. Wildl. Manage. 20(3):221–232.

Fuller, W. F. 1960. Behaviour and social organization of the wild bison of Wood Buffalo National Park, Canada. Arctic 13:3–19.

———. 1962. The biology and management of the bison of Wood Buffalo National Park. Can. Wildl. Serv. Wildl. Manage. Bull. Ser. 1, No. 16. 52 pp.

Gamble, H. B., and R. A. Bartoo. 1963. An economic comparison of timber and wildlife values on farm land. J. Farm Econ. 45(2):296–303.

Gard, R. 1971. Brown bear predation on sockeye salmon at Karluk Lake, Alaska. J. Wildl. Manage. 35(2):193–204.

Garrett, J. R., G. J. Pon, and D. J. Arosteguy. 1970. Economics of big game resource use in Nevada. Univ. of Nevada Agr. Exp. Sta. Bull. B25, Reno. 22 pp.

Gasaway, W. C. and J. W. Coady. 1974. Review of energy requirements and rumen fermentation in moose and other ruminants. Can. Nat. 101(1 and 2):227–262.

Gates, C. E. 1969. Simulation study of estimators for the line transect sampling method. Biometrics 25:317–328.

Gauthier-Pilters, H. 1974. The behaviour and ecology of camels in the Sahara, with special reference to nomadism and water management. Pages 542–551 *in* V. Geist and F. Walther, eds. The behavior of ungulates and its relation to management. Vol. 2. IUCN New Ser. Publ. 24, Morges, Switzerland.

Geer, K. 1971. Big game research. Montana Fish and Game Proj. W-120-R-2, Job L-10. 35 pp.

Geis, A. D. 1971. Population and harvest surveys. Pages 67–70 *in* A. D. Teague, ed. A manual of wildlife conservation. The Wildlife Society. Washington, D.C. 206 pp.

Geist, V. 1963. On the behavior of the North American moose in British Columbia. Behavior 20:377–416.

———. 1964. On the rutting behavior of the mountain goat. J. Mammal. 45(4):551–568.

———. 1966. Validity of horn segment counts in aging bighorn sheep. J. Wildl. Manage. 30(3):634–635.

———. 1967a. A consequence of togetherness. Nat. Hist. 76(8):24–31.

———. 1967b. On fighting injuries and dermal shields of mountain goats. J. Wildl. Manage. 31(1):192–194.

———. 1968. On the interrelation of external appearance, social behavior and social structure of mountain sheep. Z. Tierpsychol. 25:199–215.

———. 1971a. Mountain sheep—a study in behavior and evolution. Univ. Chicago Press. xv and 383 pp.

———. 1971b. A behavioural approach to the management of wild ungulates. Pages 413–424 *in* E. Duffey and A. S. Watt, eds. The scientific management of animal and plant communities for conservation. 11th Symp. Brit. Ecol. Soc., Blackwell Scientific Publications, Oxford.

———. 1975a. Mountain sheep and man in the northern wilds. Cornell Univ. Press, Ithaca, New York. 248 pp.

———. 1975b. On the management of mountain sheep: theoretical considerations. Pages 77–99 *in* J. B. Trefethen, ed. The wild sheep in modern North America. Boone and Crockett Club, Winchester Press, New York.

———, and F. Walther, eds. 1974. The behavior of ungulates and its relation to management.

2 vols. IUCN New Ser. Publ. 24, Morges, Switzerland. 940 pp.

Gilbert, A. H., and K. C. Nobe. 1969. Surveys of hunting and fishing expenditures: Uses, abuse and methodological problems. Colorado State Univ. Dep. Econ., Fort Collins. 16 pp. Multilith.

Gilbert, B. K. 1973. Scent marking and territoriality in pronghorn (*Antilocapra americana*) in Yellowstone Park. Mammalia 37(1):25–33.

Gilbert, D. L. 1975. Natural resources and public relations, 2nd ed. The Wildlife Society, Washington, D.C. 320 pp.

Gill, R. B., and O. C. Wallmo. 1973. Middle Park deer study—physical characteristics and food habits. Pages 81–103 *in* Game Research Report, July 1973, Part Two. Colorado Div. Wildl., Denver.

Gladfelter, L. 1975. Deer in Iowa, 1974. Iowa Cons. Comm. Iowa Wildl. Res. Bull. 16. 21 pp.

Goldman, E. A. 1945. A new pronghorn antelope from Sonora. Proc. Biol. Soc. 58:3–4.

Golley, F. B., and H. K. Buechner, eds. 1968. A practical guide to the study of the productivity of large herbivores. Int. Biol. Program Handbook No. 7, Blackwell Scientific Publications, Oxford. 308 pp.

Gordon, F. A. 1976. Spring burning in an aspen-conifer stand for maintenance of moose habitat, West Boulder River, Montana. Proc. Tall Timbers Fire Ecol. Conf. 14:501–538.

Graf, W. 1956. Territorialism in deer. J. Mammal. 37(2):165–170.

Graves, H. S. 1916. Game protection on the national forests. Bull. Amer. Game Prot. Assoc. 5(2):18–19.

Gray, D. R. 1970. The killing of a bull muskox by a single wolf. Arctic 23:197–198.

———. 1973. Social organization and behavior of muskoxen (*Ovibos moschatus*) on Bathurst Island, N.W.T. Ph.D. Thesis. Univ. Alberta, Edmonton. 212 pp.

Green, D. D. 1950. Predator control problems in Alaska. First Alaska Science Conference. Washington, D.C. 13 pp.

Greer, K. R. 1974. Mountain lion studies. Montana Fish and Game, Job Prog. Rep., Proj. W-120-R-5, No. L-1.2 (R). 13 pp.

Griffith, G. K. 1962. Guidelines for antelope management. Int. Antelope Conf. Trans. 5:102–114.

Grinnell, G. B. 1893. In buffalo days. Pages 155–211 *in* G. B. Grinnell and T. Roosevelt, eds. American big game hunting. Forest and Stream Publishing Co., New York.

Gross, J. E. 1972. Criteria for big game planning: performance measures vs. intuition. Trans. N. Amer. Wildl. and Nat. Resour. Conf. 37:246–259.

Gurba, J. B., and D. J. Neave. 1973. Problem wildlife management in Alberta. Joint Prog. Rep. Alberta Agr. and Lands and For. Deps., Edmonton. 16 pp. and appendices.

Guzman, G. Jr. 1961. Vegetation zones of the territory Baja, California, in relation to wildlife. Desert Bighorn Council Trans. 5:68–74.

Gwynn, J. V. 1976. The Virginia deer management program 1946–1976. Paper read at 12th Northeast Deer Study Group Meeting, Chicopee, Massachusetts. August 31–September 2, 1976.

Haber, G. C. 1977. Socio-ecological dynamics of wolves and prey in a subarctic ecosystem. Ph.D. Thesis, Univ. of British Columbia, Vancouver. 786 pp.

Hagen, H. L. 1953. Nutritive value for deer of some forage plants in the Sierra Nevada. Calif. Fish and Game 39(1):163–175.

Hahn, H. C. Jr. 1951. Economic value of game in the Edwards Plateau region of Texas. Fed. Aid Rep. Ser. No. 8, Texas Game, Fish and Oyster Comm. Austin. 49 pp.

Hailey, T. L. In Press. A handbook on pronghorn antelope management in Texas. Texas Parks and Wildl. Dep., Austin.

Haines, F. 1970. The buffalo. Thomas Crowell Co. New York. 242 pp.

Haines, W. W. 1973. Black-tailed deer populations and Douglas fir reforestation in the Tillamook burn, Oregon. Oregon State Game Comm. Game Res. Rep. No. 3. 55 pp.

Hall, E. R. and K. R. Kelson. 1959. The mammals of North America, Vol. II. The Ronald Press, New York. Pp. 547–1083.

Halloran, A. F. 1945. Five fetuses reported for *Pecari angulatus* from Arizona. J. Mammal. 26(4):434.

———. 1949. Desert bighorn management. Trans. N. Amer. Wildl. Conf. 14:527–536.

Halls, L. K. 1973. Managing deer habitat in loblolly-short leaf pine forest. J. For. 71(12):752–757.

———, and J. J. Stransky. 1968. Game food plantings in southern forests. Trans. N. Amer. Wildl. and Nat. Resour. Conf. 33:217–222.

Halls, L. K., and T. H. Ripley. 1972. Deer browse plants of southern forests. USDA For. Serv., South. and S.E. For. Exp. Stns. 78 pp.

Hamilton, R. 1962. Factors affecting dispersal of deer released in Indiana. J. Wildl. Manage. 26(1):79–85.

Hammell, H. T., T. R. Houpt, K. L. Anderson, and

S. Skjenneberg. 1961. Thermal and metabolic measurements on a reindeer at rest and in exercise. Arctic Aeromedical Lab. Rep. AAL-TDR-61-54. Seattle, Wash. 34 pp.

Hansen, C. G. 1967. Bighorn sheep populations of the Desert Game Range. J. Wildl. Manage. 29(4):693–706.

Hansen, R. M., R. L. Clark, and W. Lawhorn. 1977. Foods of wild horses, deer, and cattle in Douglas Mountain area, Colorado. J. Range Manage. 30(2):116–119.

Hanson, W. M. 1950. The mountain goat in South Dakota. Ph.D. Thesis. Univ. Michigan, Ann Arbor. viii and 92 pp.

Hanson, W. R. 1963. Calculation of productivity, survival and abundance of selected vertebrates from sex and age ratios. Wildl. Monogr. 9. 60 pp.

Harlow, R. F., and F. K. Jones Jr. 1965. The white-tailed deer in Florida. Florida Game and Fresh Water Fish Comm. Tech. Bull. 9. 240 pp.

Harlow, R. F., J. B. Whelan, H. S. Crawford, and J. E. Skeen. 1975. Deer foods during years of oak mast abundance and scarcity. J. Wildl. Manage. 39(2):330–336.

Harmel, D. E. 1975. Habitat preferences of exotics. Job Rep. R-R Project W-76-R-18. Texas Parks and Wildl. Dep. 20 pp.

Harmon, W. 1944. Notes on mountain goats in the Black Hills. J. Mammal. 25(2):149–151.

Harington, C. R. 1961. History, distribution and ecology of the muskoxen. M.S. Thesis. McGill Univ., Montreal 489 pp.

Harper., J. A. 1971. Ecology of Roosevelt elk. Oregon State Game Comm., Portland. 44 pp.

———, J. H. Harn, W. W. Bentley, and C. F. Yocom. 1967. The status and ecology of the Roosevelt elk in California. Wildl. Monogr. 165. 49 pp.

Hawkins, R. E., D. C. Autry, and W. D. Klimstra. 1967. Comparison of methods used to capture white-tailed deer. J. Wildl. Manage. 31(3):460–464.

Hawkins, R. E., and G. G. Montgomery. 1969. Movements of translocated deer as determined by telemetry. J. Wildl. Manage. 33(1):196–203.

Hawkins, R. E., and W. D. Klimstra. 1970. A preliminary study of the social organization of white-tailed deer. J. Wildl. Manage. 34(2):407–419.

Hayes, F. A., and A. K. Prestwood. 1969. Some considerations for diseases and parasites of white-tailed deer in the southeastern United States. Pages 32–36 *in* White-tailed deer in the southern forest habitat. USDA For. Serv. South. For. Exp. Sta., New Orleans, La.

Heath, R. 1974. The environmental consequences of the off-road vehicle, with profiles of the industry and the enthusiast. Defenders of Wildlife and Friends of the Earth, Washington, D.C. 36 pp.

Hebert, D. M. 1967. Natural salt licks as a part of the ecology of the mountain goat. M.S. Thesis. Univ. of British Columbia, Vancouver. 138 pp.

———, and I. McT. Cowan. 1971. Natural salt licks as a part of the ecology of the mountain goat. Can. J. Zool. 49:605–610.

Heimer, W. E. 1972. 1972 annual report. P.R. Projects W-17-3 and W-17-4, Jobs 6.1R and 6.2R. Alaska Dep. Fish and Game, Juneau.

———, and A. C. Smith III. 1975. Ram horn growth and population quality and their significance to Dall sheep management in Alaska. Alaska Dep. Fish and Game Wildl. Tech. Bull. 5. 41 pp.

Heinselman, M.L. 1973. Fire in the virgin forests of the Boundary Waters Canoe Area, Minn. Quart. Res. 3:329–382.

Hemming, J. E. 1969. Cemental deposition, tooth succession and horn development as criteria of age in Dall sheep. J. Wildl. Manage. 33(3):552–558.

———. 1971. The distribution movement patterns of caribou in Alaska. Alaska Dep. Fish and Game Wildl. Tech. Bull. 1. 60 pp.

Hendee, J. C. 1969. Appreciative versus consumptive uses of wildlife refuges: studies of who gets what and trends in use. Trans. N. Amer. Wildl. and Nat. Resour. Conf. 34:252–264.

———, and D. R. Potter. 1971. Human behavior and wildlife management: needed research. Trans. N. Amer. Wildl. and Nat. Resour. Conf. 36:383–396.

Henne, D. R. 1977. Domestic sheep mortality on a western Montana ranch. Pages 133–146 *in* R. L. Phillips and C. Jonkel, eds. Proceedings of the 1975 Predator Symposium. For. and Cons. Exp. Sta. Univ. of Montana, Missoula.

Herrero, S. M. 1970. Human injury inflicted by grizzly bears. Science 170:593–598.

———. 1972. Bears—their biology and management. IUCN New Ser. Publ. 23, Morges, Switzerland. 371 pp.

Herring, S. 1972. The role of canine morphology in the evolutionary divergence of pigs and peccaries. J. Mammal. 53(3):500–512.

Hibbs, L. D. 1966. A literature review on mountain goat ecology. Colorado Dep. Game, Fish and Parks Spec. Rep. 8. iv and 23 pp.

———, F. A. Glover, and D. L. Gilbert. 1969. The mountain goat in Colorado. Trans. N. Amer. Wildl. and Nat. Resour. Conf. 34:409–418.

Hinman, R. A. 1961. Antelope populations in southwestern Utah, with special reference to golden eagle predation. Utah State Dep. Fish and Game Info. Bull. 61–7. 61 pp.

Hjeljord, O. 1973. Mountain goat forage and habitat preference in Alaska. J. Wildl. Manage. 37(3):353–362.

Hoefs, M. 1975. Estimation of numbers and description of wild sheep in the Yukon Territory. Pages 17–23 *in* J. B. Trefethen, ed. The wild sheep in modern North America. Boone and Crockett Club, Winchester Press, N.Y.

Hoffmeister, D. F. 1962. The kinds of deer, *Odocoileus,* in Arizona. Amer. Midl. Natur. 67:45–64.

Hofman, R. R., and D. R. M. Stewart. 1972. Grazer or browser: a classification based on the stomach-structure and feeding habits of East African ruminants. Mammalia 36:226–240.

Holroyd, J. D. 1967. Observations of Rocky Mountain goats on Mount Wardle Kootenay National Park, British Columbia. Can. Field Nat. 81(1):1–22.

Holsworth, W. N. 1960. Interactions between moose, elk and buffalo in Elk Island National Park, Alberta. M.S. Thesis. Univ. British Columbia, Vancouver. 92 pp.

Holter, J. B., H. H. Hayes, and S. H. Smith. Unpubl. Protein requirement of yearling white-tailed deer. Unpubl. On file at Animal Science Dep., Univ. of New Hampshire, Durham.

Holter, J. B., W. E. Urban Jr., H. H. Hayes, and H. Silver. 1976. Predicting metabolic rate from telemetered heart rate in white-tailed deer. J. Wildl. Manage. 49(4):626–629.

Holter, J. B., W. E. Urban, and H. H. Hayes. 1977. Nutrition of northern white-tailed deer throughout the year. J. Anim. Sci. 45(2):365–376.

———. Unpubl. Predicting energy and nitrogen retention in young white-tailed deer. Unpubl. On file at Animal Science Dep., Univ. of New Hampshire, Durham.

Holter, J. B., and H. H. Hayes. 1977. Growth in white-tailed deer fawns fed varying energy and constant protein. J. Wildl. Manage. 41(3):506–510.

Hone, E. 1934. The present status of the muskox. Amer. Comm. Int. Wildl. Prot. Spec. Publ. No. 5. 87 pp.

Honess, R. F., and N. M. Frost. 1942. A Wyoming bighorn sheep study. Wyoming Game and Fish Dep. Bull. No. 1. 127 pp.

Hooven, E. F. 1973. A wildlife brief for the clearcut. J. For. 71(4):210–214.

Hoover, R. L., C. E. Till, and S. Ogilvie. 1959. The antelope of Colorado. Colorado Dep. Fish and Game Tech. Bull. No. 4, Denver. 110 pp.

Hopps, H. C. 1964. Principals of pathology, 2nd ed. Appleton-Century-Crofts, New York. 403 pp.

Hopwood, V. G. 1971. David Thompson: Travels in western North America, 1784–1812. MacMillan of Canada, Toronto. 342 pp.

Horn, E. E. 1941. Some coyote-wildlife relationships. Trans. N. Amer. Wildl. Conf. 6:283–287.

Hornaday, W. T. 1914. Wildlife conservation in theory and practice. Yale Univ. Press, New Haven, Ct. 240 pp.

———. 1931. Thirty years war for wildlife. The Gillespie Bros., Inc., Stamford, Ct. 292 pp.

Hornocker, M. G. 1969. Winter territoriality in mountain lions. J. Wildl. Manage. 33(3)457–464.

———. 1970. An analysis of mountain lion predation upon mule deer and elk in the Idaho Primitive Area. Wildl. Monogr. 21. 39 pp.

———. 1976. Cougars up close. Natl. Wildl. 14(6):42–47.

Horwitz, E. J. 1974. Clearcutting: a view from the top. Acropolis Books Ltd., Washington, D.C. 178 pp.

Houston, B. D. 1968. The Shiras moose in Jackson Hole, Wyoming. Grand Teton Nat. Hist. Assoc. Tech. Bull. 1. 110 pp.

Howard, W. E. 1974. The biology of predator control. Module in Biology, No. 11. Addison-Wesley, Reading, Pa. 48 pp.

Hubbard, B. 1887. Memorials of a half-century. G. P. Putnam, New York. 581 pp.

Hudkins, G., and T. P. Kistner. 1977. *Sarcocystis hemionilatranis* (Sp. N.) life cycle in mule deer and coyotes. J. Wildl. Dis. 13(1):80–84.

Huffaker, C. B. 1970. The phenomenon of predation and its roles in nature. Pages 327–343 in P. J. den Boer and G. R. Gradwell, eds. Dynamics of populations. Oosterbeek, The Netherlands. 611 pp.

Hunter, G. N., and L. E. Yeager. 1956. Management of the mule deer. Pages 449–482 *in* W. P. Taylor, ed. The deer of North America. The Stackpole Co., Harrisburg, Pa. 668 pp.

Huntington, D. 1904. Our big game. Charles Scribner's Sons, New York. 347 pp.

Interstate Antelope Conference. 1962. Recommended specifications for barbed wire fences (for the benefit of livestock and wildlife). Int. Antelope Conf. Trans. 13:100–101.

Jacobsen, E., and S. Skjenneberg. 1975. Some results from feeding experiments with reindeer. Pages 95–107 *in* J. R. Luick, P. C. Lent, D. R. Klein, and R. B. White, eds.

Proceedings 1st International Reindeer/Caribou Symposium. Occ. Pap. No. 2, Inst. of Arctic Biology, Univ. of Alaska, College. 551 pp.

Jennings, W. D., and J. T. Harris. 1953. The collared peccary in Texas. Pages 1–31 *in* FA report series No. 12, Texas Game and Fish Comm., Austin.

Jensen, C. H., A. D. Smith, and G. W. Scotter. 1972. Guidelines for grazing sheep on rangelands used by big game in winter. J. Range Manage. 25(5):346–352.

Jeter, L. K., and R. L. Marchinton. 1967. Preliminary report of telemetric study of deer movements and behavior on the Eglin Field Reservation in northwestern Florida. Proc. S.E. Assoc. Game and Fish Commissioners 18th Annu. Conf., 1964. 18:140–152.

Johnson, E. A., and J. S. Rowe. 1975. Fire in the subarctic wintering ground of the Beverley caribou herd. Amer. Midl. Nat. 94(1):1–14.

Johnson, H. N. 1970. The ecological approach to the study of zoonotic diseases. J. Wildl. Dis. 6(4):194–204.

Johnson, J. F. 1969. Javelina hunt information and population trend. Job Completion Rep. W-93-R-11. New Mexico Dep. Game and Fish. Santa Fe. 2 pp.

———. 1976. Javelina hunt information and population trend. Job Completion Rep. W-93-18. New Mexico Dep. Game and Fish. Santa Fe. 2 pp.

Johnson, J. 1977. New Mexico's first stratified elk hunt. Page 46 *in* R. N. Denny, ed. 1977 Western States Elk Workshop. Colorado Div. of Wildl., Denver. 84 pp. Abstr.

Johnson, M. 1966. Travel time and the price of leisure. W. Econ. J. 4(2):135–145.

Jones, J. K., Jr., D. C. Carter, and H. H. Genoways. 1973. Checklist of North American mammals north of Mexico. Texas Tech Univ. Mus., Occ. Pap. No. 12. 14 pp.

Jones, P. V. Jr. 1949. Experimental management of antelope. Texas Game, Fish and Oyster Comm. FA Rep. Ser. No. 3. 31 pp.

Jonkel, C. J. 1970. Some comments on polar bear management. Biol. Cons. 2(2):115–119.

———, and I. McT. Cowan. 1971. The black bear in the spruce-fir forest. Wildl. Monogr. 27. 57 pp.

Jonkel, C. J., P. Husby, and R. H. Russell. 1977. The reintroduction of orphaned grizzly cubs into the wild. Paper read at the 4th International Conference on Bear Research and Management, 1977, Kalispell, Montana.

Jonkel, C. J., G. B. Kolenosky, R. J. Robertson, and R. H. Russell. 1972. Further note on polar bear denning habits. Pages 142–158 *in* S. Herrero, ed. Bears—their biology and management. IUCN New Ser. Publ. 23, Morges, Switzerland.

Jonkel, C. J., D. R. Gray, and B. Hubert. 1975. Immobilizing and marking wild muskoxen in Arctic Canada. J. Wildl. Manage. 39(1):112–117.

Jonkel, C. J., P. A. Smith, I. Stirling, and G. B. Kolenosky. 1976. The present status of the polar bear in the James Bay and Belcher Islands area. Can. Wildl. Serv. Occ. Pap. No. 26. 42 pp.

Jordan, J. S., D. Hager, and W. N. Stiteler. 1965. Deer browse production and timber stand improvement in northern hardwoods. Trans. N. Amer. Wildl. Conf. 13:296–305.

Joyal, R. 1976. Winter foods of moose in Laverendrys Park, Quebec: an evaluation of two browse survey methods. Can. J. Zool. 54 (10):1765–1770.

Julander, O., W. L. Robinette, and D. A. Jones. 1961. Relation of summer range conditions to mule deer herd productivity. J. Wildl. Manage. 25(1):54–60.

Karns, P. D., H. Haswell, F. F. Gilbert, and A. E. Patton. 1974. Moose management in the coniferous-deciduous ecotone of North America. Can. Nat. 101 (1 and 2):643–656.

Kautz, M. V. 1978. Energy expenditure and heart rate of active mule deer fawns. M. S. Thesis. Colorado State Univ., Fort Collins. 68 pp.

Kearney, S. R., and F. F. Gilbert. 1976. Habitat use by white-tailed deer and moose on sympatric range. J. Wildl. Manage. 40(4):645–657.

Keiss, R. E. 1969. Comparison of eruption-wear patterns and cementum annuli as age criteria in elk. J. Wildl. Manage. 33(1):175–180.

Keith, L. B. 1974. Some features of population dynamics in mammals. Trans. XI Int. Cong. Game Biologists 11:17–58.

Kellogg, F. E. 1976. So you're not seeing deer now. Arkansas Game and Fish 8(4):12–13.

Kelsall, J. P. 1968. The migratory barren-ground caribou of Canada. Dep. of Indian Affairs and Northern Development. Can. Wildl. Ser., Ottawa. 339 pp.

———, and E. S. Telfer. 1974. Biogeography of moose with particular reference to western North America. Can. Nat. 101(1 and 2):117–130.

Kelsey, P. M. 1973. Winter deer feeding. The (New York) Conservationist. 27(5):41.

Kemp, G. A. 1972. Black bear population dynamics at Cold Lake, Alberta, 1968–1970. Pages 26–31 *in* S. Herrero, ed. Bears—their biology and management. IUCN New Ser. Publ. 23, Morges, Switzerland.

Kennedy, J. F. 1963. Introduction. Pages xi–xiii *in* S. L. Udall. A quiet crisis. Holt, Rinehart and Winston, New York. 209 pp.

Kiley, M. 1974. Behavioural problems of some captive and domestic ungulates. Pages 603–617 *in* V. Geist and F. Walther, eds. The behavior of ungulates and its relation to management. Vol. 2. IUCN New Ser. Publ. 24, Morges, Switzerland.

King, J. M. 1961. Veterinary necropsy techniques. W. Veterinarian 8:80–85.

King, R. T. 1947. The future of wildlife in forest land use. Trans. N. Amer. Wildl. Conf. 12:454–467.

Kirkpatrick, R. D., and L. K. Sowls. 1962. Age determination of the collared peccary by the tooth-replacement pattern. J. Wildl. Manage. 26(2):214–217.

Kirkpatrick, R. L. 1975. Nutrition, hormones and reproduction in white-tailed deer: a review. Paper read at Northeast Deer Study Group Meeting, Sept. 8–11, 1975, Quebec.

Kleiber, M. 1961. The fire of life. John Wiley and Sons. New York. 453 pp.

Klein, D. R. 1953. A reconnaissance study of the mountain goat in Alaska. M.S. Thesis. Univ. of Alaska, Fairbanks. 121 pp.

———. 1962. Rumen contents analysis as an index to range quality. Trans. N. Amer. Wildl. and Nat. Resour. Conf. 27:150–164.

———. 1964. Range-related differences in growth of deer reflected in skeletal ratios. J. Mammal. 45(2):226–235.

———. 1968. The introduction, increase and crash of deer on St. Matthew Island. J. Wildl. Manage. 32(2):350–367.

———. 1969. Food selection by North American deer and their response to overutilization of preferred plant species. Pages 25–44 *in* A. Watson, ed. Animal populations in relation to their food resources. Blackwell Scientific Publications, Oxford, England.

———. 1971. Reaction of reindeer to obstructions and disturbance. Science 173:393–398.

———, and S. T. Olson. 1960. Natural mortality patterns of deer in southeast Alaska. J. Wildl. Manage. 24(1):80–88.

Klein, D. R., and J. E. Hemming. 1976. Resource development and related environmental problems in arctic Alaska—impact on fish and wildlife. Paper read at the 23rd International Geographical Congress, July 24, 1976, Leningrad, USSR.

Knaus, W., and W. Schroder. 1975. Das gamswild. 2nd ed. P. Parey, Berlin. 234 pp.

Knipe, T. 1958. The javelina in Arizona. Arizona Game and Fish Dep. Wildl. Bull. No. 2.

Knorre, E. P. 1961. Itogi i perspektive adomashneniya locya. Trudy Pechora Ilych. gos. Zapos. 9:5–113.

Knowlton, F. F. 1968. Coyote predation as a factor in management of antelope in fenced pastures. Proc. Biennial Antelope States Workshop 3:65–74.

———, D. J. Carley, and R. T. McBride. 1971. Mammal damage control research—predators and predator-prey. Pages 26–32 *in* Annu. Prog. Rep., 1970–71, Work Unit DF-103.9, Denver Wildl. Res. Center, U.S. Fish and Wildl. Serv., Denver.

Kohn, B. E., and J. J. Mooty. 1971. Summer habitat of white-tailed deer in north-central Minnesota. J. Wildl. Manage. 35(3):476–487.

Kolenosky, G. B. 1972. Wolf predation on wintering deer in east-central Ontario. J. Wildl. Manage. 36(2):357–369.

Komarek, R. 1966. A discussion of wildlife management, fire and the wildlife landscape. Proc. Tall Timbers Fire Ecol. Conf. 5:177–194.

Krog, H., and M. Monson. 1954. Notes on the metabolism of a mountain goat. Am. J. Physiol. 178:515–516.

Krug, A. S. 1965. The socio-economic impact of firearms in the field of conservation and natural resources management. Proc. S.E. Assoc. Game and Fish Commissioners 19th Annu. Conf., 1965. 19:1–8.

Kuchler, A. W. 1964. Potential natural vegetation of the conterminous United States. Amer. Geog. Soc. Spec. Publ. No. 36. 116 pp.

Kufeld, R. C. 1973. Foods eaten by Rocky Mountain elk. J. Range Manage. 26:106–113.

Kufeld, R. C., O. C. Wallmo, and C. Feddema. 1973. Foods of the Rocky Mountain mule deer. USDA For. Serv. Res. Pap. RM-111. 31 pp.

Kurt, F. 1970. Rehild. Bayerischer Landwirtschafts Verlag, Munich. 174 pp.

Lambourn, L. J. 1961. Relative effects of environment and liveweight upon the feed requirements of sheep. Proc. N. Z. Soc. Animal Prod. 21:92–108.

Lang, E. M. 1957. Deer of New Mexico. New Mexico Dep. Game and Fish Bull. No. 5. 41 pp.

Lang, L. M., and G. W. Wood. 1976. Manipulation of the Pennsylvania deer herd. Wildl. Soc. Bull. 4(4):159–166.

Langer, P. 1974. Stomach evolution of the artiodactyla. Mammalia 38:295–314.

———. In Press. Anatomy of the stomach of the collared peccary, *Dicotyles tajacu* (L. 1758). Mammalia.

Laws, R. M., T. S. C. Parker, and R. C. B. Johnstone. 1975. Elephants and their habitats. Oxford University Press, London. 376 pp.

Lay, D. S. 1956. Effects of prescribed burning on forage and mast production in southern pine forests. J. For. 54:582–584.

———. 1957. Browse quality and the effects of prescribed burning in southern pine forests, J. For. 55:342–347.

Leach, H. R. 1956. Food habits of the Great Basin deer herds of California. Calif. Fish and Game 42(4):243–308.

———, and J. L. Hiehle. 1957. Food habits of the Tehama deer herd. Calif. Fish and Game 43(3):161–178.

Leege, T. A., and W. O. Hickey. 1971. Sprouting of northern Idaho shrubs after prescribed burning. J. Wildl. Manage. 35(3):508–515.

Leister, C. W. 1932. The pronghorn of North America. New York Zoo. Soc. Bull. 35(6):182–205.

Lent, P. C. 1971. Muskox management controversies in North America. Biol. Cons. 3:255–263.

———. 1974a. Mother-infant relationships in ungulates. Pages 14–55 *in* V. Geist and F. Walther, eds. The behavior of ungulates and its relation to management. IUCN New Ser. Publ. 24, Morges, Switzerland.

———. 1974b. A review of rutting behavior in moose. Can. Nat. 101 (1 and 2):307–323.

———. 1976. Testimony before Mackenzie Valley pipeline inquiry. Pages 16241–16247 *in* Proceedings of Inquiry, Vol. 106. Allwest Reporting Ltd., Burnaby, British Columbia.

———. Unpubl. Ecological and behavioral study of the Nunivak Island muskox population. Unpubl. Rep. to U.S. Fish and Wildl. Serv. On file at U.S. Fish and Wildl. Serv. offices, Anchorage and Bethel, Alaska and Univ. of Alaska, Fairbanks. 90 pp.

———, and D. Knutsen. 1971. Muskox and snowcover on Nunivak Island. Pages 50–62 *in* A. D. Haugen, ed. Symposium on snow and ice in relation to wildlife and recreation. Iowa State Univ. Press, Ames.

Lentfer, J. W. 1955. A two-year study of the Rocky Mountain goat in the Crazy Mountains, Montana. J. Wildl. Manage. 19(4):417–429.

Leopold, A. 1917. Putting the "AM" in game warden. The sportsmen's review. Clipping in Record Group 9/25/10, Wildlife Ecology, College of Agriculture, Steenbock Library Archives, University of Wisconsin-Madison.

———. 1918. The popular wilderness fallacy.

Outer's Book-Recreation 58:1, 46.

———. 1933. Game management. Charles Scribner's Sons, New York and London. 481 pp.

———, L. K. Sowls, and D. L. Spencer. 1947. A survey of over-populated deer ranges in the United States. J. Wildl. Manage. 11(2):162–177.

Leopold, A. S. 1959. Wildlife of Mexico, the game birds and mammals. Univ. California Press, Berkeley and Los Angeles. 586 pp.

———, T. Riney, R. McCain, and L. Tevis, Jr. 1951. The Jawbone deer herd. California Div. Fish and Game, Game Bull. No. 4. 139 pp.

Leopold, A. S., and F. F. Darling. 1953. Wildlife in Alaska. The Ronald Press Co. New York. 129 pp.

Leopold, A. S., and R. H. Barrett. 1972. Implications for wildlife of the 1968 Juneau Unit Timber Sale. Univ. California, Berkeley. 49 pp. and appendix.

LeResche, R. E. 1966. Behavior and calf survival in Alaska moose. M.S. Thesis. Univ. of Alaska, Fairbanks. 85 pp.

———. 1974. Moose migrations in North America. Can. Nat. 101 (1 and 2):393–415.

———. 1975. The international herds: present knowledge of the Forty mile and Porcupine herds. Pages 127–139 *in* J. R. Luick, P. C. Lent, D. R. Klein, and R. B. White, eds. Proceedings 1st International Reindeer/Caribou Symposium. Univ. of Alaska, Occ. Pap. No. 2, Inst. of Arctic Biology, Univ. of Alaska, College. 551 pp.

———, and J. L. Davis. 1973. Importance of non-browse foods to moose on the Kenai Peninsula, Alaska. J. Wildl. Manage. 37(3):279–287.

LeResche, R. E., U. S. Seal, P. D. Karns, and A. W. Franzmann. 1974. A review of blood chemistry of moose and other cervidae with emphasis on nutritional assessment. Can. Nat. 101 (1 and 2):263–290.

Lerner, L. J. 1963. Quantitative indices of recreational values. Rep. No. 11, Committee on Water Resources, West Agr. Econ. Res. Council.

Leuthold, W. 1969. Ethology and game management. Proc. IX Int. Cong. Game Biol., Moscow, USSR. 9:78–88.

Lewis, C. E., and T. J. Harshbager. 1976. Shrub and herbaceous vegetation after 20 years of prescribed burning in the South Carolina coastal plain. J. Range Manage. 29(1):13–18.

Lewis, P. 1976. The mountain lion. Colorado Outdoors 25(1):14–18.

Light, J. T. R. 1971. An ecological view of bighorn

habitat on Mt. San Antonio. N. Amer. Wild Sheep Conf. 1:150–157.

Ligon, J. S. 1927. Wildlife of New Mexico, its conservation and management. New Mexico Game and Fish Dep., Santa Fe. 212 pp.

Lindzey, J. S., R. G. Wingard and M. Ondik. 1975. Managing the whitetail. Pages 46–51 *in* R. Sievers, ed. Conservation yearbook. National Rifle Assoc., Washington, D.C.

Linke, W. 1957. Der rothirsch. Die neue brehmbucheri no. 129. A Ziemsen Verlag, Nittenberg-Lutherstadt.

Linsdale, J. M., and P. Q. Tomich. 1953. A herd of mule deer. Univ. California Press, Berkeley. 567 pp.

Liscinsky, S. A., G. O. Howard, and R. B. Waldeisen. 1969. A new device for injecting powdered drugs. J. Wildl. Manage. 33(4):1037–1038.

Lobell, C. H., and M. W. Coulter. 1969. The Maine sportsman. Univ. of Maine Agr. Exp. Sta., Misc. Rep. 124.

Long, T. A., and R. L. Cowan. 1964. Voluntary feed restriction observed in white-tailed deer. Science for the Farmer XI(4):5.

———, G. D. Strawn, R. S. Wetzel, and R. C. Miller. 1965. Seasonal fluctuations in feed consumption of the white-tailed deer. Pennsylvania State Univ. Agr. Exp. Sta., Prog. Rep. 262., University Park. 5 pp.

Longhurst, W. M. 1957. The effectiveness of hunting in controlling big-game populations in North America. Trans. N. Amer. Wildl. Conf. 22:544–569.

———, A. S. Leopold, and R. F. Dasmann. 1952. A survey of California deer herds, their ranges and management problems. California Dep. Fish and Game, Game Bull. No. 6. 136 pp.

Longhurst, W. M., H. K. Oh, M. B. Jones, and R. E. Kepner. 1968. A basis for the palatability of deer forage plants. Trans. N. Amer. Wildl. Conf. 33:181–189.

Longhurst, W. M., E. O. Garton, H. F. Heady, and G. E. Connolly. 1976. The California deer decline and possibilities for restoration. Paper read at Annual Meeting, Western Section of the Wildlife Society, Fresno, California. 41 pp. Multilith.

Lønø, O. 1960. Transplantation of the musk ox in Europe and North America. Meddel. Norsk. Polarinst. 84:3–25.

Lott, D. F. 1972. The way of the bison—fighting to dominate. Pages 321–333 *in* The marvels of animal behavior. National Geographic Society, Washington, D.C. 422 pp.

———. 1974. Sexual and aggressive behavior of adult male American bison *(Bison bison).*

Pages 382–394 *in* V. Geist and F. Walther, eds. The behavior of ungulates and its relation to management. Vol. 1. IUCN New. Ser. Publ. 24, Morges, Switzerland.

Low, W. A. 1970. The influence of aridity on reproduction of the collared peccary *(Dicotyles tajacu)* (Linn) in Texas. Ph.D. Thesis. Univ. British Columbia, Vancouver. 170 pp.

Lykke, J. 1975. Moose management in Norway and Sweden. Can. Nat. 101(1 and 2):723–735.

———, and I. McT. Cowan. 1968. Moose management and population dynamics on the Scandinavian Peninsula, with special reference to Norway. Proc. N. Amer. Moose Workshop 5:1–22.

Lyon, L. J. 1971. A cooperative research program: effects of logging on elk in Montana. Proc. Assoc. Midwest Fish and Game Commissioners Annu. Meeting. 38:447–457.

———, and W. F. Mueggler. 1968. Herbicide treatment of north Idaho browse evaluated six years later. J. Wildl. Manage. 32(3):538–541.

MacPherson, A. H. Unpubl. The caribou of Baffin Island, an unknown quantity? Unpubl. Rep. On file at Can. Wildl. Serv., Edmonton, Alberta. 13 pp.

Madson, J. 1966. The elk. Winchester-Western Press, East Alton. Ill. 125 pp.

Manning, T. H. 1971. Geographical variation in the polar bear *(Ursus maritimus* Phipps). Can. Wildl. Serv. Rep. Ser. No. 13, Ottawa. 27 pp.

Marburger, R. G., R. M. Robinson, J. W. Thomas, and K. A. Clark. 1971. Management implications of disease of big game animals in Texas. Proc. S. E. Assoc. Game and Fish Commissioners 24th Annu. Conf., 1970. 24:46–50.

Marchinton, R. L., and L. K. Jeter. 1967. Telemetric study of deer movement-ecology in the southeast. Proc. S.E. Assoc. Game and Fish Commissioners 20th Annu. Conf. 1966. 20:189–206.

Marchinton, R. L., A. S. Johnson, J. R. Sweeney, and J. M. Sweeney. 1971. Legal hunting of white-tailed deer with dogs: biology, sociology and management. Proc. S.E. Assoc. Game and Fish Commissioners 24th Annu. Conf., 1970. 24:74–89.

Markgren, G. 1969. Reproduction of moose in Sweden. Viltrery. 6(3):1–299.

———. 1974. The moose of Fennoscanda. Can. Nat. 101(1 and 2):185–194.

Marquis, D. A. 1974. The impact of deer browsing on Allegheny hardwood regeneration. USDA For. Serv. Res. Pap. NE-308. 8 pp.

Marsh, G. P. 1864. Man and nature. Charles Scribner and Co. New York. xix and 577 pp.

Martin, P. S. 1973. The discovery of America. Science 179:969–974.

Martin, R. O. R., and R. L. Hanson. 1966. Reservoirs in the United States. U.S. Geol. Surv. Water-Supply Pap. 1838. 115 pp.

Mathisen, J. 1962. Antelope trapping and transplanting. Nebraska Game Forestation, and Park Comm. Final Rep. P-R Proj. W-31-D-S. 11 pp.

Mattfeld, G. 1974. The energetics of winter foraging by white-tailed deer—a perspective on winter. Ph.D. Thesis. State Univ. of New York. 306 pp.

Matthiessen. P. 1959. Wildlife in America. The Viking Press, New York. 304 pp.

Mautz, W. W. 1969. Investigation of some digestive parameters of the white-tailed deer using the radioisotope ^{51}chromium. Ph.D. Thesis. Michigan State Univ., East Lansing. 69 pp.

———. 1971a. Comparison of the ^{51}CrCl$_3$ ratio and total collection techniques in digestibility studies with a wild ruminant, the white-tailed deer. J. Anim. Sci. 32:999–1002.

———. 1971b. Confinement effects on dry matter digestibility coefficients displayed by deer. J. Wildl. Manage. 34(2):366–368.

———. 1978. Sledding on a brushy hillside; an analogy of body fat cycle in deer. Wildl. Soc. Bull. 6(2):88–90.

———. Unpubl. Comparative digestive efficiency of hare and deer fed winter browse. Unpubl. On file at Univ. of New Hampshire, Durham.

———, and G. A. Petrides. 1971. Food passage rate in the white-tailed deer. J. Wildl. Manage. 34(4):723–731.

Mautz, W. W., H. Silver, and H. H. Hayes. 1974. Predicting the digestibility of winter deer browse from its proximate composition. Can. J. Zool. 52(10):1201–1205.

Mautz, W. W. , H. H. Silver, J. B. Holter, H. H. Hayes, and W. E. Urban. 1976. Digestibility and related nutritional data for seven northern deer browse species. J. Wildl. Manage. 40(4):630–638.

Maxwell, R. K., and J. Thorkelson. 1975. The field energetics of winter dormant bear *(Ursus americanus)* in northeastern Minnesota. Final report. U.S. For. Serv., North Cent. For. Exp. Sta. St. Paul, Mn. 50 pp. Multilith.

Maynard, L. A., and J. K. Loosli. 1962. Animal nutrition. McGraw-Hill Book Company, Inc., New York. 533 pp.

McCaffery, K. R., and W. A. Creed. 1969. Significance of forest openings to deer in northern Wisconsin. Wisconsin Dep. Nat. Resour. Tech. Bull. 44. 104 pp.

McCann, L. J. 1972. Time to cry wolf. Graphic Publ. Co., Lake Mills, Ia. 130 pp.

McCulloch, C. Y. 1973. Seasonal diets of mule and white-tailed deer. Pages 1–37 *in* Deer nutrition in Arizona chaparral and desert habitats. Arizona Game and Fish Dep. Spec. Rep. No. 3. vi and 68 pp.

———. 1974. Control of pinyon-juniper as a deer management measure in Arizona. Arizona Game and Fish Dep. Final Rep. Fed. Aid Proj. W-18-R, Work Plan 4, Jobs 2 plus 7. vii and 32 pp.

McEwen, E. H. 1970. Energy metabolism of barren ground caribou *(Rangifer tarandus)*. Can. J. Zool. 48(2):391–392.

———, and P. E. Whitehead. 1970. Seasonal change in the energy and nitrogen intake in reindeer and caribou. Can. J. Zool. 48(5):905–913.

McEwen, L. C., C. E. French, N. D. Magruder, R. W. Swift, and R. H. Ingram. 1957. Nutrient requirements of the white-tailed deer. Trans. N. Amer. Wildl. Conf. 22:119–137.

McGregor, W. G. 1974. The status of the puma in California. Pages 28–35 *in* R. L. Eaton, ed. The world's cats. Vol. III, No. 1. Proceedings of the Third International Symposium on the World's Cats. Univ. of Wash., Seattle, 95 pp.

McHarg, I. L. 1969. Design with nature. Doubleday/Natural History Press, New York. 197 pp.

McHugh, T. 1972. The time of the buffalo. Alfred A. Knopf, New York. 339 pp.

McKay, W. A., and D. A. Demarchi. 1972. Information brief on the current predator control policy for British Columbia. B.C. Fish and Wildl. Branch, File 86-00, Victoria. 3 pp.

McKnight, T. L. 1959. The feral horse in Anglo-America. Geog. Rev. 49:506–525.

McLean, D. D. 1954. Mountain lions in California. Calif. Fish and Game 40(2):147–166.

McMichael, T. J. 1970. Rate of predation on deer fawn mortality. Pages 77–83 *in* Wildlife research in Arizona, 1969–70. Arizona Game and Fish Dep. P-R Rep. Proj. W-78-14, Job No. 6.

Meagher, M. M. 1973. The bison of Yellowstone National Park. U.S. Nat. Park Serv. Sci. Monogr. No. 1. 161 pp.

———. 1976. Winter weather as a population regulating influence on free-ranging bison in Yellowstone National Park. Pages 29–38 *in* Research in the parks. Trans. of the National Park Centennial Symp. AAAS Dec. 28–29, 1971. Ser. No. 1, U.S. Govt. Printing Off. 232 pp.

Mealey, S. P. 1975. The natural food habits of free-ranging grizzly bears in Yellowstone National Park, 1973–1974. M.S. Thesis. Montana State Univ., Bozeman. 158 pp.

————, C. J. Jonkel, and R. Demarchi. 1977. Habitat criteria for grizzly bear management. Proc. XIII Int. Cong. Game Biologists. 13:276–289.

Mearns, E. A. 1907. Mammals of the Mexican boundary of the United States. Pt. 1. U.S. Nat. Bull. No. 56.

Mech. L. D. 1966. The wolves of Isle Royale. U.S. Nat. Park Serv., Fauna Ser. 7. U.S. Govt. Printing Off., Washington, D.C. 210 pp.

————. 1970. The wolf: the ecology and behaviour of an endangered species. Natural History Press, New York. 384 pp.

————, and L. D. Frenzel Jr. 1971a. An analysis of the age, sex, and condition of deer killed by wolves in northeastern Minnesota. Pages 35–51 in L. D. Mech and L. D. Frenzel, eds. Ecological Studies of the Timber Wolf in Northeastern Minnesota. USDA For. Serv. Res. Pap. NC-52, North Cent. For. Exp. Sta., St. Paul, Mn. 62 pp.

————, eds. 1971b. Ecological studies of the timber wolf in northeastern Minnesota. USDA For. Serv. Res. Paper NC-52. North Cent. For. Exp. Sta., St. Paul, Minn. 62 pp.

Mech, L. D., and P. D. Karns. 1977. Role of the wolf in a deer decline in the Superior National Forest. USDA For. Serv. Res. Pap. NC-148, North Cent. For. Exp. Sta., St. Paul, Minn.

Mendez, E. In Press. White-tailed deer in Mexico and Central America. In L. K. Halls, ed. White-tailed deer: ecology and management. The Stackpole Co., Harrisburg, Pa.

Merriam, C. H. 1901. The two bighorns and a new antelope from Mexico and the United States. Proc. Biol. Soc. 14:31–32.

Merriam, H. R. 1964. The wolves of Coronation Island. Proc. Alaska Sci. Conf. 15:27–32.

Milchunas, D. G. 1977. *In vivo-in vitro* relationships of Colorado mule deer forages. M.S. Thesis. Colorado State Univ., Fort Collins. 133 pp.

Miller, D. R. 1975. Observation of wolf predation on barren ground caribou in winter. Pages 209–220 in J. R. Luick, P. C. Lent, D. R. Klein, and R. B. White, eds. Proceedings, 1st International Reindeer/Caribou Symposium. Occ. Pap. No. 2, Inst. of Arctic Biology, Univ. of Alaska, College. 551 pp.

————. 1976. Biology of the Kaminuriak barren-ground caribou. Part 3. Can. Wildl. Serv. Rep. Ser. 36, Ottawa. 41 pp.

Miller, F. L. 1972. Eruption and attrition of man-

dibular teeth in barren-ground caribou. J. Wildl. Manage. 36(2):606–612.

————. 1974. Biology of the Kaminuriak barren-ground caribou. Part 2. Can. Wildl. Serv. Rep. Ser. No. 31, Ottawa, 88 pp.

————, R. H. Russell, and D. R. Urquhart. 1973. Preliminary surveys of Peary caribou and muskoxen on Melville, Eglinton and Byam Martin Island, Northwest Territories, 1972. Can. Wildl. Serv. Prog. Note 33:1–9.

Miller, F., C. J. Jonkel, and G. A. Tessier. 1972. Group cohesion and leadership response in barren-ground caribou to man-made barriers. Arctic 25:193–202.

Miller, F. L., and E. Broughton. 1974. Calf mortality during 1970 on the calving ground of Kaminuriak caribou. Can. Wildl. Serv. Rep. Ser. No. 26, Ottawa. 25 pp.

Miller, F. L., and R. H. Russell. 1974. Aerial surveys of Peary caribou and muskoxen on Western Queen Elizabeth Islands, Northwest Territories, 1973. Can. Wildl. Serv. Prog. Notes, No. 40. 17 pp.

————. 1975. Aerial surveys of Peary caribou and muskoxen on Bathurst Island, Northwest Territories, 1973 and 1974. Can. Wildl. Serv. Prog. Notes, No. 44. 8 pp

————, and A. Gunn. 1977. Peary caribou and muskoxen on western Queen Elizabeth Islands, Northwest Territories 1972–1974. Can. Wildl. Serv. Rep. Ser. No. 40. 55 pp.

Miller, G. 1977. The American bison (*Bison bison*): an initial bibliography. Can. Wildl. Serv. and Parks Canada. Edmonton, Alberta. 89 pp.

Miller, G. S. Jr., and R. Kellogg. 1955. List of North American mammals. U.S. Nat. Mus. Bull. 205. 954 pp.

Miller, H. A., and L. K. Halls. 1969. Fleshy fungi commonly eaten by southern wildlife. USDA For. Serv. Res. Pap. 49–50. 28 pp.

Miller, R. S., and D. B. Botkin. 1974. Endangered species: models and predictions. Amer. Sci. 62:179–181.

Moen, A. N. 1968a. Energy balance of white-tailed deer in the winter. Trans. N. Amer. Wildl. and Nat. Resour. Conf. 33:224–236.

————. 1968b. Surface temperatures and radiant heat loss from white-tailed deer. J. Wildl. Manage. 32(2):338–344.

————. 1973. Wildlife ecology. Freeman, San Francisco. 458 pp.

Moore, A. V. 1968. Effects of modified maternal care in sheep and goats. Pages 481–529 in G. Newton and S. Levine, eds. Early experience and behaviour. C. C. Thomas, Springfield.

Moore, W. G., and R. L. Marchinton. 1974. Marking behavior and its social function in white-tailed deer. Pages 447–456 *in* V. Geist and F. Walther, eds. The behavior of ungulates and its relation to management. Vol. 1. IUCN New Ser. Publ. 24, Morges, Switzerland.

Moran, R. J. 1973. The Rocky Mountain elk in Michigan. Michigan Dep. Nat. Resour. Res. Dev. Rep. 267. 93 pp.

Morrison, F. B. 1954. Feeds and feeding. Morrison Publishing Co. Ithaca, New York. 1165 pp.

Morrison, J. A., C. E. Trainer, and P. L. Wright. 1959. Breeding season in elk as determined from known-age embryos. J. Wildl. Manage. 23(1): 27–34.

Morse, W. B. 1976. Wildlife law enforcement. Paper read at the Western Association of State Fish and Game Commissioners Annual Meeting, July 28, 1976, Sun Valley, Idaho.

Morton, G. H., and E. L. Cheatum. 1946. Regional differences in breeding potential of white-tailed deer in New York. J. Wildl. Manage. 10(3):242–249.

Moyle, J. B. 1965. Big game in Minnesota. Minn. Dep. of Conserv. Tech. Bull. No. 9. 231 pp.

Müller-Schwarze, D. 1972. Responses of young black-tailed deer to predator odours. J. Mammal. 53(2):393–394.

———. 1974. Social functions of various scent glands in ungulates and the problems encountered in experimental studies of scent communications. Pages 107–113 *in* V. Geist and F. Walther, eds. The behavior of ungulates and its relation to management. Vol. 1. IUCN New Ser. Publ. 24, Morges, Switzerland.

Murie, A. 1940. Ecology of the coyote in the Yellowstone. Fauna Nat. Parks, Bull. No. 4. U.S. Govt. Printing Off., Washington, D.C. 206 pp.

———. 1944. The wolves of Mount McKinley. U.S. Nat. Park Serv. Fauna Ser. 5. 238 pp.

Murie, O. 1935. Alaska-Yukon caribou. N. Amer. Fauna No. 54. U.S. Dep of Agriculture. 93 pp.

———. 1951. The elk of North America. The Stackpole Co., Harrisburg, Pa. 376 pp.

Murphy, E. C. 1974. An age structure and reevaluation of the population dynamics of Dall sheep *(Ovis dalli dalli)*. M.S. Thesis. Univ. of Alaska, Fairbanks. 113 pp.

Murphy, D. A., and J. H. Ehrenreich. 1965. Effects of timber harvest and stand improvement on forage production. J. Wildl. Manage. 29(4):734–739.

Mutch, R. W. 1976. Fire management today: tradition and change in the Forest Service. Proc. 1975 Nat. Conv. Soc. Amer. For. 189–202.

Nagy, J. G., H. W. Steinhoff, and G. M. Ward. 1964. Effects of essential oils of sagebrush on deer rumen microbial function. J. Wildl. Manage. 28(4):785–790.

Neal, B. J. 1959a. A contribution on the life history of the collared peccary in Arizona. Amer. Midl. Nat. 61:177–190.

———. 1959b. Techniques for trapping and tagging the collared peccary. J. Wildl. Manage. 23(1):11–16.

Neal, W. A. 1968. Management of the Catfish Point deer herd. Miss. Game and Fish 27(8):8–9.

Neff, D. J. 1974. Forage preferences of trained mule deer on the Beaver Creek watersheds. Arizona Game and Fish Dep. Spec. Rep. No. 4. iv and 61 pp.

Neilson, C., and K. A. Neiland. 1974. 1974 annual report. P-R Project W-17-5 and W-17-6, Job 6.6R. Alaska Dep. Fish and Game, Juneau.

Nelson, E. W. 1912. A new subspecies of pronghorn antelope from lower California. Proc. Biol. Soc. 25:107–108.

———. 1925. Status of the pronghorned antelope, 1922–1924. U.S. Dep. Agr. Bull. No. 1346. 64 pp.

Nesbitt, W. H., and J. S. Parker, eds. 1977. North American big game. The Boone and Crockett Club and National Rifle Association of America. Washington, D.C. 367 pp.

Newberry, J. S. 1855. Report upon the zoology of the route. No. 2, Chapt. 1. Pages 70–71 *in* Abbot, H. L. 1857. Reports of exploration and surveys to ascertain the most practicable and economical route for a railroad from the Mississippi River to the Pacific Ocean. U.S. Senate, Washington, D.C. Ex. Doc. No. 78. Vol VII.

Nichols, L. 1971. 1971 annual report. P-R projects W-17-2 and W-17-3, Jobs 6.3R, 6.4R and 6.5R. Alaska Dep. of Fish and Game, Juneau.

———. 1976. An experiment in Dall sheep management: progress report. Trans. N. Amer. Wild Sheep Conf. 2:16–34.

———. In Press. Dall's sheep reproduction. J. Wildl. Manage.

Nielsen, D. B. 1975. Coyotes and deer. Utah Sci. 36(3):87–90.

Nishikawa, Y., and E. S. E. Hafez. 1968. Reproduction of horses. Pages 289–300 *in* E. S. E. Hafez, ed. Reproduction in farm animals. Lea and Febiger, Philadelphia.

Nixon, C. M., M. W. McClain, and K. R. Russell. 1970. Deer food habits and range characteristics in Ohio. J. Wildl. Manage. 34(4):870–886.

Nobe, K. C., and A. H. Gilbert. 1970. A survey of

sportsmen expenditures for hunting and fishing in Colorado, 1968. GFP-R-T-24, Colorado Div. Game, Fish and Parks, Denver. 83 pp.

Nordan, H. C., I. McT. Cowan, and A. J. Wood. 1970. The feed intake and heat production of the young black-tailed deer. Can. J. Zool. 48(2):275–282.

Nowak, R. M. 1976. The cougar in the United States and Canada. U.S. Fish and Wildl. Serv., Washington, D.C. and New York Zoological Society. 190 pp.

Odum, E. P. 1959. Fundamentals of ecology. 2nd ed. W. B. Saunders Co. Philadelphia and London. 546 pp.

Oeming, A. 1965. A herd of musk-oxen, *Ovibos moschatus* in captivity. Int. Zoo Yearbook 5:58–75.

Ogle, T. F. 1971. Predator-prey relationships between coyotes and white-tailed deer. Northwest Sci. 45(4):213–218.

O'Gara, B. W., and G. M. Matson. 1975. Growth and casting of horns by pronghorn and exfoliation of horns by bovids. J. Mammal. 56(4):829–846.

Oldemeyer, J. L. 1977. Impact of LeTourneau tree crushers on moose habitat on the Kenai National Moose Range. Paper read at 28th Annual Conference, Northwest Section of The Wildlife Society, Feb. 17–18, 1977, Kalispell, Mt.

Olson, S. T. 1952. Black-tailed deer studies-1952. Alaska Fed. Aid Proj. Rep. W-3-R-7, Work Plan E. Alaska Dep. Fish and Game, Juneau.

Ord, G. 1818. Antilocapra Ord. J. De Physique, De Chimie, D'Histoire Naturelle Et Des Arts. Paris, France. 87:149–151.

Oregon State Game Commission. 1972. Antelope respond to coyote control. Oreg. State Game Comm. Bull. 27(1):9.

Oritsland, N. A., C. Jonkel, and K. Ronald. 1976. A respiration chamber for exercising polar bears. Nor. J. Zool. 24:65–67.

Owen-Smith, N. 1974. The social system of the white rhinoceros. Pages 341–351 *in* V. Geist and F. Walther, eds. The behavior of ungulates and its relation to management. Vol 1. IUCN New Ser. Publ. 24, Morges, Switzerland.

Ozoga, J. J. 1968. Variations in microclimate in a conifer swamp deeryard in northern Michigan. J. Wildl. Manage. 32(3):574–585.

————, and E. M. Harger. 1966. Winter activities and feeding habits of northern Michigan coyotes. J. Wildl. Manage. 30(4):809–818.

Papez, N. J. 1976. The Ruby-Butte deer herd. Nevada Dep. Fish and Game Biol. Bull. No. 5. 61 pp.

Parker, G. R. 1972a. Biology of the Kaminuriak population of barren-ground caribou. Part 1. Can. Wildl. Serv. Rep. Ser. 20. Information Canada, Ottawa. 93 pp.

————. 1972b. Distribution of barren-ground caribou harvest in northcentral Canada. Can. Wildl. Serv., Occ. Pap. No. 15. 19 pp.

————. 1975. An investigation of caribou range on Southampton Island, N.W.T. Can. Wildl. Serv. Rep. Ser. No. 33. 82 pp.

————, D. C. Thomas, F. Hroughton, and D. R. Gray. 1975. Crashes of muskox and Peary caribou populations in 1973–1974 on the Parry Islands, Arctic Canada. Can. Wildl. Serv. Prog. Notes No. 56. 10 pp.

Parker, I. S. C., and A. D. Graham. 1971. The ecological and economic basis for game ranching in Africa. Pages 393–404 *in* E. Duffy and A. S. Watt, eds. The scientific management of animal and plant communities for conservation.

Parkman, F. 1872. The California and Oregon trail. 4th ed. Boston, Little, Brown and Co., New York. 448 pp.

————. 1892. The Oregon trail. Boston, Little, Brown and Co., New York. 411 pp.

Passmore, R. C. 1970. White-tailed deer. Can. Wildl. Serv. Cat. No. R69-4/7. 4 pp.

————, R. L. Peterson, and A. T. Cringan. 1955. A study of mandibular tooth-wear as an index to age of moose. Pages 223–238, Appendix A., *in* R. L. Peterson, ed. North American moose. Univ. of Toronto Press, Toronto. 280 pp.

Pasto, J. K., and D. W. Thomas. 1955. Deer economics. Pennsylvania State Univ. University Park, Pa. 29 pp.

Patton, A. 1976a. Nova Scotia deer reproduction report 1975. Nova Scotia Dep. Lands and For., For. Resour. Education, Truro, Nova Scotia. 19 pp.

————. 1976b. 1975 deer mortality report. Nova Scotia Dep. Lands and For., For. Resour; Education, Truro, Nova Scotia. 15 pp.

Patton, D. R. 1974. Patch cutting increases deer and elk use of a pine forest in Arizona. J. For. 72(12):764–766.

Paulsen, H. A. Jr., E. H. Reid, and K. W. Parker, eds. 1970. Range and wildlife habitat evaluation—a research symposium. U.S. Dep. Agr. Misc. Publ. No. 1147. 220 pp.

Pearse, P. H. 1967. A case study of big game resources in the East Kootenay. Univ. of British Columbia, Vancouver, 68 pp.

————. 1968. A new approach to the evaluation of non-priced recreational resources. Land Econ. 44(1):87–99.

————, and G. K. Bowden. 1969. Economic evaluations of recreational resources: problems and prospects. Trans. N. Amer. Wildl. and Nat. Resour. Conf. 34:283–293.

Pearson, A. W. 1975. The northern interior grizzly bear. Can. Wildl. Serv. Rep. Ser. No. 34. Information Canada, Ottawa. 84 pp.

Pearson, E. W. 1978. The 1974 coyote harvest estimate for 17 western states. Wildl. Soc. Bull. 6(1):25–32.

Pearson, H. A., H. A. Paulsen, Jr., E. H. Reid, and K. W. Parker, eds. *In vitro* techniques. Pages 85–92 *in* H. A. Paulsen, Jr., E. H. Reid, and K. W. Parker, eds. Range and wildlife habitat evaluation—a research symposium. U.S. Dep. Agr. Misc. Publ. 1147. 220 pp.

Pearson, H. A., and H. S. Sternitzke. 1976. Deer browse inventories in the Louisiana coastal plain. J. Wildl. Manage. 40(2):326–329.

Pedan, D. G., G. M. Van Dyne, R. W. Rice, and R. M. Hansen. 1974. The trophic ecology of *Bison bison L.* on shortgrass plains. J. Appl. Ecol. 11:489–498.

Peden, A. G., R. M. Hansen, R. W. Rice, and G. M. Van Dyne. 1974. A double sampling technique for estimating dietary composition. J. Range Manage. 27(4):323–325.

Pedersen, A. 1958. Der Moschusoches. A Ziemsen Verlag. 54 pp.

Peek, J. M. 1962. Studies of moose in the Gravelly and Snowcrest Mountains, Montana. J. Wildl. Manage. 26(4):360–365.

———. 1974. A review of moose food habit studies in North America. Can. Nat. 101(1 and 2):195–215.

———, D. L. Urich, and R. J. Mackie. 1976. Moose habitat selection and relationships to forest management in northeastern Minnesota. Wildl. Monogr. 48. 65 pp.

Pengelly, W. L. 1961. Factors influencing production of white-tailed deer on the Coeur d'Alene National Forest, Idaho, Ph.D. Thesis. Utah State Univ., Logan. 205 pp.

———. 1972. Clearcutting: detrimental aspects for wildlife resources. J. Soil and Water Conserv. 27(6):255–258.

Peterele, T. J. 1967. Characteristics of some Ohio hunters. J. Wildl. Manage. 31(2): 375–389.

Peterson, R. L. 1952. A review of the living representatives of the genus *Alces*. Contr. R. Ont. Mus. Zool. Palaeont. 34:1–30.

———, ed. 1955. North American moose. Univ. of Toronto Press, Toronto. 280 pp.

———. 1974a. Moose: yesterday, today, and tomorrow. Can. Nat. 101(1 and 2):1–8.

———. 1974b. A review of the general life history of moose. Can. Nat. 101(1 and 2):9–21.

Peterson, R. O. In Press. The role of wolf predation in a moose population decline. *In* Proceedings First Conference on Science in National Parks, New Orleans, La., Nov. 9–12, 1976.

———, and D. L. Allen. 1974. Snow conditions as a parameter in moose-wolf relationships. Can. Nat. 101(1 and 2):481–492.

Petrides, G. A. 1961. The management of wild hoofed animals in the United States in relation to land use. Terre et Vie 2:181–202.

———, and W. G. Swank. 1966. Estimating the productivity and energy relations of an African elephant population. Proc. 9th Int. Grassland Cong., Sao Paulo, Brazil. 9:831–842.

Pfefferkorn, I. 1795. Sonora: a description of the province. English translation by T. E. Treutlin. Univ. of New Mexico Press, Albuquerque. 329 pp.

Picton, H. D. 1962. Notes on the breeding territories of Rocky Mountain elk. Montana Fish and Game Dep., Missoula. 8 pp.

Pimlott, D. H. 1967. Wolf predation and ungulate populations. Amer. Zool. 7:267–278.

———. 1970. Predation and productivity of game populations in North America. Trans. IX Int. Cong. Game Biologists 9:63–72.

———, J. A. Shannon, and G. B. Kolenosky. 1969. The ecology of the timber wolf in Algonquin Provincial Park, Ontario. Ontario Dep. Lands and For. Res. Rep. (Wildl.) No. 87. 92 pp.

Pitzman, M. 1970. Birth behavior and lamb survival in mountain sheep in Alaska. M.S. Thesis. Univ. of Alaska, Fairbanks. 116 pp.

Platts, W. S. 1974. Environmental effects of surface-mining and the need for ecosystem management. Trans. N. Amer. Wildl. and Nat. Resour. Conf. 39:483–485.

Plummer, A. P. 1968. Restoring big game in Utah. Utah Div. Fish and Game. Publ No. 68–3. 183 pp.

Poelker, R. J. 1974. The status and management of the puma in Washington. Pages 20–27 *in* R. L. Eaton, ed. The world's cats. Volume III, No. I. Proceedings of the Third International Symposium on the World's Cats. Univ. of Wash., Seattle. 95 pp.

———, and H. D. Hartwell. 1973. Black bear in Washington. Washington State Game Dep. Biol. Bull. No. 14. 180 pp.

Post, G. 1971. An annotated bibliography of the wild sheep of North America. Rachelwood Wildl. Res. Preserve Publ. No. 1. New Florence, Pa. 86 pp.

Prestwood, A. K., S. R. Pursglove, and F. A. Hayes. 1976. Parasitism among white-tailed deer and domestic sheep on common range. J. Wildl. Dis. 12(3):380–385.

Progulske, D. R., and T. S. Baskett. 1958. Mobility of Missouri deer and their harassment by dogs. J. Wildl. Manage. 22(2):184–192.

Puglisi, M. J., J. S. Lindzey, and E. D. Bellis. 1974. Factors associated with highway mortality of white-tailed deer. J. Wildl. Manage. 38(4):799–807.

Quimby, D. C., and J. E. Gaab. 1957. Mandibular dentition as an age indicator in Rocky Mountain elk. J. Wildl. Manage. 21(4):435–451.

Rabb, G. B. 1959. Reproductive and vocal behavior in captive cats. J. Mammal. 40(4):616–617.

Rajakoski, E., and D. Kovisto. 1966, Puberty of the female moose *(Alces alces)* in Finland. Suom. Riista 18:157–162.

Ramsey, C. W. 1965. Potential economic returns from deer as compared with livestock in the Edwards Plateau region of Texas. J. Range Manage. 18(5):247–250.

Rausch, R. A. 1957. Dynamics of the railbelt moose populations. Proc. 8th Alaska Sci. Conf. 8:41–49.

———. 1967. Some aspects of the population ecology of wolves, Alaska. Amer. Zool. 7:253–265.

———. 1969. A summary of wolf studies in south-central Alaska 1957–1968. Trans. N. Amer. Wildl. and Nat. Resour. Conf. 34:117–131.

———. 1972. Predator control and bounties in Alaska. Pages 173–182 *in* S. A. Cain, chairman. Predator control—1971. Report to the Council on Environmental Quality and the Department of the Interior by the Advisory Committee on Predator Control. Univ. Michigan Press, Ann Arbor. 207 pp.

———, and A. Bratlie. 1965. Annual assessments of moose calf production and mortality in south-central Alaska. Proc. West. Assoc. Fish and Game Commissioners Annu. Meeting 45:140–146.

Rausch, R. A., R. J. Somerville, and R. H. Bishop. 1974. Moose management in Alaska. Can. Nat. 101(1 and 2):705–721.

Rausch, R. L. 1953. On the status of some arctic mammals. Arctic 6:91–148.

———. 1961. A review of the distribution of Holarctic recent mammals. Pages 29–43 *in* Proceedings 10th Pacific Science Congress, Honolulu. Bishop Museum Press, Honolulu, Ha.

Rawls, K. 1974. Scent markings in captive Maxwell's duikers. Pages 114–123 *in* V. Geist and F. Walther, eds. The behavior of ungulates and its relation to management. Vol. 1. IUCN New Ser. Publ. 24, Morges, Switzerland.

Reed, D. F., T. N. Woodard, and T. M. Pojar. 1975. Behavioural response of mule deer to a highway underpass. J. Wildl. Manage. 39(2):361–367.

Regelin, W. L. 1976. Effects of snowdrifts on mountain shrub communities. Ph.D. Thesis. Colorado State Univ., Fort Collins. 120 pp.

———, O. C. Wallmo, J. Nagy, and D. R. Dietz. 1974. Effects of logging on forage values for deer in Colorado. J. For. 72(5):282–285.

Regenstein, L. 1975. The politics of extinction. MacMillan Co., New York. 280 pp.

Reid, R. L., and S. C. Miles. 1972. Studies on carbohydrate metabolism in sheep: the adrenal response to psychological stress. Austral. J. Agr. Res. 131:282–295.

Reynolds, H. G. 1966a. Use of a ponderosa pine forest in Arizona by deer, elk, and cattle. USDA For. Serv. Res. Note RM-63. 7 pp.

———. 1966b. Use of openings in spruce-fir forests of Arizona by elk, deer and cattle. USDA For. Serv. Res. Note RM-66. 4 pp.

Richardson, A. H. 1971. The Rocky Mountain goat in the Black Hills. South Dakota Dep. Game, Fish and Parks Bull. 2:1–25.

———, and L. E. Petersen. 1974. History and management of South Dakota deer. South Dakota Dep. of Game, Fish and Parks Bull. 5. 113 pp.

Richardson, G. L. 1966. Eye lens weight as an indication of age in the collared peccary, *Pecari tajacu*. M.S. Thesis. Univ. of Arizona, Tucson. 47 pp.

Richens, V. B. 1967. Characteristics of mule deer herds and their range in northeastern Utah. J. Wildl. Manage. 31(4):651–666.

Rideout, C. B. 1973. The goats on Dome Shaped Mountain. Montana Outdoors 4(3):2–5.

———. 1974a. A radio telemetry study of the ecology and behavior of the Rocky Mountain goat in western Montana. Ph.D. Thesis, Univ. Kansas, Lawrence. ix and 146 pp.

———. 1974b. Radio tracking the Rocky Mountain goat in western Montana. Annu. Rocky Mountain Bioengr. Symp. 11:139–144.

———. 1974c. Comparison of techniques for capturing mountain goats. J. Wildl. Manage. 38(3):573–575.

———. In Press. Mountain goat home ranges in the Sapphire Mountains of Montana. *In* W. M. Samuel and W. MacGregor, eds. Proceedings of the First International Mountain Goat Symposium.

———, and R. S. Hoffman. 1975. *Oreamnos americanus*. Mammalian Species Rep. No. 63, Amer. Soc. of Mammalogists, Lawrence, Kansas. 6 pp.

Rideout, C. B., and G. L. Worthen. 1975. Use of girth measurement for estimating weight of mountain goats. J. Wildl. Manage. 39(4):705–708.

Rippin, B. Unpubl. Baffin Island caribou. Unpubl. Rep. Game Manage. Div. Northwest Territories, Can. Wildl. Serv. On file at Western Regional Library, Edmonton, Alberta. 26 pp.

Roach, B. A. 1974. Scheduling timber cutting for sustained yield of wood products and wildlife. USDA For. Serv. Gen. Tech. Rep. NE-14. 13 pp.

Robinette, W. L. 1956. Productivity—the annual crop of mule deer. Pages 415–429 *in* W. P. Taylor, ed. The deer of North America. The Stackpole Co., Harrisburg, Pa. 668 pp.

———, and O. A. Olsen. 1944. Studies of the productivity of mule deer in central Utah. Trans. N. Amer. Wildl. Conf. 9:151–161.

Robinette, W. L., and J. S. Gashwiler. 1955. Fertility of mule deer in Utah. J. Wildl. Manage. 19(1):155–136.

———, and O. W. Morris. 1959. Food habits of the cougar in Utah and Nevada. J. Wildl. Manage. 23(3):261–273.

———. 1961. Notes on cougar productivity and life history. J. Mammal. 42(2):204–217.

Robinette, W. L., C. H. Baer, R. E. Pillmore, and C. E. Knittle. 1973. Effects of nutritional change on captive mule deer. J. Wildl. Manage. 37(3):312–326.

Robinette, W. L., N. V. Hancock, and D. A. Jones. 1977. The Oak Creek mule deer herd in Utah. Utah Div. Wildl. Publ. No. 77–15. 148 pp.

Robbins, C. T., R. L. Prior, A. N. Moen, and W. J. Visek. 1974. Nitrogen metabolism of white-tailed deer. J. Anim. Sci. 38(2):186–191.

Robbins, C. T., P. J. Van Soest, W. W. Mautz, and A. N. Moen. 1975. Feed analyses and digestion with reference to white-tailed deer. J. Wildl. Manage. 39(1):67–79.

Robinson, W. B. 1943. The "human coyote-getter" vs. the steel trap in control of predatory animals. J. Wildl. Manage. 7(2):179–189.

———. 1948. Thallium and compound 1080 impregnated stations in coyote control. J. Wildl. Manage. 12(3):279–295.

Rockwell, R. H. 1971. Field notes on the preservation of big game trophies. Pages 37–45 *in* R. C. Alberts, ed. North American big game. Boone and Crockett Club, Pittsburgh, Pa. 403 pp.

Roe, F. G. 1951. The North American buffalo. University of Toronto Press. 957 pp.

Rogers, L. 1976. Effect of mast and berry crop

failures on survival, growth and reproductive success of black bear. Trans. N. Amer. Wildl. and Nat. Resour. Conf. 41:431–438.

Rohdy, D. D., and R. E. Lovegrove. 1970. Economic impact of hunting and fishing expenditures in Grand County, Colorado, 1968. Colorado State Univ. Exp. Sta. Bull. GS 916, Fort Collins. 36 pp.

Romer, A. S. 1970. The vertebrate body. W. B. Saunders Co., Philadelphia. 601 pp.

Rongstad, O. J., and J. R. Tester. 1969. Movements and habitat use of white-tailed deer in Minnesota. J. Wildl. Manage. 33(2):366–379.

Rorabacher, J. A. 1970. The American buffalo in transition: a historical and economic survey of the bison in America. North Star Press, St. Cloud, Minn. 141 pp.

Roseberry, J. L., and W. D. Klimstra. 1970. Productivity of white-tailed deer on Crab Orchard National Wildlife Refuge. J. Wildl. Manage. 34(1):23–28.

Ross, L. A., D. M. Blood, and K. C. Nobe. 1975. A survey of sportsman expenditures for hunting and fishing in Colorado, 1973. Colorado Div. of Wildl. Contract Rep. NRE-20. 102 pp.

Rowe, J. S., and G. W. Scotter. 1973. Fire in the boreal forest. Quat. Res. 3:444–464.

Rowley, I. 1970. Lamb predation in Australia: incidence, predisposing conditions, and the identification of wounds. CSIRO Wildl. Res. 15:79–123.

Roy, L. D., and M. J. Dorrance. 1976. Methods of investigating predation of domestic livestock. Alberta Agriculture, Edmonton. 54 pp.

Ruggiero, L., and J. B. Whelan. 1976. A comparison of *in vitro* and *in vivo* food digestibility by white-tailed deer. J. Range Manage. 29(1):82–83.

Runge, W., and G. Wobeser. 1975. A survey of deer winter mortality in Saskatchewan. Saskatchewan Dep. of Tourism and Renewable Resour. Wildl. Rep. 4. 22 pp.

Rush, W. M. 1944. American pronghorn. Nat. Hist. 53(7):321–323.

Russell, P. 1937. Antelope transplanting is success. New Mexico 15(6):32–33.

———. 1964. Antelope of New Mexico. New Mexico Dep. Game and Fish. Bull. No. 12, Santa Fe. 103 pp.

Russo, J. P. 1956. The desert bighorn sheep in Arizona. Arizona Game and Fish Dep. Wildl. Bull. 1. 153 pp.

Russo, J. R. 1964. The Kaibab north deer herd—its history, problems, and management. Alabama Game and Fish Dep. Wildl. Bull. No. 7. 195 pp.

Salwasser, H. 1975. The interstate wildlife

study—a fresh perspective. Mzuri Drumbeat 2(16):6–7, 18–22, 24.

Samuel, W. M., and W. A. Low. 1970. Parasites of the collared peccary in Texas. J. Wildl. Dis. 6:16–23.

Samuel, W. M., and D. R. Gray. 1974. Parasitic infection in muskoxen. J. Wildl. Manage. 38(4):775–782.

Samuel, W. M., G. A. Chalmers, J. G. Stelfox, A. Loewen, and J. J. Thomsen 1975. Contagious ecthyma in bighorn sheep and mountain goats from Western Canada. J. Wildl. Dis. 11:26–31.

Sandfort, W. W., and R. J. Tully. 1971. The status and management of the mountain lion and bobcat in Colorado. Pages 72–85 *in* S. E. Jorgensen and L. D. Mech, eds. Proceedings of a Symposium on the Native Cats of North America—their status and management. U.S. Fish and Wildl. Serv. St. Paul, Minn. 139 pp.

Schaffer, W. M., and C. A. Reed. 1972. The co-evolution of social behavior and cranial morphology in sheep and goats (Bovidae, Caprini). Fieldiana Zool. 61:1–88.

Scheffer, V. B. 1976. The future of wildlife management. Wildl. Soc. Bull. 4(2):51–54.

Schick, B. A., T. A. More, R. M. DeGraaf, and D. E. Samuel. 1976. Marketing wildlife management. Wildl. Soc. Bull. 4(2):64–68.

Schlegel, M. 1976. Factors affecting calf elk survival in north central Idaho. Proc. West. Assoc. Fish and Game Commissioners Annu. Meeting 56:342–355.

Schole, B. J., F. A. Glover, D. D. Sjogren, and E. Decker. 1973. Colorado hunter behavior, attitudes and philosophies. Trans. N. Amer. Wildl. and Nat. Resour. Conf. 38:242–248.

Schmidt, J. L. 1974a. Field care of big game. Colorado State Univ. Ext. Serv., Service in Action Leafl. No. 6.503. n.p.

———. 1974b. Cutting up a big game carcass. Colorado State Univ. Ext. Serv., Service in Action Leafl. No. 6.504. n.p.

Schmidt, R., T. Spraker, and C. Hibler. In Press. Treatment of bighorn sheep for verminous pneumonia. Trans. Northern Wild Sheep Council.

Schultz, V., L. L. Eberhardt, and J. M. Thomas. 1976. A bibliography of quantitative ecology. Dowden, Hutcheson and Ross, Stroudsburg, Pa. 362 pp.

Schwartz, C. G., and J. F. Nagy. 1976. Pronghorn diets relative to forage availability in northeastern Colorado. J. Wildl. Manage. 40(3):469–478.

Schweinsburg, R. E. 1969. Social behavior of the collared peccary *(Pecari tajacu)* in the Tuc-son Mountains. Ph.D. Thesis. Univ. of Arizona, Tucson. 115 pp.

———. 1971. The home range, movements and herd integrity of the collared peccary in southern Arizona. J. Wildl. Manage. 35(3):455–460.

———, and L. K. Sowls. 1972. Aggressive behavior and related phenomena in the collared peccary. Z. Tierpsychol. 20:132–145.

Scott, M. D., and K. Causey. 1973. Ecology of feral dogs in Alabama. J. Wildl. Manage. 37(3):253–265.

Scott, W. B. 1913. A history of land mammals in the western hemisphere. The MacMillan Co., New York. 693 pp.

Scotter, G. W. 1964. Effects of forest fires on the winter range of barren-ground caribou in northern Saskatchewan. Can. Wildl. Serv., Wildl. Manage. Bull. Ser. 1, 18. 111 pp.

———. 1967. Effects of fire on barren-ground caribou and their forest habitat in northern Canada. Trans. N. Amer. Wildl. and Nat. Resour. Conf. 32:246–259.

Seber, G. A. F. 1973. The estimation of animal abundance. Hafner Press, New York. 506 pp.

Seckler, D. W. 1966. On the uses and abuses of economic science in evaluating public outdoor recreation. Land Econ. 42(4):485–494.

Seidensticker, J. C., IV, M. G. Hornocker, W. V. Wiles, and J. P. Messick. 1973. Mountain lion social organization in the Idaho Primitive Area. Wildl. Monogr. 35. 60 pp.

Selye, H. 1950. Stress—the physiology and pathology of exposure to stress. Acta. Inc. Medical Publishers, Montreal. xx and 822 and 203 pp.

Sergeant, D. E., and D. H. Pimlott. 1959. Age determination in moose from sectioned incisor teeth. J. Wildl. Manage. 23(3):315–321.

Seton, E. T. 1909. Life histories of northern animals. 2 vols. Charles Scribner's Sons, New York. 1267 pp.

———. 1929. Lives of game animals. Vol. 3. Doubleday, Doran and Co. New York. 780 pp.

———. 1937. Lives of game animals, Vol 3. Literary Guild of America, New York. 780 pp.

Severinghaus, C. W. 1972. Weather and the deer population. The (New York) Conservationist 26(2):28–31.

———.1974. Deer population—a wildlife roller coaster. The (New York) Conservationist 28(5):36–38.

———. 1975. Advances in the science of deer management. The (New York) Conservationist 29(4):18–20.

———, and J. E. Tanck. 1964. Productivity and growth of white-tailed deer from the Adirondack region of New York. N.Y. Fish and Game J. 11(1):13–27.

Shackleton, D. M. 1973. Population quality and bighorn sheep. Ph.D. Thesis. Univ. of Calgary, Alberta. 227 pp.

———, and D. A. Hutton. 1971. An analysis of the mechanisms of brooming of mountain sheep horns. Sonderdrucke aus Z. F. Saugertierkunde Bd. 36(1971)H.6, S:342–350.

Shafer, E. L. Jr. 1963. The twig count method for measuring hardwood deer browse. J. Wildl. Manage. 37(3):428–437.

Shaw, D. and D. L. Gilbert. 1974. Attitudes of college students toward hunting. Trans. N. Amer. Wildl. and Nat. Resour. Conf. 39:157–162.

Shaw, H. G. 1977. Impact of mountain lion on mule deer and cattle in northwestern Arizona. Pages 17–32 *in* R. L. Phillips and C. Jonkel, eds. Proceedings of the 1975 Predator Symposium. For. and Cons. Exp. Sta., Univ. of Montana, Missoula.

Shaw, S. P. 1970. Forest wildlife responsibilities—what's our problem? J. For. 68(5):270–273.

———, and T. H. Ripley. 1965. Managing the forest for sustained yield of woody browse for deer. Proc. Soc. Amer. Foresters 229–233.

Shoener, W. T. 1965. An economic look at hunting. Maine Fish and Game 8(1):7–8.

Shope, R. E. 1967. The epizootiology of epizootic hemorrhagic disease of deer. Trans. N. Amer. Wildl. and Nat. Resour. Conf. 32:381–386.

Short, H. L. 1966. Methods for evaluating forages for wild ruminants. Trans. N. Amer. Wildl. and Nat. Resour. Conf. 31:122–128.

———. 1971. Forage digestibility and diet of deer on southern upland range. J. Wildl. Manage. 35(4):698–706.

———. 1972. Ecological framework for deer management. J. For. 70(4):200–203.

———. 1977. Food habits of mule deer in a semidesert grass-shrub habitat. J. Range Manage. 30(3):206–209.

———, and E. A. Epps, Jr. 1976. Nutrient quality and digestibility of seeds and fruits from southern forests. J. Wildl. Manage. 40(2):283–289.

Short, H. L., J. D. Newsom, G. L. McCoy, and J. F. Fowler. 1969. Effects of nutrition and climate on southern deer. Trans. N. Amer. Wildl. and Nat. Resour. Conf. 34:137–146.

Shuman, R. F. 1950. Bear depredations on red salmon spawning populations in the Karluk River System, 1947. J. Wildl. Manage. 14(1):1–9.

Sigman, M. J. 1977. The importance of the cow-calf bond to overwinter moose calf survival. M. S. Thesis. Univ. of Alaska, Fairbanks. 182 pp.

Silver, H., and N. F. Colovos. 1957. Nutritive evaluation of some forage rations of deer. New Hampshire Fish and Game Dep. Tech. Circ. 15. 56 pp.

———, and H. H. Hayes. 1959. Basal metabolism of white-tailed deer—a pilot study. J. Wildl. Manage. 23(4):434–438.

Silver, H., N. F. Colovos, J. B. Holter, and H. H. Hayes. 1969. Fasting metabolism of white-tailed deer. J. Wildl. Manage. 33(3):490–498.

———. 1971. Effect of falling temperature on heat production in fasting white-tailed deer. J. Wildl. Manage. 35(1):37–46.

Simkin, D. W. 1965. A preliminary report of the woodland caribou study in Ontario. Ontario Dep. Land and For. Sec. Rep. (Wildl.) No. 59. 75 pp.

Siniff, D. B., and R. O. Skoog. 1964. Aerial censusing of caribou using stratified random sampling. J. Wildl. Manage. 28(2):391–401.

Sitton, L. W., and S. Wallen. 1976. California mountain lion study. Calif. Dep. Fish and Game, Sacramento. 40 pp. Multilith.

Skinner, M. R., and O. C. Kaisen. 1947. The fossil *Bison* of Alaska and preliminary revision of the genus. Bull. Amer. Mus. Nat. Hist. 89:127–256.

Skoog, R. O. 1968. Ecology of the caribou *(Rangifer tarandus granti)* in Alaska. Ph.D. Thesis. Univ. of California, Berkeley. 699 pp.

Smith, A. D. 1949. Effects of mule deer and livestock upon a foothill range in northern Utah. J. Wildl. Manage. 13(4):421–423.

———. 1950. Sagebrush as a winter feed of deer. J. Wildl. Manage. 14(3):285–289.

———. 1952. Digestiblity of some native forages for mule deer. J. Wildl. Manage. 16(3):309–312.

———. 1959. Adequacy of some important browse species in overwintering of mule deer. J. Range Manage. 12(1):8–13.

———, and D. D. Doell. 1968. Guides to allocating forage between cattle and big game on big game winter range. Utah State Div. of Fish and Game Publ. No. 68–11. 32 pp.

Smith, B. 1863. Rudo Enseyo, 1763. (Trans. by Eusebio Guiteras.) Records of the American Catholic Historical Society, Philadelphia. Vol. V. No. 2. 1894. Republished by Arizona Silhouettes, Tucson. 1951.

Smith, H. A., T. C. Jones, and R. D. Hunt. 1972. Veterinary pathology. 4th ed. Lea and Febiger, Philadelphia. 1521 pp.

Smith, N. S., and L. K. Sowls. 1975. Fetal development of the collared peccary. J. Mammal. 56(3):619–625.

Smith, R. H., and A. LeCount. 1976. Factors affecting survival of mule deer fawns. Final Rep., Fed. Aid Proj. W-78-R, Work Plan 2, Job 4. Arizona Game and Fish Dep. 15 pp.

Smith, S. H., J. B. Holter, H. H. Hayes, and H. Silver. 1975. Protein requirement of white-tailed deer fawns. J. Wildl. Manage. 39(3):582–589.

Smith, T. E. 1976. Reproductive behavior and related social organization of the muskox on Nunivak Island. M. S. Thesis, Univ. of Alaska, College. 138 pp.

Sowls, L. K. 1961. Hunter-checking stations for collecting data on the collared peccary *(Pecari tajacu)*. Trans. N. Amer. Wildl. Conf. 26:497–505.

⸺. 1966. Reproduction in the collared peccary *(Tayassu tajacu)*. Pages 155–172 *in* I. W. Rowlands, ed. Comparative biology of reproduction in mammals. Zoological Society, London. 559 pp.

⸺. 1974. Social behavior of the collared peccary *Dicotyles tajacu* L. Pages 144–165 *in* V. Geist and F. Walther, eds. The behavior of ungulates and its relation to management. Vol. 1. IUCN New Ser. Publ. 24, Morges, Switzerland.

⸺, N. S. Smith, D. W. Holtan, G. E. Moss, and L. Estergreen. 1976. Hormone levels and corpora lutea cell characteristics during gestation in the collared peccary. Biol. Reprod. 14:572–578.

Sowls, L. K., V. R. Smith, R. Jenness, R. E. Sloan, and E. Regehr. 1961. Chemical composition and physical properties of the milk of the collared peccary. J. Mammal. 42(2):245–251.

Spalding, D. J. 1966. Twinning in bighorn sheep. J. Wildl. Manage. 30(1):207.

⸺, and J. Lesowski. 1971. Winter food of the cougar in south central British Columbia. J. Wildl. Manage. 35(2):378–381.

Spencer, H. E., Jr. 1955. The black bear and its status in Maine. Maine Dep. Inland Fish and Game Bull. No. 4. 55 pp.

Spillett, J. J., J. B. Low, and D. Sill. 1967. Livestock fences—how they influence pronghorn antelope movements. Utah Agr. Exp. Sta. Bull. 470. 79 pp.

Stearns, F. W., P. L. Schweitzer, and W. A. Creed. 1968. Deer browse production: rapid sampling and computer aided analysis. U.S. For. Serv., North Cent. For. Exp. Sta. Res. Note NC-66. 4 pp.

Steinhoff, H. W. 1971. Communicating complete wildlife values of Kenai. Trans. N. Amer. Wildl. and Nat. Resour. Conf. 36:428–438.

⸺. 1973. What North America needs is a good five-cent moose. Ontario Ministry of Nat. Resour. Trans. N. Amer. Moose Conf. and Workshop 9:232–243.

Stelfox, J. G. ed. 1976. Wood Buffalo National Park, bison research 1972–76. Section A-I *in* 1976 Annual Report. Can. Wildl. Serv. and Parks Canada, Ottawa.

Stenlund, M. H. 1955. A field study of the timber wolf *(Canis lupus)* on the Superior National Forest, Minnesota. Minnesota Dep. Cons. Tech. Bull. No. 4. 55 pp.

Stephenson, R. O., and L. J. Johnson. 1973. Wolf report. Vol. XI, Prog. Rep. Fed. Aid in Wildl. Restoration, Alaska Dep. Fish and Game, Juneau. 52 pp.

Stewart, J. A. 1964. The anatomy of the alimentary tract of the javelina, *Tayassu tajacu*. M. S. Thesis. Univ. of Arizona, Tucson. 31 pp.

Stewart, O. C. 1951. Burning and natural vegetation in the United States. Geogr. Rev. 41:317–320.

⸺. 1956. Fire as the first great force employed by man. Pages 115–133 *in* Man's role in changing the face of the earth. University of Chicago Press.

Stirling, I. 1974. Midsummer observations in the behavior of wild polar bears *(Ursus maritimus)*. Can. J. Zool. 52:1191–1195.

⸺, A. M. Pearson, and F. L. Bunnell. 1976. Population ecology studies of polar and grizzly bears in northern Canada. Trans. N. Amer. Wildl. and Nat. Resour. Conf. 41:421–430.

Stitler, W. M., and S. P. Shaw. 1966. Use of woody browse by white-tailed deer in heavily forested areas of northeastern United States. Trans. N. Amer. Wildl. and Nat. Resour. Conf. 31:205–212.

Stockstad, D. S., M. S. Morris, and E. C. Lory. 1953. Chemical characteristics of natural licks used by big game animals in western Montana. Trans. N. Amer. Wildl. Conf. 18:247–258.

Stoll, R. J., Jr., and R. W. Donohoe. n.d. White-tailed deer harvest management in Ohio. Ohio Dep. Nat. Resour. Inservice Doc. 73. 39 pp.

Stone, W., and W. E. Cram. 1902. American animals. Doubleday, Page and Company, New York. 318 pp.

Stonorov, D., and A. W. Stokes. 1972. Social behavior of the Alaskan brown bear. Pages 232–242 *in* S. Herrero, ed. Bears—their biology and management. IUCN New Ser. Publ. 23, Morges, Switzerland.

Storer, T. I. 1923. Rabies in a mountain lion. Calif. Fish and Game. 9(2):45–48.

———, and L. P. Tevix, Jr. 1955. California grizzly. Univ. of California Press, Berkeley and Los Angeles. 335 pp.

Streeter, R. G. 1970. A literature review on bighorn sheep population dynamics. Colorado Div. Game, Fish and Parks, Spec. Rep. No. 24. 11 pp.

Striton, R. A. 1959. Time, life and man. John Wiley and Sons, New York. 558 pp.

Struhsaker, T. T. 1967. Behavior of elk *(Cervis canadensis)* during the rut. Z. Tierpsychol. 24(1):30–114.

Stubblefield, T. M., J. R. Gray, and W. N. Capener. 1972. Feasibility of establishing commercial recreational enterprises on privately owned ranches and farms. New Mexico State Univ. Agr. Exp. Sta. Spec. Rep. 21, Las Cruces. 21 pp.

Sundstrom, C. 1968. Water consumption by pronghorn antelope and distribution related to water in Wyoming's Red Desert. Proc. Biennial Antelope States Workshop 3:39–46.

———, G. Hepworth, and K. L. Diem. 1973. Abundance, distribution and food habits of the pronghorn. Wyoming Game and Fish Dep. Bull. No. 12. 61 pp.

Swank, W. G. 1958. The mule deer in Arizona chaparral. Arizona Game and Fish Dep. Wildl. Bull. No. 3. 109 pp.

Swanson, E. B. 1940. The history of Minnesota game 1850–1900. Ph.D. thesis, Univ. Minn. 294 pp.

Swanson, G. A. Legislation and administration. Pages 226–255 *in* National Research Council, Land Use and Wildlife Resources. National Academy of Sciences, Washington, D.C.

———, and E. C. Waldbaver. 1967. Public hunting opportunities in the State of New York. Trans. N. Amer. Wildl. and Nat. Resour. Conf. 32:89–94.

Taber, R. D. 1956. Deer nutrition and population dynamics in the North Costal Range of California. Trans. N. Amer. Wildl. and Nat. Resour. Conf. 21:159–172.

———, and R. F. Dasmann. 1957. The dynamics of three natural populations of the deer *Odocoileus hemionus columbianus*. Ecology 38(2):233–246.

———. 1958. The black-tailed deer of the chaparral, its life history and management in the North Coast Range of California. California Dep. Fish and Game, Game Bull. No. 8. 163 pp.

Taylor, C. R. 1966. Thermoregulatory function of the horns of the family Bovidae. Report AAL-7R-63-31, Harvard Univ., Cambridge, Mass. 116 pp.

Taylor, R. A. Jr. 1962. Characteristics of horn growth in bighorn sheep rams. M. S. Thesis. Montana State Univ., Bozeman. 129 pp.

Taylor, W. P., ed. 1956. The deer of North America. The Stackpole Co., Harrisburg, Pa. 668 pp.

Teer, J. G. 1963. Texas deer herd management: problems and principles. Texas Game and Fish Comm. Bull. 44. 69 pp.

———, J. W. Thomas, and E. A. Walker. 1965. Ecology and management of white-tailed deer in the Llano Basin of Texas. Wildl. Monogr. 15. 62 pp.

Telfer, E. S. 1973. Forage yield in two forest zones of New Brunswick and Nova Scotia. J. Range Manage. 25:446–449.

———. 1974. Logging as a factor in wildlife ecology in the boreal forest. For. Chron. 50:186–190.

Tener, J. S. 1963. Queen Elizabeth Island, game survey. Can. Wildl. Serv. Occ. Pap. 4. 50 pp.

———. 1965. Muskoxen in Canada. Dep. of Northern Affairs and Nat. Resour., Can. Wildl. Serv. Monogr. Ser. No. 2., Queens Printer, Ottawa. 166 pp.

Terrel, T. L. 1973. Mule deer use patterns as related to pinyon-juniper conversion in Utah. Ph.D. Thesis. Utah State Univ., Logan. 174 pp.

Terrell, T. S., and J. J. Spillett. 1975. Pinyon-juniper conversion: its impact on mule deer, and other wildlife. Pages 105–118 *in* Proceedings of the Pinyon-Juniper Ecosystem Symposium, Logan, Utah, May 1975.

Texas Parks and Wildlife Department. 1973. Javelina status report. Texas Parks and Wildl. Dep., Austin. 2 pp.

Thomas, D. C. 1969. Population estimates of barren-ground caribou. March to May 1967. Can. Wildl. Serv. Rep. Ser. No. 9. 44 pp.

———, R. H. Russell, L. Broughton, and P. L. Madore. 1976. Investigations of Peary caribou populations on Canadian Arctic Island. Can. Wild. Serv. Prog. Note No. 64. 13 pp.

Thomas, D. W., and J. K. Pasto. 1956. Costs and benefits of the deer herd. Pennsylvania State Univ. Agr. Exp. Sta. Bull. 610, University Park, Pa. 33 pp.

Thomas, J. W., and R. G. Marburger. 1964. Mortality in deer shot in the thoracic area with the Cap-Chur gun. J. Wildl. Manage. 28(1):173–175.

Thomas, J. W., R. M. Robinson, and R. G. Marburger. 1967. Use of diazepam in the capture and handling of cervids. J. Wildl. Manage. 31(4):686–692.

Thomas, J. W., J. G. Teer, and E. A. Walker.

1964. Mobility and home range of white-tailed deer on the Edwards Plateau in Texas. J. Wildl. Manage. 28(3):463–472.

Thompson, C. B., J. B. Holter, H. H. Hayes, H. Silver, and W. E. Urban, Jr. 1973. Nutrition of white-tailed deer. I. Energy requirements of fawns. J. Wildl. Manage. 37(3):301–311.

Thompson, D. Q. 1952. Travel, range, and food habits of timber wolves in Wisconsin. J. Mammal. 33(4):429–442.

Thompson, W. R. 1957. Influence of prenatal maternal anxiety on emotionality in young rats. Science 125:698–699.

Thomson, B. R. 1972. Reindeer disturbance. J. Brit. Deer Soc. 2:882–883.

Thorne, E. T., R. E. Dean, and W. G. Hapworth. 1976. Nutrition during gestation in relation to successful reproduction in elk. J. Wildl. Manage. 40(2):330–335.

Thwaites, R. G., ed. 1905. Original journals of the Lewis and Clark expedition 1804–1806. Dodd, Mead and Co. New York. 7 vols.

Tilley, J. M. A., and R. A. Terry. 1963. A two stage technique for the *in vitro* digestion of forage crops. J. Brit. Grassl. Soc. 18:104–111.

Timm, R. M., and G. E. Connolly. 1977. How coyotes kill sheep. Rangeman's J. 4(4):106–107.

Timmermann, H. R. 1974. Moose inventory methods: a review. Can. Nat. 101(1 and 2):615–629.

Todd, J. W. 1972. A literature review on bighorn sheep food habits. Colorado Div. Game, Fish and Parks, Spec. Rep. No. 27. 21 pp.

———, and R. M. Hansen. 1973. Plant fragments in the feces of bighorns as indicators of food habits. J. Wildl. Manage. 37(3):363–366.

Toweill, D. E. and E. L. Meslow. 1977. Food habits of cougars in Oregon. J. Wildl. Manage. 41(3):576–578.

Trainer, C. E. 1975. Direct causes of mortality in mule deer fawns during summer and winter periods on Steens Mountain, Oregon. Proc. West. Assoc. Fish and Game Commissioners Annu. Meeting 55:163–170.

Trainer, D. O. 1970. The use of wildlife to monitor zoonoses. J. Wildl. Dis. 6(4):397–401.

———, and L. H. Karstad. 1971. Epizootic hemorrhagic disease. Pages 50–54 *in* J. W. Davis et al., eds. Infectious diseases of wild mammals. Iowa State Univ. Press, Ames.

Trefethen, J. B. 1961. Crusade for wildlife. The Stackpole Co., Harrisburg, Pa. 377 pp.

———., ed. 1975. The wild sheep in modern North America. Boone and Crockett Club, The Winchester Press. New York. 302 pp.

———. 1975. An American crusade for wildlife.

Winchester Press, New York. 409 pp.

———. 1976. The American landscape: 1776–1976. Two centuries of change. Wildlife Management Institute, Washington, D.C. 91 pp.

Troyer, W. A. 1960. The Roosevelt elk on Afognak Island, Alaska. J. Wildl. Manage. 24(1):15–21.

Tyson, E. 1683. Anatomy of the Mexico musk hog. Phil. Trans. 13(153):359–385 & illus.

Udy, J. R. 1953. Effects of predator control on antelope populations. Utah Dep. Fish and Game, Fed. Aid Div., Publ. No. 5. 48 pp.

Ullrey, D. E., W. G. Youatt, H. E. Johnson, P. K. Ku, and L. D. Fay. 1964. Digestiblity of cedar and aspen browse for the white-tailed deer. J. Wildl. Manage. 28(4):791–797.

Ullrey, D. E., W. G. Youatt, H. E. Johnson, L. D. Fay, and B. E. Brent. 1967. Digestiblity of cedar and jack pine browse for the white-tailed deer. J. Wildl. Manage. 31(3):448–454.

Ullrey, D. E., W. G. Youatt, H. E. Johnson, L. D. Fay, and B. L. Bradley. 1967. Protein requirements of white-tailed deer fawns. J. Wildl. Manage. 31(4):679–685.

———, and K. E. Kemp. 1968. Digestibility of cedar and balsam fir browse for the white-tailed deer. J. Wildl. Manage. 32(1):162–171.

Ullrey, D. E., W. G. Youatt, H. E. Johnson, L. D. Fay, B. L. Schoepke, and W. T. Magee. 1970. Digestible and metabolizable energy requirements for winter maintenance of Michigan white-tailed does. J. Wildl. Manage. 34(4):863–869.

———. 1971. A basal diet for deer nutrition research. J. Wildl. Manage. 35(1):57–62.

———, and K. K. Keahey. 1973. Calcium requirements of weaned white-tailed deer fawns. J. Wildl. Manage. 37(2):187–194.

Ullrey, D. E., W. G. Youatt, H. E. Johnson, A. B. Cowan, L. D. Fay, F. L. Covert, W. T. Magee, and K. K. Keahey. 1975. Phosphorus requirements of weaned white-tailed deer fawns. J. Wildl. Manage. 39(3):590–595.

Ullrey, D. E., W. G. Youatt, H. E. Johnson, L. D. Fay, R. L. Covert, and W. T. Magee. 1975. Consumption of artificial browse supplements by penned white-tailed deer. J. Wildl. Manage. 39(4):699–704.

Urness, P. J., and C. Y. McCulloch. 1974. Nutritional value of seasonal deer diets. Pages 53–64 *in* Deer nutrition in Arizona chaparral and desert habitats. Arizona Game and Fish Dep. Spec. Rep. No. 3. vi and 68 pp.

Urness, P. J., A. D. Smith, and R. K. Watkins. 1977. Comparison of *in vivo* and *in vitro* dry matter digestibility of mule deer forages. J. Range Manage. 30(2):119–121.

Urquhart, D. R. Unpubl. Oil exploration and Banks Island wildlife. A guideline for the preservation of caribou, muskox and Arctic fox on Banks Island, N.W.T. Unpubl. On file at Game Manage. Div., Govt. of Northwest Territories, Yellowknife. 105 pp.

U.S. Bureau of Land Management. 1974. Proceedings of regional fencing workshop. U.S. Bureau of Land Management, Washington, D.C. 74 pp.

U.S. Department of the Interior. 1955. National survey of fishing and hunting. U.S. Fish and Wildl. Serv. Circ. 44. U.S. Govt. Printing Office, Washington, D.C. 50 pp.

————. 1960. National survey of fishing and hunting. U.S. Bur. Sport Fish. and Wildl. Circ. 120. U.S. Govt. Printing Office, Washington, D.C. 73 pp.

————. 1966. 1965 national survey of fishing and hunting. Bur. Sport Fish. and Wildl. Resour. Publ. 27. U.S. Govt. Printing Office, Washington, D.C. 76 pp.

————. 1972a. Off-road recreation vehicles; task force study report. U.S. Govt. Printing Office, Washington, D.C. 123 pp.

————. 1972b. 1970 national survey of fishing and hunting. Bur. Sport Fish and Wildl. Resour. Publ. 95, U.S. Govt. Printing Office, Washington, D.C. 108 pp.

U.S. Fish and Wildlife Service. 1973. Threatened wildlife of the United States. Res. Publ. 114 (March 1973), Rev. Resour. Publ. 34. U.S. Govt. Printing Office, Washington, D.C. 289 pp.

————. 1976a. Wildlife and timber management. St. Marks National Wildlife Refuge, Florida. 20 pp.

————. 1976b. Federal register. 41:43340–43358.

U.S. Forest Service. 1930–1965. Annual wildlife reports. USDA For. Serv., Div. of Wildl. Manage., Washington, D.C.

————. 1969. Wildlife habitat improvement handbook. U.S. Govt. Printing Office, Washington, D.C.

————. 1971. Wildlife habitat management handbook. USDA For. Serv., Southern Region, FSH 2609.23R, Atlanta, Ga.

Vale, T.R. 1974. Sagebrush conversion projects: an element of contemporary environmental change in the western United States. Biol. Cons. 6(4):274–284.

Van Ballenberghe, V., A. W. Erickson, and D. Byman. 1975a. Ecology of the timber wolf in northeastern Minnesota. Minn. Dep. Cons. Tech. Bull. No. 4. 55 pp.

————. 1975b. Ecology of the timber wolf in northeastern Minnesota. Wildl. Monogr. 43. 44 pp.

Van Soest, P. J. 1964. Symposium on nutrition and forage and pastures: new chemical procedures for evaluating forages. J. Anim. Sci. 23(3):838–845.

————, R. H. Wine, and L. A. Moore. 1966. Estimation of the true digestiblity of forages by the *in vitro* digestion of cell walls. Proc. Int. Grassland Cong. 10:438–441.

Van Soest, P. J., and R. H. Wine. 1967. Use of detergents in the analysis of fibrous feeds. IV. Determination of plant cell wall constituents. J. Assoc. Off. Anal. Chem. 50(1):50–55.

Verme, L. J. 1963. Effect of nutrition on growth of white-tailed deer fawns. Trans. N. Amer. Wildl. and Nat. Resour. Conf. 28:431–443.

————. 1965a. Reproduction studies on penned white-tailed deer. J. Wildl. Manage. 29(1):74–79.

————. 1965b. Swamp conifer deeryards in northern Michigan: their ecology and management. J. For. 63(7):523–529.

————. 1968. An index of winter weather severity for northern deer. J. Wildl. Manage. 32(3):566–574.

————. 1969. Reproductive patterns of white-tailed deer related to nutritional plane. J. Wildl. Manage. 33(4):881–887.

————, and D. E. Ullrey. 1972. Feeding and nutrition of deer. Pages 275–291 *in* Digestive physiology and nutrition of ruminants. Vol. 3. Oregon State Univ., Corvallis. 350 pp.

Vibe, C. 1958. The muskox in East Greenland. Mammalia 22:168–174.

————. 1976. Arctic animals in relation to climatic fluctuations. Meddel. om Grønland 170(5):1–227.

Villa, B. 1951. Jabalies y berrendos. Dir. Gen. Forestal y de Caza, Dep. Caza, Mexico City, Mexico Bol 2. 30 pp.

Von Raesfeld, F. 1952. Das Deutsche waidwerk. P. Parey, Berlin. 497 pp.

Wade, D. A. 1976. The use of aircraft in predator control. Proc. Ver. Pest Conf. 7:154–160.

Wagner, F. H. 1969. Ecosystem concepts in fish and game management. Pages 259–307 *in* G. M. Van Dyne, ed. The ecosystem concept in natural resource management. Academic Press, New York.

————. In Press. Effects of livestock grazing and the livestock industry on wildlife. *In* H. Brokaw, ed. Wildlife in America. Council on Environmental Quality, Washington, D.C.

Walker, E. P., and J. L. Paradiso. 1968. Mammals of the world. Johns Hopkins Press, Baltimore. 2 vols.

Wallace, R. F. 1956. An evaluation of wildlife resources in the state of Washington. State

Coll. of Washington Bull No. 28, Pullman. 63 pp.

Wallmo, O. C. 1962. Big Bend ecological survey. Texas Game and Fish Dep. Compl. Rep. Fed. Aid Proj. LO-57-R-7, Job 9. 33 pp.

———. 1969. Response of deer to alternate-strip clearcutting of lodgepole pine and spruce-fir timber in Colorado. USDA For. Serv. Res. Note RM-141. 4 pp.

———, and D. J. Neff. 1970 Direct observations of tamed deer to measure their consumption of natural forage. Pages 105–110 *in* Range and wildlife habitat evaluation, A research symposium. U.S. Dep. Agr. Misc. Publ. No. 1147. 220 pp.

Wallmo, O. C., W. L. Regelin, and D. W. Reichert. 1972. Forage use by mule deer relative to logging in Colorado. J. Wildl. Manage. 36(4):1025–1033.

Wallmo, O. C., R. B. Gill, L. H. Carpenter, and D. W. Reichert. 1973. Accuracy of field estimates of deer food habits. J. Wildl. Manage. 37(4):556–562.

Wallmo, O. C., D. F. Reed, and L. H. Carpenter. 1976. Alteration of mule deer habitat by wildfire, logging, highways, housing development, and agriculture. Pages 34–47 *in* G. W. Workman and J. B. Low, eds. Mule deer decline in the West—a symposium. Logan, Utah, April, 1976. 134 pp.

Wallmo, O. C., L. H. Carpenter, W. L. Regelin, R. B. Gill, and D. L. Baker. 1977. Evaluation of deer habitat on a nutritional basis. J. Range Manage. 30(2): 122–127.

Walls, M. L. 1974. A dynamic white-tailed deer population simulator and lessons from its use. M. S. Thesis. Virginia Polytechnic Inst. and State Univ. Blacksburg. 167 pp.

Walters, C. J., R. Hilborn, and P. Peterman. 1975. Computer simulation of barren-ground caribou dynamics. Ecological Modeling 1:303–315.

Ward, J. L. 1972. Prenatal stress feminizes and demasculinizes the behavior of males. Science 175:82–84.

Waters, S. A., ed. 1964. Colorado year-book, 1962–1964. Colorado State Planning Div., Denver. 1,064 pp.

Webster, A. J. F., and K. L. Blaxter. 1966. The thermal regulation of two breeds of sheep exposed to air temperatures below freezing point. Res. Vet. Sci. 7:466–479.

Weeks, H. P., Jr., and C. M. Kirkpatrick. 1976. Adaptations of white-tailed deer to naturally occurring sodium deficiencies. J. Wildl. Manage. 40(4):610–625.

Wesley, D. E., K. L. Knox, and J. G. Nagy. Energy metabolism of pronghorn antelopes. J. Wildl. Manage. 37(4):563–573.

Wesson, J. A., III, P. F. Scanlon, and R. E. Mirachi. 1975. Immobilization of white-tailed deer with succinylcholine chloride: success rate, reactions of deer and some physiological effects. Proc. S. E. Assoc. Game and Fish Commissioners 28th Annu. Conf., 1974. 28:500–506.

Wetzel, J. R., J. R. Wambaugh, and J. M. Peek. 1975. Appraisal of white-tailed deer winter habitats in northeastern Minnesota. J. Wildl. Manage. 39(1):59–66.

Wetzel, R. M., R. E. Dubois, R. L. Martin, and P. Meyers. 1975. *Catagonus,* an "extinct" peccary alive in Paraguay. Science 189:379–381.

Whelan, J. B., R. L. Cowan, E. W. Hartsook, and J. S. Lindzey. 1967. Uptake and distribution of P-32 in male white-tailed deer. Federation Proc. 26(3):416. Abstr.

Whelan, J. B., K. I. Morris, R. F. Harlow, and H. S. Crawford. 1976. The bioenergetic approach to forest range management. Virginia Coop. Wildl. Res. Unit Release No. 74-25, Blacksburg, Va.

White, M. 1973. Description of remains of deer fawns killed by coyotes. J. Mammal. 54(1):291–293.

Whitehead, G. K. 1972. Deer of the world. Constable and Co., Ltd., London. 194 pp.

Wilcox, S. W. 1976. Deer production in the United States 1969–1973. Published by author at Arizona State Univ., Tempe. 7 pp. & tables and charts.

Wilcox, T. 1963. Prairie dog race. Outdoor Life 13(1):40, 43, 102.

Wildlife Management Institute. 1974. Placing American wildlife management in perspective. Wildlife Management Institute, Washington, D.C. 27 pp.

———. 1977. Organization, authority and programs of state fish and wildlife agencies. Wildlife Management Institute, Washington, D.C. 40 pp.

The Wildlife Society. 1973. 1972 fall enrollment in wildlife curricula. Wildl. Soc. Bull. 1(1):51–54.

———. 1975. Fall 1974 enrollment in wildlife curricula. Wildl. Soc. Bull. 3(1):31–33.

———. 1977. 1976 graduate placement survey. Wildl. Soc. Bull. 5(4):208–210.

Wilkinson, P. F. 1971. The domestication of the musk-ox. Polar Record 15:683–690.

———. 1974. Wool shedding in muskoxen. Biol. J. Linnean Soc. 6:127–141.

———, C. C. Shank, and D. F. Penner. 1976. Muskox-caribou summer range relations on Banks Island, N.W.T. J. Wildl. Manage. 40(1):151–162.

489

Williamson, L. L. 1973. Wildlife's corner. *In* "Gun Week" (weekly newspaper). Sidney, Ohio. Dec. 19, 1973.

———, and G. L. Doster. 1977. Socio-economic aspects of white-tailed deer diseases. Paper read at the Second International White-tailed Deer Disease Symposium, August 10, 1977, Athens, Ga.

Wilson, D. E., S. M. Hirst, and R. P. Ellis. 1977. Determination of feeding preferences in wild ruminants from trocar samples. J. Wildl. Manage. 41(1):70–75.

Wilson, E. O. 1975. Sociobioluy: the new synthesis. Belknap Press of Harvard Univ. Press, Cambridge, Mass. 697 pp.

Wobeser, G., and W. Runge. 1975. Rumen overload and rumenitis in white-tailed deer. J. Wildl. Manage. 39(3):596–600.

Wolfe, M. L. 1974. An overview of moose coactions with other animals. Can. Nat. 101 (1 and 2):437–456.

Wolters, G. L., and R. G. Schmidtling. 1975. Browse and herbages in intensively managed pine plantations. J. Wildl. Manage. 39(3):557–562.

Woodward, T. N., R. J. Gutierrez, and W. H. Rutherford. 1974. Bighorn lamb production, survival, and mortality in south-central Colorado. J. Wildl. Manage. 38(4):771–774.

Woodburne, M. O. 1968. The cranial myology and osteology of *Dicotyles tajacu,* the collared peccary, and its bearing on classification. Mem. S. Calif. Acad. Sci. 7:1–48.

Wright, G. A., and J. R. Lancaster. 1972. A spatial analysis of public attitudes toward hunting and firearm usage in middle Tennessee. Proc. S.E. Assoc. Game and Fish Commissioners 26th Annu. Meeting, 1972 26:203–205.

Wright. W. H. 1928. The grizzly bear. Charles Scribner's Sons, New York. 274 pp.

Yazan, Y., and E. Knorre. 1964. Domesticating elk in a Russian National Park. Oryx 7:301–304.

Yoakum, J. 1957. Factors affecting mortality of pronghorn antelope in Oregon. M. S. Thesis. Oregon State Coll., Corvallis. 112 pp.

———. 1968. A review of the distribution and abundance of American pronghorn antelope. Proc. Biennial Antelope States Workshop 3:4–14.

———. 1972. Antelope-vegetative relationships. Proc. Biennial Antelope States Workshop 5:171–177.

———. 1974. Pronghorn habitat requirements for sagebrush-grasslands. Proc. Biennial Antelope States Workshop 6:16–25.

Young, B. A. 1971. Application of the carbon dioxide entry technique to measurement of energy expenditure by grazing cattle. Pages 237–241 *in* 5th symposium on energy metabolism of farm animals. Joris, Druck and Verlag, Zurich, Switzerland.

———, and J. L. Corbett. 1968. Energy requirement for maintenance of grazing sheep measured by calorimetric technique. Proc. Austral. Anim. Prod. 1:327–334.

Young, B. A., and E. H. McEwan. 1975. A method for measurement of energy expenditure in unrestrained reindeer and caribou. Pages 95–107 *in* J. R. Luick, P. C. Lent, D. R. Klein, and R. B. White, eds. Proceedings, 1st International Reindeer/Caribou Symposium. Occ. Pap. No. 2. Inst. of Arctic Biology, Univ. of Alaska, College. 551 pp.

Young, E., and P. I. L. Bronkhorst. 1971. Overstrain disease in game. Afr. Wildl. 25:51–52.

Young, S. P. 1944. The wolves of North America. Dover Publications, Inc., New York. 385 pp.

———. 1956. The deer, the Indians and the American pioneers. Pages 1–27 *in* W. P. Taylor, ed. The deer of North America. The Stackpole Co., Harrisburg, Pa. 668 pp.

———, and E. A. Goldman. 1946. The puma, mysterious American cat. The Stackpole Co., Harrisburg, Pa. 358 pp.

Young, S. P. and H. H. T. Jackson. 1951. The clever coyote. The Stackpole Co., Harrisburg, Pa. 411 pp.

Zarn, M., T. Heller, and K. Collins. 1977. Wild, free-roaming horses—status of present knowledge. Bur. Land Manage. Tech. Note 294. 72 pp.

Zervanos, S. M. 1975. Seasonal effects of temperature on the respiratory metabolism of the collared peccary *(Tayassu tajacu).* Comp. Biochem. Physiol. 50A:365–371.

———, and N. F. Hadley. 1973. Adaptational biology and energy relationships of the collared peccary *(Tayassu tajacu).* Ecology 54:759–774.

Zervanos, S. M., and G. I. Day. 1977. Water and energy requirements in captive and free-living collared peccaries. J. Wildl. Manage. 41(3):527–532.

Zhigunov, P. S. 1961. Reindeer husbandry, 2nd ed. (Transl. from Russian) U.S. Dep. of Commerce Clearing House, Springfield, Va.

Zobell, R. S. 1968. Field studies of antelope movements on fenced ranges. Trans. N. Amer. Wildl. and Nat. Resour. Conf. 33:211–216.

Zyznar, E., and P. J. Urness. 1969. Qualitative identification of forage remnants in deer feces. J. Wildl. Manage. 33(3):506–510.

INDEX[a]

---

[a]For reference to ecology, habitat and management topics pertaining to particular species, readers are advised to refer directly to chapters about the species in question.